Gregory Elliott

A Cultural
Politics Book
for the Social
Text Collective

Perry Anderson

The Merciless
Laboratory of History

 Cultural Politics / Volume 15
University of Minnesota Press
Minneapolis ▸ London

The publication of this book was assisted by a bequest from Josiah H. Chase to honor his parents, Ellen Rankin Chase and Josiah Hook Chase, Minnesota territorial pioneers.

Extracts from this book originally appeared as "Olympus Mislaid? The Patience of Perry Anderson," in *Radical Philosophy*, no. 71 (May/June 1995, pp. 5–19), and a review article on the New Left, in *Radical Philosophy*, no. 68 (autumn 1994, pp. 45–48).

Published by the University of Minnesota Press
111 Third Avenue South, Suite 290
Minneapolis, MN 55401-2520
http: //www.upress.umn.edu

Printed in the United States of America on acid-free paper

Library of Congress Cataloging-in-Publication Data

Elliott, Gregory.
   Perry Anderson : the merciless laboratory of history / Gregory Elliott.
     p. cm. — (Cultural politics ; v. 15)
   Includes bibliographical references and index.
   ISBN 0-8166-2966-8 (HC/j : alk. paper)
   1. Anderson, Perry. 2. Socialists—Great Britain—Biography.
   3. Intellectuals—Great Britain—Biography. I. Title. II. Series: Cultural
politics (Minneapolis, Minn.) ; v. 15.
HX244.7.A7E48   1998
335.4'092—dc21
[B]   98-29687

10 09 08 07 06 05 04 03 02 01 00 99 98   10 9 8 7 6 5 4 3 2 1

For Neil Belton and Michael Sprinker

Deutscher's work continues to represent an irreplaceable source for the culture and politics of socialism. The reasons lie in the eminent combination of its qualities. First of all, perhaps, the serene political fortitude with which Deutscher met the contingencies of his own period—his unshakeable fidelity to the ideals of Marx and Engels, amidst so many conflagrations in which one edifice of the Left after another burnt down, or had to be rebuilt. That fortitude was the product of his absolute independence of thought—the complete freedom of his person and outlook from those fashions and phobias which have typically swayed the conformist intelligentsias of the West in one direction after another—successively Stalinist or Maoist, structuralist or post-structuralist, apostles of the New Working-Class or the New Social Movements, eurocommunism or eurosocialism. But this spiritual independence was the very opposite of sectarian or pharisaical isolation. . . . serene olympian, visionary iconoclast, shrewd politician. He had an element of each in his own make-up. A socialist movement will only flourish if it can encompass all of the ideals they represent.
▸ *Perry Anderson, preface to Isaac Deutscher,* Marxism, Wars, and Revolutions *(1984)*

Contents

XI   *Preface*

XIX   *Acknowledgements*

XXI   *Abbreviations*

1   *1. Demarcations*

41   *2. Missed Rendezvous*

111   *3. Against the Historical Current?*

192   *4. The Verdict of the World*

241   *Conclusion: The Figure in the Mirror*

245   *Notes*

301   *Select Bibliography*

317   *Index*

Preface

Longtime editor of the *New Left Review* and cofounder of New Left Books; diagnostician of English exceptionalism and historian of English Absolutism; sometime interlocutor of Trotskyism and monitor of Western Marxism; today, contributor to the *London Review of Books* and professor of history at the University of California—Perry Anderson enjoys a salience within Anglophone Marxist culture that is generally acknowledged. Writing in 1992, before the deaths of Edward Thompson and Ralph Miliband, and even as the productivity of Christopher Hill and Eric Hobsbawm showed no sign of flagging, Terry Eagleton could nominate him 'Britain's most brilliant Marxist intellectual'.[1] Whatever our estimate of that verdict, a more recent claim to the effect that Anderson is '[o]ne of the foremost contemporary Marxist thinkers'[2] would command common consent.

Yet his is a career that remains curiously underexplored. A variety of reasons might be adduced for this. Not least of them is the deterrence to detailed scrutiny afforded by the work of a polyglot polymath conversant with at least seven or eight living languages (not to mention two dead ones), and possessed of the 'olympian universalism' he has attributed to the founders of historical materialism.[3] In an age of specialists, Anderson is a generalist—but quite the reverse of an amateur. If, as one sardonic critic would have it, he has produced 'a synoptic oeuvre stretching from 800 BC to last week',[4] it is a tribute to the quality of this oeuvre that it should have commanded the respectful attention of the relevant authorities (whether on 800 B.C. or last week). Olympian, in substance and style alike, Anderson unquestionably is (the superlative has become a commentator's cliché); and, as de Gaulle once remarked, 'a summit is not a crowded place'.

Compounding inhibitions of intellectual competence, any survey of Anderson's career faces formidable obstacles of evidence and method. For a start, it risks blatant prematurity. Why should Anderson, still short of sixty, not emulate E. H. Carr, the vast bulk of whose *History of Soviet Russia* appeared after he had entered his seventh decade?[5] or—perhaps more germanely, pending resumption of the history project launched with *Passages from Antiquity to Feudalism* in 1974 and expansion of *The Ends of History* announced by Verso in 1993—Hobsbawm, who has concluded his trilogy on capitalist modernity, and rendered it a quartet, since reaching the age of seventy?

As if this—the incompletion of Anderson's exoteric oeuvre—were not enough, lest it indulge the fetish of the signature, any comprehensive account would have to trace other, quasi-esoteric dimensions of his work, in their intricate combination. These might baldly be itemized thus: (1) the overall editorial evolution of the *New Left Review* (*NLR*), which Anderson edited from 1962 for some twenty years and in whose councils he appears to have been first among equals thereafter; (2) anonymous or pseudonymous material contributed by him to the *NLR;* (3) unpublished manuscripts— some of them book-length; (4) the programme of the *NLR*'s imprint (New Left Books, subsequently Verso) from its inception in 1970, and associated publishing ventures with Fontana and Penguin; and, finally, (5) related political and cultural activities (in, say, the student movement in the late 1960s, or the Socialist Society in the early 1980s). Discriminating where necessary, and possible, between Anderson's individual and the *NLR*'s institutional positions, the totality would require proper contextualization—intellectual and political, international as well as national.

The release in spring 1992 of two substantial collections of Anderson's essays—*English Questions* and *A Zone of Engagement*—signalling a 'turning point' in his politico-intellectual development,[6] offers an opportunity for something considerably less ambitious but hopefully not devoid of all value: an elementary reconstruction of that development to date. For while neither volume affects completeness, each possibly obscures as much as it illuminates about its author's evolution since his debut in 1960.

In the foreword to *A Zone of Engagement*, Anderson notes the contrast between its first three chapters, classified as 'intra-mural surveys within the intellectual world of the revolutionary Left', and the remainder, culminating in a long essay on Francis Fukuyama that extracts a rational kernel from the mystical shell of his philosophy of modern history. Anderson's dawning scepticism about the revolutionary Marxist tradition, from the mid-1980s, attached to both its analytical resources and its political purchase. Historical materialism had come under challenge as a 'theory of historical development' from the Anglo-Weberian school of Gellner and Giddens, Runciman and Mann; revolutionary socialism had been discountenanced by the 'societal ascendancy of the West', certified by the implosion of Gorbachevite perestroika in the East.[7]

Symptoms of an altered stance were registered in the reception of Anderson's selected essays. A decade earlier, Alex Callinicos had detected an 'Americanization' of the *NLR*, observing that '[o]nce it straddled the Channel in an attempt to save us from British parochialism; now it hovers somewhere in mid-Atlantic in Olympian solitude', and he had compared

Anderson to Plekhanov.[8] Eight years later, critics were prompted to ponder whether Anderson was still a Marxist or socialist of any species, never mind a revolutionary one, and to suspect the emergence of a deutero-Anderson— one aligning himself with the Anglo-American academy while pursuing, via the European Commission, 'a kind of social-democratic Leninism'.[9] Where, some wondered, did the partisan of Lenin and Trotsky, the scourge of academicism and Eurocommunism, now stand? Had Anderson embarked upon the 'smuggler's road to socialism' reportedly decried by him in the 1980s?

Trotsky wrote of Lenin that he 'thought in terms of epochs and continents, [whereas] Churchill thinks in terms of parliamentary fireworks and feuilletons'.[10] Something similar might be said of Anderson (especially since, in the interval, a day in politics has become a long time, the latest opinion poll a historic event). In consequence, Anderson has always taken the long view, played the long game, exhibiting the 'ability to *wait*' enjoined by Trotsky,[11] in opposition to reformist pragmatism or revolutionary messianism. Indeed, it may be that part of the attraction for Anderson of a certain form of Trotskyism precisely lay in its representing, as Sartre put it in debate with Ernest Mandel in the 1950s, 'a waiting art'.[12] Whatever, in his case that art was invariably attuned to an ineluctable reality stated with typical bluntness by a professed member of the British Old Left in 1969: 'Being a revolutionary in countries such as ours just happens to be difficult'.[13]

Notwithstanding the significant discontinuities—other turning points— by which Anderson's career has been punctuated, there are equally profound continuities, disclosed by recurrent historico-political themes and patterns of response. Erstwhile Castroite sympathizer, Anderson appreciated then, and respects still, the spirit motivating the Havana Declaration of 1962: 'The role of Job does not behove a revolutionary'. Today, however, 'amidst so many conflagrations in which one edifice of the Left after another [has] burnt down'[14]—in his own time, those of Guevarism and Maoism, Eurocommunism and Eurosocialism, Trotskyism and 'actually existing socialism'—it might seem as if Anderson has heeded a version of the counsel given to disabused Communists by Deutscher in 1950. In a review of *The God That Failed*, in which he commended the trio of qualities invoked by Anderson in the passage that serves as my epigraph, Deutscher wrote:

> It seems that the only dignified attitude the ex-communist can take is to rise *au-dessus de la mêlée*. . . . This is not to say that the ex-communist . . . should retire into the ivory tower. (His contempt for the ivory tower lingers in him from his past.) But he may withdraw into a *watch-tower* instead. To watch with detachment and alertness this heaving chaos of a world, to be on

a sharp outlook for what is going to emerge from it, and to interpret it *sine ira et studio*.[15]

Interpreted thus, the author of *English Questions* and *A Zone of Engagement* would appear less a deutero- than a Deutschero-Anderson, chastened by his own previous illusions in varieties of 'Third Worldism', the potential for democratic regeneration of the Second World, and the seasonableness of revolutionary socialism in the First. But in one sense Anderson has not withdrawn to the watchtower (though he may now inhabit an ivory one). For unlike Deutscher—who was Trotsky's prewar collaborator before turning his postwar biographer—he has been stationed there all along.

Despite youthful impetuousness and occasional intemperance, the historical perspectives of Perry Anderson have been primarily secular, synchronized, if not with the *longue durée* as such, then with what he himself has called 'longer *durées*'.[16] Underlying an inconsistency of orientation, induced by the shifting imperatives of successive conjunctures in which a sharp outlook for the 'weakest link' has been a consistent feature of Anderson's politics, is a settled *attentisme*, ultimately distanced from the contingencies and vagaries of the immediate. Anderson would never subscribe to Fernand Braudel's provocation that 'events are dust'. Nor, however, would he consider a half century in politics a long time. In a passage composed a decade before Braudel coined his slogan, and which Anderson has cited approvingly, Trotsky maintained:

> Twenty-five years in the scales of history, when it is a question of profoundest changes in economic and cultural systems, weigh less than an hour in the life of man. What good is the individual who, because of empirical failures in the course of an hour or a day, renounces a goal that he set for himself on the basis of the experience and analysis of his entire previous lifetime?[17]

Almost sixty years on, and a few hours into that lifetime, Anderson's declared source of inspiration is the stoicism of Gramsci, whose 'strength of mind . . . [i]n the depths of his own defeat . . . was to bring moral resistance and political innovation together. In related circumstances, this is the combination needed today'.[18] *Comparaison n'est pas raison*—or not always. Yet whatever the identity of the figure in the Andersonian mirror, it reveals an enduring fidelity to the ideals of a lifetime: a modified yet undiminished zone of engagement in the cause of an international socialist culture and politics.

If this is an accurate depiction, it shifts the burden of attention away from suspicions of incipient heresy (e.g., hankerings after meliorist European bureaucracy), to the maintenance—in the absence of any of the political co-ordinates that might sustain it—of the 'olympian universalism' of Anderson's station in the watchtower. That posture was problematic in the past, when the existence of global socialist organizations nevertheless permitted him both to class himself among that 'portion of the bourgeoisie' which, accord-ing to the *Communist Manifesto*, 'goes over to the proletariat'—'in particu-lar, a portion of the bourgeois ideologists, who have raised themselves to the level of comprehending theoretically the historical movement as a whole'[19]—and to speak in the name of an imaginary international that never found sat-isfactory embodiment. However, with the debacle of socialist traditions in the twentieth century, and with the crisis of Marxism—at first strenuously denied, at length reluctantly conceded—Anderson's position has become more precarious, for ever more deracinated.

Contrary to Hegelian variants of Marxism, Anderson tended to conceive of 'scientific socialism' as the external conjunction of a theoretical research programme and a practical movement, rather than as 'the theoretical ex-pression of the proletarian movement'.[20] Predicated, even so, upon what the early Lukács designated 'the actuality of the revolution',[21] in its mature form Anderson's Marxism construed historical materialism as the explanatory sci-ence of history and a normative critique of capitalism. In the first register, Marxism furnished a causal knowledge of the past and present, and thereby informed the struggle for a liberated future, guiding agents in the adoption of viable strategic means toward the feasible socialist end. In the second register, without regressing to the 'utopian socialism' that Marx, Engels, and their successors reckoned to have superseded, Marxism not only provided reasons for opposing capitalism but also ought (so Anderson urged in the early 1980s) to explore the institutional shape of a desirable socialism.

What becomes of this prospectus with the *non*actuality of reformist, let alone revolutionary, socialism—at a time when (to invert Marx and Engels) 'the *real* movement which abolishes the present state of things' is not com-munism but global capitalism, and when its trophies include the traditional agencies and strategies, parties and programmes, of its historic antagonist?[22] The permissive conditions of what a critic (privately) dubbed 'Andersonian Meta-Trotskyism' have evaporated; its habits die hard. (Witness the unruf-fled serenity with which possible scenarios for socialism are scanned in 'The Ends of History',[23] for all the world as if none of its instantiations had ever elicited Anderson's own critical support.) It is the tenacious consistency and integrity of Anderson's project, resolutely focused on epochs and continents amid so many vicissitudes, that raises the most intriguing questions.

The present work essays no more (to borrow an Andersonian phrase) than a 'rudimentary diagram' of his career,[24] neither pretending to exhaust its past trajectory nor presuming to preempt its future curve, under the action of similar or different forces. It is undertaken in the belief that this career, in and through its very singularity, conforms to some of the wider contours of Anglo-Marxism since 1956; and that a portrait of the individual instance may cast some light upon the collective phenomenon. Its unfashionable approach to the history of ideas will be that of Anderson himself, articulating 'internal' and 'external' histories of his texts in their contexts (albeit with what might strike some readers as undue cross-Channel, rather than transatlantic, bias). As Anderson writes of the essays in *A Zone of Engagement*, distinguishing his own procedures from rival methodologies in intellectual history,

> They are centred on individual authors . . . whose works they aim to reconstruct, so far as possible, as an intentional unity, situated within the intellectual and political currents of their time. They assume neither automatic coherence nor inherent dispersion in the writing of their subjects. Rather they try to locate specific contradictions of argument where these occur, generally treating them not as random lapses but as symptomatic points of tension, either within the body of thought itself, or with the evidence beyond it.[25]

Like many of its subject's texts, this study is 'situated midway between the historical and the political—an attempt to mediate some of the requirements of scholarship and others of partisanship'.[26] Concerning the scholarship, it will suffice to invite correction of errors of fact, interpretation, and evaluation by others better qualified. But a further word is in order as regards the partisanship. The work of an independent Marxist, *Perry Anderson: The Merciless Laboratory of History* aims to deliver an immanent critique, measuring the 'performance' of Anderson's Marxism against its 'prediction', in its own attempts 'to approximate to a general truth of the time'[27]—an ambition intimated by my subtitle, borrowed from Trotsky.

Whether Anderson has succeeded in understanding the history he has elected to interpret is the central—though not sole—question governing my assessment. For if, for example, in view of his employment of the criterion to judge the oeuvre of others, his own failure to unite intellectual work with political activity cannot simply be ignored, neither should it be indiscriminately laboured. This is not only because to do so would deservedly court the charge of tu quoque; it also derives from the consideration (underlined by Michael Sprinker)[28] that a range of options inferior to the Lenino-Trotskyist ideal can be, and has been, pursued by figures with whom Anderson might legitimately be contrasted—for example, those directly influential in his formation and development, from Sartre and Deutscher (unaffiliated Marxists), via Althusser (critical Communist), to Mandel (Trotskyist leader). However couched, the facility of generic allegations of theoreticism, academicism, substitutionism, and so on, against Marxist intellectuals is in inverse proportion to its utility. It substitutes moralistic deprecation for materialist explanation of an objective state of affairs, incorrigible by any amount of voluntarism (as if a magical injection of 'practice' could remedy a distemper of 'theory'). Insofar as the vice is in circumstances, the fault consists more in being oblivious of that vice than in making a virtue of necessity and seeking to interpret the world aright, when changing it proves intractable. At all events, it is only fair to advise prospective readers that no set of totally correct positions will be counterposed here to Anderson's errors or misdirections. Whatever their quantity or gravity, he will often be found to have addressed the crucial problems and should not be reproved for perplexity as to their resolution—something that has not thus far been forthcoming from any other quarter.

The aspects of Perry Anderson sketched in this book would have been fewer and less rounded, were it not for the access I have had to unpublished documents, as well as the testimony of former colleagues on the *NLR*. In addition, with much conjecture (and not a little speculation), an attempt has been made, within limits, to identify texts published under another signature that may presumptively be attributed to him. (Where I have erred, I apologize to those concerned.) As one of the publisher's readers of my manuscript has suggested, the very existence of such material in the case of a journal—as opposed to a political party or group—is, at first blush, a cause for some surprise. However, it underscores the extent to which the internal life of the *NLR* assimilated certain features of the modus operandi of a semiclandestine revolutionary organization. Over and above the predilections of its sometime editor and his colleagues, such practices doubtless derive from the persistence—even amongst the anti-Stalinist Far Left—of a destructive legacy of historical Communism.

Further reflections on this score will occur as and where they seem appropriate. In utilizing the sources available to me, I have proceeded as follows. In the case of personal unpublished manuscripts that are signed, whether by Anderson or fellow editors of the *NLR*, I have not quoted but rather have paraphrased and cited page numbers. Contrariwise, where documents bear no signature and possess an institutional character, it has seemed reasonable to make direct use of them. (This applies, for example, both to the *NLR*'s constitution and charter and to three editorial reports, covering the years 1962–82, circulated within the editorial committee.) Whether this is an elegant solution may be left to the disinterested parties to determine. One obvious danger it risks is a conflation of individual and institutional positions. But in the absence of any automatic way of resolving this difficulty, it is best to engage—and then see. Given such indeterminacies of authorship, I have not included any unpublished items in the bibliography of Anderson's writings appended to this study. The bibliography does, however, encompass a good number of the anonymous or pseudonymous texts—often very brief, but no less instructive for that—I have referred to. Yet it should not be taken as infallible or complete. (More research would, for example, enhance the number of original foreign-language publications.) While on this subject, it is worth pointing out that extensive quotation from primary sources is further encouraged by the current unavailability of three of Anderson's books— *Considerations on Western Marxism* (1976), *Arguments within English Marxism* (1980), and *In the Tracks of Historical Materialism* (1983)—and by the comparative inaccessibility of some key essays (e.g., 'Problems of Socialist Strategy' [1965]).

A final disclaimer before proceeding. Readers anticipating a contribution to the black legend of the *NLR* attendant upon the various crises in its history will be frustrated. (The last, inciting charge and countercharge in the liberal and Fabian press, was amply aired.)[29] This is not simply out of tact or discretion. In 1949 Deutscher regretted that 'Clio, the Muse of History, has failed to obtain admittance to the Kremlin'.[30] Five decades on, she has been granted limited admission there but is still barred from Meard Street. It will be for a future historian to seek, and maybe to gain, entry.

Acknowledgements

Such is the depth, and breadth, of my indebtedness to others that an economy of (alphabetical) acknowledgement and exoneration seems indicated. Accordingly, excluding those who requested anonymity, I thank Neil Belton, Simon Bromley, Sebastian Budgen, Tom Hickey, Quintin Hoare, Martin Jenkins, John Kraniauskas, Francis Mulhern, Peter Osborne, Bruce Robbins, Justin Rosenberg, Michael Sprinker, and Duncan Thompson for critical advice and miscellaneous aid. Lisa Freeman, as well as her successor and colleagues, kept an editorial watch from abroad, Lucinda Tavener an affectionate one at home, where Hector and Paris resent any condescension to dead languages.

▸ *Lewes, England, May Day 1997*

Abbreviations

CGT	Confédération générale du travail
CND	Campaign for Nuclear Disarmament
CPGB	Communist Party of Great Britain
CPSU	Communist Party of the Soviet Union
CPUSA	Communist Party of the United States of America
EC	European Community
EEC	European Economic Community
FRG	Federal Republic of Germany (West Germany)
GDP	Gross domestic product
IMG	International Marxist Group
NATO	North Atlantic Treaty Organization
NLB	New Left Books
NLR	*New Left Review*
NR	*New Reasoner*
PCF	French Communist Party
PCI	Italian Communist Party
RSSF	Revolutionary Socialist Students' Federation
SPD	German Social-Democratic Party
SWP	Socialist Workers Party
ULR	*Universities and Left Review*
VSC	Vietnam Solidarity Campaign

1 ▶ Demarcations

Perry Anderson was born in London in September 1938 and subsequently taken by his aunt to China, where his father, descended from Anglo-Irish landed gentry, worked for the Imperial Maritime Customs. After spending most of the war years in the United States, the family returned to the south of Ireland.[1] Raised there, Anderson was schooled at Eton and 'went up' to Worcester College, Oxford, in 1956. This background of *dépaysements*, and what his brother, Benedict, has described as the series of cultural 'estrangements' consequent upon it, may help to account for a habitual extraterritoriality in Anderson's intellectual outlook. At any rate, as the 1968 article 'Components of the National Culture' would attest, Oxford philosophy, then at the height of its complacent insularity, proved decidedly uncongenial.

Anderson's undergraduate career was punctuated by changes of degree programme, from 'modern greats' (philosophy, politics, and economics), to philosophy and psychology, thence to modern languages (Russian and French). It coincided with the emergence and efflorescence of the British New Left, one of whose institutional matrices was the University Labour Club, dominated by the late Dennis Potter, where Anderson encountered his mentor, Isaac Deutscher.

Khrushchev's 'Secret Speech' incriminating Stalin at the Twentieth Congress of the Soviet Communist Party (CPSU), in February 1956, had precipitated a crisis in British Communism as in European Communism generally. Within weeks of Anderson's arrival at Oxford, the Soviet repression in Hungary and the Anglo-French Suez expedition were unleashed, leading to the Oxford foundation of the *Universities and Left Review* (*ULR*) as a metropolitan venue for the gathering revolt against the 'orthodoxies' of the Cold War and consumer capitalism that dominated the 'political ice-age'.[2] Edited by Stuart Hall, Gabriel Pearson, Raphael Samuel, and Charles Taylor—the last three, graduates of Balliol—the *ULR* was marked by its equidistance from Stalinism and Atlanticism, proposing, against the grain of Communism and Social-Democracy, a renascent 'humanist' socialism that would 'take socialism at full stretch—as relevant only in so far as it is relevant to the full scale of man's activities'.[3] Independent-socialist, whereas the *New Reasoner*, as late as 1959, still styled itself 'a journal of the democratic Communist opposition' intent upon the regeneration of pre-Stalinist British traditions, the *ULR* nevertheless exhibited a considerable overlap of politics and personnel with its uncle-journal. (Both Samuel and Pearson were from Communist backgrounds.) Alongside articles by the editors, the first issue of spring 1957 featured Eric Hobsbawm and Edward Thompson in the company of David Marquand and John Mackintosh, Deutscher and Claude Bourdet together with G. D. H. Cole and Joan Robinson. Accordingly, whatever the generational-experiential differences and strains, the fusion of the two journals in 1960 to form the *New Left Review* seemed an obvious economy of editorial and political energies. Under the direction of Hall, proclaiming in an inaugural editorial a 'missionary phase' on behalf of non-aligned socialism, the *NLR* constituted an alliance of many, if not quite all, the progressive talents. Its unwieldy editorial board of twenty-five or more would, however, come to exhibit the organizational vices of its cultural virtues.

Entrée

Anderson's initial contributions to the New Left project in each instance highlighted an issue of central importance to the *NLR*'s political horizons: the advent of an independent Third World; the comparative record of North European Social-Democracy; and the European reorientation of British Conservatism.

A year after the Cuban Revolution, in a student offshoot of the *NLR*— the *New University*—Anderson translated Sartre's report of a visit to Havana as the guest of its new rulers ('A Tour with Fidel Castro'), and co-authored an article with Robin Blackburn—'Cuba, Free Territory of America'—conveying for the first (but not the last) time an enthusiasm for the Castro regime. The Cuban Revolution, they wrote, 'can be called a humanism'.[4]

Anderson's debut in the *NLR* was a two-part investigation of Swedish Social-Democracy, then the subject of admiring comparisons by Labour politicians intent upon Scandinavian-style revision of their party's constitutional objectives.[5] In it he evaluated 'Mr. Crosland's Dreamland' according to normative criteria seemingly derived from a Sartrean-existentialist interpretation of Marxism, crossed with Marx's Paris *Manuscripts* (introduced to the British New Left by Charles Taylor in 1958). The relatively egalitarian character of Sweden under Social-Democratic administration was acknowledged, although rumours of a 'classless society' were firmly repudiated.[6] Notwithstanding its universal welfare state, Sweden remained a class-divided capitalist society in which the economy was humanely regulated but not humanely planned. Central planning was no programmatic optional extra of socialism, since it was designed not merely to secure allocative efficiency and equity but to institute collective social agency.[7] Just as capitalism was 'a coherent *totality*—a global mode of human existence which embraces all the diverse activities and institutions of a society and reveals the same organising principles in each of them' (p. 45)—so too a socialist society would be an expressive totality, but a disalienated one. In a Hegelian-Marxist evocation of a dereified, nonatomistic social order beyond capitalism, Anderson wrote:

> Transparency is one of the crucial defining characteristics of socialism: a community in which all the multiple mediations between our public and private existence are visible, where each social event can be seen right back to its source, and legible human intentions read everywhere on the face of the world. (P. 37)

Despite the specialist Sartrean terminology, the principles informing Anderson's critique of the Swedish road issued from the common expressive-humanist lexicon of the New Left. Rejecting the economistic visions of Communism and Social-Democracy, when it invoked Marx, the New Left invariably counterposed the ethical socialism of the young Marx, predicated upon the master category of 'alienation', to the putative determinism of his maturity, as well as his fateful posterity (Stalinism explicitly, Leninism implicitly).[8] Less conventional—indeed, a portent of subsequent wider divergences—was the statement of Andersonian dissent from a key theme of Raymond Williams's *The Long Revolution* (subject to sharp criticism by Thompson for its pacific gradualism in the same issue of the *NLR*):

> It is difficult to see in what sense the *idea* of 'a collective democratic society' . . . is specifically working-class: the literal ideas of socialism have historically mostly come from people who were not working-class themselves. . . . If it is true that 'the major cultural contribution of the working-class in this country has been the collective democratic institution', this is not obviously so: the unions and the Labour Party are in some ways markedly authoritarian structures. . . . More centrally, are working-class institutions really extendable . . . in such a way that they can be naturally enlarged to cover ever greater areas of society as a whole? . . . [I]sn't one of the most disturbing features of unionism . . . the acceptance by the unions of the sectionalism attributed to them by a middle-class 'public'? At a more fundamental level, what is surely most striking about working-class values, is that they are so often *not* transposed from the private realm to the public one: there is a typical hiatus between personal values of solidarity and humanity and public attitudes of indifference or intolerance. . . . It is [the] relative absence in the

3

working-class context [of the values involved in the arts and intellectual enquiry—'culture' in the limited sense of the term] which surely accounts for the vitiation of attitude just discussed. (Pp. 36–37)

Such intimations of a quasi-Gramscian critique of the British labour movement as yet went unelaborated. Meanwhile, a third early article was occasioned by the European suit of Macmillan's Conservative government, buffeted by the accumulating symptoms of national decline despite its third electoral triumph over a divided Labour opposition in 1959. Anderson's re-action approximated a standard socialist response to the Treaty of Rome. 'The Politics of the Common Market',[9] written with Hall, partially echoed German Social-Democrat Kurt Schumacher's denunciation of the Europe of the 'Four K's': *Konservativ, Klerical, Kapitalistich,* and *Kartellistich.* Lock-ing the United Kingdom into a Continental capitalist bloc, entry into the Common Market would severely constrain national room for reformist manoeuvre, without opening up terrain for international socialist advance (pp. 9–10). Summoning the Left to a 'real alternative', Anderson and Hall distanced themselves from any imperial patriotism of the Gaitskellite variety:

> The worst construction which could be placed upon this call is that we should rest on our splendid isolation and depend upon our traditional Empire ties, our 'Empire mission', unreconstructed and untouched, to float us through. This is the call of the past—and no less so because the Left is as susceptible to it as the Right. (P. 13)

As if to confirm the justice of Macmillan's sometime rebuke to de Gaulle— 'You want to rebuild the Holy Roman Empire. We, the Roman Empire'— Anderson and Hall feared that, in the absence of a genuinely internationalist alternative to a Common Market all too congruent with Kennedy's 'Euro-American grand design' for the prosecution of Cold War by other means, 'the British Left will find itself buried deeper and deeper in a political and economic rearrangement of world power which would be fatal to everything which we understand socialism to stand for' (p. 14).

In the event, the day of European reckoning was deferred for a decade. The U.K. application was vetoed by de Gaulle, persuaded by Macmillan's entreaties to Kennedy for donation of the dependent nuclear deterrent that perfidious Albion would function as America's Trojan horse in the Common Market. The beneficiary of Tory disarray was not the New Left, however. Two months after the joint Hall-Anderson article appeared, the Campaign for Nuclear Disarmament (CND), in which so much New Left activism and optimism had been invested as the harbinger of a 'positive neutralism', was repulsed at the Labour Party Conference. The next year, their worst fears about chauvinistic Labour reflexes were realized when Gaitskell conciliated the Left that he had disaffected with his economic and defence policies, by claiming that British membership of the European Economic Community (EEC) would signal 'the end of a thousand years of history'. Thereafter, as Wilson rallied the party on a programme of technocratic 'modernization' in a changed political conjuncture, the original New Left visibly lost compass and coherence.

By now, Anderson was on the board of the *NLR* and about to assume its editorship, following the resignation of an exhausted Hall. Prior to the parting of the ways with Thompson and company, and the germination, in effect, of a new *NLR*, he gave notice of a third distinctive strand in its formation. An affiliation to Western Marxism—originally to Sartre, soon to Gramsci—and a commitment to revolutionary Third World nationalism (Cuba) have already been noted. To these must be added the 'formative influence' of Deutscher. It first found direct expression in the introduction Anderson wrote to accompany publication of a debate on the Central Committee of the Italian Communist Party (PCI) after the Twenty-Second Congress of the CPSU in October 1961, at which Khrushchev had resumed the process of official de-Stalinization.[10] Elsewhere, Anderson notes that Italian Communism assumed the status of a 'coded contrast' with British Labourism for him in the early 1960s.[11] Not only did the intellectual contribution of the former leader of the PCI receive due recognition—the party 'enjoyed in the writings of Gramsci the unique advantage of a sophisticated and indigenous Italian Marxism' (p. 152)—but its political evolution was also singled out for commendation. After 1956, taking its cue from the 'Secret Speech' yet transcending its bureaucratic limits, the PCI had

> discreetly and gradually worked out a political style allowing for some measure of inner-party democracy, and a political stance which is now absolutely distinctive in the world Communist movement: a combination of fluent modernity and lability in the domestic Italian situation and intransigent militancy on colonial issues. . . . The independence and individuality of the PCI have made it not only the most powerful, but the only increasingly successful Communist Party in Western Europe. (P. 153)

If the French 1789 was later to be treated by Anderson as paradigmatic of the 'bourgeois revolution' that England had missed, Italian Communism—and not its Gallic counterpart, then prevaricating over the struggle for

Algerian independence while resisting the logic of de-Stalinization—demonstrated the proletarian internationalism its working-class movement lacked.

Anderson's credulity in the 'regeneration' of the 'modern prince' manqué that was the PCI, casting Amendola in the role of revolutionary renovator, would not survive for very long. As was noted in the 'Decennial Report' on the *NLR* of 1975, Anderson's judgements, converging with the outlook of Deutscher's 'worst book', *The Great Contest* (1960), had 'clearly reflected Deutscherist hopes in the rebirth of the international Communist movement by a process of internal reform' [12]—hopes that were dashed that October by Soviet diplomacy in the Cuban missile crisis and by the ensuing abrogation of domestic de-Stalinization.

Prior to this disillusionment, however, the editorial nucleus of the new *NLR* formed in 1962, with Anderson as editor, flanked by Robin Blackburn and Tom Nairn. In subsequent years they would be joined by (among others) Juliet Mitchell (1963), Quintin Hoare, Ronald Fraser, and Peter Wollen (1964), Gareth Stedman Jones and Alexander Cockburn (1965), Anthony Barnett and Ben Brewster (1966), Branka Magaš and Bob Rowthorn (1967), and Fred Halliday (1968). With the exhaustion of the original New Left, now dispersing, the transitional *NLR* was to be reorientated on the avant-garde model of *Les Temps Modernes*. Moreover, it emulated the anticolonialism and replicated the Third Worldism of Sartre and Beauvoir's journal, which, frustrated by an immobile Stalinism at home, projected its political aspirations abroad—most notoriously, in Sartre's preface to Frantz Fanon's *The Wretched of the Earth* (1961).[13]

Anderson led the way, contributing an extended study, 'Portugal and the End of Ultra-Colonialism', in three instalments, to successive issues of the journal in 1962.[14] On this occasion, the United Kingdom furnished the norm against which 'the peculiarities of Portuguese colonization in Africa', stamped by the 'twin hallmarks of extremism and archaism', were to be gauged:

> Portuguese imperialism is *not* the classic capitalist imperialism. This is not because of moral advance, but because of economic and social retardation. Portuguese colonialism is a failure to achieve the normal imperial pattern, not an option which surpasses it. In the distorting mirror of ideology, the singularity dissolves and reforms in a shape that is transformed out of all recognition.[15]

The details of Anderson's analysis, proposed as the Salazar regime battled insurgent national liberation movements in southern Africa, need not concern us (though it is worth noting his prediction, confirmed a little more than a decade later, that peripheral collapse would detonate metropolitan fascism).[16] Of more immediate moment is evidence of a methodological consciousness of the need (as Anderson put it in the Parisian terminology of the period) to synthesize 'diachronic' and 'synchronic' dimensions in any examination of social formations, if their true specificity was to be grasped. The effect, only anticipated here but soon amplified, was an explicit affiliation of the new editorial committee to Western Marxist philosophical currents, and a tacit self-demarcation from its predecessor's more ecumenical identification with native intellectual traditions. In an arresting footnote, Anderson wrote:

> [A]ny society . . . is at once a *structure* which can only be understood in terms of the inter-relationship of its parts, and a *process* which can only be understood in terms of the cumulative weight of its past. The difficulty is to synthesize the two aspects in any actual study. Liberal history and formalist sociology represent extreme opposed attempts to divorce the two dimensions altogether. . . . The co-existence of the two in the Anglo-Saxon countries marks the limits of the penetration of Marxism in these cultures. For Marxism is the only thought which has rigorously united developmental and structural analysis: it is at once pure historicity (denial of all supra-historical essences) and radical functionalism (societies are significant totalities). This synthesis remains unique.[17]

Reorientations

For the duration of the transition phase, as the new team consolidated, domestic coverage in the *NLR* tended to devolve upon members of the first New Left—for example, John Hughes on the British economy (*NLR* no. 21, October 1963)—or even figures considerably to their right—for example, Wilson's confidant Thomas Balogh on Britain and the Common Market (*NLR* no. 16, July/August 1962). In part a deliberate tactic—to provide political cover for editorial tiros—more importantly, this move reflected the displacement of attention engineered since the Andersonian succession: the profound 'internationalization', at once intellectual and political, of the *NLR*, implying a 'radical left turn'.[18]

The product of the European moment of 1956, the British New Left at the outset had sought to bridge the mutually injurious gulf between 'theory' and 'practice', culture and politics, intellectuals and workers, socialist milieu and Labourist organization. By definition, it was debarred by the mechanisms of democratic centralism from operating in the Communist Party of Great Britain (CPGB)—always numerically small, and significantly weakened by the exodus of 1956, but exercising considerable influence in the trade unions. However, it had established a network of New Left clubs and groups, supported Lawrence Daly's Fife Socialist League in Scotland, militated in the CND, and adopted a stance of 'one foot in, one foot out' vis-à-vis the Labour Party, a proportion of whose activists (and some of whose M.P.'s) were receptive to its initiatives (at a time when the CPGB, at Khrushchevite instigation, opposed unilateral nuclear disarmament).

By contrast, the 'discrepancy between cultural vitality and political weakness' identified by Michael Rustin as a trait common to both New Lefts widened in the case of the new *NLR*. Indeed, it might be said that Anderson and his colleagues made what they regarded as a virtue—although others reckoned it a vice—of necessity. The moment of 1956 having passed, they were without the national social anchorage or continental political relays of their precursors. Reacting to this dilemma, they assumed a posture of militant, self-conscious 'separatism' toward domestic socialist traditions.[19] At home, the *NLR* renounced political mobilization for cultural reformation: the induction of the French and Italian Marxisms that might engender their hitherto absent British counterpart. Abroad, it looked to a regenerated Communist movement and national liberation struggles as vectors of anticapitalist advance, subscribing to structural reformism in the North, revolution in the South.[20]

In view of the subsequent polemics, which frequently generated more heat than light, it is worth recalling that in the early 1960s the availability of what was supposedly an international culture—Marxism—was remarkably limited in Britain. Marx's early works remained untranslated or were only just beginning to appear; the *Grundrisse* would have to wait a further decade or more. For the classical Marxists, non-Russian readers were reliant upon Soviet versions of an embalmed Lenin and limited editions of an anathematized Trotsky. The reception of Luxemburg, Gramsci, and Lukács was some way off; the Western Marxist tradition was virtually unknown. As to English Marxism, of the native intellectuals directly associated with the New Left who rose to international prominence in the 1960s and 1970s, Williams's *Culture and Society* and *The Long Revolution*—both critical of historical materialism—appeared only in 1958 and 1961, respectively; Hill's *Century of Revolution* and Miliband's *Parliamentary Socialism* in 1961; Hobsbawm's *Age of Revolution* in 1962; and Thompson's *Making of the English Working Class* in 1963.

No doubt Anderson and company's peremptory dismissal, or plain neglect, of the prior national Marxist culture, from William Morris in the 1880s down to Maurice Dobb in the 1940s, was injudicious.[21] Yet their perception of a vacuum rather than a tradition, and their suspicion that, ideology abhoring a vacuum, it had all too often been filled with non- or anti-Marxist currents—these contained elements of truth. Throughout Europe a 'long night of theory' had fallen with the onset of the Cold War,[22] to whose Manichaean cultural crudities only independent Marxists were relatively immune (relatively, because, like Deutscher or Sartre, they paid the price of isolation and political impotence). In Britain the postwar reaction compounded the deficits inherited from the 1930s, sanctioning the verities and pieties attendant upon 'Victory in Europe' (not to mention Empire). As Thompson himself bitingly observed in 1960, by the end of the 1940s, 'Wordsworth's Solitary and Dickens' Mr. Podsnap . . . inhabited a single skin'.[23] Before 1956, and for some time thereafter, Britain possessed no extant, cumulative, and autonomous Marxist tradition. To all intents and purposes, 'Marxism' denoted the Soviet-sponsored doctrines of the international Communist movement—what Thompson dubbed 'diabolical and hysterical mysterialism'—and was predictably equated with Stalinism by most friends and foes, even among sections of the original New Left (whose intellectual 'eclecticism' was an explicable reaction to the desolation).[24]

The state of British Marxism had been a cause for self-chastisement in the Communist Party in the 1930s, when a pervasive 'contempt for theory' and 'our traditional and shameful theoretical level' were belaboured.[25] Upon their resignation from it, a quarter of a century later, Thompson and his fellow editor of the *Reasoner*, John Saville, had likewise raised their voices against 'the weakness of the Marxist tradition in England' and the 'shallow growth of Marxist scholarship'.[26] (At the same time, they had insisted thus in the editorial to the first issue of the *New Reasoner*: 'We have no desire to break impetuously with the Marxist and Communist tradition in Britain. On the contrary, we believe that this tradition, which stems from such men as William Morris and Tom Mann, . . . is in need of rediscovery and reaffirmation'.)[27] Whatever the immoderation and indiscrimination of its expression, Anderson's dissatisfaction could claim both precedent and pedigree. What might have passed for a youthful want of generosity soon stood accused, however, of downright hostility, when he and Nairn effectively set about razing the local heritage on account of its putative vices—'populism', 'nationalism', 'moralism', and 'empiricism' prominent among them. Here the *NLR*'s own variant of 'culturalism' disclosed its political motivation.

Reaching a nadir in Orwell's *The Lion and the Unicorn*, with its celebrated subtitle—*Socialism and the English Genius*—and its demagogic recrimination against the *marxisant* intellectuals of the 1930s, the complex targeted by Anderson served as symbolic left-wing antagonist of the dominant culture. For him, it was not completely foreign to the post-1956 New Left, given that many of its Communist representatives had been formed in the aftermath of the Seventh Congress of the Comintern, amid the extolment of national traditions, alongside international obligations, for the sake of antifascist unity—a line inflected, but not rescinded as such, during the Cold War, with the struggle for 'national independence' against U.S. imperialism decreed by the Cominform. (Hence the attempts in these years to invent a domestic line of descent for Marxism accordant with an irreproachably *British Road to Socialism*.)[28]

Anderson's own retrospect of the divergences between the first and second New Lefts illuminatingly, if tactfully, elaborates on the generational theme:

> The conditions that formed the present *New Left Review* were very different. . . . They were colder. Untouched by the afterglow of the War, we never knew the popular élan of the 40s. It was the reactionary consolidation of the 50s that dominated our consciousness. . . . In Britain its major idiom was glutinously chauvinist. . . . These coordinates determined the emergence of a type of internationalism in the NLR after 1963 quite distinct from that of its predecessors. Its relationship to English nationalism, of whatever stripe, was one of hostility rather than harmony. A fierce hatred of the reigning cultural conformism . . . inspired it from the start. We felt no inclination to delve into the native past for a more progressive or alternative tradition to counterpose to the official celebrations of English cultural empiricism and political constitutionalism. For us, the central fact which such enterprises always seemed designed to burke or minimize was the failure of British society to generate any mass socialist movement or significant revolutionary party in the 20th century—alone among major nations in Europe. . . . The internationalism that resulted was a theoretical one. . . . In a word: we did not believe in Marxism in one country.[29]

Yet this is perhaps ultimately to do something of an injustice to the profoundly *political* impulse of that *cultural* reorientation. For if the reference to a 'significant revolutionary party' risks exaggerating political differences between the generations at this stage, by backdating the remaking of the second New Left—the revolutionary 'turn' of Anderson and his colleagues— from 1967–68 to 1962–63, it is nevertheless the case that their mode of Western Marxist theorizing was far from impractically minded. To employ Williams's distinction between 'legitimating', 'academic', and 'operative' variants within postwar British Marxist theory,[30] it seems clear that, located outside party and academy, Anderson and company pertained to the 'operative' category. The burden of Anderson's objection to existing British Marxism in the early 1960s lay in its typical abstraction from the order of comparative historical analysis of contemporary social formations stipulated in the Portugal texts and elsewhere.[31] The inevitable result of such analytical dereliction, so Anderson believed, was a dearth of political—especially strategic—inspiration: disabled from understanding the contemporary world, because of inadequate intellectual resources and/or organizational constraints, British Marxism could scarcely nominate agencies, or prospect strategies, for changing it.

Socialist strategy had, of course, been an urgent concern of Thompson's, both in the pages of the *NLR* and in the volume he edited in 1960, *Out of Apathy*—a collection that exemplifies some of the weaknesses, as well as the strengths, of the first New Left. In 'Revolution', Thompson lamented 'the absence of any theory of the transition to socialism', insisting that '[t]he elaboration of a democratic revolutionary strategy . . . is the immediate task'.[32] For, as he wagered in his introduction, 'At the Point of Decay', the relevant preconditions were in place: Britain was '*over*-ripe for socialism', and there existed an 'immanent community of socialism . . . expressed in the powerful institutions of the Labour movement and in a hundred forms of democratic association and control' (pp. 9, 11). Having, however, reiterated a stock item in the postwar Communist repertoire—'It is the business of socialists to draw the line . . . between the monopolists and the people' (p. 305)—in conclusion he veered off toward a rhetoric decried by Anderson for its 'messianic nationalism':

> Of all Western countries, Britain is perhaps best placed to effect such a transition. The equilibrium here is more precarious, the Labour movement least divided, the democratic socialist tradition most strong. And it is *this* event which could at one blow break up the 'log-jam' of the Cold War and initiate a new wave of world advance. Advance in Western Europe, and further democratization in the East, may wait upon us. . . . It would be foolish to be sanguine. But foolish also to underestimate the long and tenacious tradition of the British commoner. . . . It is a tradition which could leaven the socialist world. (P. 308)[33]

In this light, Stuart Hall's verdict—that, unlike its predecessor, the new *NLR* was '*not* a project which constituted the question of political agency as in any way problematic, either theoretically or strategically'[34]—is imprecise with respect to both terms of his comparison. Anderson's attention, as he legitimately recalled in *Arguments within English Marxism*, encompassed strategic issues as a priority and did involve a problematization of Thompsonian reflections on agency and strategy, taxed with impressionism and romanticism.[35] And if they avoided Thompson's lapses into hortatory rhetoric, his fellow thinkers did not succeed in acquitting the 'immediate task' either, as consultation of Hall's contribution to the 1960 volume—an exhilarating assault on the accommodations of Croslandite revisionism—testifies. In any event, by 1963 local political realities had rendered Thompson's prospectus more than problematic. With the resurgence of the tenacious tradition of British Labourism (now equipped with a commoner for leader), new questions were posed, new answers required.

According to Anderson's critical survey 'The Left in the Fifties', the forces of resistance to the Cold War and consumer capitalism—the Labour Left, the CND, and the first New Left—had lacked the wherewithal for an alternative to them. Unequipped with a theory of the Cold War, the CND had 'objectively challenged the whole contemporary teleology of British society, but never subjectively assumed this challenge'.[36] For its part, destitute of an indigenous Marxism, the New Left had embodied the great English tradition of ethical-cultural critique of industrial civilization, reconstructed by Williams's *Culture and Society*, in which Thompson had located Morris. But it had resorted to a *'populist* and *pre-socialist* idiom' that denied it analytical leverage, 'los[ing] the virtues of cultural energy without gaining those of political efficacy' (pp. 16-17). 'The paradox', Anderson concluded, was

> that at the very moment when the suffocating situation which they had so long resisted suddenly changed, they had spent themselves. The great crisis of Conservative Britain, which exploded in depth in 1961, supervened a few months after the Left had collapsed, demobilized and exhausted. The Labour Left had ceased to provide any serious opposition to party policy. CND was visibly disintegrating. The New Left volatilized. The inheritor of the crisis had another name: Wilson. (P. 18)

Reconnaissance

Having been denationalized, as it were, in 1962, the *NLR* redirected its attention to the United Kingdom during 1963–64, a period that ushered in 'the editorial shift towards the production of a systematic Marxist theory of British history and society'[37] in the guise of what became known as the 'Nairn-Anderson theses'. Yet this preliminary programme, executed as Conservatism foundered and Labourism went over to the offensive, emphatically did not betoken a renationalization of the journal. Intent upon defamiliarization of the national physiognomy, Britain was treated by the authors as if it were a 'foreign' country,[38] and emerged from their recasting unrecognizable to many readers. Quite apart from the iconoclastic conclusions of the theses, this effect was traceable to their exotic ingredients: the transposition of a Gramscian framework, and application of Gramscian categories, to the British social formation.[39] The prior 'internationalization' of the *NLR* was thus doubly operative in this national exploration: in its Continental discourse and comparative historical optic.

As Anderson notes in the foreword to *English Questions*, and as David Forgacs has detailed,[40] Gramsci was virtually unknown to Anglophone Marxist intellectuals at the time. (Limited selections from the *Prison Notebooks*— *The Modern Prince and Other Writings*—had been published by the CPGB's imprint, Lawrence and Wishart, in 1957.) Anderson's own acquaintance with the *Notebooks* dated from his encounter with Nairn, who in 1963 contributed an essay to the PCI journal *Il Contemporaneo* that tabled the research agenda pursued in the ensuing series of articles in the *NLR*.[41]

Gramsci's stress upon 'an accurate reconnaissance of each individual country',[42] not in national isolation but from a historical vantage point of international interdependence, may be said to have furnished the standard of the kind of 'country study'—whether of First, Second, or Third World states—conducted in the *NLR* from 1962 onward. In Gramsci's own investigations of Italian history and politics, and sidelights on England and Germany, the privileged comparator was France—in particular, the contrast between the Jacobin phase of its 'bourgeois revolution' and the Italian Risorgimento: '[h]istorical relationship between the modern French state created by the Revolution and the other modern states of continental Europe. This comparison is vitally important—provided that it is not made on the basis of abstract sociological schemas' (p. 114).[43] Thus, in the passage that is the source of the Nairn-Anderson theses, he instanced '[d]ifferences between France, Germany and Italy in the process by which the bourgeoisie took power (and England)':

> It was in France that the process was richest in developments, and in active and positive political elements. In Germany, it evolved in ways which in certain aspects resembled what happened in Italy, and in others what happened in England. . . . In England, where the bourgeois revolution took place before that in France, we have a similar phenomenon to the German one of fusion between the old and the new—this notwithstanding the extreme energy of the English 'Jacobins', i.e., Cromwell's 'roundheads'. The old aristocracy

remained as a governing stratum, with certain privileges, and it too became
the intellectual stratum of the English bourgeoisie (it should be added that
the English aristocracy has an open structure, and continually renews itself
with elements coming from the intellectuals and the bourgeoisie). (Pp. 82–83)

Implicitly positioned on this spectrum of historical 'differences', the *differentia specifica* of the English case was Nairn and Anderson's explicit object.
They intended not an 'abstract sociological schema' but instead—observing
Gramsci's own injunction on the synthesis of systemic and genetic analysis
(p. 353)[44]—a 'concrete analysis of the relations of force' in contemporary
English state and society, as transmitted by their modern historical past
(p. 185).

The centrepiece of the theses was Anderson's 'Origins of the Present
Crisis', published in January 1964, whose title conveys their purpose.[45]
Regretting the absence of 'even the outline of a "totalizing" history of modern British society', Anderson argued that 'until our view of Britain today is
grounded in some vision of its effective past, however misconceived and
transient this may initially be, we will continue to lack the basis for an
understanding of the contradictory movements of our society, which alone
could yield a strategy for socialism' (p. 16). Anderson's ambition, then, was
to conceive the past accurately so as to interpret the present aright and
thereby meet a precondition for transforming it into a socialist future. Since
the past was an 'effective' one, a genealogy of the present was indispensable
to its political comprehension and transformation. Theoretical history was a
necessary condition of adequate socialist practice. Accordingly, it is not surprising that much criticism of Anderson concentrated upon his supposed
'misconce[ptions]' of the past, since they allegedly distorted the 'vision' of
contemporary Britain, therewith frustrating, rather than facilitating, a viable
'strategy for socialism'.

Methodologically, three defining Gramscian characteristics of the joint
enterprise may be isolated. The first—akin to J. S. Mill's 'method of difference'—is a focus upon the *singularities*, as opposed to the *similarities*, of
the national variant of capitalism: 'the differential formation and development of British capitalist society' (p. 16), or the 'peculiarities of the
English', as Thompson's riposte had it. The second is consideration of the
'longer *durées*'—'the distinctive overall trajectory of modern British society
since the emergence of capitalism' (p. 16)—as the key to the current conjuncture. And the third is *antieconomism*, a dual break with the orthodox
base/superstructure topography of Marx's 1859 preface to *A Contribution
to the Critique of Political Economy*. This is apparent both in the postulated

disjunction between the economic structure (capitalism) and the political-ideological structures (ancien régime/traditionalism), implying that the dominant class economically was not the ruling class politically; and in the sovereign power assigned to culture in the reproduction of the British social order—'culturalism' as the antidote to 'mechanicism', in Gramscian terms.

In 'Origins' the substantive theses on the national trajectory were assembled under four headings: the *prematurity* and *impurity* of the English 'bourgeois revolution' in the mid-seventeenth century, bequeathing a dominant agrarian capitalism and an allied mercantile capitalism, their class compact being sealed with the Glorious Revolution; the *priority* of the English Industrial Revolution, and its coincidence with counterrevolutionary nationalist mobilization against France at the end of the eighteenth century—the former polarizing, the latter sublating, a precocious proletariat and a subaltern bourgeoisie; the *supremacy* of British imperialism in the late nineteenth century, with its domestic legacy of enduring aristocratic hegemony; and the exceptional *continuity* of British state and society in the twentieth century, spared external destruction (via world war) or internal reconstruction (via reformation from above or revolution from below) (pp. 17–29). The consequent distinctiveness of the U.K. class structure was summarized thus:

> After a bitter, cathartic revolution, which transformed the structure but not the superstructures of English society, a landed aristocracy, underpinned by a powerful mercantile affinal group, became the first dominant capitalist class in Britain. This dynamic agrarian capitalism expelled the English peasantry from history. Its success was economically the 'floor' and sociologically the 'ceiling' of the rise of the industrial bourgeoisie. Undisturbed by a feudal state, frightened by the French Revolution and its own proletariat, subdued by the prestige and authority of the landed class, the bourgeoisie won two modest victories [i.e., the Reform Act and the repeal of the Corn Laws], lost its nerve and ended by losing its identity. The late Victorian era and the high noon of imperialism welded aristocracy and bourgeoisie together in a single social bloc. The working class fought passionately and unaided against the advent of industrial capitalism; its exhaustion after successive defeats was the measure of its efforts. Henceforward it evolved, separate but subordinate, within the apparently unshakeable structure of British capitalism, unable, despite its great numerical superiority, to alter the fundamental nature of its society. (Pp. 29–30)

Having reconnoitred its historical genesis, Anderson turned to the contemporary structure of British society, under a rubric—'History and Class

Consciousness: Hegemony'—that indicated the Gramscian-Lukácsian provenance and culturalist tenor of his account of hegemony, centred upon class
consciousness.[46] Three interrelated topics were treated: the character of the
dominant ideology; the distinction between hegemonic and corporate ideology or class consciousness (with a corresponding critique of Labourism); and
the configuration of class power in the United Kingdom.

In sum, the English ideology was a 'comprehensive conservatism'—a
compound of 'traditionalism' and 'empiricism', the one venerating the past,
the other abolishing any future. It inscribed the 'historical experience' of the
industrial bourgeoisie, which had been relieved of the mission of overthrowing a feudal state by the New Model Army and had, of its own accord, abdi-
cated responsibility for class rule, deferring to elders and betters whose cultural hegemony had been rejuvenated by the imperial meridian.[47] Its 'one
articulated ideology with universal claims' was a nullity: utilitarianism—an
unsuitable candidate for hegemonic status, given the 'cultural nihilism' of its
incorrigible Gradgrindery (pp. 31–32).

The bourgeoisie had contributed empiricism to the traditionalism it ea-
gerly assimilated. What of the proletariat? Replacing Marx's 'class-in-itself'/
'class-for-itself' couplet with a 'hegemonic'/'corporate' polarity, Anderson
maintained that the proletariat was dispossessed of any 'hegemonic ideology' and marked, instead, by 'an immovable corporate class consciousness'
seemingly unsusceptible to revisionism yet no less unamenable to socialism.
This 'paradox', explicable by reference to the discontinuity of its nineteenth-
century experience, divided by the watershed of 1848, was

> the most important single fact about the English working class. If a hege-
> monic class can be defined as one which imposes its own ends and vision
> on society as a whole, a corporate class is conversely one which pursues its
> own ends within a social totality whose overall determination lies outside
> it. A hegemonic class seeks to transform society in its own image, inventing
> afresh its economic system, its political institutions, its cultural values,
> its 'mode of insertion' into the world. A corporate class seeks to defend
> and improve its own position within a social order accepted as given. The
> English working class has been characterized since the mid nineteenth cen-
> tury by a disjunction between an intense consciousness of separate identity
> and a continuous failure to set and impose goals for society as a whole. In
> this disjunction lies the secret of the special nature of the labour move-
> ment in England. . . . It has not been lack of class consciousness but—
> in one sense—excess of it which has been the obstacle to the spread of
> socialism. (P. 33)

Having demoted the industrial bourgeoisie and deflated the proletariat of the *Communist Manifesto* and *Capital*, let alone orthodox Marxist historiography, Anderson embarked upon a critique of Labourism. Deprived of significant intellectual reinforcements until the end of the nineteenth century, the working class had suffered, when they finally arrived, from their boon: Fabianism, a paternalistic strain of the utilitarian bacillus. In contrast to France, where the Enlightenment was bequeathed by the *philosophes* and radicalized by their inheritors, '[i]n England, a supine bourgeoisie produced a subordinate proletariat. It handed on no impulse of liberation, no revolutionary values, no universal language. All it transmitted were the deadly germs of utilitarianism, from which the Labour Party has sickened in the twentieth century' (p. 35). Williams's assessment of working-class culture— already queried in Anderson's reflections on Swedish Social-Democracy— was now criticized for its failure to differentiate between hegemonic and corporatist institutions.[48] Not so much a modern prince as a latter-day retainer, the Labour Party, its name symbolizing its resignation to the persistence of capitalism, incarnated corporatism. Its record, whether in opposition or government, had consistently demonstrated its acceptance of a secondary station in the national life (pp. 37–39).

Finally, Anderson addressed the modalities of the hegemonic system as 'an overall order'. In any advanced capitalist society, power was 'polycentric' (a term adopted from Italian Communism). In accordance with one reading of the *Prison Notebooks*, he asserted 'the supremacy of civil society over the state' in contemporary Britain, where

> there is a very specific configuration [of class power], the product of a particular historical and geographical situation. Schematically, three main idiosyncrasies of this structure of power stand out: the relative insignificance of bureaucratic or military forms, the unusually immediate striking-capacity of economic forms, and the ultimately crucial importance of ideological and cultural forms. Together this combination may be defined . . . as the supremacy of civil society over the State. (P. 40)

Parliament—the official locus of sovereignty—was unintelligible outside this triangular constellation. The 'ransom of hegemony', parliamentary democracy was a component of the latter when Conservatism wielded power but unavailing against it when Labourism occupied office. For all the Attlee reforms, a 'permanent net superiority of the hegemonic class' constituted 'the reality of social peace and political democracy in England today' (pp. 42–43).

In a concluding section—'Increasing Entropy'—Anderson contemplated the nemesis of the pioneer. Britain was now evincing a 'general malady of the society, infrastructure and superstructure alike', its economy misshapen by the City of London, its state in thrall to 'an anachronistic economic liberalism' that transcribed the supremacy of civil society over it (pp. 43–44). Having belatedly deigned to apply for Common Market membership, Britain had been rebuffed. Therewith, Conservativism had lost the chance of 'renovating British capitalism without a major political and social crisis at home':

> The international pressures of contemporary capitalism require a radical adaptation. The unfinished work of 1640 and 1832 must be taken up where it was left off. The opportunity this crisis offers the labour movement is correspondingly great. It is clear from the preceding, or any analysis of its history and ideology, that it is incapable of tabling a socialist transformation in any immediate future. For that Labour would have to transform itself into a socialist party first. But between this perspective and the role of executor of bourgeois reform and stabilization, which some socialists are already predicting for it, there lies a wide gamut of choices. What will these choices be, and which forces will fight to determine them, are the questions which will dominate the coming years. (Pp. 46–47)

The coming year—1964—was dominated by the progress toward office of the Labour Party, which narrowly won the general election that October on a modernizing programme. Anderson's analysis of Labourism was extended by Nairn in a two-part article written for the PCI journal *Critica Marxista*, whose second instalment coincided with the formation of Wilson's minority government.[49] Contrasting Labour with its Continental sister parties of the Socialist International, Nairn's anatomy was even more scathing than 'Origins'. Ideologically, Labour was blessed with a mélange of Fabianism and Methodism, where they could boast Marxism. Politically, Labourism was the translation of trade unionism, yielding the division of labour between economism and electoralism institutionalized in the party's organizational structure by the 1918 constitution. That constitution, moreover, knew its place in the national community, the 'dead souls of Labourism' respecting the precedence of ancestral spirits in the syndrome of Burke's peerage, Carron's law.

Anderson, meanwhile, issued a 'Critique of Wilsonism', prudently dated (21 September 1964), which detected a striking contrast with Gaitskellism.[50] Labour 'now possesses a coherent analysis of British society today, a long-term assessment of its future, and an aggressive strategy based on both' (p. 4). However, although adjudging Wilson a 'dynamic and capable leader'

(p. 22), Anderson foresaw that the economic crisis enhancing Labour's chances under his leadership might well rebound upon it under his premiership. For the Labour programme was shot through with 'ambiguities and evasions':

> In every field at home Labour's present programme is radical within limits which always fall short of a serious confrontation of the power structure of British society. This is the secret of Wilson's success as a party leader and a national politician. It is also the reason why socialists must take their distances from the Labour programme and criticize it from a fully independent perspective. Anything less is an abandonment of autonomy and principle. (P. 20)

Urging the 'policy of presence' he admired in Italian Communism, Anderson insisted that autonomy should not be expressed in the form of an 'abstract maximalism' voluntaristically issuing socialist demands to Labourist governance: 'at every point the Left should try to press *demands which are firmly rooted in the present problems and perspectives of the Labour movement, but which creatively prolong and surpass them*' (p. 23). Three sectors suggested themselves: a democratization of British society; workers' control in exchange for the impending wage restraint; and a cultural policy (pp. 24–27). As to the last:

> The struggle for a liberated culture today is not in any sense a secondary or supplementary one. It is inseparable from the notion of socialism itself. The culture of a society is its consciousness of itself. In the advanced capitalist countries of our time, *consciousness* is the condition of any meaningful social change. (P. 27)

Wilson's marginal victory, less than a month later, was greeted with an *NLR* editorial,[51] which speculated that Labour would be obliged to 'act radically' or expire, and claimed that—'[f]ortunately'—the new prime minister appreciated this fact (p. 3). His radicalism was likely to differ little from widely touted recipes for the reversal of national decline. Yet its reverberations were likely to be very different:

> To a certain extent . . . , in order to survive, Labour will be forced to polarize opinion, to create polemic and a more vital struggle than the ones that have animated British political life since the end of the last Labour government in 1951. It has no choice but the tactic of divide and conquer. An era of real conflict, of partisan battles whose lines inevitably coincide at least partly

with class: this is perhaps the most hopeful prospect, in these first weeks of a new Labour government. (P. 3)

With the benefit of hindsight, we know that the only thing the Labour administration managed to divide and conquer was itself. These citations are sufficient, however, to indicate that the Nairn-Anderson theses not only possessed a political rationale, they also had an immediate political occasion—albeit they were not reducible to it. Partisans and artisans of an 'operative' Marxism, they were sponsoring in these years a form of culturalist reformism whose major premiss was that '*consciousness* is the condition of any meaningful social change'. Their work did not warrant accusations of academicism and theoreticism.[52] In his 1964 review of *The Making of the English Working Class*, Nairn had concluded, much to the disgust of its author, that '[t]he English working class, immunized against theory like no other class, by its entire historical experience, *needed* theory like no other. It still does'.[53] Provision of the requisite theory—in the first instance, by systematic experimentation with it in the British laboratory—was the strategic priority determined by the selection of cultural reformation as the precondition of social transformation. As regards the relationship between Andersonian theory and Wilsonian promise, despite unguarded optimism about the latter's radicalizing logic, Anderson and Nairn did not render socialist aspiration coterminous with Labourist ambition. '[E]xecutor of bourgeois reform and stabilization' was precisely the vocation that the government must eschew: the theses were thus no mere apologia for the 'white heat of technology'. Indeed, in his 'Critique of Wilsonism', Anderson had rebuked the 'temptation' to criticize British retardation 'from the implicit standpoint of capitalist efficiency and rationality' (p. 9), ghosting the script of the routines of Labour's 'New Britain': 'temporization with capitalism, collusion with imperialism' (p. 17).

Projections

Richard Johnson has written that the Nairn-Anderson theses, and the controversy they sparked, revolved around 'not just the "peculiarities" but . . . the "*potentialities*" of the English'.[54] Anderson's sense of those potentialities and, more generally, the strategic perspectives underlying the theses, can be better appreciated by consultation of a key related essay, 'Problems of Socialist Strategy', which we shall expound before examining their reception.

'Problems' was published in 1965 in a collective volume—*Towards Socialism*—that could be regarded as the new *NLR*'s response to *Out of Apathy*, appearing, together with 'Origins' and 'The Nature of the Labour

Party', alongside texts by figures across the left spectrum, from Labourist notables (Balogh and Crossman), via independent socialists (e.g., Williams), to a Sartrean Marxist (André Gorz).[55] As we have seen, in the foreword to *English Questions*, Anderson remarks that just as the French 1789 afforded the paradigm of the 'bourgeois revolution' England had evaded, so Italian Communism functioned as a 'coded contrast' with British Labourism in his early work.[56] In 'Problems' the contrast is uncoded. Taking his cue from an ideal-typical Continental Communism, which supplied the terms of his comparisons and contrasts with 'Leninism' and 'Labourism', Anderson sponsored the kind of structural-reformist strategy for socialism in the West that would be familiarized as 'Eurocommunism' in the 1970s.

Making Thompson's starting point in 'Revolution'—the British Left's lack of a plausible strategy for socialism—his own, Anderson suggested that this was merely the insular incidence of a European phenomenon, attributable to the paralyzing effects of the Cold War (pp. 221–22). Echoing Sartre's dilemma in *The Communists and Peace*—the inherently contradictory endeavour to theorize the practice of the French Communist Party from an 'extrinsic' standpoint—Anderson sounded a leitmotiv of his oeuvre:

> The Labour Party is unquestionably not a socialist party; yet it is the sole mass party of the working-class in England. It is thus equally impossible to formulate a strategy from 'inside' or 'outside' it. In these conditions, any attempt to consider some of the problems involved in a march towards socialism must necessarily be *abstract* and *inorganic*. For in the absence of a mass socialist party, there is no concrete coherent perspective from which to embark on such an attempt. . . . However, . . . a survey of alternatives may still be better than the void around which socialist discussion at present endlessly circulates. (P. 223)

Anderson's survey of the traditional alternatives—revolutionary/Communist (the Third International) and reformist/Social-Democratic (the Second International)—involved the adoption of a forthright position on them. And however 'abstract and inorganic' his own perspective might have been vis-à-vis British Labourism, it was both 'concrete' and 'coherent', for it was based upon a European model.

The two received conceptions of socialist strategy 'became ruling visions on different sides of the great geo-political divide which runs between Western and Eastern Europe; they correspond to two worlds and two histories'. If this was so, Western Social-Democratic condemnation of Eastern Communism as 'totalitarian' was superficial:

In Russia, and in Yugoslavia, Lenin's vision came true: in other East European
countries, it was realized artificially, and deformed. But all over a vast
area . . . socialism in the most preliminary sense was realized: the expropriators were expropriated, and social ownership of the economy achieved. To
this day, these conquests—with all their blinding accompaniment of force
and terror—remain the only indisputable monuments of the socialist movement. . . . Socialism in its full . . . sense—as the realm of freedom, the final
triumph of man over necessity and alienation—has . . . not remotely been
realized in Russia or any other Eastern country. In this sense, it is right and
necessary to repudiate the Communist states' designation of themselves as
the 'socialist countries'. At the same time, it is pedantic and parochial to
refuse a certain historical truth to the description: in a minimal-ideal sense,
these countries are socialist—their economies are socially and not privately
appropriated, and the ideology which regulates their operation is a socialist
one. It is . . . true that they are not democratic, and democracy is integral to
an authentic socialism. However, merely to denounce them as undemocratic
and therefore as historically illegitimate is a form of blindness. The categories of this criticism are simply not fundamental enough. (P. 225)[57]

The economic, political, and cultural retardation sanctioning Leninism as
a strategy entailed an environment of 'scarcity' that, by the same token,
precluded realization of an authentic socialism east of the Elbe. In this
(Deutscherite) geopolitical perspective, philosophically underwritten by
Sartre's *Critique of Dialectical Reason*, Stalinism was semidiscontinuous,
semicontinuous with Leninism. The Russian Revolution and its progeny
formed 'an immense part . . . of the common heritage of the whole socialist
movement' and could not be disowned by it (pp. 226–27).[58]

Leninism was adapted to the geopolitical realities of its own social formation where, following Gramsci, Anderson identified the state as supreme
and civil society as 'impalpable' (p. 228).[59] For precisely these reasons, it
was at once unviable and undesirable in the West:

Leninism . . . , with all its inhuman costs, represented an immense, pro-
methean progress for Russia, as it does today for China. But its very adaptation to its Eastern environment . . . radically *disadapts* it from the Western
milieu where capitalism remains supreme today. For the societies of Western
Europe constitute a wholly different universe from those of Eastern Europe,
let alone Asia. Their highly advanced economies and their complex, dense,
tessellated histories have created a social and cultural world entirely their
own. The great political achievement of this world has been democracy.

Whatever its lacunae or limitations, this democracy represents a permanent acquisition of mankind. . . . [I]t is important to emphasize that a Leninist strategy in the West is fundamentally *regressive*: it threatens to destroy a vital historical creation, when the task is to surpass it. And, in fact, Leninism as such has not had any success in Western Europe; it has never come near to doing so. Neither as norm nor as strategy is it an acceptable option. It is refused by the whole cultural texture of the advanced capitalist societies of the West. (P. 230)

Based upon an interpretation of Gramsci that Anderson would later discard, [60] this commentary yields a provisional set of conceptual and political polarities, rooted in the historic geopolitical divide, that might be depicted as in figure 1.

Eastern Europe	Western Europe
Economic backwardness	Advanced capitalism
State	Civil society
Dictatorship	Democracy
Coercion/violence	Culture/hegemony
Revolution	Reformism
Communism	Social-Democracy

Figure 1. East and West

How had Social-Democracy performed in its setting? Poorly: 'There is not one socialist society in Western Europe, in any sense of the term, after sixty years of social-democracy's existence' (p. 231). As to its reformist achievements—in pride of place the welfare state—these were not exclusive to it; postwar Christian Democracy had a comparable record. Indeed, the principal advances in the West should be accredited to liberalism in its Keynesian form. Social-Democracy in fact constituted a 'false adaptation' to its Western environment; in view of the Bad Godesberg conference of the German Social-Democratic Party (SPD), the parliamentary road seemed set to terminate not in socialism but in the 'suicide of social-democracy' (pp. 234–35).

The culprit was a strategic flaw at the heart of the Social-Democratic manifesto: 'a basic . . . misconception of the nature of power in advanced capitalist societies and the means of attaining it' (p. 235). This impinged less upon the reformism per se of Social-Democracy than upon its characteristic shape: parliamentarism. Misconstruing power in capitalist democracies as 'monocentric' and the legislature as its autonomous, sovereign instance, Social-Democracy was oblivious of the realities of the system which imprisons it. Mesmerized by the juridical sovereignty of Parliament, it utterly fails to see its sociological heteronomy. . . . [T]he attempt to win power by staking everything on the electoral contest is doomed from the outset. A social-democratic government is . . . possible; but it is always unable to realize the radical social transformation which it is ostensibly committed to achieve. The reason is two-fold. Objectively, it is circumscribed and neutralized by the immense aggregate power preserved by the hegemonic class in all the other sectors of the power structure. Subjectively . . . it has already been contained at the level of its own announced intentions. (P. 236)

Accordingly, we can add to our depiction of polarities in figure 1 'successful' under 'East', and 'unsuccessful' under 'West'. Yet these contrasting records were equally explicable by the statism common to the *frères ennemis*—the difference being that whereas the Eastern environment dictated this bias in socialist strategy, replication of it in the West neglected precisely what had to be confronted. Just as any country was a 'précis of its past' (Gramsci), so in Western countries the state was a 'résumé of civil society' (Marx). There, 'in conditions of diminishing scarcity, civil society predominates politically over the State, and determines it in its image. *The heteronomy of the State is the root cause of the failure of social-democracy'* (p. 237). The 'polycentric' power structure of advanced capitalist societies, and the 'autonomy of civil society' therein, required of socialists an alternative strategy—one that, having recognized the inadmissibility of Leninism, surmounted the naivety of Social-Democracy (pp. 237–39).

In Western Europe any socialist party must be a 'hegemonic party', based on the working class. Given that the proletariat was a social minority in most capitalist countries, however, the party would have to win the allegiance, and synthesize the aspirations, of other popular forces and social agents as well. Here a socialist intelligentsia assumed its full significance. Having identified civil society as the locus of capitalist hegemony in conditions of advanced liberal democracy, Anderson inferred a corresponding counterhegemonic role for socialist culture, articulated by an anticapitalist intelligentsia. Cultural avant-gardism was thus prescribed, even as Leninism was proscribed, in the West. The 'only full tenants of culture in a capitalist society', intellectuals were decisive in 'mediating' the relationship between the working class and culture. By dint of the preponderance of the superstructure in contemporary capitalism, 'irradiat[ing] the whole society as never before' with the dominant ideology, the 'counter-attacking role of socialist culture . . . becomes more and more crucial' (pp. 240-41). The task of a hegemonic party was to unite the potential agencies of socialism in '*a new historical bloc*', not to aggregate them in an electoral coalition. In its organization and practices, it must 'prefigure' to the present the socialist society of the future (pp. 242–44). Its predominant sphere of operations must, by definition, be civil society:

> This is the most fundamental of all the traits of a hegemonic party. . . . In Western Europe . . . capitalist hegemony is first and foremost entrenched in civil society, and must be beaten there. . . . There can be no serious talk of 'smashing' the power structure in the West. . . . In Western Europe this would mean shattering civil society itself, whereas the real task is to *free* civil society from the dominion of capital. This requires the liberating activity of the party in the *quick of social existence*—rather than in its formalized representation in Parliament. . . . This is the only way in which the consciousness of men, rather than the opinion of voters, can finally be changed. And this is the crux of the whole problem. . . . [I]t is only by changing their consciousness that socialism . . . can be achieved. (Pp. 244–45)

Socialist hegemony in civil society, where social power originated, was the precondition of meaningful electoral success, since it was the foundation of the substantive political power then exercised via state institutions (legislature and executive). Its sights set upon 'a *permanent sociological majority*' (p. 246), a successful hegemonic socialist party would not 'administer' the status quo but 'transform' society.

Judging from Anderson's earlier piece on the PCI, Italy might possess a party with the indicated hegemonic ambitions and potential. What of Britain's Labour Party? Here, extrapolating and anticipating somewhat, we may establish a subdivision within the geopolitical divide (as shown in figure 2), polarizing Britain and Italy within the West European zone.

Italy	Britain
Communism	Labourism
Hegemony/culturalism	Corporatism/economism
Marxism	Fabianism
Croce/Gramsci	Burke/the Webbs
Historicism/humanism	Traditionalism/empiricism
Polycentrism/civic socialism	Monocentrism/statism
Radical social transformation	Piecemeal social engineering

Figure 2. Italian Communism and British Labourism

Anderson's twelve-page tour of Labour (pp. 247–59) could not but itemize the consummate discrepancy between the ideal hegemonic party and the actual Labour Party. The two were virtually incommensurable magnitudes. Labour's comparative national failure could be computed by its relative Continental bonus: a social structure in which the manual working class made up a sizeable majority of the electorate. Labour could not match the Conservative performance in securing electoral loyalty from its class constituency. Internally, passive union affiliates preternaturally swelled Labour's membership totals; individual adherence was, however, dwarfed by that of the Conservative Party, which, indeed, had more workers in its ranks than did the party of the 'working man'.[61] Bereft of a viable youth movement and a reliable press, Labour displayed the many 'insignia of [its] subordination' (p. 255).

Tackling the modification of this situation, which would involve Labour converting the proletarian social majority into a socialist political hegemony, Anderson cautioned against both psephological fetishism of the pseudo-'realist' variety (predating the magical-realist genre of today) and any abstract humanism by way of left-wing response. Aiming at Thompson, as well as Gaitskell and his ilk, he wrote:

> The two approaches are apparently extreme opposites. But in fact they share a fundamental *abstraction.* Whether society is seen as a quantum of electors . . . or as a community of 'ordinary men and women' . . . its concrete, determinate reality . . . vanishes. . . . A *strategy* for socialism must be anchored in the objective structure of society, not merely in subjective sentiment. Above all, it must be based on a coherent class analysis. (Pp. 259–60)

The details of the sectoral analysis to which Anderson proceeded need not detain us. Two features of it, nevertheless, call for some comment. First, as regards the working class, Anderson was uncharacteristically insistent upon the beneficent effects of unionization. Trade union membership typically induced an alteration of class consciousness; and since consciousness—not cash—was the mainspring of political allegiance, expanding it was a vital priority (p. 263). In this connection, the trend toward 'instrumental collectivism' among the working class discerned by some contemporary sociologists (Lockwood and Goldthorpe), was to be welcomed as providing an opportunity for socialist ideology to penetrate a hitherto impervious corporatist universe; not feared as portending the waning of class and an Americanization of British politics:

> The incursion of rationalism into the hermetic world of the English working class is a necessary stage in its emancipation. . . . It is the precondition of a

genuinely ideological collectivism—founded on *ideas*, and not merely on instinct. . . . Capitalist hegemony in Britain is founded on an ideology of stupefied traditionalism and empiricism, an anti-ideology which is the enemy of all ideas and calculation. 'Instrumental collectivism' threatens to weaken its hold radically. (P. 265)

Generation of a 'genuinely ideological collectivism' was the ultimate responsibility of the intelligentsia, whose contribution to the hegemonic project would be a 'qualitative' one. Britain lacked an intelligentsia in the strict (Continental) sense but possessed intellectuals in the broad meaning of the term. (Teachers, scientists, artists, writers, academics, and students were among the categories enumerated.) As the *'sources of consciousness* in society', they potentially pulled a weight out of all proportion to their actual number:

They are . . . the artisans of the formal culture of the society. No socialist ideology which does not enlist the support and participation of significant sections of these groups has any hope of making a serious impact on society at large. These intellectuals will be the inevitable mediators of any major intellectual change in Britain. . . . In other words, the necessarily ideological contest for a permanent majority must also be fought and won where ideology originates—in the intelligentsia. (Pp. 269–70)

Following a brief discussion of the condition of women in modern Britain (pp. 276–78), which criticized the Labour Party for its failure even to recognize that 'the whole horizontal class system is cross-structured by a deep vertical system of sexual inequality' (p. 277),[62] Anderson ventured some political conclusions. Chief among them was a logical deduction from Gramscian premises: 'a systematic effort to *marry the structure of the socialist movement to the contours of civil society. . . . In effect, socialist strategy must aim at entering and inhabiting civil society at every possible point, establishing an entire alternative system of power and culture within it'* (p. 279).

As Anderson affirmed in the final section of the essay—'Ideology'—his strategic recommendations were dependent upon 'one immediate precondition: a socialist ideology' (p. 282). Labour was not, of course, the bearer of any such thing; it would have to come from elsewhere. Now, a crucial implication of Gramsci's conception of ideology was that a socialist party aspiring to hegemony would be

characterized by its integration of national cultural traditions which constitute . . . a criticism of the existing social order. In Britain, these traditions
are especially numerous and strong. . . . Any socialist ideology . . . which
does not incorporate [them] . . . as constituent elements will inevitably fail;
it will remain abstract and external, unable to affect popular sensibility or
imagination. (P. 283)

The three most obvious contenders for incorporation were those anatomized
in 'The Left in the Fifties': the antagonistic working-class consciousness of
which the Labour Left was the expression; the humanitarian liberalism that
had informed the CND; and the 'culture and society' tradition inherited by
the first New Left.

A shared theme of these three discourses—one of considerable resonance in Britain—was 'democracy'. The tendency to substitute 'democratization' for 'socialization' was pronounced in the programmes of European
Social-Democracy, bewitched, then as now, by the spectre of a Democrat in
the White House. It had a positive dimension in general—counteracting the
ideological consequences of the Cold War canard that democracy and socialism were incompatible—and in particular—spotlighting the oligarchical nature of British society. Yet since the very state that travestied democracy
flattered itself the creator and donor of it to less fortunate breeds, it was
perilous terrain for mobilization, prone to parliamentary definition and Conservative confiscation (pp. 285–86). Socialist hegemony demanded 'a much
richer and much more complex ideology' than did democracy (p. 286).
Relaying the emphases of the humanist interpretation of Marx—synthesized
in Jean-Yves Calvez's magisterial *La pensée de Karl Marx* (1956)—Anderson
proclaimed the goal of socialist thought to be nothing less than a 'philosophical anthropology—a total theory of man' (p. 287), which would lay the
foundations for a normative critique of the alienations of capitalism and a
'new model of civilization' (p. 289).

Anderson was acutely aware of the gulf separating Britannic reality from
Parisian rhapsody:

As often happens, theoretical debate has in recent years overshot the limits
of practical politics, and so inevitably remained somewhat abstract and academic. To this extent, we are in a situation not unlike that of the 1840s,
when a rarefied intellectual 'criticism', divorced from political struggle, predominated in Germany. The task now is to join the two, developing and en-
larging theory in the light of a new practice. (P. 289)

Pending that juncture, 'Problems of Socialist Strategy' ended with a statement of the young Anderson's credo:

> Socialism as a movement and a critique is based on human *needs* and these needs evolve with society itself. The great, permanent landmark of real abundance will not be the end of ideology, but the *end of necessity*. The empire of scarcity, and its curse, will be over. Integral human freedom will at last be possible. Meanwhile, elsewhere in the world, in Asia, Africa and Latin-America, men will still struggle to create a socialism of privation and duress. This must never be forgotten, in the task of creating in the advanced capitalist countries a socialism of liberty and privilege. The aims of both are ultimately the same: they are divided by all the immense distance of different historical time. The last and most vital test of an authentic European socialism is to remember this, and to maintain the fraternity between the two. (P. 290)

Generalities

Anderson would retract 'Problems of Socialist Strategy', which was never reprinted, as partaking of the 'illusions of left social-democracy' in its prioritization of civil society/culture and relegation of the state/coercion.[63] The 'Decennial Report' on the *NLR* arraigned its departure from classical Marxism, 'compromises with reformism', and endowment of Labourism with a Gramscian vocation, which had indulged the pernicious 'delusion' that a transformed Labour Party could act as the vehicle of a British transition to socialism. It attested to an 'unmistakable accommodation to Wilsonism' in the *Review* in this period (pp. 15–17).[64]

Setting this retrospective revulsion to one side, six general observations might be made on the light that 'Problems' sheds on Anderson's project. For this remarkable text anticipates many of the themes and cruces of his work thereafter.

The first concerns the principal topic: socialist strategy. Incomparably richer than anything produced on the subject by the first New Left, 'Problems', whatever its demerits, represented a concerted endeavour to complement the Gramscian diagnosis of the singularities of British history and society with a Gramscian prognosis for British socialism. In its broad outline, the strategy it sketched is a premonition of the Eurocommunism against which Anderson would set a revolutionary-Marxist face in the 1970s. *Prison Notebooks* was thus both a conceptual and a political resource, yielding proscription (Leninism) and prescription (structural reformism) alike.

'Problems' amply vindicates Anderson's judgement in *English Questions*: 'Amongst the earliest Gramscians outside Italy, we were also amongst the most thoroughgoing' (p. 3).

A second observation is that 'Problems' simultaneously discloses the centrality of Sartrean existentialism in Anderson's philosophico-political formation. *The Critique of Dialectical Reason*—and not yet Marx and Engels's *German Ideology* or Trotsky's *Revolution Betrayed*—supplied the key concept of 'scarcity', integrated into a philosophical anthropology of praxis and its alienations, and employed to differentiate the results and prospects of socialism, East and West. So much is manifest. But a directly political text by Sartre is of equal salience. *The Communists and Peace*, which essayed a concrete analysis of postwar French society from the standpoint of a fellow traveller of the French Communist Party (PCF) during the Cold War, posed the problem of the dislocation of theory and practice. Sartre's 'resolution' of the problem, and his alignment with the PCF as the incarnation of the French proletariat, provoked Merleau-Ponty's charge, in *Adventures of the Dialectic*, of 'ultra-Bolshevism'.[65] The theory/practice nexus, and the enduring dilemma it represents in the absence of a mass socialist party—a deficit founded upon the absence of a socialist proletariat— will be a recurrent concern of Anderson's. Moreover, by the end of the 1970s, it is at least arguable that his own conjunctural response to it, amid the global class struggle of the second Cold War, amounts to a further displaced variant of Sartre's option, accentuating its 'substitutionist' logic by the installation of a state—the Soviet Union—as locum tenens for party and class.

This leads to a third remark. It is readily apparent that Anderson's stance toward socialism in the East derives from Deutscher's instruction in *Stalin*, the *Trotsky* trilogy, and a host of other writings.[66] He may have wished to forget 'Problems of Socialist Strategy', but he never repented the sentiment of its closing paragraph. Revocation of any Deutscherite hopes for a 'democratic regeneration' of the Russian Revolution from above, and the shift to an orthodox Trotskyist position on the necessity of a proletarian political revolution against the ruling bureaucracy, did not entrain revision of Anderson's categorization of the USSR (and affinal states) as non-, or indeed *postcapitalist*, and therefore meriting critical support, in their contest with imperialism, from Western socialists.

Fourth, 'Problems' established the basic Andersonian problematic. The framework governing the questions posed in his work is a comprehensive polarization between East and West, within which a subdivision is inscribed: that between the insular (Britain) and the Continental (France as regards bourgeois revolution; Italy in respect of proletarian party). According to its terms, differential historical temporality generates distinct social formation and indicates specific socialist strategy. The problematic permits of further discrimination and/or significant variation. These will occur, most obviously, with a displacement of the state (East)/civil society (West) couplet, in favour of a polarity between feudal-Absolutist and capitalist-bourgeois-democratic states; and a consequent reversal of the verdicts on Leninism and vindication of a revolutionary strategy for socialism in the West. Nevertheless, these variations are internal to an invariant geopolitical problematic of the longer *durées* of European historical development. If, for Michelet, history was 'first of all geography', for Anderson it is also geography.[67]

A fifth point: 'Problems' is the first and last text of its kind released by Anderson. Portions of a manuscript dating from 1970, 'State and Revolution in the West'—its title suggestively mingling Leninist precedent and Gramscian horizon—never saw the light of day. 'The Antinomies of Antonio Gramsci', extracted from it and published six years later, for all the brilliance of its dissection of *Prison Notebooks*, its reconstruction of strategic debates in the international socialist movement, and its problematization of Eurocommunism (including the young Anderson), is more of a ground-clearing operation than an examination of the environment to which socialism in the West—let alone the United Kingdom—must be 'adapted'. Unlike 'Origins of the Present Crisis', 'The Figures of Descent' two decades later (1987) was not coupled with any strategic reflection. In this respect, the omission of 'Problems' and presentation of *English Questions* in two companionate parts—the first containing essays on British society and culture from the 1960s, the second collecting retrospectives on them—is misleading, doing less than justice to Anderson's original zone of engagement and the expressly 'operative' character of his Marxism.

Finally, 'Problems', like 'Origins', secretes a typology of the putatatively 'typical' and allegedly 'exceptional',[68] calibrating Britain against the historical gauge of France and the political gauge of Italy; and both are cast in a rhetoric that occasionally threatens to convert it into an aetiology of the normal and the pathological. Quite aside from its historical accuracy and theoretical cogency, this typology harbours problems of political efficacy. In 1992 Anderson regretted the 'national nihilism' with which Deutscher charged the theses.[69] 'Abstract cosmopolitanism' might be an equally apposite epithet.[70] In one fascinating passage, quoted earlier, Anderson displayed a shrewd awareness of the Gramscian imperative to 'integrate' the progressive components of contradictory national cultural traditions, even if—or, rather, precisely because—the primary desideratum was their sublation in a synthetic 'socialist ideology'. Failure to do so, Anderson contended, would render that ideology 'abstract and external' to its society. Despite steps in the direction of relating constructively to national traditions, this sounds like a plausible description of the *NLR* Mark 2's 'insertion' in its domestic cultural universe under Anderson's editorship. The 'sources and component parts' of Andersonian theory at the time were Sartrean and Gramscian Marxism, Italian Communism, and Deutscherism. Italian Communism would be rejected and supplanted—first by Guevarism, then by Maoism, and finally by Trotskyism. Sartre and Gramsci would be joined by Althusser and Colletti, and Western Marxism generally counterbalanced and corrected by classical Marxism. A form of Deutscherism would persist, despite Mandelian amendments in the 1970s. However, only fairly late in the day was a sui generis national tradition, as opposed to the attempt to create one by the domestication of Western Marxism, assimilated into Anderson's own synthesis: the British school of Marxist historiography. Meanwhile, throughout the 1960s, Anderson and the *NLR*'s self-conception was deliberately extranational, set as the *Review* was on a cultural revolution against local components, the polarization of national intellectuals, and the conversion of a layer of them, as potential artisans of a socialist culture, to international traditions. The stipulated 'detour' through the intellectuals necessitated their expatriation.

Dissensions

The key contemporaneous reactions to the Nairn-Anderson theses, by E. P. Thompson in the *Socialist Register* in 1965 and Nicos Poulantzas in *Les Temps Modernes* in 1966, each advanced powerful objections to them—the former to their typologism, the latter to their culturalism—whose cogency was only finally (and then rather obliquely) endorsed in 'The Figures of Descent'.[71]

In an internal memorandum of April 1963, entitled 'Where Are We Now?', Thompson had already expressed vigorous dissent from the redirection of the *Review*: 'While we strain to catch the idioms of the Third World, of Paris, of Poland, of Milan, might there not be a growing discourse around us pregnant with possibilities, not only for us but for other peoples?'.[72] Now publicly airing accumulated resentments against Anderson—'a veritable Dr. Beeching of the socialist intelligentsia'—Thompson argued that Anderson's work articulated 'an inverted Podsnappery' (pp. 35–37). Nettled by Anderson's derogation from Marxist tradition in his depreciation of English industrial capital and labour, 'supine bourgeoisie' and 'subordinate proletariat' alike, Thompson discerned an 'undisclosed model of Other Countries, whose typological symmetry offers a reproach to British exceptionalism'. At its centre was 'an ideal type of [the bourgeois] Revolution against which all others may be judged' (p. 47). Transfixed by the Gallic model, Anderson and Nairn had misconstrued the English Revolution of the seventeenth century—one of the centrepieces of that 'great arch which, in fact, in the epochal sense, make up the bourgeois revolution' (p. 47); they had under-estimated the economic supremacy and political ascendancy of the indus-trial bourgeoisie in the nineteenth century, 'hunting . . . an aristocratic Snark' (p. 56); and they had neglected the cumulative reformist achievement of the working class in the nineteenth and twentieth centuries. Lacking Bagehot's cynical clairvoyance about the British Constitution, they had been lulled into mistaking the 'dignified', aristocratic semblance, or 'theatrical show', for the 'effective'—bourgeois—real thing (p. 53). Indulging in 'com-mination' (p. 36) where they should be engaging in investigation, these 'self-appointed *illuminati*' (p. 76) were scarcely an advertisement for the wisdom of the Continental theory with which they presumed to edify the empirical 'English idiom' (p. 64). Heedless of the bourgeois cultural monuments of political economy and Darwinism in their tirades against traditionalism and empiricism, they had equally ignored the existence of Communism and Marxism in their excoriation of Labourism and obsession with Fabianism. As to their own brand of Western Marxism, the upshot was an anthropomor-phization of social class and an economic-reductionist analysis of historical process (pp. 69–70, 77ff.).

Conceptually, the antinomy structuring Thompson's influential critique was empirical history versus grand theory; on its terms, Anderson and Nairn were Platonists masquerading as Marxists. Politically, it ended with a reaffir-mation of the 'socialist humanism' of 1956 against these strange interlopers, declining the challenge to offer an alternative account of the present crisis and its origins, let alone a strategy for its socialist resolution.

Whereas the burden of Thompson's coruscating polemic was Anderson and Nairn's illicit theoretical 'schematism', Poulantzas charged them with insufficient theoretical rigorism, refusing the Marxist credentials of the the-ses for converse reasons. Anderson and Nairn had quite legitimately resorted to Gramsci as a corrective to the Anglophone 'impressionism' they de-plored. But their Lukácsian reading of *Notebooks* fundamentally vitiated its analytical framework: 'In effect, their analysis of social classes, of politi-cal superstructures, of the hegemony of class, of the power bloc, of the dominant ideology and of class consciousness reveals a perspective which is *historicist* and *subjectivist*' (p. 60). Once an authentically Marxist (i.e., Althusserian) conception of mode of production and social formation was substituted for Anderson and Nairn's expressivist totality, Marx's own analysis of the British Constitution—namely, that it involved a 'delegation of power' from mill owners to landowners—prevailed. And if the industrial bourgeoisie was indeed the hegemonic class, 'several of the concrete political analyses of the group around *New Left Review* must obviously be reconsidered' (p. 70).

Poulantzas's Althusserian criticisms mounted a challenge to Anderson and Nairn on their own chosen terrain. That this was recognized is evident from the introduction that prefaced the 1967 translation of his article in the *Review*. Relating it to Althusser's de facto manifesto, 'Contradiction and Overdetermination', which had been published two issues previously, Anderson observed that Poulantzas was primarily concerned with the '*theoretical* infrastructure of the debate', rather than the empirical disagreements of the parties to it. He promised a reply, which never materialized.[73] By now experiencing the gravitational pull of Althusserian Marxism, whose founding texts—*For Marx* and *Reading 'Capital'*—had both appeared in France in 1965, eclipsing Sartre, Anderson was presumably inhibited from redemption of his promise by a measure of concurrence with the gist of Poulantzas's critique. At any rate, his silence may be taken either as tacit endorsement of it or as evidence of uncertainty about how to refute it. For, in sharp contrast, an extended and animated counterstatement to Thompson, 'Socialism and Pseudo-Empiricism', in which Anderson's own considerable polemical skills were exhibited, was issued within months of 'Peculiarities', indignantly rebutting its each and every charge.[74]

All along the line, so Anderson remonstrated, Thompson had traduced the empirical canons he invoked. He had caricatured the status of the essays, which were avowedly 'schematic'—presenting the preliminary elements of a 'totalizing' history, not affecting to represent that history. His substantive criticisms were either misleading or plain false. He had attacked Anderson and Nairn for ignoring the capitalist character of the landowning class in the seventeenth and eighteenth centuries, when that had been a lynchpin of their reconstruction of the English trajectory; and his reassertion of the political dominance of the industrial bourgeoisie after 1832 made up in rhetoric for what it lacked by way of logic and evidence. The Thompsonian apologia for bourgeois culture was uncompelling. Oblivious of the ambiguities of Protestantism (to which he had formerly drawn attention in his account of Methodism) and of Darwinism (whose social extrapolation had spawned the Spencerite monstrosity), it was myopic as regards the limitations of political economy. Right to impugn Anderson and Nairn's excision of Communism in Britain from the record, Thompson had rushed to the opposite extreme, according it an implausible prominence. As to the methodology of the theses, he had pursued the quarry of economism, when minimal acquaintance with Western Marxism (or attention to their texts, for that matter) would have disclosed an 'idealist' bias in the angle of analytical vision.[75] Finally, Thompson had utterly ignored the declared purpose of the joint work: 'to help provide an understanding of the present' (p. 41).[76]

The Thompson-Anderson exchange was, in the first and last instance, a dialogue of the deaf; to switch to the metaphor employed in the foreword to *English Questions* (p. 4 n. 5), the duellists did not really cross swords.[77] Whereas Thompson's concentration upon the details of the interpretation of the past distorted the express motivation of the theses, Anderson's orientation to the present eluded Thompson's interrogation of an unsustainable, normative paradigm of 'bourgeois revolution'. Yet since this—the missing English 1789—was what supposedly marked off national historical development as exceptional, even aberrant, given the momentous consequences for British socialism deduced from the nonevent, Anderson's silence was redolent of difficulties sidestepped.

The principal one was that the diagnosis of English singularity was indeed made upon the basis of an abstract historical (if not sociological) schema of the optimal location and normal function of 'bourgeois revolution' in modern European development. It is not quite accurate to speak, as does Lin Chun, of 'a rigid double claim of British exceptionality (explicitly) and continental uniformity (implicitly)'.[78] For the very source of the schema—Gramsci and, behind him, the Russian Marxist tradition[79]—attests that, rather than uniformity, Continental *variability* with repect to Gallic *typicality* was the norm of European Marxist discourse: hence, for example, Plekhanov and Lenin on Russia, Gramsci on Italy, and Lukács on Germany, in addition to Anderson and Nairn on England. The rule—the French Revolution—was the exception as regards what Gramsci called 'variations in the actual process whereby the same historical development manifests itself in different countries'.[80] Notwithstanding his elective affinities with Western Marxism, via Gramsci, Anderson was (as Thompson sensed) the unwitting legatee in this respect of the orthodox historical materialism of the Second and Third Internationals, with its canonical sequence: the emergence of bourgeois society within feudalism → revolution by rising bourgeoisie against declining feudal aristocracy → dominance of industrial capitalism → proletarian revolution against bourgeois state → abolition of capitalism and transition to communism. Accordingly, it is no surprise to find earlier generations of British Marxists weighing the respective domestic shares of 'peculiarity' and 'similarity' on European Marxist scales.[81] The fact that France itself had not experienced a 'bourgeois revolution' of the stipulated (ideal) type renders it *apatride*, and the whole problematic, with its register of relative purity and maturity, explanatorily unavailing. In Ellen Meiksins Wood's blunt judgement on the 'bourgeois paradigm', 'it does not correspond to any actually existing pattern of historical development'.[82]

Anderson was to meet such objections in his later work. But over and above misspecifications of national particularity and sweeping judgements on their basis, did the original contrast between English reality and French ideality entail misconceptions of the former? The answer would seem to be, not necessarily. Yet it unquestionably did prompt the accents of what Richard Johnson later dubbed a 'rather self-indulgent anglophobia' [83]—most obviously in the 'supine bourgeoisie'/'subordinate proletariat' pairing and its handling. This fuelled interpretation of a thesis about the debility of industrial capital, and the durability of the ideological and political hegemony of a capitalist aristocracy down to the twentieth century, as an implied claim for the perennial paramountcy of a feudal class at the helm of a feudal state.

'We wrote as Marxists', Anderson was to confirm, citing textual warrant for Victorian aristocratic ascendancy in Marx and Engels themselves.[84] It would be more precise to say that Anderson and Nairn wrote as Gramscians, elaborating the Italian's notations on the 'fusion of the old and the new' and 'a kind of suture' joining landowners and mill owners;[85] or even, in Anderson's case, as a crypto-Schumpeterian, extending the Austrian's intuitions about 'an active symbiosis of two social strata'.[86] Whatever the sources of the analysis, and however accurate or inaccurate its substance, it is striking that, as Anderson remarks in his reply to Thompson, 'there is very little about straight economics in [our essays], and a great deal about ideas and institutions' (p. 30). Here were the main faults of the theses, both of them venial in this time and place, as an explanation of the 'present crisis' whose existence Anderson and Nairn correctly asserted. The first fault—one of commission—was the undue culturalist inflection of the notion of 'hegemony', issuing, in effect, in a version of the 'dominant ideology thesis'. The second— one of omission—was a concomitant neglect of the economic structures of the crisis. Not that Anderson and Nairn had access to a ready Marxist literature in this area. If Anderson was reduced to citing mainstream studies by Shonfield, Sampson, and others, it was because twentieth-century Britain had yet to become the focus of sustained attention on the part of Marxist historians.[87] To take the most relevant title, Hobsbawm's *Industry and Empire* did not appear until 1968. When it did, it could maintain, perhaps with one eye on the lack of material underpinnings to the Nairn-Anderson theses, that '[s]imple sociological explanations [of Britain's relative decline] will not do. In any case, economic explanations of economic phenomena are to be preferred if they are available'.[88] And for Hobsbawm the *priority* of England's industrial revolution—not the *prematurity* of its 'bourgeois revolution'—furnished the explanatory key. It would be left to a future instalment of the controversy to judge whether Anderson's interdisciplinary questions, if not his contentious answers, about the interrelationship between political economy, cultural formations, and state structures in the causation of the British crisis were to the point. Meanwhile, the fact that the theses 'set the agenda for much of the whole contemporary debate about the nature and causes of the British crisis'[89] was eloquent testimony to their intellectual stimulus.

Innovations

Without retracting the explanatory weight allocated to the prematurity of 1640, 'Socialism and Pseudo-Empiricism' did respond to Thompson's 'great arch' framing of the bourgeois revolution in England. This was one of two main respects in which his rejoinder developed, rather than defended, initial positions. The distinction advanced to counter Thompson is of considerable interest for the geopolitical problematic sketched earlier:

> The paradox of an unpremeditated capitalist revolution effected by a landed gentry is explicable once a clear conceptual distinction is made between an economic *order* and the social *classes* which can inaugurate, assist, subvert or resist it. . . . Capitalism does not automatically or everywhere require a victorious industrial bourgeoisie to launch it—any more than socialism necessarily requires a victorious industrial proletariat to impose it. . . . Japanese capitalism was promulgated as a national destiny by the rural warlords of the Satsuma and Choshu clans. Chinese socialism was launched by the Hunan and Yenan peasantry in arms. . . . There is no simple, technical fatality which allocates mandatory roles univocally to social groups. Within strict limits (obviously, no bourgeoisie will ever lay the foundation-stones of socialism), objective roles are separable from their agents. (P. 9)

Later qualified, at least as regards socialism in the West, this thesis of the possible symmetry of 'bourgeois revolution' and 'proletarian revolution'—more specifically, of capitalist-revolution-without-the-bourgeoisie and socialist-revolution-without-the-proletariat—infirms, among other things, rejection of the Communist social order in the East on the grounds of its nonproletarian historical agency. Its logic permits identification of Stalinism as a predictable pattern of socialist movement and regime outside the advanced capitalist world.

A second, more immediately important innovation concerned the national culture and British Marxism. Far from recanting what he came to regard as 'national nihilism', Anderson exacerbated it, implicitly spurning the project of 'integration' glimpsed in 'Problems of Socialist Strategy'. Seconding Nairn, who had written of 'the nullity of native intellectual traditions',[90] and foreshadowing the bonfire of English vanities in 'Components of the National Culture' two years later, Anderson claimed that the British intellectual configuration was defined by the correlative absence of a 'classical sociology' and an indigenous Marxism (pp. 22–23). In other words, as a result of the bourgeoisie's conceptual abdication, Britain lacked the two main traditions of 'synthetic social thought', which aspired to 'a total theory of man and society' beyond the disciplinary partitions and blinkered horizons of political economy, political philosophy, and historiography (p. 22). As Donald Sassoon has suggested, a series of 'slippages' is apparent in Anderson's argument here, from its starting point in 'Origins' in a reproach to the nineteenth-century industrial bourgeoisie for producing no 'hegemonic ideology'.[91] The stipulative redefinition of that ideology, first as a 'major *political philosophy*' and a 'total *political* vision of society' (p. 17), then as a 'comprehensive social thought' (p. 22), allows Anderson to parry Thompson's counterexample of classical political economy and to repeat the thrust of his verdict on utilitarianism, but at the price of tacitly altering his criterion from ideological efficacy (the hegemonic) to intellectual quality (the synthetic).

What of the calibre of counterhegemonic ideology? Britain had

> not produced a single major Marxist thinker in the 20th century. More than that, there has never been a Marxist culture in this country, in the sense that Marxism becomes part of the normal intellectual consensus of a great number of writers and scholars, with a thousand different inflections. How could there have been? The preconditions for a real, autonomous Marxism did not exist. (P. 26)

Whereas France could claim Jean-Yves Calvez's *La pensée de Karl Marx*, exemplifying the humanist interpretation upon which Althusser trained his sights, Britain was forced to make shift with Sir Isaiah Berlin's 'haplessly ignorant and amateur little commentary', *Karl Marx: His Life and Environment* (pp. 26–27).[92] Anderson and Nairn's work traced its lineage to the Western Marxist tradition, whose common denominator, reacting against the legacy of scientific positivism and selectively assimilating philosophical idealism, accounted for the 'predominantly political and cultural . . . emphasis' of the theses (pp. 30–31). Now anticipating *Considerations on Western Marxism* (1976), Anderson reckoned that this tradition had 'suffered immensely by its divorce from political reality and practice'. A '"counter-idealist" trend', foreshadowed by Althusserianism, was germinating within it; yet even it conformed to Continental type in part (pp. 31–32).[93] Anderson summarized the point:

> The distinctive character of Western European Marxism since 1918 has been its co-emergence and colloquy with various currents of idealism— Dilthey, Croce, Husserl, etc. The same pattern is likely to be repeated in Britain, should an 'Anglo-Marxism' ever finally emerge. The precondition for a transcendence of this dialectic is the reunification of theory and practice in a mass socialist movement. This has not yet been achieved anywhere in Europe. (P. 41)

'Socialism and Pseudo-Empiricism' ended with an invitation to solidarity on the Left.[94] In view of the vehemence of Anderson's self-defence and vigour of his retaliation, this was something of a conventional piety. As was noted in the 'Decennial Report', the article had been 'the occasion for the first clear self-definition of the review, in terms of a Western Marxist tradition hitherto absent in England, and for a sharp political demarcation between the past and present versions of NLR—the former being criticized and rejected as "populist" rather than Marxist'. It was also, however, 'the last editorial attempt at a general discourse on British society in the review' during the decade (p. 18). Thus, the 'elements' of a 'totalizing' theory remained just that, not seeding a 'systematic theory of British history and society'. Part of the explanation doubtless lies in the conceptual difficulties— unsurmounted because insurmountable amid the pyrotechnics of the original theses—isolated by Thompson and Poulantzas, whose contrasting critiques secured pervasive assent on different sections of the Marxist Left. But the desistance arguably also derived from a conjunctural political obstruction: practical refutation of the expectations of Wilsonism and volatilization of the Andersonian species of structural-reformism by the Labour government's well nigh instantaneous breach of promise, at home and abroad—a record castigated by Nairn in the *Review* in the summer of 1965.[95]

This turn of events led Anderson not to revoke the project of intellectual reformation inferred from his identification of culture as the Archimedean point from which to upturn ruling-class hegemony, but rather to requicken it. In his critique of the Nairn-Anderson theses, Johnson extrapolated two possible scenarios from them:

> At worst, allied to a New Left élitism, it points to the need for an *alternative* intelligentsia, which may secure 'the second bourgeois revolution' or technocratic revolution from above. This would be to reproduce the politics of radical liberalism as well as its analyses. At best, acceptance of the analysis tends to reduce socialist ambitions; like all good 'social democrats', we become mere 'modernizers'.[96]

As it happened, neither scenario transpired. The 1964 'Conspectus' had set the twin political objectives of eliminating Third Worldist and Western Communist aberrations internationally, and prosecuting the programme of the theses domestically (pp. 4–5). In each department what occurred was rather different. Systematic induction of the Western Marxist tradition was determined upon, in early 1966, as an editorial priority for Britain, principal responsibility for the translation and presentation of relevant material being assigned to Ben Brewster. Despite Nairn's distancing of the *Review* from the results of the Wilson administration, no examination of recent indulgence of its prospects was undertaken. Instead, as the 'Decennial Report' disapprovingly noted, there ensued 'a tacit and pragmatic displacement onto the immediate centre of resistance to the . . . regime: industrial militancy' (p. 24). But the displacement was not confined to the local scene. Quite the reverse of being eliminated from the editorial line of the *NLR*, Third Worldism was about to reach its apogee in it. Blocked in the First World, stalled in the Second, socialism was perceived to be on the advance in the Third, under the auspices initially of Cuba and Guevarism, subsequently of China and Maoism.

2 ► Missed Rendezvous

The new *NLR* editorial committee started out with a positive attitude toward revolutionary nationalism in the Third World (Cuba, Algeria, southern Africa) and to reform Communism in the Second and First (Khrushchevism, the Italian Communist Party). Hopes in the latter were dispelled by the oscillations, then ouster, of Khrushchev, coinciding with Labour's assumption of office in October 1964, and by the failure of the Centre-Left experiment in Italy.[1] Cautious expectations of Wilson were rapidly dashed (in his case, a week in politics was a long time). Sacrifice of Labour's domestic programme to exchange-rate priorities prompted a transfer of Anderson and the *NLR*'s interest to industrial militancy as the front line of resistance to economic crisis management. Of greater importance, however, was the administration's reactionary foreign policy—above all, its dutiful support for American imperialism in Southeast Asia—which had a palpable radicalizing effect on Anderson and his colleagues, in common with thousands of their contemporaries. From 1965 to 1968, Vietnam dominated the international conjuncture and decisively impacted upon the national scene, contributing to the crystallization of a student movement that supplied a significant intellectual audience and potential political constitutency for the *NLR*.

The *Review* would participate in the local Vietnam Solidarity Campaign (VSC) which, diverging from Communist and CND traditions, mobilized not for peace but for the victory of socialism in Vietnam.[2] In a keynote *NLR* article, written in the immediate aftermath of the Tet Offensive in 1968 and considered by Anderson in 1980 'the best synthesis of the historical meaning of this signal moment', the Swedish Marxist Göran Therborn argued that '[t]he dialectic of the war has transferred the ideology of the guerrillas into the culture of the metropolis':

> The international contradiction between socialism and capitalism has thus been radically redefined by the Vietnamese Revolution. After a long and inescapable detour, it has been restored to a direct and unequivocal confrontation. This is the decisive meaning of this unequal war. Its reverberations have already shaken the world. A generation is now being formed in the homelands of imperialism which has experienced the truth of their own 'democratic' and 'affluent' societies. . . . Imperialism is not a peripheral phenomenon: it is inseparable from contemporary capitalism. The Vietnamese War

has sent a searchlight to the core of the West. The result has been a *simultaneous* multiplication and radicalization of the resistance to it. . . . The end of the Vietnamese War will not be the end of imperialism, but it may herald the beginning of the end. For something unprecedented has happened. The socialist revolution in a poor Asian country has liberated the dialectic in its oppressor. Internationalism has passed into the facts.[3]

As if in punctual confirmation of Therborn's assertion, shortly after his article was published, the May events unfolded across the Channel in an apparent 'return of the repressed' to the West.[4] In 'Problems of Socialist Strategy', Anderson had drawn a theoretico-political analogy between the 1960s and the 1840s. Construing 1968 as an international-socialist equivalent of 1848 in Europe—a springtime of students, proletarians, and peasants—for him, revolution had passed into the facts: an interpretation that was to guide his and the *NLR*'s evolution for the next decade or so.

Syndicalism and Socialism

The *NLR*'s attention to British trade unionism, amid growing working-class opposition to Labour's income policies, found expression in a Penguin special: *The Incompatibles*.[5] Planned in 1966 and released the following year, the collection addressed what was to become the central issue of British politics into the 1980s. The *Review*'s input made no attempt to relate this new 'front' to the Nairn-Anderson theses, by way of either elaboration or emendation. It had as a subtext an attempt to develop 'a more practical and institutional relationship to domestic politics than afforded by the review itself'.[6] Following the failure of a scheme for a Left 'institute' in London, this desire had led to informal links and discussions with the CPGB (whose industrial organizer, Bert Ramelson, reviewed *The Incompatibles* favourably in *Comment*). These would be interrupted by the advent of student rebellion in Britain, whose prospects would preoccupy the *NLR* at home to the end of the decade, and would provide the occasion for the *Review*'s affiliation to the tradition of revolutionary socialism—a remaking, in effect, of the second New Left.

In addition to *NLR* authors, *The Incompatibles* included articles by left-wing union leaders (Jack Jones and Clive Jenkins) and Marxist journalists (Claud Cockburn and Paul Foot), exploring general issues (the role of unions under capitalism and their relationship to socialism), as well as charting recent disputes (e.g., the seamen's strike of 1966). Opening with Blackburn's survey of contemporary Britain, 'The Unequal Society', it closed with

Anderson's analysis 'The Limits and Possibilities of Trade Union Action' (pp. 263–80). In this article, Anderson was concerned firmly to demarcate socialism from syndicalism, whether of the reformist or revolutionary variety:

> Both of these currents were rejected by the central tradition of European socialism. Marx, Lenin and Gramsci were all emphatic that trade unions could not in themselves be vehicles of advance towards socialism. Trade unionism, in whatever form, was an incomplete and deformed variant of class consciousness, which must at any cost be transformed by a growth of *political* consciousness, created and sustained in a *party*. (P. 264)

Unions were subject to 'structural limitations' inherent in them by virtue of their character as economic, corporatist working-class organizations in a capitalist society. They were the 'express[ion]' of a class-divided society, not the solvent of it (p. 264). By contrast, the party was conceived, in Sartrean terms, as embodying 'a true negation of existing society and a project to overthrow it. It alone is negativity in history' (p. 265). Lenin's reproof to 'economism' in *What Is to be Done?* was endorsed, with a Gramscian gloss:

> The corporate character of trade union consciousness does not derive from the nature of trade union action or its aim. . . . It has a cultural-political basis. Trade unions only represent the working class. A revolutionary movement—a party—requires more than this: it must include intellectuals and petit bourgeois who alone can provide the essential *theory* of socialism. . . . Culture in a capitalist society is in this sense a prerogative of privileged strata: only if some members of these strata go over to the cause of the working class can a revolutionary movement be born. For without a revolutionary theory, there can be no revolutionary movement. Trade unions represent too limited a sociological base for a socialist movement. By themselves they inevitably produce a corporate consciousness. The introversion which is so striking in the British trade union movement today is the natural sign of its corporatism. It is the antithesis of the universal outlook which alone defines a socialist consciousness. (Pp. 266–67)

As well as the significant innovation of allusions to a 'revolutionary movement' and a 'revolutionary party', the first direct induction of Leninist references into Anderson's work, if through a Sartrean filter, should be noted here. The upshot is a set of specifications of the antitheses already advanced in 'Origins' and 'Problems'. Focused on the party/union polarity, they might be laid out as in figure 3.

Party	Union
Universal	Sectoral
Political	Economic
Voluntary/offensive	Spontaneous/defensive
Theoretical	Pragmatic
Working-class and petit bourgeois	Working-class
Hegemonic	Corporatist
Socialism	Syndicalism
Revolutionary actions	Strikes
'Negativity'	'Positivity'
Abolition of capitalism	Expression of capitalism

Figure 3. Party and Union

So much for the limitations of trade unionism. As to its potential, this was twofold: first, the defence and improvement of working-class living standards, negatively confirmed by Labour's efforts at placation of capital and reversal of relative economic decline by shackling its industrial 'wing'; and second, the (re)production of class consciousness in the proletariat (pp. 273–74). Delegating to trade unionism the powers attributed by Sartre to Communism, in whose absence he feared the universe would be uniformly 'bourgeois', Anderson maintained an equidistance from the outlooks of Luxemburg, champion of the mass strike, and Marcuse, analyst of working-class incorporation:

> The *socio-political identity* of the European working class is first and foremost incarnate in its trade unions. It experiences itself as a class only through its collective institutions. . . . Outside these . . . , the working class has a purely inert identity, impenetrable even to itself. It is separated from the rest of society by its characteristic occupations, customs and culture, but it is not a fused group capable of any social action. For this, it must be conscious of itself as a class. . . . [T]he very existence of a trade union *de facto* asserts the unbridgeable difference between Capital and Labour in a market society; it embodies the refusal of the working class to become integrated into capitalism on its own terms. Trade unions thus everywhere produce *working class* consciousness—that is, awareness of the separate identity of the proletariat as a social force, with its own corporate interests in society. This is not the same thing as *socialist* consciousness—the hegemonic vision and will to create a new social order, which only a revolutionary party can create. But the one is a necessary stage towards the other. (P. 274)[7]

The character of trade unionism, then, was ineliminably 'paradoxical', 'a component of capitalism that is also by its nature antagonistic to it' (p. 276).

Radicalization of the latent antagonism depended upon a renovation of unions—in the first instance, through their 'democratization' (p. 277). In the current conjuncture the imposition of wage controls by the state called for a political response in kind—a struggle against Labour's administration of British capitalism at the expense of its own constituency—and for alternative socialist policies (p. 278). Economic demands now possessed an inescapably political significance. Moreover, this put a question mark over the link between the unions and the Labour Party, professed 'wings' of a unified movement embroiled in undeclared civil war—an 'immense contradiction' likely to prove unsustainable (p. 279).

Focos and Bases

Having taken a sudden interest in industrial struggle, the *NLR* largely lost it again, turning its domestic attention from workers to students.[8] However, 1967 also marked the peak of editorial enthusiasm for a revolutionary current in the Third World—Guevarism—and its principal relay to Western intellectuals—Althusser's pupil Régis Debray, author of a semiofficial theorization of the *foco* strategy in *Revolution in the Revolution?* published and translated that year. At a time when Havana was extolling revolutionary internationalism as an alternative to the Soviet line of 'peaceful coexistence' ('create two, three, many Vietnams'), a major essay by Debray had already featured in the *Review* in 1965, generalizing from the Cuban experience to propound Castroism as the Latin American form of Leninism.[9] By the autumn of 1967, Guevara's improvization of *focismo* in Bolivia was in its death throes and Debray in a military prison in Camiri. *NLR* no. 45 carried Debray's 'Problems of Revolutionary Strategy', preceded by an introduction by Anderson and Blackburn that lauded his work as 'unquestionably . . . one of the most brilliant examples of Marxist-Leninist analysis to have appeared in many years', characterized as it was by a 'combination of an utterly intransigent revolutionary *ethics* and an extraordinarily detailed and concrete *technics* of insurrection'.[10] The inverse ratio between 'ethics' and 'technics', demonstrated by the sanguinary denouement of the Bolivian guerrilla, was not subjected to scrutiny.[11]

Instead, an *NLR* displacement mechanism came into operation, and Mao's China, engulfed since 1966 in the vortex of the Cultural Revolution, came to occupy the stellar role previously assigned Castro's Cuba. The assimilation of Maoism in the second half of the 1960s, as the ideology of a Communist regime supposedly superior in crucial respects to the tarnished USSR and a source of domestic inspiration, was evident in the *Review*'s engagement with the nascent student movement in Britain. Stirrings at the London School of Economics in March 1967 were met with two articles by members of the editorial committee,[12] and a collective volume (to which six committee members contributed) was eventually published by Penguin in 1969, entitled *Student Power*.[13] The *NLR* not only invested intellectually in the campus turbulence but also participated as a political group in a national initiative: the foundation of the Revolutionary Socialist Students' Federation (RSSF). Indeed, the federation's manifesto, adopted at its second congress in November 1968, was inspired largely by Blackburn. Designed to exclude reformist and 'centrist' socialists from the ranks of the RSSF, it marked the *Review*'s unequivocal identification with revolutionary socialism—albeit of a heterodox-Maoist, as opposed to an orthodox-Trotskyist, brand.

The RSSF programme concluded by advocating the construction of 'red bases' in British colleges and universities. This relocation of Maoist strategy from Hunan Province to Houghton Street was defended, in their respective ways, by Blackburn (under the pseudonym James Wilcox), future lecturers' union functionary David Triesman, and subsequent Charter 88 coordinator Anthony Barnett, in the issue of the *NLR* in which the manifesto was presented.[14] Anderson reportedly dissented from the hallucinatory prospectus of red bases. Yet, as was noted in the 'Decennial Report', under his direction, the '*NLR* as a whole, and *Student Power* in particular, were without question the leading exponents of "studentism", with all its enthusiasms and errors, in Britain during this phase' (p. 28).[15] Enthusiasm and error alike might be encapsulated in the German student chant cited by Gareth Stedman Jones in the Penguin anthology: 'The slogan of Berlin resounds through Europe: "Today the students—Tomorrow the workers"'.[16]

The British student movement was efficiently repressed, Blackburn and Nairn figuring among those who suffered professionally for their solidarity with it; and the RSSF rapidly withered. Once again, no analysis of this dispiriting outcome was undertaken by the *NLR*. The sole text in the *Review* of enduring value generated by the British 1968 was Anderson's 'Components of the National Culture', reprinted in *Student Power* alongside Blackburn's 'Brief Guide to Bourgeois Ideology' in a section with the Marcusean title 'The Repressive Culture'.[17]

The Ideological Front, or A Detour via the Intellectuals

Developing points made in the 1966 reply to Thompson, 'Components' was an isolated attempt in this period to resume the Nairn-Anderson theses, this time on an exclusively cultural plane. Explicitly deprecating the local intellectual heritage and implicitly recommending Continental traditions as the requisite corrective, 'Components' intensified both the culturalism of the original problematic and its tendencies to 'national nihilism'.[18] In the essays of 1964–66, Anderson's overarching evaluative criterion had been a revisionist/reformist Western Marxism, in whose name not only the hegemonic culture ('traditionalism'/'empiricism'), but also its corporatist mirror image ('Fabianism') *and* its New Left antagonist ('populism'), had been assailed. Now, however, that criterion was narrowed to revolutionary Marxism and the revolutionary socialism it grounded. In the acknowledgements to *English Questions*, Anderson confides that his early essays 'appear here shorn of some of the bombast and excess of the period to render them more readable, if not defensible'. In the case of 'Components', the effect is somewhat to moderate the insistency of its revolutionary-Marxist affiliations.

'Components' appeared in the fiftieth issue of the *NLR*, in the summer of 1968, under the banner headline 'Combat Bourgeois Ideas'.[19] The presentation of it glossed the Maoist note thus struck, pointing to the intimate connection between Anderson's bombardment of the ideological headquarters of the bourgeoisie and student rebellion. In the process it retro-projected a revolutionary vocation onto the *Review* from its Andersonian reinception:

> This . . . issue . . . opens with a critique . . . of the structures of bourgeois culture in Britain. The task of forging a revolutionary and internationalist political culture in this country has always been a central preoccupation of the Review. This involves attacking the ideas which help the ruling class to maintain its hegemony as well as a willingness to learn from advances in revolutionary theory and practice abroad. If the present stirrings of a revolutionary consciousness are not to relapse into new versions of reformism, the Left must prove itself capable of fighting the enemy both on the ideological front and in mass struggle. The student movement obviously has special responsibilities here. The emergence of a revolutionary student movement in the advanced capitalist world has upset many traditional schemas of revolution. It should now be evident to all that students are a potentially insurgent force and that they can play a key role in a general revolutionary alliance. By their struggles, students can undermine an important bastion of ruling class power (higher education) and help to detonate wider social conflicts.[20]

As reprinted in *English Questions*, still dated 1968, 'Components' ends as follows:

The chloroforming effect of this [cultural] configuration is general. Silently underpinning the social status quo, it stifles intellectual questioning of the existing order and deprives political opposition on the Left of the resources needed to understand its society, the condition of changing it. History has tied this knot, and only history can undo it. A *revolutionary* culture is not for tomorrow. But a socialist practice within culture is possible today: the student struggle is its initial form. (P. 104; my emphasis)

In the original version, the 'r' word recurred, underscoring the stance of its author:

The consequences of this total constellation for the Left need no emphasis. The chloroforming effect of such cultural configuration, its silent and constant underpinning of the social status quo, [is] deadly. British culture, as it is now constituted, is a deeply damaging and stifling force, operating against the growth of any *revolutionary* Left. It quite literally deprives the Left of any source of concepts and categories with which to analyze its own society, and thereby attain a fundamental precondition for changing it. History has tied this knot; only history will ultimately undo it. A *revolutionary* culture is not for tomorrow. But a *revolutionary* practice within culture is possible and necessary today. The student struggle is its initial form. (Pp. 56–57; my emphasis)[21]

Anderson's *maoisant* motivation, conformable to notions of ideological struggle diffused by the Chinese Cultural Revolution, was evident from his invocation of Lenin and Gramsci: 'Without revolutionary theory, wrote Lenin, there can be no revolutionary movement. Gramsci, in effect, added: without a revolutionary culture, there will be no revolutionary theory' (p. 4). The task of cultural renovation dictated a prior wave of creative destruction: 'a systematic critique of established British culture'. Congruent with such priorities, Anderson's immediate inspiration was Althusser, whose recasting of historical materialism supplied, in addition, his interpretation of the distinction between sociological and Marxist concepts of social totality: in a phrase, overdetermination and contradiction (pp. 3–4, 9). In what may be understood as a response to Poulantzas's critique of the historicism of the Nairn-Anderson theses,[22] Anderson selectively assimilated aspects of Althusserian antihistoricism and Lévi-Straussian structuralism (p. 6), signalling the philosophical ascendancy of Althusser over Sartre and Lukács, if not Gramsci, in this phase of his career.

The main postulates of 'Components' can be rapidly expounded. Anderson's remit was 'a genuinely revolutionary critique' of the national intellectual culture, excluding the natural sciences and the arts, that entailed a 'structural' analysis of it (p. 6). His typical starting point was the singularity of this ensemble—'any observed irregularities in the contours of British culture, viewed internationally' (p. 7). Framed thus, its peculiarity consisted in an 'absent centre': '*Britain—alone of Western societies—never produced a classical sociology*' (p. 7). Such totalizing sociology—a '*synthetic* social science . . . aspir[ing] to a global reconstruction of social formations' (p. 8)—was a reaction to the Continental resonance of Marxism and the working-class movement, whether in France (Durkheim), Germany (Weber), or Italy (Pareto). There and elsewhere, Marx's theory, synthesizing German philosophy, French politics, and English political economy, had germinated indigenous Marxisms (that of Lenin in Russia, Lukács in Germany, and Gramsci in Italy) with which sociology had been in constant contention. Deviating from the Continental norm, Britain had 'produced no important Marxist thinker' (p. 10). The 1930s had 'vaccinated British culture against Marxism to this day'. Whereas currents of Western Marxism had flourished on the Continent (in the Frankfurt, Della Volpean, and Althusserian schools, for instance), 'England remained unaffected. Marxist theory had never become naturalized' (p. 11).[23]

Why this allegedly unique dual absence of 'totalizing' theory—classical sociology and national Marxism? According to Anderson's theory of no theory—or 'sociology of no sociology' (p. 12)—which elaborated on 'Origins of the Present Crisis', the nonrevolutionary record of the industrial bourgeoisie in Britain was the key to the void:

> The British bourgeoisie from the outset renounced its intellectual birthright. It refused ever to put society as a whole in question. A deep, instinctive aversion to the very category of the totality marks its entire trajectory. It never had to recast society as a whole, in a concrete historical practice. It consequently never had to rethink society as a whole, in abstract theoretical reflection. Empirical, piece-meal intellectual disciplines corresponded to humble, circumscribed social action. Nature could be approached with audacity and speculation: society was treated as if it were an immutable second nature. . . . The cultural limitations of bourgeois reason in England were thus politically rational: the *ultima ratio* of the economy founded both. (P. 13)[24]

Podsnappery and Gradgrindery had mixed and matched in bourgeois ideology, reinforcing the hitherto incorrigible *vice anglais*—that 'aristocratic combination of "traditionalism" and "empiricism"' which functioned as the hegemonic ideology of a Victorian England wherein capitalist aristocracy and bourgeoisie gradually melded to form the ruling bloc (p. 12). Relieved of the obligation to construe the social totality in theory and reconstruct it in practice, the bourgeoisie was then spared the necessity of defending it against the kind of revolutionary challenge that stimulated sociology on the Continent. The result was that in the Belle Époque, 'the harmony between the hegemonic class and its intellectuals was virtually complete' (p. 15). Britain domiciled the conformist 'intellectual aristocracy' of Lord Annan's admiring portrait, where mainland countries harboured a separate, dissident intelligentsia.

Thus far, we are presented with a habitual Western Europe/Britain polarity whose terms run something as depicted in figure 4. Providentially insulated against fundamental institutional change, whether through external force (invasion) or internal agency (revolution), twentieth-century Britain had sheltered a 'white emigration' from the turbulent Continent—Popper, Berlin, Namier, and their compeers. Except in economics and literary criticism, where Keynes and Leavis respectively dominated, this levy had achieved preeminence in the major disciplines. What for Anderson was Britain's bane assumed for them the status of a privilege. Mutual complaisance ensued, the *éminences blanches* confirming 'insular reflex and prejudice', the host nation conferring nobility upon its naturalized subjects for their benediction of its effortless superiority (pp. 18–20). Whereas the English ideology of no ideology 'shunned theory even in its rejection of theory', the exiles and émigrés 'systematized the refusal of system' (p. 19).

Western Europe	Britain
Revolutionary bourgeoisie	Nonrevolutionary bourgeoisie
'Revolutionary ideology'	'Traditionalism'/'empiricism'
Marxism	Marx and Engels
Synthetic, totalizing sociology	Antisystemic social science
Separate intelligentsia	Intellectual aristocracy
Indigenous Marxism	Fabianism
Revolutionary socialism	Labourism

Figure 4. Cultural Configurations

Having identified the basic anomalies of the national culture—the absence of a classical sociology (and its concomitant: no Marxism) and the postwar dominance of a white emigration—Anderson embarked upon a swingeing 'inter-sectoral' anatomy of it (p. 20). In turn, he analyzed philosophy (Wittgenstein), political and social theory (Berlin and Popper), historiography (Namier), economics (Keynes), psychology (Eysenck), aesthetics

(Gombrich), psychoanalysis (Klein), anthropology (Malinowski), and literary criticism (Leavis). His harshest words were reserved for the Oxford philosophy of Ryle and Austin, supposedly spawned by Wittgenstein's *Philosophical Investigations*. According to the canons of its common-room complacency, virtually all Continental philosophy after Descartes, *Britannicus emeritus*, was metaphysical bunk:

> The linguistic philosophy of the forties and fifties represented a deliberate renunciation of the traditional vocation of philosophy in the West. General ideas about man and society had been the hallmark of all the great philosophers of the past. . . . English philosophy after the Second World War systematically rejected the very idea of intellectual innovation. . . . The cult of common sense accurately indicates the role of linguistic philosophy in England. It functions as an anaesthetic ideology, blotting out the very memory of an alternative order of thought. (P. 22)[25]

An 'atemporal philosophy' had its predictable correlate in Berlin and Popper's 'disembodied political theory'. Their history of ideas (e.g., in 'Two Concepts of Liberty' and *The Open Society and Its Enemies*) confected 'a manichaean morality tale, whose teleological outcome is the present: struggle of the free world against totalitarian communism' (pp. 25–26). If Keynes's *General Theory* had 'reintroduced time into orthodox economic theory' (p. 32), this had not sufficed to reconnect post-Keynesian economics with the prior, more synthetic tradition of political economy culminating in Marx. Indicative of the blinkers imposed by its short-termism was the failure to generate any plausible explanation of the British economic crisis (p. 33).[26]

Anderson's own laconic summary of his findings may stand in for any detailed paraphrase of them:

> [T]he absence of a centre produced a series of structural distortions in the character and connections of the inherited disciplines. Philosophy was restricted to a technical inventory of language. Political theory was thereby cut off from history. History was divorced from the exploration of political ideas. Psychology was counterposed to them. Economics was dissociated from both political theory and history. Aesthetics was reduced to psychology. The congruence of each sector with its neighbour is circular: together they form something like a closed system. The quarantine of psychoanalysis is an example: it was incompatible with this pattern. Suppressed in every sector at home, the idea of the totality was painlessly exported abroad, producing the paradox of an anthropology where there was no sociology. In the

general vacuum thus created, literary criticism usurps ethics and insinuates a philosophy of history. . . . The void at the centre of this culture generated a pseudo-centre—the timeless ego. . . . The price of missing sociology, let alone Marxism, was the prevalence of psychologism. A culture which lacks the instruments to conceive the social totality inevitably falls back on the nuclear psyche, as First Cause of society and history. . . . The era of revolutions is . . . unthinkable. (P. 56)

As with 'Origins of the Present Crisis', Anderson prefaced laying waste the national culture by disclaiming ambitions to comprehensiveness. Merely a 'preliminary inventory', his essay could not but contain its share of 'errors, lapses, elisions and omissions' (p. 5). Eight years later, in the foreword to *Considerations on Western Marxism*, he stated the desirability of 'modification' of certain elements, singling out the counterposition of European sociology and Marxism to English empiricism.[27] In the interim, the 'Decennial Report' had identified the culturalist modulation of the category of 'hegemony' and a 'provincialist' exaggeration of the degradation of English culture as the two principal respects in which 'Components' had compounded, rather than corrected, the errors of the Nairn-Anderson theses (p. 28). Only in 1990 did Anderson publicly revert to the subject, in the two-part article 'A Culture in Contraflow'.[28] There he wrote that his polemical propaedeutic of 1968 'had many failings':

> Written at a time of rebellion, in a spirit of *outrance*, it mounted a peremptory broadside on its chosen target. The price of this general excoriation was paid in a variety of local simplifications or misjudgements. Overstatement in critique was also accompanied by overconfidence of cure—a theoretical triumphalism that was no service to the radical alternatives advocated. (P. 193)[29]

Among the concessions Anderson now made were an excessive reliance upon Talcott Parsons's *Structure of Social Action*, with its excision of Herbert Spencer from the classical tradition;[30] an indiscriminate evacuation of sociological disciplines from the British scene; and an overly symmetrical analytical template paralleling historical materialism and 'bourgeois' sociology (pp. 205–6). Nevertheless, praying in aid Geoffrey Hawthorn's history of social theory, *Enlightenment and Despair*, he reaffirmed the overall direction of his original argument about the national culture in general, and sociology in particular, in a society exempt from the converse pressures of revolution and reaction.[31]

Anderson's comparative-historical sociology of ideas yielded a remarkable essay in cultural mapping, which was open to demur on numerous scores. 'Overstatement in critique' of particulars might, for example, include the conflation of Wittgenstein with Ryle and Austin, adopted from Gellner's *Words and Things*.[32] But of wider significance are the two faults itemized in the 'Decennial Report'—'provincialism' and culturalism—since these directly implicated the 'overconfidence of cure' prescribed on the basis of a diagnosis thus flawed. Stuart Macintyre has reminded us that a theoretical inferiority complex vis-à-vis the Continent beset an earlier generation of British Marxists, persuaded of the lamentable fragility—hence dependency—of their culture, which they explained by reference to the objective conditions of a prolonged, but now happily vanishing, global supremacy.[33] 'Components' thus possessed a precedent that its reduction of local Marxism to degree zero wrote out of the record. In this respect, its cosmopolitan composure was more redolent of an inverted cultural nationalism than provincialism. However that may be, an intellectualist conception of culture and persistent definitional ambiguity over 'hegemony' (efficacy or excellence?)[34] informed Anderson's universal specific.

'Problems of Socialist Strategy' had stipulated a 'detour' via the intelligentsia, so as to engage 'the necessarily ideological contest' to convert sections of it to socialism.[35] 'Components' repeated the prescription, with a revolutionary supplement. The remedy for a conservative national culture was an internationalist, revolutionary-Marxist culture; its vector, the student movement; its vehicle, the *NLR* and New Left Books (NLB). In the 'era of revolutions', Anderson and the *NLR*'s self-conception crossed Sartreanism—a collective of independent, avant-garde intellectuals—with Leninism—a vanguard of professional revolutionaries.[36] The advent of a revolutionary culture in Britain was the precondition for the production of the revolutionary theory indispensable to a revolutionary movement: 'A political science capable of guiding the working-class movement to final victory will only be born within a general intellectual matrix which challenges bourgeois ideology in every sector of thought and represents a decisive, hegemonic alternative to the cultural status quo' (p. 4).

The first item in the reformation programme has already been noted: the introduction of Continental Marxism to Britain via the pages of the *Review* itself. Key theoretical texts, with accompanying introductions, were translated from the summer of 1966 onward: Gorz on Sartre (no. 37), Lukács on technology (no. 39), Althusser's 'Contradiction and Overdetermination' (no. 41), Adorno's 'Sociology and Psychology' (nos. 46 and 47), Benjamin on Paris (no. 48), and Gramsci on factory councils (no. 51). This induction would continue—and accelerate—throughout the 1960s and 1970s.

Evaluation of these diverse Marxisms—whether by comparison with each other or with classical Marxism—was temporarily postponed. It would follow, with a series of articles—by Stedman Jones on Lukács, Therborn on the Frankfurt school, Norman Geras and André Glucksmann on Althusser, and others—collected in 1977 as *Western Marxism: A Critical Reader*,[37] and with Anderson's own *Considerations on Western Marxism*, released in 1976.

Meanwhile, in the spring of 1968, the decision to found NLB was taken, Ronald Fraser playing a central role in its implementation.[38] The first titles, issued in 1970, complemented the editorial programme of the *Review*, including Althusser and Balibar's *Reading 'Capital'*, Lukács's *Lenin*, Korsch's *Marxism and Philosophy*, and a biography of Gramsci. In future years, the same authors who frequented the *NLR*'s pages—Adorno, Althusser, Benjamin, Colletti, Poulantzas, Sartre—regularly featured on NLB's list.[39] By the end of the decade, when Verso had been established as its paperback imprint, NLB had published some eighty-five books, approximately half of which one way or another pertained to Western Marxist traditions. At the same time, *NLR* members were active in editing and/or translating cognate material for other publishers—most notably in the case of Quintin Hoare, who, together with Geoffrey Nowell Smith, produced a highly regarded edition of *Selections from the Prison Notebooks* for Lawrence and Wishart in 1971. Moreover, demonstrating that an orientation to Western did not preclude attention to classical Marxism, a contract was secured to construct a Pelican Marx Library, as a result of which the full range of Marx's writings was made available in scholarly paperback editions.[40]

As we have seen, in 'Components' Anderson had utilized Lévi-Strauss's conception of structural analysis, commending Edmund Leach for grasping the importance of his anthropology and 're-establish[ing] the concept of ideology as an imaginary resolution of real contradictions' (pp. 6, 50). Relatedly, an enthusiastic assessment of psychoanalysis (pp. 42–43) had quoted Althusser's quasi-Lacanian rendition of Freud's 'Copernican revolution' in his 1964 essay 'Freud and Lacan'. Anderson's positive evaluation of selected non-Marxist Continental currents had as its corollary publication of their representatives in the *NLR*—for example, Lacan on the 'mirror-phase' and an interview with Lévi-Strauss.[41] Books by them (e.g., Foucault) would figure on the subscription lists of New Left Review Editions, instituted to circulate NLB titles and similar works at discount prices. Sympathy for Freud was such as to prompt an abortive plan for remedying the inaccessibility of his writings in England. Aside from establishing the fruitful relationship with Penguin, leading to further collaboration in the 1970s—an expanded edition of Nairn's *The Left against Europe?* (1973) and the collection *Explosion in a*

Subcontinent (1975)—Blackburn would edit two substantial *NLR* anthologies for Fontana: *Ideology in Social Science* (1972), fleshing out Anderson's 'inventory' by offering critiques of academic orthodoxies in the Anglophone world; and *Revolution and Class Struggle*, a 'reader in Marxist politics'.[42]

The anathema of (post)structuralism and demotion of psychoanalysis in Anderson's *In the Tracks of Historical Materialism* (1983) thus has an incongruous air about it, given the direct or indirect role of the *NLR* in sponsoring these formations among Marxist intellectuals in the 1960s and 1970s.[43] But for now, it is important to underline the very considerable collective achievement represented by the foregoing bland enumeration of projects and titles, even while indicating its limitations.

In 'A Culture in Contraflow', Anderson points to the disparity between the popular intellectual culture of the Left in the 1930s and its socially more circumscribed successor of the 1970s and 1980s (p. 300). There is certainly no statistical equivalence. NLB's predecessor—the Left Book Club—reckoned in April 1939, three years after its launch, to have 60,000 members attending some 1,200 groups, and to have circulated 1.5 million books in that time.[44] The *NLR*'s domestic audience comprised the expanding category of cultural workers in postwar capitalism, swollen by the multiplication of institutions of higher education in Britain in the 1960s. Accordingly, rapid rerouting of its countercultural campaign to a destabilized academy was a logical step, if a vulnerable one, given the transience of the student vocation and the evanescence of its contestation. Mere statistics will not disclose the degree of the *NLR*'s penetration of this implied readership. However, as orders of magnitude, it is striking that by the mid-1980s NLB's most successful title was Paul Feyerabend's libertarian—not Marxist—*Against Method*, published in 1975, which approached sales of 35,000 a decade later; whereas the distant runners-up were Anderson's own *Passages from Antiquity to Feudalism* and *Lineages of the Absolutist State* (1974), each of which had attained just over half that total. From 1980 through 1985, NLB/Verso sold a little more than 500,000 books. But the share of the old NLB core list in the annual totals had declined from 50 percent to barely more than 10 percent by the end of the period, dramatizing the cultural retreat of classical and Western Marxism.

Nevertheless, it may be said that the 'long night of theory' lifted, and theory became a 'material force' of sorts, insofar as it gripped some of the (ex-)student masses and rather fewer of their tutors. At all events, even if the hegemonic culture on which Anderson trained his batteries in 'Components' did not yield to his bombardment, the desolate cultural panorama of the 1950s was transformed—in no small part thanks to the concerted efforts of him and his colleagues.[45] That their cultural actions were to have unintended ideological consequences is an irony of intellectual history that will detain us later.

The *Caiman*, the Chairman, and the Commissar

The long hiatus in Anderson's published work between 'Components' and his European history books has erected a major obstacle to tracking his path from the late 1960s to the mid-1970s, when he reemerged to criticize the theoreticism of Western Marxism and to advocate a Trotskyist version of classical Marxism. In fact, in a series of anonymous *NLR* pieces and unpublished documents, Anderson revised and refined the revolutionary Marxism—*dur,* if not *pur*—espoused in the 1968 essay. Initially, up to the end of the decade, this assumed the form of an Althusserian Maoism, exhibiting some credence in the official propaganda of the Cultural Revolution. Thereafter, out of growing disenchantment with Chinese foreign policy, a gradual transition to Trotskyism occurred.

The *Review*'s seeming ecumenicism in the late 1960s was belied by an emergent majoritarian position, to which Anderson fully subscribed. In the words of the 'Decennial Report', '[T]he conjoined influences of Maoism and Althusserianism were . . . in rapid ascent within NLR' (pp. 30–31). It would not be far wide of the mark to characterize the journal from 1968 to 1970 as politically quasi-Maoist and theoretically neo-Althusserian.

We have already remarked Anderson's recourse to Althusserian categories in 'Components'. Such sympathies were pronounced among other members of the editorial committee, most markedly in the cases of Brewster, Stedman Jones, and Juliet Mitchell. Mitchell's 'Women: The Longest Revolution', published in 1966, initiated the feminist appropriation of Althusser's Marxism, pioneering contemporary socialist-feminist theory in the process.[46] Maoist tendencies were rather more discreet. (A proposal to publish an NLB collection of writings by the chairman's dauphin, Marshal Lin Piao, was fortuitously scotched by his disgrace in 1972.) They first surfaced in a central episode of the period under consideration: the debate over Trotsky and his legacy between an editor of the *NLR*, Nicolas Krassó, and the Fourth International leader Ernest Mandel, which was widely noticed and translated abroad.[47]

Both Krassó's original article and his response to Mandel were significantly edited for publication by Anderson, who introduced Althusserian and Maoist motifs into the critique of Trotskyism by Lukács's former pupil.[48] In sum, 'Trotsky's Marxism' paired Stalin and Trotsky as erroneous alternatives to Lenin and contrasted the realities of the Chinese Revolution with the velleities of the Fourth International. Rejecting the theory of 'permanent revolution', Krassó contended that Trotsky's perspective was a 'falsification' of Lenin's position—one of greater magnitude, indeed, than Stalin's 'socialism in one country':

> It may be argued that Stalin, by discounting the possibility of successful European revolutions, effectively contributed to their eventual defeat. . . . However, given this criticism—which is precisely that Stalin's policies represented a debasement of Lenin's strategy—the superiority of Stalin's perspective over Trotsky's is undeniable. It forms the whole historical-practical context in which the struggle for power . . . unfolded. No matter how strong Stalin's position in the apparatus, it would have availed him little if his basic strategic line had been invalidated by the course of political events. It was . . . confirmed by history. . . . When Germany eventually invaded Russia, the Soviet State, industrialized and armed under Stalin and assisted by bourgeois allies, was able to throw back the aggressors triumphantly. There was thus no substance in Trotsky's thesis that socialism in one country was doomed to annihilation. (Pp. 79–80)

The principal theoretical error underlying the problematic of permanent revolution, and inducing Trotsky's congenital political 'voluntarism', was what Krassó dubbed 'abstract internationalism' in his reply to Mandel's rejoinder (p. 103). In an unmistakably Andersonian passage, structured around the familiar East/West geopolitical polarity, Krassó had claimed that

> Trotsky failed to understand the fundamental differences between Russia and Western Europe as social structures. For him, capitalism was one and indivisible, and the agenda of revolution was one and indivisible, either side of the Vistula. This formal internationalism . . . in fact abolished the concrete international differences between the various European countries. . . . Events vindicated [Stalin's] belief in the enduring importance of the nation, as the unit demarcating one local structure from another. Political agendas were not interchangeable across frontiers in the Europe of Versailles. History kept different times in Paris, Rome, London or Moscow. (P. 81)

Although Trotsky's position on industrialization had been superior to that of his opponents in the Bolshevik Party, he had not advanced any programme for the political implementation of his favoured economic strategy. With Lenin's death, Bolshevik Marxism had undergone a regression, of which

Stalinist 'pragmatism' and Trotskyist 'voluntarism' were the mutually inclusive symptoms. After his defeat and exile, Trotsky's abstract internationalism had achieved its apotheosis: the 'futile voluntarism' of the doomed Fourth International (p. 84).[49] His analysis of Stalin's regime had its redeeming features, however, declining—unlike his motley progeny—to 'manufactur[e] new "ruling classes" and "capitalist restorations" in the Soviet Union at will' (p. 85).

Krassó's original article concluded by proclaiming Lenin 'the one great Marxist of that epoch' (p. 86). Rebutting Mandel's criticisms, the second ended by contrasting the facts of Maoism with the dogmas of Trotskyism. The Chinese Revolution contradicted imputations of some omnipotent counterrevolutionary role to Stalin and his instruments:

> The Chinese Revolution, the fundamental turning-point in world history of these decades, focuses all the main errors which haunted Trotsky's thinking. It was a victorious revolution led by a party which never openly challenged or defied the Comintern or Stalin. This was something Trotsky believed impossible—hence his decision to found a new International. It was based on the country and its main-force strength was the peasantry, yet it never abandoned its socialist programme or ideology. . . . [T]he Chinese experience, which was to be the vortex of world revolution at mid-century, escaped him. It escaped Stalin too. . . . But this is precisely the point. Stalin's policies were not Furies, with power of life and death over the world revolutionary movement. They were the cautious and conservative moves of the Soviet state, which necessarily had only a limited influence over events elsewhere. . . . Stalin's policies were not ultimately responsible for the failure of revolution in the West. . . . The fact that Stalin was so often wrong in these years does not thereby prove that Trotsky was conversely right. Leninism had disappeared with its author. (Pp. 102–3)

The 'Decennial Report' suggests that the perspective on the fortunes of international Communism after Lenin that was adopted in these articles enjoyed majority support on the editorial committee of the NLR (with Krassó, ironically, being the most averse to the Althusserian-Maoist colouration). As a result, Mandel's second riposte was published only fifteen months after Krassó's second piece. That anticritique had a paradoxical effect, however. For, according to the report, Anderson's own attitude to Trotsky was to be 'permanently altered' by Mandel's defence of him (p. 31). A gravitation toward Trotskyism was set in train—initially on Anderson's part and then, via his imposing mediation, on other core personnel of the editorial committee.

It was to be held in a complex equilibrium *with* Maoism until the end of the decade, before being counterposed *to* Maoism in the early 1970s.[50] The valences would be reversed: Trotskyism, putative non-Leninist cousin of Stalinism, would become the legatee of Leninism; Maoism, supposed peer of Leninism, would become the oriental offspring of Stalinism. Yet, whatever the interchanges, in 1967 Anderson had collaborated on a strenuous critique of his own subsequent affiliations.

In his 'Brief History of *New Left Review*', Blackburn writes that 'Guevarist and Maoist influences were among the undercurrents of the [1966–68] period'; and in *Arguments within English Marxism*, Anderson acknowledges the *Review*'s 'interest and sympathy' for China in the late 1960s.[51] The identification with China—both its professed 'internationalist' foreign policy and its proclaimed antibureaucratic domestic course—went beyond these declarations of modest dependence. The 'Decennial Report' is more forthcoming on the *NLR*'s affinities within the ranks of international Communism:

> NLR slid towards an uncritical substitution of China for Russia in its own po-
> litical orientation. By early 1968 . . . the review's basic attitude towards the
> world Communist movement had shifted—after an interlude of reserve—
> from hopes in Khrushchevism to illusions in Maoism. The record of the
> Chinese Revolution now functioned as a kind of absolution for the disasters
> of the Russian Revolution, permitting the real problems of Stalinism as a his-
> torical phenomenon both within and beyond the USSR still to be eluded by
> NLR. (P. 32)

This substitution, it was noted, had been 'over-determined by the identifica-tion of the review's collective with Cuba and North Vietnam' (p. 36).

Maoist influence reached its zenith in 1968–69. *NLR* no. 53, whose sequence of pieces on the 'red bases' strategy—of Chinese provenance and inspiration—has been cited, further contained an enthusiastically supportive account of the Cultural Revolution, then in its third devastating year. (A promise in the 'Themes' that the *Review* would be publishing its own analysis of the upheavals in the near future went unredeemed.)[52] The following issue was 'lucky to be able to publish an informal talk Mao gave to Red Guards in Kwantung in 1967—the first time it has appeared anywhere in the Western world'.[53] And in *NLR* no. 55, a fifteen-page introduction to Marshal Tukhachevsky's 'Revolution from Without', unsigned but composed by Anderson, argued for the superiority of the Chinese prosecution of revolutionary civil war over the Russian experience, and commended the People's

Liberation Army for its conduct of the 1962 Sino-Indian War, favourably contrasting it with the Red Army's record.[54]

Anderson's current observances led him crucially to revise the stance on the potential symmetry between bourgeois and socialist revolutions adopted in 'Socialism and Pseudo-Empiricism':

> What [Tukhachevsky] did not grasp . . . was the fundamental *difference in nature* between the bourgeois and socialist revolutions. . . . [T]he political transformations of society implied by the bourgeois revolutions did not ipso facto demand mass participation from below. They can . . . be implanted bureaucratically and repressively, by a small oligarchy from above. By contrast, the socialist revolution is by definition only socialist if it involves the masses of the population taking life into their own hands and overthrowing existing society from top to bottom by themselves. . . . After the Second World War, Stalin imposed a bureaucratic 'revolution from without' . . . throughout Eastern Europe, with notorious results. These unnatural creations were at least by-products of victory over Nazi aggression and defence against the threat of Anglo-American encroachments. The ultimate debasement of the once generous traditions of the Red Army was the return of a Soviet *kommandatura* in Prague 20 years later, no longer to drive out the Germans, but simply to suppress the Czechs: reaction from without. (Pp. 84–85)

Anderson's unequivocal condemnation of the Soviet repression of the Prague Spring in August 1968 may supply one clue to the accentuation of Maoist sympathies towards the close of the decade. For the invasion of Czechoslovakia by the Warsaw Pact terminated de-Stalinization until the 1980s and therewith apparently delivered its definitive quietus to Deutscherite optimism about a regeneration of the Russian Revolution from above. It possibly also accounts for the disinclination of Anderson and his colleagues to heed Deutscher's caution about Maoism and his outright repudiation of the Cultural Revolution from its very inception.[55] Prefacing Deutscher's articles on China twenty years later, Anderson would commend their lucidity and prescience, praising their author's singular incredulity in Maoist propaganda.[56] The *NLR*'s collective—and Anderson's individual—failure to emulate such prudence was not recollected on this occasion.

Prudence was displayed in the use of a pseudonym for two Andersonian forays onto the terrain of rock music, under the signature of Richard Merton, who opted for the Stones rather than the Beatles, and the Beach Boys rather than Bob Dylan. These are curios of the counterculture.[57] A 1968 introduction to Gramsci's *L'Ordine Nuovo* articles on factory councils in postwar

Turin is of more moment.[58] For it represents Anderson's first explicit public distance taking from the Italian strategist, in the name of Leninism. Gramsci's defence of the councils against any infringement of their autonomy by either unions or party had involved a false (negative) equation between the latter and the former, whose 'radical inadequacy was soon demonstrated':

> The spontaneous wave of factory occupations in 1920 created a revolution-ary situation in Italy. But there was no revolutionary *party*—no dynamic and disciplined vanguard which alone could have seized power and destroyed the bourgeois State. . . . It [is] clear that Gramsci had telescoped the problem of the socialist State *after* the revolution with the problem of working class or-ganization *before* the revolution. The illusion of achieving dominant eco-nomic power prior to the seizure of national *political* power was dramatically exploded. . . . The absence of a theory of *insurrection* is . . . the missing link in the whole of Gramsci's early writings. (P. 26)

With due alteration of details—the illusion of achieving cultural domi-nance prior to the seizure of national political power (the now capitalized 'State')—this passage points to the missing link in Anderson's early writings, exploding what he had come to regard as their illusions. 'Insurrection'—the prohibited Leninist strategy of 1965—had become the mandatory road to socialism in the West three years later. After the defeat of the Turin occupa-tions, Gramsci had made 'the decisive shift to a Leninist problematic' (p. 27). So, by now, in the light of events even closer to home, had Anderson.

Actuality of the Revolution, or The Beginning of the End?

According to the 'Decennial Report', May 1968 'abruptly and definitively ended the previous attraction or tolerance of NLR towards Western Com-munism', as a result of the role played in the events by the PCF (p. 47).[59] By the same token, given the performance of the Maoist Union des jeunesses communistes (marxistes-léninistes), and the Guevaro-Trotskyist Jeunesse communiste révolutionnaire, it compounded the *maoisant* tendencies of the journal and initiated *trotskysant* ones among key *NLR* personnel. The Paris Spring fixed the *Review*'s revolutionary-Marxist orientation for the next decade, in a reading of contemporary history that receded only with the nor-malization of the Portuguese 'revolution of the carnations' and the mobiliza-tion of the second Cold War, in the latter half of the 1970s. The immediate consequence—indicated earlier in this chapter—was allocation of a revo-lutionary vocation to the student movement, with the London School of

Economics perhaps functioning as the domestic counterpart of the École normale supérieure, bastion of Althusserian Maoism.

A special issue of the *NLR* was devoted to France at the end of 1968 and opened with an eight-page introduction, presumably composed by the editor.[60] Despite the Gaullist June that had temporarily stifled the student and worker May, the 'May Revolution' was to be regarded 'primarily as a victory and not as a defeat' (p. 1). Revolution had been restored to the immediate agenda of Western socialists; the becalmed universe of postwar advanced capitalism had witnessed 'the return of the repressed' (p. 5).[61] Marcusean and mainstream sociological assertions about the incorporation of the working class in the metropolis had been refuted by the facts. The dynamic of May had ultimately been frustrated—not least by the PCF, officially the depository of the revolutionary tradition, which had actually hankered after 'a return to normality, to the idyll of bourgeois politics and capitalist parliaments, to the dream of electoral majority' (p. 4). French students and youth, by contrast, had furnished the revolutionary agency of May, 'detonating' the general strike. Their endeavour had been hampered, however, by the absence of organized soviets, the necessary agitation in the armed forces, and cogent political slogans, which prevented Paris in 1968 from emulating Petrograd in 1917. Three lessons were inferred from May for Britain:

> First, it underlines . . . the importance of Marxist theory and revolutionary culture. . . . The incipient revolutionary Left in Britain desperately needs . . . the capacious reservoir of ideas which were . . . available in France. The production and circulation of theory is thus itself an indispensable preliminary practice. Secondly, the May events highlighted the potential of small revolutionary groups in helping to unleash a class storm. . . . United revolutionary action is the priority today: united revolutionary organization is the horizon tomorrow. The Vietnam Solidarity Campaign and Revolutionary Socialist Students' Federation may be seen as . . . embryonic expressions of this form of politics. Thirdly, the May events vindicated the fundamental socialist belief that the industrial proletariat is the revolutionary class of advanced capitalism. . . . It has, at the same stroke, made indisputable the vital revolutionary role of intellectuals. . . . The combination of the two was precisely the chemical formula which produced the shattering explosion of May. In Britain, the working-class has visibly begun to secede from its traditional reformist party, but it has not gained any decisive new orientation. Meanwhile, a student revolt is emerging for the first time in our history. The immediate future may depend on a covergence of the two. The link between them can only be provided by revolutionary socialists. (P. 7)

There followed in that issue articles by Mandel on the 'lessons of May'; by the French Trotskyist Jean-Marie Vincent on the PCF; by his Maoist compatriot André Glucksmann on revolutionary strategy; and by the Sartrean Gorz on 'the way ahead'. To underline historical analogies and traditional models, a short text by Lenin on students was included. Glucksmann's text—a complete translation of his ultraleftist pamphlet *Stratégie et révolution en France 1968*—was hailed as 'a signal guide to action, not only in France but in Britain and every other advanced capitalist country' (p. 8).[62]

Apart from the introduction to *NLR* no. 52, the principal contribution to the analysis of May from the ranks of the *Review* itself was Nairn's contribution to a volume entitled *The Beginning of the End*, recommended in the editorial statement. In it, having located May '68 in the French revolutionary tradition, Nairn insisted:

> It is . . . not a faint re-echo of the past. . . . It is the early manifestation of a revolutionary process much greater than those of the past. Every past revolution has been 'wrong', in the sense of being in discord with the real potential of society, at that historical moment: 1640, 1789, the revolutions of the nineteenth century, and of course the socialist revolutions in backward countries of this century. May, 1968 was the precursor of the first revolution in history which can be 'right'.[63]

Thus, even as elements of the first New Left were reconvening to issue their *May Day Manifesto*, its reformism was being superseded, so their successors reckoned, by the immanence—and imminence—of revolution in the West.[64] The *NLR*'s reaction to developments across the Channel exceeded the generic 'radicalization' to which Blackburn alludes in his 'Brief History of *New Left Review*' (p. vii).

Like Nairn's 'embryonic revolution' in France, Anderson's 'embryonic expressions' of revolutionary politics in Britain—the VSC and the RSSF—would shortly be aborted, discountenancing the specifics of the second lesson of May. But their revolutionary-socialist generalities—the production and circulation of theory (cultural reformation), revolutionary organization (political vanguardism), and investment in the proletariat (transformative social agency)—defined the horizons of the *NLR*. Eight years later, in the 'Themes' to the one hundredth issue of the *Review*, the May events were cited as ushering in 'the idea of the actuality of socialism' in advanced capitalism, and a revolutionary strategy for its achievement was reaffirmed.[65]

The immediate significance of May '68 for the *NLR* collectively, and Anderson individually, can best be gauged from a sequence of unpublished documents, dating from 1968 to 1970, whose major premiss—supplied by the events—was the 'actuality of socialism' in the West. The first two are headed 'Document A—Theory and Practice: The *Coupure* of May' and 'Document B—Ten Theses'. Anonymous texts, they were submitted for editorial discussion in the autumn of 1968.

Except for its positive invocation of Maoism, 'Document A' represents a protosummary of the conclusions of *Considerations on Western Marxism*, published in 1976. Divorced from political practice by the retreat of the revolutionary wave in Europe after the First World War and the ensuing Stalinization of the Comintern, Marxist theory in the West had become 'an esoteric discipline'.[66] Untouched by the postwar turbulence, with a stunted Communist Party, an arrested Labour Party, and no Marxist tradition, Britain presented an aggravated instance of the European syndrome. 'In these circumstances', the document continued,

> the basic impossibility of an[y] unified theoretical/political practice was exactly the same in England as elsewhere, but more by reason of a weak negative vacuum . . . rather than because of solidly positive obstacles (Stalinist mass parties restraining masses and censoring theorists). Given this, the only route to a Marxist theory was to begin a theory of the *non-emergence* of a revolutionary tradition of the working class in England, and of the *non-implantation* of Marxism. . . . This task implied . . . the translation and application of much of the existing continental theory. . . . NLR from 1964 to 1968 was conceived largely as an instrument for this specific work. . . . Parenthetically, it may be said that in four years NLR has achieved a reasonable degree of success in its aims. . . . It is now probably hegemonic in its extremely limited terrain of operations. . . . The relevant point here, however, is that this success has been achieved without any direct political engagement at all. (Pp. 5–6)

The disunity of theory and practice since the First World War can thus be unequally distributed roughly as depicted in figure 5. The postwar capitalist consensus and Stalinist *Gleichschaltung* alike had now been exploded, however; and the historic rupture between theory and practice had itself been disrupted:

> [T]he May events in France have effected a profound historical *coupure*: a new epoch has . . . begun in Europe. For the first time in 40 years, a massive revolutionary upsurge occurred in the West. . . . [It] completely bypassed the French Communist Party. Thus the two crucial conditions of the historic

non-correspondence of theory and practice in Western Europe have fallen. The re-emergence of the revolutionary masses once again renders *potentially* conceivable a unified political and theoretical practice. (P. 6)

Western Europe	Britain
Marxism	No Marxism
Social-Democracy	Labourism
Defeated revolutionary upsurges	No revolutionary upsurge
Practice: mass Stalinism	Practice: negligible Communism
Theory: Western Marxism (1924–68)	Theory: *NLR* (1964–68)

Figure 5. Theory and Practice

The emergent 'revolutionary masses' contained a new component—'an auxiliary corps of the revolution who are also paradoxically for the moment its front-line troops': students (p. 7). Although deficient in the structural capacity to make the revolution, and despite being, by definition, 'fluctuating and unstable in composition', students were numerically a mass force and offered a natural locus for the reception and production of revolutionary theory—what (to vary a phrase of Trotsky's) might be called a socialist 'primitive cultural accumulation'. They thus possessed an incomparable 'strategic significance' (p. 7).

Two major currents of post-Leninist Marxism had surfaced in May— Trotskyism and Maoism:

Stalinism . . . is dead as a current in the international socialist movement. Trotskyism is not. . . . It thereby will obviously become partially transformed, since its traditional mode of existence was its symbiotic negation of Stalinism. Now that the latter is to all intents and purposes extinct, the evolution of the former has become an open question. At a minimum, it is no longer confined to a sectarian ghetto. (Pp. 8–9)

Maoism was of a different magnitude altogether, 'in certain respects . . . surpass[ing] Lenin' (p. 10).[67] Although available, until the mid-1960s Mao's thoughts had been without political echo in Europe:

It was only after . . . the Great Proletarian Cultural Revolution—allegedly isolationist and xenophobic, actually the dawn of China's internationalist presence in world politics—that it has begun to acquire any currency in small groups at all. . . . [T]he May Revolution revealed Maoism as the other great underground revolutionary current which erupted into view at the centre of the class struggle. Its penetration outside France is only just beginning now . . . ; clearly it has a long future in front of it. . . . Maoism incarnates on a macrocosmic scale that unified practice the possiblity of which the students are beginning to rediscover in the West. (Pp. 10–11)[68]

Western Marxism had crystallized in the shadow of Stalinism; Trotskyism and Maoism had emerged in its wake. Adopting the canonical Leninist formula, 'Document A' nominated Western Marxism, Trotskyism, and Maoism as the 'three sources and component parts' of the Marxist legacy inherited by the New Left (p. 11). For the purposes of revolutionary socialism in the West, each had its advantages and disadvantages. Overall, however, their conjunction in the May events had 'transformed the context and perspective of the revolutionary Left in England':

> It is not a complete exaggeration to compare them with the impact of the first French Revolution in England during the 1790's—the last historical time that the *idea* of revolution sunk home deeply into the national consciousness, producing a sizeable minority of Jacobin militants dedicated to it. Today the second French Revolution has already altered the coordinates of English socialist practice in two crucial ways. (P. 12)

These bore upon, first, the imminent availability in English of the whole corpus of Western Marxism, as bourgeois publishers rushed to fill their lists with Marcuse and company (pp. 13–14); and second, the prospects for student politics: revolutionary socialism had become 'a tangible, imaginable reality for large numbers of English youth in higher education' (p. 14). The potential for the future was considerable:

> The revolutionary left has militants in the universities today: it does not yet have a *social base* among students such as exists in France or Germany. . . . But this is an attainable objective. We are only just beginning to see the wave of politicization which would create such a base in the future. (P. 15)

What was the impending impact of these mutations upon the *NLR* itself? According to 'Document A',

> It is no longer necessary for NLR to play a 'presentational' role in its publication of theoretical texts, and it is no longer possible for NLR to remain completely aloof from a 'position-taking' role on current political issues. . . . If it is not halted, by repression or an international downswing, [student mili-

tancy] will demand of us a much greater degree of political definition than NLR ever had in the past. The narrower the gap between theoretical practice and political practice on the revolutionary Left becomes, the more our strictly theoretical practice will have to come to grips with concrete political issues, in the pages of the review. (Pp. 16–17)[69]

Any such transformation of the editorial practice of the journal implied some kind of prior consensus on the fundamental questions—past, present, and future—of socialism. Granted revolutionary-socialist sympathies, what distinguished the *NLR*'s orientation from the extant Far Left groups in Britain, whether Maoist or Trotskyist (especially the International Socialists and the International Marxist Group [IMG])?[70]

An exercise in self-clarification, 'Document B—Ten Theses' endeavoured to answer this question, demarcating the *NLR* from what it described as 'forms of sectarian politics in Britain': 'The theses below can all be derived from something like a single, initial axiom, with a multiple application, which demarcates us from all other tendencies on the Left. The Revolution is a complex totality: it is a dynamic unity of different planes and sectors, not an elementary principle'.[71]

'Document B' commenced with some preliminary tenets before proceeding to the theses proper. First, contrary to the ubiquitous tendency to 'reduce world revolution to one sector only', it was said to 'inhabit *all* four sectors of the world'—namely, advanced capitalism, the Soviet Union and Eastern Europe, China, and the Third World. In the Althusserian-Maoist terms pervasive throughout these texts, the determinant contradictions in the capitalist world system were sited in the West, but the dominant contradiction could shift from one sector to another, depending on the concrete conjuncture (pp. 1–2). Second, the revolution was not the preserve of any one social class: proletarian victory in the North was indispensable to the global triumph of socialism, but peasant victories in the South were preparing the way for it. The world over, the road to revolution involved class alliances (peasants and workers, proletarians and petit bourgeois, etc.): 'The social structure of revolution is . . . always complex, just as is its geography' (p. 2). Third, successful revolution comprised an organic combination of economic, political, and cultural class struggle, 'whose main front varies according to the situation' (pp. 3–4). Fourth, no revolutionary tradition enjoyed a monopoly on the revolution: any such movement in the West would necessarily have to be based upon a plurality of organizations (p. 3). Fifth, and finally, the socialist revolution was irreducible to its economic component: the transformation of the relations of production. Entailing cultural revolution, it encompassed the social formation in its entirety:

> The duty of every revolutionary is to fight here and now for a qualitative change not only of economy and politics, but also of education, art, sexuality and the family, and the inter-relations of all of them. . . . The radicalism of a revolution is measured by its abolition of the present notions of everyday life. (P. 4)

Turning now to the substantive theses, the first was a straightforward statement of revolutionary internationalism (p. 5). The second propounded an orthodox Trotskyist position on the USSR: a 'reactionary force' at home and abroad, its political regime (like those of its creations in Eastern Europe) was fit for proletarian 'revolution from below' (pp. 5–6). By contrast, according to the third thesis, the People's Republic of China warranted a much more positive appreciation:

> [T]he Chinese Revolution was based on the enthusiatic support of the majority class of the country—the peasantry. . . . This difference was the fundamental determinant of the subsequent outcome of the two revolutions. It allowed a decisive break with the pattern of Russian experience, which took the form, first of an open rejection of the international role of the Soviet Union, and second of an appeal to the masses to rise up and smash manifestations of bureaucratic privilege and authority within China itself. The historic merit of the Cultural Revolution . . . has been its rupture with traditional methods of inner-party political manipulation, based on the passivity of the population, and its awakening of the egalitarian initiative and creativity of the masses. (P. 7)

Thus, as between the parties to the Sino-Soviet dispute, 'Document B' sided with Maoism. This did not mean that China would or could elude the effects of a constraining economic scarcity. Nevertheless, in contrast to the Soviet Union, it constituted 'a major revolutionary pole throughout the world' (p. 8).

So much for the divided Second World, the sectors of international Communism. What of the Third World, the sector containing the colonial and ex-colonial countries? A fourth thesis vaunted the Vietnamese Revolution for 'carr[ying] the national liberation struggles of the post-war epoch to a new and unprecedented level' (p. 9). It had demonstrated that revolutionary-Marxist guidance was a precondition of successful anti-imperialism. Moreover, as Therborn had argued in 'From Petrograd to Saigon', it had brought socialist revolution back home, from periphery to metropolis: 'The renewed revolutionary upsurge in the advanced capitalist countries . . . is a direct consequence of the epic struggle of the Vietnamese' (p. 10).

Recognition of the catalytic role of the Vietnam War in rebellions on the campuses and in the ghettos did not entail demotion of the proletariat from the leading role traditionally assigned it in the transition to socialism in the West. Hence a fifth thesis:

> The socialist revolution in the West can only be achieved under the banner of the class that produces the surplus value on which all other groups live. The proletariat is the fundamental revolutionary force generated by industrial capitalism and destined to bury it. . . . [Marxism] provides the basis for the material unification of all the exploited and oppressed in a revolutionary bloc under the leadership of the working-class, capable of conquering a new hegemony. The construction of this bloc is the central task of revolutionaries in the West today. (P. 11)

This had been the historic banner of the Third International. Today, however, according to the sixth thesis, the Communist parties in the West had abandoned Leninism and were 'centrist parties of a new type . . . : anticapitalist and non-revolutionary' (p. 12). In revolutionary situations, these organizations could be expected either to split or to pass over to one of the two camps—revolution or counterrevolution. For its part, the PCF had finally opted for the latter in May '68. The Communist parties nevertheless contained socialist militants who could be detached from them, thereby 'neutralizing' their threat to revolutionary socialism (p. 13). As to revolution in the West, a seventh thesis, invoking the precedent of May, formulated the requisite relationship between vanguard and masses:

> The socialist revolution in the West will be the free work of a strategic majority of the population. Mass political activity on a decisively greater scale than the October Revolution is the only way to overthrow capitalism where it [is] institutionalized within the framework of the bourgeois-democratic state. . . . A relatively smaller vanguard is rendered possible by the symmetrically greater number and culture of the popular masses themselves. The function of this vanguard, however, is irreplaceable. It alone can provide revolutionary leadership for a broad movement of the class. (Pp. 13–14)

The organizational norm of that vanguard, so the eighth thesis had it, was 'democratic centralism' in its original Leninist form. However, the earlier point about a 'multiplicity of tendencies within the revolutionary bloc' was reiterated as a predictable and salutary correlate of the complexity of Western societies. The vanguard function was necessary; its institutional incarnation, contingent (pp. 15–16).

The comprehensively Leninist character of the theses thus far is self-evident. It logically entailed identification of the neuralgic point separating revolutionary from reformist socialists: the state. The ninth thesis stipulated:

> It is impossible to achieve socialism without the violent overthrow and de-struction of the bourgeois state machine. . . . There is only one road to social-ism—the revolutionary abolition of the state apparatus of army, police and bureaucracy which is the lynchpin of capitalist power, and the complete ex-propriation of private ownership of the means of production. The existence of bourgeois-democratic institutions in many Western countries demands the development of revolutionary tactics distinct from those pursued in October, but it [in] no way alters this fundamental tenet of Marxism. (P. 16)

Having destroyed the bourgeois state, the working class would construct a socialist state—'the transitional dictatorship of the proletariat' (p. 17)—whose task was the abolition of capitalist relations of production and the consequent suppression of the capitalist class.

What was the generic nature of the future postcapitalist social order? The tenth and last thesis maintained:

> The institutions of socialist democracy in the West . . . will inherit the legacy of the Commune and the Soviets. . . . Socialism in the highly industrialized countries will develop these historic lessons into a new civilization. Control of production by the producers will relegate the market as decisively to the past as it once did the manor. The concrete democracy of workers' assem-blies . . . will reveal the bourgeois parliaments of today to be as narrow and anachronistic an oppression as they in their day did the feudal estate. It fol-lows that a triumphant revolution will refuse the dead heritage of national egoism. It will pursue the path of international solidarity with the exploited and oppressed everywhere, until the world is free of imperialism, and with it of the realm of necessity. (Pp. 17–18)

Thus, the classic Leninist scenario was upheld: revolutionary seizure of power → destruction of the capitalist state apparatus → transitional dicta-torship of the proletariat → abolition of capitalist relations of production → communism (suppression of the market/institution of direct democracy).

The most notable feature of the 1968 theses is their optimism about revolutionary potentialities in three of the four global sectors delimited: China, the Third World, and the West. Although not officially adopted by the NLR, these documents—a 'results and prospects' at the antipodes of the May Day Manifesto—apparently accorded, in large part, with majority opinion within the editorial committee. Consequently, as we have seen, the Review committed itself to the student movement and was instrumental in fashioning the programme of the RSSF. Once the latter had been defeated, political activism was (as the 'Decennial Report' notes [p. 40]) transferred into political journalism.

By late 1969, three NLR editors—Barnett, Blackburn, and Fred Halliday— were on the staff of the Black Dwarf, and the project of creating a a revolutionary weekly to complement the Review was taking shape. In March 1970, as a result of the IMG's firm orientation to Leninism and desire to create a youth organization (the Spartacus League), the Black Dwarf editorial board split. The adherents of Trotskyism (including Tariq Ali and Blackburn) left to found the Red Mole, whereas Barnett and Halliday established Seven Days, whose staff included other members of the NLR (Cockburn, Stedman Jones, and Wollen). Seven Days survived from October 1971 to March 1972. That May, Blackburn, Hoare, and Branka Magaš joined the IMG, whose general outlook at the time is most accessibly conveyed in Tariq Ali's The Coming British Revolution, published, in a telling sign of the times, by Jonathan Cape.[72]

This phase in the NLR's existence—roughly from the autumn of 1968 to the summer of 1971—was thus marked by a mind-set that prompted some of its personnel to deduce, as a practical corollary, membership of the British section of the Fourth International, the IMG. In Anderson's case, despite the growing proximity of his own position to that of Mandel, a succession of whose publications were translated by the NLR or NLB,[73] solidarity did not prompt adherence. This can, in part at least, be explained by a determination to preserve the editorial autonomy of the Review from democratic-centralist diktat, while using it to influence the IMG milieu from without. At all events, that it did not imply fundamental dissent from IMG perspectives is apparent from two unpublished manuscripts of this period, both of which took their cue from the 'Ten Theses'. The first—'The Founding Moment' (1969)—investigated some preconditions for revolutionary socialism to manifest itself as a mass phenomenon; the second—'State and Revolution in the West' (1970)—was concerned with a critique of Gramsci's political theory and a concomitant retheorization of revolutionary-socialist strategy under conditions of advanced, bourgeois-democratic capitalism.

71

Confounding Moments

'The Founding Moment' was likewise premissed upon the imminent possibility of socialism in the West, disclosed by the French May.[74] In Western Europe, what Lenin had called the 'weak links' of imperialism were located in its southern zone: France, Italy, Spain, Portugal, and Greece (pp. 1–2). Complicating the typology of 'Problems of Socialist Strategy', the geopolitical divide beween Western and Eastern Europe was overlaid by a subdivision within the western half of the continent: between the less economically advanced and politically stable South and the more industrialized and normalized North (pp. 2–3). Whereas Social-Democracy was the dominant tradition of working-class politics in the northern belt, Communism predominated in the South. Accordingly, the prospects for socialism in the region were inseparable from the existence and performance of contemporary European Communism. 'The Founding Moment' aimed to adjudicate on leftist claims to the effect that the Communist parties had evolved into social-democratic organizations; and that their command over working-class loyalties could be displaced and replaced by the Far Left (pp. 3–5).

The full details of this remarkable text—the author's most extended reflection on the Communist movement, marshaling the full range of research on the subject in a number of languages—need not detain us. Characteristically, Anderson sought an answer to the question of a possible displacement of the parties of the Third International in the present by examining the precedent of their attempted displacement of the organizations of the Second International in the past.

The matrix of the break with reformism had been 1914–18: the explosive conjunction of the Second International's 'social patriotism', the catastrophe of the imperialist war with which it was tainted, and the positive counterexample afforded by the successful Bolshevik Revolution (p. 12). A general politicization and 'radicalization' had ensued among the proletariats of Europe, one of whose products was a 'transfer of allegiances' in 1917–21, with the foundation of Communist parties and their amalgamation into a new International.[75] However, they had arrived too late on the scene to alter the course of the abortive postwar revolutions, in a conjuncture characterized by a profound disparity between objective possibilities and subjective capacities for socialist revolution (p. 20). Concurrently, the October Revolution was isolated by external intervention and deformed by civil war (p. 22). As a result, the Communist parties had rapidly declined amid a restabilization of the capitalist order in Europe, and inevitably become subordinated to Soviet tutelage within a Comintern itself born too late to reverse the ebbing revolutionary tide. Often attributed to Stalinist manipulation, this submission derived from the Communist parties' repeated failures throughout the 1920s, magnified in the mirror of Soviet Russia's seeming success (pp. 26–27).

The Popular Front period of 1935–39 had seen the creation of Communism as a mass phenomenon in France and Spain, but in circumstances in which the Comintern functioned as a relay of the Narkomindel (p. 28). This experience anticipated what Anderson analyzed as the rebirth of European Communism during the Second World War. The refounding moment of Stalingrad at once compounded and reinflected the founding moment of Petrograd (p. 37), conjugating socialism and nationalism in the Communist-led armed resistance movements of Italy, France, Czechoslovakia, Yugoslavia, Greece, and Albania:

> That second founding moment also comprised two components which were in some ways very similar to the first. One was the impact of German occupation and popular resistance to it—the impact of political domination and repression by a foreign army, which made the national motif so important for the whole colouration of this second wave of communism. The ordeal of Nazi conquest was then overdetermined by the central role in the liberation of Europe from it played by the Red Army. Stalingrad in 1942 performs the homologous function to Petrograd in 1917. Both the negative demonstration of Nazi rule and the positive demonstration of Soviet victories over it produced once again a big mass shift leftwards.[76]

But if the shift consequent upon a second world war and a repeat redemption from Russia, in the space of a quarter century, went wider under nationalist stimulus, it cut less deeply under Stalinist auspices (pp. 46–47).

Inspection of the 'founding moments' of Communism as a political phenomenon thus indicated that nothing less than two global wars had been required to break the grip of Social-Democracy on popular loyalties, and that the 'transfer of allegiances' had not been replicated in the economically most advanced zone of Western Europe (p. 49). It was therefore safe to infer that any repetition of the cycle, this time displacing the Communist parties, would involve conditions commensurate with the moments of 1917 and 1942 (p. 52). Meanwhile, May '68 had not effected any such thing. Indeed, the PCF had survived unscathed—even enhanced, in terms of members and electors. May corroborated the inertial lessons of working-class political history in the twentieth century (pp. 54–55).

What answer did it therewith suggest to Anderson's other question: the character of contemporary European Communism? Up to the mid-1950s, for all their notorious strategic volte-faces and tactical improvizations— from United Front to Third Period, from Popular Front via neutralism to Resistance, from Tripartism to Two Camps—the Communist parties had exhibited an enduring allegiance to their original Leninist programme as regards the revolutionary destruction of the bourgeois state (if not, of course, its replacement by organs of direct proletarian democracy). They thus remained separated by a political gulf from their Social-Democratic rivals in the West (p. 72). With the Twentieth Congress of the CPSU, a new phase in their career had begun: in effect, under the rubric of official de-Stalinization, an unofficial, programmatic de-Leninization (pp. 72ff.). Regressing to the reformist positions of the pre-1914 Second International, the West European parties had embraced the peaceful, parliamentary road to socialism and were in the process, de facto if not de jure, of abrogating the dictatorship of the proletariat, touchstone of Leninism. The result was a glaring contradiction: if, programmatically, Western Communism was increasingly being assimilated to the national terrain on which it had to operate, its bureaucratic-centralist structures and international loyalties rendered it abidingly extraterritorial (p. 78).

How was this contradiction to be explained? Once the Soviet Union had attained an equality of nuclear deterrence with the United States, its diplomacy was no longer so reliant upon the external support of the Western Communist parties in fomenting interimperialist tensions (p. 96). Accordingly, their margin of national independence could be expanded and the Cominform dispensed with. Khrushchev's revelations and the Sino-Soviet split had transformed the relationship between Soviet and Western parties, releasing the latter from the old forms of institutional submission to backward socialism while making them susceptible to new forms of ideological concession to advanced capitalism (pp. 97–98). The Twentieth Congress line of 'national roads to socialism' simultaneously functioned as an apologia for preservation of bureaucratic dictatorship in the East (the Russian road) and a rationale for adaptation to parliamentary democracy in the West (the French, Italian, and other roads). It permitted the combination of international loyalty and national autonomy reflected in a traditionalist structure and a revisionist programme (pp. 102–4). The 'advanced democracy' touted by the Italian or French parties of Togliatti, Thorez, or their successors was an egregiously right-wing goal (p. 72)—part of a manifesto for a subsequent constitutional transition to socialism that erected a house of cards certain to collapse at the first gust of capitalist reality (pp. 106–8).

These astringent criticisms did not licence definition of their objects as social-democratic. The Communist parties were 'centrist'—contrary to the allegation of their leftist critics, anticapitalist (unlike Social-Democracy); but, contrary to their own designation, nonrevolutionary (unlike Maoism or Trotskyism). As such, they had a historical pedigree in the political formations out of which the Third International had been constructed (p. 111). Yet contemporary centrism was a much more formidable phenomenon than its precursor, doubly determined as it was by the tradition of historical Communism and the consolidation of postwar capitalism (pp. 112–13). Above all, it depended upon the acquiescence of the popular classes, whose radicalization, as in the aftermath of the First World War, could alone detonate its contradictions (p. 113).

In this respect, the experience of May '68 offered a decisive lesson. The PCF and its trade union arm, the Confédération générale du travail (CGT), had not behaved like social-democratic organizations during the events, which would not have escalated into a general strike and a prerevolutionary crisis without them. If the performance of the PCF had ultimately obstructed a socialist resolution, its existence had initially tabled it. Reverting to Sartrean mode, Anderson argued that, as the embodiment of revolutionary tradition and proletarian organization, French Communism was coresponsible for the effervescence displayed by the popular masses by dint of its promptings. If the French working class was of a temper different from the German, it was because the PCF was of a stamp distinct from the SPD (pp. 126–27). Given the lack of alternative (Leninist) leadership, the Gaullist restoration of order had ensued, and Communist centrism had not undergone the ordeal to which it might otherwise have been exposed (p. 128).

If, as Anderson maintained, Communism was the paramount political tradition in the weak links of the European capitalist chain; if it was not imminently about to be displaced; and if it represented a variety of centrism, what were the implications for revolutionary socialism? Were its adherents snared in the sometime dilemma identified by Sartre—namely, that it was impossible to do anything with the Communist Party but impossible to do anything without it? Anderson's first conclusion was that membership of a Communist party was a perfectly legitimate option for revolutionaries (pp. 128–29). Second, however, those socialists who declined this option were no longer confined to the margins, as they had in effect been for decades previously. The advent of the student and youth movements provided another possible venue. Yet these too had their limitations. Petit bourgeois in class character, their florescence was attributable primarily to the extraneous factor of anti-imperialism in the Third World, Havana and Hanoi performing an analogous role to Petrograd and Stalingrad in their crystallization (pp. 131–32).

The basic problem confronting revolutionary politics in the West revolved around the relations between the aspirant revolutionary organizations and the established centrist institutions (p. 132). The mutually corrective 'convergence' between the two envisioned by Magri and Althusser was a beneficial projection, compared with the mutual recriminations of Communists and *gauchistes* after May (pp. 132–34).[77] But the undemocratic centralism of the Communist parties constituted an enormous obstacle to such convergence, posing the question of whether their ingrained character simply precluded the only kind of socialist revolution that was conceivable in Western conditions (p. 135). If the Communist parties were (too) strong, the student groups were very weak. Socially, the category of students did not comprise a class, merely—even in those days—a finite occupation; politically, their ideology was internationally determined and correspondingly vulnerable to transvaluation, were anti-imperialist insurgency to damp down after the impending victory in Vietnam (pp. 135–36).

'The Founding Moment' ended by reasserting the commencement of a new historical period of revolutionary developments (p. 136). From one obviously retrospective angle, however, its penultimate notes of scepticism ghosted the future script—even the premature obituary—of scenarios for revolutionary socialism in the West. 'Paris was not Petrograd; May did not reach October', the introduction to *NLR* no. 52 observed (p. 1). Variations on the refrain could be applied to southern Europe in its entirety over the next decade—in part, for reasons ruminated by Anderson. Subject to prudent repression, student movements exhibited the indicated fragility, whereas Communist parties retained their hold on working-class loyalties and maintained their reformist trajectory (to the extent that, by the end of the 1970s, Anderson would be sharing the assessment of them proposed in Mandel's 1978 critique *From Stalinism to Eurocommunism*). Location of the 'weak links' in southern Europe proved prescient. But in each case the designs of the local Communist party, whether Brezhnevite (Portuguese and Greek) or Eurocommunist (Italian, Spanish, and French), foundered: the Spanish Communist Party's, for example, in the 'Pact of Freedom', the PCF's in the 'Union of the Left', the PCI's in the 'Historic Compromise'. The ultimate beneficiaries would be the refurbished organizations of southern European Social-Democracy, which expeditiously replicated the cycle of their northern cousins. In a 'founding moment' forgivably unforeseen by Anderson, there was indeed a transfer of working-class allegiances from European Communism—not leftward, to Trotskyism, but rather rightward, to Eurosocialism, triggering the disintegration of Far Leftism in the wake of reformist Communism.

This historical eventuation lay in the distant future. In 'The Founding Moment', Anderson had underscored that the superiority of the revolutionary-socialist programme over the reformist was quite insufficient to detach proletarian loyalties from established organizations (p. 52). Yet this did not exempt its partisans from the refinement of such a programme. The ninth of the 'Ten Theses' had averred a Leninist strategy for socialism in the West, while pointing out that bourgeois democracy there dictated 'the development of revolutionary tactics distinct from those pursued in October' (p. 16). It was as a contribution to this task that the second of the manuscripts referred to in this section—'State and Revolution in the West'—was doubtless conceived. In the absence of access to it, our comments must of necessity be rather tentative. But it would seem to have been a revolutionary rectification of 'Problems of Socialist Strategy', from which 'The Antinomies of Antonio Gramsci' was eventually extracted.[78] Given the nonrepetition of the French May and the Italian 'hot autumn' of 1969, and the waning of the student movement in Britain, certain of the conjunctural conclusions of 'State and Revolution' were apparently infirmed. Having, however, revised his West/East geopolitical problematic by replacing Gramsci's civil society/state couplet with a differentiation between capitalist/democratic and feudal/Absolutist states, Anderson undertook a lengthy detour via prehistory.

The Laboratory of Forms

In other words, 'State and Revolution in the West' was the precursor of Anderson's history project—or, more precisely perhaps, his project in comparative historical sociology—two instalments of which were published in 1974: *Passages from Antiquity to Feudalism* and *Lineages of the Absolutist State*.[79] The foreword to *English Questions* derives this project from the 'impasse' at which the debate over the Nairn-Anderson theses had arrived. Thompson's 1965 critique had harpooned the normative typology of 'Origins of the Present Crisis', but at the price of reinstating 'pluralism'. In the conviction that national specificity could be grasped only by 'a theoretical understanding of the variant national paths of capital into the world', Anderson had undertaken a 'detour through [the] prehistory' of the 'bourgeois revolutions'—the political overturns indispensable, according to Marxist tradition, for a consummate transition from feudalism to capitalism. That prehistory essentially comprised the state form of Absolutism, which

Anderson examined in its 'European matrix . . . as a whole' (pp. 6–8). As he put it in the foreword to *Lineages*:

> [T]he vertical division of the [European] continent between West and East is here taken as a central organizing principle of the materials discussed. Within each zone, of course, major social and political variations have always existed, and these are contrasted and explored in their own right. The aim of this procedure is to suggest a *regional* typology that can help to clarify the divergent trajectories of the major Absolutist States of both Eastern and Western Europe. Such a typology may serve to indicate . . . the sort of intermediate conceptual plane that is so often missing between generic theoretical constructs and particular case-histories, in studies of Absolutism as of much else. (P. 9)[80]

The 'much else' was significant: *Passages* and *Lineages* were precisely prehistories. These comparative surveys of the divergent zonal transitions to feudalism and trajectories of Absolutism were intended to issue in two further rounds of experimentation in what *Passages* called 'the "laboratory of forms" that European history provides' (p. 266): with the sequence of bourgeois revolutions that uprooted the Absolutist states, and with the capitalist states that emerged from these upheavals. In the sequels, so Anderson promised in *Lineages*, '[c]ertain of the theoretical and political implications of arguments in the present volume will . . . become fully apparent' (p. 11). If, in addition, reportedly planned volumes on the socialist revolutions and postcapitalist states had ever appeared, the implications would have been transparent.

The discrepancy between original conception and actual execution is massive; it possibly constitutes the single most important fact about Anderson's intellectual career to date. Inspecting the national culture, he had insisted that '[e]vents that fail to happen are often more important than those which do; but they are infinitely more difficult to see'.[81] The verdict may be reciprocated: Anderson's missing history books represent the 'absent centre' of his theoretico-political oeuvre. (Were some version of them to materialize in the future, the judgement would require greater or lesser qualification but not retraction: two decades or more on, they would perforce possess a quite different character.) In their absence, *Passages* and *Lineages*, for all their splendour, have something of the air of orphaned volumes.

At the same time, treatment of them as components of the original, much more ambitious programme enables us to perceive them as pentimenti. For although not all history was contemporary history for Anderson, his exploration of Absolutism was no mere antiquarianism but a genealogy, or prehistory, of the present: the prelude to a comparative history of the European capitalist states, which would permit the rigorous theorization of them and thus facilitate the formulation (and prosecution) of an adequate revolutionary strategy against them—the missing link of Leninism in the West, not found by Gramsci in *Prison Notebooks*. Hence his (Marxist and Leninist) 'history from above', taking as its object the state, or the political level at which the struggle of contending social classes is 'ultimately resolved' (p. 11).[82] Anderson's enterprise aimed to reproduce on a gigantic, continental scale the undertaking polemically discharged, in miniature, at the local level in 'Origins', correcting it in the process: reconstruction of the past in order to understand the present and master the future.

Discussing the incompletion of the *Critique of Dialectical Reason* in 1983, Anderson was at pains to explore both the intrinsic and the extrinsic obstructions that had derailed Sartre.[83] Discounting the Herculean labour involved, what frustrated Anderson can only be conjectured. But we might detect an external, political determinant in the shape of the disappointment of revolutionary expectations after 1968, climaxing with Portugal in 1975, 'when arguably the best single chance of a socialist revolution in Western Europe in this century was spectacularly missed'.[84] A major intrinsic problem—especially in view of Anderson's evident admiration for his work—was posed by Robert Brenner's renewal of the *Science and Society* 'transition debate' of the 1950s. Brenner's 1976 essay 'Agrarian Class Structure and Economic Development in Pre-industrial Europe', rejected, inter alia, the 'neo-Smithian Marxism' that accorded priority to urban development—the conjoint rise of commerce and bourgeoisie—in the transition from feudalism to capitalism; and it dissented from the Marxist orthodoxy that postulated the occurrence of a 'bourgeois revolution' as a necessary political moment in the perfection of that transition.[85] Since sophisticated versions of these received Marxist ideas were integral to Anderson's project, its architectonic thus came under challenge.

For Brenner, divergences in economic development between Eastern and Western Europe, and within Western Europe itself, were to be explained primarily by the variable balance of class forces between nobility and peasantry, and the (unintended) consequences of their conflicts, on the land itself. In the unique English instance, these had set in train a self-metamorphosis of the feudal landowners and a consequent transition to (agrarian) capitalism, which rendered superfluous a 'bourgeois revolution' against monarchy and aristocracy. Anderson's account of the 'general crisis of feudalism' in Western Europe in *Passages* (pp. 197–209) tended both to emphasize the implacable structural constraints upon the reproduction of the rural productive forces in the feudal mode of production,[86] and to allot an autonomous, dynamic role within the mediaeval economy to urban sectors engaged in commodity production and exchange. Thereafter, *Lineages* identified the mercantile 'ascendant bourgeoisie', based in those sectors, as a 'second antagonist' of the feudal aristocracy (pp. 57, 20), whose state apparatus and class power were to be contested by 'bourgeois revolutions', whether 'from below' or 'from above' (p. 431). Anderson thus subscribed to a (complex) variant of the 'bourgeois paradigm' in *Passages* and *Lineages*.[87]

Anderson's subsequent comments, in his review of Brenner's *Merchants and Revolution*, suggest that he did not find his challenge insurmountable. In the same year as Brenner's original essay, Anderson had produced a comparative paper entitled 'The Notion of Bourgeois Revolution', not published until 1992, which vindicated a reconstructed concept of bourgeois revolution.[88] Now welcoming Brenner's revised 'social interpretation' of the English Revolution while noting that in his earlier work '[t]he break with feudalism came not from any accumulation in trade or assault on absolute monarchy, but through . . . the self-conversion of the English landlords', Anderson wrote:

> For all the power of this case, there were always difficulties with its overall context. The idea of capitalism in one country, taken literally, is only a bit more plausible than that of socialism. For Marx the different moments of the modern biography of capital were distributed in a cumulative sequence, . . . before being 'systematically combined in England at the end of the 17th century'. Historically, it makes better sense to view the emergence of capitalism as a value-added process gaining in complexity as it moved along a chain of inter-related sites. In this story, the role of cities was always central. . . . Yet, even if the 'bourgeois' contribution to the economic genesis of capitalism is conceded, this does not mean that a political 'revolution' was necessary to smooth its path. . . . What converted a parliamentary revolt into an armed revolution [in England] was, on Brenner's showing, the catalytical role of the new merchants in London. Here, if ever, were revolutionary bourgeois. . . . The detractor of the significance of merchant capital in principle has been the first to establish . . . its role as demi-urge in practice. (P. 17)

It may be, then, that the European 'laboratory of forms' has not confuted Anderson's theoretico-historical hypotheses. It has, however, problematized the political implications whose elucidation was promised in the foreword to *Lineages*.

In a perceptive review of the companion volumes, appropriately entitled 'The Uniqueness of the West', Paul Hirst noted that Anderson's comparative history took the form of a 'genealogy', whereupon 'a history is a unique pattern of development made possible by the singularity of its origin'.[89] The uniqueness of the West—'the specificity of European history' (*Lineages*, p. 420)—derived from the historical 'synthesis' contained in its variant of feudalism: a hybrid socioeconomic formation engendered by the 'recombination' of the slave and 'primitive' modes of production, which preserved the legacy of antiquity—especially its cultural heritage (*Passages*, pp. 18–19). This was first and foremost of what Anderson unabashedly dubbed 'the peculiarities of the continent' (*Lineages*, p. 412). The unique emergence in Western Europe of capitalism, the 'gift and malediction of Europe to the globe', was made possible by 'the *concatenation of antiquity and feudalism there*' (pp. 415, 420):

> European feudalism proved the gateway to capitalism. It was the economic dynamic of the feudal mode of production in Europe which released the elements for primitive accumulation of capital on a continental scale, and it was the social order of the Middle Ages which preceded and prepared the ascent of the bourgeois class that accomplished it. (Pp. 414–15)

Contrariwise, the absence of the synthesis in Eastern Europe was 'the basic historical determinant of the uneven development of Europe, and of the persistent retardation of the East' (*Passages*, p. 213). It was not only in crossing continents that one changed centuries.

The differential temporalities of Western and Eastern history meant that the Absolutist states, structurally similar yet genetically distinct, had assumed a quite different character either side of the Elbe. To the West, '[t]he rule of the Absolutist State was that of the feudal nobility in the epoch of the transition to capitalism. Its end would signal the crisis of the power of its class: the advent of the bourgeois revolutions, and the emergence of the capitalist State' (p. 42). Whereas the Absolutist state in the West was 'a *compensation for the disappearance of serfdom*', its analogue in the East, demonstrating the priority of historical genesis over institutional structure,[90] was

> the repressive machine of a feudal class that had just erased the traditional communal freedoms of the poor. It was a *device for the consolidation of serfdom*, in a landscape scoured of autonomous urban life or resistance. The manorial reaction in the East meant that a new world had to be implanted from above, by main force. The dose of violence pumped into social relations

81

was correspondingly far greater. The Absolutist State in the East never lost the signs of this original experience. (P. 195)

The spectre of Stalin would seem to hover over this passage. And, indeed, the political crux of Anderson's reconstruction of the lineages and trajectories of these states was reached with his discussion of Russian Absolutism. By the advent of the First World War, the Russian social formation was economically dominated by the capitalist mode of production. Its tsarist state, however, remained a feudal-Absolutist one. Gramsci's utilization of the state/civil society couplet to pinpoint its specificity had missed its historical target. 'If all this is so', Anderson wrote,

> it is necessary to have the courage to draw the consequences. *The Russian Revolution was not made against a capitalist State at all.* The Tsarism which fell in 1917 was a feudal apparatus: the Provisional Government never had time to replace it with a new or stable bourgeois apparatus. The Bolsheviks made a *socialist revolution,* but from beginning to end they never confronted the *central enemy* of the workers' movement in the West. Gramsci's deepest intuition was in this sense correct: the modern capitalist State of Western Europe remained after the October Revolution a *new* political object for Marxist theory, and revolutionary practice. . . . The failure of the November Revolution in Germany, as momentous for the history of Europe as the success of the October Revolution . . . , was grounded in the differential nature of the State machine with which each was confronted. The mechanisms of socialist victory and defeat in these years go to the bottom of the deepest problems of bourgeois and proletarian democracy, which have still to be theoretically and practically solved in the second half of the 20th century. The political lessons and implications of the fall of Tsarism, for a comparative survey of contemporary social formations, remain to this day largely unexplored. The historical obituary of the Absolutism that expired in 1917 has in that sense yet to be completed. (Pp. 359–60)

Hinting, perhaps, at Anderson's intention to shoulder the theoretico-political burden, this conclusion had inclement implications for contemporary revolutionary socialism. It intimates that the German November was of comparable significance to the Russian October—another of those historically determinant nonevents, this time for the history of socialism in the twentieth century. It therewith qualifies Anderson's statement, in the foreword to *English Questions* (p. 7), that whereas for Nairn, August 1914 became the key date in the socialist narrative, for him—'more conventionally'—it was October 1917. Trotsky recognized that in October, 'history ha[d] moved along the line of least resistance. The revolutionary epoch has made its incursion through the least barricaded gates'.[91] Yet even so, it was 'the prologue to world revolution'. For Anderson, however, if the victorious Russian revolutionaries had not confronted a capitalist state of any sort, when their vanquished German comrades had, why should the lessons of November not loom even larger than those of October in the counsels of Western socialists half a century or more later? The unstated consequent was stark: Leninism—vindicated in principle by Anderson by negative deduction from the barren record of Social-Democracy—enjoyed no positive, practical confirmation as a strategy for socialism in social formations where the capitalist mode of production was protected and regulated by a capitalist state (let alone where that state took stable bourgeois-democratic institutional forms).

Nevertheless, the divergent trajectories of West and East, and the superiority of the former over the latter in crucial respects (advanced capitalist economy, liberal democracy), contained, so to speak, a political saving grace. The unique development of the West—the advent of an endogenous, autonomous capitalism via the synthesis of feudalism and antiquity—was also an incipiently *universal* history, a 'gift and malediction . . . to the globe'. However, the economic, political, and cultural retardation of the East facilitated the lifting of that curse there. But there is more. The Bolshevik Revolution not only wrested Russia from the universalizing dynamic and imperatives of capitalist imperialism, it therewith initiated another universal history: that of international socialism. By an irony of history traceable to its typically differential temporality and 'oblique march' (*Lineages*, p. 235), the backward East had thrown up the *postcapitalist* states.

In a stimulating review, Agnes Heller described *Passages* and *Lineages*—prefaces to what Anderson was to call the 'biography of capital'—as 'the autobiography of Europe'. Echoing Hirst, she suggested that the unique trajectory of Western Europe was not plotted, in evolutionist fashion, from the vantage point of the 'end of history': '[T]he emergence . . . of capitalism is solely the end of the *uniqueness* that led to its emergence'.[92] However, in anticipation of future controversies but without undue deformation of Anderson's problematic, it might be said that the trajectory of the East is conceived within the Marxist terms of the end of *prehistory*: the abolition of capitalism. Here, however, is the political rub, or (to mix metaphors) the menace of perdition harboured by the promise of salvation. For the Eastern retardation that induced Leninism engendered Stalinism. Quarantined, the socialist revolution had been restricted to Russia, whose legacy of scarcity and despotism had at once prompted and permitted the bureaucratic implantation of a 'postcapitalist' social order from above after the First World War, and of a revolution from without after the Second (in Eastern Europe), denaturing the socialism envisioned by Marx and Engels, Lenin and Trotsky. By contrast, the advanced Western societies that possessed the potential for a socialism of abundance—including Germany, 'strategic key to Europe'—had survived the revolutionary upsurges of 1918–20 and the Resistance movements of 1942–45. The revolution had prevailed where socialism was condemned by inherited backwardness to immersion in the 'kingdom of necessity'; it had misfired where socialism was endowed with the preconditions for attainment of the 'realm of freedom'. To this extent, the postcapitalist East did not hold up a mirror to the capitalist West. Moreover, even if, at this conjuncture, Anderson could scarcely have envisaged the converse—the West representing the future of the East—it is important to note that nothing in his problematic foreclosed the possibility of an eventual restoration of capitalism in Russia and other putatively postcapitalist states.

In his critique of Anderson, Hirst detected a homology between *Lineages of the Absolutist State* and 'Origins of the Present Crisis':

> In ['Origins'] . . . the French Revolution is the norm of political development—the classic form of a class-conscious bourgeoisie—against which English conditions and their outcomes are secretly measured. In *Lineages* it is Western development as a whole which is the norm—only in the West is there autonomous capitalist development and a bourgeois-democratic state.[93]

He then proceeded, however, by reference back to 'Problems of Socialist Strategy', to reproach Anderson with his rejection of Leninism, unaware that Anderson no longer equated it with insurrectionism and despotism. Nevertheless, Hirst is right to identify the political stake of Anderson's comparative history as a plausible Western variant of a Leninist strategy for socialism. Crudely abstracting from the intrazonal variations he explores, Anderson's revision of the European geopolitical great divide might be set out as in figure 6. If this division is approximately accurate, it means that Anderson had confronted the riddle posed by what he later named 'the Sphinx facing Marxism in the West'[94]—and aimed to solve it. As with his prestigious forerunner, Gramsci, it manifestly confounded him.

Eastern Europe	Western Europe
Backward	Advanced
No legacy from antiquity	Legacy from antiquity
Feudalism	Feudal synthesis
Crisis of feudalism: consolidation of serfdom	Crisis of feudalism: commutation of dues
Absolutist state	Absolutist state
Reimposition of feudalism	Endogenous or autonomous capitalism
Ancien régime + exogenous or heteronomous capitalism	Bourgeois revolution + full transition to capitalism
Leninism/Stalinism	Capitalist state
Abolition of capitalism/bureaucratic dictatorship over proletariat	Bourgeois-democratic institutionalization of capitalism
− − − − − − − − − − −	− − − − − − − − − − −
Political revolution from below?	Leninism?
Proletarian democracy?	Transition to communism?

Figure 6. East and West

In the *NLR* itself, indices of Anderson's strategic preoccupations could be read in the introductions to the materials by Gramsci and Tukhachevsky already cited, and to an article by Magri, who had criticized both reformism and Leninism.[95] Expounding Magri's postscript, Anderson wrote that '[t]he triangular relationship beween class, councils and party henceforth delimits the arena of the essential strategic problem of the revolution in advanced capitalism' (p. 96). And there, for the time being, the matter rested.

Published to widespread acclaim, Anderson's 'rudimentary diagrams' of 'the specificity of the European experience as a whole' (*Passages*, pp. 7–9) won the plaudits of fellow Marxists[96] and non-Marxists alike. (The back covers of *Passages* and *Lineages* featured tributes from Moses Finley, Keith Thomas, and others.) Indeed, one of the latter, D. G. MacRae, having congratulated Anderson for 'contribut[ing] to the revival of comparative studies and historical sociology in a world indifferent and hostile to such endeavours', confessed: 'I often find it hard to see reasons other than those of ideology or, perhaps, comradeship, why Anderson thinks himself a marxist'.[97] He was not alone. Theda Skocpol and Mary Fulbrook were among the many to detect a kinship with Max Weber and Otto Hintze in Anderson's emphasis upon the cultural legacy of antiquity (e.g., Roman law) to account for the unique emergence of capitalism in the West.[98] Invoking MacRae, Hirst argued that Anderson shared not only substantive theses with Weber but also methodological procedures: the 'comparative method' that we have encountered time and again in his writings.[99] In stringent Althusserian mode, Hirst further decried the 'idealism' of Anderson's conception of precapitalist modes of production, supposedly definable solely through the juridico-political and ideological superstructures that determined the

85

modality of the extraction of surplus labour by extraeconomic means within them.[100]

How Anderson might have countered such objections is imponderable. Hirst began his review by noting that Anderson had broken the 'long silence' that intervened between 'Components of the National Culture' and *Passages* and *Lineages*. Although Anderson no doubt continued to experiment in the historical 'laboratory of forms', another (as yet unbroken) silence descended.

Overboard with the Great Helmsman

Having departed from chronological sequence somewhat, we may return to the *NLR* as it entered upon its second decade, under Anderson's editorship. After 1967, the *Review* had largely abandoned analysis of its own society, ignoring the travails of the second Wilson government of 1966–70.[101] The Nairn-Anderson theses were left to lie fallow: an article by Nairn on nineteenth-century Britain in *NLR* no. 60 did not pilot the NLB book of which it was intended to form a part; and an account of the British economic crisis that underscored the strength of labour, rather than the weakness of industrial capital, was incongruent with the theses.[102] But the advent of the New Right, in the shape of Powell; the election of Heath; and the vicissitudes of his 'new course'—these were respectively examined by Nairn, Blackburn, and Barnett.[103] Nairn's 'The Left against Europe?'—a special issue of the *Review* in 1972—reversed the verdict of Hall and Anderson in 1961, predicting beneficent, unintended consequences for the British Left from Conservatism's resort to the EEC.[104] If the *NLR* was prepared to grasp this nettle, however, it evaded the issues posed by the escalating civil war in the North of Ireland.[105]

Caution on this score may have derived from a wider circumspection about nationalism and 'national liberation struggles'. At all events, generic Third Worldism was eschewed. An axiom of the 'dependency theory' associated with André Gunder Frank was refuted by Ernesto Laclau's 'Feudalism and Capitalism in Latin America'. Two years later, on the eve of the Yom Kippur War and the OPEC oil price hike, Bill Warren's famous assault on the whole problematic of the 'development of underdevelopment' was published.[106]

Since the end of 1968, a radicalized editorial stance had been attested by a series of critiques of European Communist parties. Although indulgence towards Maoism persisted, hostility to Stalinism mounted. Thus, just as the PCF's frustration of the French May provoked the *NLR*'s unequivocal rupture with Western Communism, the USSR's suppression of the Prague Spring in 1968 initiated much more critical coverage of Soviet Stalinism in its pages.[107] A little more than a year later, an article on the subject by Lucio Colletti signalled the abandonment of residual Deutscherism and sympathetic coverage of oppositional currents in Russia.[108] An orthodox Trotskyist position on the 'workers' states' was henceforth assumed. Prefacing an interview with Jiri Pelikan on Czechoslovakia in 1972, Anderson editorialized:

> The courageous resistance of the recent Czech, Russian, Polish and other East European oppositionists demands an unswerving solidarity on the part of socialists in the capitalist countries. . . . The tasks and type of the revolution to be made in Eastern and Western Europe are distinct: but the fate of each depends on the other. The complete overthrow by the masses, from below, of the total political apparatus of bureaucratic rule is the sole formula for socialist democracy in Czechoslovakia, Russia and the neighbouring countries.[109]

In the following issue of the *NLR*, Anderson presented a transcript of a meeting between striking Polish ship workers and leaders of the Communist Party, which concluded:

> [T]here can be no doubt of the unfolding logic and direction of the successive upheavals in Eastern Europe. . . . The Polish Rising of 1970 was both a direct working-class upsurge from below and aimed squarely at the indigenous bureaucratic system; and it was insurrectionary in character from the start. . . . The final demolition of its apparatus of coercion and usurpation lie ahead: only an *international* concatenation, in more than one country, will in all probability achieve it.[110]

The *NLR*'s overall development in the 1971–74 period may be summed up in three modulations of editorial line: the repudiation of Maoism; a distancing from Western Marxism; and the consolidation of Trotskyism. We can begin with Western Marxism. As we have seen, 'Document A' had envisaged an abandonment of neutrality vis-à-vis European traditions. This did not betoken any reunciation of the publication of their representatives in the *Review*, however. On the contrary, over the next five years or so, such material accounted for a substantial proportion of the contents of the journal. Althusser, for example, was carried twice and Colletti thrice; and Della Volpe, Magri, and Sebastiano Timpanaro were introduced.[111] Two interviews with Lukács appeared—one of them with Anderson.[112] Exchanges between

Adorno, Benjamin, and Brecht were translated and presented in 1973–74.[113] Nevertheless, a sequence of critiques of the postclassical theorists appeared in the *Review* concurrently. A two-part article on the first and second generations of the Frankfurt school, especially dismissive of Habermas, was contributed by the Althusserian Therborn; the early Lukács of *History and Class Consciousness* was taxed with 'Romantic anti-capitalism' by Stedman Jones; the credentials of Althusserianism were inspected by Glucksmann, Geras, and Pierre Vilar; and critical interviews were conducted by Anderson and others with Sartre, marking the philosophical break with him, and with Colletti.[114]

Of particular interest here are Anderson's unattributed introduction to Glucksmann, signalling the partial eclipse of Althusser in his intellectual affiliations, and his interview with Colletti, indicating his close proximity to the positions of Della Volpe's former pupil in these years. Associating himself with Geras's critique of Althusserian 'theoreticism' as being 'based squarely within the classical traditions of revolutionary socialism',[115] Anderson endorsed Glucksmann's interrogation of Althusser's epistemology and Balibar's theory of modes of production. As regards the latter, doubtless contra the Maoist Glucksmann himself, Anderson objected to the way in which the account of the 'property relation' in *Reading 'Capital'* erased 'the differences between capitalist and noncapitalist (postrevolutionary) modes of production'. This rendered it 'politically confusionist', licencing identification of the Soviet Union as 'state capitalist' (pp. 64–65).[116] Given Althusser's ongoing career, no definitive verdict on it could be delivered. But the innovative concepts of 'Contradiction and Overdetermination' were thought likely 'to prove the most lasting accomplishments of Althusser's "first period"' (p. 66).

Colletti had already been praised by Anderson, in an unattributed preface to Della Volpe, for 'writing a clearer language [than his teacher], which assumes its political responsibilities';[117] and his essay on Stalinism would appear in the following issue of the *NLR*. In the 1974 'Political and Philosophical Interview', when asked about Trotsky, Colletti had replied:

> What is the fundamental truth expressed by Trotsky . . . ? You could condense it . . . by saying that in any genuinely Marxist perspective, the United States of America should be the maturest society in the world for a socialist transformation. . . . In other words, Trotsky always insisted that the determinant force in any real socialist revolution would be the industrial working class, and that no peasantry could perform this function for it, let alone a mere communist party leadership. The clearest and most unequivocal devel-

opment of this fundamental thesis is to be found in the work of Trotsky. Without it, Marxism becomes purely honorific. (P. 26)

This had led, in conclusion, to some reflections on the 'dissociation' of Marxist theory and political practice in the West:

> [S]implifying greatly, we can say that in the West, Marxism has become a purely cultural and academic phenomenon; while in the East, revolutionary processes developed in an ambience too retarded to permit a realization of socialism. . . . This separation between West and East has plunged Marxism into a long crisis. Unfortunately, acknowledgement of this crisis is systematically obstructed and repressed among Marxists themselves. . . . My own view . . . is that the sole chance for Marxism to survive and surmount its ordeal is to pit itself against these very problems. . . . The only way in which Marxism can be revived is if no more books like *Marxism and Hegel* are published, and instead books like Hilferding's *Finance Capital* and Luxemburg's *The Accumulation of Capital* . . . are once again written.[118] (P. 28)

Anderson's empathy with this perspective will become fully apparent when we examine *Considerations on Western Marxism*, composed the same year that Colletti was interviewed: we might even say that Colletti had written the synopsis of *Considerations*. But whereas, within the space of a year, the Italian philosopher would have erased his version of the break between Marx and Hegel, renouncing Karl Marx for Karl Popper,[119] Anderson declined to admit the existence of a crisis of Marxism consequent upon the East/West separation. Indeed, as late as 1983, when Colletti was reproached for his conversion into 'a shrill enemy of Marxism and staunch defender of a more or less conventional liberalism', Althusser was being reproved for having, in 1977, 'propagat[ed] the notion of "a general crisis of Marxism"'.[120] Meanwhile, Timpanaro, who had replaced Colletti in Anderson's philosophical allegiances, invoked the category of 'crisis' in his 1979 postscript to *On Materialism* (first published by NLB in 1975) without inciting equivalent Andersonian censure.[121]

Why? A partial explanation for Anderson's selective disapprobation might be found in the fact that, whereas Colletti's quasi-Trotskyist outlook evinced not the least sympathy for Maoism, and Timpanaro offered due self-criticism on this score, Althusser's enthusiasm for the Chinese Revolution as a 'concrete critique' of Stalinism peaked—in the *Reply to John Lewis* (1973)—after Anderson and the *NLR* had graduated from a cognate position, publicly articulated in the Krassó-Mandel exchanges and inspired by

Althusser. Following his own turn, insufficient *anti*-Maoist zeal became a yardstick of revolutionary-Marxist rectitude for Anderson. In an NLB collection of interviews with Mandel, published in 1979 and adduced by Anderson the following year as evidence that the Trotskyist tradition 'alone ha[d] proved capable of an adult view of socialism on a *world* scale', the leader of the Fourth International was pressed to concede that 'Soviet policy [in the 1970s] has evolved positively and Chinese negatively to the point that the latter is now palpably worse'.[122] Although Mandel had revoked his erstwhile 'critical support' for the Chinese position in international policy, he resisted *NLR* enticements, evincing a comparable hostility to the bureaucracies of the People's Republic and the Soviet Union alike.[123]

The 'Decennial Report' isolated 'the rupture of NLR with the politics of Maoism' as the 'critical progress' of the 1971–74 phase in the evolution of the *Review*. Therewith, it had emancipated itself from 'any form of ideological subjection to the detachments of the international communism movement' (p. 62). The occasion for this was the switch in Chinese foreign policy in the early 1970s, traducing the internationalist slogans of the previous decade by support for Yahya Khan in West Pakistan and Sirimavo Bandaranaike in Ceylon. The first issue of 1971 (*NLR* no. 65) had carried Mao's 'Letter to Comrade Lin Piao' of 1930 (better known as 'A Single Spark Can Start a Prairie Fire'). That summer and autumn, however, articles by Tariq Ali on Bangladesh and Fred Halliday on Ceylon were prefaced by editorial condemnations of Chinese complicity with repressive regimes.[124] Criticism of China's domestic course would take longer to materialize, commencing with two articles in 1975.[125] Indeed, the *NLR* and NLB caught up with Deutscher only a decade after the official proclamation of the Cultural Revolution, whose true significance he had divined at the time. In 1976 NLB published a revised and updated translation of Fourth International leader Livio Maitan's *Party, Army, and Masses in China*, to which Hoare and especially Blackburn made a substantial contribution. According to an unpublished internal report on the *NLR* covering the years 1975–80, Halliday's extended review of the Maitan volume 'set the editorial stance towards China throughout [the] period'. In it Halliday maintained that 'Chinese foreign policy has exceeded any capitulation to imperialism effected by the Moscow "revisionists"'.[126]

Anderson never undertook the extended discussion of Maoism foreshadowed in *Considerations on Western Marxism*.[127] But his stance toward it was henceforth unremittingly—and unself-reflexively—negative. In *Arguments within English Marxism*, having quoted Althusser's naive assessment of the Chinese Revolution as a 'concrete critique' of its Russian predecessor, he wrote:

A few months earlier, Nixon was being toasted in Peking while US bombs rained on Vietnam. Within another few years, the Cultural Revolution was officially buried by the CCP as a disastrous decade of vendetta, regression and anarchy—its only durable legacy a foreign policy of ferocious reaction, far to the right even of Stalin's most cynical overtures to imperialism. (P. 110)

Two years later, reminding an American lecture audience of 'the wave of sympathy and admiration for the Cultural Revolution [that had] swept up a very broad range of socialist intellectuals', he pronounced judgement on such Sinophilia:

Already by the early seventies, the momentum of an unrestrained anti-Soviet campaign . . . led the Chinese state to an ever closer embrace with the United States government, and to an ever more accentuated abandonment of support or solidarity for national liberation movements in the Third World. . . . Domestically, it became increasingly clear that the Cultural Revolution was not only manipulated by the very bureaucratic summit it was ostensibly first aimed against, but in practice amounted to something very different from its declared goals: a gigantic purge of party and state appara-tuses, involving a huge toll of political repression . . . ; economic stagna-tion . . . ; and ideological obscurantism.[128]

Although the justice of this reckoning compels assent, there is some-thing disconcerting about the discrepancy between the ardour and the can-dour of the convert. Anderson, rather than Robinson, might have figured as a representative British socialist intellectual swept up by sympathy and ad-miration for the Cultural Revolution. Cancellation of such indulgence five years after its commencement confers no certificate of exculpation. What was enjoined upon recalcitrant cadres of the Fourth International would have been fitting: a modicum of autocritique. Instead, those who had actu-ally attached their signatures to published writings were reproved for suc-cumbing to an illusion of the epoch diffused, via the *NLR*, by its editor and their critic. *Errare humanum, perseverare diabolicum?*

Far from being an isolated incident, this was to be a recurrent syndrome. In 'private', it was a rather different story. Here Anderson and his colleagues were often their own best editorial critics. At the same time, however, in the absence of rectification, the critical notations of the 'Decennial' and other reports bring to mind a sometime insight of Trotsky's into 'the homeopathy of "self-criticism"'.   •

Results and Prospects

In the concluding balance sheet of the 'Decennial Report' on the *NLR*, the *Review*'s 'characteristic pattern of faults' was related to the consistent failures of its external political initiatives—whether involvement in the RSSF or the foundation of *Seven Days*, discussions with the CPGB or affiliations to the IMG. The 'lack of any close or binding relationship to political practice' had

> allowed the review to elude responsibility for its own errors, in a way that no periodical linked to an organizational form could do. NLR articles were never strictly submitted to the test of events, since they were not guides to an action that could have been corrected or rebuffed by them. This did not mean . . . that the political mistakes committed . . . were not exposed to the course of history. From the initial illusions in Wilsonism to the eventual indulgence towards Maoism, they invariably were. But the penalties for them were abnormally light. Because the review did not have to answer to any base engaged in practice, it was never obliged to correct or disavow its misjudgments publicly. Instead, its chacteristic response was to change the subject. . . . The political and intellectual development of NLR thus typically proceeded by consecutive displacements of interest rather than by cumulative progress in a single direction. . . . The nature of the shifts in NLR was in the main patently related to political or cultural difficulties encountered and unsolved. (Pp. 78–79)[129]

A consequence of this licence was 'a notable lack of self-criticism in the review', when it had a lot to criticize itself for:

> Perspectives falsified by events were silently relinquished rather than explicitly disavowed. New positions incompatible with former attitudes would then typically emerge at a later stage without reference to them. The succession of ideological mistakes committed, and then tacitly corrected in this way, is a lengthy one. Thus NLR could be taxed with having passed through phases of latent or incipient Third Worldism (1962–1963), Wilsonism (1964–1964 [*sic*]), Khrushchevism (1962–65), Guevarism (1967–1968), Studentism (1968–1970), and Maoism (1968–1970). Over-estimation of the peasantry and petty-bourgeoisie at the expense of the proletariat in the

class bloc necessary to make the socialist revolution was combined with ingenuous illusions in Western Social-Democracy, Soviet Communism and Chinese Communism as organizational forces working for world socialism, in different phases of the review's evolution. The political record of NLR has in this respect been very chequered. (P. 80)

Significantly, perhaps, the enumeration and dating of aberrations ends with Maoism in 1970, implying that the *Review* was thereafter on the right revolutionary-Marxist track. Yet there was no perfected variant of historical materialism waiting to be appropriated, now that the demerits of Western Marxism had been inventoried:

> For in effect Marxism, a century after *Capital*, still remained largely a system of vacuums. The immense gap between the potential of historical materialism as an explanation of the world and of history, and the actual use made of it to date, meant that there was a virtually indefinite series of problems still to be resolved or even explored for any candidate to the title of a Marxist journal. (P. 79)

Furthermore, although successive political deviations had been eliminated by the criteria of the mid-1970s,

> [t]he review . . . has in no way established a positive alternative system of theses or judgments on the critical questions where it has achieved the negative accomplishment of shedding the false answers of the past. No determinate theory of the road to a revolutionary socialist strategy in the West, of the mechanisms of imperialism in the underdeveloped South, or of the nature and future of the Communist States in the East, has yet even been broached in the review. In this sense, after a decade of publishing, everything remains to be done in NLR. (P. 81)

So much for the results of 1962–74. What of the prospects for the future?

> A political sea-change has occurred in the mid-70's that is much greater than that of the late 60's. Imperialism has been shaken by the worst series of blows for three to five decades. The spectacular victory of the Indochinese Revolution, the sudden advance of the Portuguese Revolution, and the international concatenation of workers' militancy in the advanced capitalist countries . . . have posed the most serious threats to its political stability since the loss of China and Eastern Europe in the late 40's. But at the same time, the

onset of world-wide recession and inflation, accompanied by the ascent of the oil bloc, have set off a generalized disruption of its economic stability on a scale never seen since the 30's. The combination of these two menaces . . . is creating a wholly new historical conjuncture. The chances of the Left are now much greater than at any time since the start of the Cold War, in the advanced and ex-colonial countries alike. (P. 85)

Within this synchronized political and economic crisis of the global capitalist order, events in southern Europe and Southeast Asia had thus far been fore-grounded in the *NLR*. The 'test in Portugal', initiated by the overthrow of the Caetano regime in April 1974 after thirteen years of colonial warfare in Angola and Mozambique, had been the subject of a long article by Blackburn that winter.[130] Victory in Indochina the following spring prompted an enthu-siastic editorial.[131] The two events, as predicted, were to have reverberations in their respective hemispheres: in the North, where the crisis of the capital-ist dictatorships extended to Greece and Spain; and in the South, where a wave of successful revolutions broke over the course of the decade from Southeast Asia, via southern Africa, to Central America.

Optimism, then, was understandable. Some recommendations for the future orientation of the *NLR* flowed from it. Stylistically, it could abandon its historic 'defensive posture', one of whose mandarin indices was the 'great distance . . . created and maintained between the review and its readership' (p. 92). As to its editorial programme, the Nairn-Anderson theses should be revisited, but revised by proper examination of the economic underpinnings of the British crisis; exploration of the structures of domestic bourgeois democracy that avoided the reformist inflection inherent in the former use of the category 'hegemony'; correction of the unilateralism of the account of local bourgeois culture; and detailed analysis of the intervening decade (pp. 95–96). One significant feature of those years had been the formation of a Marxist intelligentsia in the United Kingdom, whose proliferating spe-cialist journals—*Screen, Radical Philosophy,* and *Economy and Society* among them—contributed to a cultural panorama very different from that of the mid-1960s (pp. 86–87).

Sustained attention was not to be given to Britain at the expense of the rest of the advanced capitalist world—in particular, the United States and the Federal Republic of Germany (pp. 96–97). Moreover, concerning the postcapitalist states, 'Marxist theory is decades in arrear'—a deficit that the *NLR* must strive to make good (pp. 98–99). Meanwhile, in connection with the Third World, three priorities were selected: the structural inequali-ties between advanced and backward capitalisms loosely connoted by the category 'imperialism'; the character of the ex-colonial states; and the phenomenon of nationalism (pp. 99–102).

Finally, in a longer version of the stocktaking of classical Marxism subsequently appended to *Considerations on Western Marxism* for its publication by NLB, a critical agenda for engagement with the canon and corpus of historical materialism was sketched (pp. 102–17). These annotations were a response to criticisms by Anderson's colleagues of his original, 'Western Marxism: An Introduction' (1974)—in particular, its consecration of the tradition founded by a vanquished Trotsky, following its valediction of the currents induced by a victorious Stalin.

Prose of the Past, Poetry of the Future

Originally conceived as an introduction to the *Critical Reader* eventually published by NLB in 1977,[132] and focused on 'the formal structures of the Marxism that developed in the West after the October Revolution' (p. vii), *Considerations* stages a public settlement of accounts with West European Marxism. In effect, however, it comprises two autocritiques. The first—*in* the main text—retracts the counterposition in 'Components of the National Culture' of a valorized Continental tradition to a degraded national configuration at the expense of the classical Marxism superior to both. The second—*of* the main text—qualifies its counterposition of an inviolate classical historical materialism organically bound to political practice, to an unregenerate philosophical Marxism structurally divorced from working-class politics.

'Document A', devoted to 'the *coupure* of May', had already laid the guiding thread of the analysis and critique of Western Marxism as the theoretical transcription of practical frustration; and had detected a potential reunification of theory and practice after the May events, in which Maoism and Trotskyism had demonstrated their vitality as 'sources and component parts' of a renascent revolutionary Marxism. In *Considerations* the diagnosis and prognosis were reiterated, with two crucial modifications: first, disappearance of Maoism from the frame; second, identification of Trotskyism as the contemporary instantiation of classical Marxism.

The basic value system of *Considerations* was dramatized at the outset, by its antipodal epigraphs. The first, from Lenin, ruled that '[c]orrect revolutionary theory assumes final shape only in close connection with the practical activity of a truly mass and truly revolutionary movement'. The second, from Althusser's philosopher-general, Spinoza, expressed disdain for 'the multitude, and those of like passions'. Its argument is by now well known (for Anderson's own summary, see pp. 92–93). Marx had bequeathed a general theory of the capitalist mode of production, but no systematic account of historical materialism and no comparable political theory. Engels had devoted some of his efforts to the former—a task inherited and extended by the four key figures of the second generation of classical Marxism: Labriola, Mehring, Kautsky, and Plekhanov. The next cohort—Lenin and Trotsky, Luxemburg and Hilferding, Bauer and Bukharin—faced with a much more unstable political conjuncture, had sought both to develop Marxist economics by analyzing contemporary capitalism and imperialism, rather than by rehearsing *Capital*; and to elaborate the missing Marxist politics. Lenin, indeed, had 'inaugurated a Marxist science of politics', whose limitations were attributable to the backwardness of the Russian social formation (p. 12).

Frustration of socialist revolution in Europe by 1920 and its degeneration in Russia after 1924 had combined to terminate the unity of theory and practice typical of the 'classical tradition' (the title of chapter 1, pp. 1–23). They had also conduced to the 'advent of Western Marxism' (chapter 2, pp. 24–48). Intellectually predominant in capitalist Europe up until 1968, the 'hidden hallmark' of Western Marxism was '*defeat*' (p. 42), and its defining characteristic a 'structural divorce from political practice':

> The organic unity of theory and practice realized in the classical generation of Marxists before the First World War, who performed an inseparably politico-intellectual function within their respective parties in Eastern and Central Europe, was to be increasingly severed in the half-century from 1918 to 1968, in Western Europe. (P. 29)

In the immediate aftermath of World War I, the first Western theoreticians—Lukács, Korsch, and Gramsci—had still been political leaders. Thereafter, however, the twin tragedies of Stalinism and fascism had intersected to dissever theory and practice in the West for nearly a half century—an irreparable scission in the Europe of the Cold War, where a stabilized capitalism was ranged against a bureaucratized socialism. This had generated the insuperable dilemma facing, say, Sartre or Althusser and Lefebvre: adherence to the local Communist party as the de facto embodiment of socialism, at the price of bureaucratic observance; or independence of political organization and concomitant discipline, at the cost of intellectual isolation and greater or lesser practical impotence. What for Lukács amounted to an 'entry ticket to history' betokened to Adorno 'sacrifice of the intellect'.

Thus incubated by defeat and circumscribed by political history, Western Marxism had been marked by a series of 'formal shifts' (chapter 3, pp. 49–74). It had withdrawn to the academy and inverted Marx's own intellectual trajectory, regressing from economics and politics to philosophy, therewith descending from the concrete to the abstract. The main concerns of classical Marxism—understanding the politics and economics of the world of capital the better to change it—had been renounced by this latter-day *Kathedersozialismus*, which had concentrated on epistemology, producing a discourse 'on Marxism, rather than in Marxism' (p. 53). Its postwar abdication, amid the remarkable expansion of the world capitalist economy and the novel institution of representative democracy in all the main capitalist countries, was particularly grave (pp. 47–48).

A stylistic corollary of the retreat from party organization to academic seclusion was the professional deformation of a 'specialized and inaccessible idiom' (p. 53) and 'extreme forms of esotericism' (p. 105). Marxist theory became 'an esoteric discipline' that, for want of any contact with a vibrant revolutionary movement, assimilated circumjacent idealist culture, whether traditional (that of Spinoza, Kant, or Hegel) or contemporary (that of Weber, Croce, or Heidegger). In the process, it mutated into a set of mutually incommunicado national Marxisms well nigh exclusively orientated to their respective local contexts.

To the extent that Western Marxism did tackle substantive rather than methodological issues and did venture 'thematic innovations' (chapter 4, pp. 75–94), it typically inclined to 'superstructures', as opposed to 'base'; and its superstructural bias was toward culture and ideology. Only Gramsci, in his meditations on hegemony, had pursued 'a theoretical explanation of the basic historical impasse that was the origin and matrix of Western Marxism itself' (p. 80). However, even his novelties bore the impress of 'a common and latent *pessimism*', equally evident in Althusser's theory of ideology or Adorno's aesthetics, and antithetical to the confident outlook of the classical tradition (p. 88).[133]

Even so, whether sequestered from political practice by abstention or severed from it by bureaucratization, none of the Western Marxists had succumbed to the lures of reformism—unlike Kautsky, whose integrated theoretico-political labours had not immunized him in this respect. In its own specialist domains, moreover, 'this Marxism achieved a sophistication greater than that of any previous phase of historical materialism'. Accordingly, revolutionary socialists were charged with a 'necessary double movement of reconnaissance and rupture' vis-à-vis the West European constellation (p. 94).

Considerations proceeded to 'contrasts and conclusions' (chapter 5, pp. 95–106). A settlement of accounts was at once dictated and facilitated by the new conjuncture in the West, which held out the promise of a reunification of Marxist theory and revolutionary working-class political practice:

> The French Revolt of May 1968 marked . . . a profound historical turning-point. For the first time in nearly 50 years, a massive revolutionary upsurge occurred within advanced capitalism in time of peace, under conditions of imperialist prosperity and bourgeois democracy. The onset of this explosion by-passed the French Communist Party. With this, the two crucial conditions of the historic non-coincidence of theory and politics in Western Europe for the first time started to fall. The reemergence of revolutionary masses outside the control of a *bureaucratized* party rendered potentially conceivable the unification of Marxist theory and working-class practice once again. . . . The distance between revolutionary theory and mass struggle was far from abolished overnight in Paris during May–June 1968; but it closed to its narrowest gap in Europe since the general strike was defeated in Turin during the turmoil of 1920. The revolt in France, moreover, was not to remain an isolated experience. The subsequent years have seen a widening international wave of working-class insurgency in the imperialist world, unlike anything since the early twenties. (P. 95)

The first half of this passage is almost identical to the verdict of 'Document A', quoted earlier in this chapter. That document, however, had turned to a recovery of Trotskyism and discovery of Maoism as sources of a revolutionary post-May Marxism. In *Considerations*, the latter is mentioned only in passing, as a political option adopted by surviving Western Marxist thinkers and their pupils (p. 102 and n.). Contrariwise, Trotsky's legacy, as developed by Deutscher, Mandel, and Roman Rosdolsky, exacts its posthumous revenge over Stalinism, occupying centre stage:

> The tradition descended from Trotsky has . . . been a polar contrast . . . to that of Western Marxism. It concentrated on politics and economics. . . . It was resolutely internationalist. . . . It spoke a language of clarity and urgency. . . . It filled no chairs in universities. Its members were hunted and outlawed. . . . Today, this politico-theoretical heritage provides one of the central elements for any renaissance of revolutionary Marxism on an international scale. (P. 100)

For all its errors on particular issues,[134] and despite a tendency to doctrinal 'conservatism' (p. 101), the Trotskyist tradition was deemed to be in the process of revitalization, whereas Western Marxism was on the point of extinction.

Thus far, then, we are presented with two sets of 'polar contrasts': between classical historical materialism and Western Marxism, on the one hand, and between Trotskyism and postclassical historical materialism, on the other. Spanning the century from the foundation of the First International to the French May, Anderson's antitheses might be tabulated as in figure 7.

Classical Marxism/Trotskyism	Western Marxism
Union of theory and practice: revolutionary socialism	Divorce of theory and practice: theoreticism
Party/post in class struggle	Academy/professorial post
Concrete: politics and economics	Abstract: philosophy
Strategy	Methodology
Clarity	Obscurity
Intransigent materialism	Incipient idealism
Optimism	Pessimism
Rejection of Stalinism	Resignation to Stalinism
—————————————— 1968 ——————————————	
Renaissance	Extinction

Figure 7. Marxist Contrasts

In tandem with the rejuvenation of revolutionary Marxism in its former Continental heartlands, Anderson anticipated its transplantation to new geographical zones—in particular, the Anglo-Saxon world. Although England possessed an incomparable tradition of Marxist historiography, it had not as yet produced a broader Marxist culture. That, however, might rapidly change:

> For the law of uneven development governs the tempo and distribution of theory too: it can transform laggard into leading countries, benefitting from the advantages of latecomers, in a comparatively short period. At any rate, it can be said with confidence that *until* it has mastered the terrain of the United States and England . . . Marxism will not have measured itself against the full reach of the problems with which the civilization of capital confronts it, in the second half of the twentieth century. (Pp. 102–3)

A discourse in Marxism, as opposed to on it, would have to address the '*incompletion* of historical materialism' (p. 103), now that the classical tradition could be rescued from the obfuscations and corruptions of the past. Thus, the character of bourgeois democracy, a revolutionary strategy for its conquest, and the institutions of a socialist democracy—these remained terrae incognitae. Other areas—nationalism, imperialism, Communism—were

99

only just beginning to be explored. As to the resolution of the problems they posed,

> [t]he precondition . . . is . . . the rise of a mass revolutionary movement, free of organizational constraint, in the homelands of industrial capitalism. Only then will a new unity of socialist theory and working-class practice be possible, capable of endowing Marxism with the powers necessary to produce the knowledge it lacks today. (P. 104)

Pending fulfillment of this precondition, Marxism would presumably remain the kind of 'second-order' discourse (p. 53) reprehended—yet represented— by Anderson and Colletti.

Let us briefly speculate on the implications of *nonfulfillment*. Were the precondition not to be met because the organizational constraints of centrist Communist parties could not be eluded, then the theoreticians would remain impaled upon the horns of the Western Marxist dilemma. For its representatives, so Anderson had explained, the international Communist movement 'represented the central or sole pole of relationship to organized socialist politics, whether they accepted or rejected it' (p. 43). This had yielded the two optional roles—equally deleterious for any organic unity of theory and practice—of disciplined militant or 'intellectual freelance'. The former (e.g., Della Volpe) was bound to intellectual prudence and political conformity. The latter (e.g., Goldmann) secured cultural independence but sacrificed 'anchorage within the social class for whose benefit theoretical work in Marxism alone has ultimate meaning' (p. 44). If this was the unenviable choice asked of Marxist intellectuals in France and Italy—countries with mass Communist parties—how, by extrapolation, should the dilemma of British or American revolutionary socialists be formulated?

> Western Marxism . . . was always magnetically polarized towards official Communism as the only historical incarnation of the international proletariat as a revolutionary class. It never completely accepted Stalinism; yet it never actively combated it either. But whatever nuances of attitude successive thinkers adopted towards it, for all of them there was no other effective reality or milieu of socialist action outside it. (P. 96)

If this was so, then it might reasonably be concluded from such premisses that, should the post-May harvest not yield a revolutionary crop, a *repolarization* of sorts might occur (i.e., toward Eurocommunism and a reformist reunification of theory and practice). If, in turn, that proved barren; if, amid a second Cold War a decade later, a general 'crisis of Marxism' were to have crystallized, then—especially in Britain, given its miniscule Communist Party and incorrigible Labour Party—such a Marxist theoretician might be tempted to arrive at analogous conclusions regarding the 'only historical incarnation of the international proletariat as a revolutionary class', except that the only 'effective reality' now would be not a national party (the CPGB) but an international state (the USSR). Alternatively put, orthodox Trotskyism might logically be retired in favour of Deutscherism.

Obviously, we are anticipating. Such considerations were foreign to Anderson in the mid-1970s—a conjuncture of mounting, not waning, expectations on the Marxist Left. His 1974 conclusion reverted to the epigraph from Lenin, adamant that its instruction be accepted to the letter:

> Every clause here counts. Revolutionary theory can be undertaken in relative isolation . . . : but it can only acquire a *correct* and *final* form when bound to the collective struggles of the working class itself. Mere formal membership of a party organization . . . does not suffice to provide such a bond: a *close connection* with the *practical activity* of the proletariat is necessary. Nor is militancy in a small revolutionary group enough: there must be a linkage with *actual masses*. Conversely, linkage with a mass movement is not enough either, for the latter may be reformist: it is only when the masses are *themselves revolutionary*, that theory can complete its eminent vocation. These five conditions for the successful pursuit of Marxism have not been assembled anywhere in the advanced capitalist world since the Second World War. The prospects for their reappearance are now . . . at last increasing. When a truly revolutionary movement is born in a mature working class, the 'final shape' of theory will have no exact precedent. All that can be said is that when the masses themselves speak, theoreticians—of the sort the West has produced for fifty years—will necessarily be silent. (Pp. 105–6)

Now, at one level, this could be mischievously read as the motivation for a series of immediate institutional refusals: of the Second International and Social-Democracy (mass, but reformist); of the Third International and Communism (mass, but centrist); of the Fourth International and Trotskyism (revolutionary, but small)—and hence, parochially, of the Labour Party, the Communist Party of Great Britain (centrist and small to boot), and the International Marxist Group. More important, Anderson retracts with one hand what he has proferred with the other—the integration of Marxist intellectuals into working-class political organizations—and reveals, as it were, his hand. He remarks that his 'five conditions'—more stringent in sum than

Lenin's twenty-one, for amounting to a well-nigh unattainable ideal—may be about to 'reappear', having been absent from the universe of advanced capitalism since the Second World War. But the chronology is uncharacteristically gestural. When and where, in the history of twentieth-century socialism, were all these desiderata assembled in pristine form? Anderson's answer—a semi-Maoist residue tinged with quasi-Luxemburgist hues—refers us to a conjuncture in which 'the masses are *themselves revolutionary*'. Yet this resolution of the problem of the theory/practice connexion simply prompts a regress: in the absence of that '[t]riumphalism in the cause of the working class, and catastrophism in the analysis of capitalism', which Anderson notes as 'the typical vices of [the Trotskyist] tradition in its routine forms' (p. 101), whence the revolutionary masses?

In 'Components of the National Culture', written when the *NLR* itself was a Western Marxist journal in effect, revolutionary culture was the precondition of the revolutionary theory that in turn was a condition of any revolutionary movement. In *Considerations*, which publicized the break with Western Marxism, 'revolutionary masses' are the prerequisite of '*correct* revolutionary theory'. Yet Anderson's inference from a hypertrophy of 'practice' was paradoxical: occupation of a post in neither the party nor the academy, but the watchtower, whence conjunctural manifestations and institutionalizations of class struggle could be scanned.

Critical discussion of *Considerations* may be convened under three headings, bearing upon Anderson's conceptions of, and contrasts between, the traditions of classical historical materialism, Western Marxism, and Trotskyism. Anderson's notion of 'classical Marxism', and of a subsequent scission of theory and practice, would seem to derive from Deutscher. Deutscher employed it by way of comparison not with Western, but with 'vulgar Marxism'. Yet he, too, included within it figures invariably associated with the latter:

> [W]e face the problem of degeneration in Marxist thinking. We have the divorce between theory and practice, and we have a striking . . . contrast between what I call classical Marxism—that is, the body of thought developed by Marx, Engels, their contemporaries, and after them by Kautsky, Plekhanov, Lenin, Trotsky, Rosa Luxemburg—and the vulgar Marxism, the pseudo-Marxism of the different varieties of European social-democrats, reformists, Stalinists, Khrushchevites and their like.[135]

Crudely (yet conventionally) speaking, Anderson's 'classical tradition', like Deutscher's, was in fact historically divided between reformist theory and practice (that of the Second International of Kautsky, not to mention the First of Marx and Engels) and revolutionary theory and practice (that of the Third International of Lenin)—with a post–First World War current of centrist theory and practice thrown in for good measure (the 'Two-and-a-Half International' of Bauer). By spuriously unifying the founders and their successors into a singular tradition, and by performing an analogous operation on three generations of Western Marxists, Anderson is able to endow (a selected) Trotskyism with the credentials of classicism, while retrospectively casting the 'classical tradition', from Marx and Engels, via Kautsky and Plekhanov, to Luxemburg and Lenin, in its image. Even discounting indiscriminate use of the criterion of the union of theory and practice, wielded 'as a polemical bludgeon',[136] it is strange to find Anderson overlooking precisely what the founders of Western Marxism were rebelling against: namely, the massive accretions in Second International Marxist theory of 'bourgeois ideology'— most notoriously, the positivism of Kautsky or Plekhanov. This, after all, was the burden of Korsch's *Marxism and Philosophy*, Lukács's *History and Class Consciousness*, and Gramsci's later annotations on the 'philosophy of praxis' in *Prison Notebooks*.[137]

The immediate source of the category 'Western Marxism' was Merleau-Ponty's *Adventures of the Dialectic*, which retrieved Lukács's and Korsch's initiatives from the oblivion into which they had been cast, thirty years earlier, by the scientistic orthodoxies of Second and Third Internationals alike.[138] Accordingly, it is not surprising that reviewers of *Considerations* such as Jeffrey Herf alleged its conflation of 'critical' currents (Lukácsian et al.) with 'scientific' schools (Della Volpean or Althusserian) in West European Marxism.[139] More generally, Therborn has recently adjudged 'Western Marxism' 'a post hoc construction, not a self-recognized group or current'[140] and rejected the category on that basis. By contrast, in his major study *Marxism and Totality*, Martin Jay subscribes to Anderson's general thesis about a profound convergence, underlying their divergences, between West European Marxists, and treats much the same cast of characters (with the addition of Bloch and Habermas).[141] But is Anderson's elucidation of the commonalities compelling? For all the stimulus of his analysis of some of the common denominators of the West European tradition, identification of the theory/practice divorce as *definitive* of it is, by Anderson's own acknowledgement of its partial inapplicability to the originators (pp. 29–30), problematic. This is closely related, of course, to the claim that Western Marxism was the product of defeat. If anything, the reverse is true of its ultraleftist founding texts: their unconcealed hallmark was victory—Gramsci's 'revolution against *Capital*' in tsarist Russia.[142]

As we have noted, Anderson's declared focus was the 'formal structures' of Western Marxism; 'substantive judgements of the relative merits or qualities of its main representatives' (p. vii) were not his purpose. This analytical formalism exacts a price. For in view of his own affinities with classical Marxism theoretically and Leninism politically, Anderson's equation of the Della Volpean and Althusserian counterattacks on philosophical Marxism with their targets—as mere 'obsessive methodologism' (p. 53)—is incongruous. The contention that West European Marxism *tout court* was a 'prolonged, winding detour' (p. 103) both neglects the 'concrete' work in politics and economics facilitated, say, by Althusser's 'abstract' philosophical clarifications, and implies, at least, a prior state of classical grace that is disavowed on the very same page.[143]

Just as Anderson's typology of Marxism valorized a homogeneous classical tradition as the norm against which to judge undifferentiated post-classical currents, so too he idealized the Trotskyist inheritance. This move was effected in two steps. First, the theory/practice criterion was modified to signify not the demanding dialectic of Anderson's closing quotation from Lenin, but instead a disciplinary concern with economics and politics, rather than philosophy. Second, this tradition was equated with individual exemplars—Trotsky himself, Mandel, Deutscher, and Rosdolsky (the last two, of course, Trotskyists without a party)—rather than the plethora of groups vying for the mantle of legitimacy. Accordingly, the 'routinism', 'conservatism', 'catastrophism', 'triumphalism', and—a vice passed over by Anderson—sectarianism of existing Trotskyist organizations could be largely circumvented, in the name of a generic legacy.[144] So too could what Anderson elsewhere reviled as the political aberrations sponsored by the heterodox competitors of Trotskyist organizations, whether Castoriadis and Lefort's Socialisme ou Barbarie, with its denunciations of Soviet Communism as 'bureaucratic capitalism',[145] or Cliff's International Socialists and their classification of the USSR as 'state-capitalist'. Analytical indiscrimination and political discretion transformed exceptions into the rule, erecting an imaginary Trotskyism.

In the foreword to *Considerations*, Anderson indicated that the text of his 1974 introduction had been 'discussed and criticized by colleagues on *New Left Review* from a wide range of viewpoints', and that he had 'tried to take account of their reflections and criticisms' (p. viii). The topic of Trotskyism featured most prominently in collegiate reactions. Nairn objected to the way in which Anderson's 'contrasts and conclusion' plucked a Trotskyist rabbit from a Stalinized hat, relating the coup de theatre to his emphasis on failure of revolutionary leadership as the proximate cause of the setbacks in Europe of 1918–20. [146] Leninism in its Trotskyist version was not some integral, intact tradition, buried by Stalinism, but now fit for exhumation and regeneration; it too was the product of defeat, and therefore due for complementary iconoclastic considerations. Other internal critics concurred. Barnett found the assertions of the closing pages peremptory and unsubstantiated—especially a claim to the effect that Trotskyism would be perfected by impending mass revolutionary practice. Like Nairn, he probed Anderson's silence on the extant institutional forms of the tendency.[147] From an Althusserian standpoint, Stedman Jones countered Anderson's Western Marxist amalgam, his polarities between it and a classical tradition, and his absolution of the Trotskyist tradition from the theory/practice divorce (as variably defined and selectively employed). His key reservations concerned the exaltation of Trotskyism. If Western Marxism was to be measured against classical Marxism, Trotskyism should, as Krassó had maintained in 1967–68, be measured, together with Stalinism, against the Leninism that it rehearsed interminably.[148]

These criticisms provide some indication of just how controversial—and potentially divisive—Anderson's embrace of Trotskyism was within the *Review*'s editorial committee in 1974. Indeed, Nairn and Stedman Jones's positions approximated the assessment made by Eric Hobsbawm, in his review of the published text: intellectually, Trotskyism had been 'quite unable to transcend the historical framework of the communist discussions in the USSR of the 1920s'.[149] If this Communist authority was one Anderson was disinclined to accept, then that of Deutscher might have been expected to give him greater pause: 'I do not imagine that the future of communism lies in Trotskyism'.[150] For now, his colleagues' objections led him to add a lengthy passage to his manuscript for publication, isolating the 'typical vices of [the Trotskyist] tradition in its routine forms' and replacing the prospect of its perfection with that of its subjection to 'the wider criticism of mass political practice' (pp. 100–101).[151] They also possibly elicited the less sanguine appreciation of the classical tradition contained in the 1976 afterword to *Considerations*, which posed the question of the imperfections—not merely incompletion—of historical materialism.

Hobsbawm suggested that Anderson's afterword 'retract[s] much of the first 90 per cent of his essay', including its 'idealisation' of Marxism before 1914. It certainly began by revoking the 'five conditions' on the union of theory and practice—conditions whose incantation of 'the masses' incited E. P. Thompson's charge of 'anti-intellectual magic'—conceding that '[t]heir apocalyptic tone is itself a suspect sign, of difficulties evaded or ignored'.[152] His recommendations had, he now regretted, 'invite[d] an "activist" reading

of [his] theses that could be scientifically untenable and politically irrespon-
sible' (p. 109). For if, qua historical materialism, Marxism was primarily a
theory of history—hence of a past that, although susceptible to theoretical
(re)interpretation, was unamenable to practical transformation—it could not
and should not be reduced to a 'revolutionary sociology' of the present.[153]
This logically entailed revocation of 'the general and uncritical universality . . . often ascribed [by Marxists] to the union of theory and practice'
(p. 111). The results of Marxist historiography were of crucial importance
for the elaboration of Marxist theory, such that Anderson foresaw a redress-
ing of the balance between the two in the future (p. 112).

Anderson then turned to his 'polar contrast' between classical and
Western Marxisms, reaffirming its essential validity but qualifying its terms
(theory/practice). The five conditions renounced, and the rule relaxed, the
errors—not merely the lacunae—of the classical legacy were available for inspection and correction. The scientificity of historical materialism—uncom-
promisingly upheld by Anderson—precisely implied the provisionality and
fallibility of its findings, and the imperative of their rectification (p. 113).

Whereas Engels and Luxemburg are briefly treated in the 'Decennial
Report', in *Considerations* scrutiny is restricted to 'the outstanding trio of
the classical tradition—Marx, Lenin and Trotsky' (p. 113).[154] The founder
had not produced a general theory of the capitalist state and bourgeois class
power; he had neglected the phenomenon of nationalism; and his economic
theory was vulnerable with respect to the labour theory of value and the
laws of tendency (in particular, those concerning capitalist profits and class
polarization).[155] Implying internal collapse or external dissolution, these 'laws'
attested to 'a latent catastrophism' in *Capital*, which possibly accounted for
Marx's dispensing with a political theory proper (p. 116).

Lenin's limitations, on the other hand, principally attached to his political theory: his treatments of 'proletarian democracy' (in revolutionary party
and postrevolutionary state) and 'bourgeois democracy' (the indistinction
between West and East) (p. 117). Resuming a theme that had surfaced in his
1970 introduction to Magri, Anderson noted the partition in Lenin's writings between his theory of the revolutionary party and his theory of post-
revolutionary institutions (soviets). In the case of the capitalist state, reiterating the conclusions of *Lineages of the Absolutist State*, Anderson argued:

> *State and Revolution* . . . is wholly generic in its discussion of the bourgeois
> state. . . . In fact, the Russian state which had just been eliminated by the
> February Revolution was categorically distinct from the German, French,
> English or American states with which the quotations from Marx and Engels

on which Lenin relied had been concerned. By failing to delimit a feudal autocracy unequivocally from bourgeois democracies, Lenin involuntarily permitted a constant confusion among later Marxists, which was effectively to prevent them from ever developing a cogent revolutionary stategy in the West. This could only have been done on the basis of a direct and systematic theory of the representative bourgeois-democratic state in the advanced capitalist countries and the specific combinations of its machinery of consent and coercion. . . . The practical consequence of this theoretical blockage was the inability of the Third International . . . to achieve any mass implantation in the greatest centres of modern imperialism in the twenties—the Anglo-Saxon world of England and USA. Another type of party and another type of strategy were needed in these societies and were not invented. (P. 117)

As in the case of Marx, the 'tacit economic catastrophism' of Lenin's *Imperialism* had done duty for the requisite political theory and corresponding strategy (pp. 117–18).

Anderson's assessment of Marx and Lenin put serious question marks over the respective orthodoxies of both the Second and the Third Internationals. What of the Fourth? Turning to Trotsky and his legacy, Anderson queried central doctrinal tenets. The problematic of 'permanent revolution' had been confirmed in Russia itself, but its extension to the colonial and ex-colonial world in its entirety was another matter: thus far, it was 'unproven as a general theory' (pp. 118–19).[156] Trotsky's analysis of the capitalist state of Nazi Germany was exemplary. Yet his sureness of judgement had deserted him elsewhere—for example, in his adoption of a position of 'revolutionary defeatism' at the outbreak of the Second World War—and he too had failed to produce a differentiated theory of capitalist state power, resorting instead to the economic catastrophism endemic in the ranks of the Third International (pp. 119–20). Finally, despite his 'masterly achievement' in *The Revolution Betrayed*, its expansion into a general theory of the 'workers' states' and of the 'political revolutions' required to evict their usurpatory bureaucracies encountered numerous problems and paradoxes when applied to other states, such as Eastern Europe, China, Cuba, and Vietnam (e.g., the fact that, in defiance of Trotsky's predictions, external or internal bureaucracies had made the relevant revolutions in the first place) (pp. 120–21).

By way of conclusion, Anderson submitted:

The scale of [Marx, Lenin, and Trotsky's] achievements is not diminished by any list of their omissions or mistakes. Indeed, since the tradition they represent was always concerned with political and economic structures in a way

107

that Western Marxism . . . was not, the same issues re-emerge practically as universal problems before any socialist militant in the contemporary world. . . . What is the constitutive nature of bourgeois democracy? What is the function and future of the nation-state? What is the real character of imperialism as a system? What is the historical meaning of a workers' state without workers' democracy? How can a socialist revolution be made in advanced capitalist countries? How can internationalism be made a genuine practice. . . ? How can the fate of previous revolutions in comparable conditions be avoided in the ex-colonial countries? How can established systems of bureaucratic privilege and oppression be attacked and abolished? What would be the structure of an authentic socialist democracy? These are the great unanswered problems that form the most urgent agenda for Marxist theory today. (P. 121)

In the 'Decennial Report', a version of this passage tabled its questions as 'the logical agenda of the review' (p. 117). As we shall see in the next chapter, the *NLR* and Anderson—in common with Marxist theory generally—failed to supply cogent answers to them.

Before proceeding to Anderson's immediate future, a few interim observations are in order. First, he had produced, in the space of fourteen active years (1960–74), the bulk of his published output: his contributions to the common endeavour with Nairn on Britain; a book-length study of Portuguese colonialism; the two volumes of comparative European history; a survey of Western Marxism; and untold anonymous or pseudonymous editorials, presentations, and articles in the *NLR*. If to these we add the unpublished manuscripts of 1969–70 on Communism and on socialism in the West (the latter containing the substance of his major Gramsci article of 1976), it is apparent that these were Anderson's most fertile and creative years to date.

Second, the contents of Anderson's published oeuvre would gradually but perceptibly change character hereafter, becoming politically more attenuated. Like *Considerations*, *Arguments within English Marxism* (1980), and *In the Tracks of Historical Materialism* (1983) are less books *in* Marxism than books *on* it. Nevertheless, they retain the theoretico-political charge of the preceding writings. By contrast, from the later 1980s his work would shift not to the 'philosophical orientation' of Western Marxism but into a predominantly historiographical mode. Moreover, his writing would undergo a certain accentuation of the idiomatic 'esotericism' rebuked by him in the Western philosophers and construed as a 'sign of its divorce from any popular practice', in unflattering comparison with the plain parlance of the Trotskyist tradition.[157]

'Document A' remarked of Deutscher that he had 'rejected the attempt to reunite theoretical and political practice altogether and chose the logical solution—separating him entirely in language and context from his contemporaries within the different tradition of Western Marxism—of becoming a professional historian' (p. 9). Twenty years on, Anderson would take the step implicitly prepared in the afterword to *Considerations* in the defence of the historian's vocation, the relaxation of the theory/practice criterion, and the opposition to any interpretation of historical materialism as a 'revolutionary sociology', emulating Deutscher's solution—albeit this did not separate him in either context or language from Anglo-American Marxism (or it from Western Marxism). One of the prices paid would be renunciation of the habitual iconoclasm that had hitherto distinguished Anderson's work. Its zone of engagement would remain at the intersection of history and politics. Its institutional site, however, would become the academy, inducing a studied prudence most visible in the veritable gulf separating the heedless provocations of 'Components of the National Culture' from the respectful annotations of 'A Culture in Contraflow' two decades later. To suggest this is not to deny the need for some of the subsequent retractions and emendations of past hyperbole. It is, rather, to register a discontinuity and at the same time to venture the proposal that the most innovative, original Anderson is the intransigent freelance intellectual.

A third thought is suggested by Anderson's subscription to Trotskyism. From 1960 to 1974, we have remarked his successive adoption and then qualification or rejection of various alternatives to the national culture—first of all, Western Marxism, within which Anderson had approximately graduated from Sartre and Lukács to Gramsci and Althusser, thence to Colletti and Timpanaro, before issuing his blanket critique of the postclassical tradition. Concurrently, having repudiated Trotskyism in the name of Maoism, Anderson publicly reversed his verdict. Initially, an attempt was made to contrast a unified classical Marxist tradition, of which Trotskyism was the contemporary inheritor and Mandel the outstanding surviving representative, with Western Marxism. However, the classical Marxism in whose name the West European philosophers were censured proved to be both more differentiated and more problematic than depicted. By 1975, the classical tradition, whether in its primordial Marxist or later Leninist and Trotskyist mutations, was itself under searching inspection. And belying Anderson's tribute to its achievements, its 'great unanswered problems' were of such a magnitude as to render historical materialism not merely incomplete (Anderson's original judgement), not simply imperfect (his second), but 'largely a system of vacuums', such that 'everything remains to be done': the undisclosed assessment of the 'Decennial Report' (pp. 79, 81).

In 1976 Anderson staked the reviviscence of Marxist theory on the imminence of mass revolutionary practice. In the event, contemporary history mocked the promise of May '68. When the masses failed to speak the allotted lines, the theoretician was not silenced. But having postulated, in *Considerations*, 'the descendant position of capitalism on a global scale, in an epoch which despite everything saw a third of the world wrested from it' (p. 56), he could not but be disconcerted by its reascendent position in the 1980s. Consequently, for all the indemnities conferred by an intellectual autonomy akin to Sartre's and a geopolitical and historical perspective even more capacious than Deutscher's, scarred by cumulative defeats and confounded by intractable problems, Anderson's Marxism would itself slowly change colours, on the West Coast.

3 ▸ Against the Historical Current?

An unpublished editorial report, 'NLR, 1975–1980', welcomed

> the emergence of a more compact and reasoned political consensus within
> [it] than at any time in its past. Unity on fundamental questions of inter-
> national class struggle did not preclude major divergences in the national
> arena. . . . [But] no major ruptures or turns in political position occurred in
> the late 70's. In this sense, NLR might be said to have finally attained rela-
> tive ideological maturity—a stabilization of its outlook on the basis of an
> open and critical revolutionary marxism.[1]

The consensus did not embrace the nominal editorial committee of the journal in its entirety, but rather an *Aktiv* of some seven members: Anderson,
Blackburn, Barnett, Halliday, and Hoare, joined by Francis Mulhern in
November 1975, Norman Geras the following spring, and the American
Mike Davis in 1980. What Mulhern has characterized as the policy of 'integrism' advocated by Anderson[2] generated an artificial consensualism of internal regime that would implode in the crisis of 1983. That crisis, however,
was manifestly overdetermined by the acute problematization of the NLR
'outlook' itself, as the Fourth International failed 'the test in Portugal', the
regional detachments of the Third likewise came to grief in southern
Europe, and a second Cold War was mobilized on every front by the United
States, seconded by an allied regime of the radical Right in the United
Kingdom.

The cumulative impact, registered in 'NLR, 1975–1980', imposed se-
vere qualification of the optimistic conclusion of the 'Decennial Report',
which had deemed '[t]he chances of the Left . . . now much greater than at
any time since the start of the Cold War, in the advanced and ex-colonial
countries alike'.[3] By the end of the decade, socialism was off the agenda in
the First World, stalled and potentially imperilled in the Second, and tarnished and/or beleaguered in the Third. Contrariwise, despite deepening
economic recession and a sequence of Third World revolutions, the global
prospects of its historic antagonist were otherwise improving. In defiance of
Leninist and Trotskyist doctrine, the 1970s witnessed 'the first genuine extension of a stabilized capitalist order, complete with eventual bourgeois
democracy, outside the metropolitan zone since the 1890's'.[4]

The Sphinx in the West

The closest approximation we have to a statement by Anderson of the *Review*'s 'open and critical revolutionary marxism' is *Arguments within English Marxism*, provoked by E. P. Thompson's polemic against Althusser and his English publishers and progeny in *The Poverty of Theory* (1978). The closing chapter of *Arguments* is devoted to 'strategies'—a leitmotiv of Anderson's writing in the years 1975–80.

The Portuguese Revolution—neglected in the *NLR* after Blackburn's major article of 1974—had disappointed Anderson's expectations. The Communist Party's attempt to imitate the bureaucratic putschism of its Czech sister-party in February 1948 had terminated the dynamic released in April 1974; in consequence, 'arguably the best chance of a socialist revolution in Western Europe in this century was spectacularly missed'.[5] The 'dearth of strategic resource or invention'[6] had not, alas, been confined to the Portuguese transition from fascism; nor was it restricted to the Communist movement. It extended to Spain, Italy, and France, and encompassed the Fourth International. As the quinquennial report noted, Trotskyist theory and practice had not proved equal to the task of remedying the defaults of *Panzerkommunismus* in Lisbon, Eurocommunism in Rome, or Gallocommunism in Paris; their negative strategic criticisms did not sum up to positive alternative proposals.[7]

A similar verdict might be entered upon the *NLR* itself, under Anderson's editorship. Notwithstanding the critical attitude of the *Aktiv* toward the phenomenon, in its pages favourable coverage of Eurocommunism—for example, by Amendola, Claudin, and Poulantzas—outweighed critical material by, for example, Mandel or Henri Weber.[8] Moreover, as in the case of NLB's titles on the subject—pitting Étienne Balibar's *On the Dictatorship of the Proletariat* (1977) and Mandel's *From Stalinism to Eurocommunism* (1978) against Claudin's *Eurocommunism and Socialism* and Poulantzas's *State, Power, Socialism* (both 1978)—cogent interrogation of reformism did not vindicate revolutionary socialism. In the words of the quinquennial report, regretting the *Review*'s failure to reply to Poulantzas as planned, criticism 'tended to be reiteration of classical tenets, rather than creative development of new revolutionary strategies' (p. 19).[9]

Anderson's own contributions to the debates of these years basically conformed to this pattern, falsifying reformist answers, as opposed to inventing revolutionary responses, to questions of socialist strategy in the West. The first and most substantial was 'The Antinomies of Antonio Gramsci'. Published in the special one hundredth issue of the *NLR* in 1976, together with Mandel's critique of Eurocommunism, and predicated (as Anderson put it in the foreword to *A Zone of Engagement*) upon 'struggles still pending',[10] it examined the Italian Communist leader's 'contested legacy' (p. 6) with a view to preventing the Eurocommunist annexation of it for a chimerical 'third way' between Leninism and Social-Democracy.

Noting that Gramsci had utilized the concept of 'hegemony', inherited from Russian Marxism, to essay '*a differential analysis of the structures of bourgeois power in the West*' (p. 20), Anderson sought to dispel the left social-democratic 'illusions' created by one of the models of hegemony decipherable in *Prison Notebooks*—illusions which his 'Problems of Socialist Strategy' a decade earlier had exemplified (p. 27 and n. 48). In this model (p. 26), the East/West polarity was specified as in figure 8.

East	West
State/ civil society	Civil society/state
Coercion	Consent
Domination	Hegemony
(War of) Manoeuvre	(War of) Position

Figure 8. East and West

This schema was motivated by the commendable aim of foregrounding the existence of liberal-representative democracy as the specific difference of the West. However, its equation of bourgeois hegemony with cultural dominion, securing capitalist class rule by working-class consent and dictating an essentially countercultural 'war of position' by way of socialist response, contained 'a number of illusions':

The first . . . of its errors is precisely the notion that the ideological power of the bourgeoisie in Western social formations is exercised above all in the sphere of civil society, its hegemony over which subsequently neutralizes the democratic potential of the representative State. . . . In fact, it might be said that the truth is if anything the reverse: the general form of the representative State—bourgeois democracy—is itself the principal ideological lynchpin of Western capitalism, whose very existence deprives the working class of the idea of socialism as *a different type of State*, and the means of communication and other mechanisms of cultural control thereafter clinch this central ideological 'effect'. . . . The bourgeois State . . . 'represents' the totality of the population, *abstracted* from its division into social classes, as individual and equal citizens. . . . [I]t presents to men and women their unequal positions in civil society as if they were equal in the State. . . . The economic divisions within the 'citizenry' are masked by the juridical parity between exploiters and exploited, and with them the complete *separation* and *non-participation* of the masses in the work of parliament. This separation is then . . . represented to the masses as the ultimate incarnation of liberty: 'democracy' as the terminal point of history. . . . The code is all the more powerful because the juridical rights of citizenship are not a mere mirage: . . . the civic freedoms and suffrages of bourgeois democracy are a tangible reality, . . . whose loss would be a momentous defeat for the working class. (P. 28)[11]

Anderson's reiteration of Marx's anatomy of the liberal-representative state in *The Jewish Question* does not subscribe to the 'dominant ideology thesis' characteristic of Western Marxism (it does not discount the 'dull compulsion of economic relations' referred to by Marx in *Capital*).[12] It does, however, identify the ideology of the bourgeois democracy present in the West, compounded by the palpable absence of 'proletarian democracy' in the East (p. 30 n. 53), as the cultural dominant of capitalist class power; and therewith it repudiates the prioritization of consent in civil society in 'Problems of Socialist Strategy'.

An alternative model of Gramsci's, assimilating 'civil society' to the state, was likewise considered by Anderson to misconceive the uniqueness of the West and to induce political aberrations—of either a reformist-Eurocommunist genre or an ultraleftist Maoist variety—insofar as the classical notion of political revolution, directed at the state apparatus, was therein dissolved into 'cultural revolution'. Adopted by Althusser, and embodied in his notion of 'Ideological State Apparatuses', which erased the distinctions between state and social formation, 'public' and 'private' institutions, it rendered nugatory the categorical difference beween bourgeois democracy and fascism as forms of capitalist state (pp. 34–36).

What, then, was the real distribution and articulation of 'coercion' and 'consent' typical of capitalist power in the West? Gramsci's meditations were subject to the 'involuntary temptation' of occluding violence in the process of valorizing culture, thereby sanctioning 'a classical tenet of reformism' (p. 41). Insisting that only a comparative historical survey—of the kind promised in the foreword to *Lineages of the Absolutist State*—could furnish an adequate answer to the question, Anderson ventured an indicative response, whose analytical premises precluded the strategic deductions of ultraleftism and reformism:

[T]he normal structure of capitalist political power in bourgeois-democratic states is . . . dominated by culture and determined by coercion. To deny the 'preponderant' . . . role of culture in the contemporary bourgeois power system is to liquidate the most salient immediate difference between Western parliamentarism and Russian absolutism. . . . The fact is that this cultural domination is embodied in certain irrefutably concrete institutions: regular elections, civic freedoms, rights of assembly—all of which exist in the West and none of which directly threaten the class power of capital. The day-to-day system of bourgeois rule is thus based on the consent of the masses, in the form of the ideological belief that they exercise self-government in the representative State. At the same time, however, to forget the 'fundamental' . . . role of violence within the power structure of contemporary capitalism in the final instance is to regress to reformism, in the illusion that an electoral majority can legislate socialism peacefully from parliament. (P. 42)

Revolutionary crises disclosed the secret of capitalist hegemony in the West. With their intensification, the repressive apparatus of the state came to the fore, coercion assuming determinacy *and* dominance when capitalist rule was subject to concerted socialist challenge.

The strategic implications of this analysis were then drawn. Above all, it contradicted the reformist projection of any attainment of hegemony in civil society by the working class prior to—let alone in lieu of—capture of state power and demolition of the state apparatus. In other words, it ruled out any substitution of cultural revolution, in whatever inflection (by long or forced march through the institutions), for political revolution (in the state-centred, Leninist sense). The starting point for any solution to 'the problem of the specificity of a socialist revolution in the West' was an accurate distinction between East and West in which history determined political geography (pp. 50–51). This distinction had equally but conversely eluded both Lenin and Gramsci:

Lenin never mistook the class character of Tsarism. . . . Yet he also never adequately . . . contrasted the parliamentary States of the West with the autocratic State in the East. . . . Gramsci . . . was intensely conscious of the novelty of the capitalist State in the West. . . . He, however, never perceived that the Absolutism in Russia with which he contrasted it was a feudal State. . . . In the no man's land between the thought of the two, revolutionary socialism missed a theoretical junction vital for its future in Europe. (P. 51)

The immediate reflection prompted by this passage is that Anderson's essay does not effect the relevant junction either—the conjunction of Lenin and Gramsci encapsulated in the title of Anderson's 1970 manuscript 'State and Revolution in the West'. It is devoted to the reconstruction of Gramsci's 'antinomies', not their resolution; and to their historical context in the strategic debates of the Second and Third Internationals, not its supersession. Having remarked Bordiga's elucidation of the crux of the East/West opposition (feudal autocracy/bourgeois democracy) and his perception of the superiority of the second in terms of ubiquitous consent and efficacious coercion alike (pp. 52–55), Anderson proceeded to relate Gramsci's distinction between 'war of manoeuvre' (East) and 'war of position' (West) to its antecedents in the socialist movement.

These were twofold: first, the line of the 'United Front' in Western Europe promulgated by the Third Congress of the Comintern, at the behest of Lenin and Trotsky, in 1921, after it had censured the German Communist Party's theory of the 'revolutionary offensive'; and, second, Kautsky's advocacy of a 'strategy of attrition' in the West, as against a 'strategy of overthrow' in the East, inciting a controversy with Luxemburg in 1910. Gramsci's identification of his 'war of position' with the United Frontism he had opposed during 1921–24, before his assumption of the leadership of the PCI, had the effect, according to Anderson, of proscribing 'adventurism'—but at a price:

> There is no doubt that the danger of adventurism disappears in this perspective, with its overwhelming emphasis on the ideological allegiance of the masses . . . , to be gained only by the pursuit of a united front within the working class. But what happens to the phase of insurrection itself . . . ? Gramsci never relinquished the fundamental tenets of classical Marxism on the ultimate necessity for violent seizure of State power, but at the same time his strategic formula for the West fails to integrate them. The mere counterposition of 'war of position' to 'war of manoeuvre' in any Marxist strategy in the end becomes an opposition between reformism and adventurism. (P. 69)

The requisite integration would conceive a 'war of position'—united frontism in civil society—as a precondition of any subsequent transition to a 'war of manoeuvre' by the exploited, under party leadership, against the state in the West.

In conclusion, Anderson restated the political realism of revolutionary socialism, past and present, West and East: 'From beginning to end, the laws of the capitalist State are reflected and refused in the rules of a socialist revolution' (p. 77). No such revolution would transpire in the West in the absence of a prior experience—in circumstances of 'dual power'—of a 'proletarian democracy that is tangibly superior to bourgeois democracy' (p. 78). In the current conjuncture, the immediate priority for revolutionary socialists lay elsewhere:

[T]he task that the United Front was designed to acquit is still unsolved fifty years later. The masses in North America, Western Europe and Japan have yet to be won over to revolutionary socialism in their plurality. Therefore, the central problematic of the United Front . . . retains all its validity today. It has never been historically surpassed. The imperative need remains to win the working class, before there can be any talk of winning power. The means of achieving this conquest . . . are the prime agenda of any real socialist strategy today. . . . Since [the last great strategic debate in the European workers' movement,] there has been little significant theoretical development of the political problems of revolutionary strategy in metropolitan capitalism that has had any direct contact with the masses. The structural divorce between original Marxist theory and the main organizations of the working class in Europe has yet to be historically resolved. (P. 78)

The converse conclusions, within a common geopolitical problematic, of 'Antinomies of Antonio Gramsci' and 'Problems of Socialist Strategy' are self-evident: Leninism, quite the reverse of representing a mere 'insurrectionism' applicable in the backward East but inadmissible in the advanced West, is the Marxist lineage from which any cogent conception of the transition to socialism in contemporary metropolitan capitalism will descend; the left social-democratic construction of Gramscianism, quite the reverse of correcting the vices of 'parliamentarism', instils illusions in 'culturalism'.

Of equal—arguably greater—significance are the contrasting modes of the two essays. Although Anderson stresses the predominantly philological character of the later endeavour, absolving it from any direct comparison with its basically sociological predecessor, he does permit himself substantive conclusions, whose abstraction is striking. Having located the United Kingdom within the East/West great divide, 'Problems' undertook a 'concrete analysis' of the British social formation—classes, party, state—in order to ground its strategic prospectus. By contrast, 'Antinomies' deliberately proceeds at a generic level, abstaining from the 'accurate reconnaissance of [any] individual country' enjoined by Gramsci in the midst of the notes on 'state and civil society' that supply much of Anderson's matter,[13] and invoking 'the masses' as the undifferentiated agency of its unsubstantiated strategy. To borrow two phrases from Lukács, it might be said that 'Antinomies' is

117

predicated upon 'the actuality of the revolution' yet, by comparison with 'Problems', evinces an 'attenuation of actuality'.

The political accomplishment of 'Antinomies', whatever its remarkable qualities as an essay in intellectual history, is a negative one: an acute inter-rogation of reformism. Contrary to Anderson's fallacious conclusion—'The masses . . . have yet to be won over to revolutionary socialism. . . . Therefore, the central problematic of the United Front . . . retains all its validity today' (p. 78)—falsification of reformist socialism does not therewith furnish con-firmation of revolutionary socialism.[14] It may be that there is no third way: but why should the nonexecution of the United Front's task half a century or more later prove its current validity? The shackles of Stalinism in the in-tervening decades permit evasion of an equally legitimate, but much more disquieting, inference: that revolutionary socialism is no more viable in the West than its reformist rival. At all events, as Geoff Hodgson argued in a ju-dicious critique of Anderson, 'Antinomies' is marked by an absence of 'prac-tical socialist strategy' and by a resort to the 'panacea' of the United Front— a regression, in his view, from the extraparliamentary and parliamentary 'dual strategy', 'essential for a socialist revolution in the West', foreshad-owed in 'Problems'.[15]

The 'structural divorce between original Marxist theory and the main organizations of the working class in Europe' was, in fact, being repaired— however unsatisfactorily—in the reformist reunification of theory and prac-tice characteristic of Eurocommunism. Just over a year after the appearance of 'Antinomies', in the immediate aftermath of the defeat of the Union of the Left in one of the proving grounds of Eurocommunism—France— in March 1978, Anderson participated in an international colloquium in Montreal, 'The Future of Socialism in Europe', where he delivered an interim verdict on the phenomenon. In a paper tellingly entitled 'The Strategic Option: Some Questions', Anderson identified Eurocommunism, program-matically, as a reversion to the perspectives of the Second International on the eve and morrow of the First World War.[16] Its incidence was most pronounced in southern European countries that had experienced no equiva-lent of the Social-Democratic reformist administrations familiar in the northern zone of the Continent, given the hegemony of Francoism, Christian Democracy, and Gaullism in Spain, Italy, and France respectively. At the same time, for all their professions of constitutional respectability, in their traditional internal organization and international affiliation the Communist parties of Carrillo, Berlinguer, and Marchais were fundamen-tally distinct from Social-Democracy. This disjunction prompted Anderson's first question:

[I]s this tradition . . . sufficient to ensure that the experience of Euro-communism in Southern Europe . . . will not lead to a repetition of the im-passe of the Northern labour movement which, after having demonstrated a frequent ability to win elections, and after repeated experiences of govern-ment, has . . . totally failed to transform any of the North European societies in the direction of socialism? (P. 25)

The second query was the strategic riddle proper: what was the manda-tory strategy for a successful transition to socialism in the West? And what type of postcapitalist state would be required in that transition? Taking up Henri Lefebvre's emphasis on direct, 'decentralized' democracy, Anderson advised that it was vulnerable to a variety of 'negative' political deductions—for example, municipal socialism of Fabian vintage, or market socialism of Yugoslav stamp, wherein 'decentralization . . . has tended towards the re-creation of a market economy, which naturally and inevitably reproduces many of the worst vices of a capitalist market economy' (p. 25). Having ruled these out, Anderson sketched his own position:

[A] genuine transition to a much more advanced form of socialism in Western Europe would involve far more rigorously centralized institutions of economic planning than anything that exists within our capitalist societies today. It is hypocritical to gloss over or deny this fact. . . . On the other hand, and correlatively, such *economic* planning must be determined and con-trolled by organs of *political* democracy that are far more directly and locally rooted among the producers themselves than anything we know today in bourgeois democracy. . . . [E]conomic centralization, inherent in socialist planning as such, must be combined with a form of political decentralization that betokens a completely new structure of a post-capitalist state, a social-ist state. (Pp. 25-26)

Now, this combination—the obverse of the Yugoslav model—posed the question of the compatibility of direct (conciliar) and indirect (parliamen-tary) democracy. Noting that the Far Left habitually taxed Eurocommunism with straightforward parliamentarism, Anderson distinguished three stances on the issue in the workers' movement, all of which had been advocated in the years 1918–22: that of Bernstein and company, urging preservation of the existing parliamentary state, which had been transmitted to mainstream Social-Democracy; that of Kautsky and Bauer, envisaging a combination of traditional parliamentary institutions with auxiliary organs of direct democ-racy, which had been rediscovered by Eurocommunism; and that of Lenin,

119

exhorting elimination of 'bourgeois democracy' and its replacement by direct soviet democracy, which had been inherited by the Far Left. Indicating his own allegiances, Anderson conceded that

> although the [Far Left] . . . have produced many telling criticisms of the first and second options, they have done relatively little work on developing and providing any contemporary form for the third option. We all know . . . that the Soviets in Russia were extinguished very rapidly after their birth in 1917, and their life was historically imperfect and circumscribed on the rim of Eastern Europe. We know that the workers' and soldiers' councils in Central Europe . . . were also ephemeral experiences. So far, little work has been done on how . . . there could occur a resurgence of a Soviet-type state, soviet in the classical and genuine sense of the word, in the quite different social and historical conditions of contemporary Western Europe. The result is that a large question mark still remains suspended over the third alternative, which is that of the classical tradition of revolutionary socialism. (Pp. 27–28)[17]

In conclusion, Anderson turned to a third problem: the international context of any Continental transition. Of especial importance was the present and future relationship between the socialist movement in Western Europe and the Communist states of the East. Here Anderson firmly rebuked the anti-Sovietism surfacing in Eurocommunist ranks as office beckoned:

> [A]ll of us . . . will be acutely conscious of the profound historical vices and defects of the societies and states that have been constructed in the USSR . . . and Eastern Europe. But it will be vital for the future course of the West European Left that it be able to reject the fashionable equation . . . between the USSR and the USA as two 'super powers', from which a socialist Europe should be equidistant. . . . [T]his language is thoroughly unreal and unscientific. . . . [T]he myth of the two 'super powers' and of the ultimate similarity between them is a notion that has been most . . . ferociously propagated by the leadership of the Chinese Communist Party. The political logic of it has been very clear. It rapidly leads . . . to a rapprochement with the United States. . . . Any turn within the mass communist movement of Western Europe towards a similar ideological position would be very likely to have a similar diplomatic outcome. . . . Any attempt to foreclose the possibility of constructing a more positive dialectic with these societies . . . will lead only to regression and defeat. (Pp. 28–29)

Anderson's questions about the strategic option in Europe exhibited a painful honesty about their intractability. They were left hanging. But that he had not abandoned the comparative history that might afford a basis for answers to them is apparent from the paper 'The Notion of Bourgeois Revolution', contemporary with 'Antinomies' but published a decade and a half later in *English Questions*.[18] Arguing that the concept had been given its Marxist currency by the theoreticians of Russian Social-Democracy, Anderson observed that it had been coined as 'the *negative* of proletarian revolution', through a 'retro-projection' of the agency of a revolution against the bourgeois state onto the dramatis personae of any overthrow of Absolutism (p. 108). Non-Marxist historians had had little difficulty in refuting attempted applications of this false homology to England in the seventeenth century or France in the eighteenth. To escape from the resultant impasse—a theoretical norm confronting recalcitrant historical realities—Anderson proposed to contruct a general theory of the 'formal structures' of any bourgeois revolution, which would subsequently be tested against the historical evidence in each specific instance (pp. 109–13). '[P]reliminary considerations of this kind', he reflected,

> make it clear why none of the great turbulences of the transition to modernity has ever conformed to the simple schema of a struggle between a feudal aristocracy and industrial capital of the sort presupposed in the traditional Marxist vocabulary. The porous pattern of feudalism above, the unpredictable presence of exploited classes below, the mixed disposition of the bourgeoisie within, the competitive pressure of rival states without, were bound to defeat this expectation. In that sense, one could say that it was in the nature of 'bourgeois revolutions' to be denatured: these transformations could never have been the linear project of a single class subject. Here the exception was the rule—every one was a bastard birth. (Pp. 112–13)

Furthermore, it was possible to discern two distinct cycles of bourgeois revolutions. The first, essentially effected from below and conducted under the banner of a social ideology, comprised Holland, England, the American colonies, and France, stretching from the sixteenth to the eighteenth centuries, when capital was predominantly mercantile or agrarian. The second, invariably executed from above in nationalist colours, encompassed Italy, the United States, Germany, and Japan in the nineteenth century, when capital was preponderantly industrial (pp. 116-18).

As Anderson acknowledged in the foreword to *English Questions*, the credentials of the paradigm of bourgeois revolution employed in the

121

Nairn-Anderson theses had been vulnerable to the kind of objection raised by Thompson in 1965. Anderson's conceptual clarifications did not issue in any revision or reconstruction of the theses at his hands. However, Nairn did contribute an innovative, comparative restatement in 1977, 'The Twilight of the British State', which pinpointed as the matrix of Britain's postwar malaise the conjoint effects of no second 'revolution from above' by the industrial bourgeoisie in the nineteenth century and the defensive consolidation of the labour movement in the twentieth.[19] Commending it while remarking the *NLR*'s failure to cover the ejection of Labourism and assumption of Thatcherism in 1979, the quinquennial report nevertheless chided Nairn for exaggerating the centrifugal potential of peripheral nationalism in Scotland, Wales, and Northern Ireland. Yet this was no isolated occurrence in the *Review*:

> The misreading of the balance of forces involved . . . was . . . very much in the tradition of NLR. Ever since the early sixties, the review had looked with hope to one potential agent after another to unhinge the ruling political order in England—each time overestimating its radicalism or staying-power. In this sense, there was [a] direct line from the credence lent to the Labour Party in 1964 (*Towards Socialism*), to the unions in 1967 (*The Incompatibles*), to the students in 1968–69 (*Student Power*), down to the national revolts of 1974–78 (*The Break-up of Britain*). The review should . . . now learn the necessity of great political caution. (Pp. 13–14)

Nairn's association of E. P. Thompson and Raymond Williams with a 'left-nationalist popular culture', and a critique of the latter in the *NLR* by Terry Eagleton, figured in Thompson's 1978 bill of indictment, *The Poverty of Theory*, where he resumed his earlier charges.[20] Thompson's Althusserian-Andersonian amalgam, producing a composite theoreticist-academicist-elitist-(crypto-)Stalinist Marxism, indicated that he had not forgotten all the rhetorical tricks of his Communist formation during the European zenith of Stalinism. In a measured public rejoinder, Anderson described it as 'the most sustained exposition of Thompson's own credo, as a historian and as a socialist, that he has given us to date'.[21] Something similar might be said of *Arguments within English Marxism*.

The Three Sources and Two Component Parts of Andersonian Marxism

Arguments within English Marxism was a diplomatic expansion of 'Notes on "The Poverty of Theory"', which betrays Anderson's grave concern at Thompson's philippic, restaged during an acrimonious session at a History

Workshop conference in Oxford in December 1979.[22] Broadly welcoming Thompson's engagement with Althusser and the encounter thereby staged between British Marxist historiography and Western Marxist philosophy, Anderson delimited four main points of contention: the value of history, the role of human agency, the status of Marxism, and the character of Stalinism. To these he appended three areas of divergence between Thompson and the present *NLR*, ranging over questions of internationalism, utopianism, and socialist strategy. Our own discussion will be geared less to exploring Anderson's arbitration of the Thompson-Althusser dispute than to eliciting his own intellectual and political credo on the eve of the international reaction of the 1980s, two decades after the commencement of his career at the dawn of the international effervescence of the 1960s.

We can begin by noting Anderson's essential concurrence with the justice of Thompson's critique of Althusserian 'anti-empiricism' even as he stressed the necessity of theory in historiography—the construction and systematization of concepts that permit the historian's ascent from the abstract to the concrete (understood, following Marx, as 'the synthesis of many determinations'). Eschewing epistemological antinaturalism, Anderson appeared remarkably unruffled by the conventionalist critique of empiricism so pervasive in the wake of Kuhn in the Anglo-Saxon world or of Bachelard and Canguilhem in France; and he adopted a realist and falsificationist—broadly Popperian-Lakatosian—philosophy of science. Anderson insisted upon the scientificity of historiography—contra Thompson's assignment of it to the humanities—and, in particular, the scientificity of historical materialism, whose theoretical constructs were held to be subject to the acid test of the relevant historical evidence.[23]

Having briefly surveyed issues in the philosophy of history, Anderson turned to a classical dispute in social theory—the structure/agency dichotomy—and its roots in perennial philosophy: the determinism/free will debate. Noting the ambiguity of the terms *agent* and *subject* (p. 18), he rejected the converse unilateralisms of Thompson (human creativity) and Althusser (structural implacability). In their stead, he proposed a compatibilist position, seeking to reconcile intentional agency and universal causality. He attempted a discrimination within and historicization of the terms of the controversy, without displacing the structure/agency duality as such.[24] After distinguishing between two types of human agency—approximately, individual or private and collective or public—he focused upon a third:

> those collective projects which have sought to render their initiators authors of their collective existence as a whole, in a conscious programme aimed at creating or remodelling whole social structures. . . . [E]ssentially this kind of

agency is very recent indeed. . . . It is the modern labour movement that has . . . given birth to this quite new conception of historical change; and it is with the advent of . . . scientific socialism that . . . for the first time collective projects of social transformation were married to systematic efforts to understand the process of past and present, to produce a premeditated future. The Russian Revolution is in this respect the inaugural incarnation of a new kind of history, founded on an unprecedented form of agency. Notoriously, the results of the great cycle of upheavals it initiated have to date been far from those expected at their outset. But the alteration of the potential of human action, in the course of the 20th century, remains irreversible. (Pp. 20–21)

Anderson's allegiance to classical Marxist tenets is fully apparent here, in his conception of historical materialism as a 'scientific socialism' whose causal explanations facilitate collective self-emancipation and thence what Marx called the 'conscious reconstruction of human society'. Underscoring the dimension of cognition—as well as conation—in historical agency, Anderson wrote: 'The whole purpose of historical materialism . . . has . . . been to give men and women the means with which to exercise *a real popular self-determination for the first time in history*. This is . . . the objective of a socialist revolution' (p. 22). Pending the transition to Marx's 'ream of freedom', 'rational historical causality' (p. 25)—what Althusser once dubbed 'the reasons for unreason'—could be invoked to account for the fate of socialist revolutions to date, all of which had occurred under the sway of direst necessity.

Anderson's historicization of the issue of agency leads to an interrogation of the concept with which it is conjugated in *The Poverty of Theory*: experience. Arguing that Thompson's utilization of the term elides a universal or neutral denotation with a restricted or positive connotation, equating experience with illumination by definition, whereas Althusser assimilates it to illusion by fiat, Anderson obstructed the Thompsonian conclusion that the lesson learnt will necessarily be cognitively and morally valid (pp. 25–29).[25] This demotion of the claims of experience likewise applied to *The Making of the English Working Class*, whose 'subjectivist' characterization of social class was rejected in favour of the 'objectivist' definition, in terms of differential structural relationship to the means of production, recently restated in G. A. Cohen's *Karl Marx's Theory of History* (pp. 39–40).[26] This conception of class formation then underlay Anderson's assessment of Thompson's affirmation of the primacy of contending class agents in maintaining and

transforming social formations, albeit in the shape of the unintended consequences of collective social action.

Detecting in Althusser's resolution of the Hobbesian problem of social
order in the 1970 essay on ideology 'a hybrid of the positions of Parsons and
Sartre'—value integration and violent coercion, respectively—Anderson
maintained that neither was compatible with historical materialism:

> To contend that social formations typically derive their unity from the diffu-
> sion of values, or the exercise of violence . . . is to reject the Marxist insis-
> tence on the ultimate primacy of economic determinations in history. . . .
> The problem of *social order* is irresoluble so long as the answer to it is sought
> at the level of intention (or valuation). . . . It is, and must be, the dominant
> *mode of production* that confers fundamental unity on a social formation, al-
> locating their objective positions to the classes within it, and distributing the
> agents within each class. The result is . . . an objective process of class strug-
> gle. To stabilize and regulate *this* conflict, the complementary modalities of
> political power, which include repression and ideology, exercised *inside* and
> *outside* the State, are thereafter indispensable. But class struggle itself is not
> a causal prius in the sustentation of order, for *classes are constituted by
> modes of production, and not vice versa.* (Pp. 54–55)

Intentional, conflictual collective action is not the independent variable
in accounting for the maintenance of social order—the reproduction of social formations—but rather the phenomenon in need of explanation. What,
on the other hand, of social change and, a fortiori, the transformation of
social formations—that is, 'making history'? Marxists anxious to escape the
'mechanicism' of Second International orthodoxy, appealing to the 1859
Preface, have tended to have recourse, on the slender textual evidence of the
Communist Manifesto, to the class struggle as the 'motor of history'. This
was rebuffed by Anderson as a form of theoretical voluntarism. Once again,
class struggle was not the *explanans* but the *explanandum*. Contradictions
between the forces and relations of production, whose specific combinations
distinguish the various economic modes of production, were said to be 'the
deepest spring of long-term historical change' (p. 81). Reiterating points
made in *Passages from Antiquity to Feudalism*, Anderson argued that for historical materialism,

> among the most fundamental of all mechanisms of social change . . . are
> the systemic contradictions between *forces and relations of production*, not
> just social conflicts between classes generated by antagonistic relations of

production alone. The former overlap with the latter, because one of the forces of production is always labour, which simultaneously figures as a class specified by the relations of production. But they do not coincide. Crises within modes of production are not identical with confrontations between classes. The two may or may not fuse, according to the historical occasion. The *onset* of major economic crises . . . has typically taken all social classes unawares, deriving from structural depths beneath those of direct conflict between them. The resolution of such crises, on the other hand, has no less typically been the outcome of prolonged war between classes. (Pp. 55–56)

Under the stimulus of Cohen's defence of an orthodox historical material-ism, which is several times enlisted (pp. 40, 65, 72–73), and against the Althusserian-Maoist current, Anderson thus sustained the explanatory pri-macy not simply of 'base' over 'superstructure', mode of production over so-cial formation, but—by implication—of forces over relations of production.

Anderson's interpretation of the canon and corpus of historical material-ism bequeathed by Marx set its face against the rival discontinuites pos-tulated by Althusser, locating an 'epistemological break' in 1845–46, and Thompson, lamenting an immersion in 'anti-political economy' after 1848. He was more inclined, however, to side with Althusser than with his critic.[27] Crucial to Marx's theoretical construction of the capitalist mode of produc-tion in *Capital* was the couplet forces/relations of production—'the corner-stone of the theory of historical materialism as such' (p. 63)—ignored by Thompson. Classified by the latter as a category pertaining to economics, mode of production was defended by Anderson as a historical concept, whose function was precisely to 'think the *diversity* of socio-economic forms and epochs—to give us the means of *differentiating* one major type of historical structure from another in the evolution of mankind' (p. 64). Althusser and Balibar were to be credited for their clarification and systematization of the basic concepts of historical materialism in *Reading 'Capital'*, whose fertility, notwithstanding its 'anti-historicist' polemic, was evidenced by the concrete historiographical and anthropological research conducted under its aegis. From his examination of the biases of Althusser—against history—and of Thompson—against theory—Anderson, as one might expect from the au-thor of *Passages* and *Lineages*, inferred the '*mutual indispensability*' of con-ceptual and empirical perspectives: 'Marxist history is impossible without the formal constitution of theoretical concepts . . . : but these concepts will only produce real knowledge if they derive from and return to controllable historical research' (p. 66).

The fear motivating Thompson's antipathy to *Capital* was the peril of economic reductionism it allegedly harboured. Anderson regarded this as un-founded. The accusation that Althusser and Balibar had consummated eco-nomic reductionism by identifying economic mode of production with social formation was 'astonishing' (p. 67), since they had formalized the distinction between the two, proceeding to insist that any concrete social formation would invariably contain a plurality of modes of production. Contrary to Thompson's fulminations, the categorical Althusserian differentiation between theoretical object (object of knowledge) and real object—or, in Anderson's formulation, between 'epistemological procedures' and 'ontological categories' (p. 72)—precisely entailed that analytical discrimination between different social realms and practices did not imply their real separation. Rather than rending the skein of history and society, the purpose of this differentiation was to untangle it. Similar considerations prompted Anderson's endorsement of Cohen's de-fence of the base/superstructure distinction, which he himself had collapsed in *Lineages of the Absolutist State* (p. 72), and—if with reservations—of Althusser's proposition of 'differential historical temporality', adapted from the *Annales* school and central to the architectonic of *Lineages* (pp. 73–76).

The robustly political character of Thompson's practice as a historian won Anderson's admiration. Yet he dissented from Thompson's equation of history with 'the past' (*res gestae*) and his concomitant definition of histori-ography as the study of that past (*historia rerum gestarum*). Above all, he re-fused the Thompsonian assimilation of historical materialism to historiogra-phy, as a misconception of the scope and purpose of Marxism. As we have seen, in *Considerations on Western Marxism* Anderson had expressed his aversion to the tendency to conceive Marxism exclusively as a 'sociology of revolution', a strategic analysis of the present. In *Arguments*, without dis-owning that critique, it was the converse bias that he sought to redress:

[H]istorical materialism to its founders was also 'scientific socialism', in other words the enterprise of understanding the *present* and mastering the *future*. . . . In this perspective, historical materialism is not confined to . . . the past. The history with which it is concerned is equally the present. . . . [W]hat [Thompson's] whole account . . . lacks is any real sense that one of the central purposes of understanding the past is to provide a *causal knowl-edge* of historical processes capable of furnishing the basis for an adequate po-litical practice in the present, aimed at transforming the existing social order into a prepared popular future—for the first time in history. (Pp. 84–85)[28]

This raised the question for Anderson of a Marxist ethics, whose absence, he agreed with Thompson, menaced Marxist theory and socialist practice.

But against Thompson's professed 'moralism' (p. 86), *Arguments* asserted the '*difficulty* of developing a materialist ethics, at once integrally historical and radically non-utilitarian' (p. 98). Thompson's own 'extrapolation' of values from history was said to effect a 'dual simplification':

> The primary continuity between past and present, which is necessarily *causal*, is displaced from focus—risking a rhetorical rather than strategic use of history. For historical materialism, as for socialist politics, what the past bequeaths the present is first and foremost a set of *lines of force for transformation*. . . . These . . . in turn incarnate certain values that are an active part of the process of social transformation itself. . . . Marxists have no cause to abstain from judgement of these values, as they were embodied in the past. But such judgement is only possible in full historical context, which is not the same thing as the *contemporary* context of the time. (P. 98)

What, however, were the form and the criterion of such value judgements? The answer would appear to be a variety of classical Marxist, nonutilitarian consequentialism, where the relevant consequences revolve around a particular ('dialectical') conception of historical 'progress' and human emancipation. Contrary to Rankean historicism, not all epochs were equally proximate to God:

> Thompson reserves the term 'progress' for movements in the present alone, refusing it to processes in the past. More rationally, the opposite might be argued: the retrospective outcome of past conflicts is relatively settled and ascertainable, whereas the issues of the present are by their nature always fundamentally uncertain, subject to the indeterminacy of a future whose shape remains to be seen. A Marxist evaluation of the past is inseparable from an explanation of it: and an explanation must necessarily encompass its consequences, in all their ambiguity and contradiction. The present is never a fit judge of itself. Marx's conception of historical progress . . . is a hard one. But even—especially—amidst the torments of the socialist movement in the 20th century, we have no cause to revise it. (P. 99)

Tout comprendre, ce n'est pas tout pardonner: it *is* to permit due apportionment of praise and blame.[29]

Foremost among the historical phenomena demanding a Marxist explanation that will encompass all its contradictory and ambiguous consequences, and thereby conduce to an appropriate evaluation, is the greatest torment of the socialist movement in the twentieth century: the Stalinist eventuation of the Bolshevik Revolution. This was the subject of Anderson's fourth chapter. Having authoritatively despatched Thompson's demonization of Althusserianism as the philosophical correlate of Stalinism,[30] Anderson turned to his claims for the socialist-humanist critique of the phenomenon mounted in 1956. His first reservation was straightforwardly factual. Predating the official revelations of Mikoyan and Khrushchev at the Twentieth Congress of the CPSU by some thirty years, there already existed a Marxist tradition critical of Stalin, which Thompson had overlooked. Founded by Trotsky and continued by Deutscher, it was not only 'charged with a burning moral and political indignation', it was also 'an enterprise of materialist *social theory*, an attempt at a *historical explanation* of Stalinism' (p. 117). By comparison, so Anderson argued, socialist humanism substituted 'moralism for historical materialism' (p. 120), abandoning explanation for condemnation. Thompson's caricature of Althusserianism as the apotheosis of Stalinism at a stroke travestied the former and trivialized the latter:

> Its hallmark was loss of life . . . on an enormous scale. With the death of the autocrat who gave his name to the system, Stalinism in its classical sense soon came to an end in Russia. There remained a rigid party dictatorship, dedicated at once to the industrialization of a planned economy, the defence of state property against the pressure of imperialism, and the protection of its privileges from the masses of workers and peasants—still a negation of socialist democracy, but no longer an apparatus of organized terror. Stalinism in this secondary sense has proved to possess a much wider historical basis. So far this century it has constituted the format of all regimes to emerge from successful socialist revolutions, with the partial exception of Cuba. . . . Stalinism has at once been replicated and mitigated outside Russia, wherever the construction of socialism has been attempted in poor and backward social formations locked in struggle with colonial domination or imperialist aggression. (P. 121)

Kindred in spirit to the analysis in 'Problems of Socialist Strategy', the implication of this passage is that whereas, according to 'The Antinomies of Antonio Gramsci' (but contrary to 'Problems'), a version of Leninism is appropriate in the advanced West, Stalinism—in the second sense—is the explicable format of revolutionary socialism in the backward South. Accordingly, Anderson rebuked Thompson's repudiation of 'no enemies on the Left' ('I cannot conceive of any wave in the working-class movement being further to the "right" than Stalinism'):

With this dire sentence, he slips back to what is in fact a classical Cold War position. For Stalinist movements . . .—Communist parties modelled on the authoritarian traditions of the later CPSU—are not mere survivals of a reactionary past: . . . some have proved capable of still continuing to play a revolutionary role. . . . What else was the Vietnamese Revolution—the greatest epic of anti-imperialist struggle in the 20th century? . . . The drift of the declaration that there are no 'enemies to the right' of Stalinism within the labour movement is acceptance of social democracy as the lesser evil. (Pp. 122–23)

Whereas Thompson declared war on Althusserianism in particular, and Western Marxism in general, Anderson looked forward to 'a common socialist culture that ha[s] grown beyond mutual anathemas' (p. 127). Recording signs of a convergence between Anglo-Marxist historiography and Western Marxist philosophy in the work of the Centre for Contemporary Cultural Studies, he summoned Williams as a witness against Thompson's sense of 'the phantasmagoria of our time' (pp. 129–30).[31] By way of contribution to the supersession of past divisions, having sounded the differences between Thompson and Althusser, in the remainder of *Arguments* Anderson addressed those separating the two cohorts of the New Left.

Rebutting Thompson's specific allegations, Anderson submitted an anodyne account of the 1962–63 transition in the *NLR* (pp. 135–36), which opened out into a retrospective on the politico-intellectual divergences of 1964–66, inventoried in chapter 1. Anderson revoked two of the charges pressed in his 1966 counterattack on Thompson: 'nationalism' and 'moralism' (p. 140). Locating the formative moment of Thompson's 'socialist internationalism' in the Communist movement during the Second World War, when a fusion of 'internationalism' and 'nationalism' occurred, Anderson wrote of 'the emergence of a type of internationalism in the NLR after 1963, quite distinct from its predecessor': a '*theoretical* one' that renounced 'Marxism in one country' (pp. 148-49). Yet international theory had not precluded attention to national reality: on the contrary. Continental Marxism was embraced to explain national capitalism and thereby prime local socialism—albeit, Anderson ruefully admitted, amid 'the critical lack of any real popular context for Marxist theoretical work in this period' (p. 150). Whereas Thompson had invested his post-1956 political hopes in the European Communist oppositions of that year and in the CND, Anderson and his colleagues had eventually gravitated, via the Vietnam Solidarity Campaign, toward 'the main alternative heritage of revolutionary Marxism since the October Revolution'—Trotskyism, which 'became in time a central and unevadable pole of political reference within NLR' (pp. 152–53).[32]

Now, this is a somewhat abridged account. Reposing upon 'relative ideological maturity' as defined in the quinquennial report, it omits any mention of such comparative immaturities as Wilsonism or 'studentism', Guevarism or Maoism, and backdates 'an open and critical revolutionary Marxism'. Moreover, conforming to the dictates of 'integrism', it speaks on behalf of an *NLR* that extended beyond Anderson himself but reached no further than an active core considerably smaller than the official editorial committee. (Thus, the plural pronominal usage in *Arguments* is not quite royal: on the other hand, none of its subjects was *plus royaliste que le roi*.) At any rate, having cited the 'formative influence' of Deutscher and the ongoing work of Mandel, Anderson explained:

> [T]he importance of this heritage lay in the standard and model of internationalism it embodied. Throughout his life, Trotsky was an unremitting adversary of every form of social patriotism or great-power chauvinism. . . . At the same time, no socialist has had the same degree of insight into the culture and society of nations beside his own as Trotsky displayed. . . . Finally, Trotsky was the first Marxist to found a historical account of the nature, and a political strategy for the future, of his own nation on a theory of its integration into the international imperialist order. Political, cultural and theoretical, the dimensions of this internationalism overtop any before or since. It was not immune from failings or mistakes, some of them major ones. But its moral and intellectual grandeur has only grown with the passage of time. (Pp. 155–56)[33]

Rather than supplying a further source of disagreement, this nonpareil should have been a 'common element' in the politics of both New Left levies, Anderson concluded, anticipating the future coexistence of different varieties of internationalism in 'a vital political culture of the Left' (p. 156).

In the process of reclaiming 'moralism' for his brand of Marxism, in both *William Morris* and *The Poverty of Theory* Thompson had professed his affiliation to the tradition of 'utopian socialism' that Engels, in a famous pamphlet extracted from *Anti-Dühring*, sharply demarcated from 'scientific socialism'. In a chapter on the subject, Anderson made reparation for his neglect of Morris in the 1960s, acknowledging the grandeur of his transformed romanticism. However, he chided Thompson for his unwitting assimilation of 'a fashionable philosophy of Parisian irrationalism' in his discussion of desire (p. 161).[34] More importantly, citing Williams's critique of Morris, he suggested that the antithetical traditions of utopian and scientific social-ism—those of Owen, Fourier, and Saint-Simon, on the one hand, and Marx and Engels, Lenin and Trotsky, on the other—were united in one fundamen-tal respect: their conception of a communist order as a 'simplification' of so-cial relations (e.g., the Saint-Simonian projection, inherited by Engels, of the end of politics) (pp. 166–67).[35]

The utopian vision of Morris in *News from Nowhere* faithfully reproduces the romantic antipathy to the historical achievements of industrial capital-ism hymned in the *Communist Manifesto* by Marx and Engels, who construed communism as the complex supersession—not the mere suppression—of its civilization. Quoting the *Grundrisse*, Anderson reminded Thompson that Marxism sought to supersede the romanticism/utilitarianism antithesis, each of whose terms was politically labile (p. 169).[36] Meanwhile, Morris's 'futurism' possessed a merit not mentioned in Thompson's extolment of it: its role as a weapon with which to combat reformism in the present. However, it was to Rudolf Bahro's *The Alternative in Eastern Europe*—'the finest Marxist attempt yet written to think the future', translated by NLB in 1978—that credit must go for superseding the early-nineteenth-century antithesis to which Morris and, by implication, Thompson remained in thrall (pp. 174–75).

In figuring a desirable future, utopianism exhibits a generic tendency not only to discount questions of its viability but also to disregard a strategy for the transition to it from the present. Here, according to Anderson, Morris was an exception who proved the rule. In his final chapter, 'Strategies', Anderson sought to turn Morris's antireformism against the champion of his utopianism. With Morris,

> for the first time the *structural unity* of the capitalist order is clearly posed as the insurmountable obstacle to any sequence of partial reforms being capable of peacefully changing it into socialism—'it will not suffer itself to be dismembered'. The principle so firmly enunciated here was to have a long subsequent history, as a central tenet of revolutionary Marxism after Lenin. (P. 178)

Anderson suggested that Thompson's indifference to this dimension of Morris's thought, if insufficient to licence his 1966 charge of 'moralism', did indicate significant strategic divergences between the two New Lefts (p. 186). Reviewing the position adopted by Thompson in his 1960 essay 'Revolution', Anderson argued its kinship with the programme of the CPGB from the 1950s and traced a consistency in his pronouncements on the subject from

'The Peculiarities of the English' onward. To this he counterposed the collective position arrived at by *NLR* Mark 2.

As Donald Sassoon has pointed out,[37] in view of the absence of any such 'detail' from pages of the *Review* to date, Anderson prefaced his summary statement rather incongruously:

> It would not be appropriate to reiterate in detail here the strategic conceptions of the transition to socialism for which the present NLR has stood. It will be sufficient to note the major differences. For us, a socialist revolution means . . . the dissolution of the existing capitalist state, the expropriation of the possessing classes from the means of production, and the construction of a new type of state and economic order, in which the associated producers can for the first time exercise direct control over their working lives and direct power over their political government. That change will not occur without a fundamental economic crisis. . . . When it impends, the primary locus of bourgeois class power will redeploy towards the repressive rather than the representative apparatuses of the capitalist state. These apparatuses must be broken as organized institutions for any revolutionary transfer of power to occur. This can be achieved only by the creation of organs of socialist democracy, mobilizing a popular force capable of undermining the unity of the coercive machinery of the established state, and cancelling the legitimacy of its parliamentary machinery. . . . The political advent of a situation of dual power, accompanied by the onset of economic crisis, permits no gradual resolution. When the unity of the bourgeois state and the reproduction of the capitalist economy are ruptured, the ensuing social upheaval must rapidly and fatally pit revolution and counter-revolution against each other in a violent convulsion. . . . In this end-game situation, socialists will seek to avoid a conclusion by arms, but will not sow illusions as to the probablility of a resort to them. (Pp. 194–95)[38]

These perspectives belong, as Anderson observed, to the revolutionary Marxist tradition associated with Lenin and Trotsky, a reference to 'transitional goals' (p. 195) signalling an affinity with the Fourth International. By contrast, Thompson's conception of the transition to socialism amounted to a 'libertarian' variant of the alternative tradition associated with the Second International, with which some parties of the Third, in the guise of Eurocommunism, were converging. Anderson acknowledged that both scenarios contained major problems—respectively, the plausibility of the emergence of organs of 'dual power' in mature parliamentary democracies, and the verisimilitude of capitalist polity and economy pacifically submitting to their legislative transmutation. These problems were sufficient to render their arguments necessarily *'probabilistic'* (p. 197). For both were predicated on one of those events that had not thus far transpired: a 'successful transition to socialism . . . in the advanced capitalist countries' (p. 196). Nevertheless, the historical record—including the tragic counterexample of Chile in 1973—weighed decisively in the balance between them:

> There can be no axiomatics of revolutionary change. . . . The real terrain of arbitration between the two opposing conceptions . . . is *historical*—not speculation on an unknowable future, but examination of a known past. It is on that ground, the firm earth of the historian on which every Marxist should keep their feet, that evidence points to the greater cogency and realism of the tradition of Lenin and Trotsky. (P. 197)[39]

On this ground, Anderson cast a critical eye over Thompson's defence of the 'rule of law' in *Whigs and Hunters* and of the British Constitution in the essays about to be collected in *Writing by Candlelight*. Paradoxically, perhaps, in view of his later subscription to Charter 88,[40] Anderson queried Thompson's medium-term 'confinement of the *horizon* of political struggle in Britain' to campaigns against authoritarian statism:

> [I]f 'democratic practice' is separated so completely from 'socialist struggle'. . . , then 'libertarian' campaigns could imperceptibly revert to 'liberal' politics. That danger dogs any discourse which pits a new 'statism' against traditional 'freedoms'. The conception of liberty involved is always a negative one. . . . The fight for the preservation of civil liberties will only be truly successful if it is capable of *advancing* them beyond the threshold of the liberal opposition between State and individual, towards the point where the emergence of *another kind of State*—not just safeguards against the existing State—is their logical and practical terminus. For this *transitional demands*, linking immediate to ultimate, democratic to socialist, goals are essential. (Pp. 204–5)

Finally, Anderson returned to the respective emphases of Thompson and himself on 'morality' and 'strategy', maintaining that these should be regarded not as mutually exclusive but rather as standing in need of synthesis: 'What revolutionary socialism above all needs today is *moral realism*—with equal stress on each of the terms' (p. 207). To that end, he appealed to his interlocutor to 'leave old quarrels behind, and to explore new problems together':

So far, our contrasting contributions to a common socialist culture have in many ways each involved restatements or criticisms of classical inheritances, . . . more than innovative advance into unknown terrain. The reasons for that are not hard to seek: the absence of a truly mass and truly revolutionary movement in England, as elsewhere in the West, has fixed the perimeter of all possible thought in the period. But the example of Morris himself . . . shows how much can still be done in what appear to be adverse conditions. (P. 207)

Thompson made no reply to *Arguments within English Marxism*, although he did on occasion good-humouredly intimate nonrepentance, even as he accepted the invitation of its closing line.[41] Intermittently ex cathedra in tone, Anderson's text is in many ways an elegant contemporay 'restatement' of the classical inheritance, an authoritative exposition of received positions—sometimes with, sometimes without, defence—rather than an 'innovative advance'.[42] From this vantage point, both Thompson and Althusser, in their different ways, are found wanting. The possibility of social-scientific naturalism and the validity of epistemological realism; the necessity of empirically controlled theory; historical materialism as the transhistorical, cross-cultural science of social formations; mode of production as its master concept; the explanatory primacy—not exclusivity—of economic determinations as its major premiss; the systemic contradiction between forces and relations of production as the *explanans* of epochal transformations; moral realism and consequentialism; a 'dialectical' conception of historical process and progress; communism as the supersession of advanced capitalism; the ineluctability of political revolution in any transition to socialism—in these (and other) respects, Anderson's credo was that of a traditional but noncatechismal 'revolutionary Marxism'.

The degree to which it was 'open and critical' vis-à-vis the classical heritage, as the centenary of Marx's death approached, can be gauged if we compare it with the propositions of a short article by Lenin, written in 1913 to commemorate the thirtieth anniversary. There Lenin identified the three sources of Marxist doctrine as German philosophy, English political economy, and French socialism; and its three corresponding component parts as dialectical materialism, historical materialism, and scientific socialism.[43] Applying this schema to *Arguments*, we might specify the sources of Andersonian Marxism as economic and political classical Marxism (above all Marx, Lenin, Trotsky, and Gramsci); philosophical Western Marxism (predominantly Colletti and Timpanaro, subsidiarily Althusser); and historiographical and cultural British Marxism (especially Hobsbawm, Thompson, and Williams). In other words, in place of the antitheses of the past—for example, Western Marxism versus English empiricism—*Arguments* propounds the mature Andersonian synthesis of classical, Western, and Anglo Marxisms.

What are the components of this synthesis? The first point to note is that—in defiance of Lenin and Trotsky[44]—'dialectical materialism' is absent, and that this omission is not compensated by any alternative—specifically Marxist—philosophy. Under the anti-Hegelian auspices of Althusser and Colletti, Anderson had retired the Sartrean 'philosophical anthropology'— the 'total theory of man'—which he had espoused, in place of the barren 'diamat' of Communist orthodoxy, up to the mid-1960s. German philosophy—more precisely, Hegel—had been displaced as a source of Marxism; its concomitant component, however conceived, lapses with it. This leaves two of the component parts designated by Lenin: 'historical materialism' and 'scientific socialism'. Both of these loom large in *Arguments*. In each instance, however, Anderson's is a partial counterconstrual to Lenin (and Marx and Engels).

In the case of historical materialism, although Anderson prioritized *Capital*, his silence on Marx's economics proper betrayed his scepticism about what Lenin pointed to as 'the corner-stone of Marx's economic theory': 'the doctrine of surplus-value'. As already noted in connection with the afterword to *Considerations on Western Marxism*, Anderson's credence in the classics did not extend to the labour theory of value or to two of the principal laws of tendency (falling profits and class polarization) announced by Marx.[45] With historical materialism thus qualified, scientific socialism logically undergoes significant modulation.

In *The German Ideology*, Marx and Engels had made it plain that '[c]ommunism is for us not a *state of affairs* which is to be established, an *ideal* to which reality will [have] to adjust itself. We call communism the *real* movement which abolishes the present state of things.'[46] Anderson's socialism is not utopian in the canonical sense implied by this passage. For him too, 'the real movement'—the development of the productive forces, the creation of an industrial proletariat, the political and intellectual culture of capitalist civilization, and so on—furnishes the material and social premises of socialism, which is definitely not 'an ideal to which reality will have to adjust itself'. Yet it is a 'state of affairs to be established' by collective human agency, precisely because the 'laws of motion' of capitalism do not, for Anderson— as they do for Marx in the residual historical teleology of *Capital* (especially on Engels's positivist interpretation of it in *Anti-Dühring*)—spell the 'negation of the negation': the doom of capitalism and the dawn of communism.[47] Accordingly, 'scientific socialism'—socialism grounded in the knowledge imparted by historical materialism—may comprehend the past and present, and thereby inform the struggle for a liberated future. But it does not guarantee that future. And if this is the case, then—since 'the future' has deviated from its ideal image in the USSR—the burden of Engels's critique of 'utopian socialism' rebounds upon its putative 'scientific' successor. Dispensation with 'concrete' utopianism about the institutions of a postcapitalist future— dismissed as vain 'blue-printing' by the classical tradition—may conduce to an *abstract* utopianism, incanting ideals (withering away of the state, administration of things, to each according to need, etc.) to which postcapitalist reality will supposedly automatically adjust itself. In short, Anderson's conception of scientific socialism implied institutional forethought.

Arguments within English Marxism concluded with a characteristic explanation of the deficits of Marxist theory by reference to the defaults of socialist practice: 'the absence of a truly mass and truly revolutionary movement in England, as elsewhere in the West'. By the end of the 1970s, alert to the ominously changed political conjuncture, Anderson was once again thinking about capitalism and socialism in the long term.

Adverse Conditions

The editorial report on the *NLR* for 1975–80 underlined the declension of political developments in Western Europe in the period: the successful passage to bourgeois democracy in Greece, Spain, and Portugal, and the defeat of Eurocommunism in France and Italy. The *Review* had published a partial translation of Debray's ironic retrospect on the May events in 1979, accepting that the capitalist order in France, and southern Europe generally, had proved adept at withstanding its radical opponents, while contesting Debray's verdict that '[t]he French way to America passed through May '68'.[48] Nevertheless, to borrow Edmond Maire's maxim, the quinquennial report conjugated May '68 with March '78:

> The historical defeat of the European labour movement in these years was a momentous one. It was essentially the quelling of any short-range prospect of progress towards socialism in this central zone of the imperialist world itself that makes the final balance sheet of the period so equivocal—even sombre—on a world scale. . . . [E]very one of [its] chances was thrown away gratuitously. The fundamental reason, common to all these experiences, was the complete absence of any coherent *strategy* for a transition to socialism across and beyond the barrier of a bourgeois-democratic state. . . . Nor was the generalized void of practicable convictions or solutions confined to the

Communist movement. . . . The dearth of strategic inspiration proved universal. (Pp. 40–42)

While it hovered, the spectre of Communism in Western Europe had profoundly altered the ideological climate for the worse, with the concertation of 'gulagism' for an impending new Cold War:

> The sedulous build-up of Cold War hysteria about the USSR, largely sparing China, manifestly imposed new duties on the review. . . . NLR's political ability to swim against the stream, rejecting the slack conformism of most of the European and US Left, was attested here. The prescience of its emphasis on contemporary Russia, and its diagnosis of the pressures towards a new Cold War, were to be punctually vindicated at the turn of the decade with the Carter crusade over Afghanistan. (P. 24)[49]

As its official occasion indicated, the onset of the second Cold War represented a response to the setbacks, predicted in the 'Decennial Report', experienced by imperialism in the South:

> The success of the Vietnamese Revolution was swiftly followed by the Cuban expedition to Angola, which spectacularly demonstrated the new military-diplomatic balance of forces in the Third World—the first time in history a socialist regime was able to lend decisive armed assistance to a beleaguered revolution across the divide of an ocean (doubly so for the USSR, coordinating an airlift involving three continents). . . . Cuban and Soviet aid once again secured the Ethiopian Revolution from external attack in 1976, in an imposing operation revealing the importance of the USSR's new ally in South Yemen. (Pp. 33–34)

The Indochinese, Angolan, and Ethiopian revolutions had formed links of what proved to be a chain, including a Communist coup in Afghanistan in 1978 and the overthrow of the shah in Iran and Samoza in Nicaragua in 1979.[50] Yet, although coincident with 'stagflation' in the advanced capitalist order, these events had not decisively altered the global configuration of political forces. Four countervailing developments told against such a calculation: first and foremost—as already remarked—the capitalist restabilization in Western Europe; next, the alarming slowdown in the economies of Eastern Europe and the USSR, and the disastrous economic bequest of Maoism in China; third, possible emulation of the 'Spanish road' in selected countries of the underdeveloped world, eclipsing socialist victories there; and finally, armed conflicts between postcapitalist states in Southeast Asia, and 'brutality and savagery' within them (pp. 36–37).[51] The 'net ideological *perception* of these inter-related events', the report concluded with regard to the last item, 'has unquestionably been a temporary discolouration of the whole image of socialism'. Thus far, only one of the recent revolutions had eluded the 'infernal cycle'—Nicaragua, whose prospects were, however, bleak. It nevertheless pointed up the moral that 'the really decisive breakthrough for socialism can only come with the advent of a genuine revolutionary democracy, whose indispensable precondition is a comparatively advanced culture and society' (p. 39).

Meanwhile, the resurgence of the Cold War was accompanied by a regurgitation of its ideology, whose sedulous propagation in southern Europe had 'transform[ed] the cartography of contemporary Marxism' in the West (p. 43). A collapse of Latin Marxism had occurred in these years, attested either in the passage to outright anti-Communism (e.g., Colletti in Italy, Glucksmann in France) or in gravitation to a subaltern Eurocommunism (e.g., Althusser and Poulantzas) (pp. 43–47). Whereas Western Marxists had succumbed to 'Russophobia and Foucaulterie', Trotskyism had proved disappointing in its capacity 'to generate a sustained and creative alternative Marxism'—a judgement corroborated by reference to Mandel's failure to adumbrate a viable revolutionary strategy for socialism in the West. Indeed, the report concluded, 'the reserves of the Trotskyist tradition have proved far less than might have been expected: certainly insufficient to outweigh the default within Western Marxism' (pp. 47–48).

In signal contrast, it seemed that the peculiarities of the English had taken a turn that, though not utterly unanticipated,[52] was not imminently expected: a transition from negative to positive exceptionalism as regards the implantation and consolidation of Marxist culture. The quinquennial report did not substitute a reverted cultural Podsnappery for the inverted variety of 'Components of the National Culture'. Yet it was persuaded that Anglophone Marxists had 'maintained [their] numbers and morale to a far greater extent' than had their Continental peers (p. 50). Wagering that the Thatcher regime possessed little intellectual appeal (p. 49) and that Nietzsche and Heidegger were 'unlikely to take much hold' (p. 50), it deemed 'the symptoms of the "crisis of Marxism" here . . . very mild':

> So far, the basic situation indicates a remarkable strength and productivity within British Marxism—*one indeed which has reversed the historical relationship between England and Europe.* Since the early 70's, Marxist culture

in the UK has consistently been more productive and original than that of any other European country. (Pp. 50–51)[53]

In consequence, the *NLR* was in a position to engage more closely with the national culture. One sign that this process had already been set in train was the dialogue initiated with the old New Left, whether via the intensive exchanges with Williams, published (in a remarkable collective achievement) as *Politics and Letters*; or in *Arguments within English Marxism* itself; or in recent contributions to the *Review* from Raphael Samuel and Stuart Hall.[54] This confidence on the home front was publicly revealed in the foreword to *Politics and Letters*, which claimed that in the 1970s, 'active socialist culture in England has come to be predominantly Marxist'—a turn of events attributed to the flowering of Marxist historiography, the demise of Fabianism, and the diffusion of international theory. A year later, Blackburn was hailing the advent of 'a more robust and audacious Anglo-Marxism' in the pages of the *New Statesman*.[55]

What, according the quinquennial report, were the *Review*'s priorities for the future? In addition to the topics itemized in its predecessor—above all, socialist strategy in the West—a 'reanchorage in Britain' was advocated (p. 54). This was to be achieved not only by a resumption of the Nairn-Anderson theses but also by a wider communication with the local Left and an exploration, complementary to that of Western Marxism, of the traditions of 'Anglo-Marxism' (pp. 57–58). A second imperative was proper attention to the United States, whose radical intellectual culture was likewise seemingly unaffected by the 'crisis of Marxism', and whose Left was perhaps in an analogous position to its British counterpart in the mid-1960s (p. 58). Third—rendering explicit what remained implicit in the premises of the discussion of socialism, utopian and scientific, in *Arguments*—there was the whole issue of 'socialism as a future' (p. 61).

In broaching this last topic, the report recalled the prevalence of invocations of the socialist future, on the basis of a change of values, among the original New Left—and their successors' stern reaction to it:

> The focus of the redesigned journal was overwhelmingly on past and present, with scarcely anything about the future: its emphasis was deliberately *analytic*. . . . Socialism was explored along two dimensions: either as a constituted heritage of theoretical systems to be appropriated from the past . . . ; or as a variegated array of movements and regimes in the present. . . . The gain in intellectual maturity and cognitive precision achieved . . . was a very notable one. Two decades later, however, it is now

necessary to put a quite renewed emphasis on a socialism as a *future society*, that exists nowhere in the world today, or even seems very close, yet whose articulated forms it is essential to debate at once as imaginatively and as concretely as possible. For in the interim, the very notion of socialism as an alternative form of civilization has become ever more effaced and remote, within the ranks of the labour movement in the West, and fallen into popular discredit in significant zones . . . of the East. The changes in the international political conjuncture . . . have rendered this ideal crisis particularly acute. The review now has an imperative duty to make a serious contribution to the work of resolving it. (Pp. 61–62)

Tacitly dissenting from Lenin's refusal in *State and Revolution* 'to guess in the void about what cannot be known', four principal areas for concrete investigation were nominated: the structures of a socialist democracy; the character of a socialist economy; the modalities of the abolition of post-revolutionary inequalities of class and gender; and international relations between developed and underdeveloped socialist states (pp. 63–64).[56]

According to the quinquennial report, contemporary Marxism faced challenges to its radical credentials from two movements—ecology and feminism—whose discourses typically conjoined values and institutions, the quotidian and the speculative. For its part, the *NLR* had 'been very slow to adjust to the political and cultural changes' induced by the women's movement. One question it posed was the relationship between Marxism and socialism. The report affirmed the *'centrality'* of historical materialism within socialist culture, while disclaiming any monopoly. The intellectual scope, historical range, and political radicalism of historical materialism entitled it to primacy, which the *Review* should strive to reassert against philosophical and political challenges (pp. 66–68).[57]

An ideal socialism of the future and the intellectual resources to help develop it were one thing. In the present, however, the Left confronted quite another: actually existing socialism. Reminding colleagues that repudiation of anti-Communism should not issue in indulgence of the USSR, the report fixed two objectives in this domain, which demand to be quoted at length:

Firstly, we should be careful not to allow a *dissociation* to develop between projections of a rethought future for socialism in the West, and analysis of ongoing processes of socio-political development in the East. This involves both the political duty of defending the workers' states against either outright denunciation or mere dismissal on the Left, and the intellectual duty of linking the lessons of historical experience (not all of it negative) in one zone with proposals for advance in the other zone. . . . Secondly, we should be willing to entertain and think through the *longest-term* perspectives for relations between the two zones, capitalist and post-capitalist. Here it is merely worth mentioning two scenarios that we should be willing to contemplate. Is it likely that the 20th century will see *no* case of a successful capitalist restoration in any workers' state? It seems historically implausible, however jolting the prospect. After all, the bourgeois revolutions were followed by a number of absolutist restorations, even if these did not prove durable in character—1660, 1815, 1824. It may be that Yugoslavia will present such a spectacle in the next decade. Could another candidate possibly be China? . . . At the other end of the spectrum of possibilities, Marxists must be able to ask themselves whether it may not prove impossible to move towards socialism in the West until the USSR itself is democratized—a development unlikely to occur until after another major cycle of Soviet growth, at the least. To have to accept a historical priority to progress in the East over advance in the West goes against nearly all conventional thinking among socialists in the advanced capitalist countries today, and is a grim prospect. But it might also prove the most coldly realistic prediction, whose consequences—if they ensued—would have to be borne with fortitude. (Pp. 69–71)[58]

It is all here: the prospects, respectively 'jolting' and 'grim', of selective capitalist restorations in what—in standard Trotskyist idiom—are classified as postcapitalist 'workers' states'; and—a Deutscherite scenario, this—of the democratic regeneration of the Soviet Union as a prerequisite of any resumption of socialist advance in the West. Restoration is envisaged as a historical possibility by analogy with the course of the 'bourgeois revolutions' in England, France, and Spain, which also supply the consolation that it might not prove 'durable'. The USSR is excluded from the worst-case scenario— indeed, it is identified as the potential key to the future development of socialism. On this basis, the cautious enthusiasm with which Gorbachevite glasnost and perestroika are likely to have been welcomed within the *NLR* can be imagined. At the same time, unlike its Khrushchevite precursor, which appeared to justify Deutscher's sanguine outlook, Gorbachev's initiative was spurred not by a 'major cycle of Soviet growth' but by the involution of the Russian regime consequent upon deepening 'stagnation'. Where Khrushchev's de-Stalinization was a confident endeavour, undertaken as an integral part of 'peaceful coexistence and competition' with the West, Gorbachev's, three decades later, was a defensive response to Soviet defeat in that competition at the height of a second Cold War. The quinquennial report's 'most coldly realistic prediction', based upon '*longest-term* perspectives', could not envisage the ultimate jolt of a capitalist restoration in the USSR.

Having enjoined detailed attention to differential patterns of economic development in the Third World—patterns that contradicted orthodox Marxist assumptions about the postcolonial countries (pp. 71–72)—the report ended with some recommendations for the reconstruction of the *NLR*. Among them were the desirability of the recruitment of more women; a modulation of the journal's 'Olympian' tone toward its audience (expressed in 'the glacial proprieties of the Themes'); and open debate within the *Review* between the diverse positions represented on its editorial committee (p. 80). To these ends, Anderson's resignation as editor was announced:

> Today . . . the stockade mentality that inspired NLR in much of the 60's and 70's is a liability. The review must make a turn towards British culture and politics in the 80's, if only to keep the international standard of Marxism flying, and adopt a more open and popular register. . . . NLR now needs an Editor capable of reintegrating the Review into the common milieu of the Left in Britain . . . , establishing reciprocal relationships with other journals and tendencies, [and] intervening in the wider press and political arena. (Pp. 91–92)

In the event, against the backdrop of an inexorably darkening conjuncture at home and abroad, the 'stockade mentality', marked for dissolution, was set for intensification.

The Continuation of Class Politics by Other Means

Long in gestation, the second Cold War was launched by the West in response to the enhancement of Soviet power in the 1970s and its cautious support for a wave of indigenous revolutions in the South, from southern Africa and Southeast Asia to Central America, during the decade. Its official occasion was the entry of the Red Army into Afghanistan to shore up a degenerating Communist regime against a gathering Islamic jihad. This operation, however, had been preceded by a NATO decision to accelerate the nuclear arms race by installing cruise and Pershing II missiles in Europe. Primed and ignited before the formal accession to power of the New Right—Thatcher in the United Kingdom in 1979, Reagan in the United States in 1980, and Kohl in the Federal Republic of Germany (FRG) in 1983—the new Cold War escalated thereafter into wholesale revanchism against the postwar settlement.

In his study *The Making of the Second Cold War*, published by Verso in 1983, Fred Halliday summarized its significance thus:

> [T]he consolidation of Cold War II represented a comprehensive attempt to erode the consequences of the Second World War. These . . . had been: a substantial shift of resources towards the working and other disadvantaged classes in the capitalist countries, through wage and welfare policies; an acceptance of the USSR as one of the two major powers in the world as a result of its prime role in the defeat of Nazism; and the replacement of colonial rule by independence in the third world. The actions of the Reagan Administration and its allies in Europe sought to reverse these consequences by using the recession, anti-communism and historical amnesia to impose a new set of values and policies upon the world.[59]

Halliday's Deutscherite account of the new Cold War sought to develop an analytical schema proposed in Anderson's 1965 essay 'The Left in the Fifties', which anticipated the terms of the 1980s debate in the British and European peace movements:

> [T]he Cold War has *at least* four structural components, which any adequate account must synthesize: a struggle between capitalist and socialist economic systems, a conflict between parliamentary and authoritarian political systems, a contest between imperialism and indigenous national systems, and a confrontation between technologically equivalent and reciprocally suicidal military systems. International class struggle, defence of democracy, revolt against colonialism, arms race: each slogan indicates one 'moment' in the Cold War, and denies the others. The reality is their infinite imbrication and interpenetration.[60]

The meaning of the second Cold War, and the struggle of the peace movements against it, formed the international editorial priority of the *NLR* from 1980 to 1984. In this respect, the agendas of junior and senior cohorts of the New Left may be said to have coalesced in the early 1980s. Virtually silent on the subject of the nuclear arms race since the test ban treaty in 1963, two decades later the *Review* sponsored an international debate on issues of war and peace.[61] Stimulated by Thompson's urgent summons to reflection and action in 1980—'Notes on Exterminism, the Last Stage of Civilization'—the *NLR* sought not passively to reflect diversity of left-wing opinion on the issues, but actively to inflect it. It proposed its own distinctive historical interpretation and political evaluation of the new global conjuncture via both the collectively planned symposium *Exterminism and Cold War* (1982), in which Halliday and Mike Davis countered the 'exterminism' thesis, and Halliday's subsequent book-length expansion of his essay 'The Sources of the New Cold War'.[62] Anderson's role in these initiatives was decisive. In addition to corresponding at length with contributors to the *Review* (e.g., Mandel and Coates), he assumed principal responsibility for the realization of the *Exterminism* volume and, in that capacity, composed its foreword,[63] as well as making an editorial input into his colleagues' essays.

Thompson's article, its title pointedly echoing and emending Lenin's pamphlet *Imperialism, Latest Stage of Capitalism,* had focused predominant attention upon the fourth of Anderson's components of the Cold War— 'confrontation between technologically equivalent and reciprocally suicidal military systems'—in explaining its recrudescence at the close of the 1970s. Anderson dissented from explanatory emphasis and political inference alike. His foreword, although respecting the humanist prospectus of 'utopian' socialism to which Thompson adhered, refused any repudiation of the alternative, 'scientific' tradition to which he was affiliated. Such renunciation proceeded on the seemingly impeccable grounds of a universal interest, transcending class antagonisms, in preserving peace against the unprecedented perils of the age that dawned with Hiroshima:

> Socialism has . . . always promised an ultimate universalism. . . . But by and large this universalist horizon has never been centrally focused in the Marxist tradition. Utopian socialism related much more directly to it. Precisely because . . . [it] lacked either a materialist theory of historical change, or any conception of the particular transforming agency of labour, [it] could imagine socialism much more immediately as a general emancipation. . . . [Its] resources . . . will need to be drawn upon and developed again, if socialism is ever to confront with any realism the universal threat of a military explosion that would annihilate every class. At the same time, however, the advance represented by what its founders called 'scientific' socialism cannot be rescinded: class struggle . . . has not been suspended or even reduced by the thermonuclear age—it has only been deformed and displaced. Socialism still needs . . . a *historical* perspective for the transition beyond a world haunted by nuclear fear as well as divided by social misery and injustice, and such a perspective must indicate particular agencies and strategies for its realization. (Pp. viii–ix)

By implication a partisan of the 'romantic'/'utopian'—as opposed to the 'rational'/'scientific'—tradition, Thompson was to be congratulated for reviving the dormant debate on nuclear disarmament. Four main items were henceforth on the analytical agenda: explanation of the social roots of what Thompson had dubbed 'exterminism'; adjudication of the roles of the United States and the USSR in the renewal of the Cold War; examination of the comparative importance of its various geostrategic theatres; and, crucially, exploration of a political strategy for a durable peace. Thompson's scepticism about the possibility of attaining an adequate vantage point from which to survey contemporary history foreclosed the indicated route to any cogent treatment of these issues. The principal problem, Anderson maintained, resided elsewhere:

> The real difficulty . . . in the attempt to explore the nature and meaning of the Cold War . . . is not position in time but scale in space. Contemporary history is here *world* history, that of a globe now integrated into one vast field of inter-related conflicts. This poses intellectual problems of a quite new kind for any inquiry into the dangers of war or the prospects for peace. The immensity of the surface across which their fate is now decided can be encompassed only by interpretations and explanations of a truly extraordinary reach. . . . Detailed evidence and argument alone can arbitrate among them. (P. xii)

As Anderson noted in conclusion, 'Historical interpretation on this scale always implies political recommendation'. His own was emphatic. Quite the reverse of dividing or distracting the international peace movement, advocacy of socialism within its ranks conduced to its ultimate success: '[P]eace must acquire a tangible social shape capable of inspiring the positive dreams and loyalties of millions. For all the tragedies that have befallen the ideal in this century, what could that shape be if not socialist?' (p. xii).

Anderson's 'historical perspective' on the Cold War—his own implicit contemporary '*world* history'—assigned explanatory priority to the first of his structural components of 1965: the global confrontation between the contending socioeconomic systems of capitalism and Communism—a conflict conceived, in Deutscherite fashion, as the 'deformation' of international class struggle and its 'displacement' onto the actual political (and potential military) contest of Western and Eastern blocs.[64] Thus construed, the Cold War was neither technological fatality—an incongruous hypothesis from the pen of Thompson, scourge of determinism—nor human destiny. As Anderson argued in the postscript to *In the Tracks of Historical Materialism*, explanation of it required no divination of some cause in human nature that rendered hearts hard. On the contrary, it was 'the awful, but intelligible product of . . . global class struggle . . .—a conflict founded on the ceaseless determination of major capitalist states to stifle every attempt to build socialism. . . , and the deformities the resistance to it has wrought within them' (pp. 95–96).[65] Nuclear competition and diplomacy were not explicable in Thompsonian fashion by the 'isomorphism' of equivalent 'super-powers': they were rooted in the 'great contest' between capitalist and postcapitalist states, constituting the continuation of global class struggle by other means. As to the rights and wrongs of that historic contest, and the respective responsibilities of the United States and USSR for its escalation in the late 1970s, Andersonian historical interpretation implied clear political recommendation: in a word, anti-anti-Sovietism, analogous to the 'anti-anti-Communism' defended by Sartre at the height of the first Cold War.

Although not licencing Scott L. Malcomson's hyperbolic characterization of the *NLR* in this phase of its existence as 'Brezhnevite internationalist',[66] there is no doubt that Anderson's sympathies lay unequivocally, if not uncritically, with the Soviet party to the intersystemic contest. A moral-political balance sheet of the latter to date was delegated to Halliday, in his contribution to *Exterminism and Cold War*. In 'The Sources of the New Cold War', he condemned the Brezhnevite dissolution of Khrushchevite liberalization in the USSR itself, and repression of popular aspirations in Czechoslovakia (1968) and Poland (1981), identifying a 'political involution of the post-revolutionary states' that had facilitated Western mobilization of the second Cold War (pp. 306–7). Nevertheless, Halliday dismissed the warmed-up ideological leftovers of 'totalitarianism' and 'gulagism' aimed at the Soviet Union's domestic regime—but not at that of the United States' new ally, China. Moreover, if the post-Khrushchev record in Eastern Europe represented a net regression politically, the reckoning in the Third World, albeit 'deeply ambiguous', disclosed an improvement:

In the past, the main single criticism socialists always made of Soviet foreign policy in the capitalist world was its refusal to provide adequate—often indeed any—moral or material aid to revolutionary movements abroad; a refusal motivated by the determination to seek collaboration with the dominant imperial powers for the sake of narrowly national and bureaucratic interests. . . . [T]he Brezhnev epoch has seen a new Soviet willingness to help or shield revolutionary or national liberation movements across the Third World, with or without any hope of immediate material returns. . . . In [various] respects the USSR has represented a more active and progressive influence in the Third World than before. (Pp. 308–9)

The Russian intervention in Afghanistan—ceremoniously denounced by the West as evidence of Soviet expansionism—was the apparent exception that proved the postwar rule outside Eastern Europe. A 'defensive operation', it had forestalled 'an Islamic Vendée' but in the process had 'done substantial harm to the wider cause of peace and socialism' (pp. 310–11).

The Soviet Union was far from exonerated of all the charges against its internal regime and external conduct. Principal responsibility for the onset of the new Cold War nonetheless lay with the United States and its allies, aided and abetted by China (pp. 311–12). A Deutscherite examination of its contestants revealed 'not so much an isomorphism as an asymmetry of internal structure and international consequence' (p. 319). Such a verdict in turn indicated two overriding objectives for the European peace movements: West European withdrawal from NATO, which would inevitably precipitate an acute crisis of the Atlanticist order, in the process tabling socialism on the political agenda; and East European emancipation from bureaucratic tutelage and achievement of 'socialist democracy'—developments that the Western labour movements could support not by deference to the Pax Americana but by the 'creation of a freer socialism in their own countries' (pp. 322–25). For that, however,

the precondition is the overthrow of capitalism—in other words, precisely the revolutionary challenge which social democracy has always refused to contemplate. Its own accommodation to the rule of capital, and torpid administration of bourgeois society, morally incapacitate it from any full challenge to the Communist states in the East—which, whatever their other manifold defects, have historically passed beyond capitalism. . . . The Western labour movement . . . has undergone its own form of political involution since 1945. . . . It is only when it finally earns its great historical privileges in the effort and risk of actually building an advanced, emancipated socialism . . . that it will provide a real source of inspiration, or exercise a major power of attraction, in the post-capitalist states. In the field of 'freedom' as much as of 'peace', the deadlock of the Cold War can in the long run only be broken by progress towards this third term. (Pp. 325–26)[67]

The great geopolitical divide between West and East, now polarized into nuclear camps, could begin to be bridged only by the attainment in the former, where its preconditions obtained, of an advanced socialism: the future 'third term', or synthesis, which could sublate the present antithesis of advanced liberal capitalism and backward bureaucratic socialism either side of the Elbe. Furthermore, the emergence of an independent, postcapitalist Western

Europe in the North would transform the prospects of the South, releasing it from the hitherto ineluctable magnetic field of a bipolar globe (p. 326).

The Oblique March of History

To be sure, neither Halliday's interpretation nor his evaluation of the second Cold War can be attributed to Anderson. However, they—together with his revolutionary-socialist conclusion—may be taken as representative of the broad consensus of the active core of the *NLR*. For all that they point to a future 'historical alternative' to capitalism and actually existing socialism alike, therewith resisting the polarizing political logic of the international conjuncture, they refuse to equate the two on the planes of 'internal structure' or 'international consequence'. As in the case of Sartre's *The Communists and Peace*, the *NLR* and Anderson's position may (in the words of *Considerations on Western Marxism*) be described as incipiently 'polarized towards official Communism as the only historical incarnation of the international proletariat as a revolutionary class' (p. 96).[68] In view of the hopes invested in the peace movement for a political advance beyond the bounds of actually existing socialism and Social-Democracy, it was not the case that 'for . . . them there was no other effective reality or milieu of socialist action outside [official Communism]' (p. 96). That, however, was a potential inference from such political premises—with inclement implications, given the state of British Communism.

These premises, involving significant Deutscherite modification of the orthodox Trotskyist conception of Stalinism, were elaborated by Anderson in a short talk in 1982, 'Trotsky's Interpretation of Stalinism', published in the *NLR* the following year.[69] This is not the place for a detailed investigation of the disputes that rent Trotskyist milieux as the 1930s progressed and that intensified in the aftermath of the Second World War, when—contrary to confident prediction—Stalinism not only survived but prospered.[70] It will suffice for our purposes to recall that, to the end of his days, Trotsky maintained that '[t]he workers' state must be taken as it has emerged from the merciless laboratory of history'.[71] Notwithstanding its defects, the Soviet Union instantiated the expropriation of the expropriators effected after October 1917, and thereby registered historical progress over capitalism. On these grounds it was to be defended against imperialism, pending its 'regeneration' by a 'political revolution' against the usurpatory Stalinist bureaucracy. This intricate perspective, fully expounded in the study mistranslated as *The Revolution Betrayed* (1937) and vehemently reaffirmed in the writings collected as *In Defense of Marxism* (1939–40), entailed a stance of anti-Stalinism

149

without lapsing into what two of Trotsky's sometime American followers dubbed 'Stalinophobia, or vulgar anti-Stalinism'.[72] And it involved sober appreciation of the fact that, as Trotsky confided to C. L. R. James in April 1939, '[w]hen the revolutionary movement in general is declining, when one defeat follows another, . . . it is an inevitable situation that the revolutionary elements must work against the general historical current, even if our ideas, our explanations are as exact and wise as one can demand'.[73]

The problem was whether—in the light of the pre- and postwar 'general historical current'—Trotsky's ideas exhibited the requisite precision. Deutscher, for one, thought not. Having opposed the foundation of the Fourth International in 1938 as a velleity, given the iron grip of Stalinism and fascism, arguing that '[i]t is necessary to wait',[74] he questioned Trotsky's outlook on the USSR in two essential regards. According to the 'long historical perspective' entertained by Deutscher[75] and adumbrated in the postscript to his Trotsky trilogy, a 'regeneration of the Russian' was indispensable to surmounting '[t]he divorce between theory and practice—or between norm and fact': in other words, the scission between classical Marxism, predicated on the 'actuality of revolution' in the advanced West, and Stalinism, spawned by its factual realization in the backward East. The discrepancy between theoretical horizon and historical reality had widened after the Second World War: the weapons of Trotskyist criticism had been blunted by the Stalinist critique of arms, which had issued in the Eurasian extension of Communism.[76] However, regeneration was to be anticipated not from a renewal of socialist advance in the West and the catalyst it would provide to a political revolution—from below—against the Soviet bureaucracy, but from a political reformation—from above—by sections of the bureaucracy itself. For, by an irony of history, the logic of the 'modernization' of Soviet society conducted by the bureaucracy in the 1930s and 1940s worked to subvert its own dictatorship over the proletariat.[77] Trotsky had thus underestimated the *progressive* dimension of the contradictory role he attributed to Stalinism within the borders of the USSR itself.

Simultaneously, he had discounted its contradictory performance outside those borders, allocating it a unilaterally reactionary part:

> The idea that new impulses for revolution would come from the West but not from the Soviet Union was the *leitmotif* of Trotsky's advocacy of the Fourth International. Again and again he asserted that, while in the Soviet Union, Stalinism continued to play a dual role, at once progressive and retrograde, it exercised internationally only a counter-revolutionary influence. Here his grasp of reality failed him. Stalinism was to go on acting its dual

role internationally as well as nationally: it was to stimulate as well as to obstruct the class struggle outside the Soviet Union. In any case, it was not from the West that the revolutionary impulses were to come in the next three or four decades.[78]

For Deutscher, this conclusion—arguably implicit in Trotsky's own attitude toward Soviet actions in Poland and Finland in 1939–40, following the Molotov–Von Ribbentrop Pact—was one of two logically consistent political responses to the contradiction inherent in his settled characterization of Stalinism:

> How could the government of a workers' state be consistently a factor of counter-revolution? Trotsky and his disciples could deal with this problem in only one of two ways: Either they had to declare that the Soviet Union had ceased to be a workers' state; that this accounted for the anti-revolutionary direction of Stalin's policies both at home and abroad; and that consequently Marxists had no reason whatsoever to go on 'defending the Soviet Union'. Or else, they had to admit that Stalinism was continuing to act a dual or ambivalent (progressive and reactionary) role both abroad and at home; and that this was consistent with the contradictory character of the regime of the U.S.S.R., with the survival of the workers' state within the bureaucratic despotism; and that Marxists could cope with this intricate situation only *by opposing Stalinism yet defending the Soviet Union.*[79]

In the event, after the Second World War, the Fourth International declined to pursue either of these options, seeking to preserve Trotsky's original position. However, faced with accumulating practical deviations from its theoretical norm (e.g., Stalinist revolutions from without in Eastern Europe, and from within in the Balkans and Asia), its international secretary, Michel Pablo, gravitated toward an outlook that bears some resemblance to Deutscher's. In two articles published in 1951, he cautioned his comrades against 'anti-Stalinist sectarianism', insisting that Stalinism was 'a *phenomenon of contradictions,* and . . . a *self-contradictory phenomenon'.* Calibrated against the expectations of Marx and Engels, Lenin and Trotsky, it attested to the historical reality of 'a more complicated, more tortuous, longer passage from capitalism to socialism, lending transitional forms to society and proletarian power'.[80] Accordingly,

> [p]eople who despair of the fate of humanity because Stalinism still endures and even achieves victories, tailor history to their own personal measure.

151

They really desire that the entire process of the transformation of capitalist society into socialism would be accomplished within the span of their brief lives. . . . As for us, we reaffirm [that] . . . this transformation will probably take an entire historical epoch of several centuries and will in the meantime be filled with forms and regimes transitional between capitalism and socialism and necessarily deviating from 'pure' forms and norms.[81]

Pablo asserted the congruence of his 'historical perspective' on the passage to socialism—referred to in Fourth International shorthand as 'centuries of transition'—with the 'spirit' of Trotsky's writings. Moreover, so he reckoned, it had the advantage of inhibiting 'any activist impatience or impressionism' in the ranks of revolutionary Marxists.[82]

This projection entered a pessimistic qualification of the classical Marxism that was inherited by Trotskyism and which it sought to sustain 'against the general historical current'. It revised Marxism's Western norms, as it were, to accommodate its Eastern forms. Furthermore, it harboured the implication that, whereas revolutionary socialism was ultimately feasible as a strategy and goal in conditions of advanced, liberal-democratic capitalism, Stalinism was the normal incarnation—not the pathological aberration—of anticapitalist movements and postcapitalist regimes in the Third World. On a more optimistic but no less controversial note, a later intervention by Pablo—'The Rise and Decline of Stalinism', published shortly after Deutscher's *Russia after Stalin* in 1953—shared its prognostication of a de-Stalinization of the Soviet Union courtesy of the bureaucracy—a scenario that elicited unstinting denunciation of 'Pabloite-Deutscher' deviations by his more orthodox American and British comrades.[83]

This lengthy detour will enable us to appreciate the extent to which, in 'Trotsky's Interpretation of Stalinism', Anderson's own analysis of Stalinism, following a phase of orthodox Trotskyist observance and in a period of renewed Cold War when 'Stalinophobia' was endemic, had coalesced—or rather reunited—with a hybrid of Deutscherite and Pabloite perspectives.[84] Asserting that Trotsky's interpretation remained 'the most coherent and developed theorization of the phenomenon within the Marxist tradition' (p. 118), Anderson expounded it in four basic theses (pp. 120–21). First, then, as we have already remarked, Trotsky had highlighted its 'dual nature': a distinction was to be drawn between the contradictory, 'centrist' nature of Stalinism at home, and its unambiguously retrograde character abroad. Second, Stalinism comprised the political rule of a bureaucratic caste within the context of public property in the means of production: the bureaucracy was not a new class. Third, contrary to the theoreticians of 'bureaucratic collectivism' or 'state capitalism', the USSR was 'typologically a *workers' state*, precisely because these property relations . . . persisted'. As in the case of feudal and capitalist states, to confound genus and species was to confuse the burning political issue:

> The iron dictatorship exercised by the Stalinist police and administrative apparatus over the Soviet proletariat was not incompatible with the preservation of the proletarian nature of the state itself—any more than the Absolutist dictatorships over the nobility had been incompatible with the preservation of the nature of the feudal state, or the fascist dictatorships exercised over the bourgeois class were incompatible with the preservation of the nature of the capitalist state. The USSR was indeed a *degenerated* workers' state, but a 'pure' dictatorship of the proletariat—conformable to an ideal definition of it—had never existed in the Soviet Union in the first place. (P. 121)

Fourth, by way of political injunction, Trotsky had asserted the necessity of a political revolution by the dispossessed proletariat against an irredeemable bureaucracy, while asserting that the USSR merited defence against an imperialism intent upon restoration of capitalism, not elimination of despotism. In *Where Is Russia Going?*—better known under its English title, *The Revolution Betrayed*—these theses had been developed. In particular, Trotsky had rooted the bureaucratic historical phenomenon of Stalinism in 'scarcity'— the material privation of pre- and postrevolutionary Russia, which had induced 'a contradiction . . . between socialized relations of production and bourgeois norms of distribution', (re)producing the privileged bureaucratic stratum (p. 121).[85]

An approving quotation of Trotsky's stoical claim of September 1939 that '[t]wenty-five years in the scales of history, when it is a question of profoundest changes in economic and cultural systems, weigh less than an hour in the life of man'[86] prefaced Anderson's assessment of his interpretation. It had three merits. The first of these was quintessentially Andersonian:

> [I]t provides a theory of the phenomenon of Stalinism in a long *historical* temporality, congruent with the fundamental categories of classical Marxism. At every point in his account of the nature of the Soviet bureaucracy, Trotsky sought to situate it in the logic of successive modes of production and transitions between them, with corresponding class powers and political regimes. . . . Hence his insistence that the proper optic for defining the relations of the bureaucracy to the working class was the antecedent and analogous relationships between absolutism and aristocracy, fascism and bourgeoisie; just

153

as the relevant precedents for its future overthrow would be political risings such as those of 1830 or 1848 rather than a new 1789. (Pp. 123–24)

A second merit consisted in the 'sociological richness and penetration' of Trotsky's account, peerless in the left-wing literature on the topic (p. 124). Since the mid-1930s, detailed empirical analyses of the Soviet social formation had issued from such professional scholars as E. H. Carr, not other Marxists; their findings tended to corroborate Trotsky's theorization, rather than those of his Marxist critics, whether Social-Democrats (e.g., Kautsky) or heterodox Trotskyists (e.g., Cliff or Schachtman).[87]

The last—but arguably first—of the virtues discerned by Anderson was the 'political balance' displayed in Trotsky's writings—their

> refusal of either adulation or commination, for a sober estimate of the contradictory nature and dynamic of the bureaucratic regime in the USSR. In Trotsky's lifetime it was the former attitude that was unusual on the Left. . . . Today, it is the latter. . . . There is little doubt that it was Trotsky's firm insistence . . . that the USSR was in the final resort a workers' state that was the key to this equilibrium. Those who rejected this classification for the notions of 'state capitalism' or 'bureaucratic collectivism' were invariably left with the difficulty of defining a political attitude towards the entity they had so categorized. For if one thing was evident about 'state capitalism' or 'bureaucratic collectivism' in Russia, it was that it lacked any vestige of the democratic liberties to be found in 'private capitalism' in the West. Should not, therefore, socialists support the latter in any conflict between the two, as far the lesser—because 'non-totalitarian'—evil? The logic of these interpretations . . . always ultimately tended . . . to shift their adherents to the Right. (Pp. 124–25)[88]

Historically coherent, sociologically detailed, politically compelling, Trotsky's theorization nevertheless had its limitations. Revealed after his death, these revolved around his assessment of Stalinism as an *international* phenomenon. The internal dynamics of the Soviet regime over the next half century largely confirmed his interpretation, therewith—presumably— vindicating his political option of opposing Stalinism yet defending the 'workers' state'. By contrast, his analysis of its external dynamic had been falsified by the historical record. There were, Anderson argued,

> two reasons for this discrepancy in his prognostications. Firstly, he erred in qualifying the external role of the Stalinist bureaucracy as simply and unilat-

erally 'counter-revolutionary', whereas in fact it was to prove profoundly *contradictory* in its actions and effects abroad, just as much as at home. Secondly, he was mistaken in thinking that Stalinism represented merely an 'exceptional' or 'aberrant' refraction of the general laws of transition from capitalism to socialism, that would be confined to Russia itself. The structures of bureaucratic power and mobilization pioneered under Stalin proved to be both more *dynamic* and more *general* a phenomenon on the international plane than Trotsky ever imagined. (Pp. 125–26)

Regarding the first falsification, the USSR, contrary to Trotsky's predictions, had resisted and defeated German imperialism—with momentous geopolitical consequences:

> The two major forms of historical progress registered within world *capitalism* in the past fifty years—the defeat of fascism, the end of colonialism— have . . . been directly dependent on the presence and performance of the USSR in international politics. In this sense, it could be argued that . . . the exploited classes *outside* the Soviet Union may have benefited more directly from its existence than the working class inside the Soviet Union—that on a world-historical scale, the decisive costs of Stalinism have been internal, the gains external. Even the new consumer prosperity of the Western working classes, the other major advance of post-war capitalism, has owed much (not all) to the Keynesian arms economies created to meet the Soviet challenge in the Cold War. . . . [T]hese effects have . . . been largely objective and involuntary processes. . . . They testify, none the less, to the contradictory logic of a 'degenerated workers' state', colossally distorted, yet still persistently anti-capitalist. . . . By the late 1960s, the USSR had even achieved something like . . . strategic parity with imperialism . . . , and therewith proved capable of extending vital economic and military aid to socialist revolutions and national liberation movements abroad. (P. 126)

Measured 'on a world-historical scale', Trotsky's second erroneous conclusion—in sum, that Stalinism equalled Russian exceptionalism—was considered 'more radical' by Anderson. Characterizing the Stalinist parties of the Comintern as puppets of Narkomindel, Trotsky had looked to the proletariats of the West, guided by the Fourth International, for an imminent resumption of revolutionary-socialist advance. Instead,

> history took another turn. Revolution did spread, but to the backward regions of Asia and the Balkans. Moreover, these revolutions were uniformly

organized and led by local Communist Parties . . . modelled in their internal structures on the CPSU. . . . The states they created were to be manifestly cognate . . . with the USSR . . . Stalinism . . . proved to be not just an apparatus, but a *movement*—one capable not only of keeping power in a backward environment dominated by scarcity (USSR), but of actually winning power in environments that were yet more backward and destitute (China, Vietnam)— of expropriating the bourgeoisie and starting the slow work of socialist construction. . . . Stalinism as a broad phenomenon, that is, a workers' state ruled by an authoritarian bureaucratic stratum, did not merely represent a *degeneration* from a prior state of (relative) class grace: it could also be a spontaneous *generation* produced by revolutionary class forces in very backward societies, without any tradition of either bourgeois or proletarian democracy. (P. 127)[89]

Empirical refutations of Trotsky's theoretical conjectures, both these historical developments were consistent with his main premiss—namely, 'the contradictory nature of Stalinism, hostile at once to capitalist property and to proletarian liberty' (p. 127). Concerned lest his attribution of a 'revolutionary' dimension to Stalinism as a global phenomenon be misconstrued, Anderson concluded by accentuating the negative, recalling its matching '*reactionary*' consequences:

The multiplication of bureaucratized workers' states . . . has inexorably led to . . . conflicts between them. The military shield the USSR can extend to socialist revolutions or national liberation forces . . . also objectively increases the dangers of global nuclear war. The abolition of capitalism in Eastern Europe has unleashed the furies of nationalism against Russia, which has in turn responded with the most purely reactionary series of external interventions. . . . Above all, . . . while the basic Stalinist model of a transition beyond capitalism may have propagated itself . . . across the backward zones of Eurasia, its very geographical extension and temporal prolongation . . . have deeply tarnished the very idea of socialism in the advanced West, . . . thereby decisively *strengthening* the bastions of imperialism in the late twentieth century. . . . We have still to settle accounts with the immense skein of international consequences and connections, progressive and regressive, revolutionary and counter-revolutionary, that followed from the fate that befell the October Revolution, that gave rise to the phenomenon we still call Stalinism today. (P. 128)

Especially in view of Anderson's omission of this key text from *A Zone of Engagement*—published, after the deluge, in 1992—that concluding verdict may stand. The essential thing to underscore here, however, is the extent of his political investment, at the height of the second Cold War, not only in the existence of the 'workers' states'—an affiliation wholly consistent with Trotsky's options—but also in the international performance of the Soviet Union after Stalin—a balance sheet inconceivable from, say, Mandel (whose negative equation of the external records of the Soviet Union and China was being resisted at this time by Anderson and his colleagues). Directed against the 'general historical current' and delivered in Paris—'capital of European reaction'[90]—Anderson's account of Stalinism criticized it in the name of a (thus far unrealized) advanced revolutionary socialism, in a spirit analogous to the mind-set of Soviet foreign policy as encapsulated by Halliday: '[W]hat we have we hold'.[91]

Whatever the ultimate cogency of Anderson's conclusion, some scrutiny of its premises is in order. These comprise the putative three graces—historical, sociological, and political—of Trotsky's interpretation, from which a stance of anti-Stalinism, but anti-anti-Sovietism, was deduced.

Anderson's analytical optic of the *longue durée* involves historical precedents and analogies between bourgeois and proletarian revolutions, which revert to a theme of his own Marxism since his rejoinder to Thompson on the English Revolution in 1966,[92] and which are doubtless initially traceable to Deutscher's history of Bolshevism and Gramsci's annotations on Jacobinism. Its central postulate—a potential symmetry between the two—derives from a developmentalist logic of global history and depends upon a conceptual distinction between the objective class character of a post-revolutionary social order, on the one hand, and the sociological identity of the (post)revolutionary agent, on the other. These lead to classification of the USSR as a postcapitalist social formation, in transition to socialism—a passage from capitalism whose preconditions consist in further economic development to surmount the constraints of scarcity, and future instalments of political revolution (whether from below or from above, as in the case of eighteenth- and nineteenth-century processes of bourgeois revolution) to dislodge the bureaucratic estate. Although such historical-sociology-by-analogy fully accords with the Bolshevik tradition, before and after October,[93] there would seem to be less warrant for it in Marx and Engels themselves. In their work the emphasis is upon the asymmetrical nature of bourgeois and proletarian revolutions—the latter being understood as the 'self-emancipation of the working class'—for the reasons so eloquently (if anonymously) explained by Anderson during his *maoisant* phase, in 1969:

What [Tukhachevsky] did not grasp . . . was the *fundamental difference in nature* between the bourgeois and socialist revolutions. Napoleon could for a time successfully export the ideas of 1789 on his bayonets, because the political transformation of society implied by the bourgeois revolutions did not ipso facto demand mass participation from below. They can . . . be implanted bureaucratically and repressively, by a small oligarchy from above. By contrast, the socialist revolution is by definition only socialist if it involves the masses of the population taking life into their own hands and overthrowing existing society from top to bottom by themselves.[94]

The point here is less to arbitrate between Anderson's seemingly incompatible positions than to query his invocation of classical Marxism to vindicate Trotsky's interpretation of Stalinism—not to mention his qualifications of it. For Trotsky, the 'bureaucratized workers' state' of the USSR was a 'degenerated workers' state', the conjunctural national exception that proved the international historical rule. For Anderson, by contrast, Stalinism virtually *is* the rule of socialism in the East. In any event, the precedents and analogies via which Trotsky is upheld originated not with Marx or Engels but with Plekhanov, Lenin, and Trotsky himself. And they were subsequently subjected to 'geographical extension' and 'temporal prolongation' by Deutscher, in an oeuvre devoted to the misadventures of Bolshevism, lauded by Anderson as the 'greatest historical work on the fate of the revolution . . . , composed in profound continuity with [Trotsky's] legacy', but criticized by other Trotskyists on the grounds that its generalizations about revolutions made an effective socialist virtue of putative Stalinist necessity.[95] Now of course, their conformity with classical Marxist theory would no more suffice to indicate their correspondence with Stalinist reality than their derogation from it would serve to infirm them (as Anderson, adherent of a traditional realist epistemology, would be the first to concede). However, in applying an 'internalist' test of the fitness of Trotsky's interpretation of Stalinism (i.e., its logical consistency with classical Marxism) Anderson adduces few, if any, arguments on behalf of the explanatory adequacy or superiority of historical materialism. (These would require addressing two criteria for the adoption of a particular theorization of Stalinism: intertheoretical comparison and empirical confirmation.)

An incipient petitio principii—assuming, rather than demonstrating, the cogency of historical materialism—is apparent in the second of the claims staked for Trotsky: namely, the incomparable 'sociological richness and penetration' of *Where Is Russia Going?* For the attribution of both qualities is attendant upon the presumed fertility of the Marxist research programme.

Non-Marxists—Carr, Nove, Rigby—are credited with 'the major advances in detailed empirical analysis of the USSR' after Trotsky, yet are reckoned not to have achieved 'an integrated theory of it such as bequeathed by [him]' (p. 124).[96] Distinct evaluative criteria are being employed here: Marxists responsible for an alternative Marxist theory of Stalinism are faulted on empirical grounds (the works of Rizzi or Cliff are dismissed as 'strikingly thin and dated'); and non-Marxists who make the empirical grade (profundity, currency) are found wanting on theoretical grounds. The superiority of Trotsky's interpretation qua 'integrated theory' is asserted, rather than defended, since—even if Anderson is right in his estimate of its professedly Marxist competitors[97]—he neglects theoretical challenges from other quarters. And yet *tertium datur*: non-Marxist integrated theories of Stalinism.

That there might be grounds for doubting the explanatory fecundity of Marxism in this regard is inadvertently betrayed by Anderson when he pronounces *Where Is Russia Going?* 'a *topical* masterpiece to this day' (p. 124). Why, if they were armed with such an integrated theory, should Marxists have ceded the major advances in empirical scholarship in the intervening half century to their non-Marxist peers? The evident disparity in the Marxist tradition between, so to speak, historico-political 'theory' and empirical sociology of the Soviet Union is arguably symptomatic of analytical difficulties evaded and not simply attributable to pro- or anti-Soviet partisanship. Such disparity is a pronounced feature of Anderson's own writings on the subject, characterized as they are by a discrepancy between an audacity of macro-historical claim concerning Stalinism as a geopolitical agency, and a sparsity of microhistorical analysis of its internal structures and dynamics. Anderson's well-nigh exclusive focus is upon the generic nature of Stalinism as a world-historical phenomenon in the twentieth century.

Predictably, this has implications for his treatment of the third of Trotsky's merits: the political. The 'historical time-span' in which Trotsky located his analysis may have been 'epochal'. To put it crudely, however, it was considerably narrower than that of Deutscher and, following him, Anderson, who do indeed think of Stalinism in terms of continents and centuries. A regeneration of the (degenerated) revolution or, alternatively, its quietus was imminently expected by Trotsky on the morrow of the Second World War. Transition or termination could not be indefinitely adjourned. The paradox of a 'workers' state' that repressed the workers could not persist (let alone go forth and multiply): it was due for practical resolution.

Anderson disqualifies competing theoretical dissolutions of the paradox—whether proponents of 'state capitalism', 'bureaucratic collectivism', or 'bureaucratic capitalism'—as politically vitiated, tendentially. But whatever their respective demerits might be, this would seem to be a false inference: what procapitalist fatality, for example, is inscribed in the theory of state capitalism ('neither Washington, nor Moscow, but international socialism'), unless (as is the case for Anderson) the equation of the 'super-powers', whether in Maoist or Trotskyist mode, is a political enormity in and of itself? For Anderson, as we have seen, unwavering categorization of the Soviet Union as—'in the final resort'—a 'workers' state' supplied the key to Trotsky's political 'equilibrium'. It likewise provides the master key to his own political orientation vis-à-vis the 'great contest' in the 1980s. (The rightward evolution of Colletti, who in 1974 had expressed his puzzlement at the notion of a 'degenerated workers' state', doubtless fuelled Anderson's conviction that it was the political crux of the matter.)[98]

The profundity of the paradox is diminished once it is appreciated that classification of the USSR as a 'workers' state' principally refers not to its *political* 'superstructure' but to its *economic* 'infrastructure': public property in the means of production, ipso facto rendering the Soviet Union not merely a non- but a *post*capitalist social formation. This, for Anderson, is a defining characteristic of postcapitalism—an imperative prerequisite of any transition to a future socialist mode of production wherein the contradiction between socialized relations of production and 'bourgeois' norms of distribution will have been surpassed. However, setting aside any objections that might be raised against the equation of 'nationalization' (public legal ownership) with 'socialization' (actual possession and control by the associated producers), this does not dissolve the paradox. For were this to exhaust the significance of the category of 'bureaucratized workers' state', why use it? Why not discard it as potentially misleading—hence a hostage to political fortune—and substitute the notion of 'bureaucratic post-capitalist state'? Refusal of this option is logically entailed by Andersonian-Trotskyist rejection of any analysis of the postrevolutionary societies that regards them as founded upon novel, consolidated modes of production, thereby disrupting the canonical sequence—Trotsky's 'general historical scheme', however temporally protracted and politically complicated—of socioeconomic formations in historical materialism (feudalism → capitalism → socialism).[99] According to orthodox Trotskyism, the bureaucracy that dictates over the proletariat is not a new social class but a privileged stratum of an existing class—the proletariat—dependent for its material privileges upon the proletarian expropriation of the capitalist expropriators. The class character of the bureaucratic political state is thus, in the last instance, proletarian. We are back with the paradox of a workers' state that represses the working class.

It was noted earlier that Anderson's resolution of the paradox is based upon a conceptual discrimination between genus and species of state. Consonant with his historical analogies between bourgeois and proletarian revolutions, it invites similar interrogation. Can such an analogy between post-, pre-, and plain capitalist states be maintained? Can the general historical paradox formulated by Anderson—of a state (e.g., Absolutist, fascist) whose class character (feudal, capitalist) is not negated by its domination of the social class (aristocracy, bourgeoisie) whose economic dominance it preserves—be extended to postcapitalist states, without (in Marxist terms) infringing the claims advanced for the ultimate historical novelty and superiority of socialism as a societal form, whatever 'the oblique march of history'?[100] In short, are we in the presence of a paradox or a contradiction?

These questions might or might not have been answered by the collapse of historical Communism (the oblique march of history halted?). Yet it is striking testimony to Anderson's enduring commitment to his own historico-sociological version of Trotsky's epochal time span that, in one of his allusions to that collapse, he typically reverts to revolutionary history-by-analogy. The editorial report on the *NLR* for 1975–80 (pp. 69–71) had already prepared the ground, by prospecting selective capitalist restorations in the Second World and comparing these to 'absolutist restorations' in 1660 (the Stuarts in Britain), and 1815 and 1824 (the Bourbons in France and Spain). In a 1991 postscript to his 1984 preface to a collection of Deutscher's writings, Anderson wrote:

> A connoisseur of the ironies of history, his sense of the future also allowed for this one too. He is mostly thought of, with justice, as a guarded optimist for the revolution. But it was distinctive of his vision that he also contemplated, directly and calmly, the historical prospect of restoration. The peoples of the Soviet Union . . . might yet have to go through the modern experience of a capitalism they had missed. . . . If the possibility became reality, it might—like other restorations—have its redeeming place in the complicated longer-run progress towards a common human liberty, in whose resumption he never doubted.[101]

Anderson's considerations on the 'restoration' in the USSR will be examined in the final chapter of this book. Meanwhile, however, we may venture a general observation: Andersonian historical sociology, intent upon the detection of long-run, large-scale developmental patterns through comparison between different social formations, here detects a precedent that affords a *dis*analogy. In addition to the reference to 'the modern experience of a capitalism [that the peoples of the Soviet Union] had missed'—a postulate prima facie incompatible with persistent prior categorization of the 'workers' states' as *post*capitalist—the striking thing about this passage is its assimilation of *political revolution* and *economic restoration* in the East, in 1989–91, to *political restorations* in the West, in 1660 and 1815. The collapse of the Protectorate and the First Empire did not reverse the socioeconomic transformations that were furthered or facilitated by the English and French Revolutions, and were anyway rapidly followed by 1688–89 and 1830/1848. The date that dare not speak its name in Anderson's comparison is 1789. Contrary to Trotsky and Anderson, 'the relevant precedent for [the] . . . overthrow' of the bureaucracy did prove to be 'a new 1789': [102] a political revolution, from below, against the state structures of actually existing socialism, which set in train a comprehensive social transformation, with an ongoing transition to capitalism and the consequent erasure of the Second World from the geopolitical map. Judged by the criteria of Anderson's own historical materialism, connoisseurism of the ironies of history, seeking consolation in the redemptive powers of the long run, provides little immunity to the former or warrant for the latter.

Anderson's contemporaneous attitude to the second Cold War fought against the Soviet Union, and his sense of continuity with Deutscher's legacy in this, is fully evident from the original preface to *Marxism, Wars, and Revolutions,* somewhat toned down for republication in *A Zone of Engagement.* Thus, he wrote of the original Cold War that

> a virulent anti-communism . . . dominated official culture and politics in the advanced capitalist countries. In a climate of conformity and hysteria, the Soviet experience became the object of a vast ideological campaign, orchestrated through government agencies, political parties, trade-unions and intellectual institutions alike, depicting the Russian threat—of perpetual aggression and subversion—to the Free World. In other words, a period very like our own.[103]

Suggesting that '[o]ur map of the present would look very different if we had a continuity of that committed intelligence [i.e., Deutscher's] with us', Anderson commented:

> As it is, . . . the political and intellectual scene is for the moment in many ways a bleak one: amidst renewed Cold War, and unended recession, much of the Western Left is prey to every kind of fashionable temptation and illusion purveyed by the Right. . . . In the slogans of 'post-marxism' [Deutscher]

would have seen mainly . . . renegades posing as heretics. He would have mordantly analysed the continual reproduction by Brezhnevite bureaucrats of Bukovskyite dissidents, and the echo-chambers of gulagism. But he would not have exaggerated the anti-cyclones, in either East or West. The new peace movements in Europe . . . would in particular have encouraged him.[104]

'Renegades posing as heretics': such was Anderson's verdict on a new wave of revisionism, catalyzed by political setbacks, sweeping the West European Left intelligentsia in the Cold War conjuncture of the 1980s.

Some Subtleties of the Isle

Following the Conservative victory, on a neoliberal ticket, at the British general election of May 1979, the *NLR*, for the first time in a decade and a half, took a serious and sympathetic interest in developments in the Labour Party. The initiatives of domestic revolutionary socialism—whether the Socialist Workers Party's (SWP) 'Rank-and-File' strategy or the IMG's 'Socialist Unity' campaign—having foundered, the advent of a distinctive current of reformist socialism—the complex known as 'Bennism'—captured the attention of the *Review* in the early 1980s. The challenge of this new Labour Left, captained by the former industry secretary against his parliamentary peers, stimulated a debate in the *NLR*'s pages and also generated a series of Verso titles.[105]

With the exception of Anthony Barnett's major intervention against Thatcher's Falklands War in 1982,[106] the central trends in national politics— the ascendancy of 'Thatcherism' and the accelerating national economic decline of which it was the consequence—were virtually ignored in the *NLR*. The results of the New Right dispensation, confirmed in power in June 1983 against a divided opposition, were not scrutinized until the following year.[107] As if in the belief that neoliberal medicine would prove too weak for chronic ills yet too strong for electoral stomachs, the crisis of Labourism and the prospects of Bennism preoccupied the journal's home coverage. As was noted in the editorial report for the period:

> In this NLR was consistent with its own past, in which it had always sought to establish critical contact or support for whatever force appeared to threaten the status quo most immediately in national politics. . . . In this respect, there was a direct line of descent from *Towards Socialism* . . . to *Parliament, People, and Power.*[108]

As it turned out, the interviews with Benn conducted by Anderson and his fellow editors were published in the autumn of 1982, after Benn's star in the Labour Party had gone into eclipse following his defeat in the deputy leadership election the previous year. The plea for greater political caution made in the quinquennial report (pp. 13–14) was duly heeded. Although the *NLR* foreword to *Parliament, People, and Power* ascribed genuine radicalism and 'fundamental originality' to the Bennite programme, insofar as it sighted the oligarchical structures of the British state,[109] the *Aktiv* as a whole was not prepared to go as far as Tariq Ali and Quintin Hoare in championing its potential. Their 1982 article 'Socialists and the Crisis of Labourism' recommended Bennism to revolutionary socialists as the possible harbinger of 'a new model Labour Party'—'a mass socialist party', which would redeem the post-1968 disappointments of the Far Left—and it advocated membership of the old model party to that end.[110] Anxious lest this be taken to represent the official *NLR* line, Anderson pressed for qualification of what he regarded as undue optimism. When the piece did finally appear, its conclusions were contested in a response from David Coates, who argued the case for socialists preserving their independence of Labourism.[111]

In print Anderson maintained a discreet silence on such matters. However, the 1980–83 editorial report might supply a clue as to his perspective on the political conjuncture. Urging 'the construction of a clear public position on the prospects for the British Left', it argued that

> the priority, and difficulty, will be to define a stance that is at once *politically* supportive of Benn and Bennism, as the major moving force of the Left as a whole, while at the same time being *intellectually* intransigent about the nature of the Labour Party. The problem in this respect is manifest: how do we propagate the perspective of a break-up of Labourism, as the decisive precondition of any serious political change in the UK, without weakening the fortunes of the only healthy elements within it, upon whose successful exit from the old order the immediate future of any socialist prospect depends? The key notion here may well prove to be some sort of 'Alternative Political Stategy', foregrounding electoral and executive reform both within the Labour Party itself and in the bourgeois political order, as an integrated ideological package. (P. 41)

Other more or less integrated ideological packages were in the process of being assembled on the British Left, whose thrust was antipodal to this. The triennial report recalled that in 1980 the absence from Britain of the West European 'crisis of Marxism'—'in reality . . . a simple adaptation to time-worn Cold War tropes'—had been registered with relief (p. 45). Three years later, that verdict required revision. An insular strain of the 'Continental virus' was now being spread via the Communist Party monthly *Marxism Today* and its mainstream media amplifiers the *New Statesman* and the *Guardian* (pp. 45–46). What a Communist dissident subsequently dubbed 'Eurolabourism'[112]—the gradual ideological convergence of the Eurocommunist wing of the CPGB and the 'modernizing' Centre-Right of the Labour Party—was propagating an 'English permutation of the "crisis of Marxism", in the guise of the "crisis of the labour movement"' (p. 46). The unpremeditated vehicle of it was a symposium on Eric Hobsbawm's 1978 Marx Memorial Lecture, *The Forward March of Labour Halted?* published by Verso (in association with *Marxism Today*) in 1981. In 1982 the Eurolabourist consensus was still in the making; concerted expression would be given to it after Labour's disastrous showing at the polls in June 1983, in the *Marxism Today* anthology *The Politics of Thatcherism*, compiled and prefaced by its editor, Martin Jacques, in collaboration with a keynote contributor, Stuart Hall. The triennial report's reprobation of what (as the reference to 'Browderism' indicated) was considered a liquidationist enterprise was unequivocal:

> In retrospect it can now be seen that the *Labour's Foward March* debate, at least so far as some of its participants were concerned, acted to clear the ground for an increasingly outright repudiation of the very notion of an anticapitalist working-class as an historical reality at all in our epoch. The genuine processes of sectoral fragmentation, cultural disorientation, ethnic recomposition within the labour movement in Britain, Europe and the USA—eminently in need of serious and sober materialist analysis—have since been steadily utilized to undermine any principle of proletarian politics, for a more and more rightist prospect that no longer has even the dignity of the Popular Front, but is rather a shrunken and frightened latter-day Browderism. . . . Clearly related to [this] deepening pessimism and conservatism . . . has been growing capitulation to Cold War stereotypes, in their 'left' version, of the Communist states. (Pp. 46-7)[113]

Within the disputes that wracked the British Left during the first half of the 1980s, Anderson's position was that of a 'resolute socialist'; and this was the line he enjoined upon the *NLR* under Blackburn's editorship from 1983 onward. He had supported the foundation of an interdenominational Socialist Society in 1981—an initiative in which several of his colleagues (especially Blackburn and Mulhern) played a central role. Yet he fiercely opposed any ecumenicism in its charter that might permit the adhesion of intellectuals who, whatever their *marxisant* self-description, were not unambiguously anti-capitalist in a traditional Marxist sense.[114] Two years later, following Labour's second electoral defeat, he remonstrated with Blackburn over what he considered to be the *Review*'s insufficiently distinctive response to the debacle in its summer issue (no. 140, July/August 1983).[115] His reactions to a speech by Benn to the Socialist Society that autumn, after Kinnock's assumption of the Labour leadership, eloquently attest to an intransigent postelectoral mood.

Welcoming its dissociation from the ubiquitous lamentations, Anderson suggested that the *NLR* might publish Benn's speech, subject to three conditions. The first was that there be no deletion of the explicit criticisms of Eurolabourist positions. The second was that the *Review* itself should take a robust stand against British and West European revisionism. And a final caveat concerned the journal's demarcation of its own position from Benn's in two regards. Unlike him, it should concede the unpopularity of left-wing policies, responsibility for which should be laid at the door of Labourism; to pretend otherwise was counterproductive, playing into the hands of realists, ancient and postmodern. Furthermore, the *NLR* should repudiate the plurality electoral system to which Benn remained attached and—in conformity with original soviet traditions—should advocate the party-list system of proportional representation. Were the *Review* to retire its revolutionary Marxism at such a time, its very raison d'être would disappear. Quite the reverse of trimming, it should tack to the left.[116]

In a collective document drawn up in early 1984 for the information of a group of socialist-feminists who had been invited to join the editorial committee of the *Review*, [117] a set of 'substantive directions for the NLR in the coming period' was itemized. The domestic priority was

[d]evelopment of a strategic perspective on British politics clearly demarcated from the emergent consensus . . . that 'the Left went too far' in the late seventies, that the need is to adapt to existing public opinion on major issues, to trim positions to the right, to regain a 'national-popular' discourse. Against this new conformism, with its animus against the Bennite experience, and preparation for regroupment around Kinnock's leadership of the Labour Party, NLR has a duty to formulate a Marxist politics beyond Labourism, that is at once revolutionary in temper (hence inimical to the increasingly blatant moderatism of these sectors), and realistic in judgement (thus also critical of the characteristic illusions of the new Labour Left, while remaining firmly in solidarity with it against the revanchism of which it is now so frequently the object). (P. 4)

In addition to conducting critical surveys of the record of European Social-Democracy and the wider Left, engaging with feminist theory and practice, and '[r]eentering into philosophical debate' over poststructuralism and other currents (p. 5), the *Review* proposed to embark upon '[d]iscussion of models of socialism':

> The Left has typically oscillated between generalized indictments of capitalism that do no more than gesture at an ultimately superior society beyond it, which remains essentially abstract, and specific demands for concrete but highly limited reforms within capitalism. This duality has become especially untenable with the posing of civilizational questions by, among others, the ecological movement. . . . The review should be exploring . . . the alternative structures of a socialist democracy—political, economic and cultural, and the possible difficulties and dilemmas they would present, even given the breakage of bourgeois power to block them. The proper control for such 'experiments in thought' is, of course, historical experience. (P. 6)

Although Anderson and the *NLR* did maintain an orientation to 'a Marxist politics beyond Labourism', a consequent left turn proved recalcitrant to execution. A sequence of critiques of Eurosocialism and Eurocommunism was initiated in 1984, as envisaged.[118] However, no comparable account of Labourism ever materialized. The main counterstatement to the 'new revisionism' carried by the *Review* had to wait until the spring of 1985, by which time the weightiest challenge to radical right-wing administration of British capitalism—the year-long miners' strike—had gone down to defeat. It came not from the editorial committee of the *NLR* but from a veteran of the first New Left, Ralph Miliband, who took issue with former colleagues such as Hall, Hobsbawm, and Samuel in the twenty-fifth anniversary issue of the journal.[119]

In some 'Notes on the Current Outlook' drafted for collective discussion in April 1985, Anderson urged his fellow editors to capitalize upon Miliband's critique (p. 1). Yet, as he reflected, the circumstances were far from tonic: the bastions of the Left—the miners' union and the Greater London Council—were in disarray, and the Labour and Communist Parties were continuing on their rightward trajectory. Whereas the 1950s revisionism associated with Gaitskell had been contested by the New Left, the 'new realism' of the 1980s—the consensus around Kinnock—faced precious few sanctions on its left (p. 2). A major inhibition to the emergence of any consistent opposition was the much more ambitious political horizons of the opposition, fixed upon the historical goal of socialism, not the psephodrama of the next election. Anticipating the advent of a suitably normalized Labour administration, Anderson wagered on that prospect as most conducive to a revival of the Left (p. 4). For the vacuum at the heart of Eurolabourism, as of Eurosocialism on the Continent, was the lack of any alternative to Keynesianism as a formula for capitalist regulation. Social-Democracy in the 1980s was therefore set to repeat the history of its antecedents in the 1960s and 1970s, but in even more inclement objective conditions, radicalizing the disabused in the process. Accordingly, the *NLR*'s overriding responsibility was to begin to remedy the long-standing lacunae of socialist strategy and programme in preparation for a new political conjuncture (p. 5). A prerequisite of success in this undertaking was a genuine realism that shunned the damaging hyperbole to which the Labour Left was prone. Moreover, Anderson cautioned, the likely fragility of the revisionist consensus, and the recuperability of many of its adherents, should be borne in mind (p. 6). Above all, the terms of reference of left-wing controversy had to be decisively broadened, to surmount its endemic parochialism and immediatism. Advocating what may be characterized as a 'concrete utopianism', Anderson reiterated the emphasis of the 1984 'Notes' on an exploration of the 'alternative structures of a socialist democracy' that was at once desirable and viable (p. 7).

Once again, a comprehensive antirevisionist editorial programme—foreshadowed in the quinquennial report five years earlier—was not implemented by the *NLR*. In its absence, the *Review* assumed something of the appearance of what Anderson elsewhere stressed the need to avoid—a sheerly oppositional forum featuring counterpolemics that, whatever their merits as critiques of the 'new revisionism', offered little by way of alternative to it.[120] As late as the mid-1980s, Anderson was manifestly confident in a socialist revival in the foreseeable future, regarding the regression of the decade to date as a conjunctural setback that could and would be reversed. Pending the projected upturn, the *NLR*'s duty was to function as a medium of *creative* resistance to ideological conformism.

In 1981 Michael Rustin had criticized the 'separatist leftism' of the second New Left.[121] In the very process of directing its rhetorical fire at the postwar settlement, it had in effect taken it to be inviolable as the institutional form for the regulation of advanced capitalism. Therewith, it had inadvertently contributed in some ideological measure to the rise of the 'antistatist' New Right—counterrevolutionary *tertius gaudens* of the adversity between revolutionary socialism and welfarist reformism.[122] What cannot be denied is that 1968 was equally the year of the New Right—Powell's hallucination of 'Rivers of Blood' in Birmingham being as authentic an accent of the time as Vanessa Redgrave's denunciation of American imperialism in Grosvenor Square—and that, unlike its antonym, the New Right had commenced serious ideological homework on a 'revolution' against welfare capitalism. The 'resolute Left', so Anderson ruefully but candidly acknowledged, found itself on the defensive, because it increasingly lacked any feasible alternative to a Social-Democracy in disorderly retreat before the neoliberal offensive (of whose course and consequences the *NLR* offered little analysis). The strategic and programmatic deficits of decades, bemoaned by Anderson, now weighed with a vengeance; and they were not even addressed, let alone corrected, by the *Review*.

Anderson's guiding assumption seems to have been that the practical depredations of the New Right would prompt its electoral repudiation, whereas the predictable derelictions of the depleted Social-Democracy set to replace it in office—bereft of a plausible response to the economic crisis that had bred neoliberalism—would regenerate socialism. What he could not (yet) conceive was the mutual ruination of the contending parties, reformist and revolutionary: the fact that the 1980s were witnessing the global collapse of the movements and regimes that had their origins in the two principal traditions of socialist politics—the Social-Democratic Second and the Communist Third Internationals—and that the succession devolved not upon the revolutionary socialism represented by the Fourth, but with the genuinely global international of capital. Thought experiments in socialism were more readily projected than practiced amid the inexorable erosion of its existing embodiments.

It is an index of Anderson's domestic antirevisionism up to the mid-1980s that he not only repudiated all talk of a 'crisis of the labour movement' as anti-Marxist and antisocialist cant, but persevered in his commitment to the proposition that Labourism was the principal obstacle to socialist advance in Britain, whose breakup was therefore a consummation devoutly to be wished. What this outlook excluded, of course, was the possibility that the crisis of Labourism was a national symptom of profound global changes, assisted, if scarcely initiated, by the New Right, which were no less injurious to political forces to its left. The gravest was precisely the decline of the 'labour movement', rooted in that process of class 'recomposition', a 'sober materialist analysis' of which was not forthcoming from the *NLR* in general, or Anderson in particular.

This omission would be rectified after 1989, when Anderson tacitly renounced the views he had held at the time and, adopting the stance of the nonparticipant observer and bibliographer, announced that 'out of the [British] trial emerged the liveliest republic of letters in European socialism'.[123]

Transverse Movements? Conjectures and Refutations

In 1983 Anderson relinquished the titular editorship of the *NLR*. The vale-dictory overview of the editorial report for 1980–83 retracted the optimistic prognostications of its predecessor concerning the dispositions of the Anglo-phone Left intelligentsia (p. 53). Taking mild satisfaction in the *Review's* intervention over the Falklands expedition, its coverage of the second Cold War, and its novel attention to the United States,[124] the triennial report pro-posed a facultative order of priorities for the future, wondering

> if we should not consider branching out to confront and attack the noxious plethora of non- or anti-Marxist theories that have filled the ideological vac-uum left by the collapse of so much Western Marxism. . . . The popularity of most of this bric-à-brac is due to a confluence of two or three factors—the general servility to sheer fashion of most Western intellectuals, Left or Right; the *scheinradikalismus* of a 'nihilism' that ostensibly lights funeral-pyres for every philosophical convention in sight, while comfortably leaving everything material as it is; the convenience of its rancour or renegacy to-wards socialism to the bourgeois political order as such. (P. 44)[125]

In any event, the ideological conjuncture dictated vigilance against its Siren songs:

> [T]he NLR . . . must now . . . navigate with a firm compass in the dubious, perhaps soon treacherous, intellectual waters swirling about it—making no concession, either inside or outside the journal, to backward or confused political currents. The logic of such a course involves . . . a relationship to our external environment of a much more watchful and critical character than could be conveyed by any connotation of the term 'expression'. . . . Resistance as much as reflection of that milieu will be needed. Indeed, a cer-tain institutional and intellectual *Abgrenzung* might even be imposed on us in the next period, if present trends proceed unchecked. . . . The reputation of the review must be strictly guarded, in such conditions. (Pp. 49–50)

This did not entail any reversion to 'isolationism' or 'jealous integrism'; it did indicate collective discipline lest intellectual extroversion induce compro-mises of political principle.

The report ended by encouraging colleagues to focus on the issues it posed 'so that we can reconvene in 1983 collectively ready to reinvigorate the review and the imprint' (p. 60). What supervened in 1983 was the most serious crisis in the history of the *NLR* Mark 2. Before glancing at that de-nouement, we may turn to Anderson's *In the Tracks of Historical Material-ism*, in which he branched out to confront and attack contemporary anti-Marxism. The text of the René Wellek Library lectures delivered in the United States in 1982 and published with a postscript the following au-tumn, at 112 pages this opuscule constitutes the last book as such from Anderson's pen to date; and it invites an analogous verdict to that delivered on Timpanaro's *The Freudian Slip* in the quinquennial report: 'perhaps the last truly confident . . . book to be produced within [Western Marxism]' (p. 29). Yet even that apparent confidence is dependent upon something of an optical illusion, insofar as *Tracks* reiterates the sanguine prognosis of the quinquennial report, rather than the bleak diagnosis of its successor, on Anglo-Marxism. By the time Anderson's lectures were issued, announcing 'a period of overall growth and emancipation' on the basis of the available transatlantic evidence (p. 20), conformity to the cross-Channel pattern had been detected. Anglo-Marxists had contracted the European virus to which they were declared immune.

A sequel in some sort to *Considerations on Western Marxism, In the Tracks of Historical Materialism* surveyed the fortunes of Marxism in the Occident in the intervening years.[126] The earlier work, it will be remem-bered, had argued that postclassical Marxism grew out of the cumulative defeats suffered by the European workers' movement in the twentieth cen-tury. The survival and then revival of capitalism in the West, and the crystal-lization and consolidation of Stalinism in the East—these were held broadly responsible for its distinctive character vis-à-vis the classical tradition: its severance of theory from practice; its superstructural bias and philosophical bent; a series of filiations with non-Marxist intellectual formations; and a latent or overt pessimism. With the return of the revolutionary repressed to metropolitan capitalism in 1968, and the end of the long boom soon after-ward, Anderson had anticipated the emergence of a new kind of Marxism, hazarding some predictions as to its shape.

Reviewing these predictions in chapter 1 ('Prediction and Perfor-mance'), Anderson found them partially fulfilled. Western Marxism had largely run its course by the mid-1970s; subsequent historical materialism had ascended to the concrete, tackling substantive economic and political issues; and an 'Anglo-Marxism' had emerged in which the prior tradition of Marxist historiography assumed due salience (pp. 18–27).[127] On the other hand, the reunification of theory and practice in a mass revolutionary move-ment had signally failed to materialize, with the result that a 'general dearth' of socialist strategy persisted (p. 27) alongside a surfeit of Marxist literature,

171

while political opportunities came—and went. Moreover, a quite unforeseen development had ensued in their wake: the profound 'crisis of Marxism' that struck southern Europe in the second half of the 1970s (pp. 28–30).

To account for this crisis, in chapter 2 ('Structure and Subject') Anderson mooted the hypothesis that historical materialism had been challenged, worsted, and superseded as a research programme by (post)structuralism on the 'master-problem' of 'the nature of the relationships between structure and subject in human history and society' (p. 33)—but only peremptorily to reject it. 'Internal' intellectual history, so Anderson maintained, could not explain the 'veritable *débandade*' (p. 32) of Gallic Marxism. For it revealed that, quite the reverse of solving the problem that had consumed the energies of Sartre, Merleau-Ponty, and Beauvoir on the morrow of Liberation, Lévi-Strauss and Lacan, Foucault and Derrida had reproduced it on the eve of May (pp. 54–55). Imprudently conferred with Marxist credentials by Althusser, the structuralist paradigm, fallaciously extrapolating from Saussure's *Course in General Linguistics*, was vitiated by a series of crippling faults. These could be resumed as follows: first, an '*exorbitation of language*'; second, an '*attenuation of truth*'; third, a '*randomization of history*'; and fourth, in the transition to poststructuralism proper, a '*capsizal of structures*' (pp. 40–55). Accordingly, Anderson concluded:

> The unresolved difficulties and deadlocks within Marxist theory, which structuralism promised to transcend, were never negotiated in detail within this rival space. The adoption of the language model . . . , far from clarifying or decoding the relations between structure and subject, led from a rhetorical absolutism of the first to a fragmented fetishism of the second, without ever advancing a theory of their *relations*. Such a theory, historically determinate and sectorally differentiated, could only be developed in a dialectical respect for their interdependence. (P. 55)

The ascension of Parisian anti-Marxism prompted Anderson to revise his estimate of Habermas, whose omission from *Considerations on Western Marxism* he now regretted (p. 59).[128] Political pronouncements and philosophical affiliations had seemed to exclude him from a survey of historical materialism, however ecumenically conceived. This was an error for which Anderson sought to make amends, proffering a sympathetic critique of the Habermasian reconstruction of critical theory (pp. 58–67). His main concern, however, in a third chapter ('Nature and History'), was an adequate explanation for the recession of Marxism in its French and Italian postwar heartlands. Its matrix resided in 'political history'—in particular, 'the fate of the international communist movement' (pp. 67–68). In accordance with the protocols for a 'Marxism of Marxism' laid down at the outset (p. 14), which allocated explanatory primacy to the 'external environment' of Marxist theory, Anderson tracked the culprits of the crisis to the twin disappointments of Maoism and Eurocommunism (pp. 76–77). It was to these that so many southern European Marxists had successively turned in search of an alternative to Stalinism and Social-Democracy; and

> [i]t was here that the 'crisis of Marxism', so called, had its source and its meaning. Its real determinants had very little to do with its overt themes. What detonated it was essentially a *double disappointment*: first in the Chinese and then in the West European alternatives to the central post-revolutionary experience of the twentieth century so far. . . . Each of these alternatives had presented itself as a historically *new* solution, capable of overcoming the dilemmas and avoiding the disasters of Soviet history: yet each of their upshots proved to be a return to familiar deadlocks. Maoism appeared to debouch into little more than a truculent Oriental Khrushchevism. Eurocommunism lapsed into what increasingly looked like a second-class version of Occidental social-democracy. (P. 76)

For all the 'disastrous fixation with China' (p. 19), of the two, Eurocommunism was the more important. Its frustrations from 1976 to 1978 had catalyzed the 'quintessentially *Latin* phenomenon' misdescribed as 'the crisis of Marxism'.

That this was a misnomer was evident, Anderson argued, in the comparative perspective of the Anglo-American scene. Denied the tantalizing promises, yet spared the demoralizing defeats, of their European counterparts, Anglophone Marxists provided an arresting contrast to them:

> A steadier and more tough-minded historical materialism proved generally capable of withstanding political isolation or adversity, and of generating increasingly solid and mature work in and through them. This is not to say that analogous developments may not affect sectors of the Anglo-American or Nordic Lefts in the future. The popular consolidation of political regimes of imperialist reaction in Britain, or the United States, in the mid eighties may well break the nerve of some socialists, drawing them rightwards in an anxious quest for the middle ground. . . . For the moment, the contrast between the relative robustness and vitality of Marxism in this zone, and its corrosion and malady in the lands of the aborted Eurocommunist experience, is stark enough. (Pp. 77–78)

Eurocommunism had effected a 'reformist' reunification of theory and practice, contradicting Andersonian expectations of a 'revolutionary' suture of the torn halves of Marxism. Its failure, and the inability of the Fourth International to supply a credible alternative, elicited a stark political conclusion: 'The problem of . . . a [socialist] strategy remains today, as it has done now for fifty years, the Sphinx facing Marxism in the West' (p. 80).[129] Anderson did not venture an answer to a riddle—the practical analogue of the philosophical conundrum of structures and subjects—that had likewise defeated him. He turned, instead, to 'the other great crux for Marxism as a critical theory': the complex articulations of nature and history (p. 83). Urgently tabled by new political forces—feminism, ecology, and the peace movement—it signalled 'the long overdue moment of socialist morality' (p. 84).

In a postscript that developed points made in the quinquennial report (discussed earlier), Anderson addressed the relationship between historical materialism and socialism as theory and practice. Refusing Marxism any intellectual monopoly while at the same time defending its centrality, Anderson postulated 'three hallmarks that separate it from all other contributions to the culture of socialism':

> (i) The first is its sheer scope as an *intellectual system*. . . . [O]nly Marx and Engels produced a comprehensive body of theory capable of continuous, cumulative development after them. . . . (ii) [Its] second peculiar power . . . has always lain in its character as a *theory of historical development*. . . . [T]here is only one contender as a general account of human development across the centuries from primitive societies to present forms of civilization. . . . Marxism alone has produced a sufficiently general and a sufficiently differential set of analytic instruments to be able to integrate successive epochs of historical evolution, and their characteristic socio-economic structures, into an intelligible narrative. . . . There is no competing story. . . . (iii) Thirdly, Marxism has stood apart from every other tradition of socialist thought in the effect of its radicalism as a *political call to arms*, in the struggle against capitalism. . . . Capitalism has fallen to the forces fighting against it only where Marxism has risen to dominance among them. (Pp. 86–87)[130]

Marxism had not been stripped of these hallmarks. On each score, however, it now faced a challenge—from feminism, in particular. This development posed the further question of the relationship between socialism as a movement aspiring to the abolition of capitalism—ipso facto of class division—and a general human emancipation, in which the eradication of secular sexual inequality was an essential moment. Qualifying the former as a necessary condition of the latter, Anderson restated the classical case for nomination of the 'collective labourer' as the social agent of any transition to socialism (pp. 92–3).[131] In so doing, he entered a plea on behalf of 'socientific' socialism. The 'irenic universalism' of the utopian tradition

> precluded social conflict as a central principle of political change: hence its necessary resort to moral conversion as a substitute for it. The decisive advantage of 'scientific' socialism was to break this deadlock by identifying the site of a particular social agency, rooted in historically specific forms of economic production, as the Archimedean point from which the old order could be overturned—the structural position occupied by the industrial working-class created by the advent of capitalism. (P. 94)

If, in this respect—on the plane of agency—a classical Marxism was upheld, in another—vis-à-vis the goal of socialism—it was modified. Historical materialism had been impugned for an excess, and for a lack, of utopianism (pp. 97–98). On both counts Anderson met critics halfway. Regarding an excess of (abstract) utopianism: such Fourierist and Saint-Simonian residues as the notion of suppression of the division of labour, or replacement of the government of men by the administration of things, were rejected by him. Regarding a lack of (concrete) utopianism: engaging constructively with Alec Nove's professedly revisionist (promarket) *Economics of Feasible Socialism* (pp. 100–103), Anderson regretted the paucity of the 'legacy of institutional thought within classical Marxism' (p. 98).[132] In view of its tarnished record in the twentieth century, Marxism must attend to socialism as 'a *future society*' (p. 97), examining the institutional structures of a realistically conjecturable postcapitalist social formation.[133]

Marxism's traditional disabling abstention from this did not, however, controvert its enduring indispensability to the struggle for a feasible socialism:

> For historical materialism remains the only intellectual paradigm capacious enough to be able to link the ideal horizon of a socialism to come with the practical contradictions and movements of the present, and their descent from the structures of the past, in a theory of the distinctive dynamics of social development as a whole. Like any other long-term programme of research in the traditional sciences themselves, it has known periods of repetition or arrest, generated in its time errors or misdirections. But like any other such paradigm, it will not be replaced so long as there is no superior candidate for comparable overall advance in knowledge. There is no sign of that yet, and we can therefore be confident that at least as much work will

175

be done within Marxism tomorrow as it is today. The working class in the West is currently in disarray, in the throes of one of those far-reaching recompositions that have periodically marked its history since the Industrial Revolution; but it is much less defeated and dispersed than it was during the Great Depression, and—short of war—has many days still ahead of it. Marxism has no reason to abandon its Archimedean vantage-point: the search for subjective agencies capable of effective strategies for the dislodgement of objective structures. But amidst pervasive changes within world capitalism today, those three terms can only be successfully combined if they have a common end that is at once desirable and believable for millions who are now hesitant or indifferent to them. (Pp. 105–6)

As if in reminiscence of Sartre, *marxisme faute de mieux* conveys the temper, if not the letter, of the closing pages of *In the Tracks of Historical Materialism*.[134] Three aspects of Anderson's monitoring of Marxism will concern us here: the antithesis between its crisis-ridden southern European and its buoyant Anglo-American sectors; the assessment of the role of poststructuralism in the causation of the crisis; and the conjoint vindication of it and of revolutionary socialism.

Anderson is at pains to deflate the notion of a general 'crisis of Marxism', restricting the validity of the term to a theoretical 'crisis of Latin Marxism' (p. 28), set off by Maoist, and especially Eurocommunist, breach of political promise. Now, although there is no reason to dispute his perception of 'something approaching a collapse of the Marxist tradition by the late seventies' in southern Europe, the delineation of its variant forms inspires some reservations. The first—'repudiation' (e.g., the case of Colletti)—seems straightforward; the second, however—the 'dilution or diminution' of which Althusser and Poulantzas are the exemplars (pp. 29–30)—is more problematic. For by what criteria—other than their own previous claims for the scientificity of their reconstructions—are they alleged to have diminished or diluted historical materialism (as opposed to Althusserianism), when Habermas—an explicit critic of the Marxist heuristic, as he concedes (and as Anderson demonstrates)—is not? The answer would appear to be Althusser's and Poulantzas's proclamations of crisis, as against Habermas's declaration of allegiance.[135] Yet these say nothing about the substance of the theoretical matter. Nor can any political inference be made from them—although it is a safe bet that, by Anderson's standards, the Frenchman and the Greek remained some considerable distance to the left of the German. Moreover, as was noted in chapter 2, both Colletti and Timpanaro had, in their time, registered the existence of a crisis of Marxism without provoking Andersonian animus. It is certainly indiscriminate here.

Of greater significance than this lapse is its facilitating condition: the supposedly 'transverse movements of Marxist theory in the past decade' (p. 31)—a polarity between the Anglo-American and European zones in which the evaluative signs of the 1960s are inverted, and unwarranted charity to the first term of the pair is the obverse of excessive severity toward the second. The most vulnerable postulate is the alleged 'nascent Anglo-American hegemony in historical materialism today', that 'truly astonishing metamorphosis' wherein '[t]he traditional relationship between Britain and Continental Europe appears for the moment to have been reversed—Marxist culture in the UK for the moment proving more productive and original than that of any mainland state' (pp. 24–25). Notwithstanding a certain insurance clause against imminent or ultimate default—that reiterated 'for the moment'—this seems unequivocal enough. In the case of Britain, it had been privately revoked before being publicly proclaimed: there, a recognizably revisionist—and not merely reformist—nexus was forming between ex-Eurocommunist theory and Labourist practice (the phenomenon of 'Eurolabourism'). In the case of the United States, the claim was intellectually inflated—and rapidly disappointed.

It is true that Trotsky had been prey to greater credulity half a century earlier. Before being disabused by the salon intellectuals on whom we have seen Krassó and Anderson venting their contempt, he had risked the prediction that '[t]he great transoceanic "porridge" is unquestionably beginning to boil. . . . [I]t may be that we are not very far from a time when the theoretical center of the international revolution is transferred to New York'. [136] But whatever the precedent, Anderson's assessment is decidedly curious in view of a theory/practice criterion otherwise deployed by him *à tous azimuts*. It involves not the least concession to anti-intellectualism to observe that, whereas pro-Eurocommunist Marxists are rebuked for contributing to a reformist reunification of theory and practice after 1968, a bizarre bibliocentrism informs his judgement when it comes to their North American peers.[137] One does not have to subscribe to Russell Jacoby's thesis of a wholesale 'privatization' and 'professionalization' of radical intellectuals—a viewpoint neatly summed up in Paul Buhle's subheading 'American Marxism Takes a Ph.D. and So What?'—to find Anderson's evaluation incongruous.[138] Its inconsistency is patent. For whatever its temporary productivity, American Marxism replicated one of the generic vices of Western Marxism admonished in Anderson's *Considerations*, remaining corralled in the academy[139]—a site in which it was briefly insulated by political irrelevance but soon exposed to theoretical 'relevance' (i.e., post- and anti-Marxist modes). Aijaz Ahmad's verdict a decade later may enjoy the benefit of hindsight; nonetheless, it is more authentically Andersonian, for better or worse, than Anderson's own.[140] It is true that at one point Anderson issues a caveat, envisaging a failure of intellectual nerve in the face of political adversity (p. 77). Yet the overall impression remains: an indulgence toward American academics divorced from any labour movement, which is in inverse proportion to an incivility to European Marxists engaged in socialist politics—occupants of posts in the class struggle, as well as holders of chairs in the academy, to qualify Anderson's demagogic dichotomy (p. 16).

Little sign of the 'nascent hegemony' was to be seen in Britain or North America a few years later amid the crescent hegemony of poststructuralism, when—contrary to the prediction of the quinquennial report (p. 50)—Nietzsche and Heidegger took a stranglehold. Anderson is adamant that intellectual trends in France were of no moment in precipitating the crisis of Latin Marxism, whose determinants were primarily extratheoretical. Concurrent, let alone subsequent, developments provided sufficient refutation of a hypothesis that was, as Terry Eagleton commented, 'highly implausible'.[141] The advent of a comparable transatlantic crisis, under the selfsame sign of poststructuralism and afflicting intellectuals not exposed to southern European setbacks, conclusively infirms it. Anderson's exclusive resort to 'external' (political) history has precisely the effect against which he warns in his opening lecture: '[T]he recourse to the wider movement of history would tend to slip away from, or beyond, material explanation to intellectual exemption or exculpation' (p. 14). The fault lay not with Marxism but with the European Marxists.

Anderson's assertion that historical materialism was never theoretically contested, never mind vanquished, by poststructuralism cannot be accepted. For a start, it is widely *perceived* as having been (and in contemporary Western culture, misperception is nine-tenths of the law). Furthermore, the criteria governing Anderson's 'internal history' are far from neutral between the contenders. Indeed, his criteria pertain to one of those contenders as construed by him: historical materialism. In arguing that structuralism in effect aspired to resolve *Marxism's* problems (p. 33), Anderson can quite legitimately maintain that it failed to do so. If, by contrast, an alternative intrinsic history is constructed—one that revolves around the displacement, even dissolution, of those problems in French philosophical modernism—things assume a very different aspect.

This is readily apparent from the terms of vindication of historical materialism in Anderson's postscript, where it is lauded for providing an 'intelligible narrative' of 'historical evolution': '[T]here is no competing story' (pp. 86–87). For at what, if not the intellectual viability and political desirability of such 'objectivist', 'totalizing' theory and 'metanarrative', has postmodernism directed its fire? However trifling and parasitic it might (rightly) seem to Anderson, that, after all, is the whole burden of Lyotard's *Postmodern Condition* (1979); and it will avail Marxists little to accuse postmodernism of failing to vouchsafe the very thing it disavows: a 'competing story'. In any case, one antipostmodernist's meat is another's poison, as Ernest Gellner's *Postmodernism, Reason, and Religion,* published a decade after Anderson's lectures, demonstrates. In an alternative internal intellectual history, a thinker for whose Enlightenment rationalism Anderson has evinced considerable sympathy casts his rivals as accomplices, incriminating Marxism, qua 'historical subjectivism', as a 'possible intellectual ancestor' of contemporary relativism.[142]

Despite its insights, Anderson's treatment of (post)structuralism—indebted, above all, to Timpanaro[143]—is cursory, and correspondingly unlikely to convince the unconverted. Moreover, as Alex Callinicos (among others) observed at the time, there is a certain irony of intellectual history here, given Anderson's sometime sponsorship of work that he now submitted to unremitting criticism.[144] Thus, of the quartet singled out for reproof, two offenders—Lévi-Strauss and Lacan—had not only been introduced to an Anglophone Marxist audience via the *NLR*, they had been utilized in Anderson's indictment of English culture during his Althusserian phase.[145] Now, however, in a critique without nuance or qualification, characterized by sheer 'negativism'[146] and exhibiting an especial Foucaultphobia, they were cast in the role of nihilists.

In pressing his central charge—'the attenuation of truth' (p. 45)—Anderson seemed to suppose that a traditional correspondence theory of truth was unexceptionable, sufficing to refute cognitive relativism and to validate 'the ineliminable premise of any rational knowledge': namely, 'the *distinction* between the true and the false', whose 'central site is evidence' (pp. 46–47). Here, however, an excess of polemical zeal led him beyond the claims justified by the philosophy of science to which he tacitly appealed: Lakatos's 'methodology of scientific research programmes', whose radical antiempiricism renders acceptance of the falsification of a theory rationally postponable indefinitely.

Anderson mounts no case for the possiblity of objective social-scientific knowledge; he takes it for granted. No doubt this is because he is concerned less to defend epistemological naturalism and realism in general than to sustain the scientificity of one candidate in particular: an Enlightenment

Marxism. As in the case of his Trotsky article, Anderson does not specify the criteria according to which theories are to be preferred; but following *Arguments within English Marxism* (p. 12), they would appear to be broadly Lakatosian. In other words, historical materialism is vindicated as a research programme on the grounds of its greater explanatory adequacy than that of its rivals, in their multiparty, many-sided confrontation with ranges of empirical evidence. But greater than what? we might ask. For according to Anderson, Marxism has no challengers: '[T]here is no competing story'. More explanatorily comprehensive as a 'theory of historical development' than any pretenders to its title, 'it remains unchallenged not only within socialist, but also non-socialist culture as a whole' (pp. 86–87). Presumably, then, in the absence of competition, it is rational to affirm the scientificity of historical materialism—or its protoscientificity, at any rate—to the extent that (as Lakatosian and Andersonian realism dictates) at least some of its explanatory claims have been corroborated by the historical evidence. If historical materialism is to be adopted on the grounds of its incomparable theoretical ambitions relative to other historical-sociological research programmes, those ambitions must be subjected to empirical (dis)confirmation. Otherwise, its audacity might be an index not of its veracity but of its vacuity; whereas, contrariwise, their modesty might be a token of their cogency. A third possibility is that all theories of history, whatever their scope, remain empirically underdetermined or uncorroborated where not falsified. Since Anderson neither conducts an intertheoretical comparison nor presents empirical substantiation, we are given no means of arbitrating the claims he makes. We have only his authority for them.

Which authority? Anderson's affidavit for Marxism in *In the Tracks of Historical Materialism* makes for an interesting contrast with the afterword to *Considerations on Western Marxism*, where it was said to involve a series of 'great unanswered problems' (p. 121). It may be, of course, that less than a decade later he reckoned some of the problems to have been resolved. But his implicit estimate of 'scientific socialism' suggests otherwise. For the riddles of the Sphinx extend beyond the 'poverty of strategy' (p. 28) to encompass the plausibility of the proletarian agency, and the viability of the universalist goal, of socialism.

Archimedes promised to move the earth if allocated a firm spot. In his conclusion Anderson writes that Marxism 'has no reason to abandon its Archimedean vantage-point: the search for subjective agencies capable of effective strategies for the dislodgement of objective structures' (p. 105). Earlier (p. 94), he had located the superiority of 'scientific' over 'utopian' socialism in the 'Archimedean point' that the former assigned to the working class in capitalist machinofacture.[147] Here, by contrast, it is Marxism itself—not the collective labourer—which occupies that point. In any usage, the metaphor is a hazardous one in connection with historical materialism. As George Lichtheim once observed, on classical Marxist premisses the class struggle

> indicated the general direction which mankind had to take if it wanted to transcend the bourgeois horizon. Consequently there was was no need for an Archimedean standpoint outside history (of the kind philosophy has traditionally undertaken to supply), quite apart from the fact that belief in the possibility of such a location in extrahistorical space was an illusion.[148]

Anderson would justifiably deny that his 'Archimedean vantage-point' is 'extrahistorical' (albeit it contains intimations of extraterrestriality). But what cannot be gainsaid is that his closing elaboration of the conceit cancels its pretention. It simultaneously allots historical materialism firm ground and cuts the ground from under it: the vantage point turns into the quest for one—and not surprisingly, on Anderson's own reckoning. The historical agency of socialism had not performed the role assigned it in the classical scripts; its ascribed potentiality had not been redeemed in actuality. Hence, even if, notwithstanding its radical 'recomposition' (p. 105), the working class survived, that only furnished a necessary condition for the execution of its historical mission in the future. The traditional strategies for socialism—reformist and revolutionary—had each, in their different ways, misfired, without stimulating an alternative scenario for a viable transition to socialism. And the credibility and desirability of the goal of socialism—the 'common end'—was itself in question, in view of twentieth-century history. Compared with the scientific socialism of Marx and Lenin, this was the very epitome of terra infirma.

And yet—now in Galilean fashion—the earth had moved. October 1917 and its descendants offered such empirical warrant as Anderson could muster for his reaffirmation of the historical rationality of revolutionary socialism. In consequence, his estimation of the relationship between Western Marxism and historical Communism equally applied to him:

> The Western Marxist tradition had always been marked by a peculiar combination of tension and dependence in its relation to it. On the one hand, this was a filiation which from its very outset . . . had embodied hopes and aspirations for a developed socialist *democracy* which the implacable machinery of bureaucratic dictatorship crushed in the USSR with the rise of

Stalin. However mediated, sublimated or displaced . . . the ideal of a political order beyond capital that would be more, rather than less, advanced
than the parliamentary regimes of the West, never deserted it. Hence the
permanently critical distance of the Western Marxist tradition from the
state structures of the Soviet Union. . . . On other hand, this tradition
nearly always had a sense of the extent to which the Russian Revolution and
its sequels, whatever their barbarities or deformities, represented the sole
real breach with the order of capital that the twentieth century has yet
seen—hence the ferocity of the onslaughts of the capitalist states against
them. (Pp. 68–69)

Whatever the fluctuations of his political orientation within the universe of
revolutionary Marxism after 1968, by 1983 Anderson's relation to international Communism was likewise one of 'constitutive ambiguity' (p. 69),
'marked by a peculiar combination of tension and dependence'. It is not
quite accurate to speak, as did Ronald Aronson, of 'the hole at the centre
of [Anderson's] international Marxism unattached to any specific movement and not buoyed up by any current or party'.[149] For although (to
employ Aronson's terms) Anderson could not root his work in revolutionary movements or advances in the *West*, the personal authority of his text
was, in some measure, historically anchored in the *East*. Notwithstanding
its 'barbarities or deformities', Communism had enacted—and still embodied—a 'real breach with the order of capital'. The sole such rupture, its
existence rendered the prospect of future breaches, West and East, something more than mere *Zukunftsmusik*. In the absence of other (superior)
candidates, the placeholder of socialist practice, imparting ballast to Marxist theory and supplying partial (if distorted) validation of it, provisionally
reposed in historical Communism. Courtesy of Trotsky's 'merciless laboratory of history', the poetry of the future was precariously predicated on
the barbarities of the past, the deformites of the present. What little we
have, we hold.[150]

An unwitting Western Marxist even as he bid his tradition adieu,
Anderson held 'hopes and aspirations' for a 'developed socialist democracy'
whose privileged terrain would be the currently inhospitable advanced capitalist world. But he was thus left in the approximate position identified by
Aronson: '[p]rojecting the idea of socialism *against* its actual history and
outcome'.[151] The crisis of Marxism—and revolutionary socialism—could be
deflected only by a gesture to the East and a wager on the West that bespoke
its profundity.

Retrenchment

In his 'Brief History of *New Left Review*', Blackburn blandly notes that '[t]owards the end of the [1980–84] period there was a recomposition of the editorial committee, with about half of those who had joined in the mid sixties withdrawing and several new editors joining'.[152] This 'recomposition'—the resignation of two key members (Barnett and Halliday) and the departure, in solidarity with them, of half of the (mostly inactive) editorial complement—followed Anderson's relinquishment of the editorship.[153]

The details of this revealing crisis are beyond our remit. Despite surfacing tensions over developments in Britain, substantive disagreements were at a discount. Scrutiny of internal documents can even create the impression that a single spark—the misprinting of Anderson's Trotsky text—lit a prairie fire.[154] Setting aside the grievances submitted by various parties, the most acute reflections derived from Mulhern. His decipherment of the 'NLR romance' identified a self-conception that crossed Sartreanism—a collective of free-floating intellectuals exempt from sublunary determinants—with Leninism—a party of professional revolutionaries subject to 'integrist' disciplines (of a common-law, rather than statute, variety). Whatever its original rationale, this hybrid identity was now neither sustainable nor salutary.[155]

In the aftermath of this dispute, a reconstruction of the *NLR* rather different from the one eventually undertaken was attempted. It would have involved the recruitment of five prominent socialist-feminists. However, their demands were deemed unacceptable by a majority of the remaining editors.[156] Accordingly, although the *NLR* began to give sustained attention to feminism for the first time,[157] recomposition of the editorial committee integrated figures seemingly more attuned to 'resolute socialism'.[158] Its general character can be gauged from the revised constitution and charter of the *Review*, which proved an obstacle to feminist co-option and generated controversy on the existing editorial committee.

The preamble to the constitution stipulated that the *Review* was 'an independent socialist journal' whose 'general character . . . is Marxist'.[159] Its ambition was not simply to reflect left-wing opinion but to 'promote' and 'develop' its own 'coherent and distinctive theoretical positions' (p. 2). Membership of its committee was dependent upon 'a commitment to the political ideals of NLR' (p. 4), which were set out in the ten points of its charter. Therein, the *Review* was pronounced 'a Marxist journal':

> Its primary allegiance . . . is to the tradition of historical materialism. The journal does not view that tradition as composing either a closed, comprehensive

183

or completely unified corpus of ideas. Nor does it regard it as coextensive with all socialist culture of value. . . . Marxism is simply, for NLR, far the largest and weightiest body of theory to have been produced within the international socialist movement, . . . and the only one to provide a truly general paradigm for analysis of the evolution of humanity as a whole. The review holds it a duty at once to develop and to criticize the cumulative heritage of Marxist thought . . . while at the same time defending it firmly from all attacks or attempts to dissolve it from the Right.[160]

This statement of theoretical antirevisionism led into a sequence of antireformist political clauses. The first articulated a basically Deutschero-Trotskyist position on the Second World:

> The political tradition in which NLR situates itself essentially starts this century from the Bolshevik Revolution. The overthrow of capitalism in Russia . . . was the first, decisive breach in the world imperialist system. . . . Counterrevolutionary intervention and blockade, dire material and cultural scarcity, and lack of institutional foreknowledge and experience, combined to generate an authoritarian bureaucracy in the Soviet Union in subsequent years. . . . Nevertheless, the Russian Revolution and the Soviet state . . . remained a central inspiration for a series of further revolutions in backward zones over the next half century. . . . *Today post-revolutionary states . . . represent a historic progress over the capitalist or pre-capitalist societies that preceded them, and a critical bulwark against imperialism.* The review will defend them as such against every variety of capitalist attack. . . . At the same time, they also represent different forms and degrees of repressive tutelage over the working population. . . . The review will defend the cause of the ordinary working people in these countries against the institutions which stifle them at home. . . . It supports the radical democratic reconstruction of the state orders of all the post-capitalist states. It judges their actions in the light of the interests of the international socialist movement, and of humanity as a whole. (P. 5; my emphasis)

While recognizing the process of uneven capitalist development in selected capitalist countries of the South, the *NLR* was committed to anti-imperialist struggle against the 'hierarchy of power and wealth on a global scale', whose chief Western guardian was the United States (p. 6). Anti-anti-Soviet and anti-imperialist, but non–Third Worldist, the *Review*'s charter proceeded to reaffirm a revolutionary-socialist position on the First World.

In respect of agencies and strategies for socialism in the advanced capitalist zone, it rejected

> either edulcoration of the nature and mechanisms of the bourgeois state, or minimization of the capacity of the industrial working class potentially arrayed against it. At the same time, it accepts the necessarily probabilistic bounds of all strategic arguments over a transition from advanced capitalism to socialism . . . and seeks to promote serious and imaginative debate about it. In the same way it also acknowledges the need for the construction of a wide popular bloc against capital that integrates very diverse social groups—unemployed, self-employed and domestically confined, including above all those oppressed by racism and sexism—beyond the frontiers of either manual or mental wage-labour itself. (P. 7)

The traditional centrality of the working class in the movement for socialism was thus upheld. Contra contemporary Bernsteins, definition of the goal was, if anything, even more canonical:

> the elimination of all private property in the principal means of production and communication, and their collective control by the associated producers themselves, within the overall framework of freely determined central planning. . . . The political shape of such a producers' democracy will greatly enlarge the basic civil liberties . . . that exist in the advanced capitalist societies today, dissociating them from a narrow and distant parliamentary framework for a far broader, closer and more complex web of popular sovereignty covering economic, cultural and social life alike. . . . NLR regards it as a priority of its theoretical work to explore . . . the possible relations and structures of such a future socialism. (P. 8)

Raised in the quinquennial report and reprised in *In the Tracks of Historical Materialism*, the relationship between socialism and other emancipatory movements was broached in the penultimate and antepenultimate clauses of the charter. Asserting that '[t]he cause of socialism is not coextensive with that of all human emancipation', these certified the 'necessity and autonomy of the movements for peace and women's emancipation' (p. 9). In the case of the former, the Charter codified the principles that had governed collective contributions to the *Exterminism* symposium. The *NLR's* recognition of the 'historical imperative' of the struggle for peace did not entail 'equat[ion]' of

185

the military record or posture of the two major powers—the aggressive, world-wide network of American bases, the dropping of the atomic bomb on Japan, repeated nuclear menace and blackmail in Korea, Vietnam, Cuba or the Middle East by the USA, and the basically defensive reactions to these since 1945 by the USSR. Nor does it divorce the strategic confrontation between the two from its origins in the sleepless drive of international counter-revolution to crush or contain upheavals against capitalism. (P. 9)

In the case of the women's movement, resisting the political logic articulated by such texts as Sheila Rowbotham et al.'s *Beyond the Fragments*, the charter analyzed socialism and feminism as 'distinct forces', thereby insulating the former from the latter:

Sexual oppression predates class oppression, and could survive it, if this struggle [against the structures of male domination] is not successfully engaged by the Left. At the same time, socialism and feminism are distinct forces. The former has everything to gain by alliance with the latter as a movement; and owes it all practical and critical support. But neither can absorb or merge with the other: the autonomy of each is inscribed in their different, equally essential goals. Just as NLR is not a peace journal, but a socialist journal that supports the peace movement, so it is not a feminist journal but a socialist journal that supports the women's movement. (P. 10)[161]

This collective statement of principles was soon rendered more or less redundant—in part, by sharp disputes on the reconstructed committee in 1986 over institutional support for the journal *Labour Focus on Eastern Europe* (in which several *NLR* members—Hoare, Magaš, Gowan, and Camiller—played a prominent role), following which Mulhern resigned. Well might Blackburn observe that 'it is not easy to gain a perspective on the most recent period in the Review's history, NLR 143–84 [1983–90]' (p. x). Nevertheless, the charter does illuminate Anderson's own outlook at the beginning of this period. Their greater sobriety apart, its main clauses are largely consonant with the 'ten theses' a decade and a half earlier. Albeit markedly less hostile to the Soviet Union—an index of their freedom from any residual Maoist influence—their filiation remains with the tradition of revolutionary Marxism and socialism.

Anderson's limited public output from 1984 to 1986 gave expression to different aspects of this outlook. His trenchant preface to the Deutscher collection *Marxism, Wars, and Revolutions* (1984) has already been signalled. The sole text by him in the *Review* in these years was a contribution to a conference entitled 'Marxism and the Interpretation of Culture', held at the University of Illinois in 1983.[162] Responding to Marshall Berman's ambitious conjugation of 'modernization', 'modernity', and 'modernism' in *All That Is Solid Melts into Air*, Anderson challenged its account of modernist art as insufficiently differentiated, and its conception of revolutionary change as unduly diffuse. 'The echoes of sixties radicalism are unmistakeable here', he wrote with regard to the latter, refusing any substitution of Bakunin for Marx, antinomianism for historical materialism:

> Attraction to such notions has proved very widespread. But they are not . . . compatible either with the theory of historical materialism . . . , or with the record of history itself. . . . Revolution is a term with a precise political meaning: the political overthrow from below of one state order and its replacement by another. Nothing is to be gained by diluting it across time, or extending it over every department of social space. In the first case, it becomes indistinguishable from simple reform . . . ; in the second . . . , it dwindles to a mere metaphor. . . . Against these slack devaluations of the term, . . . it is necessary to insist that revolution is a punctual and not a permanent process. . . . What would be distinctive about a socialist revolution that created a genuine post-capitalist democracy is that the new state would be truly transitional towards the practicable limits of its own self-dissolution into the associated life of society as a whole. (P. 44)[163]

The historical conditions and open sociopolitical horizons that had seeded the avant-gardes of the early twentieth century, whether symbolist or expressivist, constructivist or surrealist, had largely disappeared from the West after the Second World War, with the stabilization of liberal capitalism and Stalinism either side of the Elbe. Extrapolating from them, Anderson reflected:

> In the advanced capitalist world today, it is the seeming absence of any such prospect as a proximate or even distant horizon—the lack, apparently, of any conjecturable alternative to the imperial status quo of a consumer capitalism—that blocks the likelihood of any profound cultural renovation comparable to the great Age of Aesthetic Discoveries in the first third of this century. (P. 44)

The category of 'modernism', privileged signifier of an aesthetic ideology that postdated the demise of the distinct artistic practices it homogenized, was 'vacant'—rivalled in its vacuity only by that of 'post-modernism': 'one void chasing another, in a serial regression of self-congratulatory chronology' (p. 45).[164]

Mentioned for the first time in Anderson's oeuvre here, the discourse of postmodernism was assailed by him in the 1985 postscript appended to 'Modernity and Revolution' in *A Zone of Engagement*. Lyotard's *Postmodern Condition* was now brusquely summarized, and brutally despatched, as Parisian *prêt-à-penser*:

> history without narrative; individuals without identity; discourse without meaning; art without representation; science without truth. In place of all these, Lyotard proposes the play of infinite language-games, the paralogism of incompatible conceptual planes, . . . and—above all—the cult of the unsayable intensities of the libidinal instant: in the end sole arbiter and value of post-modern existence. Politically, the consequences of this degraded ecstaticism are obvious enough. Everything else may disappear, volatilized in the mixer of post-modernism, but capitalism remains intact as the motor of its energetics. *'Le capital fait jouir'*—Lyotard's lesson—is the slogan of Dionysus in Disneyland. Intellectually, this critique of modernity is trifling. No meta-narrative is so sweeping or speculative as that of the so-called 'post-modern condition' itself. (Pp. 48–49)

Intrinsic to the 'post-modern condition' was a relativism antithetical to socialism:

> For a consequent cultural relativism must be conservative. If all cultures are in principle equally valuable . . . why fight for a better one? The energies of modernity, once generated by capitalism, are now ever more trapped and compromised by it. That is another reason for remaining true to the hope of a passage beyond this world order. (Pp. 54–55)[165]

Far from repenting classical Marxist recidivism as the 1980s progressed, Anderson adopted an *arrière-garde* stance in defiance of the recherché relativisms—cognitive, ethical, aesthetic—arrayed against it. That he did not consider socialist fidelity a political velleity is evident from a conference paper dating from summer 1984, 'On Some Postulates of an Anti-systemic Policy in Western Europe', coauthored with three members of the Stärnberg Institute for the Study of Global Structures.[166]

The paper began by exploring the causes of the capitalist stagflation of the 1970s. These had been twofold: the enhanced strength of labour vis-à-vis capital at the point of production in the 'Fordist' labour process, and the erosion of U.S. hegemony in the global economy. The end of the long boom had intersected with challenges to the metropolis from peripheral capitalism (in the shape of the oil bloc), and from socialism (the domino effect, relayed to the core states, triggered by the Vietnamese Revolution) (p. 4). Confronted with this series of interlocking (and mutually reinforcing) problems, which attested to a volatile correlation of forces both *within* capitalism and *between* it and its socialist antagonists, the American empire had struck back on all fronts (p. 6). Whatever its present limits and future prospects, Reaganite revanchism had succeeded in restoring U.S. supremacy over the capitalist world.

Of the major Western powers, only France had attempted to chart a national, social-democratic course against the international, neoliberal current. This had been wrecked by the unchecked countervailing powers of the world market, whereupon the Socialist administration had reversed direction, resorting to an austerity programme (p. 13). Its short-lived counter-cyclical experiment had foundered upon Mitterand's external option for Atlanticism and commitment to French imperial status, in a repetition of the inauspicious precedent of Wilson's Labour government two decades before (p. 14). An 'anti-systemic' politics dictated greater radicalism than Social-Democratic reformism (p. 15).

This, in turn, required the specification of a feasible programmatic alternative to the New Right and identification of political forces with the power to prosecute it. Addressing the latter issue, Anderson and his coauthors took comfort from the seeming resurgence of the labour movement in Western Europe in 1984—evidenced, for example, by the miners' defence of their industry in Britain and IG Metall's strike action for a thirty-five-hour week in West Germany. Retaining defensive strength by dint of its objective location and organizational entrenchment, the labour movement possessed offensive antisystemic potential (pp. 17–18). By contrast, the 'new social movements' were lacking in equivalent structural capacity, yet they had demonstrated their imaginative and mobilizing superiority over the labour movement. Consequently, a reciprocally beneficial anticapitalist alliance of the two was indicated, for the purposes of a contemporary universalism (pp. 18–19). The centrality, not exclusivity, of the workers' movement: such was the strategic dimension of a radical, but realistic, antisystemic politics in Western Europe, which effectively advocated a cross-fertilization—and concertation—of the long-separated traditions of 'scientific' and 'utopian' socialism.

Obviously, it would be imprudent to assume that Anderson subscribed to each and every nuance of this paper. That said, it exhibits a feature familiar from other writings we have examined: it is stronger on some premisses and postulates—the conformation of the international conjuncture and the fatal contradiction in any purely national response to it—than on others. Thus, there is not merely a marked disproportion between delineation of the adverse circumstances facing socialists, and adumbration of an antisystemic programme to surmount them (pp. 20–25); at a strategic level, there is what rapidly proved to be an unwarranted assumption about the repoliticization of the labour movement—its imminent rejuvenation, contrary to premature obituaries, under neoliberal provocation (p. 18). It is true that Anderson et al., alluding to the U.S. experience (p. 19), feared an Americanization of European trade-unionism in the absence of an anticapitalist expansion of its traditional agenda. Yet the desideratum of a new universalism, anticipated from a coalition of old labour and new social movements, pointed to the missing third term of their paper: the synthesizing role of a party, which had been foregrounded in Anderson's last extended reflection on syndicalism and socialism, in 1967 (discussed in chapter 2 of this book).

Silence on this score was perhaps inevitable. A subsequent article, published in the U.S. Trotskyist journal *Against the Current* in 1986, indicates why: the spectre of American capitalism was haunting not solely the trade unions of Europe.[167] Addressing fellow revolutionary socialists in the New World, Anderson tracked the recent misadventures of Social-Democracy in the Old. Displacing a constitutionalist Eurocommunism, the southern European parties of the Second International—Mitterrand's in the van—had formed governments throughout the Continental zone in the 1980s. They had therewith fleetingly promised to redeem the discredit that their northern cousins—Schmidt and Callaghan at their head—had incurred by capitulation to monetarist orthodoxy in the mid-1970s. The experience had proved uniformly dispiriting, portending something more profound than a mere conjunctural disorientation of reformism. In paragraphs not reproduced in *English Questions*, Anderson's analysis concluded as follows:

> The classical formations of Social Democracy in Northern Europe have exhausted their distinctive historical function. The new contingents of Southern Europe have not been able to reproduce it. . . . [T]he real approximation that could be in store is . . . the gradual conversion of European Social Democratic organizations into something like the American Democratic Party. That is, [their emasculation] of any antagonistic class content and transformation into mere substitute apparatuses of bourgeois rule. . . . The final erasure of the traditions of the Third International from the map of the European labour movement . . . was . . . a fundamental reverse for the cause of socialism. The final corruption and disappearance of the heritage of

the Second International . . . would compound a historic regression. Were it to occur, by the end of the century Western Europe could resemble the United States or Japan of today. There is still a long way to go before such a scenario is realized. . . . The Old World is not an insulated area, and any major upheavals against capital or bureaucracy elsewhere could change the situation within it—as they did . . . in the late 60s. Socialists should never forget that there is always more than one current in the sea. (P. 28)

Corroboration of Anderson's prescient worst-case scenario would arrive with greater rapidity than he feared. Like Deutscher before him, his fortitude, amid the collapse of so many edifices of the Left, is arresting. In 1986 he was undeflected from his revolutionary-socialist course by the 'historic regression' he contemplated—one in which the erasure of Communist traditions from Western traditions weighed more than that of Social-Democratic ones. Equally striking, in retrospect, is the investment of residual hopes in 'forces of ferment and resistance' within these organizations in the 1980s (p. 28) and his invocation of the happy precedent of the 'revolts against capital or bureaucracy' in Vietnam, France, and Prague in the 1960s. Socialist resistance subsided, under the impact of successive industrial, political, and electoral defeats. The revolts against bureaucracy transpired. But when they did, they betokened not the posthumous revenge of the Communist renovation interred in Prague in August 1968, but the very capitalist restoration against whose imaginary threat the Warsaw Pact had been mobilized. And with that 'fundamental reverse'—'historic regression' for a thinker who located himself in '[t]he political tradition . . . [that] essentially starts . . . from the October Revolution', whose offspring were 'a critical bulwark against imperialism', to be 'defend[ed] . . . as such against every variety of capitalist attack'—the last edifice of Anderson's revolutionary Marxism was consumed in the refining fires of historical irony. To switch metaphors (and elements): by 1986, the firm ground invoked in *Arguments within English Marxism* and staked out in *In the Tracks of Historical Materialism* had dissolved into marine cross-currents.

In his article on Berman, Anderson had cited Régis Debray's characterization of May '68 as the French route to America, travelled by cultural revolutionaries embarking for China, only to land in California.[168] There, at all events, in one of the world's largest capitalist economies—pioneer of the New Right counterrevolution—an Archimedean vantage point of sorts was to be had. And the motto of the Golden State, since the discovery in it of gold? 'Eureka!'.

4 ▸ The Verdict of the World

In the foreword to *A Zone of Engagement*, Anderson remarks the essential continuity between its first three chapters—on de Ste. Croix, Deutscher, and Berman—dated 1982–84, and 'The Antinomies of Antonio Gramsci', released in 1976.[1] 'The historical method and findings of this essay', he writes, 'seem to me to have lost none of their validity':

> But its aim was also political. Written in the wake of the Portuguese Revolution . . . [it] sought to draw a balance-sheet of the last great strategic debate of the international labour movement, for struggles still pending. That . . . was my expressed intention. When it appeared, however, I received a letter from . . . Franco Moretti . . . telling me that I had written a farewell in fitting style to the revolutionary Marxist tradition. . . . [T]his was not a verdict I was disposed to accept. But . . . his judgement proved better than mine. (P. xi)

From the mid-1980s onward, both terms in the revolutionary-Marxist couplet had been subjected to ominous challenge: its theory by a serious contender to the title of 'historical materialism', its politics by the 'societal ascendancy of the West' (p. xii). A 'turning point' in Anderson's politico-intellectual reactions was marked by the accounts of Michael Mann's sociology of power in 1986, and of Norberto Bobbio's attempted liberal-socialist synthesis in 1988, to which *A Zone of Engagement* proceeds. Indeed, after 1985, an unwontedly magnanimous note is struck in his coverage of non-Marxist oeuvres and even anti-Marxist figures. (For example, no one acquainted with the accents of 'Socialism and Pseudo-Empiricism' or 'Components of the National Culture' would associate the respectful tones of 'The Pluralism of Isaiah Berlin' [1990] with the same author.)

The Andersonian turn is not in dispute. Two features of it may be noted at the outset. First, as he makes clear (p. xii), what awoke him from something akin—in public—to a dogmatic slumber over classical Marxism was not poststructuralism (or its postmodernist pendant), but the emergence of precisely that alternative 'theory of historical development' whose absence had been confidently proclaimed as recently as October 1985.[2] Second, aided in this by the omission of 'Trotsky's Interpretation of Stalinism', which would have demonstrated the centrality of the 'workers' states' to

192

Anderson's 'particular standpoint within . . . the world of the revolutionary
Left' (p. xii), he understates the extent to which his revolutionary Marxism
must have been disconcerted by the crisis, then collapse, of the Second World,
and the consequent virtual social *exclusivity*—not merely ascendancy—of
capitalism.

The relaxation of the 'unity of theory and practice' in the afterword to
Considerations on Western Marxism had, in effect, begun to redefine 'scientific socialism' as the external conjunction of an explanatory research
programme—historical materialism—and a political tradition—socialism.
Anderson's words of intellectual solace for Marxism in the final paragraphs
of the foreword to *A Zone of Engagement* tend to consummate this process.
They also attest, however, to a continuing failure to engage with the weaknesses of the classical Marxist legacy at its very core, as intimated in
Considerations: its claim to afford not merely *a* 'critique of political economy' but *the* science of 'the natural laws of capitalist production'.[3] Suggesting the persistent or renascent vitality of structuralism, evolutionism, functionalism, and existentialism in some of the authors he examines—Ginzburg
and Runciman, Gellner and Unger—Anderson rightly infers that 'a significant research programme is never spent as soon as its critics suppose', and
extrapolates as follows:

> The future of Marxism is unlikely to be very different. Its most powerful in-
> tellectual challengers, the various historical sociologies now arrayed against
> it, share a blind side whose importance is constantly increasing. They have
> little, if anything, to say about the dynamics of the capitalist economy that
> now rules without rival over the fate of the earth. Here the normative the-
> ory which has accompanied its triumph is equally . . . bereft: the Hayekian
> synthesis, disclaiming systematic explanation of the paths of long-term
> growth or of structural crisis. The come-back of historical materialism will
> probably be on this terrain. (P. xiv)

Declining to discard historical materialism while hinting that the revenant
will not be classical Marxism, where does this leave Anderson?

Ghostlier Demarcations

In *Considerations on Western Marxism*, Anderson not only scripted his own
ulterior development but also foreshadowed the common insurmountable
dilemma of independent Marxist intellectuals after the fall:

Everything happened as if the rupture of political unity between Marxist theory and mass practice resulted in an irresistible *displacement* of the tension that should have linked the two. In the absence of the magnetic pole of a revolutionary class movement, the needle of the whole tradition tended to swing increasingly towards contemporary bourgeois culture. The original relationship between Marxist theory and proletarian practice was subtly but steadily substituted by a new relationship between Marxist theory and bourgeois theory. The historical reasons for this reorientation did not . . . lie simply in the deficit of mass revolutionary practice in the West. Rather, the blockage of any socialist advance in the nations of advanced capitalism itself determined the total cultural configuration within these societies. . . . Above all, the successful restabilization of imperialism . . . meant that major sectors of bourgeois thought retained a relative vitality and superiority over socialist thought. The bourgeois order in the West had not exhausted its historical life-span.[4]

With appropriate alteration of details, an analogous 'displacement' can be observed in Anderson's Marxism, against the backdrop of the triumphant imperialist 'restabilization' of the 1980s—a process no doubt overdetermined by his option not simply (like Deutscher) to become a professional historian but (unlike him) to pursue that vocation from a professorial chair, as any semblance of a collective project at the *Review* he had edited for two decades evaporated. It was signalled in a review of the first volume of Michael Mann's *The Sources of Social Power*, in the *Times Literary Supplement*, in December 1986; developed in successive surveys—in the *NLR*, the *London Review of Books*, and elsewhere—of non-Marxist thinkers (Norberto Bobbio and Roberto Unger, W. G. Runciman and Isaiah Berlin, Carlo Ginzburg and Fernand Braudel, Micheal Oakeshott and John Rawls); and consolidated in a forty-five-thousand-word retrospect of 'Components of the National Culture', published in the *NLR*, in two instalments, in 1990. An overly convenient way of summarizing it might be to say that in *English Questions* and *A Zone of Engagement*, there is still some importance in being Ernest, but the Ernest in question is Gellner—not Mandel.

On inspection, Anderson's assessment of the new Anglo-Weberian historical sociology—involving projects comparable in scale to Marx's *Capital* and thus far no less unfinished than it (or Sartre's *Critique of Dialectical Reason*, for that matter)—would not appear to warrant the conclusion drawn by him. Belying the ceremony accorded them, in each instance theoretical frailties and empirical fallibilities are discerned that would, by Anderson's norms, render inadmissible any claim to have surpassed Marx.[5] Indeed, as with Cohen's defence of an 'old-fashioned' Marxism in *Karl Marx's Theory of History*—erstwhile recipient of Andersonian accolades—it is reasonable to surmise that Anderson's dawning pessimism of the intelligence regarding historical materialism derived less from intertheoretical comparison than from empirical discomfiture. Faced with the concurrent 'societal ascendancy of the West' and 'structural crisis' of advanced capitalism—a combination that contradicted classical prognostications—contemporary Marxism and Weberianism alike had 'little, if anything, to say about the dynamics of the capitalist economy that now rules without rival over the fate of the earth'. The real concern, it might be ventured, was not an implausible superiority of Mann over Marx but their mutual incapacity to rise to the explanatory challenge posed them. At all events, Anderson was quite unperturbed by fashionable, broadly anti-Enlightenment critiques of Marxism. Responding to Giddens's *Contemporary Critique of Historical Materialism* (1981), for example, he contended that 'a moderately formulated evolutionism'—of the historical-materialist sort reconstructed by Erik Olin Wright, as opposed to the immoderate version propounded by Cohen, or the quasi-Spencerian variety reanimated by Runciman—'has no difficulty in defending its plausibility'.[6]

Arrayed against Marxism in one sense, the new historical sociologies are aligned with it by Anderson in another. Kindred spirits at the level of theoretical scope, they thus mounted a line of defence for the kind of historical materialism to which he was committed, against the infinitely more corrosive claims of poststructuralism. The summation in 'A Culture in Contraflow' itemizes the negative, yet accentuates the positive, in these 'totalizations':

[T]hese constructions . . . share a general architecture that derives its design from the confrontation with Marxism. Their central claim about the structure of human history is twofold. Firstly, there is no primacy of economic causation to it: military-political and ideological-cultural determinations are of equivalent significance. None of these three has any universal privilege: different societies and different epochs exhibit different dominants. . . . Secondly, this permutation in rank of importance obeys no pattern: the procession of variant institutional hierarchies . . . is contingent—not a chapter, but an encyclopedia of accidents. In their negative sense contentions like these have . . . long formed part of the critique of historical materialism in the West. What is new here is their positive instrumentation into a full-scale *alternative*. . . . In the years in which they became the bugbear of advanced opinion on the Continent, totalizations—of heroic magnitude—finally acquired *droit de cité* in Britain.[7]

'A Culture in Contraflow' reversed 'Components of the National Culture', offering a catalogue raisonné in lieu of a fusillade. Anderson rescinded the national nihilism of diagnosis and 'triumphalism' of prescription that had vitiated the latter (p. 193). Renunciation of cultural Luxemburgism did not entail dissent from Trotsky's dictum that '[h]istorical truth is not a lady-in-waiting on national pride'.[8] However, Anderson's political measurement of the cultural climate yielded a decidedly positive reading:

> The period 1968–1988 . . . saw a set of gradual changes in the historic physiognomy of the British intelligentsia. An original Marxist culture of the Left gained ground, against a background of campus unrest and industrial militancy; a combative culture of the Right . . . emerged to inform a government determined to wipe the slate clean of them; and the traditional culture of the Centre . . . was ruffled into an unaccustomed *fronde* by the outcome. The net balance of these shifts was a movement running contrary to the course taken by the state: the political and intellectual worlds went in opposite directions. . . . [A] regime of the radical Right part confronted, part created an overall cultural drift to the left. . . . [I]ts attempt at a *Gleichschaltung* of the academy tended to raise up the very adversaries it sought to stamp out, even as its drive to impose the values of the counting-house and constabulary on society swept forward elsewhere. While an authoritarian populism was redrawing the electoral contours of the country to the advantage of capital, in this domain the hegemonic legacy weakened. (Pp. 199–200)

What are we to make of this—a view from afar and above? The first thing to note is that, even were the thesis of an academic-cultural radicalization in response to the New Right to be accepted, that would not licence Anderson's conclusion that it was tantamount to a mobilization against 'capital', as opposed to neoliberal (de)regulation of it. Second, and relatedly, the sound of goalposts being moved—a revaluation of values—is unmistakable here: academic recalcitrance to political reaction is construed as intellectual radicalization. Yet it would be equally plausible to argue that, although the polity moved—to the right—the academy (if not the polytechnics, counting-houses par excellence) stood pat—in the middle of the road (where it predictably got run over). The fact that Sir Keith Joseph and his like incriminated Liberals in a collectivist conspiracy with Marxists against the propensity to truck, barter, and exchange is eloquent testimony to his radicalism (not to mention paranoia)—not that of centre opinion. In any event, third, which is it to be? A 'traditional' moderation of the Centre, acquiring credentials of heterodoxy by resistance to modern neoliberalism? Or a 'radicalization' of it, stirred up by executive repudiation of postwar orthodoxies? Anderson seems unsure. The 'large changes' he divines issue from the converse adversities of 1968 and 1988, the cultural revolution aimed at by the New Left ceding to a *'Kulturkampf'* instigated by the New Right, with all the resources of state power behind it (p. 194). On the one hand, we are informed that '[t]he great bulk of the British intellectual establishment held fast to its moderate liberal verities, indifferent or hostile to creeds of either Left or Right'. On the other, it appears that, bellicose neoliberalism having discountenanced 'peaceable conformism', 'an unmistakable radicalization of Centre opinion [ensued], within its traditional boundaries' (p. 198).

We need not ponder these uncertainties of emphasis, since, fourth, just as the Thatcher dispensation decisively altered the parameters of party-political contention in Britain in the 1980s, so too it set in train a fundamental reconfiguration *rightward* of the national intellectual culture—a shift sufficiently evidenced by a 1994 report from the Commission on Social Justice, instituted by an accommodationist Labour Party, whose philosophical premisses owed more to Robert Nozick than John Rawls, and by whose derisory criteria J. S. Mill (let alone T. H. Marshall) would count as an incorrigible 'Leveller'. (Probably attributable to sheer ignorance—or culpable amnesia—the pejorative use of an honourable term, not from 1917 or even 1789, but 1649, is itself symptomatic in this regard.) Comprehensive counterrevolution incited no *'fronde'* in the senior common rooms, but rather an increasing, if unavailing, moderation. The conformities of the English would certainly have struck the frondeur of 1968, even as they eluded the connoisseur of 1990.

Nowhere was this more apparent than in the case of the *marxisant* intelligentsia that crystallized out of the 1960s to reinforce the cohorts of the 1930s (Communist) and 1950s (New Leftist). Anderson's retrospective benediction is suggestive of the distance he himself had moved since his disparagement, but a few years before, of the pervasive 'conformism' and 'revisionism' of left-wing intellectuals:

> [T]he arrival of the Thatcher regime . . . did not undo [the] cultural gains [of the 1970s]. Put to the test, the critical zone not only resisted but grew. Although the Conservative ascendancy soon transmitted a whole series of tensions through the Left, . . . these stimulated rather than depressed theoretical debate and exploration. . . . [W]hatever the strains imposed by political adversity . . . basic solidarity on the intellectual Left was rarely breached, and out of the trial emerged the liveliest republic of letters in European socialism. (P. 197)

As has been indicated, if 'basic solidarity' was not publicly breached and 'frictions' remained 'muffled' (p. 197), it was not exactly for want of trying on Anderson's part.[9]

A similar denegation attaches to the second major transformation of the national culture since 1968 identified by Anderson: namely, the subversion of its insularity. The political yardstick of 'Components' had been revolutionary socialism, not residual meliorism. Its cultural counter to English parochialism had been European Marxism, not mere cosmopolitanism. Thereafter, it will be recalled, as Anderson turned to classical Marxism, undue propinquity to 'bourgeois theory' had figured prominently in his critical *Considerations on Western Marxism*, whereas structuralism and post-structuralism had been taken to task in *In the Tracks of Historical Materialism*. Now, however, these and other trends—the 'noxious plethora of non- or anti-Marxist theories', the 'bric-à-brac', of the triennial report on the *NLR* (p. 44)—were granted a kind of Andersonian absolution, in which the sometime 'long night of theory' was transfigured into a radical cultural dawn:

> The emergence of a substantial culture of the Left after 1968 was the key which principally unlocked the gates to Europe. A wide absorption of the corpus of continental Marxism was the main initial consequence. . . . Structuralism . . . was received in an overlapping intellectual milieu through the seventies. Hermeneutics and post-structuralism followed in the eighties, . . . by and large still issuing into a public sphere whose sympathies were with socialism and now feminism. (Pp. 201–2)

The combination of cross-Channel and transatlantic interchanges did indeed generate the 'notable'—and desirable—'mutation' divined: 'British culture became looser and more hybrid' (p. 204). It will suffice to reiterate, however, that Anderson had once looked *outre-Manche* not out of credence in the inherent virtues of cross-fertilization but because the national culture signally lacked what the Continental abundantly possessed: the totalizing theory indispensable to revolutionary politics.

Anderson prefaced his update on the disciplines reviewed in 1968 with a salutary reminder that '[a] culture may lean to the left without being lively, just as it can innovate without being radical' (p. 205). It all depends, of course, on what is meant by 'radical'—a term that had already migrated to the retributive right in Britain. The tour conducted in 'A Culture in Contraflow', classifying authors and output in an intra- rather than inter-sectoral survey, commences with the former 'absent centre': an indigenous sociology. Twenty years on, 'the most prominent change of any discipline', attributable to the provocation of a national Marxist culture after 1968, was enthusiastically recorded (pp. 206–7). Indeed, island and mainland had virtually swapped roles in the Continental configuration, Britain now boasting what France and Italy (if not Germany) disdained. The other sector in which Anderson was able to discern progress was philosophy, where the supposedly Wittgensteinian legacy codified in the routines of the Oxford faculty had been widely renounced (pp. 252–53) and political theory in particular had flourished (p. 268).[10] By contrast, economics, of whatever political stripe, bemused by British decline in the 1960s, had since failed to generate 'major structural explanations of the world crisis or its outcomes' in the 1970s and 1980s (p. 281).

In 'Components of the National Culture', the literary criticism of Leavis had been perceived as tending the social totality on behalf of an absentee sociology. Now, in a section devoted to aesthetics, its transmutation into the 'cultural studies' most prominently associated with Hall and the Birmingham Centre was tracked via the work of Williams and Eagleton. Anderson's ambivalence toward one of their main results was manifest:

> There have been two directions from which literary value has come under pressure in the recent period: one a movement towards the social, or the democracy of significations, the other a shift towards the metaphysical, or the instability of significations. These might be called the Low Road and the High Road to the dissolution of the aesthetic. . . . There can be little doubt of the audience won for the case against literature made by these two foremost theorists of the Left in English studies. But such post-critical success has inevitably also had its pyrrhic side. For aesthetic value is not to be dispatched so easily—the wish to finish with it recalling Dobrolyubov, or Bazarov, more than Marx or Morris. (Pp. 242–43)[11]

Meanwhile, in historiography—especially of Britain—where Hill, Hobsbawm, Thompson, and their colleagues had attained a certain preeminence in the 1970s, the flow of intellectual and political traffic was more nearly in the same direction a decade later. Disciplinary developments correlated inversely with the pattern elsewhere: unlike historical sociology, 'revisionist' history shunned structural macroexplanation, especially in terms of social class (pp. 282-85). As is predictable from the arraignment of poststructuralism for its 'randomization of history' in *In the Tracks of Historical Materialism*, the alleged 'generic aleatorism' (p. 286) practiced by Alan Macfarlane, J. C. D. Clark, and others is anathema to Anderson.[12] Hence it was with some relief, though perhaps less plausibility, that he ended his panorama of this sector on an optimistic military note: '[V]iewing the period as a whole, while the significant tactical gains have been made by an intellectual Right, strategically the scattered battle-field looks less unevenly divided' (p. 293).

After a snapshot of feminism, which registered its dual impact upon established disciplines and in the inception of a new one ('women's studies'), and which offered a sanguine calculation of the political balance of forces within it (p. 299),[13] Anderson delivered summary judgement:

> By and large, . . . the political changes that came over the British intellectual scene in these years were accompanied by theoretical shifts of a related . . . character. . . . Where major sociology had once been missing, it became over-arching. Anthropology and aesthetics, traditional exceptions to a purblind empiricism and insensible positivism, tilted yet further away from them. Philosophy and economics . . . regain[ed] earlier moral energies and some mutual contact. In most of these areas, historical time . . . re-entered reflection; material life took on a new referential weight; sexual difference won lodgement. . . . One of the main lessons of the period is how many diversely productive ways of allying a sense of history with a respect for material reality there are. The variety that was once capitalized played its part in this transformation. . . . But the turn itself was broader and untidier than any set of doctrinal developments. . . . The particular *Gestalt* of the post-war culture, in so many ways vacantly asocial or slackly psychologistic, had dissolved. (Pp. 299–300)

That was the good news—suspectly so. By this yardstick, much twentieth-century intellectual production could count as lower-case historical-materialist. It would thus vindicate those nontheological critics for whom what is valid in the upper-case variety has long since been absorbed into the mainstream as a non-Marxist truism—'all[iance of] a sense of history with a respect for material reality'—whereas Marx's own particular conjugation of history and materiality—the explanatory primacy of the economic—may be consigned to the Marxian mice or Humean flames.[14]

The bad news might be thought to outweigh the welcome 'disjuncture of high culture and politics' (p. 300) and advent of a nonconformist intelligentsia postulated by Anderson. The contrast here is not between student turbulence in 1968 and campus quiescence two decades later, but between the academically sequestered, oppositional 'high culture' of the 1980s and the widely diffused, socialist 'popular culture' of the 1930s (p. 300). It prompted a characteristic conclusion:

[I]f no convergence of terms or audiences like that of the thirties was in sight during the eighties, the . . . fundamental reason was the absence of any significant political movement as a pole of attraction for intellectual opposition. . . . The one bold attempt to break the political log jam . . . , Charter 88, was an initiative of socialist and liberal forces within the intellectual world, aiming at constitutional reform. Too radical for the Labour leadership, it was modest compared with Conservative designs. For the comprehensive programme of social engineering that gave the Thatcher government its dynamism . . . elicited no alternative of similar scope. Similarly, the most powerful ideological vision of the Right, the ascendant Hayekian synthesis, remained without adequate response. Situations in which cultural production fails either to reflect or affect the political direction of a country are common enough. It was Mill who wrote that 'ideas, unless outward circumstances conspire with them, have in general no very rapid or immediate efficacy in human affairs'. But circumstances may also circumscribe ideas themselves. Some of the necessary ones were, in British conditions, still missing. (Pp. 300–301)

A final, typically proleptic paragraph will be discussed later. For now, we may note the return of an Andersonian leitmotiv already familiar from 'Problems of Socialist Strategy', via 'Components of the National Culture', to *Considerations on Western Marxism* and *Arguments within English Marxism*: the theory/practice nexus or intellectual culture/political movement dialectic. According to the Gramscian-Althusserian prescription of 'Components', 'revolutionary culture' was a prerequisite of 'revolutionary theory', which in turn constituted the precondition of a 'revolutionary movement'. In *Considerations*, diluting this incipient theoreticism with a large dose of 'activism', the critical stress had fallen upon the Leninist desideratum of 'the practical activity of a truly mass and truly revolutionary movement' as the matrix of 'correct revolutionary theory'. In *Arguments*, that imperative had been reasserted, with specific reference to England: '[T]he absence of a truly mass and truly revolutionary movement in England, as elsewhere in the West, has fixed the perimeters of all possible thought in this period'.[15]

The structure of the explanation employed to account for intellectual deficiency in 'A Culture in Contraflow' is analogous. Yet there are crucial differences in its terms. The conclusion to 'Components' had been able to nominate a provisional agency for its strategy of forging a revolutionary culture: the student movement. Its ideologism of optic issued in a kind of intellectual voluntarism, locating an Archimedean point from which to move, if

201

not the earth, then at least an island, with the lever of 'revolutionary practice within culture'. Twenty years later, history (to borrow Anderson's own
figure) had untied the Gordian knot of 1968, furnishing some of the resources with which to analyze British society (in part thanks to that cultural
practice). But it had tied another no less ingenious one, for whose severance
the indicated Alexander was wanting. Despite diminished political horizons—an 'alternative of similar scope' to Thatcherism, rather than revolutionary socialism—here, as in *Considerations* and *Arguments*, the upshot is a
form of fatalism.

Quoting Mill, Anderson soberly concedes the restricted political effec-
tivity of theory per se. (The lesson, if not the language, of Marx makes its
presence felt: 'Theory becomes a material force only when it grips the
masses'.) But he adds two qualifications. The first is that 'circumstances
may . . . circumscribe ideas', where the relevant circumstances are 'the absence of any significant political movement as a pole of attraction for intellectual opposition' (and no longer 'the absence of a truly mass and truly
revolutionary movement'). The second is that 'some of the necessary [ideas]
for an effective opposition were, in British conditions, still missing'—in
other words, that an absence of theory (in particular, an 'adequate' counter
to Hayek) was itself a material force, impeding effective opposition to the
implementation of neoliberalism by the Thatcher government.[16] Accordingly, 'A Culture in Contraflow' deposits us in the political void of a circular
causality depleted of any prospective redemptive agency intermediate between high culture and low politics: without propitious circumstances (*any*
significant political movement), no fully adequate ideas; without fully adequate ideas, no propitious circumstances (effective opposition). Alternatively
put, in its own—now nonrevolutionary—terms, 'A Culture in Contraflow'
testifies to a poverty of theory, strategy, and agency. Cultural contraflow ter-
minates in political gridlock.

Hayek had received only fleeting mention in 'Components of the National
Culture'. In 'A Culture in Contraflow' he was credited with 'furnish[ing] an
encompassing philosophical carapace—cultural and historical as well as economic and political—for . . . the case for a deregulated capitalism' (p. 271).
Anderson's sense of the salience of 'the intransigent right at the end of the
century' was expressed in a fine review-article of that title, in response to a
reedition of Oakeshott's *Rationalism in Politics*, two years later.[17] Its author
was assigned to

> the quartet of outstanding European theorists of the intransigent Right
> whose ideas now shape—however much, or little, leading practitioners are

aware of it—a large part of the mental world of end-of-century politics. It is alongside Carl Schmitt, Leo Strauss and Friedrich von Hayek that Michael Oakeshott is most appropriately seen. (P. 7)

Of the four, Hayek had furnished 'the most ambitious and complete synthesis to emerge from the ranks of the post-war Right'—one 'whose scope and strength have yet to be supplanted' (pp. 8, 11), whether on Right, Left, or Centre. Such considerations opened onto a disquieting conclusion, which registered not the transverse movements but the inverse ratios of academy and polity:

> If we compare the general fortunes of these thinkers of the radical Right to that of more conventional eminences of the Centre, there is a pregnant contrast. The work of just one theorist, John Rawls, has probably accumulated more scholarly commentary than that of all four put together. Yet this veritable academic industry has had virtually no impact on the world of Western politics. (P. 11)

A subsequent contribution by Anderson to that industry—a critique of the sequel to *A Theory of Justice*, Rawls's *Political Liberalism*—instanced some of the strictly intellectual reasons for political inefficacy. In particular, Anderson reproved the practical 'indeterminacy' of the 'difference principle', indifferently serviceable to Hayek for the purposes of vindicating capitalism, or to John Roemer for legitimating (market) socialism.[18]

In a recent review of Bobbio's *Left and Right*, Anderson remarks on his approving reference to Rawls and restates the reproach to the 'formalism' of *A Theory of Justice*.[19] In 1988 Anderson and the *NLR* had avoided any postmortem of the strategies and agencies of 1968, marking the twentieth anniversary of their May Days—'the last hurrah of the old world revolution', in Hobsbawm's judgement—by ignoring it.[20] Persuaded of the advent of a 'new political conjuncture', according to the foreword to *A Zone of Engagement* (p. xii), Anderson had turned to engage a philosophical tendency with an eminent pedigree in Mill and a distinguished posterity in Bobbio: the endeavour to synthesize liberal and socialist traditions. The oeuvre of this Italian thinker of the moderate Left was submitted to admiring but uncompromising scrutiny in the *NLR* in the summer of 1988.[21] After analyzing not just the affinities but also the antinomies of Norberto Bobbio, Anderson addressed his variation on a recurrent theme in kindred literature, from Mill to Mouffe:

The reconceptualization of socialism as essentially economic democracy answers to a dual purpose. It serves at once to appropriate the central legitimation of the existing political order for the cause of social change, and to avoid the central ideological obstacle to the implementation of such change: namely, the institution of private property. Its logic is that of a circumvention—the word it would not speak is expropriation. . . . If its practical fruit to date has been relatively small, the reason is in part that major social institutions do not generally allow themselves to be painlessly bypassed. (Pp. 122–23)

Although Bobbio's own particular brand of 'liberal socialism' proved on inspection to be 'an unstable compound' (p. 128), he himself had entered damning historical judgement on the general phenomenon: 'Whereas the conjugation of liberalism and socialism has so far remained a lofty velleity, the growing identification of liberalism with market forces is an incontestable reality' (p. 128 n. 102). If it was not to remain so, it would have to confront—and contest—that reality.

'Any culture that tries to start *ex nihilo*, or take shelter in the principles of 1789 (or 1776), will be stillborn', Anderson wrote in a long essay on Francis Fukuyama in 1992.[22] At the same time, however, as he made clear in a comment on one proposal for the reinvention of the Left—Giddens's rescission of the traditional division between Left and Right as superseded—the principles of 1789 were not to be sacrificed to pervasive postmodernist travesty of them: 'The Enlightenment, in all its complexity and depth, needs to be defended and developed, rather than discarded, by the Left today'.[23] But what was left of the Left in a Europe that had produced the Enlightenment and then invented the dichotomous terms of the political discourse of modernity? As Anderson noted in respect of Bobbio's defence of their enduring pertinence:

[B]y 1994 those who argued against . . . [it] were . . . prompted to do so not just by the collapse of communism in the East but by the demoralized effacement of social-democracy in the West. The abandonment of full employment and reduction of social security, and the universality of neo-liberal doctrines for economic growth put in question the traditional contrast between Left and Right. . . . This is not to argue that the concepts should be abandoned. Bobbio's passionate call to retain them merits our fullest sympathy. But they will not be saved by shutting one's eyes to the evacuation of their content by the trend of established politics today. (In press)

In the comparative perspective of such ghostlier fin de siècle demarcations, where the political systems of the Old World seemed set for alignment with the pancapitalist polity of the New, the conformities of the English were patent.

Locus Classicus or Ukania?

'A fideist of Enlightenment': such was John Gray's sobriquet for the author of *English Questions* and *A Zone of Engagement* in his review of them.[24] Taunting Anderson with the indeterminacy of his later work as regards the agency and goal of socialism, Gray acutely observed that he was 'strangely reticent on the fiasco of Gorbachev's reformist socialism', and moved to harpoon the 'bizarre collation' made in the concluding paragraph of 'A Culture in Contraflow' (p. 301): '[T]he collapse of the Communist order in Eastern Europe and the approach of federation in Western Europe have struck away mental fixtures of the Left and Right alike'. On Gray's reading of this passage, and others in 'The Light of Europe' (1991), 'transnational capitalist institutions double as placeholders for the international class solidarity that history has persistently mocked'. This would seem a precipitate extrapolation from the letter of Anderson's texts. But what the assertion in 'A Culture in Contraflow' does do is equate the regional *modification* of the inharmonic capitalist state-system with the *elimination* of an antagonistic socioeconomic system—a conflation affording little or no consolation to socialists (even if mentally unhinging neoliberal irreconcilables such as Premier Thatcher). More to the point at this stage is Anderson's conviction, voiced in the ensuing sentence, that '[t]hese decades were the last period during which British political life could still remain intact within the traditional framework of the Ukanian state, while its economic foundations were increasingly integrated into the Common Market'.

For close on twenty years after 1968, despite his critical sympathy for Bennism in the early 1980s, Anderson had kept his own counsel on British politics in public print. Unlike Nairn, he had undertaken no development of the original *NLR* theses or their revolutionary inflection in 'Components of the National Culture'. A retrospective and update of 'Origins of the Present Crisis'—'The Figures of Descent'—was eventually published in the *Review* in 1987.[25] Urging a revision of the Nairn-Anderson theses, the 'Decennial Report' of 1975 had stipulated their 'materialist' rectification, prioritizing amends for the lack of any exploration of '[t]he economic substructures of the English crisis in their own right'.[26] That deficiency had facilitated rebuttal of Thompson's allegations of 'reductionism' in 'The Peculiarities of the

205

English' but had incurred condign charges of 'idealism' from Hinton, admitted by Anderson in 'Socialism and Pseudo-Empiricism'. 'Figures' sought to remedy it, correcting the 'culturalism' of 'Origins'.

In the interim, an abundant literature on the subject had emerged, pioneered by Hobsbawm's *Industry and Empire* in 1968, whose explanation of relative national decline eschewed noneconomic variables and tracked it to the facilities of industrial priority and consequent monopoly.[27] Hobsbawm's work merited a circumspectly positive mention in 'Components of the National Culture', in the context of an assault on the 'generalized inadequacy' of mainstream—ahistorical and monocausal—accounts of the present crisis.[28] A subsequent, more conjunctural study by Andrew Glyn and Bob Sutcliffe—*British Capitalism, Workers, and the Profit Squeeze* (1972), piloted in the *NLR* and critically reviewed there—had rooted economic malady in the burgeoning strength of industrial labour, not the increasing frailty of industrial capital.[29] Marxist reinforcements for aspects of the theses had really arrived only in the 1980s, with Andrew Gamble's *Britain in Decline* (1981) and Colin Leys's *Politics in Britain* (1983), whereas a third (para-Marxist) contribution, Geoffrey Ingham's *Capitalism Divided?* (1984), although motivated in contradiction of Marxist orthodoxy, was deemed consonant with Andersonian heterodoxy.[30] Contrasting the available approaches, Leys wrote: 'What is needed is to combine the primarily economic-historical analysis of Hobsbawm with primarily sociological, cultural and political analyses, such as those of Anderson and Nairn, so as to try to link the different aspects of the social whole'.[31] This, in sum, was what 'Figures' attempted; and various of the problems thrown up by it attach to its narrative squaring of the analytical circle implicit in the combination of methodological primacies recommended by Leys.

Whereas 'A Culture in Contraflow' overturned 'Components of the National Culture', 'Figures of Descent' basically vindicated 'Origins of the Present Crisis', so far as Anderson was concerned:

> The two principal themes of our analysis were the archaic nature of a ruling stratum, whose personnel and traditions stretched back to an agrarian and aristocratic past that had been unbroken for centuries by civil commotion or foreign defeat; and the defensive character of a labour movement intensely conscious of class but immured in acceptance of it. To the hegemonic predominance of the one . . . there corresponded the corporate subordination of the other. . . . This Gramscian polarity was given too cultural a turn. . . . The crisis was also deduced too narrowly from the character of the hegemonic order alone. But the essential intuitions were not wrong. (P. 167)

In the light of subsequent research, which corroborated Nairn and Anderson's conjectures rather than Thompson's refutations (p. 130), the theses could be reprised as follows:

> The political dome of the dominant bloc had indeed been essentially land-owning throughout most of the nineteenth century; beneath it, economically, came commerce rather than manufacturing. When agrarian property lost its weight it was not industry but finance which became the hegemonic form of capital, in a City socially and culturally in many ways closer to the wealth of estates than of factories. The arrival of modern corporations later reinforced the outward bias of London as a world financial centre, by early orientation to production overseas. . . . The combination of a Treasury determined to minimize government at home, and a Foreign Office of vice-regal horizons abroad, made [the] state eminently unsuitable for redressing the decline of British capitalism. (Pp. 167–68)

Fortified, so he reckoned, by contemporary historiography against custodians of the Marxist classics, Anderson instanced a 'glissade' in Marx and Engels's own judgements on the 'most bourgeois of nations' (p. 128), which revealed them to be less manifestly incompatible with the burden of the theses (pp. 122–26).

If the factual accuracy (not to mention doctrinal compatibility) of the depiction of national reality in the Victorian era was defensible, according to Anderson, what of the comparative credentials—hence explanatory cogency—of the case for British singularity? For it was, of course, English exceptionalism, as deduced from a (Gallic) developmental rule of 'bourgeois revolution' and capitalist modernity, that had constituted the crux of the 'origins of the present crisis'. The erstwhile peculiarity of the national trajectory was remitted (pp. 128-29). Summoning Arno J. Mayer's *The Persistence of the Old Regime* (1981) in support of his portrait of the hegemonic landowning class,[32] by the same token Anderson conceded the necessity of 'an adequately comparative perspective' on the British case (pp. 129–30). As against the fallacious, normative comparativism reproved by Thompson, the specific local cast of what was, in fact, a general Continental pattern of class power would furnish the *explanans* of British malaise—the *explanandum* of the outlines of a 'totalizing' history ventured in the 1960s (pp. 121–22). A '*lower level of individuation*' (p. 129) would do the analytical trick. Reviewing the 'collective dramatis personae whose relative importance and character were in dispute' (p. 130), Anderson successively postulated the enduring economic and political paramountcy of the agrarian capitalist aristocracy in the nineteenth century (pp. 130–36); the elevation of merchants and bankers over manufacturers within bourgeois ranks (pp. 136–40); the configuration of the minimal-liberal domestic state as 'a logical creature of this triangular constellation of land, trade and industry' (pp. 140–44); the failure of the industrial middle class to secure 'independent bourgeois representation' in 1832, and its consequent self-denying political ordinance amid 'a fundamentally unaltered aristocratic ascendancy' made immemorial as second nature by the English ideology (pp. 144–48); the evasion of the industrial challenge of the United States and Germany in the last quarter of the nineteenth century by a state whose (imperial) priorities lay elsewhere, and which survived the military challenges of the latter competitor in the twentieth century only by deferring to the former (pp. 148–56); and the consolidation of an industrial proletariat characterized by a defensive industrial organization in inverse proportion to its offensive political projection, as demonstrated by a Labour government whose reconstructions after 1945 had unfolded within the framework of an overarching restoration (pp. 157–65).

If 'Origins of the Present Crisis' had erred in attributing historical peculiarity to a 'premature' bourgeois revolution, in due comparative perspective a national 'singularity' was, after all, conspicuous here, whose consequences were analogous:

> [P]eace brought with it a record that was truly unique in the ranks of all the major capitalist powers. Among them Britain alone had now never experienced a modern 'second revolution', abruptly or radically remoulding the state inherited from the first. For between the initial bourgeois revolution that breached the old order and the final completion of bourgeois democracy as the contemporary form of the capitalist state, there typically lay violent intervening convulsions that extended the work of the original upheaval and transformed the political framework of the nation. . . . The final clearance of the social and institutional landscape that had prevailed down to the First World War . . . was only accomplished in the Second. The general significance of these 'revolutions after the revolution' was everywhere the same. They were essentially phases in the modernization of the state, which thereby permitted a reinvigoration of the economy. . . . Britain alone was exempt from this process, throughout the whole epoch of industrialization which it pioneered. (Pp. 155–56)[33]

Transferred to Conservative safekeeping, the fundamentally unreconstructed postwar British polity had disdained Common Market for Commonwealth, notwithstanding dramatization of its economic dependency on a superior imperialism in the Suez crisis. Eight years later, as Anderson issued 'Origins', the debility of British capitalism was neither gainsayable nor gainsaid (pp. 166–67).

The record of the intervening quarter century, Anderson maintained, only served to confirm the intuitions of the early 1960s. Labourism under Wilson had burked its 'modernizing' project, conforming to subaltern type before avenging itself on trade unionism for the humiliations inflicted by City and bureaucracy (pp. 169–70). Conservatism under Heath had jettisoned its precocious neoliberalism, only to succumb to the syndicalism it was pledged to stamp out (pp. 174–76). Amid intersecting global recession and national decline in the mid–1970s, Callaghan had addressed the suicide note of British Social-Democracy to the International Monetary Fund (pp. 176–78). Thereafter, Thatcherite interment of the postwar settlement and resurrection of laissez-faire—pis aller—had exacerbated the (misdiagnosed) disease it purported to cure (pp. 178–84). 'The verdict is inescapable', Anderson concluded: 'After seven years, the regime that has made the most determined effort since the war to transform the coordinates of Britain's decline has ended up reinforcing the central drift of it' (p. 184).

The reason for this denouement was the perverse futility of the Thatcherite prescription:

> The unifying principle of Thatcherite economics . . . has been the restoration of the market. But as a physic for the British illness, this was never likely to work. The starting-point for the decline of British capitalism lay in its initial conditions. As the historical first-comer, British industrialization arrived without deliberate design, and triumphed without comparable competitors. . . . The easy dominance that British industry achieved in the first half of the nineteenth century laid down certain durable lines of development. . . . Once set, these structures became progressively greater handicaps in competition with later industrial economies. . . . The combined and uneven development that is a product of the world market . . . is not amenable to correction by it. The experience of English neo-liberalism in the 1980s has in this respect merely repeated the ancestral lessons of the 1880s. . . . Deregulation . . . could only mean still more deindustrialization, in pre-established conditions. (Pp. 185–87)[34]

If relative decline was traceable to the spontaneous commercial logic of historical priority, nonredressment of it was attributable to another 'singularity': lack of the kind of premeditated, supramarket agency represented by the French technocracy, the German banking system, or the Swedish labour movement (pp. 187–89):

> [J]ust as Britain possessed a state inured to colonial military intervention yet incapable of consistent economic intervention at home, and a world capital of finance without true finance capital, so it had a corporate working class that never generated an operative corporatism. . . . The *fainéant* industrial bourgeois of modern British history found no understudies for their role. The other actors compounded rather than compensated for their abdication from the scene. (P. 190)

A do-nothing bourgeoisie was thus substituted for the 'supine' variety of 'Origins', while the industrial proletariat remained at its subordinate post.

Broadening his comparative horizons, Anderson ended by suggesting that in one ironic respect Britain retained the role of capitalist pioneer and paradigm assigned it by Marx:

> Britain . . . not only witnesses the probably early beginnings in America of something like a vaster repetition of the same historical process it has undergone, . . . but also perhaps the signs of its ultimate generalization throughout the advanced capitalist world. For the radical internationalization of the forces of production—not to speak of circulation—that defines the spearhead forms of capital in the final years of the twentieth century promises to render all national correctors . . . increasingly tenuous in the future. . . . The British crisis has no solution in the sight; and perhaps the time in which one was possible, as a national recovery, has passed. (P. 192)[35]

In response to Ellen Wood's critique of the 'bourgeois paradigm' to which the *NLR* theses pertained, Anderson objected that her work—*The Pristine Culture of Capitalism*—lacked any alternative 'developmental narrative'.[36] Paradoxically, perhaps, the opposite complaint was lodged against 'The Figures of Descent' by David Coates, whose respect for its 'richly woven narrative' was tempered by the consideration that

> neither the individual hypotheses nor the overarching argument are made at all clear. They come to us . . . only through the detailed telling of a complicated historical tale; and certainly by the time the narrative reaches the twentieth century, if not before, the story has taken over to such a degree that the thesis beneath it quite literally vanishes from view. All we have are

episodes described in a sequence, in a text which is by then almost totally devoid of explicit analytical content.[37]

It is certainly true that the option for historical narration in 'Figures', as opposed to structural analysis in 'Origins', renders identification of its methodology problematic. No mere economistic counterpart to a culturalist original, the narrative cast of the later text circumvents the explanatory protocols laid down in 'Components of the National Culture', omitting to specify the interrelation and hierarchy of the plurality of causes—economic, sociological, cultural, political—it invokes. The principles of composition are actually more complex than Coates suggests. The formal framework within which the nonlinear narrative is initially pursued is a dramatic one, encompassing the 'collective dramatis personae' of aristocrats, assorted bourgeois, state, and parties and intellectuals (pp. 130–48). This is then suspended for the years 1873–1945 ('From Sedan to Berlin', pp. 148–56), resumed with 'workers' up to 1964 (pp. 157–67), and—after a brief reprise (pp. 167–69)—definitively retired in favour of a narrative that brings us to the present ('Losing Altitude', pp. 169–84). These discontinuities of form and content complicate any arbitration of the key issues posed by Anderson's revised position, three of which will be touched on here: What are its political implications? Is it consistent with the original theses? And, however that may be, is it valid as an explanation of national malaise?

Coates is not alone among readers who, mindful of Anderson's resort to such right-wing historiography as Corelli Barnett's *Collapse of British Power* or Martin Wiener's *English Culture and the Decline of the Industrial Spirit*, have perceived in his recriminations against derelictions of industrial-bourgeois duty 'a sort of left-wing Tebbitism'—or, in the manner of 'Origins', 'cries for capitalist modernisation wrapped up in socialist language'.[38] But this would appear unduly to read the later text through the grid of the former. For if Anderson was justified in reminding his critics that the focus of the theses was the present crisis, what is most striking about his retrospect is the absence from it of the kind of political proposals inferred from them and elaborated in 'Problems of Socialist Strategy'. This was the more surprising in that the 'Themes' prefacing publication of 'Figures' in the NLR had opined: 'This is surely not the time for socialists to moderate or conceal their alternatives'—a similarly resolute note to that struck by Nairn two decades earlier, in response to Labour's instantaneous exchange of white-hot technology for Treasury entropy.[39] Having delivered a disobliging verdict on the Thatcherite version of 'there is no alternative', in conclusion Anderson instates a Marxist variant of it, leaving him somewhat in the posture of a

Sphinx without a riddle. In view of 'the effective unity between financial and industrial capital' in Britain, dramatized by the Wilson debacle, Nairn had wagered the infeasibility of a national-capitalist renovation and had tabled a socialist transformation.[40] Anderson's contrasting reticence, despite the debris of deregulation, and his scepticism about 'all national correctors' derive from the 'radical internationalization' of production and circulation in the interim (p. 192)—a theme sounded for the first time in his work here. Reverted to in 'A Culture in Contraflow' and 'The Light of Europe',[41] the putative economic tendencies and political consequences of 'international-ization'—rapidly assimilated, under the rubric of 'globalization', as la pensée unique of late-twentieth-century capitalist civilization—were shortly after-ward subjected to critical scrutiny in the pages of the NLR.[42] Above all, David M. Gordon was concerned to resist 'a spreading political fatalism in the advanced countries', induced by hasty inferences from shaky hypothe-ses.[43] In the cautiously phrased Andersonian instance, it is the blankness—not impotence—of political conclusion that impresses.

Seemingly discontinuous with 'Origins' politically, was 'Figures' consis-tent with it analytically? According to a significant secondary literature, it was not as consistent as Anderson supposed. The later analysis qualified English exceptionalism, rescinding the primacy allocated to a 'premature', 'mediated' bourgeois revolution in accounting for the failure to recast a pre-cocious capitalism. Comparatively framed, the historical turning point at which Britain failed to turn now resided not in an impure presence but in an-other absence: of the kind of 'modern "second revolution"' that had deliv-ered the ancien régime its quietus elsewhere, at once modernizing the state and rejuvenating the economy (pp. 155–56). Or, rather, British 'singularity' consisted in the virtual instantaneity of its 'revolution after the revolution' in the seventeenth century, saddling it with a premodern state ill suited to redirect a capitalist economy when historical priority backfired on it two centuries later. 'Figures' thus conjoined the original problematic of political prematurity (and senility)—the persistence of the old regime, whatever the 'lower level of individuation' (p. 129)—with a more conventional sched-ule of economic priority—'the play of comparative advantage and disadvan-tage', attendant upon the 'initial conditions' of the 'historical first-comer' (pp. 185–86).[44] In the process, argued Robert Looker, Anderson conducted 'a radical re-weighting of aristocratic hegemony in his explanation of the malady of modern Britain, relegating it to merely a supporting role in the new play',[45] whose main dramatis personae were ascendant commercial or financial capital and a congenitally liberal state. Moreover, notwithstanding its residual 'epochal scale', 'Figures' uncontroversially identified the late nineteenth century as the critical phase in shaping subsequent British descent, specifically defining the 'present crisis' as economic.[46] If both 'Origins' and 'Figures' sought to explain capitalist involution by bourgeois incompletion, there were crucial differences between their respective hypotheses:

> In the 1960s version, Anderson's explanatory focus was a process *retarding* the emergence of a fully capitalist and bourgeois social order in Britain, most notably the continuing impact of aristocratic hegemony. In his 1980s version it is the *arrested development* of that bourgeois order at an early, liberal-commercial phase, which carries the main explanatory weight. [47]

Over and above his own avowed adjustments, Anderson's consistency was thus open to doubt. But the plausibility of 'Figures' is what ultimately counts. Lest the narcissism of comparatively small differences intrude here, the common ground occupied by many parties to the Marxist controversy should be noted. Wood was not unique in 'sharing [Nairn and Anderson's] basic premiss that the priority of British capitalism provides a key to its current condition'.[48] Nor, however, was she the sole commentator to arrive at very different conclusions from Nairn and Anderson. Thus, in the pages of the *NLR* itself, Michael Barratt Brown restated a professedly 'fairly traditional Marxist view' of British capitalism, vindicating the nineteenth-century reputation of the 'workshop of the world'.[49] Alex Callinicos subscribed to Barratt Brown's 'detailed and devastating criticism' and selected the international orientation and dependency of the British economy as 'the decisive factor' in explaining a present plight that was, in any event, symptomatic of 'the general crisis of the capitalist mode of production'.[50] Both authors rebuked Anderson's recourse to Barnett's work. Barratt Brown further chided his reliance on Ingham to sustain the case for the subordination of industrial to commercial bourgeoisie, eliciting an intransigent rejoinder from the latter, who countersigned 'the substance of [Anderson's] historical account' while reiterating its incongruity with orthodox Marxist theory, whatever the empirical obiter dicta of Marx and Engels themselves.[51]

In a commanding overview of and contribution to the teeming literature on British 'economic decline' in which Anderson's essays take their place, Coates specifies the substance of that decline as comparative 'economic underperformance'—in particular, the loss of competitiveness of home-based manufacturing industry in global markets, and consequent (negative) deindustrialization; and he attributes it to 'the legacies of the past and the logics of the present'.[52] Probed by Coates where they are largely narrated by

Anderson, those legacies and logics—inherited and compounded by neo-liberalism—are substantially similar in each case. In Coates's words:

> An imperial state, internationalized capital, a moderate labour movement, and a liberal imperialist culture fused together in the brief period of UK economic and political domination, then sat there like a nightmare on the brain of the living, to block rapid and effective responses by any section of UK society to the transformation and replacement of that international domination first in the 1890s, and then after 1945.[53]

As in 'Figures', the state, although in no sense the originating cause of British decline, had functioned to reproduce it; and the labour movement, because of its political weakness despite its industrial strength, had proved incapable of checking it. But no *'fainéant* bourgeois' featured among Coates's figures of descent. For the liberal-imperialist state was the logical résumé of a civil society in which the lead industrial sectors, as well as financial institutions, were externally oriented, indicating a division *within* industrial capital (multinational/local), rather than *between* industry (national) and finance (international). The bourgeoisie had not been trapped between the hammer of premodern aristocratic hegemony and contemporary proletarian corporatism. Nor had it been symmetrically polarized between superordinate-commercial and subordinate-industrial class fractions. The reality, on Coates's interpretation of the evidence, was 'an increasing disjuncture between the British economy and British capital. British capital is alive and well. It is just British-based industry that is not'.[54]

As an earlier quotation from 'Figures' (pp. 167–68) demonstrates, on occasion Anderson registered the divisions between multinational and local industrial capital, even if, at other episodic points, the finance/industry polarity took precedence over such divisions. What renders an arguable difference in degree potentially one of kind is the *'fainéant'* flourish. Even so, the departure from Marxist orthodoxy, for which Victorian England was the locus classicus of industrial capitalism and industrial-bourgeois ascendancy—the 'classical laboratory of *Capital*', as Anderson put it (p. 122)—is arresting.

If Coates's political economy broadly coincided with Anderson's, a major recent work of non-Marxist historiography—Cain and Hopkins's *British Imperialism* (1993)—can be regarded as corroborating his miniature on an incomparably larger canvas. However, its paradigm of 'gentlemanly capitalism', although drawing upon Hilferding's insights in *Finance Capital*, derived equal inspiration from Schumpeter and Veblen.[55] In 'Figures' (p. 151

and n. 59) Anderson himself had remarked the superiority of Hilferding over Lenin and Marx in his grasp of the historical specificity of English capitalism. Anderson likewise acknowledged (p. 135 n. 40) the pertinence of Schumpeter's reflections on 'the English case' in *Capitalism, Socialism, and Democracy*, while repeating the objection he had already made in 'Origins' (p. 24) to the Austrian economist's characterization of the ruling aristocratic class as precapitalist.[56] Later, in 'The Light of Europe' (p. 334 n. 51), he would cite Veblen's excavation of 'the moss-grown situation of trade and industry in contemporary England' in *Imperial Germany and the Industrial Revolution*.[57] Since Cain and Hopkins share Anderson's critique of Schumpeter, it would be facile to conclude that a two-volume Schumpeterian history vindicates an essay in Marxist genealogy at the expense of its Marxist credentials. But it can be said that, for better or worse, Anderson's 'lower level of individuation' is not a specifically historical-materialist one.

The debate was resumed prior to publication of both Cain and Hopkins and Coates, when Anderson responded to his critics in 'The Light of Europe'.[58] A section entitled 'Economy and Chronology' (pp. 329–37) scanned 'the repertory of the Left':

> Ever since the modernity of the British economy and British State was first seriously called in question in the early sixties, socialists have been tempted to deny that the issue has reality or relevance. A long and lively literature . . . has sought to show that the whole problematic of Ukania is misconceived. . . . [T]hree tropes dominate it. . . . In one variant, the specificity of British capitalist society lies essentially in the fact that it came first in historical order. . . . In another, there is nothing special about British capitalism at all: it is rather a formation which exemplifies the international laws of development of capital as a whole. In a third, what is peculiar to the United Kingdom is the purity of its native capitalism. . . . [T]he critical test for such interpretations . . . remains . . . their capacity to provide an intelligible account of the continuing . . . decline of British capitalism. (Pp. 329–31)[59]

Anderson maintained that the third hypothesis—purity—issued in a reductio ad absurdum, whereas the second—generality—was precluded by definition (legerdemain on Anderson's part, since it was discounted because of its inability to explain what it denied: specificity). Only the first— priority—could stake a claim to explanatory purchase (pp. 331–32). But it too was rebuffed: 'banal chronology' was not a sufficient condition of British decline. The comparable Belgian experience demonstrated the contrary:

[S]imilar beginnings can have rather different endings. National fortunes are not just fates inscribed in industrial birth-certificates. They are also formed by variable natural endowments, socio-cultural structures and political institutions. The last of these can resist, as well as follow, the entries given in the first. (P. 337)

If British political institutions had proved incapable of the types of 'correction' or 'effective regulation' implemented elsewhere, it was indeed because of 'the archaic mainframe of the Ukanian state itself' (pp. 337–38), unregulated by a written constitution and powered by parliamentary sovereignty and electoral monopoly.

In the same year as that 'mainframe' came under renewed assault in Nairn's The Enchanted Glass (1988),[60] a campaign was launched against it—Charter 88—of which Anderson and Nairn were founding signatories and another former NLR editor, Anthony Barnett, the coordinator.[61] In 'A Culture in Contraflow' (p. 300), Anderson noted the comparative modesty of its programme of constitutional reform against a background of comprehensive neoliberalism.[62] Moreover, as indicated elsewhere, he was not prey to what the classical Marxist tradition decried as 'constitutional illusions'.[63] That said, former admonitions against any dissociation of democratic and socialist demands were tacitly withdrawn.[64] To borrow the terminology of the 'Themes' to the relevant issue of the NLR in 1987, whereas 'The Figures of Descent' concealed the alternative to the New Right, 'The Light of Europe' moderated it—an allusion in the latter to Wood's 'vigorous call to the pristine culture of socialism' (p. 331 n. 42) intimating the distance taken. The strategic recommendations missing from the earlier text now ensued, with Anderson's advocacy of 'social' and 'political citizenship', to be pressed upon Westminster and pursued within a federal Europe where the unbound capitalist Prometheus of the twenty-first century might be tethered to meliorist ends. By socialist standards, such horizons were limited, as he readily conceded. However, with the convulsions of Communism and the disarray of Social-Democracy, they '[held] out the best promise of practical advances in equality and emancipation in Western Europe at large' (pp. 352–53).

From one angle, 'The Light of Europe' might be seen as a return to Anderson's origins, reissuing the summons to a resumption of 'the unfinished business of 1640 and 1832' with which his essay of 1964 had ended—and doing so on the eve of a British general election in which Kinnock aspired to emulate Wilson's termination of thirteen years of Tory rule.[65] Yet as Anderson argued, if certain analogies obtained three decades on—above all, Conservative divisions in a context of economic failure and diplomatic perplexity—the political conjuncture differed decisively. Although the touted Thatcherite economic miracle had turned out to be a mirage, some far from piecemeal social engineering had significantly recast British society (pp. 303–5). Anderson avoided the extravagances of *Marxism Today*, with its ventilation of 'New Times' on the slender basis of a putative 'post-Fordism'.[66] But he split the difference on a prior dispute over the 'hegemony' of Thatcherism:

> [T]he pragmatic 'fitness to govern' that was to be the principal Conservative asset in successive elections was itself an ideological construct—its requirements set by the norms of an unabashed capitalist ethos that was new to British politics. (P. 306)[67]

Unlike the contrasting profiles of the main parties in the 1960s, Conservative ideological prepotency in the 1980s was amply attested by Labourist accommodation to it (pp. 306, 325–29).

Local normalization corresponded to Continental dispositions. Labour's trajectory conformed to the European 'parabola of Social Democracy' (pp. 307–25). The reformism of its northern wing had foundered in the mid-1970s with the end of the long boom upon which its prosperity had been predicated:

> The onset of the world recession undermined the credit of traditional Keynesian techniques for achieving macro-economic balances: first helpless before stagflation within national economies, then outflanked by the internationalization of capital flows that followed. In the new conditions, as financial markets gained increasing structural predominance over commodity and labour markets, and national monetary sovereignty declined, there was a massive general shift of power to capital-owners in the West. . . . Politically, the crisis caught the labour movements that had relied on a Keynesian environment quite unprepared. Social Democracy in Northern Europe had no alternative formulas of regulation of its own. The result was inevitably a spreading crisis of performance and direction. (P. 312)

Meanwhile, in a 'striking reversal of pattern' (p. 314), as Social-Democracy receded in the northern zone, 'Eurosocialism' advanced in the southern, displacing its Communist counterpart. Yet the promised resuscitation of the Second International evaporated, once Mitterand's countercyclical experiment in France had been sacrificed to austerity. Eurosocialism

217

failed to reproduce the two great hallmarks of the post-war cycle of Social Democracy in the North—full employment and extended welfare provision. . . . There were two basic reasons for this difference. Northern Social Democracy built its achievements during the long wave of post-war capitalist expansion. . . . The class compromise it institutionalized was the fruit of high rates of accumulation, combined with strong labour organization. Neither of these conditions obtained when Eurosocialism set out on its cycle of office. World capitalism was sunk in a long wave of recession, with low rates of accumulation and little margin for social concessions. Moreover, capital was now . . . much more radically internationalized. . . . The national economic spaces presuppposed by Keynesian demand management had been steadily reduced. (Pp. 319–20)

Cowed by Reaganomics, Eurosocialism had sponsored a substitution of liberal-democratic capitalism for welfare-statism, often via the cipher of 'modernization', which presaged 'a significant mutation': 'the gradual conversion of European Social Democratic organizations into something resembling the American Democratic Party' (pp. 323, 325). Whereas the 1986 article on which this section of 'The Light of Europe' was based concluded by invoking 'forces of ferment and resistance',[68] five years later Anderson contemplated the prospect of 'an ideological *Gleichschaltung*' in Western Europe—one compounded, not countervailed, by 'the earthquake in the East' (p. 325) in 1989.

An American or Japanese standardization of European political life would certainly not be arrested by the British Labour Party, whose socio-economic programme largely endorsed the post-postwar settlement of Thatcher (pp. 346–47), while its constitutional manifesto spurned an 'obvious and overdue line of advance for the Left' (p. 348), evading the cruces of democratization: a written constitution and proportional representation.[69] Block vote within and plurality system without vouchsafed Labour an ersatz mass membership and disproportionate parliamentary presence:

They smoothed its path and enfeebled its sinews. The regressive nature of Labourism as a political culture is rooted in the customs and privileges of this legacy. [I]f we ask why the Labour regime of Wilson and Callaghan proved so completely incapable of halting the descent of the economy, the answer lies in the extent to which the party did indeed mirror the vices of the country. . . . The agues of the national economy and parliamentary sovereignty that call for real medicine of reform in Ukania are . . . lodged in Labour's own body. (Pp. 350–51)

Nor, despite a right-wing critique of traditional Labourism that amply confirms Anderson's surmises about the Americanization—more precisely, Clintonization—of Social-Democracy, does post-1992 'New Labour', vendor of electoral confectionary, offer to dispense 'real medicine of reform'. At time of writing, Anderson has not pronounced upon it or its soundbitten leader—emperor of ice cream—and his light-minded coterie, who necessitate emendation of Robert Michels's sarcasm on reformism: 'the social-ism of non-socialists *without* a socialist past'. But such evidence as exists points to a suitable estimate: beneath contempt.[70]

'The Light of Europe' ended by affirming the 'problematic of Ukania' while articulating demands for social and political citizenship on national and Continental planes alike. 'In all probability', Anderson wrote,

> a condition of relative industrial revival in Britain is now some political reorganization, as the decline of the economy appears inseparable from the arrest of the state. Sooner or later, the Westminster system will in any case be undone by federation in Europe, which no major British party yet accepts and none will be able to resist. Various sorts of reconstruction can be envisaged, before or in that process itself. (P. 351)

In 'A Culture in Contraflow', Charter 88 had been identified as '[t]he one bold attempt to break the political logjam left by the debacle of the Wilson-Callaghan years' (p. 300). Now, there was 'no shortage of radical proposals with a strategic edge, capable of unblocking the present logjam of the Left in advanced capitalism' (pp. 351–52). Each of these avenues—company law reform, right-to-work legislation, basic income guarantees, public education provision, and maternity entitlements—[71]

> involves a set of rights, based on widespread needs. Ideologically, they share a common conception that is classically described as the idea of social citizenship. There can be little doubt that this now holds out the best promise of practical advances in equality and emancipation in Western Europe at large. But it is illusory to think that these could be realized in the United Kingdom . . . without the idea of political citizenship itself becoming for the first time a reality. . . . To think that furtherance of the one can bypass fulfilment of the other today would be an error even on a broader stage—as if in the European Community itself, with the prospect of greater concentration of bureaucratic authority in the Commission and the coming Central Bank, it will be possible to confine demands to social provision without political democratization. (Pp. 352–53)[72]

In recommending such a line of march, Anderson anticipated a standing objection from the revolutionary Left to which he had belonged, and tactfully averted it:

> What have socialists to do with the vicissitudes of any particular capitalist society, when their task is to confront the system as a whole? The question is to be respected. But national differences, however relative compared with conditions outside the metropolitan zone, continue to count for those who fall under them. . . . [N]o effective opposition to capitalism can morally neglect these contrasts. The politics of a rational Left needs to be international in a new and more radical way today: global in its conclusions. But it has not ceased to be national in its conditions. To attend to these is not to accept the limits of the present social order, as it spreads further round the world. (P. 353)

Anderson's conviction that a principal task of the Left was 'the completion of a genuine federal state in the [European] Community', or 'the construction of a true federal framework in Europe', became a leitmotiv of his writing in the early 1990s.[73] It was rooted in an appreciation of the euphemistically termed 'democratic deficit' enshrined in the Maastricht Treaty: unaccountable executive, impotent legislature, independent central bank. A sardonic allusion in the final paragraph of 'A Culture in Contraflow' to Gorbachev's wishful thinking about a 'common European home',[74] shortly after the statement on West European integration attracting Gray's incredulity, indicated that Anderson was not one of de Gaulle's 'choirboys who have drunk some of the altar wine'. It was Keynes, not Hayek, paradoxically enough, who looked forward to 'a euthanasia of politics in economic policy'.[75] But as Anderson observed in 1992, Hayek had foreseen the potential for just that, and a consequent free-fire zone for the 'artillery of commodities'—not the 'euthanasia of the rentier' provoking the sciamachy of his inheritors—in the sort of supranational arrangements ratified at Maastricht.[76] If Anderson's attitude toward 'Europe' had shifted dramatically since his last explicit intervention on the subject with Stuart Hall three decades earlier,[77] it was attributable to the perception both of the inevitability of the process of integration, and of the undesirability of its projected forms.

It is to the latter that Anderson has devoted most recent attention, in two review-articles in the *London Review of Books*, subsequently reprinted in the Verso collection *The Question of Europe*, edited by Anderson and Peter Gowan.[78] In the first, 'Under the Sign of the Interim', restoring the *Aussenpolitik* that Alan Milward's history tended to slight (pp. 55–66), he cast an unforgiving eye over the EC's institutional mould, calling it a customs union with a quasi-executive of supranational cast, without any machinery to enforce its decisions; a quasi-legislature of inter-governmental ministerial sessions, shielded from any national oversight, operating as a kind of upper chamber; a quasi-supreme court that acts as if it were the guardian of a constitution which does not exist; and a pseudo-legislative lower chamber, in the form of a largely impotent parliament that is nevertheless the only elective body, theoretically accountable to the peoples of Europe. (P. 68)

In the second, 'The Europe to Come', the cumulative impact of Soviet collapse, German reunification, and Maastricht ratification was sounded. The Hayekian consequences of Mitterrand and Kohl were much as a latter-day Keynes might describe them:

> In a system of the kind envisaged . . . , national macro-economic policy becomes a thing of the past. . . . The historic commitments of both Social and Christian democracy to full employment or social services of the traditional welfare state, already scaled down or cut back, would cease to have any further institutional purchase. This is a revolutionary prospect. . . . The protective and regulative functions of existing national states will be dismantled, leaving sound money as the sole regulator, as in the classical liberal model of the epoch before Keynes. . . . On this reading, Maastricht leads to an obliteration of what is left of the Keynesian legacy that Hayek deplored, and most of the distinctive gains of the West European labour movement associated with it. (Pp. 130–31)

Against this prospect Anderson reiterated his option for 'a genuine supranational democracy at Union level, embodying for the first time a real popular sovereignty in a truly effective and accountable European Parliament' (p. 132)—an alternative to which neither élite consensus nor public opinion was inclined, of course. Despite 'Wilhelmine' stirrings in German foreign policy (p. 135), it was their precondition—'[t]he restoration of capitalism east of the Elbe' (p. 127)—and subsequent East European applications for admission that suspended the largest question mark over the future of the Union. The widest enlargement was entertained by Major's United Kingdom, intent upon 'institutional dilution' of Maastricht and 'social deregulation' in excess of it (p. 138). Other scenarios were more or less self-serving, tenuous, and invidious (pp. 133–44). Whichever transpired, it *might* subvert Anglo designs, compelling 'a concentration of federal power in a new constitutional settlement' (p. 143). In any event, the emergent Union was being fashioned on 'political quicksands' (p. 144)—scarcely dry land or firm ground for a capitalist placeholder for socialist internationalism.

Contrary to Gray, then, Anderson's undeluded emphasis was increasingly on the impasse, rather than the escape route, of a practicable, desirable European Union. On the other hand, the 'bizarre collation' detected by Gray in 'A Culture in Contraflow' deserves retention. If any 'mental fixtures of the Left' had been 'struck away' with 'the collapse of the Communist order in Eastern Europe' (p. 301), then an obvious candidate would be Anderson's own. Although no one would have guessed it from his imperturbable postlapsarian writings, the Communist order had constituted a mental fixture of Anderson's Marxism and socialism. By his criteria, its implosion effected the zonal restoration, and ushered in the global dominion, of capitalism unbound.

Velocities of Change: The Sense of an Ending

It should not be necessary to labour this point, in view of the textual evidence presented in chapter 3. But a few reminders may be helpful. In terms of collective *NLR* documents, the quinquennial report had identified 'revived anti-communism' as 'the main danger' of the 1980s, although cautioning against 'over-reacting into an insufficiently critical stance towards the Soviet bureaucracy in particular (given its patently more progressive world role than its Chinese counterpart)'.[79] The 'workers' states' were to be strenuously defended in the face of 'hysterical Solzhenitsyniana' (p. 50). At the nadir of the second Cold War in 1983, the *Review*'s revised charter, locating the organization in the 'political tradition' stemming from the Bolshevik Revolution, had maintained that these states 'represent a historic progress over the capitalist or pre-capitalist societies that preceded them, and a critical bulwark against imperialism'.[80] The stamp of such principles was firmly impressed upon Anderson's own writings of the period, whether *In the Tracks of Historical Materialism* or (especially) 'Trotsky's Interpretation of Stalinism', both published in 1983. Most significantly of all, perhaps, October 1917, whatever its subsequent degeneration, was said in *Arguments within English Marxism* to have set in train an 'irreversible . . . alteration of the potential of historical action, in the course of the 20th century' (p. 21).

The political upshot? As a heterodox-Trotskyist critic of the Deutschero-Trotskyist position logically inferred, 'For a workers' state, however deformed or degenerate, to become a capitalist state must be a step back historically, a stage in a counter-revolutionary process which Marxists should oppose'.[81] The *NLR* Charter had espoused 'the radical democratic reconstruction of all the post-capitalist states' (p. 5). The quinquennial report had entertained 'two opposite scenarios': either 'capitalist restoration'—'however jolting the prospect'—or socialist democratization in the East (which might, in turn, unblock socialism in the West) (pp. 70–71). The first projection implicated Yugoslavia and China; the second applied to the USSR. Neither entailed cancellation of the 'irreversible alteration' postulated in *Arguments*—especially since any regression was analytically subsumed under an analogy with transient 'absolutist restorations' after the 'bourgeois revolutions' (p. 70).

Following the death of Brezhnev and gerontocratic interludes, it seemed as if the second scenario might come to pass: *ex oriente lux*. The fund of hope invested in the Gorbachev prospectus is not hard to imagine. However, doubtless mindful of the major disanalogy between Gorbachev and Khrushchev—signalled by the surmise in the quinquennial report that Soviet democratization was 'unlikely to occur until after another major cycle of Soviet economic growth, at the least' (p. 71)—the *NLR* exhibited a certain reticence on the subject. Its editors abstained from analysis of reformist prospects in the pages of the *Review* itself. Still, in a 1988 study dedicated to Boris Kagarlitsky and Boris Yeltsin, bearing the Deutscherite title *Revolution from Above*, Tariq Ali addressed the question of his Trotskyist subtitle—*Where Is the Soviet Union Going?*—and ventured the following response:

> Gorbachev represents a progressive, reformist current within the Soviet elite, whose programme, if successful, would represent an enormous gain for socialists and democrats on a world scale. The scale of Gorbachev's operation is . . . reminiscent of the efforts of an American President of the nineteenth century. . . . In order to preserve the Union, Lincoln had to push through a second American revolution based on the abolition of slavery. In order to preserve the Soviet Union, Gorbachev needs to complete the political revolution . . . , but one based on an abolition of the whole nomenklatura system of privileges on which the power of the Soviet bureaucracy rests.[82]

Ali specifically warned against the temptations of hindsight, which would be of nil benefit to the outcome of the 'debate taking place inside the USSR': 'It is much easier to worship accomplished facts' (pp. xii–xiii).

There is no reason to believe that Anderson would have endorsed Ali's outlook or analysis in all details. Even so, regardless of the felicity of the precise analogy with Lincoln's 'second revolution', it is safe to suppose a substantial measure of agreement within a shared repertory. The one direct piece of evidence we possess suggests as much. In correspondence with Norberto Bobbio arising out of his article on the Italian philosopher's attempted liberal-socialist synthesis, Anderson regretted that he had omitted 'a vital issue for the whole topic':

> That . . . is the prospect for a liberal socialism in the post-revolutionary soci-
> eties. . . . For what else . . . is the . . . aim of perestroika in the USSR? The
> 'rule of law', 'guarantee of individual rights', and 'separation of powers' are
> all part . . . of Gorbachev's own formal project. . . . Of course, the out-
> come . . . could not be less certain. Perestroika could miss a liberal socialism
> from either end . . .—that is, collapse back into the previous dictatorial
> regime, or flee forward into a de facto recreation of capitalism; possibly even
> combine these evils. But to use your own terms, a liberal socialism must now
> be reckoned—in the medium to long run—as one not unrealistic historical
> possibility, among others, in the USSR. It is difficult to see how any contem-
> porary Marxist could fail to welcome that, however inadequate the legacy of
> Marxism itself on these issues (about which I do not disagree). But if this
> were the case, the difference between our positions narrows greatly. . . . [A]
> liberal socialism would be the common aim . . . ; but reached by the *corsi e
> ricorsi* of a staggeringly illiberal historical process.[83]

The allusion is to a Viconian-cyclical, rather than Marxian-dialectical, philos-ophy of history ('*corsi e ricorsi*'); the time frame extended ('the medium to long run'); the desired outcome denoted by a double negative ('one not un-realistic historical possibility'); and 'evils'—including capitalist restoration—entertained. But a duly qualified Deutscherite cunning of reason remains op-erative here.

No worshipper of accomplished facts, Anderson otherwise reserved pub-lic judgement, pronouncing on the Gorbachev experiment—*fait inaccompli*—only in an informative report on the August 1991 Moscow coup for the *London Review of Books*.[84] The first thing to note about it is its ironic con-firmation of a statement in conclusion to 'The Ends of History': 'Historical analogies are never more than suggestive'.[85] For the analogy via which Anderson sought to illuminate the summer's momentous events was, in a charming litotes, one that 'would not occur to most politically-conscious Russians' (p. 5): Suharto's ouster of Sukarno in the aftermath of the October 1965 coup in Indonesia. It would not spring to the mind of most politically conscious previous readers of Anderson either. They would have anticipated some examination of the more traditional analogies with 1660 or 1815, and some arbitration of whether what had transpired was adjacent to

1830 and 1848 or, alternatively, the 'new 1789' repudiated in 'Trotsky's Interpretation of Stalinism'.[86] But within what Anderson dubbed 'the larger certainties of the restoration', they too were 'in for some surprises' (p. 8).

A second striking feature of the reportage was the glacial accents of its assessment of Gorbachev. Credited with Soviet withdrawal from Afghanistan and the introduction of free elections at home, he was reckoned to have bestrode the world like some cross between a pale Colossus and an ingenuous Narcissus while the lethal combination of glasnost without effective perestroika mined Soviet economy and Union: '[T]here is no other modern case of such a gap between external adulation and internal repudiation as eventually opened up in Gorbachev's government of the Soviet Union' (p. 6). Attendant upon Communist collapse in Eastern Europe, the end of the Cold War had been superinduced by 'the realities of all-round Soviet weakness'— the prevalence of the West in the 'great contest', not an accession of enlightened despotism in the East.[87] 'The central source of that weakness', Anderson observed,

has steadily worsened under Gorbachev. Perestroika turned a declining economy into a disaster zone. Disrupting the old centralised planning system, it provided no coherent alternative, leading to a spiralling breakdown of supplies and accelerating fall in output. In material provision the majority of Soviet citizens now live worse, some much worse, than under Brezhnev. For many, their personal security has deteriorated too. For perestroika also undid the old centralised administrative system that kept ethnic differences under rigid control, without putting any effective federal framework in its place. (P. 6)

Disabused of Gorbachev, Anderson was unintoxicated by Yeltsin, whose 'populism' was noted, even if he was exonerated of 'any deep-lying Russian chauvinism' (p. 7), and whose 'brutish rule' was subsequently condemned in the context of the war in Chechnya.[88] The 'wider question of the future of Russian politics as capitalism settles in' was broached. The traditionally 'nationalist and expansionist bent' of Russian liberalism was the bane that its successors would have to disavow (p. 7). An independently organized working class was forecast as a protagonist and given the lines of 'the central social question of the coming period—who are to become the proprietors of the factories and installations in which they work?' (p. 8). Notwithstanding political ebullition and 'an extraordinary psychological liberation for its people' (p. 7), however, the future socioeconomic course of Russia was set: 'restoration' (p. 8).

The coup de grâce that succeeded coup d'état in Russia in 1991 prompted Anderson's cosignature of a death certificate for Communism already issued in the *NLR* in 1989 by Ralph Miliband and Norberto Bobbio, following the bloody repression of the movement for democracy in China. These texts were later reprinted in an impressive Verso symposium, edited by Blackburn—*After the Fall: The Failure of Communism and the Future of Socialism* (1991)—containing material from the *Review* and other sources. In his obituary of 'historical communism' (to which Anderson has referred approvingly),[89] Bobbio—a veteran opponent of the phenomenon—coincided, to a degree, with Hobsbawm—a comparably veteran proponent—in his forebodings about the capitalist consequences of Communist defeat.[90] In substance, these were extrapolated from what Anderson himself had identified as the 'external gains'—as opposed to the 'internal costs'—of 'the presence and performance' of Stalinism, however involuntary those gains may have been.[91]

A month after Bobbio's 'Upturned Utopia' was published in *La Stampa*, an article on the same subject appeared in the *National Interest*.[92] Fukuyama's 'The End of History?' was not Panglossian. Yet if not all was for the best, liberal-democratic capitalism was apotheosized as the best possible—because practicable—world, within the framework of an avowedly Hegelian philosophy of history. At the New School for Social Research in 1985, Anderson had suggested to his audience that although 'a much more consciously and lucidly philosophical history' was desirable, '[w]e do not need to revive a philosophy of history today'.[93] Fukuyama's essay in substantive, rather than analytical, philosophy of history, and its subsequent expansion in *The End of History and the Last Man*, stimulated revision of that judgement. It received diverse but respectful coverage in the *NLR*,[94] in stark contrast to the virtual unanimity of negative response it elicited across the spectrum from Huntington to Hobsbawm.[95] But in what is Anderson's principal postlapsarian statement to date—'The Ends of History' (1992)[96]—it was accorded privileged treatment, on the basis that its full measure had yet to be taken. 'The charge heard on the Right, of an inverted Marxism', Anderson wrote, 'is grounds for tribute on the Left' (p. 345).

In thus dissenting from numerous critics, including Lutz Niethammer, who had reconstructed Fukuyama's antecedents in 1989, unaware of their impending afterlife,[97] Anderson was guided by the general consideration that Niethammer's

critique of the Franco-German tradition in effect concludes, not with an alternative to its diagnosis of the age, contesting its substantive theses, but with a call to eschew such ventures altogether—rejecting any macro-historical narrative as intellectually and politically overweening. Currently, the effect of such a withdrawal would be to leave the American variant in possession of the field. If this is to be questioned, it can only be on its own—legitimate, even inescapable—terrain. (P. 284)

Anderson's contestation of a terrain vacated as the preserve of speculative metaphysics, whether by Anglo-Saxon empiricism or Gallic poststructuralism, began by following Niethammer in his identification of the vision of *post-histoire* as an 'inversion' of Enlightenment teleology (p. 280). Fukuyama had reverted both this inversion (substituting optimism for pessimism) and Marx's *renversement* of Hegel (restoring idealism in place of materialism), while relocating the goal of the historical process (capitalism rather than communism). 'End-times' were, on balance, 'quality-time'; and (contrary to cheap critical victories) the purposive culmination of history was expressly not the sheer cessation of events (pp. 282, 333). Whereas Niethammer had been concerned with the twentieth-century mutation of a nineteenth-century topos at the hands of *Kulturkritiker*, in an equally imposing exercise in intellectual history Anderson reached back to Hegel (pp. 285–94) and recovered Cournot (pp. 294–308). This served to demonstrate what Fukuyama had anyway acknowledged: to borrow Régis Debray's acid remark on Michel Rocard's proclamation of the 'end of ideology' in 1989, that the 'end of history' represented a 'scoop' that was 'only two hundred years old'.[98] No mere display of antiquarian erudition, however, Anderson's essay detailed what other commentators had complained of: Fukuyama's Procrustean operation to fit Hegel to a Kojèvean frame. Moreover, it rescued from oblivion a strikingly contemporary Cournot, responsible for a 'remarkable . . . prevision of the fate of communism' (p. 307), were it to be confined to a national economic autarky that no amount of political autarchy could insulate against international pressures; and a no less remarkable divination of the imperilment of life on Earth, were capitalism to hold unregulated sway over the planet.

The ghost missing from this philosophical banquet was Marx, for whom (pace Fukuyama) communism did not consummate history but did terminate 'the prehistory of human society', and who had observed that, according to 'bourgeois' political economy, 'there has been history, but there is no longer any'.[99] Mentioned by Anderson only in passing thus far (pp. 294, 307), Marx—or, rather, Stalinist Marxism—assumed greater relief as he proceeded to Kojève's prewar lectures on the *Phenomenology* and his postwar second thoughts (pp. 309–24), which had inducted the Nietzschean motifs encapsulated in the title of Fukuyama's book. As for Hegel, 'world history' remained the relevant tribunal: *Die Weltgeschichte ist das Weltgericht.*[100] However, the goal of its finalization altered, from the differentiated freedom of the constitutional state to the '*universal* and *homogeneous* State'. And the locus of its realization shifted, from revolutionary France to revolutionary Russia (the spirit of Napoleon, the spectre of Stalin) and thence, via an evolutionary EEC (shades of Monnet), back again—albeit an incipiently classless, consumerist United States afforded the paradigm of homogeneity.[101]

Having explored 'the three major speculations on the end of history' (p. 324)—Hegel, Cournot, Kojève—and having glanced at some sequels—de Man, Gehlen, Habermas (pp. 324–31)—Anderson returned to Fukuyama's conjugation of Hegel and the late Kojève (pp. 331–57). 'The resultant synthesis', he wrote, 'is an original one, tying liberal democracy and capitalist prosperity together in an emphatic terminal knot' (p. 332). Now, Anderson did not exactly propose to play Alexander to Fukuyama's Gordius. Indeed, he largely aligned himself with the essayist against his critics. Those who had taxed him with a utopianism that imagined liberal-capitalist paradise where purgatory or inferno persisted were guilty of interpretative myopia. However complacent in several respects, Fukuyama's

> schema did not require the suppression of every significant social conflict or the solution of every major institutional problem. It simply asserted that liberal capitalism is the *ne plus ultra* of political and economic life on earth. The end of history is not the arrival of a perfect system, but the elimination of any better alternatives to this one. (P. 336)

Accordingly, his detractors were put on notice 'to show that there are powerful systemic alternatives he has discounted'.

Of the possible contenders, the first—contemporary nationalism—was devoid of the requisite universal scope, rendering apt Fukuyama's deflation of the bombast with which America's (most recent) Gulf War was infused (pp. 336–37).[102] The second—religious fundamentalism, even (or especially) the Islamic variety latched onto by superannuated Cold Warriors—was a sublimation of nationalism (pp. 338–39). And the third—a socialist phoenix from the Communist ashes—was no more availing (pp. 339–41). This last strategy of refutation took two mainstream forms. One—the positive social-democratic variant represented by Michael Mann—affirmed that socialism was

> alive and well as the most advanced form of democracy of our time—the variety that calls itself social. In Western Europe, temporary setbacks may

have checked its progress in the eighties, when international capital increasingly outflanked national governments; but the proportion of the national product absorbed by public expenditure has not qualitatively fallen, and the coming of a Federal European Union will create the conditions for renewing a forward march. (P. 339)

In other words, this was a scenario of the sort imputed to Anderson himself by Gray. An alternative—the negative social-democratic variant represented by Paul Hirst—disputed the uniformly capitalist reality of advanced liberal societies. Both proposals met with a courteous refusal:

Progressive loyalty and analytic clarity are . . . two different things. Western Europe as a zone is . . . distinct in its Social-Democracy . . . from the USA or Japan. . . . But the economies of the Community are . . . capitalist on any definition . . . of the term, structurally driven by competition between enterprises hiring wage-earners to produce profits for private owners. . . . The wish to drape a softening veil over this reality . . . is idle. The attempt to quit the realm of concepts altogether, by denying the very existence of capitalism . . . is equally fruitless. . . . What such postures really represent is a strategy of intellectual consolation. Fukuyama's inventory of the world appears unpalatable: but if it is difficult to find forces capable of altering the world, why not change the inventory? With a wand of redescription, we can dispose of capitalism or reassure ourselves of socialism. (Pp. 340–41)[103]

If the rational, empirical kernel of Fukuyama's essay survived inspection unscathed (p. 341), how did the expansion of its mystical, teleological shell in his non-Communist manifesto fare? In *The End of History and the Last Man*, the mechanisms of historical transformation were identified as the material 'desire' for the satisfaction of needs and the 'spiritual' struggle for recognition; and a fully fledged philosophy of history was elaborated, offering an account of the overall direction and meaning of the historical process— *le sens de l'histoire*—in its laborious progress toward a liberal-capitalist end state. Turning from essay to book, Anderson tracked a series of 'oscillations' (p. 349) in Fukuyama's prioritization of the causal mechanisms of his universal history, and a consequent torsion of his narrative, 'tilt[ing] the outcome of the enquiry towards the stark dichotomy between a rational hedonism and an elemental agonism with which Fukuyama's reflections conclude' (p. 350). But however problematic Fukuyama's project at the metahistorical level, the plausibility of its principal empirical contention—'the prospectus of universal capitalist democracy' presaged by the ongoing liberal economic and political revolutions of the late twentieth century—was the main bone of contention.

In picking it over, Anderson came to the point at once:

> The enormous change in the world that gives its central force to Fukuyama's case has been the collapse of the USSR. . . . Without this global turning-point, the other parts of his story . . . would remain scattered episodes. . . . If the end of history has arrived, it is essentially because the socialist experience is over. . . . But the dissolution of Stalin's empire still leaves a great question unanswered. It is clear that the primary cause of its downfall was its failure to compete in productivity with the major capitalist powers surrounding it—a fate envisaged by Stalin's opponent over half a century ago. . . . The fall of communism has brought liberal democracy [to the population], and is bringing capitalism. What levels of consumption can they expect from the change? (Pp. 351–52)[104]

Here was the Achilles' heel of Fukuyama's projection of a global liberal-capitalist cornucopia, in which a significant proportion of the world would have been levelled up to the living standards of its advanced capitalist zone. Implacable ecological constraints, of which Cournot had had due premonition, told against any such erasure of the current 'staggering inequality' between North and South and East: 'In the global ecology of capital today, the privilege of the few requires the misery of the many' (p. 353).[105] That privilege and misery require little demonstration, alas. It will suffice to note that while one-fifth of the global population lives in extreme poverty, half of it lacks regular access to essential drugs, and a third of children are undernourished, the wealth of 360 or so individual billionaires is equivalent to the annual GDP of countries whose combined population amounts to 45 percent of humanity.[106]

According to Anderson, the condition of the political term of Fukuyama's democratic-capitalist couplet was no more tonic:

> The inadequacy of . . . [Fukuyama's] response to the devitalizing of modern liberty is all too evident. That process is the outcome not just of the power of money and waning of choice within nation-states, but also of their surpassal by international markets and institutions that lack any semblance of democratic control. The European Community, so far the only attempt to transcend national forms for a higher collective sovereignty, still remains yet less accountable to its people than the states that compose it. But just as environmental balance cannot be achieved, social equity furthered, nuclear

safety assured, so too popular sovereignty cannot acquire new substance, without a different international settlement. The Hegelian problems—poverty, community, war—have not gone away, but their solutions have moved to another plane. (P. 356)[107]

The existence of these global problems and Fukuyama's failure to address them convincingly did not dispose of his denial of any *politique de rechange*. Only 'a credible alternative'—'a different international settlement'—could secure that (pp. 357–58).

The traditional name for the Left's alternative 'international settlement'—the Marxist solution to the Hegelian problems—was 'socialism', the proposal interrogated in the concluding, if not conclusive, section of Anderson's essay (pp. 357–75). Minus the extravagant philosophical framework of *Weltgeist*, Fukuyama's vision was fully in tune with the zeitgeist: 'What the end of history means, above all, is the end of socialism' (p. 358). Anderson's inventory of the cause that he had championed for more than three decades commenced, and continued, bleakly. In the last essay published before his death in 1961, just as Anderson's career was beginning, Merleau-Ponty remarked that '[t]he whole of human history is, in a certain sense, stationary'.[108] Thereafter, of course, it underwent an extraordinary acceleration. If today it had not stalled again but might be thought to have culminated, it was because the forces 'making it' were the converse of those predicted.

Lukács's sometime Fichtean defiance—'so much the worse for the facts'—was not available to Anderson.[109] Social-Democratic, Communist, and national liberation movements alike were seemingly spent, from First to erstwhile Second and Third Worlds: 'None of the political currents that set out to challenge capitalism in this century has morale or compass today' (p. 358). The 'common disarray' could be explained by the erosion of each of the cornerstones of what Anderson called 'the classical conception of socialism'. These were (1) its 'historical projection' of a socialization of the forces of production that permitted supersession of the crisis-ridden capitalist mode of production; (2) its 'subjective agency'—the organized industrial working class, endowed with the structural capacity to abolish existing relations of production; (3) its 'political objective' of the replacement of the anarchic market mechanism by planned production for historical needs in a 'free association'; and (4) its 'ethical ideal' of complex equality, beyond what Marx had called 'the narrow horizon of bourgeois right', attainable in an advanced communist society. 'Today', Anderson regretted, all of these elements of the socialist vision have fallen into radical doubt. The secular trend towards increasingly social forces of production . . . continued from the industrial revolution to the long boom. . . . Technological advances in transport and communications have since broken up manufacturing processes and decentralized plants. . . . Meanwhile the industrial working class . . . has . . . gradually declined in size and social cohesion [in the metropolitan countries]. On a world scale, its absolute numbers have grown. . . . But since global population has risen much faster, its relative size as a proportion of humanity is steadily shrinking. Centralized planning achieved remarkable feats in conditions of siege or war. . . . But in peacetime conditions, the command-administrative system in the communist countries proved quite unable to master the problem of coordination in increasingly complex economies. . . . Equality . . . is now widely discounted as either possible or desirable. Indeed, for the commonsense of the time, all the ideas that once made up a belief in socialism are so many dead dogs. (P. 359)

As it happened, the 'popular verdict' was wanting in nuance. Integration of the productive forces, expansion of waged labour, capitalist planning, legal equality—these spreading postwar phenomena dictated significant qualification of the consensus: 'The sources of socialism, as it was traditionally conceived, have not simply dried up'. Nevertheless, given that they had not flowed into the stream of a feasible socialism in the past, '[t]he test for [its] validity . . . as an alternative to capitalism lies in whether it retains a potential for solutions to the problems confronting the latter in its hour of historical triumph' (p. 360).

The intellectual culture of the Left did retain vitality, so Anderson reckoned, referring to *After the Fall* and awarding a special merit to Blackburn's account of the Marxist legacy (pp. 361–63).[110] Two common themes were discernible in reconstructive proposals: 'socialization of the market', as against its 'impossible abolition'; and a more 'developed democracy' than the standard parliamentary-capitalist fare. As to the practicability of these theoretical avenues, Anderson was less sanguine. The classical socialist economic case against capitalism—its reproduction of social inequalities within and between societies—remained valid and was even strengthened by its generation of 'ecological crisis', which indicated its long-run unsustainability as a global mode of production. But socialist silver linings were not glimpsed in acid-rain clouds. For the inviability of capitalism did not prove the viability of socialism. Indeed, the vices of the former compounded the quandaries of the latter, dramatizing its programmatic and strategic deficits: '[T]he paradox is that the terrain on which the socialist economic critique of capitalism has most contemporary power also poses it with even more difficult tasks [of planning] than those it failed to acquit in the past' (p. 364).

Similarly, at the political level, proposals for socialist advance via supranational institutions, now that capital could readily circumvent nation-states, ran into difficulties of scale:

> Western Europe contains the one significant start towards such a federation. The European Community was created principally by Christian Democrats, and the Treaty of Rome was expressly designed as the framework for a robust continental capitalism. It took a considerable time for many socialists to see it as an opportunity for long-term advance in another direction. Today that awareness is much more widespread. On any realistic reckoning, it is clear that a major task of the Left will be to press towards the completion of a genuine federal state in the Community, with a sovereign authority over its constituent parts. That . . . will require a democratically empowered European legislature. . . . Such a Union is the only kind of general will that can contest the new power of the invisible hand as the arbiter of collective destinies. But realism also dictates an awareness that, just as the larger an economy the more difficult it is to plan, so the greater the territory and population of a state, the less subject it tends to become to democratic control. (P. 365)[111]

Intimations that socialism had become utopian again, by classical Marxist criteria, were amplified in Anderson's scrutiny of the fortunes of its 'scientific' fulcrum: the social agency of the 'collective labourer'. Contemporary capitalism had impaired socialist strategy and goal. If it had not buried its allotted grave diggers, it had prepared their obsequies. With greatly reduced numbers of peasants and enhanced numbers of female waged workers, 'the human potential of opposition to the dictates of capital has become more truly universal than it was at the height of the traditional labour movement' (p. 366). Yet the result of this massive, ongoing recomposition of the world's labour force was highly ambivalent:

> The new reality is a massive asymmetry between the international mobility and organization of capital, and the dispersal and fragmentation of labour, that has no historical precedent. The globalization of capitalism has not drawn the resistances to it together, but scattered and outflanked them. . . . [F]or the moment no change in this unequal balance of forces is in sight. The potential extension of social interests in an alternative to capitalism has been accompanied by a reduction in social capacities to fight for one. (P. 366)

The inference to be drawn was stark—and unflinchingly stated in a summarizing judgement:

> All these difficulties have a common origin. The case against capitalism is strongest on the plane where the reach of socialism is weakest—at the level of the world system as a whole. . . . [T]he future belongs to the set of forces that are overtaking the nation-state. So far, they have been captured or driven by capital—as in the past fifty years, internationalism has changed sides. So long as the Left fails to win back the initiative here, the current system will be secure. (P. 367)

By way of conclusion, various historical paradigms were envisaged for the possible fate of socialism (pp. 367–75). An 'oblivion' comparable to that into which Jesuit egalitarianism in Paraguay had lapsed; a 'transvaluation' equivalent to that undergone by the ideals and idiom of the English Revolution; a 'mutation' similar to that which bred socialism out of the principles of 1789; or a 'redemption' commensurate with that experienced by liberalism itself, once the Red Army had assured the defeat of its European fascist rival in the Second World War—these were the 'analogies' that presented themselves (p. 375). Anderson's own intuition as to which eventuality was most probable is an imponderable. Yet if it is safe to infer his predisposition to the last, the nadir from which it would occur was immitigable: 'By the end of the [1980s], communism was everywhere in crisis or collapse, and social democracy was rudderless' (p. 374). As Nicholas Tredell remarked in a fine review of *English Questions* and *A Zone of Engagement*, by Anderson's own submission, '[e]vidence constrains emplotment: and it is hard to see how the history of socialism could be written as anything but tragedy'.[112]

In his calibration of the fin de siècle 'potential of socialism at large', Anderson registered 'the lesser discredit (but also lesser weight) of social democracy' (p. 374). The weightiest factor in his own revaluations—most evident in his second thoughts on the market and representative democracy (pp. 361–63)—was not the abdication of Social-Democracy but the destruction of its fraternal enemy. '[W]ith the collapse of the Soviet bloc', he wrote two years later, 'the rationale of descent from the October Revolution has all but disappeared'.[113] Made with specific reference to West European Communism, this assertion equally implicated the Far Left to which Anderson, for all his organizational aloofness, had been affiliated. To borrow the terms of his foreword to *A Zone of Engagement* (p. xii), the 1984 Ali anthology on the legacy of Stalinism in which his Trotsky text figured pertained to 'the intellectual world of the revolutionary Left, from a particular standpoint within it': the world of Trotsky, Deutscher, Mandel, and their successors, whose house journal had been the *NLR* under Anderson's editorship. By contrast, the 1991 Blackburn symposium on the future of socialism, which was commended by Anderson, featured not a single one of these successors and inhabited a different universe. No peremptory inconsistency was involved here. In accordance with Deutschero-Trotskyist perspectives, the implosion of actually existing socialism was construed as the definitive historical verdict on formerly existing revolutionary socialism, descended, like Stalinism, from the October Revolution.

In 1917 Trotsky had conceived the Russian Revolution as 'the prologue to world revolution'. A decade later, making his stand against 'socialism in one country' while awaiting the main action in the metropolitan theatre of the world, he conceded that 'if capitalism were to flourish and if its economy and culture were to be on the ascendant that would mean that we had come too early'.[114] After the outbreak of the Second World War, an even more 'onerous' prospect than Bolshevik prematurity was contemplated by him:

> [I]f the world proletariat should actually prove incapable of fulfilling the mission placed upon it by the course of development, nothing else would remain except only to recognize that the socialist programme, based on the internal contradictions of capitalist society, ended as a Utopia.[115]

Given the refutation of Trotsky's interpretation of Stalinism in the East, and notwithstanding the misfortunes of socialism in the West, Anderson could in 1976 postulate 'the descendant position of capitalism on a global scale, in an epoch which despite everything saw a third of the world wrested from it'.[116] Furthermore, although eschewing talk of the proletariat's historical 'mission', with the destabilization of imperialism he could anticipate a resurgence of socialism in the metropolis. This, rather than Deutscher's scenario of an 'obliterati[on]' of 'the old antithesis between *backward* Russia and the *advanced* West' via de-Stalinization from above, and a consequent 'regeneration of the Russian Revolution',[117] was the Andersonian wager of the time—a time which he measured much like Trotsky, who in 1932 estimated the intervening fifteen years as 'a minute on the clock of history'.[118] A little less than four minutes on, the Bolshevik past was not prologue but epilogue. Western prospects had evaporated, and the Eastern results with which they were inextricably bound up had been overturned. The 'heavy artillery' of capitalist commodities—more potent than any imperialist ordnance in Korea or Vietnam—had levelled Russian and mined Chinese walls.[119] As the bourgeoisie set about 'creat[ing] a world after its own image', putatively postcapitalist societies were rendered precapitalist overnight.

Now, as we have seen in chapter 3, Anderson's 1991 postscript to his Deutscher preface deemed him a 'connoisseur of the ironies of history', for whom any restoration of capitalism in Russia 'might—like other restorations—have its redeeming place in the complicated longer-run progress towards a common human liberty'.[120] Among the restorations specified in the quinquennial report on the *NLR* was that of the English monarchy in the seventeenth century. Granting, for the sake of argument, that the analogy held, the progress would be complicated and protracted indeed. As Anderson's discussion in 'The Ends of History' of another analogy—between the fates of Leveller radicalism and socialism—indicated, one effect of 1660 was to erase 'the radical ferment of the English Republic' from historical memory for more than three centuries (p. 369). Not 'centuries of transition', but centuries of capitalism? Or, as Bill Warren is reported to have remarked of Mandel's *Late Capitalism*, 'Capitalism—late for what?'.

The conviction that events in the East have not infirmed the classical Marxist theory of historical trajectory undergirding 'scientific socialism' led Alex Callinicos to object that there was a systemic alternative to liberal capitalism scouted in Anderson's sense of an ending: precisely revolutionary socialism.[121] But even were we to endorse his opposing interpretation of the 'key empirical issue'; to accept that Stalinism was in fact 'a particular variant of capitalism' (i.e., 'bureaucratic state capitalism'); therewith to reconceive the 'great contest' as one between competing capitalisms (liberal/state); and thus to retrieve an unvanquished socialism from a Western capitalism victorious only over its Eastern alter ego—this consolation would furnish cold comfort. For if the USSR and the Second World were not in any sense socialist, then there never has been socialism; and hence its feasibility as a systemic alternative to capitalism remains undemonstrated—an inviolate ideal, rather than a proven potential.[122]

Citing John Stuart Mill on the choice between capitalism and communism (pp. 360–61), Anderson at one point posed the question of whether socialism had as yet received 'a fair trial': '[H]ave we seen it, not as it actually existed, but as it might exist . . . ?'. More or less in the spirit of Schumpeter's admonitions about comparing 'a given reality with an *idea* . . . [or] with an *ideal*',[123] he stressed that 'real conditions'—not 'utopian circumstances'—were the requisite test bed. Those conditions exhibited a fearful asymmetry, according to him, between capital and the forces disarrayed against it. In what Blackburn termed a 'prophetic article', C. Wright Mills had regretted the New Left's subscription to the 'labour metaphysic'.[124]

In the introduction to *Mapping the West European Left* (1994),[125] Anderson returned to his apprehension of the quasi-dystopian circumstances faced by the Left at the end of the twentieth century—'a time when hopes of socialism have been struck off its agenda' (p. 11). A 'double change in its strategic situation' obtained. First there was the dispersion of its 'constituencies' with the waning of the 'centrality' of the manual working class, as wage labour increasingly disaggregated along lines of occupation, income and job security, generation, gender, and ethnicity (pp. 11–14). Having outlined the materialist analysis of class recomposition alluded to in *In the Tracks of Historical Materialism* but whose implications for working-class politics had been minimized,[126] Anderson retracted the Marxist common sense of the 1960s and 1970s for a moderate version of the sociological consensus of the 1980s: the result of this recomposition bordering upon discomposition was to 'make the task of *subjective* mobilization for any radical change inherently harder' (p. 14).

The second alteration was a circumscription of 'the *objective* space' for the governmental Left's habitual policy instruments, fiscal and monetary, by national and international exigencies—especially 'the globalization of capital' (pp. 14–15). In these conditions, reissuing the prognostication of 'The Light of Europe', Anderson foresaw '[a] farewell to the substance of social democracy . . . [without] a disappearance of the term' (p. 16). The supranational light previously glimpsed at the end of the national tunnel was itself being extinguished, as the European Union gradually adapted to the neoliberal catechism of economic correctness. Inveighing against the Maastricht Treaty, Anderson maintained:

> Reclamation both of the basic principles of representative democracy, and of any prospects of effective macroeconomic policy, requires the construction of a true federal framework in Europe. The left has on the whole been no more clear-sighted or imaginative about this than the centre or right. Indecision and confusion are still the norm. . . . Purely national strategies are vanishing for every part of the political spectrum. The West European left will acquire new contours only when this crux is resolved. (P. 22)

Meanwhile, the roll call of dishonour with which Anderson's survey opened (p. 1) dramatized not simply the political debilitation but the moral degradation of leading sectors of the Second International. With dwindling rationale, Social-Democracy was incontestably 'at an impasse' (p. 7)—reduced to appealing to a '[m]odernity voided of any content beyond market adjustment' (p. 11), implementing 'Reaganomics' under the antipodean rubric of 'Rogernomics'. Contemplating the possibility of an Americanization of West European politics less than a decade earlier, Anderson had averred: 'There is still a long way to go before such a scenario is realized'.[127] By 1994 it seemed alarmingly close at hand. In any event, the corrosion of the Second International—the 'rusty brake' from whose inhibition Trotsky had wished to release 'the masses', and hence 'the locomotive of history'[128]—had not redounded to the benefit of the non-Social-Democratic Left, to whom a solitary paragraph was devoted. It bluntly concluded thus:

> Nowhere . . . does it have any chance of forming a government: its only hope of office is in coalition with a dominant social democracy. Nor, for all the greater sharpness of its rejection of post-Reaganite capitalism, is its stock of solutions much richer. For the moment . . . , the existence of this political area does little to modify the programmatic dilemmas of the left. (P. 7)[129]

Disconcerted in government by the disintegration of the postwar conditions that had facilitated it, Social-Democracy was disorientated in opposition, in signal contrast to the record of the New Right in its wilderness years (p. 19). Anderson did not emulate the sentiment of Horkheimer's manifesto for critical theory in 1937: '[T]ruth has sought refuge among small groups of admirable men'.[130] It was, however, to 'the margins of day-to-day politics' that he looked for 'creative reflection', reprising the proposals canvassed in 'The Light of Europe' (pp. 19–21)—including 'lines of attack' on existing capitalist property relations that seem conspicuously exposed to the exact objection of political utopianism raised against Nove's *Economics of Feasible Socialism* a decade before.[131]

If, according to Anderson, Social-Democracy 'appears to have lost its compass' (p. 15), '*un monde déboussolé*'—a world that has lost both its bearings and its compass—was the all-embracing verdict on the era of 'globalitarianism' offered by one French commentator.[132] In a review of a work that came to rest on a similar note—Hobsbawm's *Age of Extremes*[133]—Anderson tactfully demurred at its catastrophist presentiments—if not the socialism or barbarism of the century's outset, then a 'changed society' or 'darkness' at its close. Underlining the 'reversal of verdicts' operated in Hobsbawm's account of the twentieth century, Anderson queried the depiction of 1945–73 as 'golden age' succeeded by a 'landslide'. Whereas Hobsbawm foregrounded the globally deleterious effects of the collapse of Communism and the diffusion of deregulated capitalism, Anderson wondered 'how far [these] have . . . been offset by the extraordinary improvement in Chinese living standards, a phenomenon of the last 20 years—a much larger historical fact than the temporary decline of Russia'. Although Anderson's summary of Hobsbawm's 'sombre prospectus for the millennium' coincided, in essentials, with his own in 'The Ends of History', his inference differed. Contrary to the title under which his review appeared, darkness had gathered; it had not fallen.

In Hobsbawm's characterization of the post-1973 period as a 'landslide', Anderson observed, 'the vision of the historian and the passion of the partisan are one'. In the case of the late Anderson, we might vary the attribution: the vision of the historian and the dispassion of the partisan are one. An earlier *Guardian* notice of Martin Bernal's *Black Athena* had advanced 'a world-historical perspective' as the necessary corrective to its audacious revisionism, and counselled that 'lively contemporary sympathies tend to be most fruitful in studies of the past when also most guarded against'.[134] Practicing what he here preached, Anderson has applied the protocol to his own studies of the present, in remarkably temperate overviews of Brazil, a long-standing and passionate interest,[135] and of South Korea, a new departure in print.[136] Such redoubtable analytical sobriety betokens no fraying of progressive loyalties on the part of a contributor to the *London Review of Books* who positions himself on 'the far left of its spectrum'.[137] Yet as Anderson remarked in *Mapping the West European Left* (p. 17), just as the *appellation mal contrôlée* of 'social democracy' could outlast the evacuation of its substance, so 'a "left" could survive within an all-capitalist system that was to the right of anything now considered in the centre'—a general theory of political relativity that presumably encompasses a 'far left'. Such a scenario has been repeated in Anderson's recent response to Bobbio's *Left and Right*.[138] In what sense is Clinton's Democratic dispensation in health and welfare more progressive than that of the Republican administration of Nixon? Or, to take the argument a stage further, who could seriously argue that today's British Labour Party is actually to the left of the official party of the Centre, the Liberal Democrats? Mitterrand, Gonzales, Blair, and their sort in Europe; Lange and Hawke in Australasia—shaking the invisible hand, these men of 'the left' have converted executive alternation into '*un jeu à risque nul*' for capital.[139]

In his letter of 12 December 1988 to Bobbio, Anderson had confided 'a deep conviction' to his correspondent:

I . . . do not believe that the listless and manipulated semi-liberty of today will be humanity's last historical word. . . . Who can really imagine the present order will just be reproduced . . . till the end of time? Things will eventually either get much worse or much better. The one safe prediction is that they will not remain the same. Of course, one is speaking of centuries rather than decades—far 'too late' for someone like me as well. But given the road covered so far, I think there are grounds for a rational optimism about the direction of this future. . . .

A few short years later, the 'rational optimism' afforded by a secular historical perspective was but dimly discernible: stoicism, rather than optimism or pessimism, had become the predominant temper of Anderson's writing.

If the role of reality instructor is the one to which Anderson currently seems most attuned, resistance to that reality is not abandoned in the act of reflecting it:

> A purely axiological defence of the idea of the Left, bereft of any historical theory or institutional attack capable of shaking the status quo, will not pass muster. Bobbio once looked to liberal socialism for such a challenge. Today he redescribes social democracy as liberal socialism, in a notable lowering of expectations. . . . The lesson of his book . . . is that the opposition between Left and Right has no axiomatic guarantee. If the Left is to survive as a meaningful force, in a world overwhelmingly dominated by the Right, it will have to fight for a real alternative to it.[140]

Anderson too has notably lowered his expectations. But aside from 'A Culture in Contraflow', he has mostly declined the consolations of redescription. Philosophers (and historians) have to interpret the world aright. The point, however, remains to change it.

Conclusion ► The Figure in the Mirror

'Jesuit, Leveller, Jacobin, Liberal—these are the figures in the mirror'.[1] So concludes 'The Ends of History', adamant that Clio can do more than amuse. When Anderson glances in his own historical mirror, what figure does he discern? Glimpsed in the disenchanted glass of *Considerations on Western Marxism*, the holder of a professorial chair at UCLA would cast an image that he has done much to make familiar. *Mutato nomine de te fabula narratur?* Tempting as it is, so trite a conclusion should be resisted. For, as has been suggested in chapter 4, Anderson's valediction of the Western Marxist tradition, polarized toward 'contemporary bourgeois culture' with the 'restabilization of imperialism',[2] can be read as a presentiment of the even more intractable dilemma of Marxist intellectuals after the fall, faced as they are with the de facto social exclusivity of the West. If, on the other hand, Anderson has retained something of the 'olympian universalism' characteristic of Marx and Engels but missing from their twentieth-century West European successors, this may in turn be attributed to his relative lack of 'concrete racination in the particular situation and life of [his] countries'[3]— the United Kingdom and United States—vis-à-vis which he remains intangibly extraterritorial.

Set upon neither 'reconciliation with reality' (Lukács) nor 'strategy of hibernation' (the Frankfurt school), Anderson's Marxism too has undergone an 'irresistible *displacement*'. Increasingly conceived as an alternative, comparative historical sociology, it is no longer the historical materialism for which, like Trotsky, he had stood—a more or less 'undiluted classical Marxism, in all its intellectual and moral strength and also in all its political weakness—a weakness which resulted from its own incompatibility with Russian backwardness and from the failures of socialism in the West'.[4] The conclusive demonstration of the political fragility *and* intellectual frailties of that Marxism has at once renewed Anderson's determination to be contemporary with both past and present,[5] and undermined his confidence in the theory of historical trajectory—cornerstone of 'scientific socialism'—of which he had been an indefatigable partisan. Intellectually, at any rate, Perry Anderson has mellowed with age. In the process, he has perhaps become contemporary with Merleau-Ponty's 1960 preface to *Signs*, published the same year as Anderson made his debut and his then master Sartre pronounced Marxism 'the untranscendable philosophy for our time': 'Marxism has definitely entered a new phase of its history, in which it can inspire and orient analyses and retain a certain heuristic value, but is certainly no longer true *in the sense it was believed to be true'*.[6]

Now, it is of course the case that 'one man's sense of concrete historical reality is another man's *trahison des clercs'*.[7] In view, however, of certain Deutscherite constants in Anderson's sense of concrete historical reality, few would dare call it intellectual treason—and not simply because it has prospered elsewhere, if often with less political reason. Reverting to a category first employed in 1969, two decades later Anderson affirmed 'a very real sense in which the life-history of any labour movement as a rule *is* chronologically differential, with certain brief "founding moments" often setting the direction of development for long decades thereafter, as in the lives of individuals'.[8] With appropriate modifications, we may posit a founding moment of Anderson's individual career in 1959–62 (Cuban Revolution, Italian reform-Communism), overdetermined by a second in 1968 (Tet Offensive, May events), which set the direction of his development for close on three decades thereafter, until the conjuncture of the late 1980s (capitalist ascendancy, Communist collapse) set in train a refoundation of whose redirections we as yet possess only initial traces.

At an inconceivably darker historical moment—during the Moscow trials—Trotsky resisted the seduction of 'pessimism': 'This would be like passively and plaintively taking umbrage at history. How can one do that? History has to be taken as she is; and when she allows herself such extraordinary and filthy outrages, one must fight her back with one's fists'.[9] Such voluntarism betrays unacknowledged difficulties within undiluted classical Marxism; and the imagery is a trifle too pugilistic to suit Anderson. The moral of resistance is nevertheless well taken. Armed with a pen, Anderson continues to wield the weapon of criticism. Paying homage to the qualities of Trotsky's biographer in 1984, he recalled

> the actual contrasts between the trio Deutscher selected for their resistance to conformity in the Napoleonic age. Goethe, Shelley, Jefferson—serene olympian, visionary iconoclast, shrewd politician. He had an element of each in his own make-up. A socialist movement will only flourish if it can encompass all of the ideals they represent.[10]

Modification of the last sentence for republication in 1992—'The culture of the Left needs them all'[11]—registers displacement within, not abandonment of, a zone of engagement. Therein, the vocation of theory—office of the 'serene olympian' stationed in the watchtower—is not to express a practical

movement of social transformation, but to explain—and criticize—the existing state of affairs, on whose abolition only a quasi-Pascalian wager may be
hazarded. Apparently resigned to the persistence of capitalism as such for
the foreseeable future, the 'shrewd politician' in Anderson is meanwhile
concerned to press practicable reforms of it while eluding the syndrome—
regularly succumbed to by half-second (ex-)social-democrats—of mistaking
these for socialism. Anderson is 'not in a mood to settle either'.[12] To vary
one of his titles, he pertains to the intransigent Left at the end of the century. Yet it might be wondered whether, by comparison with his earlier self,
he is not too much the 'serene olympian' and 'shrewd politician', too little
the 'visionary iconoclast'.

Interviewed in the *NLR* in the autumn of 1978, upon completion of his
History of Soviet Russia, E. H. Carr pondered the 'present plight' of the Left
in the advanced capitalist countries:

> It seems to me that there are two alternatives open to serious members of
> the Left today. The first is to remain communists, and to remain an educa-
> tional and propagandist group divorced from political action. [Its] func-
> tions . . . would be to analyse the social and economic transformation now
> taking place in the capitalist world; . . . and to try to draw some more or less
> realistic picture of what socialism should and could mean in the contempo-
> rary world. The second alternative for the Left is to go into current politics,
> become social-democrats, frankly recognize and accept the capitalist system,
> [and] pursue those limited ends which can be achieved within the sys-
> tem. . . . One cannot be both a communist and a social-democrat. The social-
> democrat criticizes capitalism, but in the last resort defends it. The commu-
> nist rejects it, and believes that in the end it will destroy itself. But the
> communist in western countries . . . is conscious of the strength of the forces
> which still uphold it, and the lack of any revolutionary force powerful
> enough to overthrow it.[13]

Another verdict Anderson was not inclined to accept at the time,[14] has not
Carr's judgement proved the sounder of the two? With this dispiriting qualification, of course, that in an ignominious capitulation Social-Democrats
today defend capitalism in the *first* resort, leaving 'communists' virtually
alone to *criticize* it. Anderson's pursuit of 'those limited ends which can be
achieved within the system' does not entail either that he has renounced
communism for social-democracy or that he is attempting the impossible: to
be both a communist and a social-democrat. Rather, it signifies an awareness
that the Chinese wall between revolutionary maximalism and reformist

minimalism erected by Carr is, in the current conjuncture as before, an anti-capitalist counsel of despair. In a passage that might in part stand in for the autocritique that Anderson has not delivered, a communist—Lucio Magri—has written:

> Effective political action of a mass character requires more than just a strategic perspective and an identity at the level of ideas; it cannot operate only in the *longue durée*, with regard to epochal contradictions. It must also take up position in a determinate short-term future, and acquire leverage over immediate contradictions and forces that are already in play. In fact, one of the most frequent and costly errors in the history of the workers' movement has been to confuse historical actuality with an immediate political perspective. Even great thinkers could, like Marx, see the Paris Commune as the beginning of the socialist revolution or, like Lenin, argue that the October Revolution would rapidly spread to Western Europe. In 1968 the same mistake was committed in an even more naive and unjustified manner.[15]

Recalcitrant to conformity in an age of capitalist uniformity, Anderson, however distant he may now be from an intellectual world long his own, still commends to readers of *English Questions* Gramsci's example of 'moral resistance and political innovation'.[16] Emulating it will be no easy matter; and the delay in completing a promised revision of *The Ends of History* suggests some perplexity as to how to meet so demanding a self-imposed standard. Yet we should beware of premature judgement. As the six-year interval between 'Components of the National Culture' and *Passages from Antiquity to Feudalism* and *Lineages of the Absolutist State* attests, *reculer pour mieux sauter* has proved a salutary maxim before now. Even so, predominantly concerned to avoid errors of commission in the past, Anderson will have to risk them in future, if he is to contribute to the moral-political 'combination needed today'. Invariably a waiting game, Andersonian Marxism has hitherto deferred a reckoning. Otherwise engaged, maybe its time has come.

Notes

Full bibliographic information for sources by Perry Anderson appears in the Select Bibliography that follows this section.

Preface

1. Terry Eagleton, in a review of Ellen Meiksins Wood's *The Pristine Culture of Capitalism: A Historical Essay on Old Regimes and Modern States* (Verso, London and New York, 1991), *Guardian*, 1 October 1992.
2. See the informative entry by M. A. R. Habib in Michael Payne, ed., *A Dictionary of Cultural and Critical Theory*, Blackwell, Oxford and Cambridge, Mass., 1996, pp. 27–28.
3. *Considerations on Western Marxism*, New Left Books, London, 1976, p. 13.
4. Scott L. Malcomson, 'Ten Thousand Megalomaniacs: Perry Anderson, Man of Steel', *Voice Literary Supplement*, March 1993, p. 21.
5. This is a point to which Anderson himself has drawn attention, regretting the early loss of Isaac Deutscher: see preface to Deutscher, *Marxism, Wars, and Revolutions: Essays from Four Decades*, ed. Tamara Deutscher, Verso, London, 1984, p. xviii.
6. See the foreword to *A Zone of Engagement*, Verso, London and New York, 1992, p. xii.
7. Ibid., pp. xi–xii.
8. Alex Callinicos, 'Perry Anderson and "Western Marxism"', *International Socialism* no. 23, spring 1984, pp. 113–28: here pp. 124, 125, 127.
9. The coinage is Malcomson's, in 'Ten Thousand Megalomaniacs'.
10. Leon Trotsky, quoted in Isaac Deutscher, *The Prophet Outcast—Trotsky: 1929–1940* (1963), Oxford University Press, Oxford, 1979, p. 19 n. 2.
11. Cf. Norman Geras, 'Literature of Revolution', *NLR*, nos. 113–14, January/April 1979, pp. 14ff., on 'political impatience'.
12. Jean-Paul Sartre, *The Communists and Peace* (1952–54), trans. Irene Clephane, Hamish Hamilton, London, 1969, p. 99.
13. Eric J. Hobsbawm, 'Radicalism and Revolution in Britain', in *Revolutionaries: Contemporary Essays* (1973), Phoenix, London, 1994, p. 15. This is a collection for which Anderson has expressed his admiration ('Communist Party History', in Raphael Samuel, ed., *People's History and Socialist Theory*, Routledge and Kegan Paul, London, 1981, p. 149). Significantly—and here Anderson temporarily differed—Hobsbawm continued: 'There is no reason to believe that it will be less difficult in future than it has been in the past'. For Hobsbawm's diagnosis of the revolutionary 'predicament', see pp. 16–17.
14. Preface to Deutscher, *Marxism, Wars, and Revolutions*, p. xx.
15. Isaac Deutscher, 'The Ex-Communist's Conscience' (1950), reprinted in *Marxism, Wars, and Revolutions*, pp. 49–59: here pp. 57–58.
16. See the foreword to *English Questions*, Verso, London and New York, 1992, p. 2, for Anderson's description of the analytical optic of his essays on British history. For the latest such explicit allusion in his work, see the 'Diary' devoted to South Korea, *London Review of Books*, 17 October 1996, p. 29. In the strict terms of Fernand

Braudel's employment of the distinctions in *The Mediterranean and the Mediterranean World in the Age of Philip II*, which identifies structural (geographical) *longue durée* as 'a history of constant repetition, ever-recurring cycles', and eventual (political) *temps court* as 'surface disturbances', conjunctural (socioeconomic) 'medium' time is the primary Andersonian level of analysis. In his 1958 essay 'La longue durée', Braudel reflected that if 'very long time' did indeed exist, it could be only 'the time of sages': *Écrits sur l'histoire*, Flammarion, Paris, 1969, p. 76. For Anderson's thoughts on Braudel, see *Arguments within English Marxism*, New Left Books, London, 1980, pp. 73–76, and *A Zone of Engagement*, pp. 251–78.

17. Leon Trotsky, 'The USSR in War' (1939), in *In Defense of Marxism: The Social and Political Contradictions of the Soviet Union* (1942), Pathfinder Press, New York, 1990, p. 15; cited by Anderson in 'Trotsky's Interpretation of Stalinism' (1983), in Tariq Ali, ed., *The Stalinist Legacy: Its Impact on Twentieth-Century World Politics*, Penguin, Harmondsworth, 1984, p. 123. As Deutscher notes in glossing his partial quotation of the passage, Trotsky 'applied the grand historical scale to events and to his own fate'. However, '[h]is inclination to take the long historical view did not blunt his sensitivity to the injustices and cruelties of his time—on the contrary, it sharpened it. He denounced the Stalinist perversion of socialism so passionately because he himself never lost sight of the vista of a truly humane socialist future': *The Prophet Outcast*, p. 512.

18. Foreword to *English Questions*, p. 11.

19. Karl Marx, *Selected Writings*, ed. David McLellan, Oxford University Press, Oxford, 1977, p. 229.

20. Frederick Engels, 'Socialism: Utopian and Scientific', in Karl Marx and Frederick Engels, *Selected Works*, vol. 3, Progress Publishers, Moscow, 1977, p. 151. For a valuable discussion of the implications of the self-conception of classical Marxism, see Joseph McCarney, *Social Theory and the Crisis of Marxism*, Verso, London and New York, 1990.

21. Georg Lukács, *Lenin: A Study in the Unity of His Thought*, trans. Nicholas Jacobs, New Left Books, London, 1970, p. 11.

22. Cf. Karl Marx and Frederick Engels, *The German Ideology*, in *Collected Works*, vol. 5, Lawrence and Wishart, London, 1976, p. 49.

23. 'The Ends of History', in *A Zone of Engagement*, pp. 357–75.

24. See the foreword to *Passages from Antiquity to Feudalism*, New Left Books, London, 1974, p. 9.

25. *A Zone of Engagement*, p. x. Cf. *In the Tracks of Historical Materialism*, Verso, London, 1983, p. 14, where Anderson sets down the 'protocols for a Marxist reflection on Marxism', allocating priority to 'extrinsic' (broadly political) over 'intrinsic' (theoretical) history. As we shall see, his deployment of these protocols in accounting for the fortunes of Western Marxism has something of the feared, 'reductive' result. (It follows from an overhasty conclusion—'The trajectory of the theory has thus always been *primarily* determined by the fate of [popular] practice'—inferred from an unexceptionable premiss: 'Marxist theory, bent on understanding the world, has always aimed at an asymptotic unity with a popular practice seeking to transform it'.) Application of these protocols to Anderson's own Marxism is likely to induce analogous effects, 'flattening it out on the anvil of world politics'.

26. *English Questions*, p. 11.

27. *In the Tracks of Historical Materialism*, p. 14—a set of lectures whose first chapter is entitled 'Prediction and Performance'.

28. Michael Sprinker, personal communication with author, March 1996.

29. For an account broadly sympathetic to the resigners from the *NLR*, see Patrick Wright, 'Beastly Trials of the Last Politburo', *Guardian*, 17 July 1993, p. 29. For a satirical glimpse in fictional print of the *NLR* milieu, the curious might wish to consult

the roman à clef of Tariq Ali, *Redemption*, Chatto and Windus, London, 1990—especially chap. 9, 'The *New Life Journal*' (pp. 91–106).

30. Isaac Deutscher, *Stalin: A Political Biography* (1949), 2d ed., Oxford University Press, New York, 1966, p. xiv.

1. Demarcations

1. See Benedict R. O'G. Anderson's introduction to *Language and Power: Exploring Political Cultures in Indonesia*, Cornell University Press, Ithaca and London, 1990, pp. 1–2, for an evocation of the family background, to which Perry refers readers in the foreword to *English Questions*, Verso, London and New York, 1992, p. 7 n. 6. Benedict Anderson's allusion to their father having been 'more or less disowned' by their grandfather—a general in the imperial army, stationed in China—casts an ironic light on Perry's reference, in 'The Figures of Descent', to 'career officers . . . tend[ing] to come from the neediest and least reputable branch of the [landlord] class, its Anglo-Irish extension' (ibid., p. 135).

2. For three recent accounts of the New Left in Britain, see Lin Chun, *The British New Left*, Edinburgh University Press, Edinburgh, 1993; Michael Kenny, *The First New Left: British Intellectuals after Stalin*, Lawrence and Wishart, London, 1995; and Dennis Dworkin, *Cultural Marxism in Postwar Britain: History, the New Left, and the Origins of Cultural Studies*, Duke University Press, Durham, N.C., and London, 1997. Cf. Geoffrey Foote, *The Labour Party's Political Thought: A History*, Croom Helm, London, 1985, chap. 13, 'The Challenge of the New Left' (pp. 287–307). On the *NLR* specifically, see Duncan Thompson, *The Moment of New Left Review*, Pluto Press, London and Chicago, forthcoming.

3. Editorial in *ULR* vol. 1, no. 1, spring 1957, p. 2. '[S]ocialist humanism', Edward Thompson subsequently wrote, '. . . exists by virtue of a continuing polemic, on the one hand with Communist orthodoxy, and on the other hand with liberal and social-democratic ideology': 'Where Are We Now?', internal memorandum, April 1963, p. 16 (qtd. in Kenny, *The First New Left*, p. 69).

4. Anderson and Robin Blackburn, 'Cuba, Free Territory of America', *New University* (Oxford) no. 4, 5 December 1960, pp. 17–23: here p. 22. For further evidence of the early interest, see the collective interview with Saul Landau conducted by Anderson and Blackburn, among others: 'Cuba: The Present Reality', *NLR* no. 9, May/June 1961, pp. 12–22.

5. 'Sweden: Mr. Crosland's Dreamland', *NLR* no. 7, January/February 1961, pp. 4–12; 'Sweden II: Study in Social Democracy', *NLR* no. 9, May/June 1961, pp. 34–45. Originally intended to have been published in three parts, the investigation either was never completed or simply did not appear in its entirety.

6. '[T]he stereotyped class pattern of Western capitalist countries subsists in Sweden, in the midst of overflowing welfare and abundance, almost untouched by nearly 30 years of ostensibly socialist government': 'Sweden: Mr. Crosland's Dreamland', p. 12. However, having noted that capitalism could be condemned 'either as a more or less straightforward bipolar system of exploitation, or as a social praxis in alienation from all its agents, at all its levels' (p. 10), Anderson opted for the latter as more profound.

7. 'The plan *decodes* the vast, interlocking, impenetrable, inspissated economy and ascribes a lucid meaning to every one of the myriad cryptic gestures which compose it. It renders the entire work-force transparent to itself as engaged in *one* task': 'Sweden II', p. 44.

8. In a 1988 conference paper on the New Left, Raphael Samuel quotes the young Anderson as maintaining that '[i]f there is one word which the Labour Party lacks, it is alienation': 'Born-Again Socialism', in Oxford University Socialist Discussion Group, ed., *Out of Apathy: Voices of the New Left Thirty Years On*, Verso, London and New York, 1989, pp. 39–57: here p. 43. Arbitrating the differences between E. P. Thompson and Althusser twenty years later, Anderson would note and criticize the post-1956 tendency to reduce Marx's achievement to his early writings and to seek in them the basis for a comprehensive critique of Stalinism: cf. *Arguments within English Marxism*, New Left Books, London, 1980, pp. 107–9. In 1959 Thompson himself had regretted the fact that the *ULR* milieu was 'more at ease discussing alienation than exploitation' ('Commitment in Politics', qtd. in Kenny, *The First New Left*, p. 61).
9. Anderson and Stuart Hall, 'The Politics of the Common Market', *NLR* no. 10, July/August 1961, pp. 1–14.
10. Introduction to the debate of the Central Committee of the Italian Communist Party on the Twenty-Second Congress of the CPSU, *NLR* nos. 13–14, January/April 1962, pp. 152–60. Aside from the 1984 preface to Deutscher's *Marxism, Wars, and Revolutions*, for Anderson's sense of Deutscher's stature see 'Socialism and Pseudo-Empiricism', *NLR* no. 35, January/February 1966, p. 23 ('the only Marxist intellectual of world eminence in Britain today'); and 'Components of the National Culture', *NLR* no. 50, July/August 1968, p. 20 ('the greatest Marxist historian of his time'). When 'Components' was reprinted a year later in Alexander Cockburn and Robin Blackburn, eds., *Student Power: Problems, Diagnosis, Action* (Penguin/New Left Review, Harmondsworth, 1969, pp. 214–84), the latter plaudit was rendered as 'the greatest Marxist historian in the world' (p. 234). Deutscher's 'formative influence' is declared in *Arguments within English Marxism*, p. 155.
11. *English Questions*, p. 6.
12. 'A Decennial Report', unpublished document, [1975], pp. 5–6.
13. In the words of the 'Decennial Report' (p. 6), 'The general editorial conception of the new NLR was largely inspired by *Les Temps Modernes*'. According to its current editor, in the period 1964–66 a 'certain diffuse Sartreanism also coloured the magazine's politics and *Les Temps Modernes* furnished an admired model' (Robin Blackburn, 'A Brief History of *New Left Review*, 1960–1990', in *Thirty Years of New Left Review: Index to Numbers 1–184 [1960–1990]*, London, 1992, pp. v–xi: here p. vii).
14. 'Portugal and the End of Ultra-Colonialism': part 1, *NLR* no. 15, May/June 1962, pp. 83–102; part 2, *NLR* no. 16, July/August 1962, pp. 88–123; part 3, *NLR* no. 17, winter 1962, pp. 85–114. Apparently derived from Anderson's employment at a Third World institute, African Research and Publications, the Portugal study was published in book form in France by François Maspero. The Third World focus of the new editorial team is also evident, for example, in Lucien Rey (pseudonym of Peter Wollen), 'Persia in Perspective', part 1, *NLR* no. 19, March/April 1963, pp. 32–55, and part 2, *NLR* no. 20, summer 1963, pp. 69–98; and Robin Blackburn, 'Prologue to the Cuban Revolution', *NLR* no. 21, October 1963, pp. 52–91.
15. 'Portugal', part 2, pp. 103, 99, 113.
16. See 'Portugal', part 3, p. 108.
17. Ibid., p. 113 n. 3.
18. 'A Decennial Report', p. 4. This analysis is confirmed by a contemporaneous memorandum of Anderson's: 'Conspectus', [1964], pp. 2–3. See also the editorial 'On Internationalism'—unsigned, but plausibly attributable to the editor (*NLR* no. 18, January/February 1963, pp. 3–4)—which concludes by expressing the 'hope to contribute to the necessary internationalization of British socialist thought today'.
19. The quotations are from two acute analyses by Michael Rustin, an editor of the *NLR*

until 1964: 'The New Left and the Labour Party', in *For a Pluralist Socialism*, Verso, London, 1985, chap. 2, pp. 46–75: here p. 53; and 'The New Left as a Social Movement', in Oxford University Socialist Discussion Group, ed., *Out of Apathy*, pp. 117–28: here p. 120. More recently, another former editor, Ellen Meiksins Wood, has argued that 'the adoption of Continental Marxism by the second New Left, in its *NLR* incarnation, represented a significant *political* break, marking a more decisive shift away from the labour movement and class politics than is immediately apparent in its revival of Marxist theory. That shift was . . . right from the beginning encoded in *NLR*'s anti-"populism"; and it is one of the major paradoxes of the second New Left that this transformation took the form of a renewed commitment to revolutionary Marxism': 'A Chronology of the New Left and Its Successors, or: Who's Old-Fashioned Now?', in Leo Panitch et al., eds., *Socialist Register, 1995*, Merlin Press, London, 1995, pp. 22–49: here p. 42. The general drift of this argument seems to me to read the situation of the 1990s back into the early 1960s, skirting the *post hoc, ergo propter hoc* fallacy. A related charge, 'super-theoreticism', is pressed by Lin Chun, *The British New Left*, p. xvi (cf. also p. 62).

20. These emphases are noted in one of the earliest—and best—attempts to capture the initial contrast between the cohorts: Peter Sedgwick, 'The Two New Lefts' (1964), reprinted in David Widgery, comp., *The Left in Britain, 1956–1968*, Penguin, Harmondsworth, 1976, pp. 131–53. Characterizing the 'cadres' of the new *NLR*, Sedgwick observed that '[t]hey are not so much uprooted (the common fate of the mobile intellectual) as rootless. Whereas the other New Left had preserved a notional or umbilical link between itself and the extra-intellectual sources of action in British society, this is an openly self-articulated, self-powered outfit, an Olympian *autogestion* of roving postgraduates that descends at will from its own space onto the target-terrains of Angola, Persia, Cuba, Algeria, Britain' (p. 148). The justice of much of Sedgwick's political criticism—in sum, that the new *NLR* was quasi-Jacobin as regards the Third World, and semi-Fabian vis-à-vis the First—was conceded by Anderson in the 'Conspectus', pp. 5–6. He presumably found a subsequent parody of his 'Sartrean logic and gallicized syntax' less sympathetic: Sedgwick, 'Pseud Left Review', *International Socialism* no. 15, summer 1966, pp. 18–19.

21. Anderson was to admit this in *Arguments within English Marxism*, p. 139.

22. 'Problems of Socialist Strategy', in Anderson and Robin Blackburn, eds., *Towards Socialism*, Fontana/NLR, London, 1965, p. 222.

23. E. P. Thompson, 'Outside the Whale' (1960), reprinted in *The Poverty of Theory and Other Essays*, Merlin Press, London, 1978, pp. 1–33: here p. 4.

24. The nonpejorative characterization is Kenny's, *The First New Left*, p. 2. The general atrophy of the 'dialogue on Marxism' ca. 1930–56 is powerfully underscored by Hobsbawm in a talk dating from 1966, reprinted in *Revolutionaries: Contemporary Essays* (1973), Phoenix, London, 1994, pp. 109–20.

25. Allen Hutt, 'The Revolutionary Role of the Theoretical Struggle', *Communist Review* vol. 4, February 1932, pp. 78–79 (qtd. in Neal Wood, *Communism and British Intellectuals*, Gollancz, London, 1959, pp. 170–71). As early as 1925, the Comintern had condemned the CPGB's 'aversion to theory'—an aversion reduced, but not eradicated, as the party began to recruit middle-class intellectuals in significant numbers in the 1930s. See Stuart Macintyre, *A Proletarian Science: Marxism in Britain, 1917–1933* (1980), Lawrence and Wishart, London, 1986, pp. 97, 94.

26. E. P. Thompson and John Saville, editorial, *Reasoner* no. 1, July 1956, p. 5: quoted back at Thompson with relish by Anderson in 'Socialism and Pseudo-Empiricism', p. 26. See also *Arguments within English Marxism*, pp. 138–39.

27. E. P. Thompson and John Saville, editorial, *New Reasoner* no. 1, summer 1957, p. 2. Morris was the subject of Thompson's 1955 study *William Morris: Romantic to*

Revolutionary (revised edition, Pantheon, New York, 1977); Mann, of a biography by Dona Torr, doyenne of the Communist Party Historians' Group.

28. Cf., for example, the National Cultural Congresses of the CPGB held between 1948 and 1955, which issued symposia with such titles as *The American Threat to British Culture*; *Essays on Socialist Realism and the British Cultural Tradition*; and *Britain's Cultural Heritage*. For a fine study of what might be called historiographical Popular Frontism, see Bill Schwarz, '"The People" in History: The Communist Party Historians' Group, 1946–1956', in Centre for Contemporary Cultural Studies, *Making Histories: Studies in History-Writing and Politics*, Hutchinson, London, 1982, pp. 44–95.

29. *Arguments within English Marxism*, pp. 147–49. For Anderson's reflections on the actual transfer of editorial control of the *NLR* in 1962–63, rejecting the notion of a coup as a 'legend', see pp. 135–37 (a more substantial account than that provided in 'Statement', *NLR* no. 24, March/April 1964, p. 112). Some more personal thoughts can be found in Anderson's obituary 'Diary' on Thompson, *London Review of Books*, 21 October 1993, pp. 24–25.

30. Raymond Williams, 'Notes on British Marxism since the War', *NLR* no. 100, November 1976/January 1977, pp. 84 ff.

31. See, for example, Anderson's introduction to an article by Ernest Mandel on Belgium in *NLR* no. 20, summer 1963, pp. 2–3, in which he regretted 'the fixed habit, which is deeply engrained in the Left, of conceiving capitalism as a single, undifferentiated phenomenon, whose universality is equalled only by its anonymity. . . . A general model is not denied, but enriched by the diversity of the forms which it integrates. To study the complex and particular destinies of the other advanced industrial societies is not to remove them from the relevant range of our own problems and discussion. It is[,] rather, to deepen our understanding of the fundamental structure of capitalism by exploring all its contingent possibilities, and so, reciprocally, to perceive more clearly—by contrast and similarity—the specific nature of British society today' (p. 2).

32. E. P. Thompson, 'Revolution', in Thompson et al., *Out of Apathy*, Stevens, London, 1960, pp. 287–308: here pp. 296, 305.

33. For Anderson's critique, see 'Socialism and Pseudo-Empiricism', pp. 33–39 (where 'messianic nationalism' is emphasized in the original, p. 35).

34. Stuart Hall, 'The "First" New Left: Life and Times', in Oxford University Socialist Discussion Group, *Out of Apathy*, pp. 11–38: here p. 31.

35. See *Arguments within English Marxism*, p. 186, where Anderson retracts the accusation of 'moralism' against Thompson, although noting his prioritization of 'morality' over strategy.

36. 'The Left in the Fifties', *NLR* no. 29, January/February 1965, pp. 3–18: here p. 13. Anderson's delineation of the core components of the requisite theory (p. 12), echoing Sartre's characterization of Marxism, is remarkable for foreshadowing the debate over Thompson's 'exterminism' thesis fifteen years later.

37. 'A Decennial Report', p. 13.

38. Ibid., p. 76.

39. Accordingly, the judgement of Lin Chun (*The British New Left*, p. 158)—that Gramsci was 'a hero for the British Left (save Anderson)'—is bizarre, and explicable only by reference to Anderson's later interrogation, 'The Antinomies of Antonio Gramsci' (1976). For Anderson's own observations on the assimilation, see *Arguments within English Marxism*, pp. 149–50, and *English Questions*, pp. 2–4. In the latter (p. 4), Anderson notes that in his case, 'the Gramscian palette had some Sartrean and Lukácsian subtones'. He cites chap. 1 of Lukács's *Destruction of Reason* (1954; trans. Peter Palmer, Merlin Press, London, 1980), 'On Some Characteristics of Germany's Historical Development' (pp. 35–92); but not Sartre's *The Communists and Peace* (1952–54; trans. Irene Clephane, Hamish Hamilton, London, 1969). The latter, how-

ever, is referred to, alongside Lukács's *History and Class Consciousness* and other Western Marxist texts, in 'Origins of the Present Crisis' (*English Questions*, p. 36 n. 10). For Lukács, Germany's 'ent[ry] into the modern bourgeois line of development too late' (p. 37) was demonstrable by comparison with the history not only of France but also of Britain, even though the English 'bourgeois revolution' of the seventeenth century was less comprehensive than that of the French of the eighteenth (p. 129). In an interview with Anderson conducted in 1968 but published in 1971, Lukács expressed his agreement with the gist of the *Review*'s theses: 'Lukács on His Life and Work', *NLR* no. 68, July/August 1971, p. 52.

40. David Forgacs, 'Gramsci and Marxism in Britain', *NLR* no. 176, July/August 1989, pp. 70–88 (see especially pp. 74–77)—an article cited approvingly in *English Questions*, p. 8 n. 7.

41. See *English Questions*, p. 3; and Forgacs, 'Gramsci and Marxism in Britain', p. 75.

42. Antonio Gramsci, *Selections from the Prison Notebooks*, ed. and trans. Quintin Hoare and Geoffrey Nowell Smith, Lawrence and Wishart, London, 1971, p. 238.

43. For the key relevant passages on English historical development, see ibid., pp. 18, 83–84; and on the Jacobin phase of the French Revolution, cf. pp. 77–79.

44. Cf. Anderson on the unity of 'developmental' and 'structural' analysis, quoted earlier in this chapter.

45. 'Origins of the Present Crisis', *NLR* no. 23, January/February 1964, pp. 26–53; reprinted in Anderson and Blackburn, *Towards Socialism*, pp. 11–52, and (with minor modifications) in *English Questions*, pp. 15–47. All references will be to the last unless otherwise indicated.

46. 'Hegemony was defined by Gramsci as the dominance of one social bloc over another, not simply by means of force or wealth, but by a wider authority whose ultimate resource is always cultural' ('Origins', p. 30). In 'The Figures of Descent' (*English Questions*, p. 167), Anderson conceded that the hegemonic/corporate polarity 'was given too cultural a turn'. This was perhaps more apparent in the original version, where the relevant passage reads: 'Hegemony was defined by Gramsci as the dominance of one social bloc over another, not simply by means of force or wealth, but by a social authority whose ultimate sanction and expression is a profound cultural supremacy' (*Towards Socialism*, p. 30).

47. Thus ('Origins', p. 24), 'Schumpeter's imaginary cause' of the nineteenth-century scramble for Empire—persistent aristocratic predominance in European state structures—'was a true effect' of the lion's share, in the English case. Cf. Joseph Schumpeter, 'The Sociology of Imperialism' (1919), in *Imperialism and Social Classes*, Meridian Books, New York, 1951, especially pp. 92–93; and *Capitalism, Socialism, and Democracy* (1942), Routledge, London, 1994, especially pp. 135–37.

48. The point is slightly attenuated in *English Questions*. There it is maintained that '[i]n Britain, the working class has developed . . . an adamantine social consciousness, but never a commensurate political will' (p. 37); whereas the original reads: 'In Britain the working class has generated a massive, adamantine class-consciousness—but it has never developed into a hegemonic political force' (*Towards Socialism*, p. 39).

49. Tom Nairn, 'The Nature of the Labour Party—1', *NLR* no. 27, September/October 1964, pp. 38–65, and 'The Nature of the Labour Party—2', *NLR* no. 28, November/December 1964, pp. 33–62; reprinted in Anderson and Blackburn, *Towards Socialism*, pp. 159–217, and (as 'Anatomy of the Labour Party') in Robin Blackburn, ed., *Revolution and Class Struggle: A Reader in Marxist Politics*, Fontana/Collins, Glasgow, 1977, pp. 314–73. Here too a Gramscian inspiration was apparent: cf. *Selections from the Prison Notebooks*, p. 151, where it is suggested that 'to write the history of a party means nothing less than to write the general history of a country from a monographic viewpoint' (qtd. in 'The Nature of the Labour Party—1', p. 39; and, in a striking

demonstration of methodological consistency, by Anderson in 'Communist Party History' [1979], in Raphael Samuel, ed., *People's History and Socialist Theory*, Routledge and Kegan Paul, London, 1981, p. 148; and again in the introduction to his and Patrick Camiller's edited collection *Mapping the West European Left*, Verso, London and New York, 1994, p. 9).

50. 'Critique of Wilsonism', *NLR* no. 27, September/October 1964, pp. 3–27.

51. 'Divide and Conquer', *NLR* no. 28, November/December 1964, pp. 1–3.

52. Such accusations were arguably best encapsulated before the event by Engels's epigram on the Doktorklub: 'Our actions are just words, and/long they so shall be. / After Abstraction, Practice follows as / itself'.

53. Tom Nairn, 'The English Working Class', *NLR* no. 24, March/April 1964, pp. 43–57: here p. 57.

54. Richard Johnson, 'Culture and the Historians', in John Clarke, Chas Critcher, and Richard Johnson, eds., *Working Class Culture: Studies in History and Theory*, Hutchinson, London, 1979, pp. 41–71: here p. 66—a volume (and essay) cited approvingly in *Arguments within English Marxism*, p. 127 n. 59.

55. 'Problems of Socialist Strategy', in Anderson and Blackburn, *Towards Socialism*, pp. 221–90.

56. *English Questions*, pp. 5–6.

57. As Anderson writes later ('Problems', p. 229), '[T]he conventional moral excommunication in the West of the whole experience of Leninism is parochial. Sociologically, values can never overshoot the historical and structural context which provides their sole field of substantiation. . . . This is not to say that there is a linear historical determinism, which prescribes the norms and options of every society or regime. It is rather that there is a certain negative determinism, which never produces any *one* possibility, but always eliminates several. History, in this sense, operates a permanent selectivity, which rigorously delimits the field of possibilities at any given moment, without ever finally structuring it'. The comparison between Communist and liberal violence in these pages is reminiscent not only of Sartre but also of Merleau-Ponty's *Humanism and Terror* (1947).

58. Anderson refers readers to Deutscher's 'masterly writings on the subject' ('Problems', p. 227 n. 1).

59. Cf. Gramsci, *Selections from the Prison Notebooks*, p. 238 (part of the note 'Political Struggle and Military War', pp. 229–38). The passage comparing the superstructures of civil society in the West to the 'trench-systems of modern warfare' (p. 235) is quoted by Anderson in 'Problems', p. 238.

60. See 'The Antinomies of Antonio Gramsci', *NLR* no. 100, November 1976/January 1977, p. 27 n. 48.

61. The rationale for Anderson's consistent hostility to the Labourist mechanisms of affiliated membership and bloc vote was anticipated by Gramsci, who reflected at one point that 'parties should be formed by individual memberships and not on the pattern of the British Labour Party, because, if it is a question of providing an organic leadership for the entire economically active mass, this leadership should not follow old schemas but should innovate. But innovation cannot come from the mass, at least at the beginning, except through the mediation of an *élite* for whom the conception implicit in human activity has already become to a certain degree a coherent and systematic ever-present awareness and a precise and decisive will' (*Selections from the Prison Notebooks*, p. 335).

62. Reprehending 'the vast silence which . . . lies over the whole subject', Anderson wrote that '[t]he premature death of the suffragette movement, with only the most minimal goals achieved, left women in a position of social inferiority, which, forty years later, remains in almost every aspect unchanged' ('Problems', p. 277).

63. See n. 60, this chapter. 'Problems' is mentioned neither in *Arguments within English Marxism*, where Anderson contrasts the revolutionary socialism of the second New Left with the reformist socialism of the first (see especially pp. 194–97), nor in *English Questions*.

64. Indeed, 'Problems' was deemed 'certainly the worst text produced by any e/c member throughout this period' ('A Decennial Report', p. 15).

65. Maurice Merleau-Ponty, *Adventures of the Dialectic* (1955), trans. Joseph Bien, Northwestern University Press, Evanston, Ill., 1973, chap. 5 (pp. 95–201). As is noted earlier (n. 39, this chapter), in the foreword to *English Questions*, Anderson alludes to Sartre's text but does not supply details.

66. In addition to the reference to Deutscher in 'Problems' cited earlier (n. 58, this chapter), see *Arguments within English Marxism*, pp. 117, 151, 155.

67. For Anderson, although geography is not destiny, neither is it a nugatory force. Cf. *Lineages of the Absolutist State*, New Left Books, London, 1974, p. 546 n. 79, where he writes that '[s]trictly geographical determinations of social structure were typically exaggerated by Montesquieu and his age. . . . Marxists in this century have often compensated unduly for this legacy of the Enlightenment, by ignoring the relative significance of natural milieux in history altogether. It has been left to modern historians like Braudel to lend a juster weight to them again. In fact, no truly materialist history can put geographical conditions into silent parentheses'.

68. *English Questions*, p. 6.

69. Ibid., pp. 4–5.

70. Reference to Gramsci is unavoidable here. Thus, we find him praising Croce as a 'cosmopolitan intellectual' who undertook to 'deprovincialize [Italian] culture' (qtd. in H. Stuart Hughes, *Consciousness and Society: The Reorientation of European Social Thought, 1890–1930* (1959), Harvester Press, Brighton, 1988, p. 63). But compare his depiction of the Bolshevik leadership: 'An *élite* consisting of some of the most active, energetic, enterprising and disciplined members of the society [Russia] emigrated abroad and assimilated the culture and historical experiences of the most advanced countries of the West, without however losing the most essential characteristics of its own nationality, that is to say without breaking its sentimental and historical links with its own people. . . . The difference between this *élite* and that imported from Germany (by Peter the Great, for example) lies in its essentially national-popular character' (*Selections from the Prison Notebooks*, pp. 19–20).

71. E. P. Thompson, 'The Peculiarities of the English' (1965), republished in full in Thompson, *The Poverty of Theory and Other Essays*, pp. 35–91; Nicos Poulantzas, 'Marxist Political Theory in Britain' (1966), translated in *NLR* no. 43, May/June 1967, pp. 57–74. Cf. 'The Figures of Descent', in *English Questions*, pp. 128–29, 167.

72. E. P. Thompson, 'Where Are We Now?', p. 15; qtd. in Kenny, *The First New Left*, p. 31.

73. Introduction to Poulantzas, *NLR* no. 43, May/June 1967, pp. 55–56.

74. 'Socialism and Pseudo-Empiricism', *NLR* no. 35, January/February 1966, pp. 2–42.

75. Anderson (ibid., p. 30) referred Thompson to James Hinton's recognition of his and Nairn's 'assertion of primacy to the political and ideological factors': see 'The Labour Aristocracy', *NLR* no. 32, July/August 1965, p. 77. Anderson did not, however, subscribe to Hinton's demands for a more conjuncturally differentiated history of the British labour movement and a more nuanced evaluation of the Left's heritage.

76. The 'huge gap between a brilliant, imaginative history and a vacuous political analysis is what we have tried to overcome. We have tried to link history bindingly to the present, and to reconstruct the continuity between the two. This has meant, inevitably, an attempt to "totalize" where academic historiography has compartmentalized. Conversely, it has meant a structural analysis of the present—not a journalistic evocation of it. . . . [W]e have attempted an *integrated* theory of British society, past

and present' ('Socialism and Pseudo-Empiricism', p. 39). Anderson summarizes the main contentions of his reply on pp. 40–41.

77. Cf. *Arguments within English Marxism*, pp. 139–40, where Anderson regrets the 'useless violence' of his 1966 counterpolemic.

78. Chun, *The British New Left*, p. 75.

79. See 'The Notion of Bourgeois Revolution' (1976), in *English Questions*, pp. 105–18, especially pp. 107–8.

80. Gramsci, *Selections from the Prison Notebooks*, p. 84, a passage that occurs immediately after the comments on the English variation quoted earlier in this chapter.

81. See Macintyre, *A Proletarian Science*, p. 232, where it is stated that British Marxists 'always identified the peculiarities in terms of European stereotypes'. Macintyre quotes a Communist Party pioneer, Theodore Rothstein, from 1919: 'The truth is, every country can claim exemption from the operation of social and historical forces on the plea of "peculiarities", since every country is "peculiar", but underlying all peculiarities are the same social factors—modern industry, capitalism, proletariat, and, now, world war—which are bound to produce the same effects' (p. 231).

82. Ellen Meiksins Wood, *The Pristine Culture of Capitalism: A Historical Essay on Old Regimes and Modern States*, Verso, London and New York, 1991, p. 3. For a detailed theoretical and empirical challenge to the whole problematic, in Marxist and liberal versions alike, see David Blackbourn and Geoff Eley, *The Peculiarities of German History: Bourgeois Society and Politics in Nineteenth-Century History*, Oxford University Press, Oxford, 1984.

83. Richard Johnson, 'Barrington Moore, Perry Anderson, and English Social Development' (1976), in Stuart Hall et al., eds., *Culture, Media, Language*, Hutchinson, London, 1980, pp. 48–70: here p. 61.

84. See 'The Figures of Descent', pp. 122–26. Thus, if, as Johnson claims, 'Anderson and Nairn's explanatory notion (aristocratic hegemony) *turns out to be nothing more than the principal theme of English liberal ideology*' ('Barrington Moore', p. 62), it was nevertheless a notion with prestigious—albeit partial and intermittent—precedent.

85. Gramsci, *Selections from the Prison Notebooks*, pp. 83, 18.

86. Schumpeter, *Capitalism, Socialism, and Democracy*, p. 136. In 'Origins' (p. 22), Anderson spoke of a 'systematic symbiosis of the two classes'.

87. Cf. 'Origins', pp. 15–16.

88. Eric Hobsbawm, *Industry and Empire: 1750 to the Present Day* (1968), Penguin, Harmondsworth, 1983, p. 187. In a contemporaneous lecture, 'Karl Marx and the British Labour Movement', Hobsbawm stated his view that '[t]he peculiarity of Britain is that it was the oldest, for a long time the most successful and dominant, and almost certainly the stablest capitalist society, and that its bourgeoisie had to come to terms with a proletarian majority of the population long before any other. The influence of marxism has been inevitably circumscribed by this situation' (in *Revolutionaries*, p. 102).

89. Colin Leys, *Politics in Britain: From Labourism to Thatcherism* (1983), rev. ed., Verso, London and New York, 1989, p. 14.

90. Nairn, 'The Nature of the Labour Party—1', p. 44.

91. See Donald Sassoon, 'The Silences of *New Left Review*', in *Power and Politics 3*, Routledge and Kegan Paul, London, 1981, pp. 219–54, especially pp. 223–25.

92. Writing shortly before his Althusserian turn, Anderson looked forward to the translation of Calvez's work (*La pensée de Karl Marx*, Éditions du Seuil, 1956), in which, rejecting any discontinuity between the young and the mature Marx, Marxist doctrine was conceived as an 'integral humanism'.

93. Althusser's work was 'partly subject to the common destiny' of Marxism in the West, as evidenced by its recourse to Bachelard and Lacan, 'psychoanalytic thinkers both

within the idealist tradition'. Sartre's *Critique of Dialectical Reason* remained for Anderson the 'treatise which dominates Marxist discussion today' ('Socialism and Pseudo-Empiricism', p. 31).

94. 'I trust that the debate which we have started will end by strengthening our common determination. More important battles lie ahead, in which we should be ranged together' ('Socialism and Pseudo-Empiricism', p. 42).

95. Tom Nairn, 'Labour Imperialism', *NLR* no. 32, July/August 1965, pp. 3–15, prefaced by an editorial restatement of 'the belief that socialist strategy must be founded on a unified sociological analysis of our society' (p. 1). In an implicit retraction of Anderson's 'Critique of Wilsonism', Nairn concluded: 'A maximalist programme can scarcely be opposed to a minimal programme in the classic fashion any longer, under present conditions in Britain. There can only be a maximalist programme[;] the ruins of the Labour Party's minimalist positions lie scattered all about us. Labour's aims amounted to taking over from the traditional ruling class, at least for a while, and to solving its problems for it within the general ambit of *its* vision of things. A socialist programme must envisage the replacement of that class and the structures of its power in society' (p. 15).

96. Johnson, 'Barrington Moore', p. 70.

2. Missed Rendezvous

1. Cf. *NLR*, 'The Centre-Left Moves Right', *NLR* no. 25, May/June 1964, pp. 28–29; Lucien Rey, 'The Italian Presidential Elections', *NLR* no. 30, March/April 1965, pp. 48–52; and, for the definitive hostile verdict, Jon Halliday, 'Structural Reform in Italy—Theory and Practice', *NLR* no. 50, July/August 1968, pp. 73–92.

2. Anderson was to recall this with some pride in *Arguments within English Marxism*, New Left Books, London, 1980, pp. 151–52.

3. Göran Therborn, 'From Petrograd to Saigon', *NLR* no. 48, March/April 1968, pp. 3–11: here pp. 9–11. Anderson's judgement can be found in *Arguments within English Marxism*, p. 152.

4. Introduction to special issue on France, May 1968, *NLR* no. 52, November/December 1968, pp. 1–8: here p. 5.

5. Robin Blackburn and Alexander Cockburn, eds., *The Incompatibles: Trade Union Militancy and the Consensus*, Penguin/NLR, Harmondsworth, 1967.

6. 'A Decennial Report', unpublished document, [1975], p. 25.

7. For Sartre on the relationship between party and class in France, see *The Communists and Peace* (1952–54), trans. Irene Clephane, Hamish Hamilton, London, 1969, p. 118. Anderson refers to Sartre's text in 'The Limits and Possibilities of Trade Union Action', in Blackburn and Cockburn, *The Incompatibles*, p. 280 n. 19; and to Marcuse's *One-Dimensional Man* (1964) at pp. 275, 280 n. 17. In another note (p. 280 n. 13), Anderson upheld Lenin's position, against Trotsky and Bukharin, on the autonomy of trade unions under socialism, even quoting Lenin's description of them as 'schools of communism'.

8. See, however, the interview with Hugh Scanlon, the newly elected left-wing president of the Amalgamated Engineering Union: 'The Role of Militancy', *NLR* no. 46, November/December 1967, pp. 3–15.

9. Régis Debray, 'Latin America: The Long March', *NLR* no. 33, September/October 1965, pp. 17–58; reprinted in Régis Debray, *Strategy for Revolution*, ed. with an intro. by Robin Blackburn, Jonathan Cape, London, 1970, pp. 29–99. Che Guevara's message

to the Tricontinental Solidarity Organization in Havana—'Vietnam Must Not Stand Alone'—was published in *NLR* no. 43, May/June 1967, pp. 79–91.

10. Anderson and Robin Blackburn, 'The Marxism of Régis Debray', *NLR* no. 45, September/October 1967, pp. 8–12 (here p. 8); reprinted in a *Monthly Review* symposium on 'Debrayism', Leo Huberman and Paul Sweezy, eds., *Régis Debray and the Latin American Revolution*, Monthly Review Press, New York, 1968, pp. 63–69. Debray's 'Problems of Revolutionary Strategy in Latin America', *NLR* no. 45, September/October 1967, pp. 13–41, was reprinted in *Strategy for Revolution*, pp. 135–84. Anderson and Blackburn participated, together with Tariq Ali, in a Bertrand Russell Peace Foundation mission to Bolivia to ascertain the circumstances in which Debray was being held in Camiri. See Ali, *Nineteen Sixty-Eight and After: Inside the Revolution*, Blond and Briggs, London, 1978, pp. xvii–xix. An anonymous obituary statement on Guevara—'Che'—was carried in *NLR* no. 46, November/December 1967, p. 15.

11. As the 'Decennial Report' notes (p. 35), the joint introduction 'prais[es] the general direction of Debray's theses [in "Problems of Revolutionary Strategy"], if with diplomatic qualifications and discreet reservations about his later work *Revolution in the Revolution?*—in a spirit of solidarity with an imprisoned militant. The defeat of the Bolivian guerrilla soon afterwards was not analysed in the review'.

12. Gareth Stedman Jones, Anthony Barnett, and Tom Wengraf, 'Student Power: What Is to be Done?'; and Ben Brewster and Alexander Cockburn, 'Revolt at the LSE', *NLR* no. 43, May/June 1967, pp. 3–9 and 11–25, respectively.

13. Alexander Cockburn and Robin Blackburn, eds., *Student Power: Problems, Diagnosis, Action*, Penguin/NLR, Harmondsworth, 1969.

14. *NLR* no. 53, January/February 1969. The relevant texts are Revolutionary Socialist Students' Federation, 'Manifesto', pp. 21–22; James Wilcox, 'Two Tactics', pp. 23–32; David Triesman, 'The Impermanent Stronghold', pp. 33–35; David Fernbach, 'Strategy and Struggle', pp. 37–42; and Anthony Barnett, 'A Revoltionary Student Movement', pp. 43–53. See also Paul Q. Hirst, 'Why Escalate?', in *Escalate* (the theoretical journal of the RSSF) no. 1, [1969], pp. 1–9. The ultraleftist temper of the time is conveyed by the Wilcox text—for example, in the statement (p. 28) that '[t]he pseudo-left only recognises those forms of resistance which have the blessing of the ruling order (orderly demonstrations, trade unionism etc.). It is not prepared to consider the testimony of other popular acts of resistance (industrial sabotage, absenteeism, fiddles, delinquency, shop-lifting, "madness", etc.)'.

15. Evidence of Anderson's dissent from the 'red bases' strategy is contained in 'A Decennial Report', p. 44. The existence of such tensions in the editorial committee in this period is further attested by Anderson's removal of his name from the masthead of *NLR* no. 57, September/October 1969, in protest at the acceptance for publication therein of an Arab nationalist text (Fawwaz Trabulsi, 'The Palestinian Problem: Zionism and Imperialism in the Middle East', pp. 53–90). Readers of the *Review* were informed simply that 'Perry Anderson is temporarily engaged in other work, and will not be editing *New Left Review* for the next few months' (p. 2). The offending item having been reproved in the same issue by Blackburn, under the pseudonym M. A. Malik ('Comment', pp. 93–96), the 'other engagements' were rapidly fulfilled and Anderson returned as editor for the following issue.

16. Gareth Stedman Jones, 'The Meaning of the Student Revolt', in Cockburn and Blackburn, *Student Power*, pp. 26–56: here p. 54.

17. 'Components of the National Culture', *NLR* no. 50, July/August 1968, pp. 3–57; reprinted in Cockburn and Blackburn, *Student Power*, pp. 214–84, and in *English Questions*, Verso, London and New York, 1992, pp. 48–104. All references will be to the original version unless otherwise specified. See also Robin Blackburn, 'A Brief

Guide to Bourgeois Ideology', in *Student Power*, pp. 163–213. Other articles criticizing domestic academic disciplines were Gareth Stedman Jones, 'The Pathology of English History', *NLR* no. 46, November/December 1967, pp. 29–43; and David Godard, 'The Limits of British Anthropology', *NLR* no. 58, November/December 1969, pp. 79–89. These were collected, with related material, in Robin Blackburn, ed., *Ideology in Social Science: Readings in Critical Social Theory*, Fontana/Collins, Glasgow, 1972, pp. 96–115 and 61–75, respectively.

18. This fact is registered in the 'Decennial Report', p. 28.

19. Reflecting the preoccupations of the conjuncture, the fiftieth issue of the *NLR* also contained reports on student struggles at Hull, Hornsey, and Essex (pp. 59–71); the development of the Cultural Revolution in Canton (pp. 93–104); further contributions to a debate on Trotsky (pp. 113–23, 127–28); and the critical stocktaking 'Structural Reform in Italy', referred to in n. 1 of this chapter.

20. 'Themes', *NLR* no. 50, July/August 1968, p. 1.

21. Concomitantly, Anderson's revisions touch upon the status of Marxism and the bond between science and class. Thus, '[a] political science capable of guiding the working-class movement to final victory' ('Components', p. 4) becomes '[a] politics capable of overcoming capital' (*English Questions*, p. 49). Anderson's remarks in 1980 on Thompson's revisions of *William Morris* might, mutatis mutandis, be applied to his own: '[T]he original version of the book contains a number of passages that recall the militant temper of the time . . . and which have—significantly, or otherwise—been omitted from the revised edition. Above all, the first *William Morris* was informed by a fierce polemic against *reformism*, that is notably mitigated in the second' (*Arguments within English Marxism*, pp. 188–89).

22. This connection was shrewdly noticed by Michael Gane, 'Althusser in English', *Theoretical Practice* no. 1, January 1971, pp. 10–11.

23. The argument is summarized in 'Components', pp. 11–12.

24. Cf. E. H. Carr's comments on empiricism, quoted by R. W. Davies in the second (post-humous) edition of *What Is History?* (Penguin, Harmondsworth, 1987, pp. 159–60): 'The tradition of the English-speaking world is profoundly empiricist. Facts speak for themselves. . . . The difference has its historical roots. Not for nothing has the English-speaking world remained so obstinately empirical. In a firmly established social order, whose credentials nobody wishes to question, empiricism serves to effect running repairs. . . . Of such a world nineteenth-century Britain provided the perfect model'. A prewar foreign observer of the intellectual scene had already written of British empiricism that it 'was once as it were justified by the position the country once occupied, that is, in the days when it was leader of capitalistic progress. But today, . . . that empiricism has become one of the symptoms of the diseased backwardness of British capitalism in general': Dmitri Mirsky, *The Intelligentsia of Great Britain*, trans. Alec Brown, Victor Gollancz, London, 1935, pp. 173–74. Note, however, Mirsky's caustic verdict on the contemporary overreaction to the syndrome (p. 214): 'System, system, system—this is what British intellectuals run crying after as soon as they lose faith in aforementioned Nanny empiricism'.

25. Those inclined to suspect sheer caricature here might wish to consult Gilbert Ryle's ineffable Introduction to A. J. Ayer et al., *The Revolution in Philosophy*, Macmillan, London, 1956, pp. 1–4. Although in 'Components' (pp. 22–23) Anderson cites only Ernest Gellner's 1959 critique of ordinary language philosophy, *Words and Things*, his disdain for 'the parish-pump positivism of interbellum Vienna' (p. 18) and its therapeutic Oxbridge relatives is powerfully anticipated in Marcuse. See the latter's *One-Dimensional Man: Studies in the Ideology of Advanced Industrial Society*, Beacon Press, Boston, 1964, chap. 7, 'The Triumph of Positive Thinking: One-Dimensional Philosophy' (pp. 170–99, where Gellner is cited at p. 173 n. 2). Cf. Jonathan Rée,

'English Philosophy in the Fifties', *Radical Philosophy* no. 65, autumn 1993, pp. 3–21; and, for further evidence of Anderson's especial animus against Wittgenstein, his unsigned introduction to an article entitled 'Wittgenstein and Russia', *NLR* no. 73, May/June 1972, pp. 83–84.

26. In a footnote ('Components', p. 35 n. 55), Anderson writes: 'It is perhaps not surprising that the one reasonably comprehensive and cogent account of the crisis has been produced by an economic historian, not an economist—Eric Hobsbawm's *Industry and Empire*' (retouched to read 'the most cogent account of the crisis' in *English Questions*, p. 80 n. 55). The reason for Anderson's original reservation is no doubt to be found in Hobsbawm's assertion of the self-sufficiency of an economic explanation. In Althusserian fashion, Anderson, by contrast, maintains (p. 35): 'It is as plain as day that Britain's economic crisis has more than one major cause; that these causes are not randomly or equivalently related, but form a complex *hierarchy*; and that they englobe the socio-political structure of contemporary Britain. But orthodox economics has proved completely unable *either* to construct a hierarchical model of the causality of the crisis (not merely a plural one), *or* to integrate the economic end-product into the political and historical totality from which it is so manifestly articulated'. Cf. *English Questions*, p. 80, for a less idiomatically Althusserian version of the passage.

27. *Considerations on Western Marxism*, New Left Books, London, 1976, p. viii and n. 1.

28. 'A Culture in Contraflow', part 1, *NLR* no. 180, March/April 1990, pp. 41–78, and part 2, *NLR* no. 182, July/August 1990, pp. 85–137; reprinted in *English Questions*, pp. 193–301 (to which all references will be made).

29. Needless to say, these alternatives did not encompass the scenario ascribed to Anderson by an overwrought Roger Scruton: 'Like the National Socialist, Anderson looks to youth for our redemption, hoping to mobilise the cultural brownshirts against the reactionary status quo' ('Perry Anderson', in *Thinkers of the New Left*, Longman, London, 1985, pp. 129–43: here p. 134).

30. Cf. Talcott Parsons, *The Structure of Social Action* (1937), 2d ed., vol. 1, Free Press, New York, 1968, pp. 3–4 (qtd. in 'Components', p. 7 n. 4).

31. See Geoffrey Hawthorn, *Enlightenment and Despair: A History of Social Theory* (1976), 2d ed., Cambridge University Press, Cambridge, 1987, p. 170 (qtd. in 'A Culture in Contraflow', p. 206); and cf. pp. 88–89, 110–11.

32. Considering his glancing remarks on Wittgenstein in the 1990 retrospective ('A Culture in Contraflow', pp. 253–54), this is not a judgement Anderson himself would accept.

33. See Stuart Macintyre, *A Proletarian Science: Marxism in Britain, 1917–1933* (1980), Lawrence and Wishart, London, 1986, pp. 233–34. Macintyre's distillation of the conclusions of Maurice Dobb and company preechoes the Andersonian prescription: '[T]he backward state of British socialism corresponded to the backwardness and insularity of the national culture, and could only be overcome by challenging the whole of that culture'.

34. See Donald Sassoon, 'The Silences of *New Left Review*', in *Politics and Power 3*, Routledge and Kegan Paul, London, 1981, pp. 226–30. For Sassoon, Anderson's indictment of bourgeois ideology is drafted in much the spirit attributed by its critics to the Imperial German Civil Service, whose mind-set was said to run, That is all very well in practice, but does it work in theory?

35. 'Problems of Socialist Strategy', in Anderson and Robin Blackburn, eds., *Towards Socialism*, Fontana/NLR, London, 1965, p. 270.

36. Cf. also Antonio Gramsci's description of 'what happens on the editorial committees of some reviews, when these function at the same time both as editorial committees and as cultural groups': *Selections from the Prison Notebooks*, ed. and trans. Quintin Hoare and Geoffrey Nowell Smith, Lawrence and Wishart, London, 1971, pp. 28–29.

Might this passage have supplied Anderson with an ideal image of the evolution and function of the *NLR*?

37. *New Left Review*, ed., *Western Marxism: A Critical Reader*, New Left Books, London, 1977.

38. According to the Verso Constitution (unpublished document, n.d., p. 1), '[i]n 1970 the publishing company NLB was founded as an extension of the political and cultural work of New Left Review. . . . The principal objectives of the new house were: (1) to further New Left Review's established policy of making available to English-language readers major works of the European Marxist tradition, within a framework designed to aggregate their intellectual impact and appeal; (2) to make possible the extension of the work of NLR's editors and contributors as authors in their own right, and therewith to provide a point of assembly for other socialists writing in English, so as to help create an English-language sector of Marxist work eventually comparable in concentration to NLB's European Marxist translations; (3) to promote book production of a more directly political and interventionist character under the direction of NLR'.

39. Thus, for example, Adorno, *Minima Moralia* (1974); Althusser, *Lenin and Philosophy* (1971) and *Politics and History* (1972); Benjamin, *Understanding Brecht* and *Charles Baudelaire* (both 1973); Colletti, *From Rousseau to Lenin* (1972) and *Marxism and Hegel* (1973); Poulantzas, *Political Power and Social Classes* (1973) and *Fascism and Dictatorship* (1974); and Sartre, *Between Existentialism and Marxism* (1974) and *Critique of Dialectical Reason* (1976).

40. From 1973 onward, eight volumes of Marx appeared: the early writings, including the *Economic and Philosophical Manuscripts*, introduced by Lucio Colletti; three collections of political writings, from the *Communist Manifesto*, via the *Eighteenth Brumaire*, to the *Critique of the Gotha Programme*, edited by David Fernbach; the *Grundrisse*, translated in full for the first time by Martin Nicolaus; and a retranslation of *Capital* in its entirety by Ben Fowkes and Fernbach, introduced by Ernest Mandel.

41. Jacques Lacan, 'The Mirror-Phase as Formative of the Function of the I', trans. Jean Roussel, *NLR* no. 51, September/October 1968, pp. 71–78 (preceded by 'Themes' describing the essay as 'seminal' and stating that 'Lacan's work is widely influential outside his discipline. . . . [I]t is time it received its due international currency': p. 2); and Claude Lévi-Strauss, 'A Confrontation', *NLR* no. 62, July/August 1970, pp. 57–74. Althusser's 'Freud and Lacan' appeared in *NLR* no. 55, May/June 1969, pp. 49–65, and was adjudged 'perhaps the best Marxist theorization of psychoanalysis that has ever been written' ('Themes', p. 2).

42. In the 'further reading' appended to *Ideology in Social Science* (pp. 378–82), Blackburn commenced with 'advanced posts of academic social theory', including works by Lévi-Strauss, Barthes, and Foucault.

43. A single index: the Lévi-Straussian formula for ideology (or myth), lauded in 'Components' (p. 50), was dismissed as weightless and unoriginal in *In the Tracks of Historical Materialism*, Verso, London, 1983, p. 49.

44. Statistics according to Neal Wood, *Communism and British Intellectuals*, Victor Gollancz, London, 1959, p. 61.

45. In *Arguments within English Marxism* (pp. 129–30), Anderson cites Raymond Williams's testimony as to the positive contrast between the cultural contexts of the late 1960s and the late 1930s, against E. P. Thompson's declaration of 'unrelenting war' on '[t]heoretical practice (and allied Marxisms)', sponsored by the *NLR*. Compare Thompson, 'The Poverty of Theory: or An Orrery of Errors', in *The Poverty of Theory and Other Essays*, Merlin Press, London, 1978, pp. 380–84, with Williams, *Marxism and Literature*, Oxford University Press, Oxford, 1978, pp. 4–5. Cf. Stuart Hall, 'The Emergence of Cultural Studies and the Crisis of the Humanities', *October* no. 53, summer 1990, p. 16.

46. Juliet Mitchell, 'Women: The Longest Revolution', *NLR* no. 40, November/December 1966, pp. 11–37.

47. The relevant texts are Krassó, 'Trotsky's Marxism', *NLR* no. 44, July/August 1967, pp. 64–86; Mandel, 'Trotsky's Marxism: An Anti-Critique', *NLR* no. 47, January/February 1968, pp. 32–51; Krassó, 'Reply to Ernest Mandel', *NLR* no. 48, March/April 1968, pp. 90–103; and Mandel, 'Trotsky's Marxism: A Rejoinder', *NLR* no. 56, July/August 1969, pp. 69–96.

48. This according to the 'Decennial Report', pp. 29–30, where it is said that the original piece was 'mediated through the subediting of the NLR office', with an 'intromission of elements of a critique of Trotsky drawn from the ideas of Althusser'; and that its sequel was '[m]ore heavily processed than the first essay in the review office' and 'correspondingly more Althusserian in inspiration'.

49. 'By a supreme irony, [Trotsky] often found himself at the end of his life in the midst of precisely those salon intellectuals—the antithesis of the Leninist revolutionary—whom he had always detested and despised. For many of them were political recruits to his cause, especially in the United States—the Burnhams, Schachtmans and others. It was pathetic[,] of course, that Trotsky should have entered into serious argument with creatures such as Burnham. His very association with them was graphic evidence of how lost and disoriented he was in the unfamiliar context of the West' (Krassó, 'Trotsky's Marxism', p. 84).

50. Cf. Robin Blackburn's reference of Lin Chun (*The British New Left*, Edinburgh University Press, Edinburgh, 1993, p. 175 n. 21) to the Krassó-Mandel exchange as evidence of the *NLR*'s non-Trotskyist orientation.

51. Robin Blackburn, 'A Brief History of *New Left Review*, 1960–1990', in *Thirty Years of New Left Review: Index to Numbers 1–184 (1960–1990)*, London, 1992, pp. v–xi: here p. vii; and Anderson, *Arguments within English Marxism*, p. 109 and n. 25.

52. See Bill Jenner, 'The New Chinese Revolution', *NLR* no. 53, January/February 1969, pp. 83–96; and cf. 'Themes', p. 2.

53. Mao Tse-tung, 'Talk on Strategic Dispositions', *NLR* no. 54, March/April 1969, pp. 33–40; cf. 'Themes', p. 1.

54. 'Introduction to Tukhachevsky', *NLR* no. 55, May/June 1969, pp. 74–89. (Anderson's authorship is confirmed by the 'Decennial Report', p. 49.) The piece bruited André Glucksmann's exposition of Maoist military strategy in *Discours de la guerre* (1967), a chapter of which had been translated in *NLR* no. 49, May/June 1968, pp. 41–57.

55. See Isaac Deutscher, 'Maoism—Its Origins and Outlook' (1964) and 'The Meaning of the Cultural Revolution' (1966), both reprinted in Deutscher, *Marxism, Wars, and Revolutions: Essays from Four Decades*, ed. Tamara Deutscher, Verso, London, 1984, pp. 181–211 and 212–17. Contrariwise, Deutscher's enduring optimism about the future of the Soviet Union, up until his premature death in 1967, is evident from the title of the Trevelyan Lectures delivered by him at Cambridge that year to mark the fiftieth anniversary of the Bolshevik Revolution: *The Unfinished Revolution: Russia, 1917–1967*, Oxford University Press, London, 1967. (The second lecture was published in *NLR* no. 43, May/June 1967, pp. 27–39.)

56. 'Credulity in the official propaganda of the Chinese regime, as purge succeeded purge in the ranks of party and state and of the population at large, often persisted until the death of Mao himself. Deutscher was totally untouched by such fashionable illusions': Anderson, preface to *Marxism, Wars, and Revolutions*, p. xiii. Anderson's first positive mention of Deutscher in connection with the Cultural Revolution is found in 'The Antinomies of Antonio Gramsci', *NLR* no. 100, November 1976/January 1977, p. 36 n. 72.

57. Richard Merton, 'Comment on Beckett's "Stones"', *NLR* no. 47, January/February 1968, pp. 29–31; and 'Comment on Chester's "For a Rock Aesthetic"', *NLR* no. 59,

January/February 1970, pp. 88–96. In the former, Anderson extended his depreciation of Britain's intellectual culture to its arts: 'Britain today is a society stifling for lack of any art that expresses the experience of living in it. Our theatre is a quaint anachronism, our novel is dead, and our cinema a mere obituary of it. Perhaps the only art form which has an authentic expressive vitality in England is pop music. It at least reflects back to us the immediate constituents of experience, even when it does not illuminate them. It is no accident that it is the one product of contemporary British culture which has any international currency' (p. 31). Two years later, Anderson was contrasting the Stones' 'Street Fighting Man' with the Beatles' 'lamentable petty bourgeois cry of fear "Revolution"' (p. 93); lambasting Dylan's 'self-pitying verse and prophetic posturings' (p. 95); and concluding that although, say, the Stones' *Beggar's Banquet* and Telemann's *Tafelmusik* were aesthetically incomparable, '[t]he true merit and significance of rock lies elsewhere: it is the first aesthetic form in modern history which has asymptotically started to close the gap between those who *produce* and those who *appropriate* art. It alone thereby prefigures, amidst its innumerable poverties and confusions, the structure of future art, in a liberated social formation: communism. It is in this deepest sense of all that it deserves to be called a people's music' (p. 96). See also the original version of 'Components', pp. 43–45 n. 72, for a long footnote suggesting that Marxist and Freudian science had subverted the possibility of the novel as a literary form in contemporary capitalist society.

58. 'Introduction to Gramsci, 1919–1920', *NLR* no. 51, September/October 1968, pp. 22–27. The contents page of the issue attributed the piece to 'P. A.', but this was retracted in *NLR* no. 52, November/December 1968, p. 66, as an 'editorial error'. The 'Decennial Report' (p. 37) recorrects the 'erratum'.

59. The result was a succession of critical analyses of West European Communist parties in the *Review*, of which the most substantial were probably Bill Warren, '"The British Road to Socialism"', *NLR* no. 63, September/October 1970, pp. 27–41; and Lucio Magri, 'Italian Communism in the Sixties', *NLR* no. 66, March/April 1971, pp. 37–52, preceded by Anderson's unsigned introduction, pp. 35–36.

60. Introduction to *NLR* no. 52, November/December 1968, pp. 1–8.

61. Cf. the verdict of a Marxist historian above any suspicion of ultraleftist leanings: E. J. Hobsbawm, 'May 1968', in *Revolutionaries: Contemporary Essays* (1973), Phoenix, London, 1994, pp. 234–44; and for a retrospective view, *Age of Extremes: The Short Twentieth Century, 1914–1991*, Michael Joseph, London, 1994, p. 298.

62. The *NLR* had already published Glucksmann's 'Politics and War in the Thought of Mao Tse-tung' (see n. 54 in this chapter) and would carry his 1967 critique of Althusser, 'A Ventriloquist Structuralism', positively (if anonymously) prefaced by Anderson, in *NLR* no. 72, March/April 1972, pp. 68–92 (reprinted in its *Western Marxism: A Critical Reader*, pp. 282–314). By 1980, after Glucksmann's metamorphosis from anti-Communist *enragé* to anti-Communist *nouveau philosophe*, Anderson was castigating him while inculpating Althusser by association with him (see *Arguments within English Marxism*, p. 110, and *In the Tracks of Historical Materialism*, p. 29).

63. Tom Nairn, 'Why It Happened', in Angelo Quattrocchi and Tom Nairn, *The Beginning of the End: France, May 1968*, Panther, London, 1968, pp. 103–75: here p. 155.

64. Cf. Raymond Williams, ed., *May Day Manifesto, 1968*, Penguin, Harmondsworth, 1968, synthesizing the contributions of (among others) Michael Barratt Brown, Stuart Hall, Mike Rustin, and Edward Thompson. Williams and company maintained that '[i]t is only at the level of unthinking repetition that the choice between "revolution", in its traditional sense of a violent capture of state power, and "evolution", in its traditional sense of the inevitability of gradual change towards socialist forms, can survive. These are not, and have not for some time been, available socialist strategies, in societies of this kind' (p. 152). This and other passages were cited by Anderson in

Arguments within English Marxism (p. 193), in a chapter on strategic differences between the first and second New Lefts, to which we shall attend in chap. 3.

65. 'Themes', *NLR* no. 100, November 1976/January 1977, p. 1.
66. 'Document A—Theory and Practice: The *Coupure* of May', unpublished document, [1968], p. 4.
67. The following respects are listed: Mao's theory of contradictions, alliances, practices, and cultural revolution (ibid., p. 10).
68. The 'allegations' against the Cultural Revolution cited here were the burden of Deutscher's 1966 article (see n. 55 above). 'Document A' continued: '[Mao's thought] has, of course, like all historical phenomena its own determinate limits. Western Marxism is the theory of a renunciation of [any] political practice. Trotskyism is the theory of past political practice, recorded in the absence of any present political practice by the masses. Mao Tse Tung's thought is the only contemporary theory of a mass political practice; but it has emerged in a social formation radically distant and distinct from West European capitalism' (p. 11). Significantly, in an interview with Sartre conducted in 1969 by Anderson, Ronald Fraser, and Quintin Hoare, in which the philosopher was probed on the subject of China and Maoism, one of his interlocutors suggested: 'Perhaps the paradox of a cultural revolution is that it is ultimately impossible in China, where it was invented, but is somewhat more possible in the advanced countries of the West?' ('The Itinerary of a Thought', *NLR* no. 58, November/December 1969, pp. 43–66: here p. 62; reprinted in Sartre, *Between Existentialism and Marxism*, trans. John Mathews, New Left Books, London, 1974, pp. 33–64).
69. For a muted public echo of this, see the editorial in *NLR* no. 60, March/April 1970: recording ten years of the *Review*'s existence, and announcing the launch of NLB, it promised future improvements in the journal, 'rendering [it] more politically active and responsible' ('Themes', p. 2).
70. For an overview of these formations, see John Callaghan's *The Far Left in British Politics*, Blackwell, Oxford, 1987; and cf. the same author's *British Trotskyism: Theory and Practice*, Blackwell, Oxford, 1984.
71. 'Document B—Ten Theses', unpublished document, [1968], p. 1.
72. Tariq Ali, *The Coming British Revolution*, Jonathan Cape, London, 1972. See pp. 203–7 for a 'critical but fraternal' assessment of the *NLR* to date, which concludes with 'the general thesis that from now on the struggle for theoretical advance will become increasingly intertwined with the struggle to build an international revolutionary party' (p. 207).
73. NLB issued the following volumes by Mandel during the 1970s: *Europe versus America* (1970); *The Formation of the Economic Thought of Karl Marx* (1971); *Late Capitalism* (1975); *From Stalinism to Eurocommunism* and *The Second Slump* (both 1978); and *Revolutionary Marxism Today* and *Trotsky* (both 1979).
74. 'The Founding Moment', unpublished manuscript, [1969], p. 1. In accordance with the procedure set down in the preface, paraphrase will have to substitute for direct quotation in the case of this document, with page references given in parentheses as and where appropriate. However, in a paper delivered to a History Workshop conference in Oxford in 1979, Anderson drew on elements of 'The Founding Moment', permitting occasional quotation from it rather than the 1969 manuscript. See 'Communist Party History', in Raphael Samuel, ed., *People's History and Socialist Theory*, Routledge and Kegan Paul, London, 1981, pp. 145–56. The notion of 'founding moments' recurs in two other brief late pieces by Anderson: a review of Charles Bergquist's *Labor in Latin America*, in *In These Times*, 6–12 April 1988, p. 7; and a contribution to a discussion of the same topic, 'The Common and the Particular', in *International Labor and Working-Class History* no. 36, fall 1989, pp. 31–36 (at p. 36).
75. 'Communist Party History', p. 153.

76. Ibid., pp. 153–54. Cf. *Arguments within English Marxism*, pp. 142–43.

77. Anderson singled out Lucio Magri's *Considerazioni sui fatti di Maggio* (Bari, 1968; partially translated by Chiara Ingrao and Chris Gilmore as 'The May Events and Revolution in the West', in Ralph Miliband and John Saville, eds., *Socialist Register, 1969*, Merlin Press, London, 1969, pp. 29–53) and Althusser's 'A propos de l'article de Michel Verret sur "Mai étudiant"' (*La Pensée* no. 145, June 1969, pp. 3–14) as the two best analyses of May '68 to date—evidence, indeed, of the continuing theoretical fertility of Western Communism ('The Founding Moment', p. 130). He did not mention a key work by two members of the Trotskyist Jeunesse communiste révolutionnaire: Daniel Bensaïd and Henri Weber, *Mai 68: Une répétition générale*, François Maspero, Paris, 1968. It should be noted that the introduction to *NLR* no. 52 itself had looked forward to a 'convergence' between students and workers in Britain (p. 7).

78. The reference to 'State and Revolution in the West' in the 'Decennial Report' (p. 70) tends to bear out this supposition.

79. *Passages from Antiquity to Feudalism* and *Lineages of the Absolutist State*, both New Left Books, London, 1974.

80. Anderson defines his study as '[a]n attempt . . . to explore a mediate ground' between an empirically removed, 'abstract' Marxist theory and a theoretically disengaged, 'concrete' Marxist historiography (*Lineages*, pp. 8–9).

81. 'Components of the National Culture', p. 7.

82. '[I]t is the construction and destruction of States which seal the basic shifts in the relations of production, so long as classes subsist. A "history from above"—of the intricate machinery of class domination—is thus no less essential than a "history from below". . . . The abolition of the State altogether remains . . . one of the goals of revolutionary socialism. But the supreme significance accorded to its final disappearance, testifies to all the weight of its prior presence in history' (*Lineages*, p. 11).

83. See *In the Tracks of Historical Materialism*, pp. 36–37, 70–71.

84. 'Communist Party History', p. 155. Cf. *In the Tracks of Historical Materialism*, pp. 79–80: 'The fall of Portuguese fascism created the most favourable conditions for a socialist revolution in any European country since the surrender of the Winter Palace'.

85. Robert Brenner, 'Agrarian Class Structure and Economic Development in Pre-industrial Europe', originally published in *Past and Present* no. 70, February 1976; reprinted, together with a 1982 reply to critics, 'The Agrarian Roots of European Capitalism', in T. H. Aston and C. H. E. Philpin, eds., *The Brenner Debate: Agrarian Class Structure and Economic Development in Pre-industrial Europe*, Cambridge University Press, Cambridge, 1985, pp. 10–63 and 213–327, respectively. (Anderson's contribution to the second piece is acknowledged at p. 213 n.) See also Brenner's 'The Origins of Capitalist Development: A Critique of Neo-Smithian Marxism', *NLR* no. 104, July/August 1977, pp. 25–92. Anderson's high estimation of Brenner is expressed in his review of the latter's *Merchants and Revolution: Commercial Change, Political Conflict, and London's Overseas Traders, 1550–1653* (Cambridge University Press, Cambridge, 1993) in the *London Review of Books*, 4 November 1993, pp. 13–17, under the title 'Maurice Thomson's War'; and cf. his contribution to 'Agendas for Radical History', *Radical History Review* no. 36, 1986, p. 34. The original 'transition debate' was reprinted by NLB, with later contributions, as Rodney Hilton et al., *The Transition from Feudalism to Capitalism*, London, 1976.

86. Although upholding a classical Marxist conception of structural contradictions between forces and relations of production in a mode of production, and refusing any 'inflect[ion of] Marx's theory of complex objective contradictions into a simple subjective contest of class wills' (*Passages*, p. 197 n. 3), Anderson distanced himself from a common interpretation of this conception, sponsored by Marx's 1859 preface: '[T]he characteristic "figure" of a crisis in a mode of production is not one in which vigorous

(economic) forces of production burst triumphantly through retrograde (social) relations of production, and promptly establish a higher productivity and society on their ruins. On the contrary, the forces of production typically tend to *stall* and *recede* within the existent relations of production; these then must themselves first be radically changed and reordered *before* new forces of production can be created and combined for a globally new mode of production. In other words, the relations of production generally change *prior* to the forces of production in an epoch of transition, and not vice versa' (p. 204).

87. See Ellen Meiksins Wood, *The Pristine Culture of Capitalism: A Historical Essay on Old Regimes and Modern States*, Verso, London and New York, 1991, chap. 1 (pp. 1–19). The English and French Revolutions, for example, are explicitly defined as 'bourgeois' in *Lineages* at pp. 142 and 112, respectively.

88. 'The Notion of Bourgeois Revolution', in *English Questions*, pp. 105–18.

89. Paul Hirst, 'The Uniqueness of the West—Perry Anderson's Analysis of Absolutism and Its Problems' (1975), reprinted in Hirst, *Marxism and Historical Writing*, Routledge and Kegan Paul, London, 1985, pp. 91–125: here p. 100.

90. For Anderson's critique of Marx on the relationship between the 'genesis' and 'structure' of modes of production, see *Lineages*, pp. 420–21.

91. Leon Trotsky, qtd. in Isaac Deutscher, *The Prophet Armed—Trotsky: 1879–1921* (1954), Oxford University Press, Oxford, 1979, p. 455.

92. Agnes Heller, review of *Passages* and *Lineages*, *Telos* no. 33, fall 1977, pp. 202–10: here pp. 202–3. Cf. Hirst, 'The Uniqueness of the West', pp. 94–98.

93. Hirst, 'The Uniqueness of the West', p. 120.

94. *In the Tracks of Historical Materialism*, p. 80.

95. Introduction to Magri, and Lucio Magri, 'Problems of the Marxist Theory of the Revolutionary Party', *NLR* no. 60, March/April 1970, pp. 92–96, 97–128. See also 'Presentation of Blanqui', and Auguste Blanqui, 'Instructions for an Uprising', *NLR* no. 65, January/February 1971, pp. 27–29, 30–34. Significantly or otherwise, one of the first NLB titles was 'A. Neuberg', *Armed Insurrection* (1928), trans. Quintin Hoare, London, 1970—a Comintern manual whose actual authors included Tukhachevsky and Ho Chi Minh.

96. See, for example, E. J. Hobsbawm, 'From Babylon to Manchester', *New Statesman*, 7 February 1975, pp. 177–78; and Ralph Miliband, 'Political Forms and Historical Materialism' (1975), reprinted from *Socialist Register, 1975* in Miliband, *Class Power and State Power: Political Essays*, Verso, London, 1983, pp. 50–62.

97. D. G. MacRae, 'Chains of History', *New Society*, 30 January 1975, pp. 269–70: here p. 269. In 'Components of the National Culture' (p. 48), MacRae had been held up as a 'symbol of British sociological orthodoxy'.

98. Theda Skocpol and Mary Fulbrook, 'From Antiquity to Late Capitalism', *Journal of Development Studies* vol. 13, no. 3, April 1977, pp. 290–95, especially p. 295. For Anderson's analysis of Roman law, see *Passages*, pp. 65–67, and *Lineages*, pp. 24–28. Anderson was at pains to acknowledge these predecessors: on Hintze, see, e.g., *Passages*, p. 131 n. 10, and *Lineages*, pp. 410 n. 22, 418–19; and on Weber, *Lineages*, pp. 24 n. 14, 29 n. 21, 424 and n. An English edition of the latter's *The Agrarian Sociology of Ancient Civilizations*, trans. with an intro. by R. I. Frank, was published by NLB in 1976.

99. Hirst, 'The Uniqueness of the West', pp. 96–97.

100. See ibid., pp. 106–19, and cf. *Lineages*, pp. 403–4. Relatedly, we might note the role attributed by Anderson to warfare under feudalism: *Lineages*, pp. 31–32. In response to a later critic, Anderson conceded his error in conflating legal superstructure and economic infrastructure: see *Arguments within English Marxism*, p. 72, commenting

on G. A. Cohen's, *Karl Marx's Theory of History: A Defence*, Oxford University Press, Oxford, 1978, pp. 247–48.

101. For an indication of the depth of the revulsion, see Robin Blackburn's preelection intervention, 'Let It Bleed', *Red Mole* vol. 1, no. 3, April 1970.

102. Tom Nairn, 'The Fateful Meridian', *NLR* no. 60, March/April 1970, pp. 3–35; Andrew Glyn and Bob Sutcliffe, 'The Critical Condition of British Capital', *NLR* no. 66, March/April 1971, pp. 3–33.

103. Tom Nairn, 'Enoch Powell: The New Right', *NLR* no. 61, May/June 1970, pp. 3–27 (reprinted in Nairn, *The Break-up of Britain: Crisis and Neo-Nationalism* [1977], 2d ed., Verso, London, 1981, chap. 6 [pp. 256–90]); Robin Blackburn, 'The Heath Government: A New Course for British Capitalism', *NLR* no. 70, November/December 1971, pp. 3–26; Anthony Barnett, 'Class Struggle and the Heath Government', *NLR* no. 77, November/December 1973, pp. 3–41.

104. 'The Left against Europe?', *NLR* no. 75, September/October 1972; revision published as Tom Nairn, *The Left against Europe?* Penguin/*NLR*, Harmondsworth, 1973.

105. Criticizing the *NLR*'s 'culpable silence' on the issue after 1970, the 'Decennial Report' suggested that 'Ireland . . . remained the great unanswered question of this period of the review, by common consent avoided' (p. 61). In the event, the period stretched up to 1987, when an article entitled 'Women's Rights and Catholicism in Ireland' was published in *NLR* no. 166, November/December 1987, pp. 53–77. Prior coverage had included Liam Baxter et al., 'Discussion on the Strategy of People's Democracy', and Peter Gibbon, 'The Dialectic of Religion and Class in Ulster', both in *NLR* no. 55, May/June 1969, pp. 3–19, 20–41, respectively; and an interview with Cathal Goulding, 'The Present Course of the IRA', *NLR* no. 60, March/April 1970, pp. 51–61. Well might Anderson write in his 'Reader's Note' to Jane Hindle, ed., *London Review of Books: An Anthology* (Verso, London and New York, 1996): 'The *London Review*'s record of publication, on this least popular of all topics, puts to shame many journals to the left of it' (p. xv). Anderson's own comments on contemporary Ireland are few and far between. But for a clear sign of hostility to the Provisional IRA, see *Arguments within English Marxism*, p. 203 n. 56. For its current editor's view of the *Review*'s record, see Robin Blackburn, 'Ireland and the *NLR*', *NLR* no. 212, July/August 1995, pp. 151–55.

106. Ernesto Laclau's article, 'Feudalism and Capitalism in Latin America', published in *NLR* no. 67, May/June 1971, pp. 19–38, was reprinted as chap. 1 of his *Politics and Ideology in Marxist Theory: Capitalism—Fascism—Populism*, New Left Books, London, 1977, pp. 15–50; Bill Warren's 'Imperialism and Capitalist Industrialization', *NLR* no. 81, September/October 1973, pp. 3–44, formed the basis of his posthumously published *Imperialism: Pioneer of Capitalism*, ed. John Sender, New Left Books, London, 1980. The latter elicited some anxious notes from Anderson, conceding the superiority of its case over that of the 'dependency' theorists while arguing that Warren's true antecedent was not, as he supposed, Lenin, but the capitalist apologists of 'Legal Marxism' (Struve and company): '"Imperialism—Pioneer of Capitalism"', unpublished notes, [1980–81], p. 1. Against these converse distorting mirrors, Anderson insisted upon the conjoint development of capitalism and persistence of imperialism in the South (p. 5).

107. See 'Themes', *NLR* no. 53, January/February 1969, p. 1, expressing '[a]bsolute condemnation of the Soviet invasion' by way of introduction to two articles on the subject (pp. 3–12, 13–20); and Anderson's introduction to Tukhachevsky, cited in n. 54, this chapter.

108. Lucio Colletti, 'The Question of Stalin', *NLR* no. 61, May/June 1970, pp. 61–81. Cf. Tamara Deutscher, 'Soviet Oppositions', *NLR* no. 60, March/April 1970, pp. 52–58; Robin Blackburn, 'The Politics of "The First Circle"', *NLR* no. 63, September/

October 1970, pp. 56–65; and Anderson's later introduction to Roy Medvedev's, 'Problems of Democratization and Détente', NLR no. 83, January/February 1974, pp. 25–26.

109. 'Themes', NLR no. 71, January/February 1972, pp. 1–2.

110. 'Polish Document—Presentation', NLR no. 72, March/April 1972, pp. 31–34: here pp. 33–34.

111. See Anderson's respective introductions in NLR no. 59, January/February 1970, pp. 97–100 (Della Volpe); NLR no. 60, March/April 1970, pp. 92–96, and NLR no. 66, March/April 1971, pp. 35–36 (Magri); and 'Themes' in NLR no. 85, May/June 1974, p. 1 (Timpanaro).

112. 'Lukács on His Life and Work' (1968), NLR no. 68, July/August 1971, pp. 49–58.

113. For Anderson's own contributions, see the introductions to Adorno, NLR no. 81, September/October 1973, pp. 46–53; Brecht on Lukács, NLR no. 84, March/April 1974, pp. 33–38; and Lukács on Benjamin and Brecht, NLR no. 110, July/August 1978, pp. 81–82. These were incorporated, together with prefatory material by Rodney Livingstone and Francis Mulhern, into Ernst Bloch et al., *Aesthetics and Politics*, New Left Books, London, 1977. See also the 'Publisher's Note', penned by Anderson, in Walter Benjamin, *One-Way Street and Other Writings*, New Left Books, London, 1979, pp. 29–42.

114. See Göran Therborn, 'Critique of the Frankfurt School', NLR no. 63, September/October 1970, pp. 65–95, and 'Jürgen Habermas: A New Eclecticism', NLR no. 67, May/June 1971, pp. 69–83 (both reprinted in NLR, *Western Marxism*, pp. 83–139); Gareth Stedman Jones, 'The Marxism of the Early Lukács: An Evaluation', NLR no. 70, November/December 1971, pp. 27–64 (reprinted in *Western Marxism*, pp. 12–60); Norman Geras, 'Althusser's Marxism: An Account and Assessment', NLR no. 71, January/February 1972, pp. 57–86 (reprinted in *Western Marxism*, pp. 232–72); André Glucksmann, 'A Ventriloquist Structuralism' (1967), NLR no. 72, March/April 1972, pp. 68–92 (reprinted in *Western Marxism*, pp. 282–314); Pierre Vilar, 'Marxist History, a History in the Making: Towards a Dialogue with Althusser', NLR no. 80, July/August 1973, pp. 65–106; Jean-Paul Sartre, 'Itinerary of a Thought', NLR no. 58, November/December 1969, pp. 43–66; and Lucio Colletti, 'A Political and Philosophical Interview', NLR no. 86, July/August 1974, pp. 3–28 (reprinted in *Western Marxism*, pp. 314–50).

115. 'Introduction to Glucksmann', NLR no. 72, March/April 1972, pp. 61–67 (here p. 61); reprinted in *Western Marxism*, pp. 273–81. Anderson also presented Vilar's essay on Althusser: see NLR no. 80, July/August 1973, p. 64.

116. In a note ('Introduction to Glucksmann', p. 65 n. 4), Anderson observed that 'Balibar has since taken the step implicitly prepared above; see his collaboration in Bettelheim's [*Economic Calculation and Forms of Property*] . . . , a volume devoted to the divination of "capitalism" in the USSR today (China tomorrow?)'. The question received an affirmative response from Bettelheim five years later, following Mao's death and the suppression of the Gang of Four. See Charles Bettelheim, 'The Great Leap Backward', in Bettelheim and Neil G. Burton, *China since Mao*, Monthly Review Press, New York, pp. 37–130.

117. See p. 100 of the introduction to Della Volpe cited in n. 111, this chapter.

118. For some analogous reflections on the 'gulf between East and West', see Isaac Deutscher, 'On Socialist Man' (1966), in *Marxism in Our Time*, Ramparts Press, Berkeley, Calif., 1971, p. 247.

119. See Colletti's 'Marxism and Dialectic', NLR no. 93, September/October 1975, pp. 3–29.

120. *In the Tracks of Historical Materialism*, pp. 28–30. Contemporaneously, Anderson's fellow NLR editor Francis Mulhern was referring to 'the misnamed "crisis of

Marxism"', specifying that it was more accurately designated as 'a crisis of Maoism, or of culpably lingering illusions in Stalinism': introduction to Régis Debray, *Teachers, Writers, Celebrities: The Intellectuals of Modern France*, Verso, London, 1981, p. xix n. 13.

121. Cf. Sebastiano Timpanaro, *On Materialism* (1970), trans. Lawrence Garner, rev. ed. Verso, London, 1980, p. 261. For Anderson's acknowledgement of Timpanaro's inspiration, see the foreword to *In the Tracks of Historical Materialism*, p. 8.

122. *Arguments within English Marxism*, p. 156; Mandel, *Revolutionary Marxism Today*, ed. Jon Rothschild, New Left Books, London, 1979, pp. 189–90. The interviews were conducted by Blackburn and Hoare, among others. For Althusser's position, see his 'Note on "The Critique of the Personality Cult"' (1972), trans. Grahame Lock, in *Essays on Ideology*, Verso, London, and New York, 1993, pp. 114–32; and, for Anderson's assessment, *Arguments within English Marxism*, pp. 109–11.

123. Cf. Mandel, *Revolutionary Marxism Today*, pp. 191–98.

124. See *NLR* no. 68, July/August 1971, 'Themes', p. 1, and Tariq Ali, 'Bangla Desh— Results and Prospects', pp. 27–48; and *NLR* no. 69, September/October 1971, 'Themes', pp. 1–2, and Fred Halliday, 'The Ceylonese Insurrection', pp. 55–90. In each instance, compromising diplomatic messages from Chou En-Lai were published to underline the point of Chinese counterrevolutionary collusion. (The articles by Ali and Halliday were subsequently collected in Robin Blackburn, ed., *Explosion in a Subcontinent: India, Pakistan, Bangladesh, and Ceylon*, Penguin/NLR, Harmondsworth, 1975, pp. 151–220, 293–347, respectively.) All this proved too much for Ben Brewster, who resigned from the *NLR* in protest at its departure 'from what I regard as a Marxist-Leninist political and theoretical position'—a position he sought to advance via the Althusserian-Maoist journal *Theoretical Practice* (1971–73) with Paul Hirst, Barry Hindess, and their colleagues. See Brewster's 'Communication', *NLR* no. 70, November/December 1971, pp. 110–11.

125. Cf. Gilbert Padoul, 'China 1974: Problems Not Models', and Claude Aubert, 'People's Communes—How to Use the Standard Visit', *NLR* no. 89, January/ February 1975, pp. 73–84 and 86–97, respectively. The accompanying 'Themes' (pp. 1–2) condemned 'blindness . . . to the reality' of the 'post-capitalist societies'.

126. 'NLR, 1975–1980', unpublished report, [1980], p. 22, commenting on Halliday, 'Marxist Analysis and Post-revolutionary China', *NLR* no. 100, November 1976/ January 1977, pp. 165–92 (the quotation is from p. 167). Cf. Livio Maitan, *Party, Army, and Masses in China: A Marxist Interpretation of the Cultural Revolution and its Aftermath* (1969), trans. Gregor Benton and Marie Collitti, New Left Books, London, 1976.

127. 'The nature and influence of Maoism fall outside the scope of this essay: discussion of it at length will be necessary elsewhere': *Considerations on Western Marxism*, p. 102 n. 12.

128. *In the Tracks of Historical Materialism*, p. 73. Note that of the eleven Maoist sympathizers instanced there, Enzensberger, Poulantzas, Glucksmann, Arrighi, and Robinson had all been published in the *NLR*—Robinson and Glucksmann, indeed, on the subject of Maoism—and the *Review*'s relations with a sixth—Rossana Rossanda of *Il Manifesto*—were close into the 1970s.

129. The coincidence with the verdict of a Trotskyist critic is striking: see Ian Birchall, 'The Autonomy of Theory: A Short History of *New Left Review*', *International Socialism* no. 10, winter 1980, pp. 51–91, especially p. 86.

130. Robin Blackburn, 'The Test in Portugal', *NLR* nos. 87/88, September/December 1974, pp. 5–46.

131. 'Victory in Indochina', *NLR* no. 91, May/June 1975, pp. 3–4.

132. See the foreword to the 4th ed. of *Considerations on Western Marxism*, Verso, London, 1984, p. ix.

133. Among the innovations, Anderson cited Sartre's discussion of 'scarcity' in the *Critique of Dialectical Reason*, which Anderson himself had deployed in 'Problems of Socialist Strategy'. Noting Trotsky's reference, in *The Revolution Betrayed*, to Marx and Engels's invocation of it in *The German Ideology* (*Considerations*, p. 86 n. 30), Anderson elucidated its Sartrean implications for the prospects of a postcapitalist order thus: 'The bureaucratization and repression of all post-revolutionary States produced by history so far is . . . linked to the very nature and condition of the proletariat as a social ensemble, so long as global scarcity and class divisions exist. Bureaucracy remains an ineliminable accompaniment and adversary of socialism in this epoch' (p. 88).

134. Anderson cites, inter alia, Trotsky's problematic of 'permanent revolution' and Deutscher's 'unfounded optimism' about the USSR after Stalin.

135. Deutscher, 'Marxism in Our Time' (1965), in *Marxism, Wars, and Revolutions*, pp. 243–55: here p. 245.

136. This is the judgement of Richard D. Wolff, in his review of *Considerations*: 'Western Marxism', *Monthly Review*, vol. 30, no. 4, September 1978, pp. 58–64: here p. 58.

137. See, for example, *Selections from the Prison Notebooks*, pp. 381 ff., where Gramsci notes Bauer, Adler, et al.'s resort to neo-Kantianism in response to the 'orthodox tendency' represented by Plekhanov.

138. See Maurice Merleau-Ponty, *Adventures of the Dialectic* (1955), trans. Joseph Bien, Northwestern University Press, Evanston, Ill., 1973, chap. 2, '"Western" Marxism' (pp. 30–58) and chap. 3, 'Pravda' (pp. 59–73). Cf. Karl Korsch, 'The Present State of the Problem of "Marxism and Philosophy"—an Anti-Critique' (1930), in *Marxism and Philosophy*, trans. Fred Halliday, New Left Books, London, 1970, pp. 98–144 (especially pp. 119–20), for Korsch's own employment of the category 'West European Marxism'.

139. Jeffrey Herf, 'Science and Class or Philosophy and Revolution: Perry Anderson on Western Marxism', *Socialist Revolution* no. 35, September/October 1977, pp. 129–44, especially p. 134.

140. Göran Therborn, 'Dialectics of Modernity: On Critical Theory and the Legacy of Twentieth-Century Marxism', *NLR* no. 215, January/February 1996, pp. 59–81: here p. 70.

141. See Martin Jay, *Marxism and Totality: The Adventures of a Concept from Lukács to Habermas*, Polity Press, Cambridge, 1984—in particular, 'Introduction: The Topography of Western Marxism', pp. 1–20. Published two years later, J. G. Merquior's *Western Marxism* (Paladin, London, 1986) likewise treats the same figures as *Considerations*. But since it defines its subject as 'by and large a *Kulturkritik* sublimated into empty theoreticism' (p. 250), it is far from clear what many of the authors discussed are doing in its pages.

142. Cf. Therborn, 'Dialectics of Modernity', pp. 71–72. It is also worth noting in this context Robin Blackburn's much more 'activist' reading of Western Marxist production in his 'Brief Guide to Bourgeois Ideology', p. 213.

143. This was Russell Jacoby's bone of contention with *Considerations*, in a study that identified the Western tradition with 'critical Marxism', as against 'conformist Marxism' (including Althusser): 'The predominance of philosophical works signified not a retreat but an advance to a reexamination of Marxism. . . . I do not view Western Marxism as an unfortunate detour from "classical" Marxism; nor do I look forward to its extinction. The myth of a heroic Marxism, harmonizing philosophy, economics, science, and praxis, overwhelms the feeble efforts to rethink Marxism' (*Dialectic of Defeat: Contours of Western Marxism*, Cambridge University Press,

Cambridge, 1981, pp. 6–7). In his review ('Goodbye to All That?', *Radical Philosophy* no. 16, spring 1977, pp. 39–41), John Mepham further noted that in the very year *Considerations* was announcing the end of Western Marxism, NLB was going to the trouble of translating one of its monuments: Sartre's *Critique*. Subsequently, hailing 'a new appetite . . . for the concrete' among Marxist intellectuals, Anderson would register the salience of the 'Althusserian current' therein, citing work by Poulantzas, Therborn, Aglietta, and others, therewith subverting his verdict of 'obsessive methodologism': see *In the Tracks of Historical Materialism*, pp. 21–23. Similarly, rejecting E. P. Thompson's kindred allegations against Althusser, he would insist in *Arguments within English Marxism* that 'Althusserianism has proved remarkably *productive—generating an impressively wide range of works dealing with the real world, both past and present*' (p. 126).

144. A token: Workers Revolutionary Party spokesman Cliff Slaughter convicted *Considerations* of 'a rejection of *all* the fundamental theories of Marxism' ('Anderson's "Western Marxism"', *Labour Review* vol. 1, no. 3, August 1977, p. 175).

145. In a furious review, Paul Piccone upbraided Anderson for his failure to mention Socialisme ou Barbarie, 'the most intellectually alive post–World War II Trotskyist group': *Telos* no. 30, winter 1976/1977, pp. 213–16 (here p. 215).

146. Tom Nairn, 'Comments on "Western Marxism: An Introduction"', unpublished document, September 1974, pp. 2–10. For Nairn, as he goes on to make clear, and as Anderson observes in the foreword to *English Questions* (p. 7), the crucial turning point settling the fate of revolution in the West was August 1914. Notoriously, the 1938 founding programme of the Fourth International—*The Death Agony of Capitalism and the Tasks of the Fourth International*, written by Trotsky—had maintained that '[t]he historical crisis of mankind is reduced to the crisis of the revolutionary leadership' (qtd. in Alex Callinicos, *Trotskyism*, Open University Press, Milton Keynes, 1990, p. 20).

147. Anthony Barnett, 'Introduction to Western Marxism: Some Preliminary Comments', unpublished document, July 1974, pp. 3–5; Tom Nairn, 'Comments', p. 10.

148. Gareth Stedman Jones, 'Comment', [1974/75], pp. 8–10.

149. Eric Hobsbawm, 'Look Left', *New Statesman*, 24 September 1976, pp. 408–11.

150. Deutscher, *The Prophet Armed*, p. ix: 'I see [Trotsky] as the representative figure of pre-Stalinist communism and the precursor of post-Stalinist communism. Yet I do not imagine that the future of communism lies in Trotskyism. I am inclined to think that the historic development is transcending both Stalinism and Trotskyism and is tending towards something broader than either of them'. For Deutscher's verdict on the foundation of the Fourth International itself, see *The Prophet Outcast—Trotsky: 1929–1940* (1963), Oxford University Press, Oxford, 1979, pp. 210–12; and cf. Victor Serge, 'On Trotskyism', in David Cotterill, ed., *The Serge-Trotsky Papers*, Pluto Press, London and Boulder, Colo., 1994, pp. 210–12.

151. The twenty-five or so lines from 'The combination of enforced isolation . . .' down to '. . . the wider criticism of mass proletarian practice' (*Considerations*, pp. 100–101) were added for publication in 1976. Cf. the original 'Western Marxism: An Introduction', [1974], p. 127.

152. Hosbawm, 'Look Left'. Anderson's original conclusion ('Western Marxism', p. 134) had struck a somewhat more apocalytic, and even more antiacademic, note. For Thompson's reproof, see his review 'The Marx Claimants', *Guardian*, 16 September 1976, p. 7.

153. Anderson makes a sharp rejoinder (*Considerations*, p. 110 n. 1) to Hindess and Hirst's dismissal of historiography in their *Pre-capitalist Modes of Production* (Routledge and Kegan Paul, London, 1975, p. 312) as 'not only scientifically but also politically valueless'.

154. Concerning Engels, the 'Decennial Report' (pp. 107–8) cited Gareth Stedman Jones's essay on his philosophical constructions—'Engels and the End of Classical German Philosophy', *NLR* no. 79, May/June 1973, pp. 17–36—as a model of the necessary type of criticism. In the case of Luxemburg (p. 111), the report instanced articles by Norman Geras (in *NLR* no. 82, November/December 1973, pp. 17–37, and *NLR* no. 89, January/February 1975, pp. 3–46), later collected in his *The Legacy of Rosa Luxemburg*, New Left Books, London, 1976, chaps. 1 and 2 (pp. 13–109).

155. The laws in question were precisely 'the framework of classical Marxist categories' that Mandel's *Late Capitalism* (1972; trans. Joris De Bres, New Left Books, London, 1975) had been lauded for employing in the main text of *Considerations* (p. 98). Anderson specifies that '[t]he most hazardous conclusions . . . were the general theory of the falling rate of profit, and the tenet of an ever-increasing class polarization between bourgeoisie and proletariat. Neither has yet been adequately substantiated' (p. 115). In the 'Decennial Report' (p. 106), they are straightforwardly dubbed '[t]he most evident errors of conclusion'.

156. The 'Decennial Report' (p. 113) deems the theory 'unsubstantiated'.

157. Cf. *Considerations*, pp. 53–54 and 100; and Anderson's comments on Deutscher's prose style in his preface to *Marxism, Wars, and Revolutions*, p. xx.

3. Against the Historical Current?

1. 'NLR, 1975–1980', unpublished report, [1980], pp. 3–4.

2. In an internal memorandum of 1983, to which we shall return.

3. 'A Decennial Report', unpublished report, [1975], p. 85.

4. 'NLR, 1975–1980', p. 36. The report continues: 'How many countries can emulate . . . the Spanish road remains to be seen: perhaps only a minority of the present candidates. But the regional demonstration effect of even selected such successes is likely to be very great in the last two decades of this century, endowing capitalism with an ideal dimension—as the model of a feasible and desirable society—that it has so far radically lacked in the underdeveloped world. Any such scenario would quickly relativize socialist victories in the series of very backward countries like Ethiopia or Afghanistan which were so much more ostensive in the late 70's' (pp. 36–37).

5. 'Communist Party History', in Raphael Samuel, ed., *People's History and Socialist Theory*, Routledge and Kegan Paul, London, 1981, p. 155.

6. *In the Tracks of Historical Materialism*, Verso, London, 1983, p. 80.

7. Mandel's revealing failure to produce a projected study, 'Revolution in Western Europe', is cited in 'NLR, 1975–1980', p. 47.

8. Cf. Giorgio Amendola, 'The Italian Road to Socialism', and Fernando Claudin, 'Democracy and Dictatorship in Lenin and Kautsky', both in *NLR* no. 106, November/December 1977, pp. 39–50, 59–78, respectively; Nicos Poulantzas, 'Towards a Democratic Socialism', *NLR* no. 109, May/June 1978, pp. 75–87; Ernest Mandel, 'Revolutionary Strategy in Europe—a Political Interview', *NLR* no. 100, November 1976/January 1977, pp. 97–132; and Henri Weber, 'Eurocommunism, Socialism, and Democracy', *NLR* no. 110, July/August 1978, pp. 3–14.

9. See the 'Themes' to *NLR* no. 109, p. 2. This issue also contained Althusser's swingeing critique of the PCF, 'What Must Change in the Party', pp. 19–45.

10. 'The Antinomies of Antonio Gramsci', *NLR* no. 100, November 1976/January 1977, pp. 5–78. Cf. *A Zone of Engagement*, Verso, London and New York, 1992, p. xi.

11. In a footnote ('Antinomies', p. 28 n. 49), Anderson continues: 'In other words, it is

quite wrong simply to designate parliament an "ideological apparatus" of bourgeois power without further ado. The ideological function of *parliamentary sovereignty* is inscribed in the formal framework of every bourgeois constitution, and is always central to the cultural dominion of capital. However, parliament is also, of course, a "political apparatus", vested with real attributes of debate and decision, which are in no sense a mere trick to lull the masses. They are objective structures of a once great—still potent—historic achievement, the triumph of the ideals of the bourgeois revolution'.

12. Cf. Nicholas Abercrombie et al., *The Dominant Ideology Thesis*, Allen and Unwin, London, 1980.

13. Antonio Gramsci, *Selections from the Prison Notebooks*, ed. and trans. Quintin Hoare and Geoffrey Nowell Smith, Lawrence and Wishart, London, 1971, p. 238.

14. In his closing paragraph ('Antinomies', p. 78), Anderson invokes Régis Debray. Interestingly, the gravamen of Althusser's critique of his pupil's theorization of *focismo* in Latin America, arguing that his 'negative demonstration' of the inviability of the strategic alternatives did not constitute a 'positive demonstration' of the feasibility of *focos*, holds true, with obvious alterations of detail, for 'Antinomies'. See 'Letter from Louis Althusser', in Debray, *A Critique of Arms* (1974), trans. Rosemary Sheed, Penguin, Harmondsworth, 1977, pp. 258–67.

15. Geoff Hodgson, 'The Antinomies of Perry Anderson', in *Socialism and Parliamentary Democracy*, Spokesman Press, Nottingham, 1977, pp. 105–37, especially pp. 122 ff. Without replying to Hodgson's criticisms, Anderson commended this volume, together with Poulantzas's *State, Power, Socialism*, as 'the two most intelligent and original expositions' of the 'dual strategy' perspective on offer (*Arguments within English Marxism*, New Left Books, London, 1980, p. 197). 'Anderson', Hodgson wrote (p. 134), 'shares his trajectory, from being a Marxist within the mainstream labour movement to the relative isolation of the far-left grouplets, with a whole generation of socialists in Britain. The tragedy of this useless exodus is made more intense in that it involves a man of intellectual brilliance'.

16. 'The Strategic Option: Some Questions', in André Liebich, ed., *The Future of Socialism in Europe?* Interuniversity Centre for European Studies, Montreal, 1978, pp. 21–29.

17. Cf. the long question to Raymond Williams on the subject of socialist democracy, in the interviews conducted with him by Anderson and others around this time: *Politics and Letters: Interviews with New Left Review*, New Left Books, London, 1979, pp. 426–28. It concluded by suggesting that 'in our much more advanced societies [than Russia] we have no model of socialist democracy that is more advanced, we have an absence of any such experience at all—whereas in that backward society sixty years ago certain kinds of institutions were adumbrated which even today remain imaginatively and practically beyond our ordinary range of political discussion in the West' (p. 428).

18. 'The Notion of Bourgeois Revolution' (1976), in *English Questions*, Verso, London and New York, 1992, pp. 105–18.

19. Tom Nairn, 'The Twilight of the British State', *NLR* nos. 101–2, January/April 1977, pp. 3–61 (reprinted as chap. 1 of *The Break-up of Britain: Crisis and Neo-Nationalism* [1977], 2d ed., Verso, London, 1981, pp. 11–91). In an otherwise very critical review, Eric Hobsbawm paid tribute to the 'often brilliant enquiry into the "crisis of England"': 'Some Reflections on "The Break-up of Britain"', *NLR* no. 105, September/October 1977, pp. 3–23 (here p. 15). According to 'NLR, 1975–1980' (p. 3), Nairn's key essay on nationalism, 'The Modern Janus', provoked keen dissension within the editorial committee; it was published in *NLR* no. 94, November/December 1975, pp. 3–29 (and reprinted as chap. 9 of *The Break-up of Britain*, pp. 329–63).

20. See Nairn, *The Break-up of Britain*, pp. 303–4, taken exception to by E. P. Thompson in the foreword to his *The Poverty of Theory and Other Essays*, Merlin Press, London,

1978, pp. iii–iv. Terry Eagleton's essay, 'Criticism and Politics: The Work of Raymond Williams', was published in *NLR* no. 95, January/February 1976, pp. 3–23, and incorporated into his *Criticism and Ideology: A Study in Marxist Literary Theory*, New Left Books, London, 1976, chap. 1 (pp. 11–43). It occasioned considerable controversy within the *Aktiv*, of which Anthony Barnett's 'Raymond Williams and Marxism: A Rejoinder', *NLR* no. 99, September/October 1976, pp. 47–64, is the muffled echo, and *Politics and Letters* the welcome ultimate outcome. Cf. the foreword to the latter (pp. 7–10), coauthored by Anderson, for a typically discreet reference at p. 9.

21. *Arguments within English Marxism*, pp. 2–3.

22. See E. P. Thompson, 'The Politics of Theory', in Samuel, *People's History and Socialist Theory*, pp. 396–408, responding intransigently to judicious papers by Stuart Hall ('In Defence of Theory', pp. 378–85) and Richard Johnson ('Against Absolutism', pp. 386–96). The occasion is evoked by Anderson in his obituary 'Diary' on Thompson, *London Review of Books*, 21 October 1993, p. 24.

23. See *Arguments within English Marxism*, pp. 5–15; and cf. *Lineages of the Absolutist State*, New Left Books, London, 1974, pp. 7–8. Anderson had thus abandoned his erstwhile antinaturalist position on the ontological and methodological differences between the natural and social or human sciences: cf. 'Socialism and Pseudo-Empiricism', *New Left Review* no. 35, January/February 1966, p. 19. Richard Johnson has remarked that *Arguments*, whatever its cogency as a response to Thompson's critique of Althusser, '. . . leaves history-writing and research relatively unquestioned': 'Reading for the Best Marx: History-Writing and Historical Abstraction', in Centre for Contemporary Cultural Studies, ed., *Making Histories: Studies in History-Writing and Politics*, Hutchinson, London, 1982, p. 153. Cf. Paul Hirst's conventionalist rejoinder to *The Poverty of Theory*, 'The Necessity of Theory' (1979), reprinted as chap. 4 of Hirst, *Marxism and Historical Writing*, Routledge and Kegan Paul, London, 1985, pp. 57–90.

24. See Ted Benton, *The Rise and Fall of Structural Marxism: Althusser and His Influence*, Macmillan, London, 1984, pp. 210–11.

25. Cf. Oscar Wilde: 'Experience is the name everyone gives to their mistakes' (*Lady Windermere's Fan*). See also the long question on experience to Williams in *Politics and Letters*, pp. 168–70. In a footnote to *Arguments* (p. 29 n. 36), Anderson cites Sartre's critique of 'l'expérience-qui-comporte-sa-propre-interprétation' in his 'Reply to Claude Lefort': see Sartre, *The Communists and Peace* (1952–54), trans. Irene Clephane, Hamish Hamilton, London, 1969, pp. 207–64. For a defence of Althusser against the imputation of hyperrationalism, see Benton, *The Rise and Fall of Structural Marxism*, pp. 203–9.

26. In addition to the critique of *The Making of the English Working Class* in *Arguments* (pp. 30–49), see Anderson's review of Charles Bergquist's *Labor in Latin America* ('Laboring under Various Pretences in Latin America', *In These Times*, 6–12 April 1988), on the need to combine 'political economy with social history'; and his contribution to a symposium on the subject, 'The Common and the Particular' (*International Labor and Working-Class History* no. 36, fall 1989, pp. 31–36), which praises Bergquist's work for its 'synthesis of experience and structure' (p. 35). Cf. G. A. Cohen, *Karl Marx's Theory of History: A Defence*, Oxford University Press, Oxford, 1978.

27. See *Arguments*, pp. 62–63. An interesting partial inversion of positions between Thompson and Anderson has occurred here, relative to the antagonisms of 1965–66. In 'The Peculiarities of the English', Thompson had selected political economy as the quintessential English ideology—one that refuted Anderson's concentration upon utilitarianism and its miseries—expressing his surprise that Anderson and Nairn should have neglected it, 'when Marx himself . . . devoted his life's work to overthrowing it'

(*The Poverty of Theory and Other Essays*, p. 63). In response, Anderson rebuked 'the incredibly impoverished vision of Marx's work this reveals', citing Marx's philosophical writings by way of refutation ('Socialism and Pseudo-Empiricism', p. 21). The contrast with Anderson's emphasis on *Capital* in *Arguments* is attributable to his graduation from the philosophical humanism of his Sartrean formation.

28. Cf. *Considerations on Western Marxism*, New Left Books, London, 1976, pp. 109–11, to which Anderson refers the reader.

29. Marx's own nonutilitarian consequentialism is most evident in his overall attitude toward capitalism: for him, as Fredric Jameson has observed, it is 'at one and the same time the best thing that has ever happened to the human race, and the worst' ('Postmodernism, or The Cultural Logic of Late Capitalism', *NLR* no. 146, July/August 1984, p. 86). See, for example, the notorious closing lines of Marx, 'The Future Results of the British Rule in India' (1853; in *Surveys from Exile*, Penguin/NLR, Harmondsworth, 1973, p. 325); and cf. the conclusion of Isaac Deutscher's Trotsky trilogy, *The Prophet Outcast—Trotsky: 1929-1940* (1963), Oxford University Press, Oxford, 1979, pp. 522–23. Anderson's adherence to what Jameson calls Marx's 'dialectical imperative' is evident in his unpublished notes on Bill Warren, '"Imperialism— Pioneer of Capitalism"', pp. 1–3. For a recent instance, see his 'Diary' on South Korea (*London Review of Books*, 17 October 1996, pp. 28–29), where he writes that '[t]he toll of empire in [postwar] Korea was huge, but privileges perversely went with it' (p. 28). And cf. the questioning of Williams on the subject of historical processes and historical progress in *Politics and Letters*, pp. 308–11. An extremely illuminating discussion of Marx's own relation to 'progressivism' can be found in Étienne Balibar, *The Philosophy of Marx*, trans. Chris Turner, Verso, London and New York, 1995, chap. 4, 'Time and Progress: Another Philosophy of History?' (pp. 80–112).

30. See *Arguments*, pp. 100–114. In the process (p. 108), Anderson effectively retracted the praise lavished on Calvez for his philosophical-anthropological interpretation of Marx (cf. 'Socialism and Pseudo-Empiricism', p. 27), and took a swipe at Alasdair MacIntyre's Anglicanism. More generally, he commended the Althusserian 'reinstatement of serious study of *Capital* and of *Pre-capitalist Economic Formations* as the core of historical materialism', against the stream of the late 1950s and early 1960s, with which the young Anderson had swum. Later in chap. 4 (pp. 125–26), Anderson issued a peremptory dismissal of English Althusserianism, to which one of its proponents— Paul Hirst—later responded, more in sorrow than in anger: see 'Anderson's Balance Sheet', chap. 1 of Hirst, *Marxism and Historical Writing* (pp. 1–28).

31. Doubtless with an eye on Thompson, and Hindess and Hirst, respectively, the foreword to *Politics and Letters* maintained that the *NLR*'s dual commitment to the exposition and evaluation of Continental Marxism 'has set the Review apart from two reactions to be found among older and younger generations to the broadening of Marxist culture in England: vehement anathemas on foreign doctrines as alien intrusions of theory into the national tradition, or hierophantic espousals of one school at the expense of all the others, as the site of a privileged knowledge' (p. 9). Cf. the 'Editorial Note', penned by Anderson, in *NLR*, ed., *Western Marxism: A Critical Reader*, New Left Books, London, 1977, p. 7. In *Politics and Letters* (p. 317), Williams credits the *Review* with 'an unalterable achievement' in expanding the domestic range of Marxist culture.

32. Anderson relates Thompson's neglect of Trotsky after 1956 to the latter's rejection of antifascist war in 1939 as an imperialist conflict—'a major political error', in Anderson's view—and to the Fourth International's hostility to 'united frontism' from 1941 to 1947 (*Arguments*, pp. 154–55). He further remarks, in passing (p. 155 and n. 39), that *NLR* editors 'varied widely among themselves in their particular assessments of [Trotsky's heritage], and none was ever uncritical of it', referring readers to *Considerations on Western Marxism*, pp. 118–21, for his own evaluation.

33. 'So far', Anderson continued (*Arguments*, p. 156), 'it is this tradition alone that has proved capable of an adult view of socialism on a world scale, as anyone who reads Mandel's recent *Revolutionary Marxism Today* may see for themselves'. Earlier, Anderson had praised Mandel's *From Stalinism to Eurocommunism* for its 'surgical sharpness and clarity' (pp. 115–16).

34. 'The catch-word of Desire has . . . been one of the slogans of the subjectivist *Schwarmerei* that followed disillusionment with the social revolt of 1968—celebrated in such writings as Jean-Paul Dollé's *Désir [de] Révolution* and Deleuze and Guattari's *Anti-Oedipe*, the expression of a dejected post-lapsarian anarchism. Intellectually, the category operates as a licence for the exercise of any fantasy freed from the responsibility of cognitive controls' (*Arguments*, p. 161).

35. For Williams's views, see *Politics and Letters*, pp. 128–29.

36. The relevant passage from the *Grundrisse* can be found in the Penguin/NLR ed., trans. Martin Nicolaus, Harmondsworth, 1973, p. 162. Anderson also refers readers to Stedman Jones's 'The Marxism of the Early Lukács', in *Western Marxism*, pp. 23–24.

37. See Donald Sassoon, 'The Silences of *New Left Review*', in *Politics and Power 3*, Routledge and Kegan Paul, London, 1981, pp. 249–51, where Anderson's perspective is derided as a 'Big Bang conception of revolution'.

38. Cf. the critical probing of Williams's notion of the 'long revolution' in *Politics and Letters*, pp. 419–20. And note also Anderson's later objection to Roberto Unger: 'Intimations of harmony discount considerations of strategy, in a reminder of the other side of the utopian tradition' ('Roberto Unger and the Politics of Empowerment', *A Zone of Engagement*, pp. 130–48: here p. 148).

39. As we have noted, Anderson cited Poulantzas's *State, Power, Socialism* and Hodgson's *Socialism and Parliamentary Democracy* as 'the two most intelligent and original expositions' of the reformist prospectus, and Mandel's *From Stalinism to Eurocommunism* as the 'most effective critique' (*Arguments*, p. 197). Earlier, he had credited Morris with having 'effectively [written] the script of the Chilean tragedy nearly a century in advance' (p. 179; see also pp. 196, 206). And for the same lesson from the destruction of Popular Unity's reformist experiment, cf. 'A Political and Philosophical Interview' with Colletti, in *Western Marxism*, p. 345; *Politics and Letters*, pp. 418–19; and *In the Tracks of Historical Materialism*, p. 103. Note also the premonitions of disaster in the 'Themes' to *NLR* no. 78, March/April 1973, p. 1.

40. The paradox is perhaps compounded by the fact that Thompson declined to sign Charter 88. Cf. his *Writing by Candlelight*, Merlin Press, London, 1980.

41. See E. P. Thompson's 'Notes on Exterminism, the Last Stage of Civilization', *NLR* no. 121, May/June 1980, pp. 3–31, for his registration of 'an ulterior difference of stance', based upon 'generational experience' (p. 27). And cf. his contribution to a 1985 symposium at the New School for Social Research, in which Anderson also participated: 'Agendas for Radical History', *Radical History Review* no. 36, 1986, pp. 37–41, where Thompson confided that 'I feel no need to reply to Perry. I think he had many important and interesting things to say. I think we'd call it a draw' (p. 39). Anderson recalls the event in his 1993 *London Review of Books* 'Diary', p. 24.

42. See the laudatory reviews by John Dunn, 'An English Marxist Faces His Inquisitor', *New Society*, 12 June 1980, pp. 235–36; and Christopher Hitchens, 'Theory and Experience', *New Statesman*, 13 June 1980, pp. 906–8.

43. V. I. Lenin, 'The Three Sources and Three Component Parts of Marxism' (1913), in his *Collected Works*, vol. 19, Progress Publishers, Moscow, 1968, pp. 23–28.

44. See, for example, Trotsky's 'Open Letter to Comrade Burnham' (1940), in *In Defense of Marxism: The Social and Political Contradictions of the Soviet Union* (1942), Pathfinder Press, New York, 1990, p. 74.

45. In November 1978, a conference on the validity of Marx's labour theory of value, in

the light of Piero Sraffa's *Production of Commodities by Means of Commodities*, was held in London, jointly organized by the *NLR*, the *Cambridge Journal of Economics*, and the Conference of Socialist Economists. From it emerged Ian Steedman et al., *The Value Controversy*, Verso, London, 1981, intended (according to the 'Editorial Note', p. 7) as 'a contribution to an ongoing debate'. For Lenin's claim, see 'The Three Sources and Three Component Parts of Marxism', p. 26.

46. Karl Marx and Frederick Engels, *The German Ideology* (1845–46), in *Collected Works*, vol. 5, Lawrence and Wishart, London, 1976, p. 49.

47. See Karl Marx, *Capital*, vol. 1, trans. Ben Fowkes, Penguin/*NLR*, Harmondsworth, 1976, part 8, chap. 32, 'The Historical Tendency of Capitalist Accumulation' (pp. 927–30); and Frederick Engels, *Anti-Dühring*, trans. Emile Burns, Progress Publishers, Moscow, 1947, part 1, chap. 13, 'Dialectics: The Negation of the Negation' (pp. 159–74). Cf. Eric Olin Wright, 'Class Analysis, History, and Emancipation', *NLR* no. 202, November/December 1993, pp. 15–35.

48. See *NLR* no. 115, May/June 1979: 'Themes', pp. 1–2; Régis Debray, 'A Modest Contribution to the Rites and Ceremonies of the Tenth Anniversary', pp. 45–65; and Henri Weber, 'Reply to Debray', pp. 66–71. Debray (p. 59) remarked the 'phantasmagoria' of André Glucksmann's *Stratégie et révolution en France*—a text translated in full (and lauded) in the *NLR* special issue on May '68.

49. Among the *NLR* publications on the USSR were interviews with Ernest Mandel, 'On the Nature of the Soviet State' (*NLR* no. 108, March/April 1978, pp. 23–45); with E. H. Carr, 'The Russian Revolution and the West' (*NLR* no. 111, September/October 1978, pp. 25–36); and with Zhores Medvedev, 'Russia under Brezhnev' (*NLR* no. 117, September/October 1979, pp. 3–29)—'accompanied', it is noted, by 'firm editorial statements in the Themes'.

50. The principal *NLR* analyst of these events was Fred Halliday: 'Revolution in Afghanistan', *NLR* no. 112, November/December 1978, pp. 3–44; 'The War and Revolution in Afghanistan', *NLR* no. 119, January/February 1980, pp. 20–41; *Iran: Dictatorship and Development*, Penguin, Harmondsworth, 1979; and (with Maxine Molyneux) *The Ethiopian Revolution*, New Left Books, London, 1981. See also his *Threat from the East? Soviet Policy from Afghanistan and Iran to the Horn of Africa*, Penguin, Harmondsworth, 1982.

51. Reflecting on the last point, the quinquennial report commented (pp. 37–38): 'The Cambodian revolution is a case apart, surpassing Stalinism in Russia itself in its wholesale extermination of social groups, but without any of the transforming and liberating aspects of the Russian experience. The terrible blow it has dealt to the name of communism has no common measure with any other upheaval of these years. But in their own way the Angolan, Ethiopian, Yemeni and Afghan revolutions have all been tarnished with very ugly episodes of fratricide and repression. Shootouts in Presidential palaces have occurred in Luanda, Addis, Aden and Kabul alike— a pattern of murderous settling of accounts that is a reminder of how backward the political culture in each of these societies still remains compared even with the norms of Stalinist Russia in the 20s. The use of mass terror by the Mengistu and Amin regimes, once besieged in national civil wars, has likewise been far worse than anything committed by the Bolsheviks in the Russian Civil War. Finally, the two processes of military adventurism and political brutalization appeared to fuse with the Russian intervention in the degenerating crisis in Afghanistan. The result was to permit the USA to unleash the greatest ideological-political offensive against the USSR since the Truman Doctrine, ushering in the 80's with a full-scale re-edition of the Cold War. In reality, the two processes above were not, of course, identical or even essentially similar. Paradoxically, indeed, the Vietnamese attack on Cambodia and the Soviet entry into Afghanistan were in large part designed to put an end to

intolerably terrorist regimes that were endangering or disgracing the cause of socialism in their region'.

52. Cf. the reflections on the 'uneven development' of theoretical production in the afterword to *Considerations on Western Marxism*, p. 102.

53. The quinquennial report proceeded (pp. 51–52) to an enumeration of book and journal titles to substantiate the point.

54. Raphael Samuel, 'British Marxist Historians, 1880–1980', *NLR* no. 120, March/April 1980, pp. 21–96; Stuart Hall, 'Nicos Poulantzas: "State, Power, Socialism"', *NLR* no. 119, January/February 1980, pp. 60–69. These were soon followed, of course, by Thompson's 'Notes on Exterminism' (see n. 41, this chapter). Mention should also be made here of a fundamental work on twentieth-century British intellectual culture by one of Williams's *NLR* interlocutors, Francis Mulhern: *The Moment of 'Scrutiny'*, New Left Books, London, 1979.

55. *Politics and Letters*, pp. 7–8. Cf. Robin Blackburn, 'Theory and Experience', *New Statesman*, 18 July 1980, pp. 23–24 (here p. 24)—a tetchy response to Alex Callinicos's critical reception of *Arguments* in the same periodical, 27 June 1980, pp. 969–70.

56. Cf. *In the Tracks of Historical Materialism*, pp. 97–100. It is interesting to find Ralph Miliband, in 'Thirty Years of *Socialist Register*', regretting that 'we did not address the question of socialist construction with anything like the detailed and rigorous concern which it requires' (*Socialist Register, 1994*, Merlin Press, London, 1994, pp. 1–19: here p. 6).

57. Cf. *In the Tracks of Historical Materialism*, pp. 85–89.

58. In terms of *NLR*'s and NLB's editorial programme, the report refers to a projected series of articles on Eastern Europe, and to forthcoming books on the USSR (by Bogdan Kravchenko) and Indochina (by Anthony Barnett). Significantly, perhaps, none of the books (including a study by Blackburn of Cuba) appeared, and few of the articles materialized. Note, however, Oliver MacDonald's (i.e., Peter Gowan's) major piece 'The Polish Vortex: Solidarity and Socialism', *NLR* no. 139, May/June 1983, pp. 5–48.

59. Fred Halliday, *The Making of the Second Cold War* (1983), 2d ed., Verso, London, 1986, pp. 242–43.

60. 'The Left in the Fifties', *NLR* no. 29, January/February 1965, p. 12 (qtd. in Halliday, ibid., p. 36 n. 13).

61. The key interventions were E. P. Thompson, 'Notes on Exterminism, the Last Stage of Civilization'; Raymond Williams, 'The Politics of Nuclear Disarmament', *NLR* no. 124, November/December 1980, pp. 25–42; Roy Medvedev and Zhores Medvedev, 'The USSR and the Arms Race', *NLR* no. 130, November/December 1981, pp. 5–22; Lucio Magri, 'The Peace Movement and European Socialism', *NLR* no. 131, January/February 1982, pp. 5–19; Rudolf Bahro, 'The SPD and the Peace Movement', *NLR* no. 131, pp. 20–31; Alexander Cockburn and James Ridgeway, 'The Freeze Movement versus Reagan', *NLR* no. 137, January/February 1983, pp. 5–21; Ernest Mandel, 'The Threat of War and the Struggle for Socialism', *NLR* no. 141, September/October 1983, pp. 23–50; and Ken Coates, 'The Peace Movement and Socialism', *NLR* no. 145, May/June 1984, pp. 88–121. The earlier items were collected, together with texts by Etienne Balibar, Noam Chomsky, and others, in *NLR*, ed., *Exterminism and Cold War*, Verso, London, 1982.

62. See Mike Davis, 'Nuclear Imperialism and Extended Deterrence', and Fred Halliday, 'The Sources of the New Cold War', in *Exterminism and Cold War*, pp. 35–64, 289–328, respectively. (Anderson's imprimatur is affixed to his fellow editors' essays in *In the Tracks of Historical Materialism*, p. 96 n. 10.) In addition to this volume, in 1984 Verso published Diana Johnstone's *The Politics of Euromissiles*.

63. Foreword to *Exterminism and Cold War*, pp. vii–xii.

64. Cf., for example, Deutscher, *The Prophet Outcast*, p. 518: 'On both sides of the [post-

war] great divide . . . the international balance of power swamped the class struggle. As in the Napoleonic era, revolution and counter-revolution alike were the by-products of arms and diplomacy. . . . All [Trotsky's] habits of thought made it difficult . . . for him to imagine that for a whole epoch the armies and diplomacies of three powers [Russia, America, and Britain] would be able to impose their will upon the social classes of old Europe; and that consequently the class struggle, suppressed at the level on which it had been traditionally waged, would be fought at a different level and in different forms, as rivalry between power blocs and as cold war'.

65. For 'amplification', Anderson refers readers to the essays by Davis and Halliday in *Exterminism and Cold War*, proceeding to a restatement of the political conclusion in his foreword to the collection. Anderson notes Rudolf Bahro's convergence with Thompson's 'universalist' perspective (*In the Tracks of Historical Materialism*, p. 95)— a position from which he and his fellow interviewers (Monty Johnstone and Fred Halliday) failed to shake the author of *The Alternative in Eastern Europe*, in the exchanges published as Bahro, *From Red to Green: Interviews with New Left Review*, trans. Gus Fagan and Richard Hurst, Verso, London, 1984.

66. Scott L. Malcomson, 'Ten Thousand Megalomaniacs: Perry Anderson, Man of Steel', *Voice Literary Supplement*, March 1993, p. 21. Such exaggeration derives from the *Review*'s unfashionable emphasis on what it deemed 'the progressive dimension of the Soviet Union—most strikingly attested in recent years by its international policy from Vietnam to Afghanistan' ('Themes', *NLR* no. 110, July/August 1978, p. 1).

67. Halliday reiterated this perspective at the essay's conclusion ('Sources of the New Cold War', p. 327): 'The New Cold War that threatens us all is the distorted product of the conflict between a militaristic capitalism and an involuted and bureaucratic socialism. It can only be transcended by a socialism that, whilst not equating these two international forces, seeks to be a historical alternative to both'.

68. This renders the verdict of Lin Chun—namely, that 'Anderson was quite a fundamentalist of post-war leftist anti-communism'—mystifying (cf. Chun's *The British New Left*, Edinburgh University Press, Edinburgh, 1993, p. 175 n. 20).

69. 'Trotsky's Interpretation of Stalinism', published in the same issue of the *Review* as Gowan's major article on Poland (see n. 58, this chapter): *NLR* no. 139, May/June 1983, pp. 49–58; reprinted in Tariq Ali's anthology *The Stalinist Legacy: Its Impact on Twentieth-Century World Politics*, Penguin, Harmondsworth, 1984, pp. 118–28. (Given the unfortunate misprints in the conclusion to the *NLR* version, all references, unless otherwise indicated, will be to the Ali volume.) Anderson's talk was one of three brief overviews of the results and prospects of socialism that he attempted in the early 1980s. A second—'The Social Democratic Parabola'—though never published in its original form, possibly formed the basis for a subsequent article, 'Social Democracy Today', carried in the American Trotskyist journal *Against the Current* (vol. 1, no. 6, November/December 1986, pp. 21–28). This piece was in turn incorporated (with revisions) as sec. 1 ('The Parabola of Social Democracy') of 'The Light of Europe', in *English Questions*, pp. 307–25. The third item—'On the Relations between Existing and Alternative Socialisms'—was originally scheduled for publication in the *NLR* in 1983 but then withdrawn in favour of the Trotsky text. Unfortunately, it has not been possible to obtain access to a copy of it.

70. For a lucid summary, see Alan M. Wald, *The New York Intellectuals: The Rise and Decline of the Anti-Stalinist Left from the 1930s to the 1980s*, University of North Carolina Press, Chapel Hill, 1987, pp. 296–97: 'Faced with the contradiction between theory and reality, the Trotskyists were posed with four alternatives: they could abandon building the Fourth International and organizations such as the [American] SWP; they could correct, update, and adjust Marxism and Trotskyism in the light of the unexpected phenomena; they could attempt to demonstrate how all the post–World

War II social transformations actually *did* occur according to Trotsky's pre-1940 perspectives; or they could deny that authentic revolutions had occurred'. In the event, of course, different groups and individuals pursued each of these options. See Alex Callinicos, *Trotskyism*, Open University Press, Milton Keynes, 1990, chap. 2, 'Crisis' (pp. 23–38), containing a helpful genealogy of Anglo-American Trotskyism down to the mid-1980s.

71. Leon Trotsky, 'Balance Sheet of the Finnish Events' (1940), in *In Defense of Marxism*, pp. 170–78: here p. 178.

72. Max Schachtman and James Burnham, writing in 1939, prior to their own terminal attack of 'Stalinophobia'. Castigating Sidney Hook and his ilk, they observed that 'the main intellectual disease from which these intellectuals suffer may be called Stalinophobia, or vulgar anti-Stalinism. The malady was superinduced by the universal revulsion against Stalin's macabre system of frame-ups and purges. And the result has been that most of the writing done on the subject since then has been less a product of cold social analysis than of mental shock, and where there is analysis it is moral rather than scientific or political' (qtd. in George Novack and Joseph Hansen, introduction to *In Defense of Marxism*, pp. xix–xx).

73. Qtd. in Callinicos, *Trotskyism*, p. 19.

74. See *The Prophet Outcast*, p. 421, where Deutscher quotes from the arguments drafted by him and advanced by the Polish delegates to the 'foundation congress' of the Fourth International in September 1938.

75. Ibid., p. 510.

76. Ibid., p. 516. According to Deutscher, '[T]o the end Trotsky's strength and weakness alike were rooted in classical Marxism. His defeats epitomized the basic predicament by which classical Marxism was beset as doctrine and movement—the discrepancy and divorce between the Marxist vision of revolutionary development and the actual course of class struggle and revolution. . . . The conflict between the Marxist norm and the reality of revolution came to permeate all the thinking and activity of the ruling party. Stalinism sought to overcome the conflict by perverting or discarding the norm. Trotskyism attempted to preserve the norm or strike a temporary balance between norm and reality until revolution in the West resolved the conflict and restored harmony between theory and practice. The failures of revolution in the West were epitomized in Trotsky's defeat' (p. 514).

77. Ibid., pp. 521–22.

78. Ibid., p. 212.

79. Ibid., pp. 461–62; my emphasis.

80. Michel Pablo, 'Where Are We Going?' (1951), reprinted in *Struggle in the Fourth International: International Secretariat Documents, 1951–1954*, vol. 1, Pathfinder Press, New York, 1974, pp. 4–12: here pp. 7–8.

81. Ibid., pp. 9–10.

82. Michel Pablo, 'On the Duration and Nature of the Transition from Capitalist to Socialism' (1951), reprinted in *Struggle in the Fourth International*, pp. 12–16: here pp. 14–15. Pablo wrote: 'It . . . conforms to Trotsky's spirit (if not to the very letter of his writings) that *the transformation of capitalism into socialism will actually take an entire historical epoch, filled with bureaucratically deformed transitional regimes, and that these inevitable bureaucratic deformations (which have basically economic causes) will disappear only to the extent that the Revolution conquers in the advanced countries and the level of the productive forces reaches and surpasses that of the most advanced capitalism*' (p. 14). In an article from 1939 ('Again and Once More Again on the Nature of the USSR'), Trotsky had indeed acknowledged that '[t]he real passage to socialism cannot fail to appear incomparably more complicated, more heterogeneous, more contradictory than was foreseen in the general historical scheme': in *In Defense*

of Marxism, p. 31. Whether under the inspiration of Trotsky or simply as a logical development of his own historico-political vision, Deutscher himself was to argue that classical Marxism had been unduly optimistic about the character and duration of the transition to socialism, underestimating its complexity and longevity. See his essay 'The Roots of Bureaucracy' (1960), reprinted in *Marxism, Wars, and Revolutions: Essays from Four Decades,* ed. Tamara Deutscher, Verso, London, 1984, pp. 221–42, especially p. 237; and cf. 'On Socialist Man' (1966), in *Marxism in Our Time,* Ramparts Press, Berkeley, Calif., 1971, p. 249 (the version reprinted in *Marxism, Wars, and Revolutions* omits the discussion that followed Deutscher's paper and hence the relevant passage). By contrast, Ernest Mandel—Pablo's postwar protégé in the secretariat of the Fourth International—subsequently dissented from his position: cf. *Revolutionary Marxism Today,* ed. Jon Rothschild, New Left Books, London, 1979, pp. 159–61, where Mandel is explicitly questioned about 'centuries of transition'.

83. On 'Pabloism' in the international Trotskyist movement, see Callinicos, *Trotskyism,* pp. 33–34. For its British reception, see John Callaghan, *British Trotskyism: Theory and Practice,* Blackwell, Oxford, 1984, pp. 59–62, and *The Far Left in British Politics,* Blackwell, Oxford, 1987, p. 68. According to Callaghan (*British Trotskyism,* p. 220 n. 17), the first draft of the offending document was actually drafted by Mandel.

84. The Deutscherite perspective underlying 'Trotsky's Interpretation of Stalinism' is noted and reproved by Michael Cox, 'The Revolutionary Betrayed: The *New Left Review* and Leon Trotsky' (1987), in Cox and Hillel Ticktin, eds., *The Ideas of Leon Trotsky,* Porcupine Press, London, 1995, pp. 289–304 (especially pp. 289, 303). A possible subterranean influence of 'Pabloism' on Anderson has eluded most commentators, with the exception of the eagle-eyed veteran Ian Birchall, who uses it, however, in a rather different context: see 'The Autonomy of Theory: A Short History of *New Left Review*', *International Socialism* no. 10, winter 1980, p. 91 n. 72.

85. Anderson suggests that the category of 'scarcity' has been 'basic to historical materialism since Marx's formulation of it in *The German Ideology*'. As we have observed, it has certainly been basic to Anderson's Marxism since its deployment, in a Sartrean inflection, in 'Problems of Socialist Strategy' to account for the advent of 'Leninism' in Russia.

86. Trotsky, *In Defense of Marxism,* p. 15.

87. In *Arguments within English Marxism* (p. 117), Anderson had claimed that '[t]he fundamental hypotheses of *The Revolution Betrayed* . . . remain unsurpassed to this day as a framework for investigation of Soviet society'.

88. A hostile reference to Schachtman, who categorized the USSR as 'bureaucratic-collectivist', follows. Schachtman had already been derided, along with Burnham, in Nicolas Krassó, 'Trotsky's Marxism', *NLR* no. 44, July/August 1967, p. 84. A specific reference to him and Alasdair MacIntyre as partisans of the 'anti-communist crusade', in the manuscript of Anderson's 'Social Democracy Today' (p. 7), was cut for its publication in *Against the Current*—a Schachtmanite journal. For a portrait of American Trotskyists, see Wald, *The New York Intellectuals,* chap. 6, 'Cannonites and Schachtmanites' (pp. 164–92).

89. Cf. *Arguments within English Marxism,* p. 121.

90. *In the Tracks of Historical Materialism,* p. 32.

91. Halliday, 'The Sources of the New Cold War', in *Exterminism and Cold War,* p. 311.

92. Cf. 'Socialism and Pseudo-Empiricism', p. 9

93. See, for example, E. J. Hobsbawm, *Echoes of the Marseillaise: Two Centuries Look Back on the French Revolution,* Verso, London and New York, 1990, chap. 2, 'Beyond the Bourgeoisie', (pp. 33–66). Cf. Anderson, 'The Notion of Bourgeois Revolution', in *English Questions,* pp. 107–8.

94. Introduction to Tukhachevsky, *NLR* no. 55, May/June 1969, pp. 84–85. See also 'The

Antinomies of Antonio Gramsci', p. 46, for a critical comment on Gramsci's 'occasional assimilation of the bourgeois and proletarian revolutions in his writings on Jacobinism'.

95. For Anderson's evaluation of Deutscher's oeuvre, see 'Trotsky's Interpretation of Stalinism', *NLR* no. 139, p. 55 (the sentence from which this quotation is extracted does not appear in the corresponding paragraph of Ali's *The Stalinist Legacy*, p. 124). Among Deutscher's critics was Schachtman, who deprecated his 'obsess[ion]' with 'analogies between the bourgeois revolutions . . . and the Bolshevik revolution': see Callinicos, *Trotskyism*, pp. 49–54, where Schachtman is quoted (p. 50) in the course of a discussion of Deutscher and Anderson. Also of interest in the context of historical-reasoning-by-analogy are Lukács's 1935 essay 'Hölderlin's Hyperion' (on which see Michael Löwy, *Georg Lukács—From Romanticism to Bolshevism* [1976], trans. Patrick Camiller, New Left Books, London, 1979, pp. 196–98); and Régis Debray, *Loués soient nos seigneurs: Une éducation politique*, Éditions Gallimard, Paris, 1996, pp. 534–38. Another Trotskyist critic of Deutscher was Alasdair MacIntyre, who accused him of historical determinism. See his review of *The Prophet Outcast*, 'Trotsky in Exile' (1963), reprinted in MacIntyre, *Against the Self-Images of the Age: Essays on Ideology and Philosophy*, Duckworth, London, 1971, pp. 52–59 (especially pp. 58–59); and also 'Is a Science of Comparative Politics Possible?', in ibid., pp. 272–73. In his assessment of Deutscher's trilogy, E. H. Carr detected a voluntaristic strain in biographer and subject alike: see 'The Tragedy of Trotsky', in Carr, *The October Revolution: Before and After*, Knopf, New York, 1969, pp. 139–66, especially p. 158. For Anderson, to the contrary, Deutscher's 'Stalin and Trotsky are preeminently products of history, subject to the determinations of wider social forces that they expressed or rejected: but they are also moral agents, accountable for their actions and the consequences of them' ('The Legacy of Isaac Deutscher', in *A Zone of Engagement*, pp. 56–75: here p. 73).

96. The plaudit to Deutscher follows immediately after this judgement in the *NLR* version of 'Trotsky's Interpretation of Stalinism'.

97. For a more ecumenical Trotskyist assessment, see Wald, *The New York Intellectuals*, pp. 188–89, who nonetheless concludes that 'the weight of contemporary scholarship . . . seems to support Trotsky's "transitional" analysis as the best guide to an *overall* assessment of the Soviet Union. Moreover, adherents of the transitional society approach, such as . . . Ernest Mandel, have been most successful in outlining laws of motion . . . peculiar to that society'. (Mandel's 'On the Nature of the Soviet State', in *NLR* no. 108, was adjudged 'probably the best general statement of the nature of Soviet society to have been written since the war', in 'NLR, 1975–1980', p. 23.) For a late but representative instalment of the debate, see Mandel's critique of the state-capitalist position, 'A Theory Which Has Not Withstood the Test of the Facts', and Chris Harman's rejoinder, 'Criticism Which Does Not Withstand the Test of Logic', in *International Socialism* no. 49, winter 1990, pp. 43–64, 65–88, respectively.

98. See Lucio Colletti, 'A Political and Philosophical Interview', in *Western Marxism*, pp. 349–50.

99. Unlike Anderson, Wald was at least prepared to concede the 'confusing' character of Trotsky's terminology: *The New York Intellectuals*, p. 189. And cf. the recent work by one of Mandel's French followers, Daniel Bensaïd, *Marx l'intempestif: Grandeurs et misères d'une aventure critique (xixè–xxè siècles)*, Éditions Fayard, Paris, 1995, pp. 43–44 n. 42, for the more radical option of revoking the claim that the bureaucratic states were ever '*post*-capitalist'. A postlapsarian judgement, it is perfectly possible that Anderson would share it today.

100. *Lineages of the Absolutist State*, p. 235. In the first chapter of this work, Anderson

had indicated the need to proceed with caution as regards historical analogies between states, precisely reminding Christopher Hill that '[t]he general and epochal character of Absolutism renders any formal comparison of it with the local, exceptionalist regimes of fascism inappropriate' (p. 18 n. 8).

101. 'The Legacy of Isaac Deutscher', in *A Zone of Engagement*, p. 75. Cf., for example, Deutscher's *The Prophet Unarmed—Trotsky: 1921–1929* (1959), Oxford University Press, Oxford, 1982, p. 462, where an analogy with the English and French restorations is entertained but reckoned 'extremely remote'.

102. 'Trotsky's Interpretation of Stalinism', pp. 123–24.

103. *Marxism, Wars, and Revolutions*, p. vii. In *A Zone of Engagement* (p. 61), the 'anti-communism' is 'comprehensive' (rather than 'virulent'), and the 'climate' one of 'conformity and fear' (as opposed to 'conformity and hysteria').

104. *Marxism, Wars, and Revolutions*, p. xix. (This passage is omitted from *A Zone of Engagement*.)

105. For the *NLR* debate, see Michael Rustin, 'The New Left and the Present Crisis', *NLR* no. 121, May/June 1980, pp. 63–89, and 'Different Conceptions of Party: Labour's Constitutional Debates', *NLR* no. 126, March/April 1981, pp. 17–42; Francis Cripps, 'The British Crisis—Can the Left Win?', *NLR* no. 128, July/August 1981, pp. 93–97; David Coates, 'Labourism and the Transition to Socialism', *NLR* no. 129, September/October 1981, pp. 3–22; Ken Coates, 'The Choices before Labour', *NLR* no. 131, January/February 1982, pp. 32–43; Tariq Ali and Quintin Hoare, 'Socialists and the Crisis of Labourism', *NLR* no. 132, March/April 1982, pp. 59–81; Geoff Hodgson, 'On the Political Economy of the Socialist Transformation', *NLR* no. 133, May/June 1982, pp. 52–66; David Coates, 'Space and Agency in the Transition to Socialism', *NLR* no. 135, September/October 1982, pp. 49–63; Raymond Williams, 'Problems of the Coming Period', *NLR* no. 140, July/August 1983, pp. 7–18; Ken Livingstone, 'Why Labour Lost', *NLR* no. 140, pp. 23–39; and Eric Heffer, 'Socialists and the Labour Party', *NLR* no. 140, pp. 40–49. The relevant book titles were Martin Jacques and Francis Mulhern, eds., *The Forward March of Labour Halted?* Verso/*Marxism Today*, London, 1981; Tony Benn, *Parliament, People, and Power: Agenda for a Free Society—Interviews with New Left Review*, Verso, London, 1982; Tariq Ali and Ken Livingstone, *Who's Afraid of Margaret Thatcher? In Praise of Socialism*, Verso, London, 1984; and Michael Rustin, *For a Pluralist Socialism*, Verso, London, 1985.

106. Anthony Barnett, 'Iron Britannia', *NLR* no. 134, July/August 1982, pp. 5–96. An expanded version was published under the title *Iron Britannia: Why Parliament Waged Its Falklands War* by Alison and Busby, London, 1982.

107. See Bob Jessop et al., 'Authoritarian Populism, Two Nations, and Thatcherism', *NLR* no. 147, September/October 1984, pp. 32–60; and cf. Stuart Hall's riposte, *NLR* no. 151, May/June 1985, pp. 115–20. Prior to this, the only stocktaking in the *Review* was Tom Nairn's brief 'The Crisis of the British State', *NLR* no. 130, November/December 1981, pp. 37–44. See also his 1981 postscript, 'Into Political Emergency', in *The Break-up of Britain*, pp. 365–404.

108. 'NLR, 1980–1983', unpublished report, [1982], p. 18.

109. *Parliament, People, and Power*, p. x. Two respects in which Benn was found wanting were over abolition of the monarchy and the expropriation of capital: pp. 44–49, 127–31.

110. See Ali and Hoare, 'Socialists and the Crisis of Labourism', especially pp. 79–81, 61–62. In his introduction to *Who's Afraid of Margaret Thatcher?* two years later, Ali resumed the central theme of the argument as follows (p. 37): 'The post-1979 period has made two basic truths abundantly clear. The days of old SDP-style reformism . . . are over, but so are all the dreams which kept many of us high during

the sixties and seventies, when we visualized bypassing the established institutions of the Labour Movement in one big leap. The alliances which need to be fought for . . . are between the new breed of socialist politicians exemplified by Livingstone and the generation of Marxists brought up on the writings of Miliband, Mandel and Anderson. Perhaps the attempt to reconstruct Labour along socialist lines will come to grief. . . . It would be foolish to become as dogmatic over this possibility as one was over its polar opposite in 1968 and after. What can be said with certainty is that a serious socialist project in Britain requires a fusion of the theoretical reach and grasp of a wide layer of Marxists with the practical skills, abilities and courage of leaders able to communicate with millions such as Benn, Scargill and Livingstone'.

111. See Coates, 'Space and Agency in the Transition to Socialism', especially pp. 62–63.

112. See the pseudonymous Lee Pitcairn, 'Crisis in British Communism: An Insider's View', NLR no. 153, September/October 1985, pp. 102–20.

113. On 'Browderism'—the line of collaboration between class and nation, highly influential in Latin American Communist parties, espoused by CPUSA leader Earl Browder toward the end of the Second World War ('Communism is twentieth-century Americanism')—see, for example, Paul Buhle, Marxism in the USA from 1870 to the Present Day: Remapping the History of the American Left, Verso, London, 1987, pp. 193–94. Official condemnation of it was penned by PCF leader Jacque Duclos, in Cahiers du Communisme, in April 1945. For Eric Hobsbawm's response to the charge, subsequently made against Marxism Today by CPGB traditionalists, see 'The Retreat into Extremism' (1985), in his Politics for a Rational Left: Political Writing, 1977–1988, Verso/Marxism Today, London and New York, 1989, p. 98 n. 9.

114. 'A Problem in Defining the Socialist Society', unpublished memorandum, 1981, p. 1. Foundation of the society was motivated in Robin Blackburn's 'Notes on the English Political Crisis', unpublished document, [1981].

115. Letters of 4 August and 8 August 1983 from Anderson to Blackburn.

116. Letter of 5 October 1983 from Anderson to the NLR.

117. 'Notes for Meeting, 21/1/84', unpublished document, 17 January 1984. With suitable emendation, the historical section of these notes (pp. 1–3) formed the basis of Robin Blackburn's 1991 'Brief History of New Left Review, 1960–1990', in Thirty Years of New Left Review: Index to Numbers 1–184 (1960–1990), London, 1992, pp. v–xi.

118. See, inter alia, Jonas Pontussen, 'Behind and beyond Social Democracy in Sweden', NLR no. 143, January/February 1984, pp. 69–96; Niels Finn Christiansen, 'Denmark: End of the Idyll', NLR no. 144, March/April 1984, pp. 5–32; Tobias Abse, 'Judging the PCI', NLR no. 153, September/October 1985, pp. 5–40; Patrick Camiller, 'Spanish Socialism in the Atlantic Order', NLR no. 156, March/April 1986, pp. 5–36; James Petras, 'The Contradictions of Greek Socialism', NLR no. 163, May/June 1987, pp. 3–25; and Jane Jenson and George Ross, 'The Tragedy of the French Left', NLR no. 171, September/October 1988, pp. 5–44. Some of these texts were updated and collected, together with an introduction by Anderson and other material, in Anderson and Camiller, eds., Mapping the West European Left, Verso, London and New York, 1994.

119. See Ralph Miliband, 'The New Revisionism in Britain', NLR no. 150, March/April 1985, pp. 5–26, and the preceding 'Themes' (p. 2), in which the Review's concurrence with this critique of 'an anti-left spectrum' is indicated. Miliband's article had been preceded by a survey entitled 'The British Women's Movement', in NLR no. 148, November/December 1984, pp. 74–103, by two oppositionist Communists, Angela Weir and Elizabeth Wilson, who developed arguments contained in the anti-revisionist pamphlet Class Politics: An Answer to Its Critics, by Ben Fine et al., London, 1984.

120. 'NLR Perspectives', unpublished document, [1985], p. 2. Here (p. 3) Anderson proposed that the *NLR* carry a series of editorial statements articulating its outlook on national and international politics and explaining its predominantly Marxist self-conception.

121. See Michael Rustin, 'The New Left and the Labour Party', chap. 2 of *For a Pluralist Socialism* (pp. 46–75): here p. 53.

122. Cf. former *NLR* editor Ronald Fraser et al.'s twentieth-anniversary retrospective, *Nineteen Sixty-Eight: A Student Generation in Revolt*, Chatto and Windus, London, 1988, pp. 313–14.

123. See 'A Culture in Contraflow', in *English Questions*, pp. 196–97.

124. 'NLR 1980–1983', pp. 20–21, 23–24, 27. Mike Davis's articles on the United States, published in the *NLR* from 1980 to 1986 and subsequently collected in *Prisoners of the American Dream: Politics and Economy in the History of the US Working Class* (Verso, London, 1986), were considered by Anderson to be the North American equivalent of the *Review*'s theses on Britain.

125. Cf. Gramsci, *Selections from the Prison Notebooks*, p. 369: 'That all those Nietzschean charlatans in verbal revolt against all that exists, against conventionality, etc., should have ended up by accepting it after all, and have thus made certain attitudes seem quite unserious, may well be the case, but it is not necessary to let oneself be guided in one's judgements by charlatans'.

126. In a 1984 foreword to a new edition of *Considerations on Western Marxism* (Verso, London, 1984, p. ix), Anderson suggests that *In the Tracks of Historical Materialism* may be read as its 'continuation'; or that, in conjunction with *Arguments within English Marxism*, the three works may be taken to compose 'an unpremeditated trilogy'.

127. In addition to Anderson's remarks on historiography in *Tracks*, pp. 24–27, see his contemporaneous review of Geoffrey de Ste. Croix's *Class Struggle in the Ancient Greek World*, in *History Workshop Journal* no. 16, autumn 1983, pp. 57–73 (reprinted as chap. 1 of *A Zone of Engagement* [pp. 1–24]). Cohen's *Karl Marx's Theory of History*, meanwhile, was 'clearly the landmark of the decade' in philosophy (p. 23).

128. A rapprochement with Habermas, revising the damning assessment by Therborn in the *NLR* in 1971, had been initiated in 1979, with Anderson's noticeably warm introduction to an interview entitled 'Conservativism and Capitalist Crisis', *NLR* no. 115, May/June 1979, p. 72. It would be continued in the interviews conducted by Anderson and Peter Dews in 1984–85: see 'A Philosophico-political Profile', *NLR* no. 151, May/June 1985, pp. 75–105 (reprinted in Dews, ed., *Habermas: Autonomy and Solidarity*, Verso, London, 1986, pp. 149–89); and 'Life-Forms, Morality, and the Task of the Philosopher', in *Habermas: Autonomy and Solidarity*, pp. 191–216.

129. As regards revolutionary Marxism, represented by the Trotskyist movement, Anderson noted that such 'negative demonstrations' of the 'implausibility' of Eurocommunism as Mandel's critiques 'were not accompanied by any sustained positive construction of an alternative scenario for defeating capitalism in the West' (*Tracks*, p. 79).

130. Two years later, before an audience of one thousand people at the New School for Social Research in New York, Anderson reiterated the point: 'The great advantage enjoyed by Marxism, the reason it continues to be the central paradigm within a radical history that is in fact much wider than it, is its possession of a comprehensive and articulated set of concepts and hypotheses about the principal lines of historical development as a whole. . . . It still has no real rivals in that sense, and its potential is far from exhausted; indeed in some respects it is only starting to be realized' (Anderson et al., 'Agendas for Radical History', *Radical History Review* no. 36, 1986, pp. 32–37: here pp. 33–34). However, in conclusion (p. 37), he drew attention to 'a peculiar paradox of our situation now': 'For never has radical or socialist

work—including a major, increasing corpus of Marxist historiography—enjoyed such authority in a common understanding of the past as in the last twenty-five years. But never too have radicals or socialists been more uncertain about the direction of the present, and diffident—even despondent—about the shape of the future, than they are very widely today'.

131. Anderson's discussion of the decentralized character of women's oppression (pp. 91–92)—criticized by socialist-feminists (e.g., Lynne Segal in *Is the Future Female? Troubled Thoughts on Contemporary Feminism* [1987], 2d ed., Virago, London, 1994, pp. 211–12)—has an interesting affinity with Beauvoir's reflections in the introduction to *The Second Sex* (1949), trans. and ed. H. M. Parshley, Penguin, Harmondsworth, 1987, p. 19. Beauvoir's work is classified as 'the central text of modern feminism' in *A Zone of Engagement*, p. 372.

132. Utopian residues had already been noted in *Arguments within English Marxism*, p. 167. In *Tracks* (p. 22), Anderson likewise repeats his praise for Bahro's *Alternative*—a work in whose programme, however, abolition of the division of labour is central. See *The Alternative in Eastern Europe* (1977), trans. David Fernbach, New Left Books, London, 1978, e.g., pp. 177, 182, 436; and cf. p. 253 for Bahro's own defence of 'utopian thought'. Citing Anderson's discussion of Nove, J. G. Merquior (*Western Marxism*, Paladin, London, 1986, p. 197) comments: 'One should not be too hasty . . . in applying the label "post-Marxist". Anderson would reject it, settling, perhaps, for the more ambiguous "neo-Marxist"'. Anderson is acknowledged in Merquior's foreword (p. vii), in the unlikely company of Raymond Aron, Leszek Kolakowski, and others, for 'many a pithy conversation on Marxism and its problems with a number of first-rate minds'.

133. These structures are political order, economic system, 'egalitarian levelling', and international relations (*Tracks*, pp. 99–100).

134. See Sartre's memoir 'Merleau-Ponty', in *Situations IV,* Éditions Gallimard, Paris, 1964, pp. 200–201. This would seem to capture the spirit of *Tracks* better than either Merquior or Alex Callinicos, who compared Anderson to Plekhanov, characterizing him as 'an erudite, elegant guardian of Marxist orthodoxy' ('Perry Anderson and "Western Marxism"', *International Socialism* no. 23, spring 1984, pp. 113–28: here p. 127).

135. Cf. *Tracks*, pp. 29–30, 59 and n. 4, where an unwontedly graceless reference is made to 'Althusser's asseverations' (i.e., 'The Crisis of Marxism' [1977], trans. Grahame Lock, in *Il Manifesto*, ed., *Power and Opposition in Post-revolutionary Societies*, Ink Links, London, 1979, pp. 225–37). For Althusser's own firm response to like charges from Communist quarters, see the posthumously published manuscript 'Marx dans ses limites' (1978), in François Matheron, ed., *Écrits philosophiques et politiques, Tome I*, Éditions Stock/IMEC, Paris, 1994, pp. 362–64. The degree of Anderson's intransigence on the topic may be gauged from the fact that at an international socialist conference held at Cavtat, Yugoslavia, in 1983, he had found himself aligned (as he reported to colleagues) with representatives of the Soviet, Chinese, and Greek Communist parties in deprecating reactionary talk of a 'crisis of Marxism': 'Cavtat 1983', unpublished memorandum, 1983, p. 1.

136. Leon Trotsky, qtd. in Wald, *The New York Intellectuals*, p. 94.

137. The imputation of bibliocentrism is adapted from Kate Soper, who spotted 'a somewhat bibliocentric conception of history' in *Arguments within English Marxism*. See her *Humanism and Anti-Humanism*, Hutchinson, London, 1986, p. 117 n. 79.

138. See Russell Jacoby, *The Last Intellectuals: American Culture in the Age of Academe*, Basic Books, New York, 1987, especially, pp. 112–90; and Paul Buhle, *Marxism in the USA*, pp. 221–57, 264–70. Cf. the exchange between Lynn Garafola and Jacoby in *NLR* no. 169, May/June 1988, pp. 122–28, and no. 172, November/December

1988, pp. 125–27; Bruce Robbins, *Secular Vocations: Intellectuals, Professionalism, Culture*, Verso, London and New York, 1993; and Wald, *The New York Intellectuals*. There are analogies between the U.S. debate and the controversy sparked across the Atlantic by Thompson's castigation in 1978 of 'those barrels of enclosed Marxisms which stand, row upon row, in the corridors of Polytechnics and Universities' ('The Poverty of Theory', p. 383).

139. Anderson implicitly recognizes this: see *Tracks*, p. 26. Interestingly, the mutually injurious absence of any points of organizational contact between a volatile intelligentsia and the working class in the United States is emphasized by him in some comments on a draft article by Mike Davis: 'Notes on "Why the American Working-Class Is Different"', unpublished document, [1980?], p. 13.

140. Cf. the introduction to Aijaz Ahmad, *In Theory: Classes, Nations, Literatures*, Verso, London and New York, 1992, pp. 1–42. For a very readable political retrospective, see Todd Gitlin, *The Sixties: Years of Hope, Days of Rage*, Bantam Books, Toronto, 1987, which remarks the widespread perception that by the 1980s, 'a whole generation had moved en masse from "*J'accuse*" to Jacuzzi' (p. 433).

141. See Terry Eagleton's review 'Marxism, Structuralism, and Post-Structuralism' (1984), reprinted in Eagleton, *Against the Grain: Essays 1975–1985*, Verso, London, 1986, pp. 89–98: here p. 92.

142. See Ernest Gellner, *Postmodernism, Reason, and Religion*, Routledge, London and New York, 1992, pp. 31–35; and for his own alternative to historical materialism, *Plough, Sword, and Book: The Structure of Human History*, Collins Harvill, London, 1988 (where Marxism is classified as 'one of the major world religions': see pp. 143–44). Anderson's view of Gellner is conveyed in 'Max Weber and Ernest Gellner: Science, Politics, Enchantment' (1992), in *A Zone of Engagement*, pp. 182–206. And for his attitude to Lyotard, see the postscript (1985) to 'Marshall Berman: Modernity and Revolution' (1983), in ibid., pp. 48–49.

143. See Anderson's acknowledgements in *Tracks*, p. 8, where he also thanks Peter Dews 'for more local reflections'. Cf. Sebastiano Timpanaro, *On Materialism* (1970), trans. Lawrence Garner, rev. ed., Verso, London, 1980, chap. 4, 'Structuralism and Its Successors', (pp. 135–219); and Dews, *Logics of Disintegration: Post-structuralist Thought and the Claims of Critical Theory*, Verso, London and New York, 1987.

144. Cf. Callinicos, 'Perry Anderson and "Western Marxism"', p. 121. The 'seriously belittling' nature of Anderson's critique of French theory is the burden of Eagleton's review of *Tracks* (p. 98). The epilogue of Martin Jay's contemporaneous study *Marxism and Totality: The Adventures of a Concept from Lukács to Habermas* (Polity Press, Cambridge, 1984) is precisely devoted to 'The Challenge of Post-Structuralism' (pp. 510–37).

145. See chap. 2 of this book. Anderson's mounting scepticism, even hostility, toward psychoanalysis—especially the Lacanian variety—is publicly expressed not only in *Tracks* (e.g., p. 88) but also in the preface to Deutscher, *Marxism, Wars, and Revolutions*, pp. xvii–xviii. Trotsky had adjudged Freudianism 'sometimes ingenious and instructive, but more often whimsical and arbitrary' (qtd. in Deutscher, *The Prophet Outcast*, p. 229); and this was the burden of Sebastiano Timpanaro's epistemologico-philological critique *The Freudian Slip: Psychoanalysis and Textual Criticism* (1974), trans. Kate Soper, New Left Books, London, 1976. Timpanaro's critique is endorsed in Anderson's review of Carlo Ginzburg's *Ecstasies*, in *A Zone of Engagement*, p. 216; as is Gellner's *The Psychoanalytic Movement*, in 'Max Weber and Ernest Gellner', in ibid., p. 202.

    The inaccuracy of Anderson's account of Althusser (*Tracks*, pp. 37–38) is also worth remarking here: cf., for example, Althusser, 'Sur Lévi-Strauss' (1966), in François Matheron, *Écrits philosophiques et politiques, Tome II*, Éditions Stock/IMEC,

Paris, 1995, pp. 418–30, which makes the same point about Lévi-Straussian 'formalism' on pp. 425–26 as does Anderson on his pp. 48–49.

146. See Anders Stephanson and Cornel West, 'The British and the Rational', *Socialist Review* no. 84, November/December 1984, pp. 123–29.

147. This was a usage consistent with Trotsky's allusion of 1931: 'I am a Marxist. . . . I stand on the ground of the reality of bourgeois society, in order to find in it the forces and the levers with which to overthrow it' ('Factory Councils and Workers' Control of Production' [1931], in Trotsky, *The Struggle against Fascism in Germany* [1971], Penguin, Harmondsworth, 1975, p. 46). It may be recalled that in *Arguments* (p. 197), Anderson had referred to 'the firm earth of the historian on which every Marxist should keep their feet'.

148. George Lichtheim, *Marxism in Modern France*, Columbia University Press, New York and London, 1966, pp. 155–56.

149. Ronald Aronson, 'Historical Materialism, Answer to Marxism's Crisis', *NLR* no. 152, July/August 1985, pp. 74–94: here p. 78.

150. Cf. Karl Korsch, writing in 1935: '*One cannot protest against a reality simply in the name of an abstract principle*' (qtd. in Jay, *Marxism and Totality*, p. 131 n. 10); or again in 1928: '[E]ven the worst reality would be better than merely standing in thought' (qtd. in ibid., p. 142 n. 52).

151. Aronson, 'Historical Materialism, Answer to Marxism's Crisis', p. 82.

152. Blackburn, 'A Brief History of *New Left Review*, 1960–1990', p. x. For a marginally less obfuscatory formula, see the 'Themes' to *NLR* no. 142, November/December 1983, p. 4.

153. Anderson's resignation as editor was effective from *NLR* no. 137, January/February 1983, in whose 'Themes' (p. 4) it was announced. The other resigners in the autumn were Jon Halliday, John Merrington, Juliet Mitchell, Roger Murray, Tom Nairn, Lucien Rey (i.e., Peter Wollen), Bob Rowthorn, and Gareth Stedman Jones.

154. Anderson's complaints about this and other matters led to a commission of inquiry into the *Review*'s internal affairs, conducted by Norman Geras and Tariq Ali, in September 1983. It generated a typically extensive literature, comprising submissions from the main protagonists—Anderson, Barnett, Blackburn, Davis, Halliday, and Mulhern—and issued in a report in October, which substantially upheld Anderson. Discussed at a committee meeting on 6 November 1983, it was narrowly adopted—whereupon Barnett and Halliday resigned.

155. Submission to the *NLR* commission of inquiry, 16 September 1983.

156. The five were Cathy Porter, Lynne Segal, Kate Soper, Barbara Taylor, and Hilary Wainwright. The demands, with which Soper was not associated, included: a declaration that the *NLR* was a Marxist-feminist journal; eventual gender parity on the editorial committee; and regular readers' meetings (letter from Cathy Porter, Lynne Segal, Barbara Taylor, and Hilary Wainwright to *NLR*, 6 February 1984, registering strong objections to the *NLR* Charter's assertion of the autonomy of socialism from feminism). In a 'Memo on Socialism and Feminism', penned after the misfired reconstruction (12 February 1984), Anderson proposed a *Review* symposium on the subject, equivalent to the *Exterminism and Cold War* volume (pp. 4–5).

157. Among its fruits was a series surveying the international women's movement, beginning with Britain in *NLR* no. 148, November/December 1984, and proceeding to Spain (no. 151), India (no. 153), West Germany (no. 155), Greece (no. 158), the Arab world (no. 161), Ireland (no. 166), Japan (no. 167), Bangladesh (no. 168), Brazil (no. 173), and France (no. 180). Some of these are now available, together with other material, in Monica Threlfall, ed., *Mapping the Women's Movement: Feminist Politics and Social Transformation in the North*, Verso, London and New York, 1996. The *Review*'s neglect of feminism after publication of Juliet Mitchell's

'Women: The Longest Revolution' in 1966 (no. 40) can be gauged from consultation of its index for 1960–90. Of the sixty-one items listed under the rubric 'Women's Oppression and Sexual Politics' for nos. 41–184 (1967–90), there are only twenty-seven for 1967–82 (nos. 41–141), of which several are brief comments and rejoinders (*Thirty Years of New Left Review*, pp. 112–14). Cf. Donald Sassoon, 'The Silences of *New Left Review*', pp. 242–45. Meanwhile, an equivalent neglect on the part of NLB/Verso began to be seriously remedied from the mid-1980s onward, with the establishment of the Questions for Feminism series.

158. They included Victoria Brittain and Ellen Meiksins Wood, specialist on black Africa and political theorist, respectively; IMG members Peter Gowan and Patrick Camiller; and the philosopher Peter Dews. Wood was subsequently responsible for one of the key antirevisionist texts of the period, *The Retreat from Class: A New 'True' Socialism*, Verso, London, 1986.

159. 'Constitution', unpublished document, [1983], pp. 1–2.

160. 'Charter', unpublished document, [1983], p. 2.

161. In an undated submission to his fellow editors, Mulhern argued that this clause of the charter effectively adopted a radical-feminist stance in its partitioning of feminism and socialism. Anderson replied that for classical Marxism the goal of socialism was a classless society, not (as Mulhern supposed) a general human emancipation. The analytical and practical relations between the two movements required intensive future investigation ('NLR's Charter: Socialism and Feminism', [1984/85], pp. 1–3). Anderson's own interim position had been stated in *In the Tracks of Historical Materialism*, pp. 89–93; Mulhern's perspective of a 'feminized socialism' was indicated in 'Towards 2000, or News from You-Know-Where', *NLR* no. 148, November/December 1984, pp. 5–30, especially pp. 19–23. Of the feminist material published in the *Review*, Anderson expressed particular enthusiasm for Johanna Brenner and Maria Ramas, 'Rethinking Women's Oppression', *NLR* no. 144, March/April 1984, pp. 33–71.

162. 'Modernity and Revolution', *NLR* no. 144, March/April 1984, pp. 96–113; reprinted as 'Marshall Berman: Modernity and Revolution', in *A Zone of Engagement*, pp. 25–45, together with a postscript from 1985 (pp. 46–55), originally presented to a colloquium on postmodernism in Spain. All references will be to the latter version.

163. Cf. the long question to Raymond Williams, distinguishing between political revolution and postrevolutionary social transformation, in *Politics and Letters*, pp. 419–20.

164. In the discussion that followed Anderson's delivery of his paper and is reproduced in the conference proceedings (Cary Nelson and Lawrence Grossberg, eds., *Marxism and the Interpretation of Culture*, Macmillan, Basingstoke, 1988, pp. 334–38), he was taxed with 'economism' by Cornel West. His response was revealing: 'What you are calling classical Marxism is not something I'm particularly ashamed of; actually, I think it's a kind of common sense' (p. 337).

165. Very much in the spirit of Trotsky's view, as described by Deutscher, that revolutionary socialism was 'the consummation, not the repudiation, of great cultural traditions' (*The Prophet Armed—Trotsky: 1879–1921* [1954], Oxford University Press, Oxford, 1979, p. 49), Anderson criticized aesthetic relativism to his audience at Urbana-Champaign and refused any comparison between such films as Hawks's *Rio Bravo* and Proust's *Remembrance of Things Past* (conference proceedings in Nelson and Grossberg, *Marxism and the Interpretation of Culture*, pp. 335, 338). For an example of his own literary judgements, see his comments on Powell's *A Dance to the Music of Time* at p. 337, as well as his earlier review of James Tucker's *The Novels of Anthony Powell*, in the *Guardian*, 26 August 1976, p. 7.

A substantial new text on postmodernism by Anderson—*The Origins of Postmodernity*, Verso, London and New York, 1998—appeared while the present book was in production, too late to be properly taken into account here. Focused on Fredric Jameson's anatomy of postmodernism as the 'cultural logic of late capitalism', it was, initially conceived as a preface to Jameson's collection *The Cultural Turn: Selected Writings on the Postmodern, 1983–1998*, Verso, London and New York, 1998, in which a brief foreword by Anderson now appears. *The Origins of Postmodernity* is comparable in method and design to 'The Ends of History', tracing Jameson's antecedents, surveying his innovations, and arbitrating the claims of his critics in a beguiling elaboration and emendation of the analytical framework of the Berman article. Jameson's oeuvre emerges from it as the consummation of the tradition treated in *Considerations on Western Marxism*.

166. Perry Anderson, Folker Fröbel, Jürgen Heinrichs, and Otto Kreye, 'On Some Postulates of an Anti-systemic Policy in Western Europe', unpublished conference paper, [1984]. According to the title page, it was delivered at two conferences—in Warsaw and Paris—in June 1984.

167. 'Social-Democracy Today', *Against the Current* vol. 1, no. 6, November/December 1986, pp. 21–28; incorporated (with modifications) as 'The Parabola of Social Democracy' into 'The Light of Europe' (1991), in *English Questions*, pp. 307–25.

168. See 'Marshall Berman', pp. 39–40; cf. Régis Debray, 'A Modest Contribution to the Rights and Ceremonies of the Tenth Anniversary', *NLR* no. 115, May/June 1979, especially pp. 58–62.

4. The Verdict of the World

1. *A Zone of Engagement*, Verso, London and New York, 1992, p. xii.

2. See Anderson et al., 'Agendas for Radical History', *Radical History Review* no. 36, 1986, pp. 33–34. Cf. *In the Tracks of Historical Materialism*, Verso, London, 1983, pp. 86–88 (cited in *A Zone of Engagement*, p. xii and n.), where the Weberian paradigm (if not Weber's work) is curtly dismissed.

3. Cf. Karl Marx's preface to the first edition of *Capital*, vol. 1, trans. Ben Fowkes, Penguin/NLR, Harmondsworth, 1976, pp. 90–91.

4. *Considerations on Western Marxism*, New Left Books, London, 1976, p. 55.

5. See *English Questions*, Verso, London and New York, 1992, pp. 205–31; and *A Zone of Engagement*, pp. 76–86, 149–68, 182–206, for appreciations of Mann, Runciman, and Gellner. Thus, vol. 1 of Michael Mann's *The Sources of Social Power* (Cambridge University Press, Cambridge, 1986) is adjudged '[n]ot lesser than *Economy and Society* itself in analytic stature, [but] superior as literature' (*A Zone of Engagement*, p. 86) and 'the commanding single work of the new British sociology, and a landmark in the discipline *tout court*' (*English Questions*, pp. 214–15). However, its disavowal of *comparative* sociology is criticized as severely disabling on the characteristically Andersonian grounds that 'true difference can only be established by contrast' (see *English Questions*, p. 216; and cf. *A Zone of Engagement*, p. 85).

6. *English Questions*, pp. 210–11. Anderson refers to Erik Olin Wright's article 'Giddens's Critique of Marxism', *NLR* no. 138, March/April 1983, pp. 11–35—subsequently incorporated into Wright, Andrew Levine, and Elliott Sober, *Reconstructing Marxism: Essays on Explanation and the Theory of History*, Verso, London and New York, 1992.

7. 'A Culture in Contraflow', *NLR* no. 180, March/April 1990, pp. 41–78, and no. 182, July/August 1990, pp. 85–137; reprinted in *English Questions*, pp. 193–301 (to which all references will be made): here pp. 230–31. Anderson's admiration for the

philosophy and methodology of social science set out in vol. 1 of W. G. Runciman's *Treatise on Social Theory* (Cambridge University Press, Cambridge, 1983) should also be noted (pp. 221–22).

8. Leon Trotsky, qtd. in Isaac Deutscher, *The Prophet Armed—Trotsky: 1879–1921* (1954), Oxford University Press, Oxford, 1979, p. 189.

9. The principal unmuffled antirevisionist statement from within the *NLR* was Ellen Meiksins Wood, *The Retreat from Class: A New 'True' Socialism*, Verso, London, 1986.

10. Note the critical side glance at psychoanalysis ('A Culture in Contraflow', pp. 258–59), no longer accorded a subsection in its own right, where the various epistemological and cultural deflations of Cioffi, Grunbaum, and Gellner are cited. (The salience of psychoanalysis within the culture of British feminism is noted at pp. 296–97.) As regards political philosophy, the 'prolific output' of analytical Marxism is neutrally remarked (p. 267). But cf. Ellen Meiksins Wood, 'Rational Choice Marxism: Is the Game Worth the Candle?', *NLR* no. 177, September/October 1989, pp. 41–88, for a thoroughgoing critique in tune with Anderson's own views.

11. See also 'A Culture in Contraflow', pp. 251–52 on Eagleton's *Ideology of the Aesthetic* (1990); and cf. Raymond Williams, *Politics and Letters: Interviews with New Left Review*, New Left Books, London, 1979, pp. 325ff., for some intensive interrogation of the 'Low Road'.

12. Anderson's 1990 verdict thus qualified the closing judgement of his 1985 contribution to 'Agendas for Radical History', p. 37. Cf. his critique of the 'linguistic turn' in historiography, especially the 'discursive idealism' preponderant in accounts of the French Revolution, in 'The Common and the Particular', *International Labor and Working-Class History* no. 36, fall 1989, pp. 32–33, where the influence of Ernesto Laclau is noted. (Laclau and Chantal Mouffe's *Hegemony and Socialist Strategy* [1985] had been scathingly criticized by Wood in *The Retreat from Class*, chap. 4, pp. 47–75, and then by Norman Geras in 'Post-Marxism?', *NLR* no. 163, May/June 1987, pp. 40–82; reprinted as chap. 3 of his *Discourses of Extremity: Radical Ethics and Post-Marxist Extravagances*, Verso, London and New York, 1990, pp. 61–125.) Revival of the social interpretation of the English Revolution in Robert Brenner's *Merchants and Revolution* is celebrated in Anderson's reception of it, 'Maurice Thomson's War', *London Review of Books*, 4 November 1993, pp. 13–17.

13. Cf. Lynne Segal, *Is the Future Female? Troubled Thoughts on Contemporary Feminism* (1987), 2d ed., Virago, London, 1994; and 'Generations of Feminism', *Radical Philosophy* no. 83, May/June 1997, pp. 6–16.

14. Cf. Anderson's comment on Mann, *The Sources of Social Power* ('A Culture in Contraflow', p. 215): 'Historical in its conception and materialist in its application, Mann's work is at the same time a rejection of historical materialism—or a reminder that there may be more than one of them'. And see W. G. Runciman, *A Treatise on Social Theory—Volume II: Substantive Social Theory* (Cambridge University Press, Cambridge, 1989), e.g., pp. 12, 39.

15. *Arguments within English Marxism*, New Left Books, London, 1980, p. 207. Cf. 'Components of the National Culture', *NLR* no. 50, July/August 1968, p. 4; and *Considerations on Western Marxism*, pp. 105–6.

16. Consider Theodor Adorno's supplement to Marx: 'Not only theory, but also its absence, becomes a material force when it seizes the masses' (qtd. in Fredric Jameson, *Late Marxism: Adorno, or, The Persistence of the Dialectic*, Verso, London and New York, 1990, p. 40).

17. 'The Intransigent Right at the End of the Century', *London Review of Books*, 24 September 1992, pp. 7–11. For a critique of tributary contemporary works by Ferdinand Mount and Shirley Letwin, see 'High Jinks at the Plaza', *London Review of Books*, 22 October 1992, pp. 16–19.

18. 'On John Rawls', *Dissent*, winter 1994, pp. 139–44 (here pp. 139–40)—the journal in which Irving Howe's celebrated blast of 1965, 'New Styles in "Leftism"', had appeared.
19. 'The Future of the Left', *NLR*, in press.
20. Eric Hobsbawm, *Age of Extremes: The Short Twentieth Century, 1914–1991*, Michael Joseph, London, 1994, p. 446. The May events were not so much as alluded to in *NLR* no. 169, May/June 1988. For an excellent brief balance sheet by a former editor, see Fred Halliday, 'The Legacy of 1968', *Interlink*, April 1988, pp. 22–23. Two other works of relevance from the *NLR* milieu were Ronald Fraser et al., *Nineteen Sixty-Eight: A Student Generation in Revolt*, Chatto and Windus, London, 1988; and Tariq Ali, *Street Fighting Years: An Autobiography of the Sixties*, Fontana, London, 1987—a volume that might be compared with the same author's tenth-anniversary reflections, *Nineteen Sixty-Eight and After: Inside the Revolution*, Blond and Briggs, London, 1978.
21. 'The Affinities of Norberto Bobbio', *NLR* no. 170, July/August 1988, pp. 3–36; reprinted in *A Zone of Engagement*, pp. 87–129 (references will be to the latter).
22. *A Zone of Engagement*, p. 362.
23. 'Comment: Power, Politics, and the Enlightenment', in David Miliband, ed., *Reinventing the Left*, Polity Press, Cambridge, 1994, pp. 39–44: here p. 40 (where Hayek's work is once again instanced as 'the most powerful theoretical version of contemporary liberalism'). Cf. Anthony Giddens, *Beyond Left and Right: The Future of Radical Politics*, Polity Press, Cambridge, 1994. And see also Anderson's 'The Future of the Left': 'In the wake of the collapse of communism, it is above all on the Left—or former thinkers of the Left—that the temptation to deny the distinction can be observed. The real reason for the new scepticism is . . . a move of self-protection, compensating for an experience of defeat with a rhetoric of supersession' (in press).
24. John Gray, 'Enlightenment Projects', *Times Literary Supplement*, 14 August 1992, pp. 4–5.
25. 'The Figures of Descent', *NLR* no. 161, January/February 1987, pp. 20–77; reprinted in *English Questions*, pp. 121–92. All references will be to the latter.
26. 'A Decennial Report', unpublished document, [1975], pp. 94–96: here p. 95.
27. E. J. Hobsbawm, *Industry and Empire: From 1750 to the Present Day* (1968), Penguin, Harmondsworth, 1983: pp. 187–88 for the rejection of '[s]imple sociological explanations'; and p. 14 for Hobsbawm's thesis: '[T]he relative decline of Britain is, broadly speaking, due to its early and long-sustained start as an industrial power. Nevertheless this factor must not be analysed in isolation. What is at least equally important is the . . . unique . . . position of this country in the world economy, which was partly the cause of our early success and which was reinforced by it. . . . Britain always had a line of retreat open when the challenge of other economies became too pressing. We could retreat further into both Empire and Free Trade—into our monopoly of as yet undeveloped regions. . . . We did not have to compete but could evade. And our ability to evade helped to perpetuate the archaic and increasingly obsolete industrial and social structure of the pioneer age'.
28. See 'Components of the National Culture', p. 35 and n. 55; and cf. the nuancing of the original in *English Questions*, p. 80 and n. 55.
29. See Andrew Glyn and Bob Sutcliffe, 'The Critical Condition of British Capital', *NLR* no. 66, March/April 1971, pp. 3–33; and cf. David Yaffe, 'The Crisis of Profitability', *NLR* no. 80, July/August 1973, pp. 45–62.
30. Geoffrey Ingham's differences with a Marxist problematic are conveyed in *Capitalism Divided? The City and Industry in British Social Development*, Macmillan, Houndmills, 1984, chap. 1 (pp. 15–39). His 'succinct and fundamental work' is lauded by Anderson as 'perhaps the most important single contribution—at once historical and

theoretical—to a better understanding of the British fate to have appeared in the eighties', in *English Questions*, p. 138 n. 43 (where readers are referred to Colin Leys's review of it, 'The Formation of British Capital', *NLR* no. 160, November/December 1986, pp. 114–20). Gamble's study is characterized as 'admirable' in *English Questions*, p. 152 n. 60; and Leys's as 'the best single synthesis on the British crisis and its contemporary consequences that now exists', in ibid., p. 185 n. 89.

31. Colin Leys, *Politics in Britain: From Labourism to Thatcherism* (1983), rev. ed., Verso, London and New York, 1989, p. 39. For Leys's assessment of 'Figures', see p. 14 n.

32. Arno J. Mayer, *The Persistence of the Old Regime: Europe to the Great War*, Croom Helm, London, 1981, in whose preface (p. x) Anderson is acknowledged.

33. Britain's 'revolution after the revolution' in 1688–89, tellingly dubbed 'glorious', predated industrial capitalism: 'The singularity of the British case lay . . . in the rapidity and finality of the sequel' ('Figures', p. 155).

34. As regards the 'ancestral lessons' of the previous century, Anderson (ibid., p. 186 n. 91) cites Hobsbawm's discussion of the collective suboptimality of individual capitalist rationality in *Industry and Empire*, pp. 187–92—an analysis immediately preceded by his repudiation of '[s]imple sociological explanations'.

35. The closing lines ('Figures', p. 192) invoke Marx's citation of Horace in the preface to the first Penguin /NLR edition of *Capital*, vol. 1, p. 90: 'At the zenith of English capitalism, Marx declared that his portrait of it in *Capital* held a mirror of the future to the rest of the world. Now, towards its nadir, the superscription may be read once again: *De te fabula narratur*'. Anderson acknowledges (p. 191 n. 96) the indebtedness of his discussion of the American case to a forthcoming text by Robert Brenner, and further cites Brenner's research on the world economy in 'The Light of Europe' (*English Questions*, pp. 334–35) and in 'Maurice Thomson's War' (p. 17). The work in question, 'Uneven Development and the Long Downturn', was finally published in *NLR* no. 229, May/June 1998, and was glowingly prefaced by Anderson.

36. *English Questions*, p. 332 n. 45.

37. David Coates, 'In Pursuit of the Anderson Thesis', in Colin Barker and David Nicholls, eds., *The Development of British Capitalist Society: A Marxist Debate*, Northern Marxist Historians Group, Manchester, 1988, pp. 69–75: here p. 73.

38. Ibid., p. 74. See 'The Figures of Descent', pp. 154 n. 62, 155 n. 63 on Barnett; pp. 147–48 on Wiener.

39. See 'Themes', *NLR* no. 161, January/February 1987, p. 1; and cf. Tom Nairn, 'Labour Imperialism', *NLR* no. 32, July/August 1965, p. 15.

40. Nairn, 'Labour Imperialism', pp. 10, 14–15.

41. See *English Questions*, pp. 201, 301, 312, 319–20, 353.

42. See David M. Gordon, 'The Global Economy: New Edifice or Crumbling Foundations?', *NLR* no. 168, March/April 1988, pp. 24–64, where the relevant passage from 'Figures' is glossed as 'lucidly apprehend[ing] the spirit of the prevailing views' (p. 30). For an excellent digest, see Simon Bromley, 'Globalization?', *Radical Philosophy* no. 80, November/December 1996, pp. 2–5.

43. Gordon, 'The Global Economy', p. 64. The conclusion to one of the Marxist studies cited by Anderson is similar to his own: cf. Andrew Gamble, *Britain in Decline: Economic Policy, Political Strategy, and the British State* (1981), 2d ed., Macmillan, Houndmills, 1985, pp. 223–31.

44. Ellen Meiksins Wood's elucidation is very helpful here: *The Pristine Culture of Capitalism: A Historical Essay on Old Regimes and Modern States*, Verso, London and New York, 1991, pp. 11–17.

45. Robert Looker, 'Shifting Trajectories: Perry Anderson's Changing Account of the Pattern of English Historical Development', in Barker and Nicholls, *The Development of British Capitalist Society*, pp. 7–32: here pp. 8–9. In 'The Light of Europe', Anderson

pays tribute to this text as 'probably . . . [t]he best direct critique' of his position (*English Questions*, p. 330 n. 39).

46. For this respecification of the 'crisis', see Looker, 'Shifting Trajectories', pp. 13–16.

47. Ibid., p. 21.

48. Wood, *The Pristine Culture of Capitalism*, p. 17.

49. Michael Barratt Brown, 'Away with All the Great Arches: Anderson's History of British Capitalism', *NLR* no. 167, January/February 1988, pp. 22–51 (the self-description occurs on p. 24).

50. Alex Callinicos, 'Exception or Symptom? The British Crisis and the World System', *NLR* no. 169, May/June 1988, pp. 97–106 (the quotations are from pp. 98, 103, 105).

51. Geoffrey Ingham, 'Commercial Capital and British Development: A Reply to Michael Barratt Brown', *NLR* no. 172, November/December 1988, pp. 45–65: here p. 46.

52. David Coates, *The Question of UK Decline: The Economy, State, and Society*, Harvester Wheatsheaf, Hemel Hempstead, 1994: here p. 279.

53. Ibid., pp. 274–75; cf. Gamble, *Britain in Decline*, pp. 77–78.

54. Coates, *The Question of UK Decline*, p. 167.

55. See the introduction to P. J. Cain and A. G. Hopkins, *British Imperialism: Innovation and Expansion, 1688–1914*, Longman, London and New York, 1993, especially pp. 13–17. The debate sparked by 'Origins of the Present Crisis' is cited as 'very stimulating' at p. 117 n. 41; the controversy over Ingham's *Capitalism Divided* at p. 201 n. 77. The authors' historical argument is summarized in *British Imperialism: Crisis and Deconstruction, 1914–1990*, Longman, London and New York, 1993, pp. 300–310. Significantly, they conclude by posing the question of 'whether the particular configuration of interests we have identified was both present and of equal importance elsewhere, or whether it was specific to the British case' (p. 314).

56. Cf. Joseph Schumpeter, *Capitalism, Socialism, and Democracy* (1942), Routledge, London and New York, 1994, pp. 135–37; and—a text not explicitly referred to by Anderson but quoted by Cain and Hopkins—'The Sociology of Imperialism' (1919), in Schumpeter, *Imperialism and Social Classes*, Meridian Books, New York, 1951, pp. 92–93. Schumpeter's celebrated phrase for the dynamic of capitalism—'the perennial gale of creative destruction' (*Capitalism, Socialism, and Democracy*, p. 84)—is borrowed in 'The Figures of Descent' (p. 156) to mark the absence of a 'modern "second revolution"' in the United Kingdom.

57. See Thorstein Veblen, *Imperial Germany and the Industrial Revolution* (1915), Augustus M. Kelley, New York, 1964, chap. 4, 'The Case of England' (pp. 88–149), especially pp. 129–32 (the quotation is from p. 193). Veblen noted 'very substantial survivals' from the English historical past, instancing state, church, and nobility (p. 120), and pithily observed that a 'superfluity of inanities' (e.g., polo) 'has in the course of time been worked into the British conception of what is right, good and necessary to civilised life' (p. 143). His main concern was with 'the peculiar features of the German case'—the theme, common to liberals and Marxists, of an alleged *Sonderweg* deviating from the Western-bourgeois norm, which is the target of David Blackbourn and Geoff Eley, *The Peculiarities of German History: Bourgeois Society and Politics in Nineteenth-Century Germany*, Oxford University Press, Oxford, 1984.

58. 'The Light of Europe', in *English Questions*, pp. 302–53.

59. For more precise references and rejoinders to the critical literature, see ibid., pp. 330–32 and nn. 39, 42–45.

60. Tom Nairn, *The Enchanted Glass: Britain and Its Monarchy* (1988), 2d ed., Vintage, London, 1994; and see also Nairn, 'The Sole Survivor', *NLR* no. 200, July/August 1993, pp. 41–47. For Anderson's appreciation, cf., e.g., *English Questions*, pp. 10, 194, 197, 340 n. 60; and *A Zone of Engagement*, pp. 144, 173–74.

61. A major essay by Anthony Barnett motivating Charter 88's constitutional proposals—

'The Empire State', in Barnett, ed., *Power and the Throne: The Monarchy Debate*, Vintage/Charter 88, London, 1994, pp. 1–53—conjoined the problematics of Ukania and 'gentlemanly capitalism'. (It is characterized as 'remarkable' in the introduction to Anderson and Patrick Camiller, eds., *Mapping the West European Left*, Verso, London and New York, 1994, p. 21 n. 25.) The major attempt to develop an economic programme to complement those proposals—Will Hutton's *The State We're In* (1995; rev. ed., Vintage, London, 1996)—likewise deployed Cain and Hopkins's historical argument. Predictably scorned as far too radical by 'New' Labour, it is exactingly reviewed by Colin Leys in 'A Radical Agenda for Britain', *NLR* no. 212, July/August 1995, pp. 3–13.

62. A member of Charter 88's council, also an editor of the *NLR*, put the point succinctly: '[T]he radical agenda appears to have regressed about a century to an operative definition of citizenship that excludes economic and social dimensions' (Michael Rustin, 'Citizenship and Charter 88', *NLR* no. 191, January/February 1992, pp. 37–42: here p. 42). For an even sharper verdict, see Lynne Segal, 'Whose Left? Socialism, Feminism, and the Future', *NLR* no. 185, January/February 1991, pp. 81–91: 'Today we face a cultural climate where much of the Left, like those associated with *Charter 88*, has moved so far to the right that nineteenth-century liberalism has become its centre' (p. 91).

63. Thus, note Anderson's reminder to Roberto Unger in 1989 that 'the effect of [constitutional arrangements] is always subject to the objective structure of the state and the actual balance of social forces' (*A Zone of Engagement*, p. 144).

64. Cf. *Arguments within English Marxism*, p. 205.

65. See also Robin Blackburn's preelectoral statement, 'The Ruins of Westminster', *NLR* no. 191, January/February 1992, pp. 5–35.

66. See Stuart Hall and Martin Jacques's collection *New Times: The Changing Face of Politics in the 1990s*, Lawrence and Wishart/*Marxism Today*, London, 1989. Of the various critiques, the most immediately relevant are Michael Rustin, 'The Politics of Post-Fordism: Or, The Trouble with "New Times"', *NLR* no. 175, May/June 1989, pp. 54–77; and Bob Jessop et al., 'Farewell to Thatcherism? Neo-liberalism and "New Times"', *NLR* no. 179, January/February 1990, pp. 81–102.

67. Anderson singles out Stuart Hall's collection *The Hard Road to Renewal: Thatcherism and the Crisis of the Left* (Verso/*Marxism Today*, London and New York, 1988) as the most fluent representative of the case for ideological dominance ('The Light of Europe', p. 305 n. 10). Hall's category of 'authoritarian populism' is utilized in 'A Culture in Contraflow', p. 200. Hobsbawm's rationale for an anti-Tory front (see his *Politics for a Rational Left: Political Writing, 1977–1988*, Verso/*Marxism Today*, London and New York, 1989) is cited in 'The Light of Europe', p. 329 and n. 38. Throughout *English Questions* (pp. 8–9, 196–97), Anderson's allusions to the debates of the 1980s on the British Left are unfailingly respectful to all concerned, betraying little or nothing of his own parti pris of the period. For some less guarded reactions, see my own *Labourism and the English Genius: The Strange Death of Labour England?* Verso, London and New York, 1993, especially pp. 146–52, in a chapter devoted to the vicissitudes of Labourism (and, subsidiarily, Communism), in the years 1979–92.

68. 'Social Democracy Today', *Against the Current* vol. 1, no. 6, November/December 1986, p. 28.

69. The underlying reason, so Anderson argued, was that Labour 'is itself . . . far less democratic even than the unreformed Ancien Régime at Westminster' ('The Light of Europe', p. 349).

70. Just as the *NLR* has avoided the generalized credulity (see, for example, no. 219, September/October 1996, headlined 'New Labour, Old Danger'), the home periodical with which Anderson has been consistently involved of late—the *London Review of*

Books—has firmly distanced itself from the Blair phenomenon. See Ross McKibbin's preelection overview, 'Very Old Labour', *London Review of Books*, 3 April 1997; and cf. Anderson's 'Reader's Note' in Jane Hindle, ed., *London Review of Books: An Anthology*, Verso, London and New York, 1996, pp. ix–xxi (especially pp. xi–xiii), as well as 'A Culture in Contraflow', pp. 199, 203.

71. See 'The Light of Europe', p. 352 and n. 78 (and note the reappearance of a very attenuated version of the 'Archimedean point' figure in connection with the education strategy).

72. It is to Michael Mann's *Socialism Can Survive* (1985), rather than T. H. Marshall's *Citizenship and Social Class* (1949), that Anderson looks for the foregrounding of 'social citizenship' as 'the most effective ideological vision of the Left' ('The Light of Europe', p. 352 n. 79). Cf. his 1994 'Comment: Power, Politics, and the Enlightenment' for an acute awareness that '"[s]ocial citizenship" universalized welfare benefits, ostensibly to avoid stigmatization of the poor, actually to purchase the consent of the better-off. . . . Is the result really to the advantage of the worse-off today? These are the kinds of hard question the Left needs to ask itself' (p. 43).

73. 'The Ends of History' (1992), in *A Zone of Engagement*, p. 365; introduction to Anderson and Camiller, *Mapping the West European Left*, p. 22.

74. '[W]hatever shape the coming European home acquires, with its probable train of homeless . . .': *English Questions*, p. 301.

75. J. M. Keynes, qtd. in Robert Skidelsky, *John Maynard Keynes: Hopes Betrayed, 1883–1920*, Macmillan, London, 1983, p. 228.

76. 'High Jinks at the Plaza', p. 19.

77. See Anderson and Stuart Hall, 'The Politics of the Common Market', *NLR* no. 10, July/August 1961, pp. 1–14. Since then, of course, Nairn had developed the pro-European case argued at length in a special issue of *NLR*, no. 75, September/October 1972, pp. 5–120.

78. 'Under the Sign of the Interim', *London Review of Books*, 4 January 1996, pp. 13–17, reviewing books by Alan Milward and François Duchenne, and 'The Europe to Come', *London Review of Books*, 25 January 1996, pp. 3–8, occasioned by works by Bernard Connolly and Keith Middlemass; reprinted in Peter Gowan and Anderson, eds., *The Question of Europe*, Verso, London and New York, 1997, pp. 51–71 and 126–45, respectively. (All subsequent references will be to the latter.) The Verso volume features contributors from across the political spectrum: 'The one trait they have in common', note Gowan and Anderson in their preface, 'is to give short shrift to *bien-pensant* discourse about the [European] Community, of any kind. . . . In this sense, the book can be read as a series of interconnected debates about the nature and future of European unity' (p. x).

'The Europe to Come' incited some prickly correspondence from Timothy Garton Ash (*London Review of Books*, 8 February and 7 March 1996), to which Anderson responded (*London Review of Books*, 22 February and 21 March 1996). 'Under the Sign of the Interim' once again employs the Archimedean trope—this time in connection with the manoeuverings of deputies of the soi-disant Section française de l'internationale ouvrière in the National Assembly after the Suez fiasco.

79. 'NLR, 1975–1980', unpublished report, [1980], p. 69. Here, as the subsequent triennial report observed, the test case was Poland ('NLR, 1980–1983', unpublished report, [1982], p. 32). Peter Gowan's major article 'The Polish Vortex: Solidarity and Socialism', *NLR* no. 139, May/June 1983, pp. 5–48 (reprinted in Tariq Ali, ed., *The Stalinist Legacy: Its Impact on Twentieth-Century World Politics*, Penguin, Harmondsworth, 1984, pp. 463–515), sought to discharge the responsibility.

80. 'Charter', unpublished document, [1983], pp. 4–5.

81. Chris Harman, 'Criticism Which Does Not Withstand the Test of Logic', *International*

Socialism no. 49, winter 1990, pp. 65–88 (here p. 80), responding to Ernest Mandel's reiteration of the 'post-capitalist economy'/'transitional society' analysis—'A Theory Which Has Not Withstood the Test of the Facts'—in ibid., pp. 43–64 (the quoted phrases appear on p. 47). It might be noted here that in *Arguments within English Marxism* (p. 121), Anderson had identified Cuba as a 'partial exception' to the uniformly Stalinist 'format' of postrevolutionary socialist regimes; and in 'Laboring under Various Pretenses in Latin America' (*In These Times*, 6–12 April 1988, p. 7), he had reminded readers that 'the impact of the Cuban Revolution [was] comparable in its effects on the Latin American left only to that of the Russian Revolution on the European Left . . . —transforming all the horizons of possible discussion and action'.

82. Tariq Ali, *Revolution from Above: Where Is the Soviet Union Going?* Hutchinson, London, 1988, p. xiii. Having acknowledged fellow *NLR* editors Robin Blackburn and Peter Gowan, as well as Tamara Deutscher and Daniel Singer (p. vii), Ali confides that his 'own political formation had been greatly influenced by the writings of Isaac Deutscher, Leon Trotsky and Ernest Mandel (in that order)' (p. ix). Mandel's own analysis is contained in his *Beyond Perestroika: The Future of Gorbachev's USSR*, trans. Gus Fagan, Verso, London and New York, 1989. And for the enthusiastic reaction to Gorbachev of a former *NLR* editor, see Anthony Barnett, *Soviet Freedom*, Picador, London, 1988. The *Review*'s first article on the subject was Zhores Medvedev, 'Innovation and Conservatism in the New Soviet Leadership', *NLR* no. 157, May/June 1986, pp. 5–26, preceded by cautious remarks in the 'Themes', pp. 1–2.

83. Letter of 12 December 1988, in 'Un carteggio tra Norberto Bobbio e Perry Anderson', *Teoria Politica* vol. 5, nos. 2–3, 1989, pp. 293–308.

84. 'August in Moscow', *London Review of Books*, 26 September 1991, pp. 5–8.

85. 'The Ends of History', in *A Zone of Engagement*, p. 375.

86. Cf. 'Trotsky's Interpretation of Stalinism', in Ali, *The Stalinist Legacy*, pp. 123–24.

87. In his 'Diary' on E. P. Thompson (*London Review of Books*, 21 October 1993, pp. 24–25), Anderson denied the laurels to the peace movement: '[Thompson] proved to be the prophet of [the Cold War's] end. That is remarkable enough. How far the peace movement contributed to the ending is another issue. . . . On this we differed. Between the ideals of END and the realities of Soviet breakdown was a large gap. It is not a belittlement of the advocates of the end of the Cold War to distinguish them from its agents. The First World War was not terminated by the Zimmerwald Left or the Stockholm Appeal, but by the victory of the Entente. We do not honour them the less for that. Was the conclusion of the Cold War very different?' (p. 25). Cf. Fred Halliday, 'The Ends of Cold War', *NLR* no. 180, March/April 1990, pp. 5–23; E. P. Thompson, 'The Ends of Cold War', and Fred Halliday, 'A Reply to Edward Thompson', *NLR* no. 182, July/August 1990, pp. 139–46, 147–50, respectively. These texts were reprinted in Robin Blackburn, ed., *After the Fall: The Failure of Communism and the Future of Socialism*, Verso, London and New York, 1991, pp. 78–114. Anderson's subscription to the thrust of Halliday's intersystemic analysis may be presumed.

88. 'Reader's Note', in Hindle, *London Review of Books: An Anthology*, p. xii. In the interim Anderson praised Jonathan Steele's work *Eternal Russia: Yeltsin, Gorbachev, and the Mirage of Democracy* (Faber and Faber, London and Boston, 1994; rev. ed., 1995) as '[a] tour de force of contemporary history. No other account of the failure of Gorbachev's *perestroika* and the prospects for Yeltsin's rule comes close to it' (back cover endorsement).

89. 'The Future of the Left', in press.

90. Compare Norberto Bobbio, 'The Upturned Utopia', trans. Patrick Camiller, in Blackburn, *After the Fall*, pp. 3–5 (especially p. 5), with Eric Hobsbawm, 'Goodbye to All That' (originally published in *Marxism Today*, October 1990), in ibid., pp. 115–25 (especially pp. 122–23).

91. See 'Trotsky's Interpretation of Stalinism', p. 126.
92. Francis Fukuyama, 'The End of History?', *National Interest* no. 16, summer 1989, pp. 3–18.
93. 'Agendas for Radical History', p. 34.
94. See *NLR* no. 193, May/June 1992, pp. 89–113, for reactions from Fred Halliday, Michael Rustin, and Ralph Miliband; and *NLR* no. 202, November/December 1993, pp. 37–53, for Joseph McCarney, 'Shaping Ends: Reflections on Fukuyama' (reprinted in Christopher Bertram and Andrew Chitty, eds., *Has History Ended? Fukuyama, Marx, Modernity,* Avebury, Aldershot, 1994, pp. 13–30). Cf. the same author's consistently illuminating sequence of texts: 'History under the Hammer', *Times Higher Education Supplement,* 1 December 1989, p. 3; 'The True Realm of Freedom: Marxist Philosophy after Communism', *NLR* no. 189, September/October 1991, pp. 19–38; and 'Endgame', *Radical Philosophy* no. 62, autumn 1992, pp. 35–38—all of them rooted in the conviction that '[t]he philosophy of history is *our* subject' ('Endgame', p. 38). For my own thoughts, see 'The Cards of Confusion: Reflections on Historical Communism and the "End of History"', *Radical Philosophy* no. 64, summer 1993, pp. 3–12 (reprinted in *Has History Ended?* pp. 46–64).
95. Cf., for example, Hobsbawm's offhand dismissal in 'Goodbye to All That', p. 124. And note also Jacques Derrida's comments in *Specters of Marx: The State of the Debt, the Work of Mourning, and the New International,* trans. Peggy Kamuf, Routledge, New York and London, 1994, pp. 14–16, 56–57, 59–64, 66–68, 70, 74, 100 (a work extracted, in a sign of straitened times, in *NLR* no. 205, May/June 1994, pp. 31–58).
96. 'The Ends of History', in *A Zone of Engagement,* pp. 279–375.
97. Lutz Niethammer, *Posthistoire: Has History Come to an End?* (1989), trans. Patrick Camiller, Verso, London and New York, 1992.
98. Régis Debray, *Que vive la République,* Éditions Odile Jacob, Paris, 1989, p. 118.
99. Karl Marx, preface to *A Contribution to the Critique of Political Economy* (1859), in Marx and Frederick Engels, *Selected Works,* vol. 1, Progress Publishers, Moscow, 1969, p. 108; *The Poverty of Philosophy* (1847), in Marx and Engels, *Collected Works,* vol. 6, Lawrence and Wishart, London, 1976, p. 174.
100. Alexandre Kojève, *Introduction to the Reading of Hegel: Lectures on 'The Phenomenology of Spirit'* (1947), ed. Allan Bloom, trans. James H. Nichols Jr., Cornell University Press, Ithaca, N.Y., and London, 1980, p. 185: '"*Weltgeschichte ist Weltgericht*" ("World History is a tribunal that judges the world"). History is what judges men, their actions and their opinions, and lastly their philosophical opinions as well. To be sure, History is, if you please, a long "discussion" between men. But this *real* historical "discussion" is something quite different from a philosophic dialogue or discussion. The "discussion" is carried out not with verbal arguments, but with clubs and swords or cannon on the one hand, and sickles and hammers or machines on the other'. Schiller's maxim is invoked in Francis Fukuyama, *The End of History and the Last Man* (1992), Penguin, Harmondsworth, 1993, p. 137; Kojève's depiction of 'historical "discussion"' is cited in Anderson, 'Comment: Power, Politics, and the Enlightenment', p. 42 (see n. 119, this chapter).
101. See 'Note to the Second Edition', in Kojève, *Introduction to the Reading of Hegel,* pp. 159–62.
102. 'Fukuyama's cool refusal of certain kinds of conventional wisdom is nowhere more striking than in his judgement of this issue. The conflict in the Gulf which excited so many of his critics, igniting enthusiasm on Right and Left alike for the battle to uphold the cause of national independence and democracy in the Middle East against the menace of a new Hitler, he was to compare with the quarrel between a fifteenth-century condotterie and a thirteenth-century clerical seigneurie': 'The Ends of

History', p. 337. Elsewhere, Anderson has remarked that '[t]he hypocrisies of the "international community" as a code word for the dominant powers are plain enough' ('Comment: Power, Politics, and the Enlightenment', p. 43); and see also 'Reader's Note', p. xiii, where the *London Review*'s 'escape from the hypocrisies of the "international community"' is noted. In 'An Open Letter to *New Left Review*' (*International Socialism* no. 50, spring 1991, pp. 101–3), Alex Callinicos and his colleagues expressed their anxiety that the Review was succumbing to those hypocrisies, adducing Fred Halliday's 'The Crisis of the Arab World: The False Answers of Saddam Hussein' (*NLR* no. 184, November/December 1990, pp. 69–74) as evidence. Cf., however, Robert Brenner, 'Why Is the United States at War with Iraq?', *NLR* no. 185, January/February 1991, pp. 122–37 (acknowledging Anderson's 'political collaboration throughout the crisis' at p. 123 n.); and Peter Gowan, 'The Gulf War, Iraq, and Western Liberalism', *NLR* no. 187, May/June 1991, pp. 21–70.

103. In his review of Rawls's *Political Liberalism*, Anderson has brusquely despatched an analogous syndrome by reference to Marx's Eleventh Thesis on Feuerbach: '. . . as if the office of the philosopher was neither to interpret the world nor to change it, but simply to change its interpretations' ('On John Rawls', p. 141). The 'strategy of consolation' involved is similar to that of asserting the supersession of the Left/Right dichotomy.

104. Anderson cites Trotsky, *The Revolution Betrayed: What Is the Soviet Union and Where Is It Going?* (1937), trans. Max Eastman, Pathfinder Press, New York, 1980, chap. 4, 'The Struggle for Productivity', p. 78. In *The Third International after Lenin* (1929; trans. John G. Wright, Pathfinder Press, New York, 1982), Trotsky had averred that 'it is impossible to build a socialist paradise, like an oasis in the hell of world capitalism' (p. 68). Three years later, he execrated 'socialism in one country' as a 'reactionary, national-socialist utopia' (qtd. in Isaac Deutscher, *The Prophet Outcast—Trotsky: 1929–1940* [1963], Oxford University Press, Oxford, 1979, p. 102).

105. Anderson's readers are referred to 'a fundamental map of our time' ('The Ends of History', p. 353 n. 153): Giovanni Arrighi, 'World Income Inequalities and the Future of Socialism', *NLR* no. 189, September/October 1991, pp. 39–64.

106. The indices of misery are drawn from the 1995 World Health Organisation Report *Bridging the Gap*; those of privilege, from the 1996 *UN Development Report*.

107. Anderson proceeds ('The Ends of History', pp. 356–57) to criticize Fukuyama's silence on inequalities between the sexes in flagrant contradiction of the official ideology of liberal societies: 'The end of history may see the last men, as they now are. Women willing to see themselves as the ultimate exemplars of their sex are likely to be fewer' (p. 357).

108. Maurice Merleau-Ponty, 'The Eye and the Mind', qtd. in Martin Jay, *Marxism and Totality: The Adventures of a Concept from Lukács to Habermas*, Polity Press, Cambridge, 1984, p. 377.

109. See Georg Lukács, 'What Is Orthodox Marxism?' (1919), in *Political Writings, 1919–1929: The Question of Parliamentarism and Other Essays*, trans. Michael McColgan, New Left Books, London, 1972, pp. 19–27: here p. 27.

110. See Robin Blackburn, 'Fin de Siècle: Socialism after the Crash', *NLR* no. 185, January/February 1991, pp. 5–66; reprinted in Blackburn, *After the Fall*, pp. 173–249.

111. This passage is preceded by the statement that 'the construction of effective supranational sovereignties is the obvious remedy to the loss by national states of so much of their substance and authority' ('The Ends of History', p. 365). Significantly or not, in a paper presented to an Actuel Marx conference in Paris in autumn 1995, which otherwise reproduces a slightly abridged version of the 'The Ends of History', pp. 358–67, the main verb in this sentence is rendered 'appears to be' (*paraît être*), and what

follows is 'an essential remedy' (*un remède indispensable*): 'Le capitalisme après le communisme', in Jacques Bidet, ed., *Cent ans de marxisme: Bilan critique et perspectives*, Presses Universitaires de France, Paris, 1996, pp. 253–59: here p. 257.

112. Nicholas Tredell, 'Modern Tragedy', *P. N. Review* vol. 19, no. 1, September/October 1992, pp. 66–70: here p. 70. Tredell is alluding to Anderson's essay 'On Emplotment—Andreas Hillgruber' (1990), in *A Zone of Engagement*, pp. 169–81 (especially p. 180).

113. Introduction to *Mapping the West European Left*, p. 7.

114. Leon Trotsky, qtd. in Isaac Deutscher, *The Prophet Unarmed—Trotsky: 1921–1929* (1959), Oxford University Press, Oxford, 1982, p. 301.

115. Leon Trotsky, 'The USSR in War' (1939), in *In Defense of Marxism: The Social and Political Contradictions of the Soviet Union* (1942), Pathfinder Press, New York, 1990, pp. 3–21: here p. 9.

116. *Considerations on Western Marxism*, p. 56.

117. Cf. Deutscher, *The Prophet Outcast*, pp. 521–22: here p. 522.

118. Trotsky, qtd. in ibid., p. 185.

119. See Marx and Engels, 'Manifesto of the Communist Party' (1848), in *Selected Works*, vol. 1, p. 112. The passage is invoked by Anderson in 'Comment: Power, Politics, and the Enlightenment', where, having cited Kojève's characterization of '*real* historical discussion' (see n. 100, this chapter), he remarks: 'The imagery remains a trifle old-fashioned, as befitted a Hegelian. Marx was more modern: it was "the artillery of commodities" that would convince the world of the truth of capital' (pp. 42–43).

120. 'The Legacy of Isaac Deutscher', in *A Zone of Engagement*, pp. 56–75: here p. 75. Anderson writes that Deutscher 'is mostly thought of, with justice, as a guarded optimist for the revolution'. In Deutscher's obituary notice, E. H. Carr had observed that '[n]o charge was more frequently made against his journalistic writings than that of an excessive optimism': 'Isaac Deutscher: In Memoriam' (1967), in Carr, *The October Revolution: Before and After*, Knopf, New York, 1969, pp. 177–78: here p. 178.

121. See Alex Callinicos, *Theories and Narratives: Reflections on the Philosophy of History*, Polity Press, Cambridge, 1995, chap. 1, 'Sympathy for the Devil? Francis Fukuyama and the End of History' (pp. 15–43)—especially pp. 17–22, which criticizes the Deutscherite reactions of Anderson, Halliday, and me. Callinicos (pp. 215 n. 23, 218–19 n. 92) cites Anderson's response to his criticisms during a seminar held at the Center for Social Theory and Comparative History, University of California at Los Angeles, in April 1993. On the Marxist theory of historical trajectory, see Erik Olin Wright, 'Class Analysis, History, and Emancipation', *NLR* no. 202, November/December 1993, pp. 15–35.

122. Cf., however, Alex Callinicos, *The Revenge of History: Marxism and the East European Revolutions*, Polity Press, Cambridge, 1991, for an argument to the contrary.

123. Schumpeter, *Capitalism, Socialism, and Democracy*, p. 200.

124. See C. Wright Mills, 'Letter to the New Left', *NLR* no. 5, September/October 1960, pp. 18–23; cited by Robin Blackburn, 'A Brief History of *New Left Review*, 1960–1990', in *Thirty Years of New Left Review: Index to Numbers 1–184 (1960–1990)*, London, 1992, p. vi. In *Arguments within English Marxism* (p. 47), Anderson quotes Thompson's qualified invocation of Mills with implicit disapprobation, and alludes to him again in 'The Common and the Particular', p. 31.

125. Anderson and Camiller, *Mapping the West European Left*, pp. 1–22.

126. Cf. *In the Tracks of Historical Materialism*, p. 105.

127. 'Social Democracy Today', p. 28.

128. See Leon Trotsky, 'What Next? Vital Questions for the German Proletariat' (1932),

in *The Struggle against Fascism in Germany* (1971), Penguin, Harmondsworth, 1975, p. 122.

129. Cf. the very pertinent reflections by a leading member of one of the organizations to which Anderson refers, Lucio Magri, of Rifondazione Comunista: 'The European Left between Crisis and Refoundation', *NLR* no. 189, September/October 1991, pp. 5–18.

130. Max Horkheimer, 'Traditional and Critical Theory' (1937), qtd. in Jay, *Marxism and Totality*, p. 209.

131. Cf. *In the Tracks of Historical Materialism*, pp. 102–3.

132. See Ignacio Ramonet, 'Régimes globalitaires', *Le Monde Diplomatique*, January 1997, p. 1.

133. 'Darkness Falls', *Guardian*, 8 November 1994, supplement, p. 12.

134. 'The Myth of Hellenism', *Guardian*, 13 March 1987, p. 21.

135. 'The Dark Side of Brazilian Conviviality', *London Review of Books*, 24 November 1994, pp. 3–8. Cf. the unattributed introduction 'Brazil', *NLR* no. 25, May/June 1964, pp. 39–41; and the likewise unattributed 'Historical Introduction, 1930–64: The Legacy of Vargas', in João Quartim, *Dictatorship and Armed Struggle in Brazil*, trans. David Fernbach, New Left Books, London, 1971, pp. 19–51. According to the notes on contributors in Alexander Cockburn and Robin Blackburn, eds. *Student Power: Problems, Diagnosis, Action* (Penguin/NLR, Harmondsworth, 1969), Anderson was at the time 'preparing a thesis on Brazilian politics'. More recently, see 'Dictadura y democracia en América Latina' (1987), in Anderson, *Democracia y Socialismo: La lucha democrática desde una perspetiva socialista*, Editorial Tierra del Fuego, Buenos Aires, 1988, pp. 43–66. And cf. Emir Sader, 'The Workers' Party in Brazil', *NLR* no. 165, September/October 1987, pp. 93–102, in which Alex Callinicos has detected 'suspiciously Andersonian tones' (*Trotskyism*, Open University Press, Milton Keynes, 1990, p. 53).

136. 'Diary', *London Review of Books*, 17 October 1996, pp. 28–29. If Anderson's report registered the pressures that were shortly to ignite massive labour unrest in South Korea, his encomium to the convenience and cleanliness of Seoul (p. 28) suggests a somewhat sheltered experience. According to a 1996 UN report, it is one of the most expensive and polluted cities in the world, tap water there rarely being drinkable on account of contamination by heavy metals. See Laurent Carroué, 'Les travailleurs coréens à l'assaut du dragon', *Le Monde Diplomatique*, February 1997, pp. 1, 18–19.

137. 'Reader's Note', p. ix.

138. See 'The Future of the Left', in press.

139. See Serge Halimi's fine report 'La Nouvelle-Zélande éprouvette du capitalisme total', *Le Monde Diplomatique*, April 1997, pp. 10–11: here p. 10.

140. 'The Future of the Left', in press.

Conclusion: The Figure in the Mirror

1. 'The Ends of History', in *A Zone of Engagement*, Verso, London and New York, 1992, p. 375.

2. See *Considerations on Western Marxism*, New Left Books, London, 1976, pp. 55–56.

3. Cf. ibid., p. 13. And note also the comments on Jean Monnet in 'Under the Sign of the Interim', in Peter Gowan and Anderson, eds., *The Question of Europe*, Verso, London and New York, 1997, pp. 59–62.

4. Isaac Deutscher, *The Prophet Unarmed—Trotsky: 1921–1929* (1959), Oxford University Press, Oxford, 1982, p. 465.

5. Cf. 'The Antinomies of Antonio Gramsci', *NLR* no. 100, November 1976/January 1977, p. 78, alluding to Régis Debray, *Revolution in the Revolution? Armed Struggle and Political Struggle in Latin America* (1967), trans. Bobbye Ortiz, Penguin, Harmondsworth, 1968, p. 19.

6. Maurice Merleau-Ponty, qtd. in Martin Jay, *Marxism and Totality: The Adventures of a Concept from Lukács to Habermas*, Polity Press, Cambridge, 1984, p. 382. Cf. Jean-Paul Sartre, *Critique of Dialectical Reason* (1960), vol. 1, trans. Alan Sheridan-Smith, New Left Books, London, 1976, p. 822.

7. Ernest Gellner, *Nations and Nationalism*, Blackwell, Oxford, 1983, p. 133.

8. 'Laboring under Various Pretenses in Latin America', *In These Times*, 6–12 April 1988, p. 7—a proposition that resumes 'The Founding Moment', unpublished manuscript, [1969], pp. 46–47.

9. Leon Trotsky, qtd. in Isaac Deutscher, *The Prophet Outcast—Trotsky: 1929–1940* (1963), Oxford University Press, Oxford, 1979, p. 363.

10. Preface to Isaac Deutscher, *Marxism, Wars, and Revolutions: Essays from Four Decades*, ed. Tamara Deutscher, Verso, London, 1984, p. xx. Cf. the evocation of Hobsbawm's 'distinctive temper' in Anderson, 'Darkness Falls', *Guardian*, 8 November 1994, supplement, p. 12.

11. *A Zone of Engagement*, p. 73.

12. See Anderson's 'Diary' on E. P. Thompson, *London Review of Books*, 21 October 1993, p. 25.

13. E. H. Carr, 'The Russian Revolution and the West', *NLR* no. 111, September/October 1978, p. 36.

14. Cf. Anderson's comments on Franco Moretti's reaction to 'The Antinomies of Antonio Gramsci', in *A Zone of Engagement*, p. xi; and see the 'Themes' to *NLR* no. 111, p. 1.

15. Lucio Magri, 'The European Left between Crisis and Refoundation', *NLR* no. 189, September/October 1991, p. 13.

16. Foreword to *English Questions*, Verso, London and New York, 1992, p. 11.

Select Bibliography

Texts by Perry Anderson

Texts are listed in chronological order.

1960

Cuba, Free Territory of America' (with Robin Blackburn), *New University* (Oxford) no. 4, 5 December, pp. 17–23.

1961

'Sweden: Mr. Crosland's Dreamland', *New Left Review* no. 7, January/February, pp. 4–12.
'Cuba: The Present Reality', interview with Saul Landau (with Ralph Samuel et al.), *New Left Review* no. 9, May/June, pp. 12–22.
'Sweden II: Study in Social Democracy', *New Left Review* no. 9, May/June, pp. 34–45.
'The Politics of the Common Market' (with Stuart Hall), *New Left Review* no. 10, July/August, pp. 1–14.

1962

Introduction to the debate of the Central Committee of the Italian Communist Party on the Twenty-Second Congress of the CPSU, *New Left Review* nos. 13–14, January/April, pp. 152–60.
'Portugal and the End of Ultra-Colonialism, Part 1', *New Left Review* no. 15, May/June, pp. 83–102.
'Portugal and the End of Ultra-Colonialism, Part 2', *New Left Review* no. 16, July/August, pp. 88–123.
'Portugal and the End of Ultra-Colonialism, Part 3', *New Left Review* no. 17, winter, pp. 85–114.

1963

'On Internationalism' (unattributed), *New Left Review* no. 18, January/February, pp. 3–4.
Introduction to Mandel on Belgium (unattributed), *New Left Review* no. 20, summer, pp. 3–4.

1964

'Origins of the Present Crisis', *New Left Review* no. 23, January/February, pp. 26–53. Reprinted in Anderson and Robin Blackburn, eds., *Towards Socialism*, Fontana/New Left Review, London, 1965, pp. 11–52; and in Anderson, *English Questions*, Verso, London and New York, 1992, pp. 15–47.
'Brazil' (unattributed), *New Left Review* no. 25, May/June, pp. 39–41.
'Critique of Wilsonism', *New Left Review* no. 27, September/October, pp. 3–27.
'Divide and Conquer' (unattributed), *New Left Review* no. 28, November/December, pp. 1–3.

1965

'The Left in the Fifties', *New Left Review* no. 29, January/February, pp. 3–18.
Towards Socialism (with Robin Blackburn, eds.), Fontana/*New Left Review*, London, 397 pp.
'Problems of Socialist Strategy', in Anderson and Blackburn, *Towards Socialism*, pp. 221–90.

1966

'Socialism and Pseudo-Empiricism', *New Left Review* no. 35, January/February, pp. 2–42.

1967

'The Limits and Possibilities of Trade Union Action', in Robin Blackburn and Alexander Cockburn, eds., *The Incompatibles: Trade Union Militancy and the Consensus*, Penguin/ *New Left Review*, Harmondsworth, pp. 263–80.
Introduction to Poulantzas (unattributed), *New Left Review* no. 43, May/June, pp. 55–56.
'The Marxism of Régis Debray' (unattributed; with Robin Blackburn), *New Left Review* no. 45, September/October, pp. 8–12. Reprinted in Leo Huberman and Paul Sweezy, eds., *Régis Debray and the Latin American Revolution*, Monthly Review Press, New York, 1968, pp. 63–69.

1968

'Comment on Beckett's "Stones"' (as Richard Merton), *New Left Review* no. 47, January/ February, pp. 29–31.
'Components of the National Culture', *New Left Review* no. 50, July/August, pp. 3–57. Reprinted in Alexander Cockburn and Robin Blackburn, eds., *Student Power: Problems, Diagnosis, Action*, Penguin/*New Left Review*, Harmondsworth, 1969, pp. 214–84; and in Anderson, *English Questions*, pp. 48–104.
'Introduction to Gramsci, 1919–1920', *New Left Review* no. 51, September/October, pp. 22–27.
Introduction to special issue on France, May 1968 (unattributed), *New Left Review* no. 52, November/December, pp. 1–8.

1969

Introduction to Tukhachevsky (unattributed), *New Left Review* no. 55, May/June, pp. 74–89.
Introduction to Colletti (unattributed), *New Left Review* no. 56, July/August, p. 18.
'The Itinerary of a Thought', interview with Jean-Paul Sartre (with Ronald Fraser and Quintin Hoare), *New Left Review* no. 58, November/December, pp. 43–66. Reprinted in Sartre, *Between Existentialism and Marxism* (1972), trans. John Mathews, New Left Books, London, 1974, pp. 33–64.

1970

'Comment on Chester's "For a Rock Aesthetic"' (as Richard Merton), *New Left Review* no. 59, January/February, pp. 88–96.
'Presentation of Kautsky, 1914' (unattributed), *New Left Review* no. 59, January/February, pp. 39–40.
Introduction to Della Volpe (unattributed), *New Left Review* no. 59, January/February, pp. 97–100.
Introduction to Magri (unattributed), *New Left Review* no. 60, March/April, pp. 92–96.

1971

'Presentation of Blanqui' (unattributed), *New Left Review* no. 65, January/February, pp. 27–29.

Introduction to Magri on Italian Communism (unattributed), *New Left Review* no. 66, March/April, pp. 35–36.

'Lukács on His Life and Work' (1968), interview with Georg Lukács (unattributed), *New Left Review* no. 68, July/August, pp. 49–58. Reprinted in Georg Lukács, *Record of a Life: An Autobiographical Sketch*, Verso, London, 1983, pp. 171–82.

'Historical Introduction, 1930–64: The Legacy of Vargas' (unattributed), in João Quartim, *Dictatorship and Armed Struggle in Brazil*, trans. David Fernbach, New Left Books, London, pp. 19–51.

1972

'Polish Document—Presentation' (unattributed), *New Left Review* no. 72, March/April, pp. 31–34.

Introduction to Glucksmann on Althusser (unattributed), *New Left Review* no. 72, March/April, pp. 61–67. Reprinted in *New Left Review*, ed., *Western Marxism: A Critical Reader*, New Left Books, London, 1977, pp. 273–81.

Introduction to Moran on Wittgenstein and Russia (unattributed), *New Left Review* no. 73, May/June, pp. 83–84.

1973

Presentation of Vilar on Althusser (unattributed), *New Left Review* no. 80, July/August, p. 64.

Introduction to Adorno (unattributed), *New Left Review* no. 81, September/October, pp. 46–53. Incorporated into Ernst Bloch et al., *Aesthetics and Politics*, New Left Books, London, 1977, pp. 100–109.

Introduction to Davies's 'The White Working-Class in South Africa' (unattributed), *New Left Review* no. 82, November/December, pp. 38–39.

1974

Introduction to Medvedev's 'Problems of Democratization and Détente' (unattributed), *New Left Review* no. 83, January/February, pp. 25–26.

Introduction to Brecht on Lukács (unattributed), *New Left Review* no. 84, March/April, pp. 33–38. Incorporated into Bloch et al., *Aesthetics and Politics*, pp. 60–67.

Passages from Antiquity to Feudalism, New Left Books, London, 304 pp.

Lineages of the Absolutist State, New Left Books, London, 573 pp.

'A Political and Philosophical Interview', interview with Lucio Colletti, *New Left Review* no. 86, July/August, pp. 3–28. Reprinted in *New Left Review*, ed., *Western Marxism*, pp. 315–50.

1975

'Victory in Indochina' (unattributed), *New Left Review* no. 91, May/June, pp. 3–4.

1976

'The Measure of His Dance', review of James Tucker's *The Novels of Anthony Powell*, *Guardian*, 26 August, p. 7.

'Cold Waugh', review of *The Diaries of Evelyn Waugh*, *Guardian*, 2 September, p. 7.

Considerations on Western Marxism (1974–76), New Left Books, London, 125 pp.

303

1977

'The Antinomies of Antonio Gramsci', *New Left Review* no. 100, November 1976/January 1977, pp. 5–78.

Introduction to Sartre's *Critique of Dialectical Reason* (unattributed), *New Left Review* no. 100, November 1976/January 1977, pp. 138–42.

'Editorial Note' (unattributed), in *New Left Review*, ed., *Western Marxism*, p. 7.

1978

Introduction to articles on Ethiopia and Somalia (unattributed), *New Left Review* no. 107, January/February, pp. 38–39.

Introduction to Lukács on Benjamin and Brecht (unattributed), *New Left Review* no. 110, July/August, pp. 81–82.

'The Russian Revolution and the West', interview with E. H. Carr (unattributed; joint), *New Left Review* no. 111, September/October, pp. 25–36.

'The Strategic Option: Some Questions', in André Liebich, ed., *The Future of Socialism in Europe?* Interuniversity Centre for European Studies, Montreal, pp. 21–29.

1979

'Publisher's Note' (unattributed), in Walter Benjamin, *One-Way Street and Other Writings*, New Left Books, London, pp. 29–42.

Introduction to Habermas (unattributed), *New Left Review* no. 115, May/June, p. 72.

Foreword to Raymond Williams, *Politics and Letters: Interviews with New Left Review* (unattributed; joint), New Left Books, London, pp. 7–10.

Interviews with Raymond Williams (with Anthony Barnett and Francis Mulhern), in Williams, *Politics and Letters*.

'Russia under Brezhnev', interview with Zhores Medvedev (unattributed), *New Left Review* no. 117, September/October, pp. 3–29.

1980

Arguments within English Marxism, New Left Books, London, 218 pp.

Presentation of Deutscher on Poland and the USSR (unattributed), *New Left Review* no. 124, November/December, p. 85.

1981

'Communist Party History' (1979), in Raphael Samuel, ed., *People's History and Socialist Theory*, Routledge and Kegan Paul, London, pp. 145–56.

1982

Foreword to *New Left Review*, ed., *Exterminism and Cold War* (unattributed), Verso, London, pp. vii–xii.

Interviews with Tony Benn (unattributed; with Robin Blackburn and Francis Mulhern), in Benn, *Parliament, People, and Power: Agenda for a Free Society—Interviews with New Left Review*, Verso, London.

1983

'Trotsky's Interpretation of Stalinism', *New Left Review* no. 139, May/June, pp. 49–58. Reprinted in Tariq Ali, ed., *The Stalinist Legacy: Its Impact on Twentieth-Century World Politics*, Penguin, Harmondsworth, 1984, pp. 118–28.
'Class Struggle in the Ancient Greek World', *History Workshop* no. 16, autumn, pp. 57–73. Reprinted as 'Geoffrey de Ste. Croix and the Ancient World', in Anderson, *A Zone of Engagement*, Verso, London and New York, 1992, pp. 1–24.
In the Tracks of Historical Materialism, Verso, London, 112 pp.

1984

'Modernity and Revolution' (1983), *New Left Review* no. 144, March/April, pp. 96–113. Reprinted (together with the ensuing discussion) in Cary Nelson and Lawrence Grossberg, eds., *Marxism and the Interpretation of Culture*, Macmillan, Houndmills, 1988, pp. 317–38; and with a postscript as 'Marshall Berman: Modernity and Revolution', in Anderson, *A Zone of Engagement*, pp. 25–55.
Interviews with Rudolf Bahro (with Fred Halliday and Monty Johnstone), in Bahro, *From Red to Green: Interviews with New Left Review*, Verso, London.
Preface to Isaac Deutscher, *Marxism, Wars, and Revolutions: Essays from Four Decades*, ed. Tamara Deutscher, Verso, London, pp. i–xx. Reprinted with a postscript as 'The Legacy of Isaac Deutscher', in Anderson, *A Zone of Engagement*, pp. 56–75.
Foreword to the 4th ed. of *Considerations on Western Marxism*, Verso, London, p. ix.

1985

'A Philosophico-political Profile', interview with Jürgen Habermas (with Peter Dews), *New Left Review* no. 151, May/June, pp. 75–105. Reprinted in Dews, ed., *Habermas: Autonomy and Solidarity*, Verso, London, 1986, pp. 149–89.

1986

'Agendas for Radical History' (with E. J. Hobsbawm, Christopher Hill, and E. P. Thompson), *Radical History Review* no. 36, pp. 26–45.
'Life-Forms, Morality, and the Task of the Philosopher', interview with Jürgen Habermas (with Peter Dews), in Dews, *Habermas: Autonomy and Solidarity*, pp. 191–216.
'Social Democracy Today', *Against the Current* vol. 1, no. 6, November/December, pp. 21–28. Incorporated (with modifications) into Anderson, 'The Light of Europe', in *English Questions*, pp. 307–25, as 'The Parabola of Social Democracy'.
'Those in Authority', review of Michael Mann's *The Sources of Social Power*, vol. 1, *Times Literary Supplement*, 12 December, pp. 1405–6. Reprinted as 'Michael Mann's Sociology of Power', in Anderson, *A Zone of Engagement*, pp. 76–86.

1987

'The Figures of Descent', *New Left Review* no. 161, January/February, pp. 20–77. Reprinted in Anderson, *English Questions*, pp. 121–92.
'The Myth of Hellenism', review of Martin Bernal's *Black Athena*, *Guardian*, 13 March, p. 21.

1988

'Laboring under Various Pretenses in Latin America', review of Charles Bergquist's *Labor in Latin America*, *In These Times*, 6–12 April, p. 7.

'Dictadura y democracia en América Latina', in Anderson, *Democracia y socialismo: La lucha democrática desde una perspetiva socialista*, Editorial Tierra del Fuego, Buenos Aires, pp. 43–66.

'The Affinities of Norberto Bobbio', *New Left Review* no. 170, July/August, pp. 3–36. Reprinted in Anderson, *A Zone of Engagement*, pp. 87–129.

1989

'A Dream of Change', review of Roberto Unger's *Politics, a Work in Constructive Theory*, *Times Literary Supplement*, 13 January, pp. 37–38. Published in expanded form as 'Roberto Unger and the Politics of Empowerment', *New Left Review* no. 173, January/February 1989, pp. 93–107; reprinted in Anderson, *A Zone of Engagement*, pp. 130–48.

'Societies', review of W. G. Runciman's *A Treatise of Social Theory*, vol. 2, *London Review of Books*, 6 July, pp. 6–9. Reprinted as 'W. G. Runciman: A New Evolutionism', in Anderson, *A Zone of Engagement*, pp. 149–68.

'The Common and the Particular', *International Labor and Working-Class History* no. 36, fall, pp. 31–36.

Letters to Norberto Bobbio, in 'Un carteggio tra Norberto Bobbio e Perry Anderson', *Teoria Politica* vol. 5, nos. 2–3, pp. 293–308.

1990

'A Culture in Contraflow—I', *New Left Review* no. 180, March/April, pp. 41–78. Reprinted in Anderson, *English Questions*, pp. 193–238.

'A Culture in Contraflow—II', *New Left Review* no. 182, July/August, pp. 85–137. Reprinted in Anderson, *English Questions*, pp. 239–301.

'Witchcraft', review of Carlo Ginzburg's *Ecstasies: Deciphering the Witches' Sabbath*, *London Review of Books*, 8 November, pp. 6–11. Reprinted as 'Nocturnal Enquiry: Carlo Ginzburg', in Anderson, *A Zone of Engagement*, pp. 207–29.

'England's Isaiah', review of Isaiah Berlin's *The Crooked Timber of Humanity*, *London Review of Books*, 20 December, pp. 3–7. Reprinted as 'The Pluralism of Isaiah Berlin', in Anderson, *A Zone of Engagement*, pp. 230–50.

1991

'Nation-State and National Identity', review of Fernand Braudel's *The Identity of France*, *London Review of Books*, 9 May, pp. 3–8. Reprinted as 'Fernand Braudel and National Identity', in Anderson, *A Zone of Engagement*, pp. 251–78.

'Diary' (on the Russian coup d'état), *London Review of Books*, 26 September, pp. 5–8.

1992

'The Notion of Bourgeois Revolution' (1976), in Anderson, *English Questions*, pp. 105–18.

'The Light of Europe' (1991), in Anderson, *English Questions*, pp. 302–53.

'On Emplotment—Andreas Hillgruber' (1990), in Anderson, *A Zone of Engagement*, pp. 169–81.

'Science, Politics, Enchantment' (1990), in John Hall and Ian Jarvie, eds., *Transition to Modernity: Essays on Power, Wealth, and Belief*, Cambridge University Press, Cambridge, pp. 187–212. Reprinted as 'Max Weber and Ernest Gellner: Science, Politics, Enchantment', in Anderson, *A Zone of Engagement*, pp. 182–206.

'The Ends of History', in Anderson, *A Zone of Engagement*, pp. 279–375. Revised and expanded version announced as Anderson, *The Ends of History*, Verso, London and New York, forthcoming.

English Questions, Verso, London and New York, 370 pp.

A Zone of Engagement, Verso, London and New York, 384 pp.

'The Intransigent Right at the End of the Century', review of Michael Oakeshott's *Rationalism in Politics and Other Essays*, *London Review of Books*, 24 September, pp. 7–11.

'High Jinks at the Plaza', review of Ferdinand Mount's *The British Constitution Now*, *London Review of Books*, 22 October, pp. 16–19.

1993

Review of Geoffrey Elton's *The English*, *Guardian*, 12 January, supplement, p. 8.

Storia d'Europa (et al., eds.), vol. 1, Einaudi, Turin.

'Diary' (on E. P. Thompson), *London Review of Books*, 21 October, pp. 24–25.

'Maurice Thomson's War', review of Robert Brenner's *Merchants and Revolution*, *London Review of Books*, 4 November, pp. 13–17.

1994

'Comment: Power, Politics, and the Enlightenment', in David Miliband, ed., *Reinventing the Left*, Polity Press, Cambridge, pp. 39–44.

Mapping the West European Left (with Patrick Camiller, eds.), Verso, London and New York, 276 pp.

Introduction to *Mapping the West European Left*, pp. 1–22.

'Darkness Falls', review of E. J. Hobsbawm's *Age of Extremes*, *Guardian*, 8 November, supplement, p. 12.

'The Dark Side of Brazilian Conviviality' (on the Brazilian presidential elections), *London Review of Books*, 24 November, pp. 3–8.

'On John Rawls', review of Rawls's *Political Liberalism*, *Dissent*, winter, pp. 139–44.

1995

'The Invention of the Region', European University Working Papers Series, Florence.

'Fantasmi', *Il Manifesto*, 1 November, p. 10.

'Il fantasma della destra eversiva', *Il Manifesto*, 30 November, p. 21.

1996

'Under the Sign of the Interim' (on the European Community), *London Review of Books*, 4 January, pp. 13–17. Reprinted in Peter Gowan and Perry Anderson, eds., *The Question of Europe*, Verso, London and New York, 1997, pp. 51–71.

'The Europe to Come', *London Review of Books*, 25 January, pp. 3–8. Reprinted in Gowan and Anderson, *The Question of Europe*, pp. 126–45.

'Le capitalisme après le communisme', in Jacques Bidet, ed., *Cent ans de marxisme: Bilan critique et perspectives*, Presses Universitaires de France, Paris, pp. 253–59.

'Diary' (on South Korea), *London Review of Books*, 17 October, pp. 28–29.

'Reader's Note', in Jane Hindle, ed., *London Review of Books: An Anthology*, Verso, London and New York, pp. ix–xxi.

1997

The Question of Europe (with Peter Gowan, eds.), Verso, London and New York, 399 pp.

1998

'Themes' (on Tovert Brenner on the world economy), New Left Review no. 229, May/June, pp. i–v.

'A Belated Encounter' (on Anderson's father), *London Review of Books*, 30 July, pp. 3, 6–10

'My Father's Last Years in China', *London Review of Books*, 20 August, pp. 28–31, 34.

Foreword to Fredric Jameson, *The Cultural Turn: Selected Writings on Postmodernism, 1983–1998*, Verso, London and New York, pp. xi–xiv.

The Origins of Postmodernity, Verso, London and New York, 143 pp.

In Press

'The Future of the Left', review of Norberto Bobbio's *Left and Right, New Left Review*.

Forthcoming

The Ends of History, Verso, London and New York.

Letter to Norberto Bobbio, *New Left Review*.

Secondary Texts

Texts for each author are listed in order published.

Ahmad, Aijaz, *In Theory: Classes, Nations, Literatures*, Verso, London and New York, 1992.

Ali, Tariq, *The Coming British Revolution*, Jonathan Cape, London, 1972.

———, *Nineteen Sixty-Eight and After: Inside the Revolution*, Blond and Briggs, London, 1978.

———, ed., *The Stalinist Legacy: Its Impact on Twentieth-Century World Politics*, Penguin, Harmondsworth, 1984.

———, *Revolution from Above: Where Is the Soviet Union Going?* Hutchinson, London, 1988.

———, *Redemption*, Chatto and Windus, London, 1990.

Ali, Tariq, and Ken Livingstone, *Who's Afraid of Margaret Thatcher? In Praise of Socialism*, Verso, London, 1984.

Ali, Tariq, and Quintin Hoare, 'Socialists and the Crisis of Labourism', *New Left Review* no. 132, March/April 1982, pp. 59–81.

Althusser, Louis, *For Marx* (1965), trans. Ben Brewster, Allen Lane, Harmondsworth, 1969.

———, 'The Crisis of Marxism' (1977), trans. Grahame Lock, in *Il Manifesto*, ed., *Power and Opposition in Post-revolutionary Societies*, Ink Links, London, 1979, pp. 225–37.

Althusser, Louis, and Étienne Balibar, *Reading 'Capital'* (1968), trans. Ben Brewster, New Left Books, London, 1970.

Aronson, Ronald, 'Historical Materialism, Answer to Marxism's Crisis', *New Left Review* no. 152, July/August 1985, pp. 74–94.

Bahro, Rudolf, *The Alternative in Eastern Europe* (1977), trans. David Fernbach, New Left Books, London, 1978.

Barker, Colin, and David Nicholls, eds., *The Development of British Capitalist Society: A Marxist Debate*, Northern Marxist Historians Group, Manchester, 1988.

Barnett, Anthony, *Iron Britannia: Why Parliament Waged Its Falklands War*, Alison and Busby, London, 1982.

————, 'The Empire State', in Barnett, ed., *Power and the Throne: The Monarchy Debate*, Vintage/Charter 88, London, 1994, pp. 1–53.

Barratt Brown, Michael, 'Away with All the Great Arches: Anderson's History of British Capitalism', *New Left Review* no. 167, January/February 1988, pp. 22–51.

Benn, Tony, *Parliament, People, and Power: Agenda for a Free Society—Interviews with New Left Review*, Verso, London, 1982.

Benton, Ted, *The Rise and Fall of Structural Marxism: Althusser and His Influence*, Macmillan, London, 1984.

Berman, Marshall, *All That Is Solid Melts into Air: The Experience of Modernity*, Verso, London, 1983.

————, 'The Signs in the Street: A Response to Perry Anderson', *New Left Review* no. 144, March/April 1984, pp. 114–23.

Birchall, Ian, 'The Autonomy of Theory: A Short History of *New Left Review*', *International Socialism* no. 10, winter 1980, pp. 51–91.

Blackburn, Robin, 'Prologue to the Cuban Revolution', *New Left Review* no. 21, October 1963, pp. 52–91.

————, ed., *Ideology in Social Science: Readings in Critical Social Theory*, Fontana/Collins, Glasgow, 1972.

————, 'The Test in Portugal', *New Left Review* nos. 87/88, September/December 1974, pp. 5–46.

————, ed., *Revolution and Class Struggle: A Reader in Marxist Politics*, Fontana/Collins, Glasgow, 1977.

————, 'Theory and Experience', *New Statesman*, 18 July 1980, pp. 23–24.

————, ed., *After the Fall: The Failure of Communism and the Future of Socialism*, Verso, London and New York, 1991.

————, 'Fin de Siècle: Socialism after the Crash', in Blackburn, *After the Fall*, pp. 173–249.

————, 'A Brief History of *New Left Review*, 1960–1990', in *Thirty Years of New Left Review: Index to Numbers 1–184 (1960–1990)*, New Left Review, London, 1992, pp. v–xi.

————, 'The Ruins of Westminster', *New Left Review* no. 191, January/February 1992, pp. 5–35.

Blackburn, Robin, and Alexander Cockburn, eds., *The Incompatibles: Trade Union Militancy and the Consensus*, Penguin/New Left Review, Harmondsworth, 1967.

Brenner, Robert, 'Agrarian Class Structure and Economic Development in Pre-industrial Europe' (1976), in T. H. Aston and C. H. E. Philpin, eds., *The Brenner Debate: Agrarian Class Structure and Economic Development in Pre-industrial Europe*, Cambridge University Press, Cambridge, 1985, pp. 10–63.

————, 'The Agrarian Roots of European Capitalism' (1982), in T. H. Aston and C. H. E. Philpin, eds., *The Brenner Debate: Agrarian Class Structure and Economic Development in Pre-industrial Europe*, Cambridge University Press, Cambridge, 1985, pp. 213–327.

————, 'Why Is the United States at War with Iraq?', *New Left Review* no. 185, January/February 1991, pp. 122–37.

————, 'Uneven Development and the Long Downturn', *New Left Review* no. 229, May/June 1998.

Buhle, Paul, *Marxism in the USA from 1870 to the Present Day: Remapping the History of the American Left*, Verso, London, 1987.

Cain, P. J., and A. G. Hopkins, *British Imperialism: Innovation and Expansion, 1688–1914*, Longman, London and New York, 1993.

————, *British Imperialism: Crisis and Deconstruction, 1914–1990*, Longman, London and New York, 1993.

Callaghan, John, *British Trotskyism: Theory and Practice*, Blackwell, Oxford, 1984.

————, *The Far Left in British Politics*, Blackwell, Oxford, 1987.

Callinicos, Alex, 'Theory and Experience', *New Statesman*, 27 June 1980, pp. 969–70.
———, 'Perry Anderson and "Western Marxism"', *International Socialism* no. 23, spring 1984, pp. 113–28.
———, 'Exception or Symptom? The British Crisis and the World System', *New Left Review* no. 169, May/June 1988, pp. 97–106.
———, *Trotskyism*, Open University Press, Milton Keynes, 1990.
———, *Theories and Narratives: Reflections on the Philosophy of History*, Polity Press, Cambridge, 1995.
Callinicos, Alex, et al., 'An Open Letter to *New Left Review*', *International Socialism* no. 50, spring 1991, pp. 101–3.
Carr, E. H., *The October Revolution: Before and After*, Knopf, New York, 1969.
———, 'The Russian Revolution and the West' (interview), *New Left Review* no. 111, September/October 1978, pp. 25–36.
Charter 88, *Prospects and Plans for the Nineties*, Charter 88, London, 1990.
Chun, Lin, *The British New Left*, Edinburgh University Press, Edinburgh, 1993.
Coates, David, 'Labourism and the Transition to Socialism', *New Left Review* no. 129, September/October 1981, pp. 3–22.
———, *The Question of UK Decline: The Economy, State, and Society*, Harvester Wheatsheaf, Hemel Hempstead, 1994.
Cockburn, Alexander, and Robin Blackburn, eds., *Student Power: Problems, Diagnosis, Action*, Penguin/*New Left Review*, Harmondsworth, 1969.
Cohen, G. A., *Karl Marx's Theory of History: A Defence*, Oxford University Press, Oxford, 1978.
Colletti, Lucio, 'A Political and Philosophical Interview', *New Left Review* no. 86, July/August 1974, pp. 3–28.
Cox, Michael, 'The Revolutionary Betrayed: The *New Left Review* and Leon Trotsky' (1987), in Cox and Hillel Ticktin, eds., *The Ideas of Leon Trotsky*, Porcupine Press, London, 1995, pp. 289–304.
Davis, Mike, 'Nuclear Imperialism and Extended Deterrence', in *New Left Review*, ed., *Exterminism and Cold War*, pp. 35–64.
———, *Prisoners of the American Dream: Politics and Economy in the History of the US Working Class*, Verso, London, 1986.
Debray, Régis, *Revolution in the Revolution? Armed Struggle and Political Struggle in Latin America* (1967), trans. Bobbye Ortiz, Penguin, Harmondsworth, 1968.
———, *Strategy for Revolution*, ed. Robin Blackburn, Jonathan Cape, London, 1970.
———, *Modeste contribution aux discours et cérémonies officielles du dixième anniversaire*, François Maspero, Paris, 1978; partially translated in *New Left Review* no. 115, May/June 1979, pp. 45–65.
Deutscher, Isaac, *Russia after Stalin*, Hamish Hamilton, London, 1953.
———, *The Great Contest: Russia and the West*, Oxford University Press, London, 1960.
———, *The Unfinished Revolution: Russia, 1917–1967*, Oxford University Press, London, 1967.
———, *The Prophet Armed—Trotsky: 1879–1921* (1954), Oxford University Press, Oxford, 1979.
———, *The Prophet Unarmed—Trotsky: 1921–1929* (1959), Oxford University Press, Oxford, 1982.
———, *The Prophet Outcast—Trotsky: 1929–1940* (1963), Oxford University Press, Oxford, 1979.
———, *Marxism, Wars, and Revolutions: Essays from Four Decades*, ed. Tamara Deutscher, Verso, London, 1984.
Dews, Peter, *Logics of Disintegration: Post-structuralist Thought and the Claims of Critical Theory*, Verso, London and New York, 1987.

Dunn, John, 'An English Marxist Faces His Inquisitor', *New Society*, 12 June 1980, pp. 235–36.

Dworkin, Dennis, *Cultural Marxism in Postwar Britain: History, the New Left, and the Origins of Cultural Studies*, Duke University Press, Durham, N.C., and London, 1997.

Eagleton, Terry, *Criticism and Ideology: A Study in Marxist Literary Theory*, New Left Books, London, 1976.

———, 'Marxism, Structuralism, and Post-Structuralism' (1984), in Eagleton, *Against the Grain: Essays, 1975–1985*, Verso, London, 1986, pp. 89–98.

Elliott, Gregory, *Labourism and the English Genius: The Strange Death of Labour England?* Verso, London and New York, 1993.

———, 'Missing Ingredients', *Radical Philosophy* no. 68, autumn 1994, pp. 45–48.

———, 'Olympus Mislaid? A Profile of Perry Anderson', *Radical Philosophy* no. 71, May/June 1995, pp. 5–19.

Forgacs, David, 'Gramsci and Marxism in Britain', *New Left Review* no. 176, July/August 1989, pp. 70–88.

Fraser, Ronald, et al., *Nineteen Sixty-Eight: A Student Generation in Revolt*, Chatto and Windus, London, 1988.

Fukuyama, Francis, 'The End of History?', *National Interest* no. 16, summer 1989, pp. 3–18.

———, *The End of History and the Last Man* (1992), Penguin, Harmondsworth, 1993.

Gamble, Andrew, *Britain in Decline: Economic Policy, Political Strategy, and the British State* (1981), 2d ed., Macmillan, Houndmills, 1985.

Geras, Norman, 'Althusser's Marxism: An Account and Assessment' (1972), in Geras, *Literature of Revolution: Essays on Marxism*, Verso, London, 1986, pp. 91–131.

———, *Discourses of Extremity: Radical Ethics and Post-Marxist Extravagances*, Verso, London and New York, 1990.

Glucksmann, André, 'Strategy and Revolution in France, 1968', *New Left Review* no. 52, November/December 1968, pp. 67–121.

———, 'A Ventriloquist Structuralism' (1967), in *New Left Review*, ed., *Western Marxism: A Critical Reader*, pp. 282–314.

Gowan, Peter, 'The Polish Vortex: Solidarity and Socialism' (1983), in Ali, ed., *The Stalinist Legacy*, pp. 463–515.

———, 'The Gulf War, Iraq, and Western Liberalism', *New Left Review* no. 187, May/June 1991, pp. 21–70.

Gramsci, Antonio, *Selections from the Prison Notebooks*, ed. and trans. Quintin Hoare and Geoffrey Nowell Smith, Lawrence and Wishart, London, 1971.

Gray, John, 'Enlightenment Projects', *Times Literary Supplement*, 14 August 1992, pp. 4–5.

Hall, Stuart, 'Introducing NLR', *New Left Review* no. 1, January/February 1960, pp. 1–3.

———, 'The Supply of Demand', in E. P. Thompson et al., *Out of Apathy*, Stevens, London, 1960, pp. 56–97.

———, *The Hard Road to Renewal: Thatcherism and the Crisis of the Left*, Verso/*Marxism Today*, London and New York, 1988.

———, 'The "First" New Left: Life and Times', in Oxford University Socialist Discussion Group, *Out of Apathy*, pp. 11–38.

Hall, Stuart, et al., editorial, in *Universities and Left Review* vol. 1, no. 1, spring 1957, pp. i–ii.

Hall, Stuart, and Martin Jacques, eds., *The Politics of Thatcherism*, Lawrence and Wishart/*Marxism Today*, London, 1983.

———, eds., *New Times: The Changing Face of Politics in the 1990s*, Lawrence and Wishart/*Marxism Today*, London, 1989.

Halliday, Fred, 'Marxist Analysis and Post-revolutionary China', *New Left Review* no. 100, November 1976/January 1977, pp. 165–92.

———, 'The Sources of the New Cold War', in *New Left Review*, ed., *Exterminism and Cold War*, pp. 289–328.

———, *The Making of the Second Cold War* (1983), 2d ed., Verso, London, 1986.

———, 'The Legacy of 1968', *Interlink*, April 1988, pp. 22–23.

———, 'The Ends of Cold War' (1990), in Blackburn, *After the Fall*, pp. 78–99.

———, 'Reply to Edward Thompson', in Blackburn, *After the Fall*, pp. 110–14.

Heller, Agnes, Review of *Passages from Antiquity to Feudalism* and *Lineages of the Absolutist State*, by Perry Anderson, *Telos* no. 33, fall 1977, pp. 202–10.

Herf, Jeffrey, 'Science and Class or Philosophy and Revolution: Perry Anderson on Western Marxism', *Socialist Revolution* no. 35, September/October 1977, pp. 129–44.

Hinton, James, 'The Labour Aristocracy', *New Left Review* no. 32, July/August 1965, pp. 72–77.

Hirst, Paul Q., 'Anderson's Balance Sheet', in Hirst, *Marxism and Historical Writing*, Routledge and Kegan Paul, London, 1985, pp. 1–28.

———, 'The Uniqueness of the West—Perry Anderson's Analysis of Absolutism and Its Problems' (1975), in Hirst, *Marxism and Historical Writing*, Routledge and Kegan Paul, London, 1985, pp. 91–125.

Hitchens, Christopher, 'Theory and Experience', *New Statesman*, 13 June 1980, pp. 906–8.

Hobsbawm, Eric J., 'From Babylon to Manchester', *New Statesman*, 7 February 1975, pp. 177–78.

———, 'Look Left', *New Statesman*, 24 September 1976, pp. 408–11.

———, *Industry and Empire: From 1750 to the Present Day* (1968), Penguin, Harmondsworth, 1983.

———, *Politics for a Rational Left: Political Writing, 1977–1988*, Verso/*Marxism Today*, London and New York, 1989.

———, *Age of Extremes: The Short Twentieth Century, 1914–1991*, Michael Joseph, London, 1994.

———, *Revolutionaries: Contemporary Essays* (1973), Phoenix, London, 1994.

Hodgson, Geoff, *Socialism and Parliamentary Democracy*, Spokesman Press, Nottingham, 1977.

———, 'The Antinomies of Perry Anderson', in Hodgson, *Socialism and Parliamentary Democracy*, pp. 105–37.

Ingham, Geoffrey, *Capitalism Divided? The City and Industry in British Social Development*, Macmillan, Houndmills, 1984.

———, 'Commercial Capital and British Development: A Reply to Michael Barratt Brown', *New Left Review* no. 172, November/December 1988, pp. 45–65.

Jacoby, Russell, *Dialectic of Defeat: Contours of Western Marxism*, Cambridge University Press, Cambridge, 1981.

———, *The Last Intellectuals: American Culture in the Age of Academe*, Basic Books, New York, 1987.

Jacques, Martin, and Francis Mulhern, eds., *The Forward March of Labour Halted?* Verso/*Marxism Today*, London, 1981.

Jameson, Fredric, *Postmodernism, or The Cultural Logic of Late Capitalism*, Verso, London, 1990.

Jay, Martin, *Marxism and Totality: The Adventures of a Concept from Lukács to Habermas*, Polity Press, Cambridge, 1984.

Jessop, Bob, Kevin Bonnett, Simon Bromley, and Tom Ling, *Thatcherism: A Tale of Two Nations*, Polity Press, Cambridge, 1988.

Johnson, Richard, 'Barrington Moore, Perry Anderson, and English Social Development' (1976), in Stuart Hall et al., eds., *Culture, Media, Language*, Hutchinson, London, 1980, pp. 48–70.

Kenny, Michael, *The First New Left: British Intellectuals after Stalin*, Lawrence and Wishart, London, 1995.

Krassó, Nicolas, 'Trotsky's Marxism', *New Left Review* no. 44, July/August 1967, pp. 64–86.

———, 'Reply to Ernest Mandel', *New Left Review* no. 48, March/April 1968, pp. 90–103.

Laclau, Ernesto, and Chantal Mouffe, *Hegemony and Socialist Strategy: Towards a Radical Democratic Politics*, Verso, London, 1985.

Leys, Colin, 'The Formation of British Capital', *New Left Review* no. 160, November/ December 1986, pp. 114–20.

———, *Politics in Britain: From Labourism to Thatcherism* (1983), rev. ed., Verso, London and New York, 1989.

Lukács, Georg, *The Destruction of Reason* (1954), trans. Peter Palmer, Merlin Press, London, 1980.

McCarney, Joseph, *Social Theory and the Crisis of Marxism*, Verso, London and New York, 1990.

MacIntyre, Alasdair, *Against the Self-Images of the Age: Essays on Ideology and Philosophy*, Duckworth, London, 1971.

Macintyre, Stuart, *A Proletarian Science: Marxism in Britain, 1917–1933* (1980), Lawrence and Wishart, London, 1986.

MacRae, D. G., 'Chains of History', *New Society*, 30 January 1975, pp. 269–70.

Magri, Lucio, 'The May Events and Revolution in the West' (1968), trans. Chiara Ingrao and Chris Gilmore, in Ralph Miliband and John Saville, eds., *Socialist Register, 1969*, Merlin Press, London, 1969, pp. 29–53.

———, 'The European Left between Crisis and Refoundation', *New Left Review* no. 189, September/October 1991, pp. 5–18.

Malcomson, Scott L., 'Ten Thousand Megalomaniacs: Perry Anderson, Man of Steel', *Voice Literary Supplement*, March 1993, p. 21.

Mandel, Ernest, 'Trotsky's Marxism: An Anti-Critique', *New Left Review* no. 47, January/ February 1968, pp. 32–51.

———, 'Trotsky's Marxism: A Rejoinder', *New Left Review* no. 56, July/August 1969, pp. 69–96.

———, *From Stalinism to Eurocommunism: The Bitter Fruits of 'Socialism in One Country'* (1977), trans. Jon Rothschild, New Left Books, London, 1978.

———, 'On the Nature of the Soviet State' (interview), *New Left Review* no. 108, March/ April 1978, pp. 23–45.

———, *Revolutionary Marxism Today*, ed. Jon Rothschild, New Left Books, London, 1979.

Mayer, Arno J., *The Persistence of the Old Regime: Europe to the Great War*, Croom Helm, London, 1981.

Mepham, John, 'Goodbye to All That?', *Radical Philosophy* no. 16, spring 1977, pp. 39–41.

Merleau-Ponty, Maurice, *Adventures of the Dialectic* (1955), trans. Joseph Bien, North-western University Press, Evanston, Ill., 1973.

Merquior, J. G., *Western Marxism*, Paladin, London, 1986.

Miliband, Ralph, *Parliamentary Socialism: A Study in the Politics of Labour* (1961), 2d ed., Merlin Press, London, 1972.

———, 'Political Forms and Historical Materialism' (1975), in Miliband, *Class Power and State Power: Political Essays*, Verso, London, 1983, pp. 50–62.

———, 'The New Revisionism in Britain', *New Left Review* no. 150, March/April 1985, pp. 5–26.

Mitchell, Juliet, 'Women: The Longest Revolution', *New Left Review* no. 40, November/ December 1966, pp. 11–37.

Mulhern, Francis, *The Moment of 'Scrutiny'* (1979), Verso, London, 1981.

———, 'A Welfare Culture? Hoggart and Williams in the Fifties', *Radical Philosophy* no. 77, May/June 1996, pp. 26–37.

Nairn, Tom, 'Why It Happened', in Angelo Quattrocchi and Tom Nairn, *The Beginning of the End: France, May 1968*, Panther, London, 1968, pp. 103–75.

——, 'The English Working Class' (1964), in Blackburn, *Ideology in Social Science*, pp. 187–206.

——, *The Left against Europe?* (1972), Penguin/*New Left Review*, Harmondsworth, 1973.

——, 'Anatomy of the Labour Party' (1964), in Blackburn, *Revolution and Class Struggle*, pp. 314–73.

——, *The Break-up of Britain: Crisis and Neo-Nationalism* (1977), 2d ed., Verso, London, 1981.

——, 'The Sole Survivor', *New Left Review* no. 200, July/August 1993, pp. 41–47.

——, *The Enchanted Glass: Britain and Its Monarchy* (1988), 2d ed., Vintage, London, 1994.

New Left Review, ed., *Western Marxism: A Critical Reader*, New Left Books, London, 1977.

——, ed., *Exterminism and Cold War*, Verso, London, 1982.

Oxford University Socialist Discussion Group, ed., *Out of Apathy: Voices of the New Left Thirty Years On*, Verso, London and New York, 1989.

Pablo, Michel, 'On the Duration and Nature of the Transition from Capitalism to Socialism' (1951), in *Struggle in the Fourth International: International Secretariat Documents, 1951–1954*, vol. 1, Pathfinder Press, New York, 1974, pp. 12–16.

——, 'Where Are We Going?' (1951), in *Struggle in the Fourth International: International Secretariat Documents, 1951–1954*, vol. 1, Pathfinder Press, New York, 1974, pp. 4–12.

Poulantzas, Nicos, 'Marxist Political Theory in Britain' (1966), *New Left Review* no. 43, May/June 1967, pp. 57–74.

——, *State, Power, Socialism*, trans. Patrick Camiller, New Left Books, London, 1978.

Rowbotham, Sheila, Lynne Segal, and Hilary Wainwright, *Beyond the Fragments: Feminism and the Making of Socialism*, Merlin Press, London, 1979.

Rustin, Michael, *For a Pluralist Socialism*, Verso, London, 1985.

——, 'The New Left as a Social Movement', in Oxford University Socialist Discussion Group, *Out of Apathy*, pp. 117–28.

——, 'The Politics of Post-Fordism: Or, The Trouble with "New Times"', *New Left Review* no. 175, May/June 1989, pp. 54–77.

——, 'Citizenship and Charter 88', *New Left Review* no. 191, January/February 1992, pp. 37–42.

Samuel, Raphael, 'Born-Again Socialism', in Oxford University Socialist Discussion Group, *Out of Apathy*, pp. 39–57.

Sartre, Jean-Paul, *The Communists and Peace* (1952–54), trans. Irene Clephane, Hamish Hamilton, London, 1969.

——, *Between Existentialism and Marxism* (1972), trans. John Mathews, New Left Books, London, 1974.

——, *Critique of Dialectical Reason*. Vol. 1, *Theory of Practical Ensembles* (1960), trans. Alan Sheridan-Smith, New Left Books, London, 1976.

——, *Critique of Dialectical Reason*. Vol. 2, *The Intelligibility of History* (1985), trans. Quintin Hoare, Verso, London and New York, 1991.

Sassoon, Donald, 'The Silences of *New Left Review*', in *Politics and Power 3*, Routledge and Kegan Paul, London, 1981, pp. 219–54.

Schwarz, Bill, '"The People" in History: The Communist Party Historians' Group, 1946–1956', in Centre for Contemporary Cultural Studies, ed., *Making Histories: Studies in History-Writing and Politics*, Hutchinson, London, 1982, pp. 44–95.

Scruton, Roger, 'Perry Anderson', in Scruton, *Thinkers of the New Left*, Longman, London, 1985, pp. 129–43.

Sedgwick, Peter, 'The Two New Lefts' (1964), in Widgery, *The Left in Britain, 1956–1968*, pp. 131–53.

Skocpol, Theda, and Mary Fulbrook, 'From Antiquity to Late Capitalism', *Journal of Development Studies* vol. 13, no. 3, April 1977, pp. 290–95.

Sprinker, Michael, 'Between Science and Ideology: Historical Determination in the Work of Perry Anderson', in Sprinker, *Imaginary Relations: Aesthetics and Ideology in the Theory of Historical Materialism*, Verso, London and New York, 1987, pp. 207–36.

———, ' "Dancing in the Dark": Perry Anderson on Socialism's Impasse', *Radical History Review* no. 57, 1993, pp. 98–115.

Stedman Jones, Gareth, 'The Marxism of the Early Lukács' (1971), in *New Left Review*, ed., *Western Marxism*, pp. 12–60.

Stephanson, Anders, and Cornel West, 'The British and the Rational', *Socialist Review* no. 84, November/December 1984, pp. 123–29.

Therborn, Göran, 'From Petrograd to Saigon', *New Left Review* no. 48, March/April 1968, pp. 3–11.

———, 'The Frankfurt School' (1970–71), in *New Left Review*, ed., *Western Marxism*, pp. 83–139.

———, 'Dialectics of Modernity: On Critical Theory and the Legacy of Twentieth-Century Marxism', *New Left Review* no. 215, January/February 1996, pp. 59–81.

Thompson, Duncan, 'The Moment of *New Left Review*, 1960–1992', D. Phil. thesis, University of Brighton, 1997.

Thompson, Edward P., 'At the Point of Decay', in Thompson et al., *Out of Apathy*, Stevens, London, 1960, pp. 3–15.

———, 'Revolution', in Thompson et al., *Out of Apathy*, Stevens, London, 1960, pp. 287–308.

———, 'The Marx Claimants', *Guardian*, 16 September 1976, p. 7.

———, 'Through the Smoke of Budapest', *Reasoner* no. 3, November 1956, supplement, pp. 1–7; reprinted in Widgery, *The Left in Britain, 1956–1968*, pp. 66–72.

———, *William Morris: Romantic to Revolutionary* (1955), rev. ed., Pantheon, New York, 1977.

———, 'Outside the Whale' (1960), in Thompson, *The Poverty of Theory and Other Essays*, Merlin Press, London, 1978, pp. 1–33.

———, 'The Peculiarities of the English' (1965), in Thompson, *The Poverty of Theory and Other Essays*, Merlin Press, London, 1978, pp. 35–91.

———, 'The Poverty of Theory: or an Orrery of Errors' (1978), in Thompson, *The Poverty of Theory and Other Essays*, Merlin Press, London, 1978, pp. 193–397.

———, *The Making of the English Working Class* (1963), 3d ed., Penguin, Harmondsworth, 1980.

———, *Writing by Candlelight*, Merlin Press, London, 1980.

———, 'The Politics of Theory' (1979), in Raphael Samuel, ed., *People's History and Socialist Theory*, Routledge and Kegan Paul, London, 1981, pp. 396–408.

———, 'Notes on Exterminism, the Last Stage of Civilization' (1980), in *New Left Review*, ed., *Exterminism and Cold War*, pp. 1–33.

———, 'The Ends of Cold War: A Rejoinder' (1990), in Blackburn, *After the Fall*, pp. 100–109.

Threlfall, Monica, ed., *Mapping the Women's Movement: Feminist Politics and Social Transformation in the North*, Verso, London and New York, 1996.

Timpanaro, Sebastiano, *The Freudian Slip: Psychoanalysis and Textual Criticism* (1974), trans. Kate Soper, New Left Books, London, 1976.

———, *On Materialism* (1970), trans. Lawrence Garner, rev. ed., Verso, London, 1980.

Tredell, Nicholas, 'Modern Tragedy', *P. N. Review* vol. 19, no. 1, September/October 1992, pp. 66–70.

Trotsky, Leon, *The Revolution Betrayed: What Is the Soviet Union and Where Is It Going?* (1937), trans. Max Eastman, Pathfinder Press, New York, 1980.

———, *In Defense of Marxism: The Social and Political Contradictions of the Soviet Union* (1942), Pathfinder Press, New York, 1990.

Wald, Alan M., *The New York Intellectuals: The Rise and Decline of the Anti-Stalinist Left from the 1930s to the 1980s*, University of North Carolina Press, Chapel Hill, 1987.

Warren, Bill, *Imperialism: Pioneer of Capitalism*, ed. John Sender, New Left Books, London, 1980.

Widgery, David, comp., *The Left in Britain, 1956–1968*, Penguin, Harmondsworth, 1976.

Williams, Raymond, ed., *May Day Manifesto, 1968*, Penguin, Harmondsworth, 1968.

———, 'Notes on British Marxism since the War', *New Left Review* no. 100, November 1976/January 1977, pp. 81–94.

———, *Politics and Letters: Interviews with New Left Review*, New Left Books, London, 1979.

———, *Culture and Society, 1780–1950* (1958), Penguin, Harmondsworth, 1984.

———, *The Long Revolution* (1961), Penguin, Harmondsworth, 1984.

Wolff, Richard D., 'Western Marxism', *Monthly Review* vol. 30, no. 4, September 1978, pp. 55–64.

Wood, Ellen Meiksins, *The Retreat from Class: A New 'True' Socialism*, Verso, London, 1986.

———, 'Rational Choice Marxism: Is the Game Worth the Candle?', *New Left Review* no. 177, September/October 1989, pp. 41–88.

———, *The Pristine Culture of Capitalism: A Historical Essay on Old Regimes and Modern States*, Verso, London and New York, 1991.

———, 'A Chronology of the New Left and Its Successors, or: Who's Old-Fashioned Now?', in Leo Panitch et al., eds., *Socialist Register, 1995*, Merlin Press, London, 1995, pp. 22–49.

Wood, Neal, *Communism and British Intellectuals*, Victor Gollancz, London, 1959.

Index

absolutism, 78, 79, 81, 82, 85, 115, 121, 153, 161, 281
Adorno, Theodor, 53, 54, 88, 96, 97, 289
aesthetic relativism, 287
aesthetics, 50, 51, 97, 199
Afghanistan, 138, 143, 148, 225, 270, 275
Africa, 6, 29; southern, 6, 41, 94, 143
Against the Current, 190, 277
Ahmad, Aijaz, 178
Albania, 73
Algeria, 6, 41
Ali, Tariq, 164, 223, 234, 286; *The Coming British Revolution*, 71; *Revolution from Above*, 223; 'Socialists and the Crisis of Labourism', 164
Althusser, Louis, xvii, 32, 34, 38, 45, 48, 53, 54, 56, 76, 87–89, 90, 95, 96, 97, 104, 105, 109, 112, 114, 122–27, 130, 135, 136, 139, 172, 176, 260, 261, 267, 270, 285; 'A propos de l'article de Michel Verret sur "mai étudiant" ', 263; 'Contradiction and Overdetermination', 34, 53, 88; 'The Crisis of Marxism', 284; *Ecrits philosophiques et politiques, Tome I*, 284; *Ecrits philosophiques et politiques, Tome II*, 285; *Essays on Ideology*, 267; *For Marx*, 34; 'Freud and Lacan', 54; *Lenin and Philosophy*, 259; 'Letter from Louis Althusser', 271; 'Marx dans ses limites', 284; 'Note on "The Critique of the Personality Cult" ', 267; *Politics and History*, 259; *Reading 'Capital'*, 34, 126; 'Reply to John Lewis', 89; 'Sur Lévi-Strauss', 285; 'What Must Change in the Party', 270
Althusserianism, 33, 34, 39, 48, 56, 85, 88, 123, 129, 130, 176
Amendola, Giorgio, 6, 112, 270
Anderson, Benedict, 1, 247
Anderson, Perry, works by: 'The Affinities of Norberto Bobbio' (1988), 203; 'Agendas for Radical History' (1986), 263, 274, 283, 289; 'The Antinomies of Antonio Gramsci' (1976), 31, 77, 112–18, 121, 129, 192, 250, 260, 270,

271, 280, 300; *Arguments within English Marxism* (1980), xviii, 12, 41, 59, 90, 108, 112, 122–37, 140, 180, 191, 201, 202, 222, 223, 246, 248, 249, 250, 252–57, 259–65, 267, 269, 271, 273, 279, 283, 284, 293, 295, 298; 'Comment on Beckett's "Stones" ' (1968), 60; 'Comment on Chester's "For a Rock Aesthetic" ' (1970), 60; 'Comment: Power, Politics, and the Enlightenment' (1994), 294, 296, 297, 298; 'The Common and the Particular' (1989), 262, 272, 289, 298; 'Communist Party History' (1981), 245, 252, 262; 'Components of the National Culture' (1968), 1, 38, 46–53, 54, 55, 56, 86, 95, 102, 109, 139, 192, 194, 196, 198, 199, 201, 202, 205, 206, 211, 244, 248, 257, 261, 264, 289; *Considerations on Western Marxism* (1976), xviii, 39, 52, 54, 64, 89, 90, 95–108, 109, 110, 127, 136, 149, 171, 172, 177, 180, 193, 198, 201, 202, 241, 268, 269, 270, 273, 276, 283, 288, 299; correspondence with Bobbio (1989), 224, 239; 'Critique of Wilsonism' (1964), 18–20; 'Cuba, Free Territory of America' (1960), 2; 'A Culture in Contraflow' (1990), 52, 55, 109, 193–203, 205, 206, 212, 216, 219, 220, 222, 240, 289, 293, 294; 'Darkness Falls' (1994), 238, 300; 'The Dark Side of Brazilian Conviviality' (1994), 239; *Democracia y Socialismo: La lucha democrática desde una perspectiva socialista* (1988), 299; 'Diary' (on E. P. Thompson) (1993), 250, 272, 274, 295; 'Diary' (on South Korea) (1996), 239, 245, 273; 'Editorial Note', *Western Marxism: A Critical Reader* (1977), 273; 'The Ends of History' (1992), xv, 204, 222–39, 241, 288; *The Ends of History*, xi, 244; *English Questions* (1992), xii, xiv, 13, 21, 31, 35, 47, 48, 82, 121, 190, 194, 195, 205, 234, 244,

247, 250, 251, 253, 256, 257, 258, 277, 288, 290–94; 'The Europe to Come' (1996), 219–222; 'The Figures of Descent' (1987), 31, 205–16, 247, 251, 291; 'The Founding Moment' (1969), 71–77, 262, 263; 'The Future of the Left' (1998), 290; 'Geoffrey de Ste. Croix and the Ancient Greek World' (1983), 283; 'High Jinks at the Plaza' (1992), 289; ' "Imperialism—Pioneer of Capitalism" ' (1980–81), 265, 273; *In the Tracks of Historical Materialism* (1983), xviii, 55, 108, 146, 171–83, 185, 191, 198, 199, 222, 237, 246, 259, 261, 263, 267, 269, 274, 276, 277, 283, 285, 287, 288, 298; 'The Intransigent Right at the End of the Century' (1992), 202; introduction to Adorno (1971), 266; introduction to Brecht on Lukács (1974), 266; introduction to Central Committee of PCI (1962), 5; introduction to Della Volpe (1970), 88, 266; introduction to Glucksmann (1972), 88, 266; introduction to Gramsci (1968), 60, 85; introduction to Lukács on Benjamin and Brecht (1978), 266; introduction to Magri (1971), 106, 266; introduction to Medvedev (1974), 266; introduction to NLR no. 52 (1968), 62; introduction to Timpanaro (1974), 266; introduction to Tukhachevsky (1969), 59, 85, 265; introduction to Vilar (1973), 266; introduction to 'Wittgenstein in Russia' (1972), 258; 'Laboring under False Pretences in Latin America' (1988), 262, 295; 'Le capitalisme après le communisme', 298; 'The Left in the Fifties' (1965), 12, 28, 144; 'The Legacy of Isaac Deutscher' (1984), 60, 162, 186, 245, 248, 260, 270, 280, 281, 285; 'The Light of Europe' (1991), 205, 212, 215–19, 237, 238, 277, 291, 293; 'The Limits and Possibilities of Trade Union Action' (1967), 43–45, 255; *Lineages of the Absolutist State* (1974), 55, 77–86, 106, 114, 126, 127, 244, 253, 264, 272; *Mapping the West European Left*, 237, 239, 252, 282, 293; 'Marshall Berman: Modernity and Revolution' (1983), 186–87, 191, 287; 'Maurice Thomson's War' (1993), 263,

289, 291; 'Max Weber and Ernest Gellner: Science, Politics, Enchantment' (1992), 285; 'Memo on Socialism and Feminism' (1986), 286; 'Michael Mann's Sociology of Power' (1986), 194; 'NLR's Charter: Socialism and Feminism' (1984/5), 287; 'Nocturnal Enquiry: Carlo Ginzburg' (1990), 285; 'Notes on the Poverty of Theory', 122; 'Notes on "Why the American Working Class Is Different" ' (1980), 285; 'The Notion of Bourgeois Revolution' (1992), 80, 121–22, 279; 'On Emplotment— Andreas Hillgruber' (1990), 298; 'On John Rawls' (1994), 297; 'On Some Postulates of an Anti-systemic Policy in Western Europe', 188; 'On the Relations between Existing and Alternative Socialism' (1983), 277; *The Origins of Postmodernity* (1998), 287–88; 'Origins of the Present Crisis' (1964), 14–18, 20, 31, 38, 43, 49, 52, 77, 79, 84, 205, 206, 208, 209, 210, 211, 212, 213, 215, 251, 254, 292; *Passages from Antiquity to Feudalism* (1974), xi, 55, 77–86, 125, 126, 244, 263–64; 'The Pluralism of Isaiah Berlin' (1990), 192; 'Polish Document: A Presentation' (1972), 87; 'The Politics of the Common Market', 4; 'Portugal and the End of Ultra-colonialism' (1962), 6–7, 11; 'Postscript to "Modernity and Revolution" ' (1985), 188, 285; 'Postscript to Preface, *Marxism, Wars and Revolutions*' (1991), 161, 236; Preface, 'An Interview with Jiri Pelikan' (1972), 87; 'Problems of Socialist Strategy' (1965), xviii, 20–32, 38, 42, 43, 53, 72, 77, 84, 113, 114, 117, 118, 129, 201, 211, 253, 268, 279; 'Publisher's Note' (1979), 266; *The Question of Europe*, 220, 294; 'Reader's Note' (1996), 265, 294, 297; 'Roberto Unger and the Politics of Empowerment' (1989), 274, 293; 'Social Democracy Today' (1986), 277; 'The Social-Democratic Parabola' (1992), 277; 'Socialism and Pseudo-Empiricism' (1966), 34, 37–40, 60, 157, 192, 206, 248, 249, 250, 254, 255, 272, 273, 279; 'State and Revolution in the West' (1970), 31, 71, 77, 115–16, 263;

'The Strategic Option: Some Questions' (1978), 118–21; 'Sweden: Mr Crosland's Dreamland' (1961), 2–3, 247; 'Sweden II: Study in Social Democracy', 2–3, 247; 'Trotsky's Interpretation of Stalinism' (1982), 149, 152, 180, 183, 192, 222, 225, 234, 246, 279, 280, 295; 'Under the Sign of the Interim' (1996), 219–22, 294, 299; 'Western Marxism: An Introduction' (1974), 95, 269; *A Zone of Engagement* (1992), xii, xiv, xvi, 113, 156, 162, 188, 192, 193, 194, 203, 205, 234, 246, 270, 274, 280, 281, 284, 285, 288, 292, 293, 298, 300
Anglo-Marxism, xvi, 39, 140, 171
Angola, 94, 138
Annales, 127
Annan, Lord, 50
Anse, Tobias: 'Judging the PCI', 282
anticapitalism, 24, 75, 88, 155, 165, 189, 190, 222
anticommunism, 139, 141, 144, 162
anti-imperialism, 68, 75, 76, 184
anti-Marxism, 168, 170, 171, 172, 179, 192, 198
antinaturalism, epistemological, 123
antinomianism, 187
antipostmodernism, 179
antiquarianism, 79
antiquity, legacy from, 81, 85
antireformism, 132, 184
antirevisionism, 168, 169
antirevolutionism, 151
anti-Sovietism, 120
anti-Stalinism, xvii, 149, 150, 157
antisystemic politics, 189, 190
aristocracy, 13, 36, 116, 121, 153, 161, 208, 211: hegemonic, 15, 212, 213, 214
Aron, Raymond, 284
Aronson, Ronald, 182
Arrighi, Giovanni: 'World Income Inequalities and the Future of Socialism', 297
Ash, Timothy Garton, 294
Asia, 29, 42, 151, 155
assembly, rights of, 115
Atlanticism, 1, 148, 189
atomic bomb, 186
Attlee, Clement, 17
attrition, strategy of, 116

Aubert, Claude: 'People's Communes— How to Use the Standard Visits', 267
Aussenpolitik, 220
Australasia, 239
Australia, 238
autocritique, 91, 95, 244
axiomatics, 134
Ayer, A. J.: *The Revolution in Philosophy*, 257

Bachelard, Gaston, 123
Bad Godesberg, 23
Bagehot, Walter, 33
Bahro, Rudolf: *The Alternative in Eastern Europe*, 132, 277, 284; *From Red to Green: Interviews with New Left Review*, 277; 'The SPD and the Peace Movement', 276
Bakunin, Mikhail, 187
Balibar, Etienne, 54, 112, 126, 127; *On the Dictatorship of the Proletariat*, 112; *The Philosophy of Marx*, 273; *Reading 'Capital'*, 54, 88
Balkans, 151, 155
Balogh, Thomas, 7, 21
Bandaranaike, Sirimavo, 90
Bangladesh, 90
Barbarism, 238, 286
Barker, Colin: *The Development of British Capitalist Society: A Marxist Debate*, 291–92
Barnett, Anthony, 6, 46, 70, 86, 105, 111, 163, 183, 213, 216, 276, 292: 'The Empire State', 292–93; 'Introduction to Western Marxism: Some Preliminary Comments', 269; *Iron Britannia*, 163, 281; *Power and the Throne: The Monarchy Debate*, 292–93; 'Raymond Williams and Marxism: A Rejoinder', 272; 'A Revolutionary Student Movement', 256; *Soviet Freedom*, 295
Barnett, Corelli: *Collapse of British Power*, 211
Barratt Brown, Michael, 213, 261
Bauer, Otto, 96, 103, 119
Baxter, Liam: 'Discussion on the Strategy of People's Democracy', 265
Beach Boys, 60
Beatles, 60
Beauvoir, Simone de, 6, 172: *The Second Sex*, 284

Benjamin, Walter, 53, 54: *Charles Baudelaire*, 259; *One-Way Street and Other Writings*, 266; *Understanding Brecht*, 259
Benn, Tony, 164, 166, 205, 281, 282; *Parliament, People and Power: Agenda for a Free Society—Interviews with New Left Review*, 163, 164, 166, 281
Bensaïd, Daniel: *Mai 68: Une répétition générale*, 263; *Marx l'intempestif: Grandeurs et misères d'une aventure critique (xixè–xxè siècles)*, 280
Benton, Ted: *The Rise and Fall of Structural Marxism*, 272
Bergquist, Charles: *Labor in Latin America*, 262, 272
Berlin, Germany, 46, 50, 51, 211
Berlin, Sir Isaiah, 194; *Karl Marx: His Life and Environment*, 38
Berlinguer, Enrico, 118
Berman, Marshall, 187, 191, 192; *All That Is Solid Melts into Air*, 187
Bernal, Martin, 239
Bernstein, Eduard, 185
Bertram, Christopher: *Has History Ended? Fukuyama, Marx, Modernity*, 296
Bettelheim, Charles: *China since Mao*, 266; *Economic Calculation and Forms of Property*, 266; 'The Great Leap Backwards', 266
Bidet, Jacques: *Cent ans de marxisme: Bilan critique et perspectives*, 298
Birchall, Ian: 'The Autonomy of Theory: A Short History of *New Left Review*', 267, 279
Birmingham Centre, 199
Blackbourn, David: *The Peculiarities of German History: Bourgeois Society and Politics in Nineteenth-Century Germany*, 254, 292
Blackburn, Robin, 6, 42, 45, 46, 55, 63, 71, 86, 90, 94, 111, 140, 165, 166, 183, 186, 226, 232, 235, 236: *After the Fall: The Failure of Communism and the Future of Socialism*, 226, 232, 234, 295; 'Brief Guide to Bourgeois Ideology', 46, 256–57, 268; 'Brief History of *New Left Review*', 59, 63, 183, 248, 282; 'Cuba, Free Territory of America', 2; *Explosion in a Subcontinent: India, Pakistan, Bangladesh and Ceylon*, 54–55, 266;

Ideology in Social Science, 55, 257, 259; *The Incompatibles*, 42, 122, 255; 'Ireland and the NLR', 265; 'Let It Bleed', 265; 'Notes on the English Political Crisis', 282; 'The Politics of "The First Circle" ', 265; 'Prologue to the Cuban Revolution', 248; *Revolution and Class Struggle*, 55, 251; 'The Ruins of Westminster', 293; 'Theory and Experience', 276; *Towards Socialism*, 20, 122, 163, 251; 'The Unequal Society', 42
Black Dwarf, 71
Blair, Tony, 239
Bloch, Ernst, 103; *Aesthetics and Politics*, 266
Bobbio, Norberto, 192, 194, 203, 204, 224, 226, 240; *Left and Right*, 203, 239; 'Upturned Utopia', 226, 295
Bolivia, 45
Bolshevism, 57, 72, 82–83, 157–58, 184, 222
Bordiga, Amadeo, 116
Bourbons, 161
Bourdet, Claude, 2
bourgeois culture, 34, 47
bourgeois democracy, 77, 82, 84, 98, 99, 106, 107, 108, 137, 208
bourgeois ideology, 49, 53, 103
bourgeois paradigm, 36, 80, 210
bourgeois politics, 62, 164, 167, 170
bourgeois revolution, 5, 13, 15, 21, 30, 33, 35–37, 60, 70, 74, 77, 78, 79, 80, 81, 85, 121, 142, 190, 207, 208, 212, 223
bourgeois state, 61, 121, 137
bourgeois theory, 194, 198
bourgeoisie, 13–17, 32, 37, 47, 49, 50, 113, 121, 122, 153, 156, 161, 210, 214, 236
Braudel, Fernand, xiv, 194, 245–46; *Écrits sur l'histoire*, 246; *The Mediterranean and the Mediterranean World in the Age of Philip II*, 246
Brazil, 239, 286, 299
Brecht, Bertolt, 88
Brenner, Johanna: 'Rethinking Women's Oppression', 287
Brenner, Robert, 79, 80: 'Agrarian Class Structure and Economic Development in Preindustrial Europe', 79, 263; *Merchants and revolution*, 80, 263, 289;

'The Origins of Capitalist Development: A Critique of Neo-Smithian Marxism', 263; *Uneven Development and the Long Downturn*, 291; 'Why Is the United States at War with Iraq?', 297
Brewster, Ben, 6, 40, 56, 267
Brezhnev, Leonid, 147, 223, 225
Brezhnevism, 76, 163
Britain, 7, 9, 11, 13, 18, 25, 28, 30, 38, 39, 42, 47, 49, 53, 55, 62, 63, 64, 65, 67, 77, 94, 101, 108, 134, 143, 152, 165, 169, 173, 178, 189, 195, 197, 198, 199, 208, 210, 212, 219; capitalism in, 14, 15, 18, 167, 207, 209, 213, 215; culture of, 48, 49, 143, 198; decline of, 36, 199, 209, 214; economy of, 7, 51, 86, 213, 214, 215; history of, 12, 29, 210, 245; politics in, 26, 205, 216, 217; relationship with continental Europe, 177; society in, 10, 15, 18, 28, 31, 39, 202, 217. *See also* United Kingdom
British Constitution, 33, 34, 134
British Labour Movement, 4
British Left, 4, 21, 86, 164, 165
British Marxism, 9, 10, 11, 32, 35, 38
Bromley, Simon: 'Globalization?', 291
Browderism, 165
Buhle, Paul, 177; *Marxism in the USA from 1870 to the Present Day: Remapping the History of the American Left*, 282, 284
Bukharin, Nikolai, 96
Bukovskyite dissidents, 163
bureaucratized socialism, 96
Burke, Edmund, 25
Burnham, James, 260, 278, 279
Burton, Neil G.: *China since Mao*, 266

Caetano, 94
Cain, P. J., 214, 215; *British Imperialism: Crisis and Deconstruction, 1914–1990*, 292; *British Imperialism: Innovation and Expansion, 1688–1914*, 214, 292
California, 191
Callaghan, James, 190, 209, 218
Callaghan, John: *British Trotskyism: Theory and Practice*, 262, 279; *The Far Left in British Politics*, 262, 279
Callinicos, Alex, xii, 179, 213, 236, 276, 284, 297, 299: 'Open Letter to *New Left Review*', 297; 'Perry Anderson and

"Western Marxism" ', 284, 285; *The Revenge of History: Marxism and the East European Revolutions*, 298; *Theories and Narratives: Reflections on the Philosophy of History*, 298; *Trotskyism*, 278, 279, 299
Calvez, Jean-Yves: *La pensée de Karl Marx*, 28, 38, 254
Cambodian revolution, 275
Cambridge Journal of Economics, 275
Camiller, Patrick, 287: *Mapping the West European Left*, 237, 239, 252, 282, 293; 'Spanish Socialism in the Atlantic Order', 282
Campaign for Nuclear Disarmament (CND), 4
campus unrest, 69, 196
Canguilhem, Georges, 123
Cape, Jonathan, 71
capital, 182, 188, 191, 196, 233, 234, 236; agrarian, 121; globalization of, 237; industrial, 121; internationalization of, 217, 233; labour and, 44; mercantile, 121
capitalism, 15, 20, 22, 23, 28, 37, 41, 42, 44, 57, 69, 102, 136, 137, 146, 148, 149, 160, 161, 162, 188, 189, 193, 227, 230, 235, 236, 247; abolition of, 35, 44, 83, 85, 156; advanced, 135, 148, 152, 195; contemporary, 233; continental, 4, 233; deregulated, 238; eastern, 236; industrial, 132; liberal, 236; metropolitan, 117; national, 130; overthrow of, 148; post-Reaganite, 238; postwar, 55, 155; private, 154; state, 160, 236; Western, 236; Western European, 262
capitalist countries, advanced, 134, 144, 162
capitalist economies, 191, 193, 195, 212
capitalist mode of production, 82, 83, 96, 213, 231
capitalist power, 70, 208, 230
capitalist restoration, 161, 191, 223, 224
capitalist revolution, 37
capitalist society, 24, 152, 184, 220, 222, 235
capitalist state, 81, 82, 83, 85, 106, 107, 153, 208, 222
capitalist world, 147, 189, 210, 230
Carr, E. H., xi, 154, 159, 243, 244, 298: *History of Soviet Russia*, xi, 243;

'Interview', 243; 'Isaac Deutscher: In Memoriam', 298; *The October Revolution: Before and After*, 280; 'The Russian Revolution and the West', 275; 'The Tragedy of Trotsky', 280; *What Is History?* 257

Carrillo, Santiago, Communist party of, 118

Carron's law, 18

Carroué, Laurent: 'Les travailleurs coréens à l'assaut du dragon', 299

Carter, Jimmy, 138

Castoriadis, Cornelius, 104

Castro, Fidel, xiii, 2, 45

Central America, 94, 143

Central Bank, 219, 220

Central Europe, 96, 120

Centre for Contemporary Cultural Studies, 130; *Making Histories: Studies in History-Writing and Politics*, 250, 272

Ceylon, 90

Charter 88, 46, 134, 201, 216, 219

Chechnya, 225

Chile, 134

China, 1, 22, 40, 45, 56, 59, 60, 65, 67, 68, 71, 90, 93, 107, 138, 142, 147, 148, 156, 157, 173, 191, 222, 223, 226, 235, 238, 247, 262, 266

Chinese communism, 93, 284

Chinese revolution, 57, 58, 59, 68, 89, 91

Chinese socialism, 37

Chitty, Andrew: *Has History Ended? Fukuyama, Marx, Modernity*, 296

Chomsky, Noam, 276

Choshu clan, 37

Christian Democracy, 23, 118, 221, 233

Christiansen, Niels Finn: 'Denmark: End of the Idyll', 282

Chun, Lin, 35; *The British New Left*, 247, 249, 250, 260, 277

Churchill, Winston, xiii

civil society, 17, 18, 22, 23, 24, 25, 27, 29, 31, 113, 116, 117, 214

Clark, J. C. D., 199

class, 30, 44, 67, 76, 115, 117, 125, 126, 145, 149, 152, 153, 155, 206

class character, 157, 160, 161

class consciousness, 15–16, 26, 33, 43, 44, 84, 206

class forces, 79, 156

class power, 16, 80, 133, 153, 207

class structure, 15, 66, 102, 125, 145, 151, 178, 181

class struggle, 67, 111, 144, 146, 147

class system, 27

classical tradition, 105, 171

Claudin, Fernando: 'Democracy and Dictatorship in Lenin and Kautsky', 270; *Eurosocialism and Communism*, 112

Cliff, Tony, 104, 154, 159

Clinton, Bill, 239

Clio, 241

Coates, David, 164, 210, 211, 213, 214, 215; 'Labourism and the Transition to Socialism', 281; 'Space and Agency in the Transition to Socialism', 281

Coates, Ken, 145; 'The Choices before Labour', 281; 'The Peace Movement and Socialism', 276

Cockburn, Alexander, 6, 71; 'The Freeze Movement versus Reagan', 276; *The Incompatibles*, 42, 122, 255; *Student Power: Problems, Diagnosis, Action*, 46, 122, 248, 256, 257, 299

Cockburn, Claud, 42

Cohen, G. A., 124, 126, 127, 195; *Karl Marx's Theory of History*, 124, 195, 265, 272, 283

Cold War, 1, 4, 9, 10, 11, 12, 21, 28, 30, 94, 96, 130, 144, 145, 147, 152, 155, 162, 163, 225; new, 138, 148; second, 30, 61, 101, 111, 142, 143, 144, 147, 149, 157, 162, 170, 222; stereotypes, 165; theory of, 12

Cole, G. D. H., 2

collective labourer, 175, 181, 233

collectivism, bureaucratic, 152, 154

collectivist conspiracy, 196

Colletti, Lucio, 32, 54, 87, 88, 100, 109, 135, 136, 139, 160, 176; *From Rousseau to Lenin*, 259; *Marxism and Hegel*, 89, 259; 'A Political and Philosophical Interview', 88, 266, 274; 'The Question of Stalin', 87, 88

colonialism, 144, 155

Colossus, 225

Cominform, 10, 74

Comintern, 10, 58, 64, 72, 73, 116, 155

Commission on Social Justice, 197

Common Market, 4, 7, 18, 205, 208

communism, 1, 3, 21, 23, 25, 33, 34, 70, 72, 99, 101, 105, 108, 122, 135, 136,

138, 146, 181, 197, 216, 217, 226, 227, 231, 236, 243, 244; British, 149; collapse of, 161, 204, 205, 222, 225, 230, 234, 238; contemporary, 72; European, 72, 73, 86, 130; French, 6, 75, 98; international, 9, 58, 59, 68, 90, 100, 172, 182; Italian, 6, 13, 18, 25, 41, 74, 76, 116; official, 100, 149; second wave of, 73; Western, 40, 61, 87; West European, 234
communist parties, 69, 72–76, 101, 112, 118, 165, 167; Chinese, 120; Czech, 112; German, 116; Greek, 284; Latin American, 282; Spanish, 76; Western European, 261
Communist Party of Great Britain (CPGB), 7, 8, 9, 13, 42, 64, 92, 132, 165; *The British Road to Socialism*, 10
comparative history, 81, 84, 108
competition, 142, 209, 229, 180
Conference of Socialist Economists, 275
Connolly, Bernard, 294
consciousness, 19, 20, 25, 26; corporate, 43; national, 66; political, 43; revolutionary, 47; socialist, 43–44; working-class, 44
consequentialism, 128, 135
conservatism, 17, 18, 86, 104, 165, 209, 212
constitutional reform, 201, 206
constitutionalism, 10
Continental theory, 33, 64
conventionalism, 123
Corn Laws, repeal of, 15
corporate ideology, 16
corporate working class, 210
corporatism, 17, 25, 26, 43, 47
corporatist institutions, 17
cosmopolitanism, 31, 198
Cotterill, David: *The Serge-Trotsky Papers*, 269
counterrevolution, 15, 69, 133, 151, 155, 156, 184, 197, 222
Cox, Mick: *The Ideas of Leon Trotsky*, 279; 'The Revolutionary Betrayed: *The New Left Review* and Leon Trotsky', 279
Cripps, Francis: 'The British Crisis—Can the Left Win?' 281
Critica Marxista, 18
critical theory, 174, 238
Croce, Benedetto, 25, 39, 97

Croix, Geoffrey de Ste.: *Class Struggle in the Ancient Greek World*, 192, 283
Cromwell, Oliver, 13
Croslandite revisionism, 12
Crossman, Richard, 21
Cuba, 5, 6, 40, 41, 45, 59, 107, 129, 138, 186, 242, 276, 295
Cultural Revolution, 32, 45, 48, 56, 59, 60, 65, 68, 90, 91, 191, 197, 260, 262
culturalism, 9, 15, 16, 25, 32, 36, 47, 52, 53, 117, 206, 211
Czechoslovakia, 60, 73, 87, 147

Daly, Lawrence, 8
Darwinism, 33, 34
Davis, Mike, 111, 145, 277, 285, 286; 'Nuclear Imperialism and Extended Deterrence', 145, 276, 277; *Prisoners of the American Dream: Politics and Economy in the History of the U.S. Working Class*, 283
De Gaulle, Charles, xi, 4, 220
de Man, Paul, 228
Debray, Régis, 45, 137, 191, 227; *A Critique of Arms*, 271; *Loués soient nos seigneurs: Une éducation politique*, 280; 'A Modest Contribution to the Rites and Ceremonies of the Tenth Anniversary', 275, 288; 'Problems of Revolutionary Strategy', 45, 256; *Revolution in the Revolution? Armed Struggle and Political Struggle in Latin America*, 45, 256, 300; *Strategy for Revolution*, 255, 256; *Teachers, Writers, Celebrities: The Intellectuals of Modern France*, 267
de-industrialization, 209, 213
Deleuze, Gilles: *Anti-Oedipe*, 274
democracy, 22, 23, 28, 114; bourgeois, 111, 113, 114, 116, 117, 119, 120, 144, 156; representative, 237; socialist, 129, 133, 148
Democratic party, 28, 190, 218, 239
dependency theory, 86
deregulation, 209, 212
Derrida, Jacques, 172, 296; *Specters of Marx: The State of the Debt, the Work of Mourning, and the New International*, 296
Descartes, René, 51
despotism, 84, 151, 153
de-Stalinization, 5, 6, 60, 74, 152, 235

determinism, 3, 123, 146
Deutscher, Isaac, xiv, xvii, xviii, 1, 2, 5, 9,
31, 60, 90, 98, 102, 104, 105, 109, 110,
129, 131, 142, 150, 151, 152, 157, 158,
159, 161, 162, 184, 186, 191, 192, 194,
235, 236, 242, 260, 287, 295, 298; *The
Great Contest*, 6; *Marxism in Our Time*,
266, 279; *Marxism, Wars, and
Revolutions: Essays from Four Decades*,
279; 'On Socialist Man', 266, 279; *The
Prophet Armed—Trotsky, 1879–1921*,
287; *The Prophet Outcast—Trotsky,
1929–1940*, 269, 273, 276–77, 280,
298; *The Prophet Unarmed—Trotsky,
1921–1929*, 281; 'The Roots of
Bureaucracy', 279; *Russia after Stalin*,
152; *Stalin*, 30; *Trotsky* trilogy, 30, 150;
The Unfinished Revolution, 260
Deutscher, Tamara, 295; 'Soviet
Oppositions', 265
Deutscherism, 6, 22, 30, 32, 60, 87, 101,
142, 144, 146, 148, 149, 152, 223, 224,
242
Dews, Peter, 285, 287; *Logics of
Disintegration: Post-structuralist
Thought and the Claims of Critical
Theory*, 285
dialectical materialism, 136
dialectics, 128, 135
Dickens, Charles, 9
Dilthey, Wilhelm, 39
Disneyland, 40, 45, 146, 188, 242
Dissent, 290
Dobb, Maurice, 8
Dollé, Jean-Paul: *Désir [de] Révolution*,
274
dominant ideology thesis, 36, 114
Dunn, John: 'An English Marxist Faces His
Inquisitor', 274
Durkheim, Émile, 49
Dworkin, Dennis: *Cultural Marxism in
Postwar Britain*, 247
Dylan, Bob, 60

Eagleton, Terry, xi, 122, 178, 199;
*Criticism and Ideology: A Study in
Marxist Literary Theory*; 'Criticism and
Politics: The Work of Raymond
Williams', 272; *Ideology of the Aesthetic*,
289
East/West opposition, 116, 113

economic development, 79, 143
economic theory, 51, 106
economics, 36, 50, 51, 97, 98, 99, 126,
136, 199, 200
Economy and Society, 94
ecumenicism, 56, 166
Elbe, 22, 81, 148, 187, 221
Eley, Geoff: *The Peculiarities of German
History: Bourgeois Society and Politics
in Nineteenth-Century Germany*, 254,
292
Elliott, Gregory, 298; 'The Cards of
Confusion: Reflections on Historical
Communism and the "End of History" ',
296; *Labourism and the English Genius:
The Strange Death of Labour England*,
293
empiricism, 9, 10, 16, 25, 27, 33, 47, 49,
50, 52, 123, 136, 227
Engels, Friedrich, xv, 36, 50, 84, 96, 102,
103, 106, 131, 132, 136, 137, 151, 157,
158, 174, 207, 213, 241, 268, 269; *The
German Ideology*, 30, 136, 246, 268,
279
England, 13, 66, 99, 106, 107, 121, 122,
135, 137, 139, 140, 142
English Marxism, 8
English Revolution, 33, 80, 157, 162, 234
English working class, 16, 20, 26
enlightened despotism, 225
Enlightenment, 17, 204, 205
Enlightenment Marxism, 179
Enlightenment rationalism, 179
Enlightenment teleology, 227
Ethiopia, 138, 270, 275
ethnicity, 237
Eton, 1
Eurasia, 156
Eurocommunism, xiii, 21, 29, 31, 76, 100,
112, 113, 114, 118, 119, 120, 133, 137,
139, 167, 173, 174, 176, 190
Euro-labourism, 165, 166, 168, 177
Europe, 64, 72, 81, 96, 121, 139, 143,
144, 148–49, 163, 165, 190, 198, 204,
219, 220, 221, 237, 239; eastern, 21,
22, 23, 60, 67, 68, 72, 78, 79, 81, 84,
85, 87, 93, 96, 107, 138, 146, 147, 148,
151, 156, 205, 221, 222, 225, 276;
southern, 76, 94, 111, 118, 119, 137,
176, 190; western, 11, 21, 22, 23, 24,
25, 50, 65, 72, 78, 79, 82, 87, 96, 98,

112, 116, 119, 120, 137, 138, 164, 173, 189, 191, 205, 218, 219, 220, 221, 228, 229, 233, 234, 244
European Commission, xiii, 74, 76
European community, 219, 220, 229, 230, 233
European Economic Community (EEC), 5, 86, 228
European history, 78, 81, 108
European labour movement, 190
European Social Democracy, 28, 102, 167, 218
European socialism, 29, 169, 197
European Union, 221, 222, 237
European workers' movement, 171
Eurosocialism, xiii, 77, 167, 168, 217, 218
evolutionism, 83, 193, 195
exceptionalism, 33, 139, 155, 207, 225
exterminism, 145, 146
Eysenck, Hans, 50

Fabianism, 17, 18, 25, 33, 47, 50, 119, 140
factory councils, 53, 60
Falklands War, 163, 170
Fanon, Frantz: *The Wretched of the Earth*, 6
Far Left groups, xvii, 67, 72, 77, 119, 120, 164, 234, 239
fascism, 7, 96, 114, 150, 155, 161
February Revolution, 106
Federal Republic of Germany, 94, 143
feminism, 141, 167, 174, 183, 186, 198, 200
Fernbach, David: 'Strategy and Struggle', 256
feudalism, 35, 81, 83, 85, 121, 153, 160, 161; feudal class, 36, 81; feudal estate, 70, 79; feudal mode of production, 80, 81; feudal state, 15, 16, 31, 36, 153
Feyerabend, Paul: *Against Method*, 55
Fichtean defiance, 231
Fife Socialist League, 8
Fine, Ben: *Class Politics: An Answer to Its Critics*, 282
Finland, 151
Finley, Moses, 85
First Empire, 162
First International, 99
Foot, Paul, 42
Foote, Geoffrey: *The Labour Party's Political Theory: A History*, 247
forces of production, 210, 231

Fordist labour process, 188
Foreign Office, 207
foreign policy, 91; internationalist, 59; reactionary, 41; Soviet, 147
Forgacs, David, 13
formalism, 203
formalist sociology, 7
Foucault, Michel, 54, 139, 172, 179
Fourier, Charles, 132
Fourierism, 175
Fourth International, 56, 57, 58, 71, 90, 91, 101, 107, 111, 112, 133, 150, 151, 152, 155, 169, 174, 269, 273, 277, 279
France, 13, 30, 31, 35, 38, 49, 62, 63, 66, 72, 73, 100, 112, 118, 121, 123, 137, 139, 142, 161, 178, 189, 191, 199, 217, 228, 248, 286
Frank, André Gunder, 86
Frankfurt school, 49, 54, 88, 241
Fraser, Ronald, 6, 54, 262; *Nineteen Sixty-Eight: A Student Generation in Revolt*, 283, 290
French Communist Party (PCF), 21, 30, 61, 62, 63, 64, 69, 73, 74, 75, 76, 86
French Revolution, 15, 21, 35, 66, 84, 162, 264; second, 66
Freud, Sigmund, 54
Fröbel, Folker: 'On Some Postulates of an Anti-systemic Policy in Western Europe', 188
Fukuyama, Francis, xii, 204, 226, 227, 228, 229, 230, 231, 296, 297: 'The End of History?' 226; *The End of History and the Last Man*, 226, 229, 296
Fulbrook, Mary, 85
functionalism, 193
futurism, 132

Gaitskell, Hugh, 4, 5, 18, 26, 167
Gamble, Andrew, 206; *Britain in Decline: Economic Policy, Political Strategy, and the British State*, 291, 292
Gane, Mike: 'Althusser in English', 257
Gang of Four, 266
Gauchistes, 76
Gaullism, 118
Gaullist restoration, 75
Gellner, Ernest, xii, 53, 179, 193, 194; *Plough, Sword, and Book: The Structure of Human History*, 285; *Postmodernism, Reason and Religion*, 179; *The*

Psychoanalytic Movement, 285; *Words and Things*, 53
geopolitical problematic, 31, 37, 77
Geras, Norman, 54, 88, 111, 286; 'Althusser's Marxism: An Account and Assessment', 266; *Discourses of Extremity: Radical Ethics and Post-Marxist Extravagances*, 289; *The Legacy of Rosa Luxemburg*, 270; 'Literature of Revolution', 245; 'Post-Marxism?' 289
German Social Democratic Party (SPD), 23
Germany, 13, 28, 49, 57, 66, 84, 121, 199, 208; banking system in, 210; foreign policy of, 221; imperialism of, 155; reunification of, 221; working class in, 75
Gibbon, Peter: 'The Dialectic of Religion and Class in Ulster', 265
Giddens, Anthony, xii, 195, 204; *Beyond Left and Right: The Future of Radical Politics*, 290; *A Contemporary Critique of Historical Materialism*, 195
Gilmore, Chris: 'The May Events and Revolution in the West', 263
Ginzburg, Carlo, 193, 194; *Ecstasies*, 285
Gittlin, Todd: *The Sixties: Years of Hope, Years of Rage*, 285
glasnost, 142, 225
Gleichschaltung, 64, 196
globalitarianism, 238
globalization, 233, 237
Glorious Revolution, 15
Glucksmann, André, 54, 63, 88, 139; *Discours de la guerre*, 260; 'Politics and War in the Thought of Mao Tse-tung', 261; *Stratégie et révolution en France 1968*, 63, 275; 'A Ventriloquist Structuralism', 261, 266
Glyn, Andrew, 206; *British Capitalism, Workers, and the Profit Squeeze*, 206; 'The Critical Condition of British Capital', 290
Godard, David: 'The Limits of British Anthropology', 257
Goethe, Johann Wolfgang von, 242
Goldmann, Lucian, 100
Gonzales, Felipe, 239
Gorbachev, Mikhail, 142, 205, 220, 223, 224, 225
Gordon, David, 212
Gorz, André, 21, 53, 63

Goulding, Carol: 'The Present Course of the IRA', 265
Gowan, Peter: *The Question of Europe*, 186, 220, 287, 294, 295, 297
Gradgrindery, 16, 49
Gramsci, Antonio, xiv, 13, 14, 22, 23, 24, 25, 27, 32, 33, 35, 43, 48, 49, 53, 54, 60, 61, 71, 77, 79, 82, 84, 85, 96, 97, 103, 108, 109, 113, 114, 115, 116, 117, 135, 157, 244, 268, 280: *The Modern Prince and Other Writings*, 13; *Selections from the Prison Notebooks*, 13, 17, 29, 33, 54, 79, 103, 113, 251, 252, 258, 283
Gramscianism, 13, 15, 27, 29, 30, 31, 32, 36, 43, 117
Gramscian-Lukacsianism, 16
Gray, John, 205, 220, 222, 229; 'Review of *A Zone of Engagement*', 205
Great Depression, 176
Greater London Council, 167
Greece, 72, 73, 94, 286
Grossberg, Lawrence: *Marxism and the Interpretation of Culture*, 287
Guardian, The, 165, 239
Guattari, Félix: *Anti-Oedipe*, 274
Guevara, Ernesto (Che), 45; 'Vietnam Must Not Stand Alone', 256
Guevarism, xiii, 32, 40, 45, 59, 92, 131
Guevaro-Trotskyism, 61
gulagism, 138, 147, 163
Gulf War, 228

Habermas, Jürgen, 88, 103, 172, 176, 228; 'Conservatism and Capitalist Crisis', 283; *Habermas: Autonomy and Solidarity*, 283; 'Life-Forms, Morality and the Task of the Philosopher', 283; 'A Philosophico-political Profile', 283
Halimi, Serge: 'La Nouvelle-Zélande: éprouvette du capiatalisme total', 299
Hall, Stuart, 1, 2, 4, 5, 11, 12, 86, 140, 165, 167, 199, 220, 272, 276, 259, 261, 293; 'The Emergence of Cultural Studies and the Crisis of the Humanities', 259; *The Hard Road to Renewal: Thatcherism and the Crisis of the Left*, 293; 'In Defence of Theory', 272; 'Nicos Poulantzas: *State, Power, Socialism*', 276; 'The Politics of the Common Market', 4

Halliday, Fred, 6, 71, 90, 111, 144, 145, 147, 149, 157, 183; 'The Ceylonese Insurrection', 267; 'The Crisis of the Arab World: The False Answers of Saddam Hussein', 297; 'The Ends of Cold War', 295; *The Ethiopian Revolution*, 275; *Iran: Dictatorship and Development*, 275; 'The Legacy of 1968', 290; *The Making of the Second Cold War*, 144, 145, 276, 277; 'Marxist Analysis and Post-revolutionary China', 267; 'A Reply to Edward Thompson', 295; 'Revolution in Afghanistan', 275; 'The Sources of the New Cold War', 145, 147, 276; *Threat from the East? Soviet Policy from Afghanistan and Iran to the Horn of Africa*, 275; 'The War and Revolution in Afghanistan', 275

Halliday, Jon, 277, 286, 296, 298: 'Structural Reform in Italy—Theory and Practice', 255, 257

Harman, Chris: 'Criticism Which Does Not Withstand the Test of Logic', 280, 294–95

Havana, Cuba, 2, 45, 75

Hawke, Bob, 239

Hawthorn, Geoffrey, 52

Hayek, Friedrich von, 201, 202, 203, 220, 221

Heath, Edward, 86, 209

Heffer, Eric: 'Socialists and the Labour Party', 281

Hegel, G. W. F., 89, 97, 136, 226, 227, 228; *Phenomenology*, 227

hegemonic ideology, 16, 17, 38, 50

hegemony, 15, 16, 17, 18, 23, 25, 27, 33, 36, 47, 52, 53, 64, 69, 94, 97, 113, 115

Heidegger, Martin, 97, 139, 178

Heinrichs, Jürgen: 'On Some Postulates of an Anti-systemic Policy in Western Europe', 188

Heller, Agnes, 83

Herf, Jeffrey, 103

hermeneutics, 198

high culture, 200, 202

Hilferding, Rudolf, 89, 96, 214, 215; *Finance Capital*, 89, 214

Hill, Christopher, xi, 199, 281; *Century of Revolution*, 8

Hilton, Rodney: *The Transition from Feudalism to Capitalism*, 263

Hindle, Jane: *London Review of Books: An Anthology*, 265

Hindness, Barry: *Pre-capitalist Modes of Production*, 269

Hinton, James, 206

Hintze, Otto, 85

Hiroshima, 145

Hirst, Paul, 81, 83, 84, 85, 86, 229, 273; *Marxism and Historical Writing*, 272, 273; *Pre-capitalist Modes of Production*, 269; 'The Uniqueness of the West', 81, 264; 'Why Escalate?' 256

historical materialism, 8, 48, 52, 93, 95, 96, 97, 99, 105, 106, 109, 123–29, 135, 136, 137, 141, 158, 160, 162, 171, 172, 173, 174, 177, 178, 180, 181, 183, 187, 192, 193, 195, 241

historical sociologies, 85, 161, 193, 195, 199, 241

historical subjectivism, 179

historical trajectory, theory of, 241

historicism, 25, 33, 48

historiography, 38, 50, 123, 126, 127, 135, 199, 207, 269, 289; Anglo-Marxist, 130; British Marxist, 123; Marxist, 140

History Workshop, 122–23

Hitchens, Christopher: 'Theory and Experience', 274

Hoare, Quintin, 6, 54, 71, 90, 111, 164, 186, 262, 267; 'Socialists and the Crisis of Labourism', 164

Hobbes, Thomas, 125

Hobsbawm, Eric, xi, 2, 36, 37, 105, 135, 165, 167, 199, 203, 206, 226, 238, 239, 282, 291, 293, 296, 300; *Age of Extremes*, 238, 261; *Age of Revolution*, 8; *Echoes of the Marseillaise: Two Centuries Look Back on the French Revolution*, 279; 'From Babylon to Manchester', 264; 'Goodbye to All That', 295; *Industry and Empire*, 36, 206, 258, 291; 'May 1968', 261; *Politics for a Rational Left: Political Writing, 1977–1988*, 282, 293; 'The Retreat into Extremism', 282; *Revolutionaries: Contemporary Essays*, 249, 261; 'Some Reflections on *The Break-up of Britain*', 271

Ho Chi Minh, 264

Hodgson, Geoff, 118; 'On the Political Economy of the Socialist

Transformation', 281; *Socialism and Parliamentary Democracy*, 271, 274
Holland, 121
Holy Roman Empire, 4
Hook, Sidney, 278
Hopkins, A. G., 214, 215; *British Imperialism: Crisis and Deconstruction, 1914–1990*, 292; *British Imperialism: Innovation and Expansion, 1688–1914*, 214, 292
Horkheimer, Max, 238
Howe, Irving: 'New Styles in "Leftism" ', 290
Huberman, Leo: *Régis Debray and the Latin American Revolution*, 256
Hughes, H. Stuart: *Consciousness and Society*, 253
Hughes, John, 7
humanism, 2, 25, 26, 38, 145
Hunan Province, 37, 46
Hungary, 1
Huntington, Samuel, 226
Husserl, Edmund, 39
Hutton, Will: *The State We're In*, 293

iconoclasm, 13, 109, 242, 243
idealism, 35, 39, 85, 136, 206, 227
ideologism, 201
IG Metall, 189
Il Contemporaneo, 13
Il Manifesto, 267
imperialism, 10, 15, 20, 30, 41, 42, 70, 90, 91, 93, 95, 96, 99, 108, 129, 138, 144, 149, 153, 155, 156, 184, 191, 194, 209, 222, 235, 241
imperialist order, international, 131
India, 286
Indochina, 93, 94, 138, 276
Indonesia, 224
industrial bourgeoisie, 15, 16, 17, 33, 34, 37, 38, 49; nineteenth-century, 38
industrial capital, 32, 36, 86, 206, 212, 214
industrial capitalism, 15, 35, 69, 100, 214
industrial militancy, 40, 41, 196
industrial proletariat, 37, 208, 210
Industrial Revolution, 15, 37, 176, 232
industrial working class, 88, 175, 185, 231, 232
industrialization, 57, 129, 208
Ingham, Geoffrey, 206, 213; *Capitalism Divided? The City and Industry in*

British Social Development, 206, 290, 292
Ingrao, Chiara: 'The May Events and Revolution in the West', 263
instrumental collectivism, 26, 27
insurrectionism, 84, 117
integration, 28, 31, 38, 44, 116, 131, 220
integrism, 111, 131, 170
intelligentsia, 27, 50, 53
international markets, 230
International Marxist Group (IMG), 67, 71, 92, 101, 163
International Monetary Fund, 209
International Socialists, 67, 104
internationalism, 4, 10, 42, 45, 57, 58, 108, 123, 131, 234, 248
Ireland, 1, 265, 286
Islamic jihad, 143
Islamic Vendée, 148
isolationism, 65, 170
Italy, 13, 25, 30, 31, 35, 41, 49, 61, 72, 73, 100, 112, 118, 121, 137, 139, 199; communism in, 5, 17, 19, 21, 25, 32; Marxism in, 5, 8, 32

Jacobinism, 13, 157
Jacoby, Russell, 177; *Dialectic of Defeat: Contours of Western Marxism*, 268; *The Last Intellectuals: American Culture in the Age of Academe*, 284
Jacques, Martin, 165; *The Forward March of Labour Halted?* 165, 281
Jameson, Fredric: *The Cultural Turn: Selected Writings on Postmodernism, 1983–1998*, 288; *Late Marxism: Adorno, or, The Persistence of the Dialectic*, 289; 'Postmodernism, or, The Cultural Logic of Late Capitalism', 273
Japan, 37, 117, 121, 186, 191, 218, 229, 286
Jay, Martin, 103; *Marxism and Totality: The Adventures of a Concept from Lukács to Habermas*, 103, 285
Jefferson, Thomas, 242
Jenkins, Clive, 42
Jenson, Jane: 'The Tragedy of the French Left', 282
Jessop, Bob: 'Authoritarian Populism, Two Nations, and Thatcherism', 281; 'Farewell to Thatcherism? Neo-liberalism and "New Times" ', 293

Johnson, Richard, 20, 36, 40; 'Against Absolutism', 272; 'Reading for the Best Marx: History-Writing and Historical Abstraction', 272
Johnstone, Diane: *The Politics of Euromissiles*, 276
Jones, Jack, 42
Joseph, Sir Keith, 196

Kagarlitsky, Boris, 223
Kant, Immanuel, 97
Kathedersozialismus, 97
Kautsky, Karl, 96, 97, 102, 103, 154, 119
Kennedy, John F., 4
Kenny, Michael: *The First New Left: British Intellectuals after Stalin*, 247
Keynes, John Maynard, 50, 51, 220, 221
Keynesianism, 23, 168, 217, 218, 221
Khan, Yahya, 90
Khrushchev, Nikita, 1, 5, 41, 74, 129, 142, 147, 223
Khrushchevism, 41, 59, 92, 102, 142
Kinnock, Neil, 166, 167, 216
Klein, Melanie, 51
Kohl, Helmut, 143, 221
Kojève, Alexander, 227, 228, 298; *Introduction to the Reading of Hegel: Lectures on 'The Phenomenology of Spirit'*, 227
Kolakowski, Leszek, 284
Korea, 186, 235, 245, 273
Korsch, Karl, 54, 96, 103, 268, 286; *Marxism and Philosophy*, 54, 103; 'The Present State of the Problem of Marxism and Philosophy—An Anti-Critique', 268
Krassó, Nicolas, 56, 57, 58, 89, 105, 177; 'Trotsky's Marxism', 56–58, 89, 260, 279; 'Reply to Ernest Mandel', 58, 89, 260
Kravchenko, Bogdan, 276
Kreye, Otto: 'On Some Postulates of an Anti-systemic Policy in Western Europe', 188
Kuhn, Thomas, 123
Kwantung, 59

Labour Focus on Eastern Europe, 186
Labour movement, 11, 16, 18, 19, 122, 124, 141, 165, 178, 190, 206, 217, 218, 242, 249, 282; decline of, 169; European, 137; moderate, 214; north-

ern, 119; resurgence of, 189; western, 148; West European, 221
Labour Party, 3, 8, 17, 18, 20, 21, 25, 26, 27, 42, 44, 45, 101, 122, 163, 164, 189, 197, 239, 248; British, 218; new model, 164; programme, 19
labour theory of value, 106, 136
Labourism, 5, 7, 12, 16, 17, 18, 21, 25, 33, 50, 65, 122, 163–64, 166, 167, 169, 209, 217–19, 293
Labriola, Antonio, 96
Lacan, Jacques, 54, 172, 179
Laclau, Ernesto, 86, 289; 'Feudalism and Capitalism in Latin America', 86; *Hegemony and Socialist Strategy*, 289; *Politics and Ideology in Marxist Theory*, 265
Lakatos, Imre, 123, 179
Lakatosian realism, 180
Landau, Saul: 'Cuba: The Present Reality', 247
landowning classes, 34, 36
La Stampa, 226
Latin America, 29, 45, 271
Latin Marxism, 176, 178
Leavis, F. R., 50, 51, 199
Lefebvre, Henri, 96, 119
Left, 47, 48, 196, 197, 203, 205, 218, 219, 222, 226, 231, 234, 240, 243, 290, 293, 294, 296; collapse of the, 191; culture of the, 198, 242; intellectual culture of the, 55, 232; Labour, 12, 28, 163, 166, 168; Latin American, 295; politics of the, 220; reinvention of the, 204; revival of the, 168; theorists, 199; U.S. and European, 138; Western European, 120, 237
Lenin, V. I., xiii, 8, 22, 35, 43, 48, 49, 57, 58, 63, 65, 72, 84, 95, 96, 101, 103, 104, 106, 107, 115, 116, 119, 132, 133, 134, 135, 136, 141, 145, 151, 158, 181, 215, 244, 265, 275; *Imperialism*, 107; *State and Revolution*, 106, 141; 'The Three Sources and Three Component Parts of Marxism', 135, 274, 275; *What Is to Be Done?* 43
Leninism, xiii, 3, 21, 22, 24, 29, 31, 43, 45, 53, 58, 61, 66, 69, 70, 71, 74, 79, 83, 84, 85, 104, 105, 111, 113, 117, 129, 183, 201, 279; programme of, 74; strategy of, 23, 77, 84
Letwin, Shirley, 289

Lévi-Strauss, Claude, 54, 172, 179, 286; 'Claude Lévi-Strauss: A Confrontation', 54
Levine, Andrew: *Reconstructing Marxism: Essays on Explanation and the Theory of History*, 288
Leys, Colin, 206; 'The Formation of British Capital', 291; *Politics in Britain: From Labourism to Thatcherism*, 206; 'A Radical Agenda for Britain', 293
liberal capitalism, 187, 218, 226, 228
liberal democracy, 24, 83, 228, 230
Liberal Democrats, 239
liberal socialism, 204, 224
liberalism, 23, 89, 204, 234
libertarianism, 55, 134
Lichtheim, George, 181
Lin Chun, 260, 277
Lincoln, Abraham, 223
Lisbon, Portugal, 112
literary criticism, 50, 51, 52, 199
Livingstone, Ken: 'Why Labour Lost', 281
Lockwood, David, 26
London, England, 57, 207
London Review of Books, xi, 220, 224, 239, 265, 293–94, 297
London School of Economics, 46, 61–62
Looker, Robert, 212; 'Shifting Trajectories: Perry Anderson's Changing Account of the Pattern of English Historical Development', 291–92
L'Ordine Nuovo, 60
Löwy, Michael: *Georg Lukács—From Romanticism to Bolshevism*, 280
Lukács, Georg, xv, 8, 35, 48, 49, 53, 54, 56, 87, 88, 96, 109, 117, 231, 241; *Destruction of Reason*, 250; *History and Class Consciousness*, 88, 103, 251; 'Hölderlin's Hyperion', 280; interview, on his life and work, 87, 251; *Lenin*, 54
Lukacsianism, 33
Luxemburg, Rosa, 8, 44, 89, 96, 102, 103, 106, 116; *The Accumulation of Capital*, 89
Lyotard, J.-F., 179, 188, 285; *The Postmodern Condition*, 179, 188

Maastricht Treaty, 220, 221, 237
MacDonald, Oliver (P. Gowan): 'The Polish Vortex: Solidarity and Socialism', 199, 276, 277

MacIntyre, Alasdair, 273, 279; *Against the Self-Images of the Age: Essays in Ideology and Philosophy*, 280; 'Is a Science of Comparative Politics Possible?' 280; 'Trotsky in Exile', 280
Mackintosh, John, 2
Macmillan, Harold, 4
MacRae, D. G., 85
Magas, Branca, 6, 71, 186
Magri, Lucio, 76, 87, 106, 244; *Considerazioni sui fatti di Maggio*, 263; 'The European Left between Crisis and Refoundation', 299; 'Italian Communism in the Sixties', 261; 'The Peace Movement and European Socialism', 276; 'Problems of the Marxist Theory of the Revolutionary Party', 85
Mahon, Evelyn: 'Women's Rights and Catholicism in Ireland', 265
Maire, Edmond, 137
Maitan, Livio, 90; *Party, Army, and Masses in China*, 90, 267
Major, John, 221
Malcomson, Scott L., 147
Malik, M. A.: 'Comment', 256
Malinowski, Bronislav, 51
Mandel, Ernest, xiii, xvii, 32, 56, 57, 58, 63, 71, 76, 89, 90, 98, 104, 109, 112, 113, 131, 139, 145, 157, 194, 235, 236, 274, 279, 280, 282, 283, 295; *Beyond Perestroika: The Future of Gorbachev's USSR*, 295; *Europe versus America*, 262; *The Formation of the Economic Thought of Karl Marx*, 262; *From Stalinism to Eurocommunism*, 76, 112, 113, 262, 274; *Late Capitalism*, 236, 262, 270; 'On the Nature of the Soviet State', 275, 280; *Revolutionary Marxism Today*, 90, 262, 267, 274, 279; 'Revolutionary Strategy in Europe—A Political Interview', 270; 'Revolution in Western Europe', 270; *The Second Slump*, 262; 'A Theory Which Has Not Withstood the Test of the Facts', 280, 295; 'The Threat of War and the Struggle for Socialism', 276; *Trotsky*, 262; 'Trotsky's Marxism: An Anti-Critique', 260; 'Trotsky's Marxism: A Rejoinder', 58, 260
Mann, Michael, xii, 192, 194, 195, 228; *Socialism Can Survive*, 294; *The Sources of Social Power*, 194, 288, 289

Mann, Thomas, 9
manufacturing, 207, 208, 213, 232
Mao Tse-tung, 45, 59, 260, 262, 266:
'Letter to Comrade Lin Piao', 90
Maoism, xiii, 32, 40, 45, 46, 47, 56, 58,
59, 61, 63, 64, 65, 66, 67, 75, 86, 88,
89, 90, 92, 93, 95, 98, 109, 131, 138,
160, 173, 176, 262, 267; Althusserian,
56, 126; illusions in, 59; repudiation of,
87; ultraleftist, 114
Marchais, Georges, Communist party of,
118
Marcuse, Herbert, 44, 66; One-
Dimensional Man, 255, 257
Marcuseanism, 46, 62
Marquand, David, 2
Marshall, T. H., 197; Citizenship and
Social Class, 294
Marx, Karl, xv, 3, 14, 24, 34, 36, 43, 49,
50, 54, 80, 84, 89, 96, 97, 102, 103,
106, 107, 114, 123, 124, 126, 132, 135,
136, 151, 157, 158, 174, 181, 187, 194,
195, 199, 200, 207, 210, 213, 215, 227,
231, 241, 244, 268, 289, 291, 298;
Capital, 17, 93, 96, 103, 106, 114, 126,
136, 194, 214, 259, 263, 264, 273, 274,
288, 291; Communist Manifesto, xv, 17,
125, 132, 259; Critique of the Gotha
Programme, 259; Economic and
Philosophical Manuscripts, 259;
Eighteenth Brumaire, 259; 'The Future
Results of the British Rule in India', 273;
The German Ideology, 30, 136, 246,
268, 279; Grundrisse, 8, 132, 259, 274;
The Jewish Question, 114; Paris
Manuscripts, 2; Pre-capitalist Economic
Formations, 273; Preface to A
Contribution to a Critique of Political
Economy, 14, 125, 263; Surveys from
Exile, 273
Marxism, 7, 10, 12, 18, 25, 33, 38, 39, 49,
50, 52, 55, 65, 69, 70, 79, 89, 99, 100,
101, 104, 105, 108, 110, 123, 127, 131,
134, 140, 152, 157, 159, 161, 173, 174,
176, 179, 181, 182, 184, 186, 222, 241,
244, 268, 277, 285; alternative, 139;
Anglo-American, 109, 136; autonomous,
9, 38; Bolshevik, 57; British, 139; classical, 8, 29, 32, 54, 55, 56, 95–97, 99,
105, 106, 116, 124, 128, 135, 136, 150,
152, 153, 158, 175, 181, 188, 192, 198,
233, 241, 242, 246; contemporary, 139,
141, 195; continental, 130, 198, 249;
European, 35, 178, 198; French, 8; indigenous, 12, 38, 49, 50; Gramscian, 32;
international, 182; Latin, 139; orthodox,
143; revolutionary, 29, 47, 56, 68, 98,
111, 112, 130, 131, 132, 166, 191–93,
283; Russian, 113; Stalinist, 227;
Swedish, 41; traditional, 121; Western,
xi, 5, 7, 10, 32, 35, 49, 54, 55, 56, 65,
66, 93, 96, 97, 99, 103, 104, 106, 108,
109, 114, 130, 136, 140, 171, 174, 181,
246; Western European, 39
Marx memorial lecture, 165
Marxism Today, 165, 217; The Politics of
Thatcherism, 165
Marxist culture, 273
Marxist historiography, 17, 32, 99, 106,
171, 263, 284
Marxist intellectuals, 13, 100, 101, 193,
248
Marxist theory, 10, 62, 64, 82, 89, 94, 98,
106, 108, 127, 137, 173, 177, 182, 194,
213, 246, 249, 263
Marxist tradition, 77, 133, 145, 152, 176,
216
Masparo, François, 248
materialism, 135, 227, 237
May 1968, 42, 61, 63, 65, 66, 69, 72, 73,
75, 76, 86, 95, 98, 110, 191, 242
Mayer, Arno J., 207
McCarney, Joseph: 'Endgame', 296;
'Shaping Ends: Reflections on
Fukuyama', 296; Social Theory and the
Crisis of Marxism, 246; 'The True
Realm of Freedom: Marxist Philosophy
after Communism', 296; 'Under the
Hammer', 296
Mcintyre, Stuart, 53; A Proletarian
Science: Marxism in Britain,
1917–1933, 249
McKibbin, Ross: 'Very Old Labour', 294
mechanicism, 15, 125
Medvedev, Roy: 'Problems of
Democratization and Détente', 266;
'The USSR and the Arms Race', 276
Medvedev, Zhores: 'Innovation and
Conservatism in the New Soviet
Leadership', 295; 'Russia under
Brezhnev', 275; 'The USSR and the
Arms Race', 276

Mehring, Franz, 96
Meiksins Wood, Ellen, 249, 268, 287
meliorism, xiv, 198, 216
Mepham, John: 'Goodbye To All That?' 269
Merleau-Ponty, Maurice, 103, 172, 231, 241; *Adventures of the Dialectic*, 103; *Humanism and Terror*, 252; *Signs*, 241
Merquior, J. G.: *Western Marxism*, 268, 284
Merrington, John, 286
Merton, Richard, 60
Methodism, 18, 34
Michel, Pablo, 151
Michelet, Jules, 31
Michels, Robert, 219
Middle East, 186, 296
Middlemass, Keith, 294
Miliband, Ralph, xi, 167, 226, 282, 296; *Class Power and State Power*, 264; *Parliamentary Socialism*, 8; 'Political Forms and Historical Materialism', 264; 'Thirty Years of *Socialist Register*', 276
Mill, John Stuart, 14, 197, 201, 202, 203, 236
Mills, C. Wright, 236
Milward, Alan, 220, 294
Mirsky, Dmitri: *The Intelligentsia of Great Britain*, 257
Mitchell, Juliet, 6; 'Women: The Longest Revolution', 56, 286–87
Mitterand, François, 189, 190, 217, 221, 239
modernism, 187
modernity, 5, 121, 187, 188, 204, 237
modernization, 150, 187, 218
Molotov-Von Ribbentrop Pact, 151
Molyneux, Maxine: *The Ethiopian Revolution*, 275
Monnet, Jean, 228, 299
Monthly Review, 256
moralism, 9, 128, 129, 130, 131, 132
Moretti, Franco, 192, 300
Morris, William, 8, 9, 12, 131, 132, 135, 199; News from Nowhere, 132
Mouffe, Chantal, 203; *Hegemony and Socialist Strategy*, 289
Mozambique, 94
Mulhern, Francis, 1, 111, 165, 183, 186, 266, 286, 287; *The Forward March of Labour Halted?* 28, 165; *The Moment of*

'*Scrutiny*', 276; 'Towards 2000, or News from You-Know-Where', 287

Nairn, Tom, 9, 13, 14, 18, 20, 33, 34, 35, 36, 38, 39, 40, 46, 54, 63, 82, 104, 122, 286; 'Anatomy of the Labour Party', 251; *The Beginning of the End*, 63; *The Breakup of Britain*, 122, 271, 281; 'Comments on "Western Marxism: An Introduction" ', 269; 'The Crisis of the British State', 281; *The Enchanted Glass*, 216; 'The English Working Class', 20; 'The Fateful Meridian', 86; 'Into Political Emergency', 281; 'Labour and Imperialism', 291; 'The Labour Aristocracy', 253; *The Left against Europe?* 54, 86, 294; 'The Modern Janus', 271; 'The Nature of the Labour Party', 20, 251; 'The Sole Survivor', 292; 'The Twilight of the British State', 122, 271
Nairn-Anderson theses, 6, 12, 13, 20, 32, 36, 40, 42, 46, 48, 52, 77, 86, 94, 122, 140, 205, 206, 207, 211, 212, 213, 216
Namier, Lord, 50
Napoleon, 158, 228
Napoleonic age, 242, 277
Narkomindel, 73, 155
National Interest, 226
national liberation movements, 6, 8, 68, 88, 91, 231
nationalism, 9, 10, 11, 15, 41, 86, 95, 99, 106, 121, 130, 156
nation-states, 230, 233; function and future of, 108
naturalism, 135, 179
Nazism, 60, 73, 107, 144
Nelson, Cary: *Marxism and the Interpretation of Culture*, 287
neo-Althusserianism, 56
neoliberalism, 163, 169, 190, 202, 204, 205, 209, 214, 216; English, 209; resistance to, 197
Neuberg, A.: *Armed Insurrection*, 264
New Labour, 219
New Left, 1, 3, 4, 5, 7, 8, 10, 47, 66, 130, 131, 167, 197, 236, 248; first, 7, 9, 11, 12, 28, 63, 167; original, 140; second, 42, 168, 249
New Left Books, xi, xii, 53, 71
New Left Clubs, 8

New Left Review: 'Brazil', 299; 'Cavtat 1983', 284; charter, xvii, 183, 185, 186, 222; 'Conspectus', 40, 248; constitution, xvii, 183; 'Decennial Report, 1965–1975', 6, 29, 39, 40, 46, 52, 53, 56, 58, 59, 61, 71, 90, 91, 92–95, 106, 108, 110, 111, 138, 205, 248, 253, 256, 260, 261, 263, 265, 269, 270; 'Document A-Theory and Practice: The *Coupure* of May', 64–70, 87, 95, 98, 109, 262; 'Document B-Ten Theses', 64–70, 71, 77, 186; *Exterminism and Cold War*, 145, 147, 185, 276, 277, 286; fiftieth issue, 257; foreword to *Parliament, People and Power*, 164; 'Historical Introduction, 1930–64: The Legacy of Vargas', 299; 'NLR Perspectives', 283; 'Notes on the Current Outlook', 167, 168; 'Quinquennial Report, 1975–1980', 90, 111, 112, 122, 131, 137–43, 161, 164, 168, 171, 174, 178, 185, 222, 223, 236, 270, 276, 294; Socialist Feminist Document, 166; 'Statement', 250; *Thirty Years of New Left Review*, 248, 282; 'Triennial Report, 1980–1983', 163, 164, 165, 170–71, 198, 294
New Left Review Editions, 54
new revisionism, 167, 168
New Right, 86, 143, 163, 169, 189, 191, 196, 197, 216, 238
New Statesman, 140, 165
Nicaragua, 138, 139
Nicholls, David: *The Development of British Capitalist Society: A Marxist Debate*, 291–92
Niethammer, Lutz, 226, 227
Nietzsche, Friedrich, 139, 178, 227
nihilism, 47, 170, 179
Nixon, Richard, 91, 239
North Atlantic Treaty Organization (NATO), 143, 148
Nove, Alec, 159, 175; *Economics of Feasible Socialism*, 175, 238
Nozick, Robert, 197
nuclear arms race, 143, 147
nuclear deterrence, 74
nuclear disarmament, 146

Oakeshott, Michael, 194, 202, 203; *Rationalism in Politics*, 202

objectivism, 79, 124
Oriental Khrushchevism, 173
Orwell, George:*The Lion and the Unicorn*, 9
Owen, Robert, 132

Pablo, Michel, 151, 152
Padoul, Gilbert: 'China 1974: Problems Not Models', 267
Pakistan, 90
pancapitalist polity, 205
Panzerkommunismus, 112
Paraguay, 234
Pareto, Elfredo, 49
Paris, France, 32, 53, 57, 62, 76, 112, 157
Paris Commune, 70, 244
parliamentarism, 23, 117, 119; Western, 115
Parsons, Talcott, 52, 125; *Structure of Social Action*, 52, 258
peace movements, 144, 146, 148, 149, 163, 174, 295
Pearson, Gabriel, 1, 2
peasantry, 37, 42, 58, 67, 68, 79, 88, 92, 233
Pelican Marx Library, 54
Pelikan, Jiri, 87
People's Liberation Army, 59–60
perestroika, xii, 142, 224, 225
Petras, James: 'The Contradictions of Greek Socialism', 282
Piao, Marshal Lin, 56
Plekhanov, Georgii, xiii, 35, 96, 102, 103, 158
Poland, 15, 32, 87, 147, 294
political economy, 33, 34, 38, 214
political philosophy, 38
political radicalism, 141
political relativity, general theory of, 239
political revolution, 80, 107, 114, 153, 157, 162, 223, 230
political right, 154, 162, 196, 197, 201, 203, 204, 205, 237, 240
political theory, 19, 51, 96, 106, 107
Pontussen, Jonas: 'Behind and Beyond Social Democracy in Sweden', 282
pop music, 261
Popper, Karl, 50, 51, 89, 123
Popular Front, 73, 74, 165
populism, 9, 12, 39, 47, 196, 225
Porter, Cathy, 286

Portugal, 6, 72, 79, 94, 108, 111, 137, 263
Portuguese Communist Party, 76
Portuguese Revolution, 61, 93, 112, 192
postcapitalism, 30, 70, 78, 84, 94, 137, 160, 162, 175, 187, 223, 236, 268
postclassical theorists, 88
post-Fordism, 217
post-Marxism, 162, 178
postmodernism, 179, 187, 188, 204, 192, 287
postrevolutionary institutions, 106, 160, 224
poststructuralism, 55, 167, 172, 176, 178, 179, 192, 195, 198, 199
postwar capitalism, 62, 64, 75
postwar culture, 200
Potter, Dennis, 1
Poulantzas, Nicos, 32, 33, 34, 39, 48, 54, 112, 139, 176, 267, 289; *Fascism and Dictatorship*, 259; 'Marxist Political Theory in Britain', 32; *Political Power and Social Classes*, 259; *State, Power, Socialism*, 112, 271, 274; 'Towards a Democratic Socialism', 270
Powell, Anthony: *A Dance to the Music of Time*, 287
Powell, Enoch, 86, 168
Prague, Czechoslovakia, 60, 191
Prague Spring, 60, 87
precapitalism, 85, 184, 222, 236
presocialism, 12
private property, 185, 204
production: forces of, 135; internationalization of, 212; means of, 124, 133, 152, 160; mode of, 127, 135, 126, 160; overseas, 207; relations of, 126, 135
progressivism, 151, 273
proletarian corporatism, 214
proletarian democracy, 82, 85, 106
proletarian internationalism, 6
proletarian party, 3
proletarian revolution, 30, 35, 37
proletarianism, 160
proletariat, 15, 16, 17, 24, 32, 42, 67, 92, 153, 160, 268; industrial, 136; international, 149; Soviet, 153
proportional representation, 166, 218
Protestantism, 34
Proust, Marcel: *Remembrance of Things Past*, 287

psychoanalysis, 51, 54, 55, 265
psychology, 50, 51, 52

Quartim, Joao: *Dictatorship and Armed Struggle in Brazil*, 299

racism, 185
radicalism, 122, 164, 174, 196
Ramas, Mari: 'Rethinking Women's Oppression', 287
Ramelson, Bert, 42
Ramonet, Ignacio, 299
Rawls, John, 194, 197, 203; *Political Liberalism*, 203, 297; *A Theory of Justice*, 203
Reagan, Ronald, 143, 144
Reaganomics, 218, 237
realism, 123, 134, 135, 168, 179, 233; epistemological, 135
recession, economic, 94, 111, 144, 162, 218
Red Army, 23, 46, 59, 60, 73, 143
Red Mole, 71
Redgrave, Vanessa, 169
Rée, Jonathan: 'English Philosophy in the Fifties', 257–58
Reform Act of 1832, 15
Reform Communism, 41; Italian, 242
reformism, 21, 23, 29, 47, 63, 72, 74, 85, 97, 112, 114, 115, 116, 118, 132, 190, 217, 219, 281
reformist theory, 102
relativism, 188
representative democracy, 97, 234
Republican party, 239
revanchism, 143, 166
revisionism, 12, 16, 163, 166, 175, 197, 239
revolution: sociology of, 127; traditional schemas of, 47
revolutionary change, concept of, 187
revolutionary culture, 6, 48, 102, 201
revolutionary Left, 48, 62, 66, 67, 193, 220, 235
revolutionary politics, 76, 198
revolutionary practice, 82, 202
Revolutionary Socialist Students' Federation, 46, 62, 63, 71, 92: 'Manifesto', 256
revolutionary socialists, 62, 97, 100, 164, 190

revolutionary strategy, 13, 79, 99, 107
revolutionary theory, 47, 48, 65, 95, 101, 102, 103, 201
revolutionary tradition, 64, 67, 75
Rey, Lucien: 'Persia in Perspective', 248, 286
Ridgeway, James: 'The Freeze Movement versus Reagan', 276
Rigby, T. H., 159
right-to-work legislation, 219
Risorgimento, 13
Rivers of Blood speech, 168
Rizzi, Bruno, 159
Robbins, Bruce: Secular Vocations: Intellectuals, Professionalism, Culture, 285
Robinson, Joan, 2, 91
Rocard, Michel, 227
rock music, 60, 261
Roemer, John, 203
Rolling Stones, 60, 261
Roman Empire, 4
Roman law, 85
romanticism, 12, 131, 132
Rome, Italy, 57, 112
Rosdolsky, Roman, 98, 104
Ross, George: 'The Tragedy of the French Left', 282
Roundheads, 13
routinism, 104
Rowbotham, Sheila: Beyond the Fragments, 186
Rowthorn, Bob, 6, 286
Runciman, W. G., xii, 193, 195, 194, 288; Treatise on Social Theory, 289
Russia, 35, 57, 59, 83, 84, 87, 107, 120, 129, 138, 153, 154, 155, 184, 225, 226, 236, 239, 228, 275, 277; absolutism in, 82, 115; Marxist tradition in, 35; politics, 225. See also USSR
Russian Revolution, 22, 30, 59, 69, 70, 76, 77, 82, 83, 95, 124, 129, 131, 149, 156, 157, 181, 182, 191, 222, 234, 235, 244, 275, 295
Russophobia, 139
Rustin, Michael, 8, 168, 261, 296; 'Citizenship and Charter 88', 293; 'Different Conceptions of Party: Labour's Constitutional Debates', 281; For a Pluralist Socialism, 281; 'The New Left and the Present Crisis', 281; 'The

Politics of Post-Fordism: Or, the Trouble with "New Times" ', 293
Ryle, Gilbert, 51, 53

Sader, Emir: 'The Workers' Party in Brazil', 299
Saint-Simon, Claude Henri de, 132, 175
Salazar, Antonio de Oliveira, 6
salon intellectuals, 177
Sampson, Anthony, 36
Samuel, Raphael, 1, 2, 140, 167, 248; 'Born-Again Socialism', 248; 'British Marxist Historians, 1880–1980', 276; People's History and Socialist Theory, 245, 252, 262, 272
Sartre, J. P., xiii, xvii, 2, 9, 21, 32, 34, 44, 48, 53, 54, 56, 75, 79, 88, 96, 109, 110, 125, 136, 149, 172, 176, 194, 241, 262, 268; Between Existentialism and Marxism, 259, 262; The Communists and Peace, 21, 30, 149, 250, 255, 272; Critique of Dialectical Reason, 22, 30, 79, 194, 255, 259, 268, 269, 300; 'An Itinerary of a Thought', 262, 266; Situations IV, 284; 'A Tour with Fidel Castro', 2
Sartreanism, 2, 3, 21, 30, 43, 53, 63, 75, 183, 248
Sassoon, Donald, 38, 133; 'The Silences of New Left Review', 274, 287
Satsuma clan, 37
Saussure, Ferdinand de, 172
Saville, John, 9
Scanlon, Hugh: 'The Role of Militancy', 255
scarcity, 24, 30, 84, 153, 156, 157, 268, 279
scepticism, 76, 146, 212, 285
Schachtman, Max, 154, 260, 278, 279
scheinradikalismus, 170
Schmidt, Carl, 190, 203
Schumpeter, Joseph, 214, 215, 236, 292; Capitalism, Socialism, and Democracy, 215, 251; Imperialism and Social Classes, 251, 292; 'The Sociology of Imperialism', 251, 292
Schwartz, Bill: ' "The People" in History: The Communist Party Historians' Group, 1946–1956', 250
Science and Society, 79
scientific socialism, xv, 175, 180, 181, 189, 193, 236, 241

scientificity, 106, 179
Scotland, 8, 122
Scruton, Roger: *Thinkers of the New Left*, 258
Second International, 21, 35, 72, 101, 103, 107, 133, 118, 169, 190, 217, 237; corrosion of, 238; orthodoxy of, 125
sectarianism, 104, 151
Sedgwick, Peter: 'Pseud Left Review', 249; 'The Two New Lefts', 249
Segal, Lynne: 'Generations of Feminism', 286, 289; *Is the Future Female? Troubled Thoughts on Contemporary Feminism*, 284, 289; 'Whose Left? Socialism, Feminism, and the Future', 293
separation of powers, 224
separatism, 8
separatist leftism, 168
serfdom, consolidation of, 81, 85
Serge, Victor: 'On Trotskyism', 269
Seven Days, 71, 92
sexism, 185
sexual difference, 200
sexual inequality, 27, 174
sexual oppression, 186
sexuality, 68
Shah of Iran, 138
Shelley, Percy Bysshe, 242
Shonfield, Anthony, 36
short-termism, 51
Singer, Daniel, 295
Sino-Indian War (1962), 60
Sino-Soviet relations, 68, 74
Sinophilia, 91
Skocpol, Theda, 85
Slaughter, Cliff, 269
slavery, abolition of, 223
Smith, Geoffrey Nowell, 54
Sober, Elliott: *Reconstructing Marxism: Essays on Explanation and the Theory of History*, 288
social class, 33, 37, 67, 79, 161, 199, 277
social conflict, 47, 175, 228
Social Democracy, 1, 3, 21, 23, 24, 65, 72, 74, 75, 101, 113, 118, 119, 130, 148, 149, 168, 169, 173, 190, 221, 229, 234, 238, 239, 240, 243; barren record of, 83; breaking the grip of, 73; classical formations of, 190; Clintonization of, 219; disarray of, 216; effacement of, 20; fail-ure of, 24; left-wing, 117; postwar cycle of, 218
social engineering, 201, 217
social formation, 7, 11, 13, 22, 33, 49, 68, 83, 113, 114, 125, 126, 127, 129, 135, 161; British, 117; postcapitalist, 157, 160; Soviet, 154
social order, 28; limits of present, 220; postrevolutionary, 157; reproduction of, 15
social relations, 81, 132
social services, 221
social theory, 52, 129
social totality, 16, 48, 50, 199
socialism, 11, 16, 19, 22, 29, 30, 31, 37, 41, 42, 43, 44, 53, 67, 70, 77, 84, 108, 111, 115, 119, 122, 132, 136, 137, 139, 142, 145, 146, 147, 148, 152, 160, 162, 169, 175, 180, 185, 186, 188, 189, 190, 193, 198, 204, 219, 222, 223, 228, 229, 231, 233, 234, 236, 238, 243, 274, 276, 277, 287; advanced, 119, 148; authen-tic, 22; culture of, 24, 32, 140, 174, 180, 184; European, 43; failures of, 241; fate of, 234; feasibility of, 232, 236; French, 135; future, 140, 141, 175, 235; history of, 82, 234; ideology of, 22, 26, 27, 28, 31; international, 31, 65, 83, 160, 184; liberal, 240; local, 130; peace and, 148; progress toward, 137; recon-ceptualization of, 204; resurgence of, 235; revolutionary, xiv, xv, 42, 47, 63, 66, 67, 69, 70, 71, 75, 76, 82, 88, 99, 112, 115, 116, 117, 118, 120, 134, 149, 152, 163, 168, 169, 176, 181, 182, 198, 202, 235, 236, 263, 287; scientific, 124, 127, 131, 132, 135, 136, 137; theory, 43, 174; transition to, 117, 119, 133, 134, 135, 137, 151, 152, 157, 175; utopian, 131, 132, 137, 140; viability of, 232; Western, 30, 62, 83
socialist demands, 19, 216
socialist democracy, 70, 87, 99, 108, 141, 167, 181, 182
socialist-feminists, 56, 166, 183
socialist hegemony, 25, 28
socialist humanism, 33, 247
Socialist International, 18
socialist movement, 22, 27, 116, 120, 128, 242
socialist party, 18, 21, 24, 27

socialist politics, 169, 178
socialist programme, 235
Socialist Register, 32
socialist revolution, 42, 60, 63, 67, 69, 72, 76, 78, 79, 82, 84, 93, 96, 108, 112, 116, 118, 124, 133, 158, 187, 244
socialist society, xii, 23, 24, 165, 166
socialist strategy, 11, 21, 24, 27, 29, 31, 33, 118, 168, 171, 174, 233
socialist theory, 100
Socialist Unity campaign, 163
Socialist Workers' Party (SWP), 163
socialists, 46, 133, 142, 147, 154, 173, 190, 191, 205, 223
society, 7, 18, 43, 52, 114, 115, 127, 131, 158
socioeconomic forms, 126
socioeconomic structures, 174
sociology, 26, 50, 51, 117; absentee, 199; bourgeois, 52; classical, 49, 50; European, 52; totalizing, 50
Solzhenitsyniana, 222
Somoza, Anastasio, 138
Soper, Kate: Humanism and Anti-Humanism, 284, 286
South Korea, 239, 299
South Yemen, 138
Southeast Asia, 41, 94, 139, 143
Soviet bureaucracy, 153, 222, 223
Soviet collapse, 221
Soviet communism, 93, 104, 284
Soviet economy, 223, 225
Soviet Union, 6, 58, 67, 74, 88, 90, 142, 143, 147, 148, 151, 152, 155, 157, 160, 161, 162, 166, 173, 182, 221, 223, 260; defects of, 149; weakness of, 225; withdrawal from Afghanistan by, 225
Spain, 72, 73, 94, 112, 118, 137, 142, 161, 286
Spartacus League, 71
Spencer, Herbert, 52
Spencerism, 34
Spinoza, Baruch, 95, 97
Sprinker, Michael, xvi
Sraffa, Piero: Production of Commodities by Means of Commodities, 275
stagflation, 138, 217
Stalin, Josef, 1, 56, 57, 58, 91, 95, 129, 155, 157, 181, 228, 230, 268, 278; opponents of, 230; policies of, 151; spectre of, 82

Stalingrad, Russia, 73, 76
Stalinism, 1, 3, 6, 9, 22, 37, 59, 65, 66, 83, 85, 88, 96, 98, 100, 105, 118, 122, 123, 129, 130, 150, 151, 152, 155, 156, 157, 158, 171, 173, 187, 226, 235, 236, 248, 269, 275, 278; assessment of, 154; critique of, 89; costs of, 155; interpretation of, 235; legacy of, 234; Marxist theory of, 159; nature of, 152, 156; opposition to, 151, 154; rejection of, 99; Soviet, 87; theorization of, 153
Stalinization, 64
Stalinophobia, 150, 152, 278
state apparatus, 70, 80, 114, 115
state capitalism, 88, 115, 116, 133, 154
state power, 115, 116, 197
statism, 25, 134
Stedman Jones, Gareth, 6, 46, 54, 56, 71, 88, 105, 286; 'Comment', 269; 'Engels and the End of Classical German Philosophy', 269–70; 'The Marxism of the Early Lukács', 266, 274; 'The Pathology of English History', 257; Western Marxism: A Critical Reader, 54, 261, 266, 273, 274
Steedman, Ian: The Value Controversy, 275
Steele, Jonathan: Eternal Russia: Yeltsin, Gorbachev, and the Mirage of Democracy, 295
Stephanson, Anders: 'The British and the Rational', 286
structuralism, 48, 172, 178, 193, 198
student and youth movements, 46, 47, 53, 61, 66–67, 71, 75, 76, 77
studentism, 46, 92, 131
students, 27, 45, 63, 65, 66, 76, 122; French, 62; German, 46
subjectivism, 33, 124
Suez crisis, 1, 209
superpowers, 120, 147, 160
supertheoreticism, 249
Sutcliffe, Bob, 206; British Capitalism, Workers, and the Profit Squeeze, 206; 'The Critical Condition of British Capital', 290
Sweden, 247; labour movement in, 210; social democracy in, 2, 17
Sweezy, Paul: Régis Debray and the Latin American Revolution, 256
syndicalism, 43, 44, 190, 209

Taylor, Barbara, 286
Taylor, Charles, 1, 2
Tebbitism, 211
technology, 20, 53
teleology, 12, 51, 136
Test Ban Treaty, 144
Tet Offensive (1968), 41, 242
Thatcher, Margaret, 139, 143, 163, 197, 201, 202, 205, 218
Thatcherism, 122, 163, 202, 209, 217
Theoretical Practice, 257, 267
theoreticism, 20, 56, 99
Therborn, Göran, 41, 42, 54, 68, 88, 103; 'Critique of the Frankfurt School', 266; 'From Petrograd to Saigon', 41, 68; 'Jürgen Habermas: A New Eclecticism', 266
Third International, 21, 35, 69, 72, 75, 101, 103, 107, 111, 133, 169, 190
Third World, 13, 32, 40, 41, 45, 67, 68, 71, 75, 91, 94, 111, 138, 143, 144, 147, 152, 231, 248
Third Worldism, xiv, 6, 40, 86, 92
Thomas, Keith, 85
Thompson, Duncan: *The Moment of New Left Review*, 247
Thompson, E. P., xi, 2, 3, 5, 9, 11, 12, 14, 20, 26, 32–39, 46, 77, 105, 112, 122, 123, 124, 126, 127, 128, 129, 130, 132, 133, 134, 135, 144, 145, 146, 147, 157, 199, 205, 207, 248, 261, 269, 273, 277, 295, 298; 'At the Point of Decay', 11; 'The Ends of Cold War', 295; *The Making of the English Working Class*, 8, 20, 124, 272; 'The Marx Claimants', 269; 'Notes on Exterminism, The Last Stage of Civilisation', 144, 274, 276; *Out of Apathy*, 11, 20, 248; 'Peculiarities of the English', 32, 34, 133, 205–6, 272; 'The Politics of Theory', 272; 'The Poverty of Theory', 259, 285; *The Poverty of Theory*, 112, 122, 124, 131, 259, 271, 272, 273; 'Revolution', 11, 21, 132; 'Where Are We Now?' 32, 247; *Whigs and Hunters*, 134; *William Morris*, 131, 249–50, 257; *Writing by Candlelight*, 134, 274
Thompsonianism, 12, 34
Thorez, Maurice, 74
Threlfall, Monica: *Mapping the Women's Movement: Feminist Politics and Social Transformation in the North*, 286

Ticktin, Hillel: *The Ideas of Leon Trotsky*, 279
Timpanaro, Sebastiano, 87, 89, 109, 135, 171, 176, 179; *The Freudian Slip*, 171, 285; *On Materialism*, 89, 267, 285
Togliatti, Palmiro, 74
Tory rule, 216
totalitarian communism, 51
totalitarianism, 21, 147
Trabulsi, Fawwaz: 'The Palestinian Problem: Zionism and Imperialism in the Middle East', 256
trade unionism, 8, 18, 42, 43, 44, 122, 209
traditionalism, 15, 16, 25, 27, 33, 47, 49, 50
Treaty of Rome, 4, 233
Tredell, Nicholas: 'Modern Tragedy', 234
triangular constellation (land, trade, and industry), 17, 208
Triesman, David, 46; 'The Impermanent Stronghold', 256
tripartism, 74
triumphalism, 52, 102, 104, 196
Trotsky, Leon, xiii, xiv, xvi, 8, 56, 57, 58, 65, 83, 84, 88, 89, 92, 95, 96, 98, 102, 104, 106, 107, 116, 129, 131, 132–36, 149–60, 162, 161, 177, 179, 182, 183, 184, 196, 234, 235, 238, 241, 242, 246, 268, 269, 277, 279, 286, 287, 295, 297; 'Again and Once More Again on the Nature of the USSR', 278–79; *The Death Agony of Capitalism and the Tasks of the Fourth International*, 269; 'Factory Councils and Workers' Control of Production', 286; *In Defence of Marxism: The Social and Political Contradictions of the Soviet Union*, 149, 274, 278–79; 'Open Letter to Comrade Burnham', 274; *The Revolution Betrayed: Where Is Russia Going?* 30, 107, 149, 153, 158, 159, 268, 279, 297; *The Struggle Against Fascism in Germany*, 286; *The Third International after Lenin*, 297
Trotskyism, xiii, 32, 56, 59, 65, 66, 67, 71, 75, 76, 95, 98, 99, 101, 103, 109, 111, 112, 131, 139, 142, 152, 160, 262, 269, 278; consolidation of, 87; dogmas of, 58; French, 63; heterodox, 154; international, 279; orthodox, 101, 149, 160
Truman Doctrine, 275

Tsarism, 82, 115; class character of, 115; fall of, 82
Tsarist state, 82
Tucker, James: *The Novels of Anthony Powell*, 287
Tukhachevsky, Marshal, 59, 60, 85, 158, 264
Turin, Italy, 60–61, 98
Two-and-a-Half International, 103
typologism, 32

Ukania, 205, 215, 216, 218, 219
Unger, Roberto, 193, 194, 274, 293
unilateralism, 94, 123
Union des Jeunesses Communistes (marxistes-léninistes), 61
Union of the Left, 76, 118
unions, 3, 42, 44, 45, 61
United Front, 11, 74, 116, 117
United Kingdom, 4, 6, 12, 16, 31, 94, 111, 117, 140, 143, 177, 214, 219, 221, 241, 264. *See also* Britain
United States of America, 1, 74, 88, 91, 94, 99, 106, 107, 111, 120, 121, 137, 140, 143, 146, 147, 152, 165, 170, 171, 173, 177, 178, 186, 190, 191, 208, 210, 223, 228, 229, 241, 260, 275, 277, 283, 285; hegemony of, 189; imperialism of, 10
universalism, 145, 189, 190, 241
Universities and Left Review (ULR), 1
University Labour Club, 1
USSR, 30, 45, 68, 87, 101, 104, 105, 120, 137, 138, 142, 143, 150, 153–56, 158, 159, 181, 186, 224, 236, 266, 268, 276, 280; acceptance of, 44; collapse of, 230; responsibilities of, 147; role in Cold War, 146. *See also* Russia
utilitarianism, 16, 17, 38, 132, 272
utopian socialism, xv, 145, 180, 189

values, 128, 140, 141
vanguardism, political, 63
Veblen, Thorstein, 214, 215, 292; *Imperial Germany and the Industrial Revolution*, 215
Versailles, 57
Vietnam, 41, 45, 59, 69, 76, 91, 107, 156, 186, 191, 235
Vietnam Solidarity Campaign (VSC), 41, 62, 63, 130

Vietnamese Revolution, 41, 68, 130, 138, 189
Vilar, Pierre, 88; 'Marxist History, a History in the Making: Towards a Dialogue with Althusser', 266
Vincent, Jean-Marie, 63
violence, 23, 114, 115, 125
voluntarism, xvii, 57, 58, 125, 242

wage and welfare policies, 144
wage controls, 45
wage labour, 185, 232, 237
Wainwright, Hilary, 286
Wald, Alan: *The New York Intellectuals: The Rise and Decline of the Anti-Stalinist Left from the 1930s to the 1980s*: 277, 279, 280, 285
Wales, 122
war, 146, 176, 231
Warren, Bill, 86, 236; 'The British Road to Socialism', 261; 'Imperialism and Capitalist Industrialization', 265; *Imperialism: Pioneer of Capitalism*, 265
Warsaw Pact, 60, 191
Washington D.C., 160
Webb, Beatrice, 25
Webb, Sidney, 25
Weber, Henri: 'Eurocommunism, Socialism, and Democracy', 270; *Mai 68: Une répétition générale*, 263; 'Reply to Debray', 275
Weber, Max, 49, 85, 97, 112; *The Agrarian Sociology of Ancient Civilizations*, 264; *Economy and Society*, 288
Weberianism, 195, 288
Weir, Angela: 'The British Women's Movement', 282
welfare capitalism, 169
welfare state, 23, 218, 221
Weltgeist, philosophical framework of, 231
West: advanced, 117, 129, 150, 156, 235; capitalist, 84; development of, 83, 84; revolution in the, 58, 63, 115; societal ascendancy of, 195; transition to socialism in, 119
West, Cornel: 'The British and the Rational', 286
Western Europe, 11, 21–25, 50, 65, 72, 78, 79, 82, 87, 96, 98, 112, 116, 119, 120, 137, 138, 164, 173, 189, 191, 205, 218–21, 228, 229, 233, 234, 244; com-

munist parties in, 74; left intelligentsia in, 163; Marxism in, 95, 103, 104; politics, 238
Western history, 81
Western intellectuals, 170
Western left, 162
Western Marxism, xi, 5, 7, 10, 32, 35, 47, 49, 54, 55, 56, 65, 66, 93, 96, 97, 99, 100, 102, 103, 104, 106, 108, 109, 170, 171, 181, 182, 246, 269; tradition, 8, 38, 39, 40, 181, 182, 241
Westminster system, 219
white emigration, 50
Widgery, David: *The Left in Britain, 1956–1968*, 249
Wiener, Barnett, 211
Wiener, Martin: *English Culture and the Decline of Industrial Spirit*, 211
Wilcox, James, 46; 'Two Tactics', 256
Williams, Raymond, 10, 17, 122, 130, 131, 136, 140, 199, 261, 273; *Culture and Society*, 8, 12; *The Long Revolution, 3; Marxism and Literature*, 259; *May Day Manifesto, 1968*, 63, 71, 261; *Politics and Letters: Interviews with New Left Review*, 140, 271, 272, 273, 274, 287, 289; 'The Politics of Nuclear Disarmament', 276; 'Problems of the Coming Period', 281
Wilson, Elizabeth: 'The British Women's Movement', 282
Wilson, Harold, 5, 7, 12, 18, 19, 40, 41, 189, 209, 212, 216, 219
Wilsonism, 29, 39, 92, 131
Wittgenstein, Ludwig, 50, 51, 53, 199
Wolff, Richard D.: 'Western Marxism', 268
Wollen, Peter, 6, 71, 286
women's emancipation, 185
women's movement, 141, 186, 286
women's studies, 36, 200, 210, 213, 216
Wood, Ellen Meiksins: 'A Chronology of the New Left and Its Successors; or, Who's Old-Fashioned Now?' 249; *The Pristine Culture of Capitalism*, 210, 291; 'Rational Choice Marxism: Is the Game Worth the Candle?' 289; *The Retreat from Class: A New 'True' Socialism*, 287, 289
Wood, Neal: *Communism and British Intellectuals*, 249, 259

Worcester College, Oxford, 1
Wordsworth, William, 9
workers: assemblies, 70; control, 19; democracy, 108; militancy, 93; movement, 82, 119, 189, 244
workers' state: 107, 141, 142, 153, 154, 155, 156, 157, 158, 159, 160, 162, 192, 222
working class, 21, 24, 26, 33, 62, 64, 70, 102, 114, 115, 165, 176, 180; centrality of, 185; culture, 17; European, 44; history of, 176; institutions, 3; insurgency of, 98; leadership of, 69; living standards of, 44; loyalties, 72, 76; movement, 49, 53; organization, 61; political history, 73; politics, 72, 95, 237; representation of, 43; struggles of, 101; values, 3; Western, 155
world capitalism, 67, 97, 176, 218
World Communist Movement, 5, 59
world market, 189, 209
world revolution, 67, 83
World War I, 64, 75, 82, 84, 96, 103, 118, 208, 295
World War II, 10, 51, 60, 73, 84, 101, 102, 107, 130, 144, 149, 150, 151, 159, 187, 208, 234, 235
Wright, Erik Olin, 195; 'Class Analysis, History, and Emancipation', 275, 298; 'Giddens's Critique of Marxism', 288; *Reconstructing Marxism: Essays on Explanation and the Theory of History*, 288
Wright, Patrick: 'Beastly Trials of the Last Politburo', 246

xenophobia, alleged, 65

Yaffe, David: 'The Crisis of Profitability', 290
Yeltsin, Boris, 223, 225, 295
Yemeni revolution, 275
Yenan peasantry, 37
Yom Kippur War, 86
youth movement, 26
Yugoslavia, 22, 73, 119, 142, 223

zeitgeist, 231
Zimmerwald Left, 295
zones, backward, 156

Gregory Elliott is senior lecturer in humanities at the University of Brighton. His publications include *Althusser: The Detour of Theory, Labourism and the English Genius,* and *Althusser: A Critical Reader.*